College English and Communication

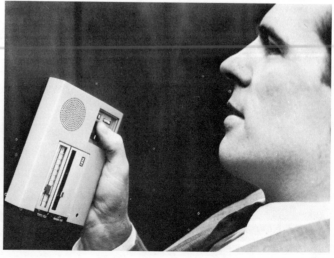

College English and Communication

SECOND EDITION

Marie M. Stewart, Ph.D.
Executive Assistant to the Director
Edmundite Development Program
Mystic, Connecticut

Frank W. Lanham, Ph.D.
Professor of Business and
Distributive Education
Wayne State University
Detroit, Michigan

Kenneth Zimmer, Ed.D.
Chairman of the Department of
Business Education
and Office Administration
California State College at
Los Angeles, California

GREGG DIVISION   McGRAW-HILL BOOK COMPANY
NEW YORK ST. LOUIS DALLAS SAN FRANCISCO TORONTO LONDON SYDNEY MEXICO PANAMA

Book and cover design by Richard W. Stalzer.
Composition by Beissel Company.
The text type—10/12 Laurel, with News Gothic, and
special headings in Baskerville, Horizon Bold Condensed,
and Headline Open.

College English and Communication, Second Edition

2 3 4 5 6 7 8 9 HDBP 8 7 6 5 4 3 2 1 0 9

61330

Preface

College English and Communication, Second Edition, provides the student with a comprehensive program tailored to develop the communication competence needed to enter upon and to progress in a business career. Success in secretarial, marketing, accounting, managerial, and all other types of business careers depends on relevant education and training in all four language arts: writing, speaking, listening, and reading.

The success of a salesman, for example, depends on his proficiency in *listening* to his customers describe their product and service requirements; in *speaking* to his customers about his company's ability to satisfy their needs; in *writing* to his supervisor to report the results of discussions with customers; and in *reading* to keep himself up to date on a wide variety of matters related to his work. In other words, the success of a salesman—or any other business employee—is predicated on his success as an effective communicator.

LAYING THE FOUNDATION

An effective communicator owes much of his competency in reading, writing, listening, and speaking to the thorough training in fundamentals that prepared him for polished application of the specific knowledge and skills applicable to each of those communication arts. In *College English and Communication,* the foundation for total communication competence is built through a comprehensive presentation of the practical principles of word usage, language structure, and writing mechanics.

Using Words Effectively

The effective use of words is implicit in communication. Consequently, Chapter 1 (Sections 1 through 4) provides both a framework and a reference point for a program of continual vocabulary expansion and refinement—a program that includes a special exercise for the development of spelling or some other vocabulary skill among the activities at the end of each remaining section of the textbook.

Language Structure

The presentation of language structure in Chapter 3 (Sections 7 through 21) concentrates only on those traditional grammar principles that will have a direct, immediate bearing on the student's proficiency in writing, speaking, listening, and reading for business purposes. As in the previous edition, any principle that is frequently misunderstood or often forgotten is reinforced by a "Memory Hook." In addition, the statements and illustrations of principles are followed immediately by "Checkup" exercises.

One of the features of this edition is the recognition of contradictory but equally acceptable language-usage principles. In Chapter 3, any non-traditional principle that has gained widespread acceptance among business writers and speakers is presented and discussed under the heading "Twilight Zone." However, the instructor has the option of accepting or refusing to accept any principle that is in the transitional, or "Twilight Zone," stage.

The Mechanics of Style

The mechanics of style presented in Chapter 4 (Sections 22 through 30) are those applied in written business communications, specifically, the use of punctuation, capitalization, and abbreviations and the expression of numbers. Throughout the discussion, the emphasis is placed on using the rules to guide readers in interpreting correctly the messages intended by the writer.

WRITING

Because good writers are scarce and the demand is great, approximately one-third of this edition of *College English and Communication* is devoted to written business communication. The student who masters the specialized principles and techniques presented in Chapters 5 through 8 (Sections 31 through 48) will be well prepared for any writing assignment he may encounter in his career.

Writing Craft

Chapter 5 (Sections 31 through 33) emphasizes the structural principles of writing that ensure a reader's quick, correct, and exact interpretation of a business communication. In essence, this chapter is a meaningful, down-to-earth treatment of rhetoric that in the past has too often left the student completely befuddled.

Creative Business Writing

If a business correspondent is a master of business-writing principles, he will do a job that is more than adequate; but if he is a creative writer as well, he will rank among those at the top of his profession or career. In Chapter 6 (Sections 34 and 35), the student prepares himself for creatively writing the various types of business communications covered in Chapters 7 and 8.

Section 34 gives the student an insight into the fundamental psychological drives that affect human behavior. He learns when and how to appeal to those drives in order to evoke the favorable response that is his main purpose in writing. Section 35 deals with procedures for planning messages to achieve effectiveness through creative means.

Writing Business Letters

Chapter 7 (Sections 36 through 44) provides thorough coverage of the principles and procedures applicable to the effective creative writing of business letters for special purposes. The elements of style that are characteristic of all business letters are covered in Section 36.

Other Written Communications

Chapter 8 (Sections 45 through 48) gives special emphasis to the writing of intracompany communications and features an expanded treatment of informal and formal reports. Section 46 provides complete and thorough training in the writing of informal reports, the type for which there is the most frequent demand in any business office; Section 47 prepares the student for writing formal reports.

SPEAKING

This edition of *College English and Communication* prepares the student to meet his immediate and long-range oral communication needs. Chapter 9 (Sections 49 through 54) follows a practical approach to the mastery of speaking techniques needed for top performance in such situations as these: ordinary conversation, receiving callers, telephoning, acting as the leader of a group, and contributing as a group member.

READING AND LISTENING

Skill in receiving communications is vitally important in the classroom as well as on the job; therefore, Chapter 2 (Sections 5 and 6) establishes guidelines for continuing improvement in reading and listening.

LOOKING TO THE FUTURE

Education has been defined as "what remains and is of value after graduation." In terms of that definition, this edition of *College English and Communication* does indeed educate: it takes the student far beyond the confines of the classroom.

Chapter 10 (Sections 55 and 56) deals with the very important subject of obtaining a job, with particular emphasis on the principles and techniques of using communication skills when writing and when interviewing for a job.

Chapter 11 (Sections 57 and 58) identifies and discusses the communication skills that provide the basis for successful performance on the job and for advancement from one job to another.

COMMUNICATION PROJECTS

To become a master of the communication arts, the student must be able to put into practice the principles he has learned. This vital practice is supplied by a variety of Communication Projects at the end of each section of *College English and Communication,* Second Edition.

Practical Application

Each section of the text provides Practical Application exercises that apply the principles covered in the particular section and that reinforce the principles presented in previous sections.

Editing Practice

The Editing Practice at the end of each section fills a very real need to develop the critical faculty that will enable the student to produce polished letters, memos, reports, and other communications. As mentioned previously, this activity typically includes a vocabulary-improvement exercise in the form of a paragraph that deals with a business subject.

Case Problem

The purpose of the Case Problem at the end of each section is to enrich the student's background and to promote his ability to make sound judgments and decisions.

SUPPORTING MATERIALS

In addition to the textbook, the *College English and Communication* program includes a book of correlated communication problems, a set of objective tests, and an instructor's guide and key.

Communication Problems

This book provides carefully planned learning experiences correlated section by section with the textbook. The variety and wealth of exercises make possible the achievement of its purpose—reinforcement and enrichment.

Objective Tests

The tests that accompany *College English and Communication,* Second Edition, consist of an inventory test for use at the outset of the course, eleven end-of-chapter tests (one for each chapter of the text), and a final examination for use at the end of the course.

Instructor's Guide and Key

The *Instructor's Guide and Key for College English and Communication,* Second Edition, is much more than an answer book for the textbook, the communication problems, and the objective tests. It is also a source of helpful suggestions for planning and presenting a highly successful course.

Marie M. Stewart
Frank W. Lanham
Kenneth Zimmer

Illustrations

The photographs that appear in this book show a wide variety of on-the-job working situations in a highly diversified group of actual business organizations. We wish to acknowledge the cooperation of the many companies that have supplied these illustrations for *College English and Communication*. We wish particularly to acknowledge the active support of the National Urban League in helping us obtain photographs for this book.

Title Spread

Page ii, top left: Donald L. Miller, special assistant to the president, Interchemical Corporation, examines a report on company procedures. *Courtesy Interchemical Corporation.*

Page ii, top right: An executive secretary pauses during her transcription while her employer asks her to edit a speech he has prepared. *Courtesy E. I. du Pont de Nemours & Company, Inc.*

Page ii, bottom left: Benjamin Franklin's printing press represents the midpoint of progress between the first machine, invented by Gutenberg in the 1400's, and the automated presses of today.

Page ii, bottom right: A traveling executive uses a portable dictaphone to reply to letters forwarded to him by his secretary. *Courtesy IBM.*

Page iii: A young businesswoman explains to visiting executives the merits of her company's training program. *Courtesy Today's Secretary.*

Introduction

Page xvi: An office manager shows her assistant how the appeal of a letter may be strengthened by using a "you" approach. *Courtesy American Can Company.*

Page 2: Two trainees learn their new jobs by using their listening skills. *Courtesy New York Life Insurance Company.*

Page 3: An executive trainee pauses in her work to greet a telephone caller pleasantly. *Courtesy Moser Secretarial School.*

Page 4: An executive explains to visitors the fast, accurate communications needed to control air traffic at a major airport. *Courtesy The Ford Foundation.*

Page 5: Ludy Lee (left), product merchandising assistant in the Household Products Division of Lever Brothers Company, dictates to her secretary, Gloria Musel. *Courtesy Lever Brothers Company.*

Page 6: A young businesswoman explains the office filing system to a newcomer with whom she will be working closely. *Courtesy Chas. Pfizer & Company, Inc.*

Page 7: A secretary uses her editing skills to check and retype her employer's work. *Courtesy Union Carbide Corporation.*

Page 8: A secretary needs the ability to read quickly and accurately even when she is working with files. *Courtesy New York Life Insurance Company.*

Page 9: Mary Tortovete feeds information into a small computer with guidance from her boss, Stanley Sumlin, senior financial analyst at Mobil Oil Corporation. *Courtesy Mobil Oil Corporation.*

Page 10: Western Electric executive Eugene Keough and Doris Mayers, executive secretary, confer on the results of a study they have conducted. *Courtesy Western Electric Company.*

Page 11: Ruby Lightbourne (right), a secretary at Sterling Drug's Winthrop Laboratories, checks a reference source with Assistant Librarian Janet Stevenson. *Courtesy Sterling Drug.*

Page 12: Arthur Jackson, a television technician at CBS, films a television broadcast. *Courtesy CBS.*

Page 13: A secretary listens carefully to a message a caller wishes to leave for her boss. *Courtesy American Airlines.*

Chapter 1 — Using Words Effectively
Pages 14-15

Top left: An executive secretary verifies the wording of a message being left by a caller. *Courtesy AT&T.*

Top right: Guy E. Noyes (left), a senior vice-president and economist at Morgan Guaranty Trust Company, discusses economic indicators with Dr. Henry E. Finley, professor of economics at Florida A. & M. University, Tallahassee, Florida. *Courtesy Morgan Guaranty Trust Company.*

Center left: James Sermons, a personnel specialist at Ethicon, Inc., clarifies an instruction for his secretary, Gelsomina Riccioni. *Courtesy Ethicon, Inc.*

Center right: An efficient executive secretary pleasantly greets callers and fellow workers. *Courtesy CBS.*

Bottom left: Many signs compete for the attention of potential customers on a New York City street. *Photo by Ann Grifalconi.*

Bottom center: A lab technician takes precise notes of her observations. *Courtesy The Ford Foundation.*

Bottom right: Philip Gordon, an assistant treasurer in Personnel Administration at The Chase Manhattan Bank, lectures to a group of Chase Manhattan employees from branch offices around the world. *Courtesy The Chase Manhattan Bank. Photo by Raymond Juschkus.*

Chapter 2 — Receiving Communications
Pages 40-41

Top left: Secretary Jean Stonitsch listens to and records instructions dictated by her boss, Donald L. Miller, special assistant to the president, Interchemical Corporation. *Courtesy Interchemical Corporation.*

Top right: An executive catches up on articles his secretary has marked for his attention.

Center left: A secretary skims a discussion of managerial techniques for points appropriate for a speech her boss has been asked to deliver before a college group. *Courtesy Young & Rubicam, Inc.*

Center right: Alfred Broderick, CBS news assistant, listens carefully while Douglas Edwards, CBS news commentator, gives instructions on preparing the script for a news broadcast. *Courtesy CBS.*

Bottom left: Yvonne Bertie, director of the secretarial training program at the National Urban League, and Juanita Levy, a secretary at Lever Brothers Company, review a new training manual. *Courtesy National Urban League.*

Bottom right: Members of the Advisory Board on Community Relations of Teaneck, New Jersey, discuss the merits of a new community action program.

Chapter 3 — Language Structure
Page 57

Top: A young professor uses the modern equipment of a language laboratory to provide individualized instruction for his students. *Courtesy The Ford Foundation.*

Center: To verify the wording of a report she is typing, Anita Flintall, a finance clerk in the News Division at CBS, checks the original data that she has on file. *Courtesy CBS.*

Bottom left: A secretary pauses to check the grammar of a letter her boss has dictated to her. *Courtesy The Prudential Insurance Company of America.*

Bottom right: Benjamin Franklin's printing press represents the midpoint of progress between the first machine, invented by Gutenberg in the 1400s, and the automated presses of today.

Chapter 4 — Mechanics of Style
Page 145

Top: To save time, a secretary checks the copy she has typed and corrects an error before she removes the paper from the typewriter.

Center: Gloria Rojas, a CBS reporter-writer trainee, proofreads a news bulletin before she submits it to her supervisor. *Courtesy CBS.*

Bottom left: Interchangeable type, such as the Selectric elements, provides a broad choice for the secretary who must prepare particularly attractive copy. *Courtesy IBM.*

Bottom right: A secretary keeps at her fingertips the references she needs most frequently—such as a dictionary, a thesaurus, an English handbook, a company directory and an almanac.

Chapter 5 — Writing Craft
Page 207

Top: Two executives discuss the effectiveness of visual aids in a report they are preparing. *Courtesy The Ford Foundation.*

Center: A secretary prepares camera-ready copy from manuscript recorded by typewriter on magnetic tape. *Courtesy IBM.*

Bottom left: Francee Covington, an apprentice in the CBS Journalism Program, checks late news bulletins while Ralph Blumberg, reporter-assignment editor, telephones field reporters. *Courtesy CBS.*

Bottom right: In all his business correspondence, an executive must apply the principles of effective writing. *Courtesy Olin Mathieson Chemical Corporation.*

Chapter 6 — Creative Business Writing
Pages 234-235

Top left: A young businesswoman checks the effectiveness of her writing in a news release she has prepared for her boss. *Courtesy Cunningham & Walsh, Inc.*

Top right: Jack Carter (left), news services supervisor at AT&T, reviews a script with James G. Barringer, network radio-TV coordinator. *Courtesy AT&T.*

Center left: Wesley Swint, administrative trainee, proofreads a business procedures report that he is preparing for his supervisor at CBS. *Courtesy CBS.*

Center right: An office manager shows her assistant how the appeal of a letter may be strengthened by using a "you" approach. *Courtesy American Can Company.*

Bottom left: Three writers confer about the wording of an important advertising circular to be used in a nationwide promotion program. *Courtesy AT&T.*

Bottom center: Mrs. Henrie Robinson (left), a personnel clerk at Lever Brothers Company, and Winifred Richardson, personnel assistant, check a file record in order to assemble facts before writing a memorandum. *Courtesy Lever Brothers Company.*

Bottom right: Two business writers check their facts before they begin the draft of a key report. *Courtesy The Ford Foundation.*

Chapter 7 — Writing Business Letters
Pages 254-255

Top left: Many business offices today use postage meters to seal envelopes and imprint the postage. *Courtesy Pitney-Bowes, Inc.*

Top right: Neatly written shorthand makes a secretary's job easier.

Center left: ZIP-Coded mail may be sorted rapidly by optical scanning equipment now being installed in many post offices; however, noncoded mail must still be sorted by hand. *Courtesy United States Post Office.*

Center right: A typist's hands should be relaxed and comfortably positioned over the typewriter.

Bottom left: Wallace W. Price, manager of procedures at Olin Mathieson Chemical Corporation, dictates a response letter to his secretary, Carolanne Carroll. *Courtesy Olin Mathieson Chemical Corporation. Photo by George W. Martin.*

Bottom center: A secretary transcribes the letters her boss dictated while she was preparing the minutes of his weekly sales meeting. *Courtesy IBM.*

Bottom right: A group of workers in the same office answer inquiries, request information, send reminder notices, promote sales, and write many other kinds of letters. *Courtesy Employers Insurance of Wausau. Photo by John F. Hornyak.*

Chapter 8 — Other Written Communications
Pages 364-365

Top left: A secretary gathers background material for a speech she is to present at a company-wide meeting of secretarial personnel. *Courtesy The Ford Foundation.*

Top right: Nelson Freeman (right), dean of students at Savannah State College, discusses a report with John Sibbald, a college relations specialist of Chas. Pfizer & Company. *Courtesy Chas. Pfizer & Company, Inc.*

Center left: A well-organized administrative assistant turns to his file of important business papers for facts needed in the memorandum he is writing. *Courtesy American Airlines.*

Center right: A public relations assistant checks the final draft of a news release while his colleague verifies a change in the data reported by the release. *Courtesy The Ford Foundation.*

Bottom left: A secretary uses a teletypewriter for communication with branch offices located throughout the country. *Courtesy AT&T.*

Bottom center: Using her draft of the minutes of a meeting, an efficient secretary alerts her boss to matters requiring follow-up. *Courtesy Chas. Pfizer & Company, Inc.*

Bottom right: With the help of modern automated equipment, a computer trainee quickly processes large volumes of data. *Courtesy IBM.*

Chapter 9 — Communicating Orally
Pages 410-411

Top left: A trainee carefully files a reel of magnetic tape in its proper place on the rack. *Courtesy The Prudential Insurance Company of America.*

Top right: A secretary telephones the travel agent for her company in order to verify the final details of her employer's travel arrangements. *Courtesy AT&T.*

Center left: Management analyst Andy Byers explains to a group of new employees the organization chart of The Port of New York Authority. *Courtesy The Port of New York Authority.*

Center right: Whitney M. Young, Jr., executive director of the National Urban League, delivers an address in Los Angeles before the National TV and Radio Editors. *Courtesy National Urban League.*

Bottom left: Dr. Sidney McNairy, professor of biochemistry at Southern University in Baton Rouge, Louisiana, chats with former student Marian Simien, who is a research assistant in virology at Chas. Pfizer & Company, Inc. *Courtesy Chas. Pfizer & Company, Inc.*

Bottom center: A visitor gives the receptionist his name and the details of his appointment with an executive of the company. *Courtesy Employers Insurance of Wausau. Photo by John F. Hornyak.*

Bottom right: A radio broadcaster speaks to audiences across the nation. *Courtesy AT&T.*

Chapter 10 — Obtaining a Job
Pages 460-461

Top left: A modern office building soars high above the street in an urban business district.

Top right: Many large companies administer employment tests to job applicants. *Courtesy AT&T.*

Center right: A job hunter circles an ad for a position that sounds right for her interests and qualifications.

Bottom left: Clerks, typists, secretaries, salesmen, managers, storekeepers, and other business workers make their ways to their offices in companies of all sizes and types.

Bottom right: Evelyn Davis (right), a placement supervisor at CBS, interviews prospective employee Virginia Cuppett before hiring her as a CBS executive secretary. *Courtesy CBS.*

Chapter 11 — Advancing on the Job
Pages 482-483

Top left: Gean Howard, an employee of American Oil Company, and Professor Harry Turner, Virginia State College, Norfolk, Virginia, examine a reference source for a research project. *Courtesy American Oil Company.*

Top right: A bank executive, who began her career as a secretary, reviews a mortgage application. *Courtesy Libby-Owens-Ford Glass Company.*

Center left: Without prompting from her boss, an executive secretary calls for cost figures she knows he will need for a meeting he must attend. *Courtesy AT&T.*

Center right: Jeanette Civale, an executive secretary at The Chase Manhattan Bank, records a personnel memorandum dictated by Philip Gordon, an assistant treasurer in Personnel Administration. *Courtesy The Chase Manhattan Bank. Photo by Raymond Juschkus.*

Bottom left: A junior executive asks the boss's executive assistant for help in clearing up a discrepancy in the sales figures reported to him. *Courtesy Burroughs Corporation.*

Bottom center: Because she doesn't know the answer, an alert trainee turns a call over to her supervisor and listens carefully while her supervisor tactfully refuses the caller's unreasonable request. *Courtesy Eastman Kodak Company.*

Bottom right: CBS attorney Eleanor Applewhaite telephones to check the accuracy of information that she will use in writing a legal brief. *Courtesy CBS.*

Contents

INTRODUCTION

| | Communicating in the World of Business |

Many of you will soon be embarking upon a business career—a career for which you have been preparing yourself for many years by acquiring the skills and knowledge that will help you become successful as a secretary, as an accountant, as a salesman, or as a worker in one of many other business occupations. Each business occupation has its own skill and knowledge requirements—although some of the requirements are common to more than one of these occupational fields. Skill in typewriting, for example, is necessary in many different business positions—but not in all of them.

However, there is one ability that is essential in every business position—and that is the ability to communicate. Whether you are a typist in a typewriting pool or the president of a large corporation, you make frequent use of communication skills—although not always in the same way or to the same degree.

As a beginning worker, you won't even get your foot in the door of the company for which you would like to work if you cannot successfully communicate your qualifications for a position. Indeed, we could go back much further into your life to illustrate the need for being able to communicate effectively. On the day you drew your very first breath, you communicated your presence and your needs by crying—and you have been communicating in one way or another ever since!

Of course, the method used for communicating in one situation is not always the method that should be used in another situation. We must tailor our communication to fit the situation. As a business worker, you must learn not only *how* to communicate in the world of business but also how to communicate *effectively*. As a matter of fact, the degree of success you achieve in the business world often depends upon how effectively you are able to communicate your ideas.

Much of the groundwork in communication already has been laid—in your activities at home, in your social life, and, perhaps most of all, at school. You now have an opportunity to reappraise your communication ability, to remedy any deficiencies that may still exist, and to learn how to apply the basic principles of communication to the world of work.

The primary objective of this book is to help you use your communication skills as effectively as possible in performing your daily activities in business —regardless of the type of position you hold or the level on which you function—and to show you how you can use your communication abilities to assist you in moving up the ladder of success.

THE SCOPE OF BUSINESS COMMUNICATION

You may have been laboring under the illusion that business communication is limited to letter writing, that only the executive needs to know how to write letters, and that he does so solely by direct dictation to a stenographer. You have been misled if that is your understanding of the scope of business communications. If you will glance through the pages of this book, you will see that the world of business communications is not limited to the writing of letters but that business uses all the areas of communication that you use at school, at home, and in your social life—writing, reading, listening, and speaking.

Let us take a close look at a large business that makes its home office in Chicago, Illinois. This business may obtain raw materials from South Africa and Mexico, conduct manufacturing operations in North Carolina and California, and ship its products to customers all over the world—and all of this activity emanates from a ten-story building in Chicago. Business is today far more dependent on communication than at any other time in history. An international chemical firm (see page 13) advertised that it had 45 plants in 12

countries and research laboratories and technically trained representatives in 71 countries. Without extensive, effectively used communications systems, such a business organization could not function. But even the small business is dependent on effective communication to carry on its everyday affairs.

Regardless of the nature and the size of the business, most modern businesses have one problem in common: effective and efficient communication must be accomplished between the employee and his supervisor, between one employee and another, and between the business and its customers, its suppliers, and the general public. Communication is necessary for evoking action, for obtaining cooperation, and for maintaining the day-to-day working equilibrium necessary for business stability. Poor communication can create misunderstandings and loss of business, of time, and of money.

HOW WE COMMUNICATE

Communications began, of course, with face-to-face conversation. The first written communication took the form of symbols and was used by the caveman as a means of sending messages when face-to-face conversation was not possible. As writing systems developed, letters, journals, and reports eventually became part of man's rather simple means of communicating with others. Today, with the benefit of hundreds of years of experimentation behind him, man now has available several means for communicating around the world every kind of oral or written message imaginable. Messages in the form of all types of conversations, speeches, and meetings are transmitted by telephone, radio, television, Telefax, film, and voice-recording devices as well as face to face. Written messages are transmitted through letters, telegrams, radiograms, cablegrams, advertisements, newspapers, books, and periodicals. Effective mail delivery systems and other systems of distribution ensure delivery of written messages. The effort needed for an employee to communicate with a

business associate on the other side of the globe is very little more than is required for him to send a message to a fellow employee in his own office building.

Sending Messages Orally

Face-to-Face Contact   Face-to-face communication is particularly important in dealing with customers, with salesmen, and with co-workers. Often face-to-face conversation is taken for granted and treated with the attitude that communicating orally requires little or no skill. As a matter of fact, this method requires an exceptional amount of skill if the message is to be transmitted clearly and convincingly.

The Telephone   The telephone is used by every business worker to communicate with others both inside and outside the business office. The use of the telephone facilitates receiving messages from outside the office and sending messages to other locations with speed and with less effort than other means of communicating. Telephone conferences may be arranged among several people in different locations. When great distances are involved, however, the use of the telephone is expensive; the communicator must determine whether the cost is justified. Where a great many calls are placed between various branch offices of one firm or between two or more separate firms, direct telephone lines may be installed to connect the firms. By using these direct lines, calls do not have to be transmitted through the telephone office.

Interoffice Communication Devices   Although the telephone is frequently used for interoffice communication, other devices are available. Loudspeaker systems enable a person to speak to an entire unit at one time, rather than requiring him to speak to each individual separately. Some interoffice communication systems are designed to connect two or more offices in the same building.

Meetings Meetings or conferences are an integral aspect of every business office. They are used to orient new employees, to train both new and experienced personnel, and to provide information on new policies and products. Sometimes they are used for "brainstorming," a technique often used for developing new ideas. Because business leaders must often lead conferences as well as participate in them, they should be familiar with discussion-leading techniques and parliamentary procedure. These techniques can save valuable time and make conferences more productive.

Speeches Though not all business workers are called on to give formal speeches, many of them are required to do so at one time or another. This activity is not limited to the top executives of a business firm; secretaries, salesmen, accountants, and others are called on from time to time to address school groups, professional and civic organizations, and church and social groups. Even the fields of radio and television are within the realm of possibility. A businessman or woman must remember that when he or she speaks to a group, the firm—not the individual—is being represented. Often members of the audience will have little or no other contact with the company; therefore, they will judge the firm by the impression given by the speaker. Here is a valuable public-relations opportunity. The person who can make the most of this type of opportunity is almost certain to enhance his chances for success in business.

Dictation Devices While the dictation disc, tape, belt, cylinder, or wire is usually thought of as a means of recording dictation that a stenographer will later transcribe into letter or report form, the practice of mailing these recordings directly to the correspondent is growing in popularity. Of course, this technique is most informal and should be used only for communicating within one company or with business associates with whom the dictator is well

acquainted. The disadvantage of sending the recorded message directly to the addressee is that no written record of the message is provided.

Sending Written Messages

Memorandums   A memorandum is actually a form of letter or report, even though it differs in appearance from either of these forms of communication. Memorandums are usually neither so formal nor so long as either the business letter or the report, but this fact does not decrease their importance as communication media. They are used more frequently in interoffice communication than any other written media.

Letters   Letters are used for every conceivable type of business communication. They are used to communicate with those who buy from a firm and with those who sell to a firm. They are used for sales promotion, for giving or requesting information, for requesting credit, for granting (or refusing) credit, for requesting payment on overdue accounts, and for social-business purposes. A complete list of the purposes served by business letters would be almost endless. Letters may be written and prepared individually, or they may be written in a "form letter" style designed for a mass mailing.

Telegrams, Radiograms, and Cablegrams   Telegrams, radiograms (messages sent over radio, usually between ships), and cablegrams (messages sent between continents via cables on the floor of the ocean) are used by businessmen when speed is essential in transmitting written messages and where the use of the telephone is either impractical or impossible. In domestic communications, telegrams are often used because they attract more attention than other types of messages. Because the cost of telegrams, radiograms, and cablegrams is based on the number of words used, special skill in writing highly condensed, yet clear, messages is required.

Reports The modern business world depends heavily on reports to give facts or to report progress to business owners and to individuals at various operating levels. The length and formality of a report will vary with its purpose. One report may be a hundred pages long; another may be only one page long. The skillful writer must know the form and style most suitable for his particular report. There are several types of reports that business workers may have to prepare, but one special type of report with which they should be familiar is the report of what transpires at meetings, usually referred to as *minutes*.

Business Literature Books, newspapers, magazines, and pamphlets provide excellent opportunities for the creative business writer to express his views on various phases of business. Executives often contribute to books and periodicals; in fact, some magazines depend entirely on the contributions of executives for the articles they publish.

News Releases A business likes to keep its name before the public. One way of doing so is by letting the public know about changes in personnel, new product or service innovations, participation of its personnel in business or civic activities, and other such newsworthy items. Such events call for the writing of news releases to be sent to newspapers and to radio and television stations. Naturally, news releases will receive more favorable attention if they are prepared in a style acceptable to the medium to which they are sent.

Advertising Copy Advertising copy for newspapers, magazines, radio, television, pamphlets, folders, and sales letters accounts for an enormous volume of business communications. While this material is usually prepared by people especially trained for this kind of writing, the business worker in the fields

of advertising, marketing, or sales is very frequently given this responsibility. Even if he does not actually prepare the copy, such an employee must evaluate the material prepared by someone else.

DATA COMMUNICATION IN BUSINESS

The development of automation and electronic data processing has led to a new aspect of communication called *data communications*. The American Telephone and Telegraph Company has published a book entitled *Data Communications in Business*[1] that attempts to explain this new field of communication.

What makes data communications different from any other form of communication? First of all, whatever information is transmitted must first be translated into a special code, of which there are over sixty in operation today. This code, usually referred to as *language*, takes the place of the words that you and I would ordinarily use in sending a message. In reality, the code is the language of the machine, just as English is the language of people.

The second distinguishing characteristic of data communications is that the data are transmitted by some electronic means—for example, a telephone line that may connect two computers. One computer is sending the information and the other is receiving it. Here are some examples of data communications at work in business:

- The Statler Hotel in New York City confirms an executive's room reservation in Los Angeles by teleprinter communication with the Statler's central office.
- The branch office manager submits sales information to the company's home office computer, using a punched-card transmission system.

[1]Edgar C. Gentle, Jr., Editor, *Data Communications in Business*, American Telephone and Telegraph Company, New York, 1965.

- On the first of the month, a sales manager receives a report of the preceding month's sales by means of a teleprinter service from the company's data processing center.

Data communications make possible the storing of vast amounts of information in one place and the rapid transmission of this information to another place. The information that is stored, therefore, must be accurate and must also be clear to the user. Otherwise, costly mistakes may result. If the Statler Hotel makes a reservation for an executive when there actually is no space available, ill will and the loss of that company's future business may be the outcome.

The effectiveness of any data communications system depends on accuracy and clarity at the time the information is programmed, as well as at the time the information is retrieved. Undoubtedly, the person who needs the information wants it in order to make some important decision that must be put into writing, probably in the form of a report. Therefore, the business worker should be familiar with business report writing and should be able to communicate data in a manner that will be understood by his reader. One of the functions of this book is to teach you how to write such reports.

YOU AS A BUSINESS COMMUNICATOR

No matter how extensive or elaborate a communication system may be, effective communication still depends on the individual's skill in using written and spoken words.

In addition, nearly every business employee is involved in communicating. Hence, as a business worker, you must be able to speak and write with clarity, confidence, and knowledge; and you must be able to read and listen with understanding. To ensure personal success, as well as the success of your company, you and every other employee must be a skilled business communicator.

In recent years, business has become increasingly aware of the need for improvement of every business worker's communication skills and particularly the skills of workers who come in contact with the public. Today, courses in effective speaking and writing, as well as in reading improvement, are offered not only by colleges and universities but also by companies themselves. Businesses know that the time and money spent to improve the communication skills of their employees represent dollars saved in time and understanding in day-to-day business operations.

DEVELOPING COMMUNICATION SKILLS

A skilled communicator is a person who can communicate facts, ideas, opinions, and instructions with a minimum of effort. To become a skillful communicator, you must know how to use language correctly. Therefore, you must command a broad vocabulary, which involves not only the ability to spell but also the knowledge of how to use words precisely. You must be able to speak and write without error, as clearly as possible, and in the fewest words necessary. Not only must you be familiar with the many media available for communicating, but also you must have the ability to select the best medium to convey a particular message. If you are to be considered a skilled business communicator, you must be well read and well informed about your field of work, your company, and your particular function in that company. You must be able to think creatively. You must use research techniques effectively when resource materials are called for and you must know how to outline, draft, and perfect your message so that it is well fitted to both the purpose you wish to achieve and the medium you have chosen to convey it.

HUMAN RELATIONS AND COMMUNICATION

Your work in this course and your study of this book will be directed toward helping you achieve this goal—becoming a skillful communicator. However, one skill that cannot be overlooked and that is essential to success in all aspects of your job, not just in communication, is the human relations skill, the ability to understand and deal with people. Skill in human relations cannot be learned mechanically as can structure and usage or vocabulary and spelling. Although these mechanics contribute to human relations skill, they are basically tools for making communication in any human relations situation more effective.

The employee who is skilled in human relations has learned to consider carefully each situation in which he is dealing with others, taking time to consider the feelings and goals of those with whom he is dealing. He remembers that every person believes that his own opinion is founded on good reasons. He gives instructions clearly and carefully, taking time to make sure that they are correct. We might say that he practices "business diplomacy."

A salesman dealing with an irate customer hears the customer out and then tries to satisfy both the customer and his company by understanding both sides of the issue. An employer dealing with an employee who has a grievance tries to show the worker that he understands his problem, and he remembers to give reasons for the company policies he must uphold. The supervisor who must change the job of one of his employees lets the worker know why he is being given a different kind of work. In all phases of activity today, business is interested in improving human relations. That is why

studies of personnel relations, labor relations, management relations, and public relations are receiving a great deal of attention.

WHY COMMUNICATION SKILL IS IMPORTANT TO YOU

Perhaps the best way you can prove your ability to accept leadership responsibilities is through communication. By your facility in expressing ideas, you can convince others of your merits. Your adept use of communication techniques accomplishes two things:

- It demonstrates your ability to communicate with others—an essential skill for a leader who must gain acceptance for ideas, facts, and ways of behavior.
- It enables you to win acceptance for ideas, facts, and ways of behavior that will contribute to the success of the organization in which you are employed.

As you study the material presented in this book and obtain valuable practice in building your communication skill, keep in mind the important role that communications can play in helping you achieve a successful future in the business world. And remember, too, that every hour of study is time spent in working for yourself, for your own personal, individual advancement.

MONSANTO—*Basic Source of Creative Chemistry*

Monsanto is one of the world's largest and foremost chemical companies, producing thousands of chemicals, fibers, plastics and petroleum products. With 45 plants in 12 countries, 13 research laboratories and technically trained representatives in 71 countries, Monsanto is an invaluable source of creative chemistry for industry and agriculture.

A large and increasing proportion of today's industrial problems are chemical problems—solved by familiarity with chemically made materials—by knowledge of the application of chemistry to processing or manufacturing. Generally, the chemical or the technology for solving these problems is available from Monsanto.

MONSANTO COMPANIES

U.S.A.	Monsanto Chemical Company
ARGENTINA	Monsanto Argentina S.A.I.C.; Buenos Aires
AUSTRALIA	Monsanto Chemical (Australia) Ltd.; Melbourne
BELGIUM	Monsanto Europe, S.A.; Brussels
	Monsanto Belgium, S.A.; Ghent
CANADA	Monsanto Canada Ltd.; Montreal
ENGLAND	Monsanto Chemicals Ltd.; London
	Chemstrand Ltd.; London
FRANCE	Societe Monsanto; Paris
INDIA	Monsanto Chemicals of India Private Ltd.; Bombay
JAPAN	Mitsubishi Monsanto Chemical Co., Ltd.; Tokyo
MEXICO	Monsanto Mexicana, S.A.; Mexico, D.F.
REPUBLIC OF PANAMA	Monsanto Overseas S.A.; Panama
SPAIN	Monsanto Iberica, S.A.; Barcelona
	Etino-Quimica S.A.; Barcelona
SWITZERLAND	Monsanto Overseas S.A.; Geneva
	Monsanto Research, S.A.; Zurich

Using Words Effectively

Word References for Vocabulary Building

Primitive man depended entirely on pictures to express his thoughts in writing. The early American Indian used an elaborate sign language to communicate with the early settlers. Young children who have not learned to read words can put together a fairly accurate story from pict .res ' ' see in books, newspapers, and magazines. Some alphabets, such as the Japai. ese alphabet, really consist of pictures. Although pictures, sign language, and "picture" alphabets carry more dramatic power than mere alphabet characters that do not tell a story, the modern writer and modern speaker v '1 find these methods of communication laborious and slow. Only a.1 .cient modern language can cope with the volume of communication that must be handled daily. And the communicator must depend primarily on his skill in the use of words to create in the mind of his reader or listener the pictures he wishes to paint.

The artist creates a picture by using paints. The writer and the speaker create pictures by using words. The greater the number of words in the communicator's vocabulary, the clearer the picture he can present. Before he begins to paint, the artist must know exactly what effect he wishes his picture to have; and he must have the skill to apply the precise colors and shades that will produce this effect. So, too, must the writer or speaker know the impression he wishes to leave on his reader or listener; and he must have the skill to select the right words to create the intended effect.

THE DICTIONARY

The most useful reference for those who deal in words is the dictionary. The sooner the writer or speaker learns to make the best use of the dictionary, the sooner he learns to use words precisely. Every successful writer, secretary, editor, proofreader, and executive, regardless of the extent of his vocabulary, experience, or writing craftsmanship, keeps a dictionary within easy reach—and uses it often.

Those who work extensively with the written and spoken word—students and employed persons alike—should select a reliable dictionary. For ordinary office and school use, a standard abridged (concise) dictionary is adequate. A pocket-sized dictionary is not recommended for business use. Besides having a limited number of word entries, a pocket-sized dictionary gives little word information and lacks the "extras" provided in a larger dictionary.

In addition to all kinds of word information, dictionaries provide a great deal of miscellaneous information that is of invaluable help in all types of communication.

Word Information

The dictionary is used primarily, of course, to look up information about words—spelling, definitions, synonyms, and the like. As an example of the extensive information provided by a good dictionary, consider the word *business*. The dictionary gives the following:

busi·ness \'biz-nəs, -nəz\ *n, often attrib* **1** *archaic* : BUSYNESS **2 a** : OCCUPATION, CALLING **b** : an immediate task or objective : MISSION **3 a** : a commercial or industrial enterprise **b** : TRADE, COMMERCE; *esp* : PATRONAGE **4** : AFFAIR, MATTER <a strange —> **5** : movement or action (as lighting a cigarette) by an actor intended esp. to establish atmosphere, reveal character, or explain a situation **6** : a rightful interest : personal concern <none of your —> **7 a** : a maximum effort; *esp* : a damaging assault **b** : DOUBLE CROSS

syn BUSINESS, COMMERCE, TRADE, INDUSTRY, TRAFFIC mean activity in supplying commodities. BUSINESS may be an inclusive term but specifically designates the activities of those engaged in the purchase or sale of commodities or in related financial transactions; COMMERCE and TRADE imply the exchange and transportation of commodities; INDUSTRY applies to the producing of commodities, esp. by manufacturing or processing, on so large a scale that capital and labor are significantly involved; TRAFFIC applies to the operation and functioning of public carriers of goods and persons **syn** see in addition WORK

Spelling First, the dictionary tells how the word *business* is spelled. Many persons, however, are unable to use a dictionary because they do not know what letters stand for specific sounds. The topics presented in the spelling section, Section 4, provide the hearing and seeing skills needed for finding words in the dictionary. Some additional tips for verifying the spelling of words are these:

- Be sure that you actually see the letters in their correct order; for example, *gauge,* not "guage."
- Be sure that you have not inserted letters that are not there, as "similiar" instead of *similar.*
- Be sure that you have included all the letters that are supposed to be in the word; for example, *occurrence,* not "occurence."
- Be sure that the word is not some other word that is spelled somewhat like the one you are seeking. *Read the definition.* Suppose you are writing this sentence: "The office manager ordered embossed station?ry." Perhaps you need to verify the spelling of *station?ry.* In the dictionary you will find *stationAry,* but the definition reads "fixed in a station, course, or mode." This definition is not the meaning intended. Looking under *stationEry,* you will find "materials (as paper, pens, and ink) for writing or typing." Now you know that the word you seek is spelled *stationery.*
- When two spellings are given for a word, the first is preferred. *Judgment* and *judgement* are both listed in the dictionary, but *judgment* is preferred.
- Pay particular attention to compound words to determine whether they are written as one word (*topcoat*), two words (*postal card*), or as a hyphenated word (*soft-spoken*).
- Be sure to use any accent marks that are part of a word. Some words have different meanings with and without accent marks. For example, *résumé* is a noun that means "a summary"; but *resume* is a verb that means "to assume or take again."

Hyphenation Sometimes a word must be divided at the end of the line of writing, and the writer must know where it can be correctly divided. The dictionary indicates, by centered periods, where words can be hyphenated;

busi·ness (divided only after the *i*), but *busi·ness·man* (divided after the *i* or after *business.*)

Capitalization   The dictionary shows the capitalization of a word when it is not the first word in a sentence. The word *business* is not capitalized unless it is the first word in a sentence. The word *south* by itself is not capitalized, but in *South African* it is capitalized.

Pronunciation and Syllabic Division   Immediately after the regular spelling of a word appears the phonetic spelling of the word, indicating also where the word is accented and where syllabic divisions occur in pronunciation. If you are unfamiliar with phonetic symbols, refer to the dictionary section that explains them. The dictionary shows that the pronunciation of *business* is *'biz-nəs.* The hyphen indicates the syllables.

Part of Speech   The abbreviation *n* indicates that the word *business* is a noun. By knowing the part of speech, the writer often can tell whether he is correct in his use of a word. For example, "He put a *lean* on the property," cannot be correct because *lean* is either a verb (*to lean against*) or an adjective (*lean meat*); and the sentence in question requires a noun. With additional searching the writer finds that *lien* is a noun. After reading the definition, he knows that the word he needs is spelled *lien.*

Inflectional Forms and Derivatives   The dictionary shows irregular plurals of nouns, past tense and participial forms of irregular verbs, and the comparative and superlative forms of irregular adjectives and adverbs. For instance, after the word *shake* come the forms *shook, shaken,* and *shaking.* After the definition of the word *contract* come the derivative noun *contractibility* and the adjective *contractible.*

Synonyms   For many words, the dictionary also indicates numerous synonyms (words that mean almost the same). For example, some synonyms listed for *business* are *commerce, trade, industry,* and *traffic.*

Illustrations   For many words, the dictionary provides illustrations in the form of drawings, tables, or charts, particularly where such illustrations will help to clarify the definition of a word. For example, a writer preparing a paper on money systems used in various countries would find helpful the chart of money names, symbols, and subdivisions following the definition of the word *money.*

Remember that the dictionary does not attempt to show what usage should be, but rather what the present usage is. It is a guide and an essential business tool.

Miscellaneous Information

A good dictionary provides much more than word information. For instance, the front section of a typical abridged dictionary contains the following kinds of information: a guide to the organization and use of the dictionary; an explanation of details given about word entries; a key to phonetic symbols; a guide to correct punctuation; a list of abbreviations used in the word entries.

The section at the back of the book contains many extra aids for the writer and speaker, as illustrated by the following listing.

Abbreviations   Hundreds of abbreviations are used in modern life, not only in business but also in government, education, science, politics, and various other areas of human endeavor. In this section are given the meanings of commonly used abbreviations, such as *B/L* (bill of lading).

Arbitrary Signs and Symbols and Proofreader's Marks   Signs and symbols frequently used in such fields as astronomy, biology, books, business, chemistry, mathematics, medicine, music, and physics are included under this heading. For example, the dictionary tells the writer that ‰ means "per thousand." The various proofreader's marks used in preparing copy for the printer and instructions on how to use them are also included in this section.

Biographical Names   The spelling and pronunciation of the names of famous people are listed under the heading *Biographical Names*. Such biographical data as dates of birth and death, nationality, and occupation are also given. A businessman can refer to this section, for example, when he prepares a speech in which reference is made to famous persons; he can also use this section for quick identification of names found in business reading or heard in a business conversation.

Gazetteer   The gazetteer gives the pronunciation of the names of places, as well as information on their location, population, and so on. This section, therefore, can be used for checking the spelling of names of places to which correspondence is sent.

Forms of Address   This list includes a wide variety of alternate forms of address acceptable in formal correspondence—to government officials, clergy, military officers, and so on. It is a useful reference for addressing many types of business correspondence.

Vocabulary of Rhymes   This section is more helpful to the poet than to the business writer. However, an advertising copywriter may find this section useful when he is writing jingles for his clients.

Rules for Punctuation, Compounds, Capitalization, and Italicization   The sections on punctuation, compounds, capitalization, and italicization are excellent summaries of the rules governing these details of style. The writer who prepares reports will find these sections of great value.

THESAURUS

A thesaurus is a book of words arranged according to *ideas*. Whereas the dictionary can help the writer find the meaning of a specific word, the thesaurus can help him find a specific word that will express exactly an idea that he has in mind. *Roget's International Thesaurus* is the classic thesaurus.

To illustrate the use of a thesaurus, suppose that a writer is composing copy that advertises new spring styles. The word *smart* has been used so much that it has lost its effectiveness. The writer would like to use some other adjective. He looks up *smart* in the Index Guide of his thesaurus and finds the following different adjective meanings of that word: *intelligent, alert, stylish, quick, witty, impudent.* The meaning he is looking for is, of course, *stylish.* Turning to the number written after *stylish,* 642, he finds this list:

ADJS. **11. fashionable, in fashion, in style, in vogue,** being done; **all the rage,** all the go [coll.]; **popular,** prevalent, current; **up-to-date,** up-to-datish, up-to-the-minute, up-to-dick [slang], up [coll.], abreast of the times; **in the swim,** on the boat [slang]; new-fashioned, new-fashion [dial.].

12. stylish, modish, vogueish; **alamode,** in the mode; *à la française, à la parisienne, à l'anglaise, à l'americaine* [all F.].

13. smart, chic; well-dressed, well-groomed, dressed to advantage; **spruce,** natty, neat, trim, sleek, smug, trig, tricksy; **dapper,** dashing, jaunty, braw [Scot.]; **sharp,** spiffy, classy, nifty [all slang]; **dressy** [coll.], **sprucy** [slang], **sporty** [coll.]; swank, swanky [both coll.]; swell [slang], nobby [slang, esp. Eng.]; chichi, *recherché* [F.].

14. ultrafashionable, ultrastylish, ultrasmart.

15. faddish, faddy [coll.], fadmongering.

Note how the number of adjectives having different shades of meaning gives the writer a wide variety of words from which to choose.

Experienced writers, when stymied for the exact words needed to express what they have in mind, solve their problem by consulting Roget. Here are some situations in which the thesaurus is particularly useful.

Finding the Most Suitable Word for a Given Idea

Suppose that you wish to describe a fellow employee to whom time seemingly means nothing. The word *slow* comes to mind. You look up *slow* in the Index Guide of your thesaurus, and you are referred to numbered sections containing words and phrases that convey the idea of *slow.* Here you find *leisurely, creeping, crawling, poking, slow-going, slow-moving, slow-footed, dawdling, lingering, loitering, tarrying, dallying, dillydallying, lagging,* plus the descriptive phrases *creeping like a snail* and *slow as molasses.*

Finding a Word That Will Prevent Your Being Repetitious

Suppose that you have previously used the word *trained* and you wish to use some other word to say that your firm hires only *trained* office workers. In the Index Guide, the numbered sections under *trained* give the following possible substitutions: *skilled, skillful, dexterous, adroit, expert, handy, deft, proficient, accomplished, practical, competent, efficient, qualified, capable.* You might choose *skilled, competent,* or *qualified.*

Finding the Correct Word for Something Vaguely Remembered

Perhaps you are writing a letter about raincoats and wish to use the word that identifies the kind of raincoat worn by cowboys, but you cannot think of the term. In the Index Guide under *clothes* is listed the numbered section containing the word that slipped your memory—*poncho.*

Finding an Appropriate Phrase for a Given Subject

Suppose that you are preparing a speech about good work habits, and you wish to make a point about the desirability of being on time for work or of completing assignments on time. You think that a phrase of some kind will help to strengthen your point. In your thesaurus under *work*, the numbered section for *at work* provides the following phrases: *not let the grass grow under one's feet, make the most of one's time, improve the shining hour.*

DICTIONARY OF SYNONYMS

A reference book like *Webster's Dictionary of Synonyms* is extremely valuable to the business writer and to anyone who prepares speeches, as well as to the writer of advertising copy. How to use synonyms and antonyms is explained fully in Section 3.

COMMUNICATION PROJECTS

Practical Application

A From your employer's very rough notes, you are to type a report. Of necessity, he used some abbreviations; but you know that he expects you to write out the terms. Consult a dictionary; then write the complete words for the following abbreviations in the rough draft.

1. the agcy. fee
2. the canc. order
3. his LL.B. degree
4. attached to the B/L
5. pfd. methods

6. cv. bonds
7. f.o.b. Chicago
8. sent a M.O.
9. a ten-year mtg.
10. interest at 5 pc per an.

B For a speech he was preparing, the president of a company was making reference to the following persons. He used a dictionary to check his pronunciation. Using your dictionary, write the pronunciation as he found it and give some identifying information.

1. Cellini
2. Fessenden
3. Kaiser, Henry John
4. Malthus, Thomas Rob
5. Thyssen

C A sales manager for a firm doing business throughout the world was uncertain of his pronunciation (and sometimes of the location) of places where the company operated. To avoid embarrassment, he used his dictionary to determine the correct pronunciation and the location of the following places. What did he find?

1. Worcester
2. Wichita
3. Ypsilanti
4. Tientsin
5. Poughkeepsie

D The following words should be part of your vocabulary. For each, write the correct pronunciation and the definition. Use each word in a sentence.

1. lien
2. mortgage
3. bimetallism
4. depreciate
5. incumbent

6. emanate
7. franchise
8. monopoly
9. accrual
10. cartel

E In the following sentences, the writer has not used the correct word to convey his thought. Identify the incorrect word and indicate the word that should have been used. Define both the correct and the incorrect word.

1. The manager selected the factory sight yesterday.
2. The personal were selected by the vice-president.
3. Our supervisor does not advice the employees.
4. Bill was formally employed by another firm.
5. We have not hired a full compliment of staff as yet.

In each of the following pairs of words, which of the two spellings is preferred?

1. judgement, judgment
2. acknowledgement, acknowledgment
3. envelope, envelop (noun)
4. canceling, cancelling

5. advisor, adviser
6. instalment, installment
7. theatre, theater
8. traveller, traveler

Editing Practice

Synonyms or Antonyms?   In each of the items below, two words can be matched because they are similar or opposite in meaning. Identify the correct pair for each item and indicate whether they are synonyms or antonyms.

Example: (a) joy   (b) spree   (c) party   (d) sorrow   (e) failure
Answer: a,d   antonyms

1. (a) vestige   (b) dress   (c) underwear   (d) hope   (e) trace
2. (a) armor   (b) hirsute   (c) formerly   (d) humorous   (e) bearded
3. (a) listless   (b) perfunctory   (c) shy   (d) thoroughness   (e) amiable
4. (a) deny   (b) alleviate   (c) aggravate   (d) solder   (e) obfuscate
5. (a) wretched   (b) rotated   (c) obsolete   (d) antiquated   (e) old
6. (a) celebrate   (b) celibate   (c) double   (d) martial   (e) unwedded
7. (a) fireplace   (b) deceased   (c) bravery   (d) dearth   (e) abundance
8. (a) placate   (b) practice   (c) nettle   (d) retaliate   (e) nodule
9. (a) imitative   (b) exemplary   (c) demeanor   (d) deplorable   (e) showy
10. (a) nativity   (b) digestion   (c) indigence   (d) tolerance   (e) poverty

Case Problem

Problem Solving   You are a pool supervisor; and Mr. Edgar, who draws on the pool for stenographic assistance, has asked you not to send him Patricia or Ann. His reason is that they change his punctuation and wording; consequently, time is wasted and nerves are frayed because he insists that they retype the letters exactly as he dictated them.

What steps would you take to solve this problem and to insure that there will be no similar problem in the future?

---

2 | Precision in Word Usage

Words stir the emotions. They can lift the heart, persuade one to act, or enlighten the mind. They can bewilder, cause despair, or evoke anger. The words you use in writing and speaking can build the respect and admiration of those with whom you are communicating; or they can mark you as unimaginative—and uneducated. If your word resources are limited, you have no stockpile from which you can choose words that will communicate precise shades of meaning. However, having a good vocabulary is not simply a matter of knowing many words. The skillful business communicator knows that he must use the *right* word at the *right* time. He must be concerned with correctness in the words he uses, and he must also be concerned with the interpretations that readers or listeners will make of the words he uses. Therefore, he follows certain guides that help him use words precisely.

THE CORRECT WORD

The communicator is careful to choose correct words; that is, he avoids illiterate usages. He must be careful not to use words that do not exist. In the sentence *Mr. Clark expects to attend the meeting in Chicago irregardless of the weather,* *irregardless* is incorrect because there is no such word. The correct word is *regardless.* Probably the writer has confused *irregardless* with *irrespective,* which is similar in meaning and is an acceptable word.

Some illiterate words develop because the true words are mispronounced (and therefore are often misspelled). For example, if a speaker pronounces the word *irreparable* as *irrepair'able* instead of *irrep'arable,* he is using a word that does not exist. Other examples are *revelant* for *relevant, strinth* for *strength; hunderd* for *hundred; drownded* for *drowned; infame'ous* for *in'famous; compare'able* for *com'parable;* and *merchantile* for *mercantile.*

Homonyms

A common error in word usage is choosing a word that looks or sounds like another word that means something else. For instance, writing a vendor and telling him that he "did not send the *stationary* with the shipment" would cause a writer to lose prestige. *Stationary* and *stationery* sound alike, but their meanings are different. If this correspondent had known his homonyms, he would have written *stationery.* Below are some of the homonyms with which business writers should be familiar:

allowed, aloud	mail, male
attendance, attendants	medal, meddle
bail, bale	metal, mettle
bare, bear	miner, minor
berth, birth	overdo, overdue
born, borne	pain, pane
brake, break	passed, past
cereal, serial	patience, patients
cite, site, sight	peace, piece
coarse, course	presence, presents
complement, compliment	principal, principle
dependence, dependents	residence, residents
fair, fare	role, roll
forth, fourth	sail, sale
grate, great	shear, sheer
hear, here	sole, soul
indict, indite	stake, steak
instance, instants	strait, straight
intense, intents	their, there, they're
know, no	threw, through
lean, lien	to, too, two
leased, least	undo, undue
lessen, lesson	waive, wave
lesser, lessor	ware, wear
loan, lone	weak, week

Pseudohomonyms

Pseudohomonyms are words that sound somewhat alike but have different meanings. They are called *pseudo* because, when pronounced correctly, these words do not sound exactly alike. For example, the statement *Smith, Jones, and Hill earned $300, $500, and $800, respectfully* does not convey the meaning intended. The communicator has confused the word *respectfully* (meaning "courteously") with *respectively* (meaning "in the order given"). The pseudohomonyms that give the most trouble are listed here.

accede, exceed	elicit, illicit
accept, except	eligible, illegible
access, excess	emigrate, immigrate
adapt, adopt	eminent, imminent
addition, edition	expand, expend
adverse, averse	extant, extent
advice, advise	facilitate, felicitate
affect, effect	fiscal, physical
appraise, apprise	formally, formerly
carton, cartoon	ingenious, ingenuous
cooperation, corporation	later, latter
dairy, diary	liable, libel
decent, descent, dissent	persecute, prosecute
deceased, diseased	personal, personnel
deference, difference	peruse, pursue
desert, dessert	reality, realty
detract, distract	recent, resent
device, devise	respectfully, respectively
disburse, disperse	statue, statute
disprove, disapprove	suit, suite

Spelling

Confusing homonyms or pseudohomonyms leads easily to incorrect spelling, a word fault that will surely mark the communicator as careless. Business executives complain more about employees' poor spelling than about any other single language handicap. There is little excuse for misspelling words. Careful attention to the similarities and differences between homonyms or pseudohomonyms and to the suggestions in Section 4 of this chapter and the frequent use of a dictionary will improve your spelling.

WORDS SUITED TO THE AUDIENCE

An expert in building construction would be unwise, in talking to a women's garden club, to dwell on technical aspects of his subject and to use terms like *stress, porosity, interstice,* and *tenon.* Such words would be meaningless to this audience. The speaker would be understood, however, if he discussed nontechnical phases of his subject, using words like *comfort, safety, ventilation,* and *cost.* In other words, a speaker should use words geared to the knowledge and interests of his audience.

In written communications, however, knowing one's readers is not so easy. Even so, the expert correspondent finds out as much as possible about those who will read his messages, and he selects words that are appropriate and meaningful.

WORDS WITH SHADES OF MEANING

The skilled communicator is specific in his choice of words. For example, only the unskilled writer or speaker uses the word *cheap* when he really means *inexpensive.* These words do not mean exactly the same thing to most persons. To many, *cheap* means *worthless* or *shoddy*. However, one could purchase an inexpensive suit that is definitely not worthless or shoddy. Even the word *inexpensive* can have several meanings. What is considered inexpensive by one person may be thought expensive by another, and the term may have to be qualified. During a summer sale of winter coats, a shopper can often save a great deal by taking advantage of a *bargain;* but this does not mean that the coat he buys is necessarily an *inexpensive* one.

The sentence *We are sorry to advise you that we cannot make delivery until next month* demonstrates an all-too-common lack of precision in word usage. To *advise* means to *counsel* or to *warn.* The writer meant to say *We are sorry to tell you* (or simply *We are sorry that . . .).* The skillful communicator always uses specific words that convey the exact shade of meaning he intends.

WORDS TO AVOID

One of the aims of communicating in business is the building of goodwill. Because words play an important part in building business friendships, a communicator must use words that are positive and that are pleasant to hear or to read.

Negative Words

Which of the following paragraphs is better from the standpoint of building goodwill?

> In your letter you failed to indicate the size and color of the lampshades you want. Your carelessness will cause delay in getting the shipment to you.
>
> Just as soon as you tell us the size and color of lampshades you prefer, we will ship them to you.

Although the second paragraph is the obvious selection, note that the topic is the same for both paragraphs. Note also that the second paragraph is positively worded and avoids such unpleasant expressions as *you failed* and *your carelessness.* Negative words are almost sure to evoke a negative response.

Words have negative effects usually because they are used to blame or accuse. Most expert business writers consider *failed, careless, delay,* and *inexcusable* negative words, regardless of how they are used, and they recommend that these words be avoided. Actually, such words are unpleasant primarily when they are accompanied by *you* (*you failed*) or *your* (*your delay*). *Your oversight, your error, your claim* will wrinkle the reader's brow, but *our oversight, our error*—while not necessarily wise choices of words— carry a different impression entirely.

The following words become negative when used with *you* or *your* and thus do not achieve the aim of promoting good business relationships.

blunder	defective	inability	regret
claim	delay	inadequate	trouble
complaint	dissatisfaction	inferior	unfavorable
criticism	error	mistake	unfortunate
damage	failure	neglected	unsatisfactory

Unnecessary Word Repetitions

Some writers and speakers spoil otherwise correct English by throwing in unnecessary and repetitious words—words that merely clutter the message. The italicized words in the following expressions are unnecessary.

at about	connect *up*
up above	continue *on*
both alike	*and* etc.
new beginner	*past* experience
cooperate *together*	*free* gratis
same identical	my *personal* opinion
lose *out*	rarely (seldom) *ever*
modern methods *of today*	repeat *back* or *again*
over *with*	refer *back*
customary practice	*true* facts

Antiquated Words

The up-to-date communicator avoids using words that convey an out-of-date impression. For example, he does not use words such as these:

advise (for *say, tell*)	kindly (for *please*)
beg	party (for *person,* except in legal work)
duly	same ("and we will send you same")
esteemed	state (for *say* or *tell*)
favor (for *letter*)	trust (for *hope, know, believe*)
herewith (except in legal work)	via

BUILDING AN EFFECTIVE VOCABULARY

A rich vocabulary is always an asset. The possessor of a better-than-average vocabulary can be a better conversationalist and a better writer because he is able to express his ideas and opinions effectively. His vocabulary skills give him poise and confidence. Numerous opportunities for daily improvement of vocabulary are present all around us. Here are a few suggestions that can noticeably increase word power.

Become Word-Conscious

Be alert to new and different words; learn how they are spelled, how they are pronounced, what they mean, and what their correct usage is. Listen for new words in classes, on the job, on radio and television, in the movies, and in the theater. When you are reading textbooks, newspapers, magazines, fiction, or nonfiction, watch for new words that will enrich your vocabulary. Often it is helpful to keep a special notebook in which new words are recorded for future reference.

Sometimes you will learn a new and specialized group of words because you need them as the working vocabulary for a new subject that you are studying or for a new job that you are learning. At other times you will learn words almost by accident, simply because you see or hear them so often. Frequently you will find yourself learning a new word merely because it interests you. Take advantage of every opportunity for expanding your word power. But also remember to discriminate between good English and slang—in business situations, a large vocabulary of slang expressions reflects poorly on the quality of anyone's speech or writing.

Learn to Use Word Tools

The dictionary, the thesaurus, and the special dictionary of synonyms and antonyms are the tools needed for vocabulary building. You should use these tools in order to increase your word power. (See Section 1 for a discussion of these references.)

Practice Using New Words

Unless new words are practiced, they will become lost. Practice them when you speak. When you are writing any kind of material, business or social, edit it for the purpose of using new and different words. Aim constantly for variety and precision in the use of words.

COMMUNICATION PROJECTS

Practical Application

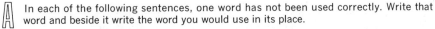

In each of the following sentences, one word has not been used correctly. Write that word and beside it write the word you would use in its place.

1. Our costs acceded our income.
2. We are unable to except any additional orders until next month.
3. The teller could not gain excess to the bank vault.
4. The secretary was quite adapt in typewriting.
5. Which addition of the newspaper carried that article?
6. He was adverse to approving the order without checking with his superior.
7. What advise can you give to the college graduate going into business?
8. Did you canvas all the staff regarding vacation preferences?
9. His behavior in the office was not very discrete.
10. The decision reached by the arbitration board was an equable one.

In each of the following sentences, select the word in parentheses that correctly completes the thought intended.

1. The work was done without the (assistance, assistants) of the clerks.
2. Did you (appraise, apprise) the manager of the difference in cost?
3. Mr. Kent was asked to prepare a (bibliographical, biographical) description to be used to introduce the speaker to the audience.
4. He waited (awhile, a while) before reporting her tardiness.
5. His advertisement showed (insight, incite) into mass psychology.
6. Statements are prepared at the end of the (fiscal, physical) year.
7. Our treasurer cannot (disperse, disburse) any additional funds this month.
8. Your account is long (passed, past) due.
9. Will you serve as the (disinterested, uninterested) party in the arbitration?
10. The printer made a (sleight, slight) change in the style of type.

Study the following paragraphs selected from advertisements, and note on a separate sheet of paper the descriptive words used.

1. Appointments are individually designed in the taste and true tradition of a fabulous hostelry. Whether your stay is overnight or longer, you will find each spacious room designed for your comfort, relaxation, and enjoyment.
2. Carmel-by-the-Sea . . . a moment of enchantment trickling down the sides of pine-studded slopes to the sandy fringes of the capricious Pacific. Entertaining, fairy-tale-fronted shops rub close elbows with assorted, myriad craft studios, art galleries, small theaters, and patioed coffeehouses.
3. A unique and breathtaking display of original and exclusively designed Christmas decorations that bring old-fashioned warmth and eye excitement to your Christmas season.

The following sentences were written by someone with little or no imagination. Rewrite the sentences, using a variety of descriptive words such as those used in Practical Application C.

1. We have such gift items as tables, lamps, candles, linens, etc. Visit our shop today.
2. Our stock of merchandise includes clothes for infants and for boys and girls.
3. Our food is delicious—try our pancakes, steaks, salads, and pastries. We give good servings, but our prices are cheap.

Select a product that you would like to sell if you were a salesman. List as many words and phrases as you can to describe that product.

Prepare a one- or two-minute oral description of the product selected in Exercise E. In your presentation to the class, use as many descriptive words and phrases as possible.

Editing Practice

Make the Blanks Make Sense   In each sentence there is a blank space indicating that a word has been omitted. On your paper write a word that you think would make sense if inserted in the blank space.

1. We understand that you have . . a desire to become located in this area.
2. In times of . . , our employees receive a bonus at Christmas time.
3. We have your request for . . of material for covering porch furniture.
4. We are working as hard as possible to discover the . . of the trunk that should have been delivered to you on Monday.
5. Have your . . draw up your will so that it is clear and legally correct.

Case Problem

Tactful Words   The office manager of the Pompton Company found, when he examined letters written by Jack Lester, that Jack was not very tactful when he wrote to customers of the company. He frequently used expressions like *your error, you claim,* and *you failed.* In discussing this problem with Jack, the office manager learned that Jack did not understand that these expressions were negative and could result in the loss of goodwill—or even customer business. "After all," said Jack, "when the customer is at fault, why shouldn't we tell him so?" How should the office manager answer Jack?

---

3 Variety in Word Usage

Whether you are writing or speaking, you desire the undivided attention of your audience. You can win and keep this attention only if you reach for variety in the words you use. Nothing is more deadly than hearing or seeing the same trite words and expressions over and over, because they kill the sparkle that your message may otherwise convey. Success in business communication also depends to a large extent on imaginative variety of expression.

AVOID HACKNEYED WORDS AND EXPRESSIONS

A writer or speaker who has been working at the same job for many years sometimes loses his enthusiasm and freshness of outlook. When this happens, his communications reflect his loss of spirit. Every writer and every speaker must be alert to ways of avoiding stale communications. One way to skirt this communication hazard is to avoid using hackneyed words and expressions.

Hackneyed Words

Some communications fall flat because they contain overworked words. The adjective *nice* is an example: a nice-looking hat; a nice time at a party; a nice person to work with; a nice steak for dinner. How much more interesting would be these word choices: a *stunning, chic, smart,* or *lovely* hat; *lively, gay, stimulating, jolly,* or *splendid* party; *amiable, good-natured, friendly, cooperative,* or *pleasant* person to work with; *tender, delicious, mouth-watering,* or *sizzling* steak.

Many persons also overuse such adjectives as *good, awful, bad,* and *fine.* The following sentences show how meaningless these words can be.

1. We had a *good* time at your party, and the food was so *good.*
2. I have an *awful* headache.
3. The accountant located a *bad* error in that statement.
4. Our company had a *fine* Christmas party for the office staff.

Now see what words could have been substituted—words that take the flatness out of the sentences.

Sentence 1: *delightful, enjoyable, pleasant* time; *delicious, savory, palatable, delectable, tasty, appetizing, rich* food

Sentence 2: *wretched, painful, dismal, unbearable, annoying* headache

Sentence 3: *unfortunate, troublesome, flagrant, costly* error

Sentence 4: *enjoyable, pleasant, sparkling, magnificent, splendid* party

Hackneyed Expressions

Just as generalized, overworked words are ineffective in communication, so also are hackneyed or trite expressions. Such phrases as *better late than never, free and easy, let's face it, last but not least, at all times, in the near future,* and a host of similar clichés have little meaning. They show a definite lack of imagination, and their use should be avoided.

Some of the commonly overused words and expressions, together with suggested substitutions, are listed below and on page 30.

For	*Substitute*
along the lines of	like
asset	advantage, gain, possession, resource
at all times	always
deal	agreement, arrangement, transaction
factor	event, occurrence, part
field	branch, department, domain, point, question, range, realm, region, scene, scope, sphere, subject, theme
fix	adjust, arrange, attach, bind, mend, confirm, define, establish, limit, place, prepare, repair
inasmuch as	since, as
in the near future	soon (or state the exact time)

For	Substitute
line	business, merchandise, goods, stock
matter	situation, question, subject, point (or mention what is specifically referred to)
our Mr. Smith	our representative, Mr. Smith
previous to, prior to	before
proposition	proposal, undertaking, offer, plan, affair, recommendation, idea
say	exclaim, declare, utter, articulate, express, assert, relate, remark, mention
reaction	opinion, attitude, impression
recent communication	letter of (give exact date)
run	manage, direct, operate

STRIVE FOR VARIETY

Hackneyed words and expressions can easily be identified and therefore avoided. Putting variety into word usage, however, requires creativity; and that is a quality that must be developed by understanding, studying, and applying the following suggestions for achieving variety.

Using Synonyms

One way to achieve variety in word usage is through the use of synonyms. A synonym, as you know, is a word that has the same or nearly the same meaning as another word; for example, *level, smooth, even,* and *flat* are synonymous. Although synonyms have the same basic meaning, each synonym has a different shade of meaning. Word discrimination and language sense are needed to enable the communicator to select the synonym that will be the best substitute for the word he has in mind.

For example, you wish to use a synonym for *famous.* Your dictionary gives as synonyms the words *renowned, celebrated, noted, notorious, distinguished, eminent, illustrious.* These are synonyms, but they do not mean exactly the same thing. In addition to listing synonyms, your dictionary gives a full explanation of the different shades of meaning, like this:

syn RENOWNED, CELEBRATED, NOTED, NOTORIOUS, DISTINGUISHED, EMINENT, ILLUSTRIOUS: FAMOUS implies little more than the fact of being, sometimes briefly, widely and popularly known; RENOWNED implies more glory and acclamation, CELEBRATED more notice and attention esp. in print; NOTED suggests well-deserved public attention; NOTORIOUS frequently adds to FAMOUS an implication of questionableness or evil; DISTINGUISHED implies acknowledged excellence or superiority; EMINENT implies even greater conspicuousness for outstanding quality or character; ILLUSTRIOUS stresses enduring honor and glory attached to a deed or person

By permission. From Webster's Seventh New Collegiate Dictionary, copyright 1963 by G. & C. Merriam Co., Publishers of the Merriam-Webster Dictionaries.

Synonyms, therefore, must be used with care. If you were describing a famous scientist, for instance, you would not refer to him as *notorious,* which means "widely and unfavorably known." Nor would you describe a criminal as *eminent,* even though it is a synonym for *famous*—because your criminal is famous for infamy.

Sometimes reference is made to another word under which synonyms are given. For example, after the word *exact,* the dictionary refers you for synonyms to the word *correct.* Not all words have synonyms; however, for words without synonyms, a phrase can be used to achieve variety. The dictionary does not list synonyms for *explore;* but it does offer such definitions as "to search through or into; to penetrate; to examine minutely, esp. for diagnostic purposes; to make or conduct a systematic search." Thus, as a substitution for *explore,* expressions like *search the area thoroughly, penetrate the woods, examine the records minutely,* or *systematically search the files* could be used.

Another excellent source of synonyms, of course, is the thesaurus. The thesaurus will be of help in avoiding trite expressions and in developing variety in word usage. For instance, suppose you are preparing a report in which you state, "Capable office workers are few and far between." You wish to avoid the expression *few and far between,* partly because it is trite and partly because it does not exactly express the thought you would like to convey.

The dictionary will provide limited assistance. The word *few* is defined as "not many; consisting of or amounting to a small number." The thesaurus, on the other hand, gives many additional similar words; for example, *sparseness, handful, meager, small number, hardly any, scarcely any, scant, rare,* and *minority.*

Using Antonyms

An antonym is a word that means exactly the opposite of another word. For example, *light* is an antonym of *dark.* Antonyms may also be "created" by using such prefixes as *in, ir, non,* and *un* before a word. For instance, *popular, unpopular; conforming, nonconforming; responsible, irresponsible;* and *capable, incapable.*

Facility in the use of antonyms sometimes helps the communicator to make a telling point; for example, an advertisement for a reference book might read, "The illiterate become literate."

Using Picture-Making Words

Use of picture-making words requires imagination as well as creativity. Ability to use words that make a listener or a reader actually see what is being described or that make him see himself in the picture is word usage raised to the highest level. A thesaurus is a treasure house for picture-making words. Even when the exact word you are looking for is not in this book, some other word or words listed will furnish the spark that brings to mind the very word you need. A thesaurus specializes in ideas, and ideas are needed to make pictures.

To an advertising copywriter, every word must serve a useful purpose, because each word is very costly to his client. The copywriter makes pictures for readers and does so in the fewest possible words. Notice the colorful words used in the following advertisements.

Stock up on this *tangy, zestful* sauce.
Take *easy-chair* comfort . . . add sports-car *sizzle* . . .
Splash in *rolling* surf or *placid* fresh-water lakes.

Opportunities for using picture-making words are present whenever and wherever the communicator talks or writes. For instance, in a letter to a business associate of long standing, the sentence *We appreciate the cordial relationship that exists between us* creates a picture of warmth.

Skill in using picture-making words requires hard work and much practice.

COMMUNICATION PROJECTS

Practical Application

The following sentences were selected from various types of business communications. They contain italicized words or phrases that are weak or colorless. Substitute a more meaningful word or phrase for each.

1. The salesman had a *fine* record of sales last month.
2. Our supervisor had a *good* plan for reducing tardiness in the office.
3. The accountant had a *big* problem to solve.
4. There is *an awful lot* to learn on this job.
5. Our office has a very *nice* staff.
6. Miss Jameson had her typewriter *fixed* last week.
7. The office manager *said* that he would not tolerate office gossip.
8. At our office picnic, *a good time was had by all.*
9. A *bad* error must have been made in coding the letter.
10. The mail clerk *walked slowly* through the office.

Complete each of the following sentences by supplying, at the point marked by a question mark, the best descriptive word at your command.

1. Our systems analyst developed a(n) ? record-keeping plan that pleased the president.
2. The interior decorator selected ? draperies for the office windows.
3. She is a(n) ? typist.
4. Sue dislikes working with numbers, so her records are usually ?
5. Mr. Graves has a(n) ? record of attendance that should be emulated by others.

Match each word in Column I with a Column II word or phrase that has a similar meaning.

I	II
a. honest	1. merchandise
b. obtain	2. develop
c. occurrence	3. unsafe
d. goods	4. principle
e. great	5. virtuous
f. materialize	6. trustworthy
g. dogmatic	7. reluctant
h. precarious	8. considerable
i. praiseworthy	9. incident
j. procrastinate	10. put off
	11. opinionated
	12. acquire

The verb *fix* is overused by many persons, as are the adjectives *fine* and *good*. In the following phrases, substitute a precise word for *fix* and list substitute descriptive terms for *fine* and *good*.

1. fix typewriter margins
2. a fine meal
3. a good worker
4. fix the dinner
5. a fine speaker
6. a fine supervisor
7. a good secretary
8. fix the broken space bar
9. a fine building
10. fix this error

E What words or phrases may be used for each of the following italicized expressions? For each expression, write a sentence using the word or phrase suggested.

1. to learn the *ABCs* of your job
2. remarks that *go against the grain*
3. *put one's shoulder to the wheel*
4. *take a fancy* to the work
5. *go the whole hog*
6. *get on one's high horse*
7. *rack one's brains*
8. *set no store by*
9. *make short work of*
10. *toot one's own horn*

F Write an antonym for each of the following words.

1. include 2. suave 3. accurate 4. win 5. pretentious

Editing Practice

Picture-Making Words Rewrite these sentences, substituting an exact, picture-making word for the italicized word or words in each item.

1. A career in aviation demands *fine* young men.
2. Consider carefully *all the sides* of the situation.
3. Mr. Wilson is a *grand* boss.
4. We all thought that Fred's arguments were *funny*.
5. The incentive plan gave the entire staff a *big* boost in morale.

Case Problem

The Uninformed Employees The Warner Paper Manufacturing Company makes cardboard boxes, as well as other paper products. The vice-president in charge of production, Tom Stewart, saw a demonstration of a new machine that folds boxes more efficiently than the one now owned by the company. While this new machine would not reduce labor, it would do a better job of folding. Mr. Stewart decided to try the new machine and ordered one on a trial basis. When the machine arrived, it was delivered to the room where it was going to be used. It was not unpacked because the manufacturer's representative could not set it up until the following week. Of course, most of the employees noticed the box and could see from the markings on the crate that it was a new machine. Soon rumors began to spread that this new machine would replace many of the employees and that they had better start looking for new positions.

Within one week after the machine arrived, Bill Brown, the head supervisor, came to Tom Stewart and told him of the discontent arising in the department because of lack of information about the new machine. Bill emphasized that the employees had many reasonable questions about the machine and the effect it would have on their work.

1. Who should handle this problem—Bill Brown or Tom Stewart?
2. What can he tell the employees in order to allay their fears?
3. What should have been done to prevent this problem from occurring?

Spelling Improvement

Why is correct spelling essential for a business communicator? Well, let's see.

In many cases, our opinions and judgments are often influenced by the visual impressions we receive. For instance, a rumpled sports jacket worn by a job applicant would probably cause the interviewer to make this eye-mind connection: sloppy appearance—sloppy work. Although such a judgment may not necessarily be sound, the applicant would nevertheless have little chance of being considered for the job opening.

Similarly, a spelling error in any business communication—be it a letter, an advertisement, a promotion leaflet, or whatever—runs the risk of setting up this eye-mind association: low-grade writing—low-grade company and product.

As a business writer, then, your status and your advancement possibilities may be affected by your ability, or inability, to spell words correctly. Therefore, to overcome your spelling difficulties, you should study and apply the principles presented in this section. You need to learn some guides to correct spelling; but more than that, you need to be alert to the spelling pitfalls that make consulting a dictionary imperative.

GUIDES TO CORRECT SPELLING

Because there are so many variations in the spelling of English words, a writer must command a knowledge of the principles that almost always hold true. He must know and be able to apply the following guides to correct spelling.

Final Y

Many of our common nouns end in *y: sky, company, attorney, valley.* The spelling of the plurals of these common nouns depends on whether the *y* is preceded by a consonant or a vowel. If preceded by a consonant, the *y* is changed to *i* and *es* is added: *sky, skies; company, companies.* If preceded by a vowel, only *s* is added: *attorney, attorneys; valley, valleys.*

Ei *and* Ie *Words*

Among the most frequently misspelled words are these: *receive, receipt, deceive, deceit, perceive, conceive, conceit, believe, belief, relieve,* and *relief.* The word *Alice* is the clue to their correct spelling. In *Alice* we see the combinations *li* and *ce.* These combinations can help you remember that the correct spelling after *l* is *ie;* after *c, ei*—*believe,* but *receive.*

Endings Ful, Ous, Ally, Ily

To spell correctly the endings *ful, ous, ally,* and *ily,* a writer needs to know that:

- The suffix *ful* has only one *l: careful, skillful, sorrowful.*
- The adjective ending with the sound *us* is spelled *ous: monotonous, serious, tremendous.*
- The ending *ally* has two *l*'s: *accidentally, generally, usually.*
- The ending *ily* has one *l: family, necessarily, readily.*

Doubling a Final Consonant

Knowing when to double and when not to double a final consonant is easy for the person who can spell by sound. The only hearing aid he needs is this: If the last syllable of the base word is accented, if the vowel sound in the last syllable is *short,* and if the suffix to be added begins with a vowel, double the final consonant. For example:

compel	compelled, compelling	omit	omitted, omitting
equip	equipped, equipping	prefer	preferred, preferring
occur	occurred, occurrence, occurring	regret	regretted, regretting

In the following words, the accent is on the *first* syllable; therefore, in the preferred spelling, the final consonant is *not* doubled.

benefit	benefited, benefiting
cancel	canceled, canceling (but *cancellation*)
differ	differed, differing
equal	equaled, equaling
marvel	marveled, marveling, marvelous
travel	traveled, traveler, traveling

Words of One Syllable

Ability to hear long and short sounds of vowels is needed to determine whether or not to double the final consonant of a one-syllable word. If the vowel sound is long, do not double; if short, do double the final consonant.

gripe	griping (long vowel sound)	grip	gripping (short sound)
hope	hoping (long vowel)	hop	hopping (short vowel)
mope	moping (long)	mop	mopping (short)
plane	planing (long)	plan	planning (short)

CHECKUP 1

Correct any spelling errors in these sentences.

1. We are not permitted to release the figures you requested.
2. Retailers have had a very successfull year.
3. Mr. Lynch's reference is not quite clear.
4. Unless we recieve your check by May 1, we must take legal action.
5. The strikers are hopping for an early settlement.
6. We hope your latest venture turns out satisfactorily.
7. Do you have all the supplys you need for this project?
8. Your action placed us in a most ridiculus position.

DICTIONARY "ALERTS"

Good spellers are not necessarily those who can pluck out of their memories the correct spelling of all words they write. A much more likely possibility is that they know where the spelling pitfalls lie and therefore are alert to the need for consulting a dictionary.

The most common spelling pitfalls are presented here so that you, too, will be alert to the tricky combinations that are the nemesis of so many writers. Remember: If you are not positive of the spelling of words containing these prefixes and suffixes, *use your dictionary.*

Word Beginnings

Words beginning with the prefixes *per, pur* and *ser, sur* present a spelling obstacle because they sound alike. If you are not absolutely sure of the correct spelling of any given word, check a dictionary. Study the following words.

percolate	purchase	sermon	surface
perplex	purpose	servant	surplus
persist	pursuit	service	surtax

Word Endings

There are ten groups of word endings that are tricky because they have similar sounds or because they may be pronounced carelessly. The spelling of these endings, however, differs. Do not try to guess at the spelling of words with the following endings.

Unt, Uns   If these endings were clearly enunciated as *ant, ance, ent, ence,* they would present no problem for the person who can spell by ear. However, because they are so often sounded *unt* and *uns* and because there are so many words with these endings, they are a spelling danger spot. They must be spelled by eye, not by ear. Some common words having these endings are the following:

accountant	avoidance	competent	absence
descendant	perseverance	dependent	existence
reluctant	remittance	obedient	interference
tenant	resistance	permanent	violence

Uhble, Uhbility   *Uhble,* which might be *able* or *ible,* is another spelling trap. The alert writer consults a dictionary in order to avoid misspelling this ending. Some common *uhble* and *uhbility* words are the following:

attainable	acceptability	collectible	feasibility
payable	availability	deductible	flexibility
receivable	mailability	indelible	plausibility
returnable	probability	reversible	visibility

Shun, Shus   The ending *shun* might be spelled *tion, sion,* or even *cian, tian, sian, cion,* or *xion.* The ending *shus* might be *cious* or *tious.* Learn the spelling of the words listed here; but at the same time, remember never to trust a *shun* or a *shus* ending.

attention	complexion	conscious	audacious
collision	extension	precious	conscientious
connection	suspension	suspicious	pretentious
ignition	suspicion	technician	propitious

Shul, Shent   The ending that sounds like *shul* is sometimes spelled *cial* and sometimes *tial.* A *shent* ending might be *cient* or *tient.* Look at the following words and learn how they are spelled, but never take chances on the spelling of any word ending in *shul* or *shent.*

artificial	essential	ancient	patient
beneficial	partial	deficient	proficient
judicial	substantial	efficient	quotient

Ize, Kul   The ending *ize* might be spelled *ize* or *ise,* or even *yze*—as in *analyze.* A *kul* ending could be *cal* or *cle.* An expert writer, therefore, never trusts the spelling of these word endings. If he has the slightest doubt as to their spelling, he checks a dictionary. Study the following *ize* and *kul* words.

apologize	advertise	electrical	article
criticize	enterprise	identical	obstacle
realize	merchandise	mechanical	spectacle
specialize	surprise	technical	vehicle

Ar(y), Er(y), Or(y) *Stationary* and *stationery* end with the same sound, but they are spelled differently. Words that end in *ar(y), er(y),* or *or(y)* should be recognized as spelling hazards, and the business communicator should check their spelling. He should memorize the spelling of the following words.

calendar	advertiser	debtor
grammar	adviser	exhibitor
customary	transformer	inventory

Seed Although only a few words have *seed* endings, they are frequently written incorrectly because the ending has three different spellings. When studying the following list of *seed* words, memorize these facts: (1) The only word ending in *sede* is *supersede,* and (2) the only words ending in *ceed* are *exceed, proceed,* and *succeed.* All other *seed* words, then, must be spelled *cede.*

sede	*ceed*	*cede*	
supersede	exceed	accede	precede
	proceed (but *procedure*)	cede	recede
	succeed	concede	secede
		intercede	

CHECKUP 2

What is the correct spelling of the words enclosed in parentheses?

1. You are to (proseed) in accordance with the (preseeding) directions.
2. (Reversuhble) raincoats do double duty.
3. We are all prone to (critisize) public officials.
4. Bill's outstanding characteristic is his (perseveruns).
5. We are unable to grant you any (extenshun) of time.
6. Are those signatures (identikul)?

YOUR SPELLING VOCABULARY

A business writer cannot afford the time-consuming interruptions that are caused by having to verify spellings frequently. He must, therefore, be sure of the correct spelling of the words used most often in his communications.

The "Spelling 400" listed in the Appendix of this textbook will serve as a foundation for developing a good spelling vocabulary. But knowing how to spell these words requires more than rote memorization. You must analyze each word and fix in your mind its peculiarities, as illustrated by the analyses of the following twenty words.

accommodate (two *c's*—two *m's*)	occasion (two *c's*—one *s*)
aggressive (two *g's*—two *s's*)	occurred (two *c's*—two *r's*)
believe (*ie*)	precede (*cede*)
chief (*ie*)	privilege (*vile*)
convenient (*ven*—*ient*)	proceed (*ceed*)
definite (*fi*)	receive (*ei*)
develop (no final *e*)	recommend (one *c*—two *m's*)
embarrass (two *r's*—two *s's*)	repetition (*pe*)
forty (only *four* word without *u*)	separate (*par*)
ninth (only *nine* word without *e*)	until (only one *l*)

COMMUNICATION PROJECTS

Practical Application

A Without using a dictionary, write the required derivatives of the words enclosed in parentheses.

1. (Incident), we talked with your buyer at the convention.
2. Your (defer)-payment plan is excellent.
3. We are now (scrape) the bottom of the files for promotional ideas.
4. Mirrors with (bevel) edges were missing from the June 8 shipment.
5. The (pulley) we ordered have not yet been delivered.
6. We think that your advertisement is (deceive) the public.
7. Your front counter should display jewelry, scarves, and like (sundry).
8. This is a most (moment) decision for us to make.
9. We are (scrap) manual machines and replacing them with electric machines.
10. A correspondence consultant can make many (help) suggestions.
11. You would do well not to act too (hasty).
12. Your account is (pay) on the first of each month.
13. We did not intend that our statement be taken (literal).
14. Our freezer is filled with (turkey).
15. There is no substitute for (care) checking.

B Make any needed spelling corrections in these sentences.

1. Although the scolding was embarrassing to all of us, the incident called for a reprimand.
2. You are to be congratulated on your perserverence.
3. We are grateful to you for accomodating us so quickly.
4. Make a list of the accounts that we consider uncollectible.
5. This is the ninth application we have received from persons over fourty.
6. At that price, the retailer will realise very little profit.
7. We recommend that you make a servay.
8. Eleanor is an exceptionally competant secretary.
9. All advertisers will be exhibitors at the boat show.
10. Mr. O'Brien's contention is that the expansion plans are not complete.
11. Please write the city and the state on seperate lines.
12. A definite trend will develope very soon.
13. On file cards, the last name preceeds the first name.
14. Mr. Gray handles all our technicle problems.
15. Doing business with you is indeed a privelege.

C Correct any spelling errors you find in this letter.

Dear Mr. Adams:

We were sorry to learn that you were inconvenienced by delayed shipment of your order No. 267.

Immediately upon receipt of your letter, we proceeded to check; and we found that the shipping date on your invoice was incorrect. But our chief shipping clerk has now devised a system for insuring that no such mistake can be made in the future.

You can be sure, Mr. Adams, that there will be no repetition of this unfortunate occurrence.

Sincerely,

Editing Practice

Why Be Trite?   Rewrite these sentences, using fresh and different words for the italicized trite expressions.

1. *After all is said and done,* there is little that we can do to reduce excise taxes.
2. For the past month, Mr. Miller has looked as if he were *dead on his feet.*
3. There is more to Cooper's plan than *meets the eye.*
4. Unless we receive your check by June 1, we shall be forced to take *drastic action.*
5. Writers who are experts in their profession are *few and far between.*

Case Problem

Leading a Discussion   Jim Ford was chairman of the dance committee for the Business Club at Miller Business College. The committee was meeting to plan the annual graduation dance, and Donna Allen made a suggestion to get a name band to play for the dance. Jim did not think the suggestion was feasible, since a name band would cost more than they would take in through the sale of tickets. However, Jim, as chairman, did not want to oppose any suggestions made by the members of the committee. He hoped someone in the group would say something in opposition to the suggestion, but nothing was said by any of the committee members except that they thought it was a good idea.

1. What is the function of a chairman?
2. Should Jim let the group go ahead with the suggestion even though it will certainly be a failure?
3. What can Jim say to get the group to see the fallacy of the suggestion without appearing as though he is trying to force his own opinion on the group?

CHAPTER

2

Receiving
Communications

5 | Developing Listening Skill

All communication consists of a two-way process—the sending of a message and the receiving of that message. In written communication, the sender is the writer; the receiver, the reader. There can be no communication, of course, when a written message is not read. In oral communication, the sender is the speaker; the receiver, the listener. If the listener does not hear and understand what is spoken, again there is no communication. The effectiveness of all communication depends upon the proper functioning of the sending and the receiving units.

THE NEED FOR LISTENING SKILL

Surveys of communication habits reveal that the majority of people spend most of their communication time listening. One survey found that in a typical working day, communication time was used as follows: 9 percent for writing, 16 percent for reading, 30 percent for speaking, and 45 percent for listening. Another survey showed that 11 percent of communication time was spent in writing, 4 percent in reading, 22 percent in speaking, and 63 percent in listening. Although the results of these surveys do not agree exactly, one fact is significant: *Listening occupies more time than any other communication activity.* The average business employee spends approximately 70 percent of his working day in some communication activity, and nearly half of this communication time is spent in listening. Yet research indicates that most of us listen with only about 25 percent efficiency! [1]

Listening and the Business Worker

Efficient listening habits contribute to business success. In fact, many business workers must rely on listening skill to carry out their daily assignments. The telephone operator, for example, must listen carefully to be able to fulfill correctly the many instructions she receives daily from people placing calls.

The salesman must listen carefully to determine the desires of his customers. Have you ever had an experience similar to this one? You enter a store and ask the salesclerk for a cardigan sweater. The clerk appears to have received your message, and he soon returns with a sweater in your size. Much to your annoyance, however, he has brought you a pullover sweater. Now you have to tell him again that you want a sweater that buttons down the front. The clerk's poor listening habits have caused you unnecessary delay and have made extra work for him. Such incidents are much too frequent in the business world today. For example, a survey by a large retail stores organization indicated that 68 percent of the customers lost by the stores took their business elsewhere because sales personnel were indifferent to customers' needs. [2]

[1] Ralph G. Nichols and Leonard A. Stevens, *Are You Listening?* McGraw-Hill Book Company, New York, 1957, pp. ix, 6, 8.
[2] Ibid., pp. 167-168.

No business worker is immune to the need for effective listening, because every business worker—whether secretary, accountant, machine operator, or clerk—receives oral instructions and information from co-workers, superiors, and customers. Failure to listen properly results in misunderstandings and errors, both of which are costly to businesses in terms of goodwill, time, and money.

Management, too, can benefit from effective listening practices. An article in *Fortune* magazine, dealing with the importance of communication in business management, called listening "the most overlooked tool of management!" [1] Many prominent individuals and groups agree with this premise. There is common agreement that leadership can be demonstrated best through effective listening and that the employer who gives orders but does not listen to his men does not know what his employees think. When employees feel they have no voice with management, they may turn to their fellow employees to express themselves.

Effective listening by management usually results in many benefits for business. Sympathetic listening can help to establish good employee relations and to settle grievances arising from real or imagined irritants. Furthermore, employees often contribute time- and money-saving ideas to business when they know that management will listen to their suggestions. "By far, the most effective method of tapping the ideas of subordinates is sympathetic listening in the many day-to-day informal contacts within the department and outside the work place." [2]

ACTIVE VERSUS PASSIVE LISTENING

There are two types of listening: active and passive. When we listen passively, we absorb just enough of the speaker's words to keep the conversation going. We can get by with passive listening in a casual conversation with friends, in a telephone chat with a relative, or in a discussion while playing cards. In such situations, it makes little difference whether or not we actually hear and absorb every word. However, in the business office and in all business settings, active listening is required.

Active listening means concentrating on what is being said, absorbing as much as possible, and *participating mentally* in what is heard. Participating mentally calls for mentally summarizing the speaker's words while you are listening to him.

You must be able to determine when you can get by with passive listening and when you must be an active listener. Will it be to your advantage to remember what is being said? Are the speaker's remarks likely to result in your taking some sort of action? If the answer to either of these questions is "Yes," you must listen actively. The salesman who must know the customer's wishes, the bank teller who needs to know what denomination of bills and coins the depositor wants in change, the clerk at the airline reservation desk who needs to know where the traveler is going and when he would like to arrive—all must listen actively.

[1] "Is Anybody Listening?" *Fortune*, vol. 42, pp. 77-83ff., September, 1950.
[2] Earl G. Planty and William Machaver, "Stimulating Upward Communication," in M. Joseph Dooher and Vivienne Marquis, *Effective Communication on the Job*, American Management Association, New York, 1956, p. 155.

LISTENING AND READING

The average person speaks between 125 and 150 words per minute; the good listener, on the other hand, can comprehend speech at a rate of more than 300 words per minute.[1] Thus, it is easy for the brain to take a nap or to indulge in mental side trips while it is waiting to receive more information!

People find it nearly impossible to read thoughtfully while they are daydreaming or while their minds are crowded with problems. They know they must concentrate on what they are reading, or they will have to reread to comprehend the message fully. However, most people find it easy to focus their attention on things other than the speaker's words while they listen. They assume that they can receive the spoken message without participating actively in the communication process. The listener often listens halfheartedly, even though he knows he cannot go back and listen again to a spoken message.

During the last two decades much progress has been made toward improving reading habits and comprehension. In fact, it's now possible for the alert reader to speed up his reading rate and, hopefully, to raise his level of comprehension. Because skill in listening is now recognized by many as an equally important aspect of communication, steps are being taken to improve the ability to listen. Listening-improvement programs are being included as part of high school and college courses, as well as part of executive and supervisory development courses. In addition, books and magazine articles are being written about the techniques of correct listening.

HOW TO IMPROVE YOUR LISTENING SKILLS

The first step toward becoming an effective listener is to determine your listening strengths and weaknesses. As a start in this direction, answer the following questions so that you can decide where to begin your self-improvement program.

1. Have you recently had your hearing acuity tested?
2. Do you avoid being distracted by outside sights and sounds when listening to someone speak?
3. Do you make it a point not to interrupt a speaker before he finishes a thought?
4. Do you avoid listening and doing something else (reading, for example) at the same time?
5. When people talk to you, do you concentrate on what they are saying instead of taking brain naps and mental excursions?
6. Do you listen for ideas and for feelings as well as for facts?
7. Do you look at the speaker when he is talking to you?
8. Do you feel that other people have something to contribute to your knowledge?
9. If something said by the speaker is not clear to you, do you ask him to repeat or to explain the point again?
10. Do you avoid being prejudiced by words and phrases used by the speaker?

[1]Nichols and Stevens, *op. cit.*, p. 78.

11. When someone is talking to you, do you try to make him think that you are paying attention even if you are not?
12. Can you tell by a person's appearance and delivery that he won't have anything to say that will be of interest to you?
13. Do you turn your attention elsewhere when you believe a speaker will not have anything of interest to say to you?
14. Do you have to ask the speaker to repeat what he has said because you cannot remember?
15. If you feel that it takes too much time and effort to understand something, do you try to avoid hearing it?

You should have answered "Yes" to the first ten questions and "No" to the last five questions. If you did not have a perfect score, perhaps the following suggestions can help you to begin your own listening-improvement program.

Develop the Proper Attitude Toward Listening

Listening is a strictly voluntary activity; no one can make a person listen unless he wants to listen. The main purpose of a lecture or a class discussion is learning; if a student wants to learn, he listens. If a stenographer wants to record all the words of the dictator, she listens. If a supervisor is eager to help employees solve their problems, he listens. A good listener tries to find something of interest in the speaker's message and attempts to sustain this interest. The supervisor who listens halfheartedly to employees' complaints doesn't really listen. He doesn't have a desire to listen, and he cannot be forced to listen.

To be a good listener—to want to hear what the other person has to say— you must first respect the speaker and his right to have his own point of view. Sometimes you will find it difficult to go along with ideas that are contrary to yours. Whether or not you should stick to your own point of view or change your thinking can be determined only after you have listened to what the speaker has to say. If you can learn the reasons for the ideas presented, you will be in a better position to make a decision. Such decisions may call for either changing your own thinking or influencing the thinking of the other person by showing him specifically where his ideas are factually inaccurate or illogical.

Finally, a good listener is objective about personalities. He does not let mannerisms, voice, speech patterns, or other personality characteristics distract him from what the speaker is saying. His attention is focused on the *words* and *ideas* of the speaker rather than on the speaker's appearance or manner of speaking.

Prepare Yourself Physically for Effective Listening

Here are some suggestions that you can easily follow in physically preparing yourself to listen effectively.

- If you have difficulty hearing, have a doctor check your hearing acuity and suggest any necessary remedial steps.
- Sit where the conditions for hearing will be the best for you. If your mind wanders easily, try to find a place where you will not have visual or auditory distractions.
- Look at the speaker while he is talking.
- Have the seating arrangement and room ventilation as comfortable as possible.

Prepare Yourself Mentally for Effective Listening

An effective listener is mentally prepared to listen. This statement implies several things. The listener must understand what the speaker is saying. Therefore, he must have a vocabulary that includes not only words in general usage but also words common to his trade or profession. One unfamiliar word can mean that the listener will not understand the whole message or that he will incorrectly interpret all or part of the message. For example, a secretary asked an office boy to bring her a *ream* of typewriting paper. The office boy did not know the meaning of the word *ream*—all the packages in the supply room were marked "500 Sheets." The office boy, therefore, had to go back to the secretary to ask her what *ream* meant. An efficient listener should, if possible, ask a speaker to explain unfamiliar words. However, if such interruptions are frequent, the listener will be embarrassed.

The efficient listener prepares ahead of time for attending a lecture or a speech where the subject is known in advance. By doing as much reading about the topic as possible, he prepares himself to listen better and to derive greater benefit from the speaker's message.

Many words in the English language have multiple meanings, and the efficient listener realizes that it isn't always possible to know which of several meanings the speaker intends. For example, a secretary may be requested to *duplicate* a letter for her boss. Of course, a letter may be duplicated by using carbon paper, by photocopying, or by running off copies on a fluid or a stencil duplicator. To make certain that he understands the intention of the speaker, a good listener should ask questions rather than make assumptions that may be incorrect. By asking either "Is this what you mean?" or "Did I understand you correctly?" the listener avoids problems that may arise because of misinterpretation. The secretary in the example above should have asked her boss a question such as, "Would you like five photocopies?"

Develop Habits That Contribute to Effective Listening

Skill in any activity is based on acquiring habits that contribute to the development of that skill. A skilled typist develops correct habits of sitting, key stroking, and reaching, among others. A skilled swimmer practices correct habits of movement and breathing. So, too, the effective listener must develop certain habits that will contribute to the development of his listening skill. What do these habits include?

> Ability to concentrate
> Alertness in grasping ideas
> Ability to coordinate ideas
> Ability to take notes when necessary

Concentrating Because the typical listener can comprehend at a much faster rate than most speakers talk, the listener frequently has difficulty in concentrating and, as a result, "tunes out" the speaker. The listener takes mental excursions, daydreams, and relaxes his brain during these lapses. In addition, he permits distractions, such as noises and movements, to take his attention away from the speaker's words. A distracted listener, therefore, can become hopelessly confused when he tries to "tune in" again, because he has lost part of what was said. Concentration, therefore, requires discipline and sustained, undivided attention. What, then, *should* you be doing during the time when your mind is waiting for the speaker's words to catch up to it?

Grasping Ideas When you listen to a speaker, try to think along with him and to look for the main points of his message. When he conveys an essential idea, fact, or piece of information, rephrase it mentally in your own words. This process will help you to understand and to remember what you hear. For example, the following selection demonstrates what you might be thinking while the speaker is talking.

What the Speaker Is Saying

I have read many books on selling. There are books that bring up every possible selling situation and give you ways and means to meet those situations—several hundred of them perhaps. But when you get in the presence of a prospect, you cannot recall any of them. However, you *can* remember this formula: ask yourself the simple question, "Just what does this prospect *want*?" If you cannot find out any other way, ask him. It is often that simple. Too many salesmen think they must do *all* of the talking. Avoid it. Listen at least half the time and ask questions. It is only in this way you can uncover unsatisfied wants.[1]

What You Are Saying to Yourself

You can't memorize ways of meeting every selling situation presented in books. You should find out what the prospect wants. Ask him what he wants, if necessary. You don't need to do all the talking—listen half the time and ask questions.

As you hear each idea presented, weigh it in terms of its validity. To yourself, you might ask and answer such questions as "What has this to do with me?" "Are things exactly as he says they are?" "Is he leaving anything out? If so, why?" "How can I use this material?" "Why is the speaker so aroused that he is pounding his fist on the table?" "Has he confused solid evidence with emotionalism?" "Is his illustration typical or is it an exaggerated example?" "Is the illustration out of date and no longer applicable?"

When the speaker takes time to move from one point to another, review mentally what he has said. In this way, you can improve both your comprehension and your retention of the message while keeping your mind from wandering.

Another way to use extra listening time is to think ahead and to anticipate what the speaker is going to say next. If you select a point that is actually made by the speaker, you will remember it longer. If you select a point that the speaker does not make, you can compare the speaker's point with the one you selected. In this way, you will learn by comparison and contrast.

Coordinating Ideas Another useful activity that the listener can perform is the coordination of ideas and information that contribute to the main idea. For example, read the speech excerpt shown at the top of page 48. Note that only the italicized words in the paragraph are part of the main idea. The other sentences are not separate ideas but are sidelights that add color, interest, and details to the main idea.

[1]William Phillips Sandford and Willard Hayes Yeager, *Effective Business Speech*, McGraw-Hill Book Company, New York, 1960, p. 176.

One of the major cost factors in operating a modern business office is absenteeism and tardiness. For instance, if an office with one thousand employees averages fifty absences a month and the average daily rate of pay is $25, the company loses $1,250 a month or $15,000 a year. Such a loss takes a big bite out of company profits.

In this paragraph, notice the words *For instance.* Speakers often provide the listener with cues that indicate whether an idea is a new one or whether it merely adds support to an idea already presented.

Note-taking   In many instances, the listener must take notes in order to retain for future reference the information he hears. The student who attends a lecture, the secretary who takes a message over the telephone for her boss, and the accountant who receives a set of oral instructions from his supervisor are but a few examples of people who must take notes as they listen. Taking notes is actually an extension of active listening participation and consists of putting on paper, in your own words, the essential ideas and information provided by the speaker. Do not spend too much time taking notes, or you will miss the heart of the message. Above all, you should never attempt to take verbatim notes. Proper note-taking, however, can contribute to effective concentration, to learning, and to remembering. Here are some suggestions for taking notes.

- Prepare in advance by reading as much as you can about the subject on which you are to hear someone speak.
- Sit in a location where you can hear and see without strain.
- Come equipped for note-taking with plenty of notepaper, a good pen, and an extra pencil or two.
- Use a firm, uncluttered writing surface.
- Label your notes so that you can identify them later without difficulty.
- Listen for such speaker's cues as "first," "second," and "third"; "another important consideration"; "finally"; "the most significant thing"; "on the other hand"; "in summary"; as well as questions posed by the speaker, pauses, voice intonations, and gestures.
- Flag important parts of your notes with brackets, underscores, arrows, or indentions.
- Listen for special instructions.
- Read over your notes promptly.

Efficient listening, like efficient reading, requires practice. Now that you have been provided with several suggestions for improving your listening skill, you should avail yourself of every opportunity to put these suggestions into practice.

COMMUNICATION PROJECTS

Practical Application

A   Reexamine the questions (pages 44-45) used to determine your listening strengths and weaknesses. Indicate the reason for the "Yes" or "No" answer to each question.

B　Your instructor will read a selection to you. Listen very carefully, taking no notes as you listen. After the reading, your instructor will ask you to write the answers to several questions about the selection.

C　A good listener is able to distinguish facts from opinions. On a separate sheet of paper indicate which of the following statements are opinions and which can be verified as facts.

1. You will enjoy using our product.
2. You are in good hands when you use our insurance protection.
3. This clock will run for 40 hours without rewinding.
4. Mary is wearing the prettiest hat I have ever seen.
5. This car gets up to 36 miles per gallon of gasoline.
6. The weather today is pleasant.
7. No other typewriter has such beautiful lines as this one.
8. Our electric light bulb is guaranteed to burn a minimum of 350 hours.
9. The textbook we are using in American history is very interesting.
10. The textbook we are using in American history is accurate.

D　Your instructor will give you a set of directions. Listen to them very carefully, but take no notes. You will then follow the directions given.

E　List twenty words that affect you emotionally by evoking such feelings as pleasure, sadness, satisfaction, or horror. Be prepared to discuss the following questions:

1. Why do certain words emotionally affect individuals?
2. Why might words of this type have different connotations to different students?

F　Your instructor will give you directions for an exercise to determine your span of listening attention.

Editing Practice

Contextually Speaking　Some of the following sentences contain words that are out of context. Correct each sentence that contains a contextually incorrect word. Write *OK* for any correct sentence.

1. Personality is one of the most important facts in securing and in holding a position.
2. Another infringement of your installment payment was due last Friday.
3. We are counting on your continued corporation.
4. Unless we receive payment within ten days, we shall have to discriminate filling your orders.
5. The codicil is most specific about the form of payment.

Case Problem

The Careless Clerk　Tom Williams was a reservation clerk for Westcoast Airlines. One afternoon he answered the telephone in his customary fashion by asking, "May I help you?" He was told that a Mr. Robert Powell would like to make reservations on a flight to Seattle, Washington, that would get him there in time for a 5 p.m. dinner meeting with a very important client. Tom checked the flight bookings for the date and time requested and found that the only space he had available was on a flight leaving at 7 a.m. the same day. There was a 2:10 p.m. flight, arriving in Seattle at 4:15 p.m., but there was no space available. Mr. Powell had a meeting to attend that morning and could not leave before noon.

Tom said he would put Mr. Powell's name on the waiting list for the 2:10 flight and would notify him if there were any cancellations. He told Mr. Powell that there was a good chance of getting a seat on the 2:10 flight, since his name would be the first one on the waiting list. Mr. Powell thought this arrangement would be fine, gave Tom the necessary information about contacting him, and hung up. Just as soon as Tom hung up, the customer standing in front of him started asking for information regarding other flights; and Tom neglected to record Mr. Powell's name on the proper waiting list.

When Mr. Powell had not received any word regarding his reservation by the day preceding the flight, he asked his secretary to check with the airline office. The clerk who answered the telephone referred to the waiting list but, of course, did not find Mr. Powell's name among the nine or ten names listed. Because there were so many names already on the waiting list, it was extremely doubtful whether more than the first two or three could be accommodated on that flight. When Mr. Powell heard the news from his secretary, he became extremely angry and telephoned the general manager of Westcoast Airlines to register his complaint.

1. Was Mr. Powell justified in his complaint? Why or why not?
2. What should the general manager say to Mr. Powell in an attempt to smooth out the situation?
3. What advice should the general manager give to Tom Williams?

 # Developing Reading Skill

One communication skill—reading—has played a major role in your educational achievement throughout your scholastic life. How effectively you read has determined to a great extent how well you performed in nearly every subject you have taken and, therefore, has determined what kind of final grade you have received. Even typewriting skill is affected by reading skill. Inefficient readers seldom make good typists because they cannot read the copy fast enough or do not read it accurately.

Reading will continue to play an important role in determining how efficiently you perform. Whether you are in a clerical position that requires you to check one set of figures against another or in an executive position and can't see the top of your desk because it is covered with periodicals, reports, and a multitude of other reading matter awaiting your attention, reading is certain to be an essential part of your job.

So whether you are a student or a business worker, your skill in reading is just as important as other communication skills—perhaps even more important! The guides to reading improvement presented in this section will help you develop your reading skill.

ELEMENTS OF READING SKILL

First, what is involved in reading skill? Two elements make up reading skill—speed and comprehension. How fast you are able to read will determine how much material you can cover in the time you are able to devote to reading. As a student, you have often been required to read a great deal for your courses. The slow reader must spend every evening and many hours on weekends to cover all the assigned reading—and still he might not be able to complete it all! The fast reader would undoubtedly have time left over for personal pleasure and relaxation.

The business worker is paid for producing, whether what he produces is a typewritten business letter or decisions to establish a branch store in Kalamazoo. Therefore, he cannot devote his entire working day to reading only, no matter how important the reading matter may be. And, of course, the more a business worker can read and absorb, the more information he can acquire to help him make decisions or perform particular tasks.

Another element of reading skill that is even more important than reading speed is comprehension—understanding what you read. Regardless of how fast you read, if you don't comprehend what you are reading, no worthwhile purpose is served. Therefore, you must fully understand the meanings of the words used and the implications of the thoughts being expressed by the writer.

Are you able to read as fast as it is possible for you to read? Do you fully comprehend the material that you read, or do such factors as a poor vocabulary or improper reading habits block your ability to receive accurately the message conveyed? Unless you can answer "Yes" to both these questions, you should attempt to improve your reading skill, for any improvement you can make will contribute to your success as a business worker.

Is it too late to improve your reading skill? Not if you are willing to work at it. Many people have vastly improved both their reading speed and their comprehension through reading-improvement courses offered by schools, by business organizations, and by private institutes devoted specifically to reading improvement. Those who have serious reading deficiencies or those who wish to make great strides in reading improvement should enroll in one of these organized programs. However, there are several things you can do on your own to improve your reading skill.

GUIDES TO READING IMPROVEMENT

Study the following five-step program for improving reading skill.

Check Physical Factors

The condition of your eyes plays an important role in reading effectiveness. You should have your eyes checked regularly by a competent eye specialist, particularly if you wear glasses or show any signs of eye difficulty, such as blurred vision, smarting eyes, or the need to hold copy either very close to your eyes or at arm's length.

Lighting conditions also affect the ease with which copy can be read. Natural light, of course, is preferred. The best artificial light for reading is an indirect light. In either case, the light should fall on the copy, not on your eyes, and care should be taken that there are no glaring or shiny spots anywhere near you.

For the best reading conditions, you should sit comfortably in a well-ventilated, not overheated, room. The room should be free of distracting sights and sounds.

Whether or not you wear glasses, you should practice good eye hygiene. Here are some suggestions.

- Rest your eyes every half hour or so either by looking into the distance or by closing them for a few minutes.
- Exercise your eyes, especially when you are doing close work and your eyes begin feeling tired. One good exercise for strengthening the eye muscles is to rotate the eyes slowly without moving your head. Move your eyes far to the right; then to the left; then up; and finally, down.
- Avoid reading when you are in bright sunlight or while you are riding in a vehicle.
- Have eye injuries or sties attended to immediately by a physician.

Select Proper Reading Technique

The way you read should be adapted to the material you are reading and to your purpose in reading it. In particular, you should adjust your reading speed to your purpose in reading.

Reading for Pleasure   If you are reading materials such as novels, magazine articles, and newspaper items, you do not need to absorb every detail or remember many specific facts. Therefore, you should be able to read quite rapidly, at a rate of around 400 words a minute.

Reading for Specific Data   When you are looking for a specific name, date, or other item of information, you should be able, by skimming a page, to locate the item without reading every word. When you wish to determine the principal ideas in reading matter, perhaps because you want to decide whether or not to read it, skim each page and stop only to read significant phrases.

Reading for Retention or Analysis   This kind of reading includes textbook reading or other study reading requiring either the memorization of facts or a thorough understanding of the meaning that you can interpret, explain, or apply to other situations. Reading for such retention or analysis calls for active participation by the reader and may call for slower reading. Active participation in reading will be discussed later.

Copying and Checking   This kind of reading includes work such as proofreading typewritten or printed copy or the checking of invoices or the copying necessary to prepare punched cards or tapes. Such reading must be carefully done, with concentration and attention to meaning and accuracy. One undetected error can be very costly. Unless the following were read for meaning, the error would not be discovered:

> The principle of $324 must be paid by January 5.

Checking one copy against another or one column of figures against another calls for a high degree of concentration, for one must read two sets of items simultaneously.

Develop a Wide Vocabulary

The greater your vocabulary, the faster you will be able to read and the better you will be able to understand what you read. You will not need to stop to look up word meanings so often, and you will not be so likely to misinterpret the meaning that is intended, particularly if a word has many shades of meaning. Refer to Section 1 for suggestions on building your vocabulary.

Increase Reading Speed

As previously discussed, how rapidly you should read depends upon the type of material you are reading and the purpose for which you are reading. Most "light" reading should be at the rate of at least 400 words a minute. Most studying and other serious reading should be at the rate of at least 200 to 250 words a minute. Here are five suggestions for helping you improve your reading speed.

Read in Thought Units   Reading in phrases, rather than word by word, forces your eyes to take in more words at each pause. With fewer pauses on each line of print, you naturally read faster. For example, read the following lines:

1. t m l q w z
2. books chair driver down
3. read in thought units

Certainly you had no difficulty in reading each of these lines, but each succeeding line should have been read faster. In the first line, you had to read individual letters; in the second, you read individual words; but in the third, your eyes could encompass and read the whole phrase with one glance.

You should be able to read a line in a newspaper column with only one or two eye pauses and to read a book-width line with not more than four or five pauses. Read the following sentence, noticing the difference in speed when you read word by word and when you read in phrases.

Word by Word   A / good / reader / is / more / likely / to / understand / and / remember / what / he / reads / if / he / actively / participates / in / what / he / is / reading.

Phrases   A good reader / is more likely / to understand and remember / what he reads / if he actively participates / in what he is reading.

Keep Your Eyes Moving From Left to Right   Do not allow yourself to go back and read a phrase a second time. These backward movements of the eyes, called *regressions*, slow the reader and are often habit-forming. Force yourself to concentrate and to get the meaning of a phrase the first time. To do so demands practice, discipline, and the elimination of all distractions that might interfere with your reading.

Avoid Vocalization   Don't spell or pronounce the words you are reading, not even silently. Such vocalization means you can read silently only as fast as you can read aloud.

Read Only Word Beginnings   Many words can be identified by reading only the beginnings. For example, you can easily identify the complete words from these first syllables: *remem—, sepa—, funda—, educa—*. You can tell from the rest of the sentence what the exact ending of each word should be; for example, *remembering, remembrance; separate, separately, separation: He remem—(remembered) how to sepa—(separate) the parts.*

Practice Rapid Reading   By exercising your willpower and by continually practicing rapid reading, you are certain to increase your reading speed. Reading, like any other skill, will improve with proper practice.

Increase Reading Comprehension

Even more important than reading speed to the student and business worker are comprehension (understanding) and retention (remembering). Many of the suggestions made for increasing reading speed will also contribute to greater comprehension. Some additional aids follow.

Scan or Preview the Material   Look over the material to be read, noting the main headings and subheadings, looking at illustrations, and reading captions and numbered portions. This preliminary survey will help you determine your purpose in reading, and it will also help reinforce the important points you want to remember.

Participate Actively in Your Reading   Try to relate what you are reading to what you already know. Keep in mind the problem you wanted to solve when you started to read. Not only do you need a high degree of concentration, but also you must search for the main ideas and for the way the author arranges these ideas to reach a conclusion.

Study all illustrative material, such as pictures, graphs, and charts, and also the footnotes; all these are designed to explain and amplify main ideas. Be sure, too, to read examples presented by the author. Often these examples will help to clarify an idea that at first may seem hazy to you. They will also help you remember main ideas.

Take Notes   If you own the book or magazine you are reading, you may wish to underline or otherwise mark some key words or phrases. You may also want to make marginal notes. If the publication is not yours, you may want to take notes in a notebook that you can refer to later.

How do you select the essential material for note-taking? Just record main ideas and related ideas. Never take verbatim notes, even if you know shorthand.

How do you find the main ideas? Usually, writers convey only one idea per paragraph. Often this main idea is in the first sentence, but sometimes it may be in the last sentence. Occasionally there may be two central ideas expressed in a key phrase or sentence within the paragraph. If you have difficulty finding a central idea, you may need to read the paragraph carefully two or three times. In addition to the central idea, you should also note facts, examples, and other ideas that explain, support, and develop the main idea.

Reread and Review   How often you reread or review the material you read will depend on its difficulty and on the use you plan to make of it. Often a quick skimming or rereading of your notes will be adequate for review if the first reading was done carefully.

If you will follow the suggestions made in this section and immediately begin a definite plan for reading improvement, you will find that not only will you be able to read more in the same amount of time, but you will also get more from what you read.

COMMUNICATION PROJECTS

Practical Application

 To test your reading speed, have someone time you with a stopwatch (or a watch with a second hand) as you read the following selection:

> Hot-rodders were once a menace to safety on the public highways, but most of them have now become both respectable and well respected for their help to other motorists. As a sport, hot-rodding got off to a hazardous start in the forties, when old cars were made into steel rams and the young drivers collected dents the way the outlaws used to collect notches on their guns. Some aimed their rolling junk heaps at one and all, and even at each other. A driver who might flinch from a collision was called a quitter. It

was a bad nightmare, and it was getting worse until, at last, parents and their friends got excited and began corrective actions.

One step taken in some towns was to set up, on a local airfield, a drag strip where hot-rodders could hold driving contests and exhibits. Civic leaders in some cities formed clubs at whose meetings young drivers could get help in the mechanics of building and driving a hot rod safely; some of the clubs issued neat plaques for the cars of members. Fine new magazines, with as much stress on safety and on service to stranded motorists as on the inventing of new paint jobs and body angles, caused interest in the sport to jump ahead and did much at the same time to attract many of the finest young drivers into a legion of Sir Galahads of the highway.

But the fate of our hot-rodders is a question mark for the future. Each time there is a driving discourtesy or an accident involving a young driver, fuel is lent to the fury of those who feel that hot-rodding is a hazard, that it expands to the danger point the ego of its fans, that it must be suppressed. Yet there are others who believe this sport can be kept safe and useful and that it should be developed further. They protest that it is not fair to criticize the entire field for the bad judgment of a few mavericks. They point proudly to the thousands of "wreckless" young drivers who star in the campaign to bring courtesy back into motoring and who know infinitely more than most of their dads do about what goes on under the hood of the modern automobile.[1] (380 words)

Note how long you took to read the selection above. Check your reading speed with the following chart. For example, if you read the above paragraphs in one minute, your reading speed is 380 words per minute; if it took you two minutes, your speed is 190 words per minute.

30 seconds	760 wpm	2½ minutes	152 wpm
1 minute	380 wpm	3 minutes	127 wpm
1½ minutes	260 wpm	3½ minutes	109 wpm
2 minutes	190 wpm	4 minutes	95 wpm

One good reading habit that will help you gain speed is to look only at the beginnings of familiar words rather than at the entire words. Test your ability to do this by reading as rapidly as possible the following paragraph, in which the endings of some familiar words have been omitted.

Prod__ improve__ is a widespread form of compet__ in the Amer__ econ__. Creat__ new prod__ and improv__ old prod__ have freq__ taken the pl__ of price compet__ as the princi__ bas__ for econ__ rivalry. Accord__, over the ye__ the range of prod__ and the oppor__ for the exer__ of consumer choi__ have stead__ broad__. For ex__, wool suits now com__ not on__ with other wool suits but al__ with ray__, Dac__, and cot__ suits. Contin__ multiplic__ of grades and varie__ of prod__ has incr__ the range of substit__ and inter-prod__ riv__.

Secretaries, typists, clerical workers, copy editors, and advertising copywriters must learn how to proofread carefully. Proofreading calls for the reading of each word not only for spelling but also for its meaning within the sentence. Proofread the following paragraphs, and on a separate sheet of paper, make a list of all the errors. Then rewrite the paragraphs so that they are free from error.

You letter of February 20 and the check for $506 were received today. We appreciates you promt attention in the handling of this paynent.

Please send us the letterhead stationary and have our account credit for the amount of our return.

[1]Rowe, Lloyd, and Winger, *Vocational Office Typing*, 191 Series, Second Edition, Book 2, McGraw-Hill Book Company, New York, 1967, p. 20.

The checking of amounts of money and other figures often results in errors because of reading carelessness. Compare the following two lists. Indicate which pairs of items do not agree.

List A	List B
1. 838754B	838754B
2. 2243887	2243387
3. $4697.54	$46979.54
4. 6833T79	6833T79
5. SM178871	SM178187
6. 654V133	645V133
7. WTRZK	WTZRK
8. January 17, 1946	January 17, 1964
9. 115 dozen at 61¾¢	115 dozen at 63¼¢
10. T168V142L987	T168V142L897

Editing Practice

Digesting a Letter   Secretaries and administrative assistants often read all incoming letters for their employers. When the employer is especially busy, he may ask his assistant or secretary to prepare a short digest (or summary) of each letter so that he won't have to read the entire message. Using incomplete sentences, write a digest of the following letter. Add a brief note to the effect that the typewriters were left for a trial period of one week and that they were returned at the end of the trial period.

Gentlemen:

Our client, the Reliable Typewriter Exchange, has placed in our hands for collection your account of $485 due on the purchase of two typewriters.

This bill should have been paid four weeks ago. In view of this fact, we must insist on a remittance by return mail. Otherwise, we shall be compelled to resort to legal proceedings, in accordance with my instructions.

Very truly yours,

Case Problem

The Bothersome Visitor   Sally Bowman is a receptionist and switchboard operator at the Lincoln Electrical Supply Company. One afternoon Michael Graham, who had an appointment to discuss a new product with Sally's boss, arrived at the office. However, because Sally's boss was in conference and would not be available for about ten minutes, Sally asked Mr. Graham to be seated until her boss was free. For a minute or two, Mr. Graham thumbed through one of the magazines lying on the table in the reception room. Then he started talking to Sally, who was not occupied at the switchboard that moment. Soon, however, the board lit up; but Mr. Graham continued talking to Sally. The flashing of the lights indicated that the calling parties were getting impatient because of the delay, but Sally did not know how to get Mr. Graham to stop talking to her so that she could attend to her duties.

1. What could Sally say to Mr. Graham so that he would not be offended when she interrupted him?
2. Suppose Mr. Graham continued talking. What should Sally do?

CHAPTER

3

Language
Structure

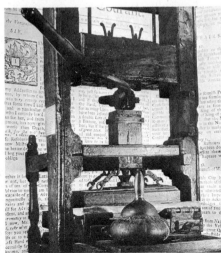

7 | These Changing Times

Would you go along with the statement that there can be little progress without some change? If you accept this generalization, you would also agree that the economic progress of our nation has involved—and, indeed, is still involving—multitudinous changes. In fact, if you were required to write a report on the business and industrial changes of even the past fifty years, you would be out of circulation for quite some time.

For instance, the accountant of earlier years computed in his head and recorded by hand. When calculators appeared on the market, they were thought to be the ultimate in rapid and accurate reckoning. But now we have computers that perform complex operations in seconds, and the potential of these computers is almost in the realm of science fiction.

Now consider all the changes that have occurred in methods of transportation, in various mass-communication areas, in service professions, in food packaging and distribution, and in many other sectors of our economy. Teenagers have seen some progress-making changes that seem miraculous to the older generation, such as faster and faster planes capable of carrying more and more passengers and freight. "Live by Satellite" television programs enable people to see what is going on in foreign countries when those events are taking place.

Without communication, however, there can be no progress. Every change, no matter how slight, is dependent on language—writing, speaking, reading, listening. You can readily understand that changing the design of an automobile, for instance, requires more than blueprints. Numerous letters and reports are written; whatever is written must be read; frequent conferences are held; and when you consider that planning is concerned with marketing as well as with manufacturing the product, the number and kinds of communications almost overwhelm the imagination.

Logically, then, we must expect that language itself has also seen some revisions that are in tune with changing times. Therefore, whenever you hear the term *standard English,* you will know that reference is being made to the clear, but also correct, English used by expert modern communicators.

STANDARD ENGLISH

Progress-making changes are worthwhile only when they serve a purpose—producing better goods more quickly, reducing the margin of error, promoting efficiency, building goodwill, and so on. Consequently, we can assume that there are good reasons for any changes made in the English language.

The assumption is correct. The purpose of standard English, the language of today, is to ensure the utmost clarity and accuracy of communication. Achievement of this purpose will increase profits by saving the time and money wasted on messages that confuse a listener or reader. The ability to communicate clearly and accurately prevents incidents that cause ill will and therefore helps to build goodwill.

If you will read thoughtfully the following discussion of standard English, you will know what it is—and what it is *not*.

Out-of-Style Usages

Some of the English principles that were taught in the early years of this century are no longer a part of our English courses—and with good reason. There were some principles that required the learning of many rules for alternate usages; but the differences were so unimportant that insistence on learning and following these rules fell into the category of "nitpicking." Because the intelligent mind rejects any unnecessary learning burden, the rules for unimportant differences were promptly forgotten, and the words whose usages they governed were used interchangeably.

As an illustration, consider the use of *shall* and *will*. The writer of today does not have to stop to review rules before he decides which is correct— "*Shall* (or *Will*) you attend the banquet on Friday?" Furthermore, if you received a letter containing the question "Shall you attend the banquet on Friday?" the *shall* would strike you as being a little stilted. Yet, according to one out-of-style rule, *shall* would be the correct choice for this particular question.

There are other types of rules that are also now out of style; for instance, this rule: "Do not use the apostrophe and *s* to form the possessive of inanimate things; use an *of* phrase." Application of the rule would mean that the title *Today's Secretary* is incorrect and must be written *The Secretary of Today*. Observing this apostrophe rule would destroy the effectiveness, the pungency, of much of our writing, as evidenced by having to write "You would do well to study the business of our nation," instead of the smoother and more forceful "You would do well to study our nation's business."

In the Twilight Zone

Just as each day has a period that is neither night nor day, but somewhere between, so are there English principles that are in the process of changing from "definitely incorrect" to "well, maybe," and in time to come they may very well be considered "correct." Their place in the Twilight Zone is dictated by common usage, which means their increasing use by educated persons.

Changes in the English language, however, take place very slowly; it may be many years before common usage is universal enough to promote any principle to the status of being correct. In the meantime, a knowledgeable communicator conforms to a common-usage trend only when such conformity suits his audience or when it accomplishes some clearly formulated purpose.

Using the preposition *like* for the conjunction *as* is a prime example of a Twilight Zone principle. As you probably know, a conjunction, not a preposition, must be used to introduce a clause; yet frequently you hear or read such expressions as these: *like I said before, like you did yesterday, like it was going to rain*. Although quite commonly heard, the use of *like* for *as* is not universally accepted, as witness the nationwide storm of criticism that arose when a leading tobacco company used as part of its slogan, "like a cigarette should" instead of "as a cigarette should." And most interesting is the thought that an enormous amount of free advertising resulted from seeing in print an English violation that many of the protesters probably violated in their everyday speech.

A lesson to be learned here is that a Twilight Zone expression might pass unnoticed when used orally, but that the same expression when written could expose the writer to censure.

Nonstandard English

Do not let the preceding discussion lead you into thinking that, as far as English usage is concerned, "Anything goes." While it is true that some principles are no longer in use and that other principles may be in the process of change, it is also true that a standard of quality in English usage does exist.

In fact, the business world puts a premium on the ability to write and speak Standard English. Why? Well, a business writer or speaker wants his readers or audience to pay attention to his message, not to his grammar. Hence he uses Standard English, the usage customarily associated with business communication and the usage that is the least likely to attract attention to itself. For these reasons, mastery of Standard English is a key factor to success in business.

YOU AND YOUR ENGLISH

The fact that you are college-trained will weigh heavily in your favor when you are applying for a position and will also be of advantage whenever you are being considered for an on-the-job promotion. Remember, though, that a high quality of performance will be expected of you.

Communication of some kind—speaking, writing, listening, or reading—will play an important part in your job performance; and the basis of all communication is language. Therefore, the excellence of your performance will depend to a great extent on your command of the English language.

The language-structure presentation in this chapter of your textbook will provide you with a solid foundation in modern English usage. You will find no mention of principles that have fallen into disuse. Twilight Zone principles will be pointed out to you, and you may wish to use them in *informal* writing or speech. Your *formal* communication efforts, however, must be couched in language that cannot be debated or criticized.

To paraphrase the slogan of a leading newspaper, "All the News That's Fit to Print," this chapter teaches "All the Language Principles You Need to Know."

regards - as
regard - to

COMMUNICATION PROJECTS

Practical Application

A In the following paragraphs, see whether you can "spot" any instances of substandard English. If you do, write your corrections. This exercise previews the points of grammar that will be discussed in Sections 8-21.

1. Thank you very much for the courtesy you showed Mr. Hill and I during our visit to your office on June 3. Installing a Telefax in our plant would involve a great deal of money, and we felt that we must be sure of its value to our particular operation before considering such a step. The opportunity of seeing your Telefax and its picture-sending advantages was of real help to us, and we come away with much valuable information.

2. Because you have not recently used your Blanton charge-account privileges, we have been wondering if you was unhappy with our goods or services. We look upon our charge-account customers as friends, and each of you are important to us. So, on this friend-to-friend basis, would you please tell us why you have not been in to see us lately. We would be most grateful.

3. You did us a real favor by reporting the poor service you received when shopping in our shoe department. We have been able to prevent any more of them distressing incidents by retraining the clerk who waited on you. You may be sure, Mrs. Gates, that the next time you shop at Blanton's—which we hope will be soon—all of we "Blantonites" will give you interested, personal attention.

B Correct any spelling errors you find here.

Thank you for reccomending me for a secretarial position at Morse Industries. I felt sure that, as both teacher and friend, you would be able to give a picture of me as a person as well as a worker. If anything developes, I'll let you know.

Editing Practice

The Right Word in the Right Place   The words *complete, operation, further,* and *running* are used in the following letter; but are they used in the right places? Rewrite the letter and, if these words are not in the right places, put them where they belong.

Gentlemen:

Last January we sold you one of our Rapid Knitting machines. We guarantee our machines, for we know that they are in perfect operation condition when they leave our factory. We presume that your machine is giving further satisfaction.

We should be grateful to you, however, for filling out the enclosed blank form. You will note that the form asks for details about the running of the machine. If you have complete details or if you have any remarks, please write them on the back of the form.

Very sincerely yours,

Case Problem

Embarrassing Moment   Raymond Mullins belongs to one of the local civic clubs and attends its meetings regularly. During the social hour at one of the meetings, one of his best customers greets Mr. Mullins by name. However, Mr. Mullins has to return the greeting without mentioning the customer's name—he cannot remember it. During the conversation with the customer, another member of the organization, Frank Whelan, approaches both men. "Hello, Ray; it's good to see you again—and I'd like to welcome your guest to our meeting." Now Mr. Mullins must introduce the two men, and he still cannot remember the name of the customer whom Frank Whelan has mistaken for his guest.

1. What should Mr. Mullins say?
2. What might the customer have said, when he first appeared, to protect Mr. Mullins from being embarrassed?
3. What is a good way to remember names?

The Sentence

The sentence is the thought unit by means of which a writer or a speaker expresses himself. Quite possibly he may be able to identify nouns, verbs, and other parts of speech. He may know the principal parts of verbs, the case forms of pronouns, the rules governing parallel construction, and many other pertinent details. His knowledge is worthless, however, unless it can be used effectively to express his thoughts, ideas, and convictions. Effective expression can be achieved only through the medium of the sentence. Logically, then, a review of the mechanics of communication should start with the sentence.

The topics presented in this section, although few in number, are important because their correct usage lays the foundation for both written and oral communication.

DEFINITION

The traditional definition of a sentence, "A sentence is a group of words expressing a complete thought," cannot be improved upon. However, because so many writers write sentence fragments instead of complete sentences, the following Memory Hook is presented as an aid to immediate understanding and correct application of the definition of a sentence.

MEMORY HOOK

A group of words starting with a capital letter and ending with a period is a sentence only if the words express a complete thought—that is, make sense. This principle may be condensed to *No Sense—No Sentence*. The sentence-fragment error is frequently made because the writer does not see that the fragment is part of a preceding or a following sentence.

> As requested, we are shipping your order No. 468 on Thursday of this week. (These words make sense, have meaning, express a complete thought; therefore, this is a sentence.)

> As requested. We are shipping your order No. 468 on Thursday of this week. (The first group of words is a "no sense" group. The writer did not see that his sentence fragment was the introduction to the main thought.)

> Your appointment has been changed to 10 a.m. on May 6. Because Mr. Ames will not return to the office until May 5. (The sentence fragment is the explanatory part of the main message, and the sentence should be written as follows: *Your appointment has been changed to 10 a.m. on May 6 because Mr. Ames will not return to the office until May 5.*)

SUBJECT AND PREDICATE

In order to construct a sentence correctly, a speaker or a writer must be able to recognize its subject and predicate. Every sentence has a subject and a predicate. Once you select the subject, you know that the predicate is the rest of the sentence. The subject is that part of the sentence that shows who *is speaking* or *is spoken to* or *is the person or thing spoken about*. The predicate, then, is what is being said about the subject.

The complete subject may be a single word or a group of words, such as:

I appreciate your thoughtfulness. (*I* is the complete subject of the sentence, the *person speaking*.)

You have a reputation for integrity. (*You* is the complete subject, the *person spoken to*.)

The secretary in the outer office also acts as receptionist. (*The secretary in the outer office* is the complete subject, the *person spoken about*.)

Pictures for the new brochure will be taken tomorrow. (*Pictures for the new brochure* is the complete subject, the *things spoken about*.)

CHECKUP 1

Checkups appear at intervals throughout Chapters 3 and 4. The purpose of these Checkups is to help you measure your knowledge of the rules covered and to pinpoint the areas to which additional study should be devoted.

Indicate whether the following groups of words are sentences or sentence fragments. Then rewrite the sentence fragments to make sentences.

1. Apartments for senior citizens are available here in Bellville.
2. Another satellite is to be launched on August 24.
3. If you wait a few months.
4. Asia is indeed the "hot spot" of the world.
5. We are thinking of hiring an additional store detective.
6. When you address by electronic tape.
7. Information for our files is on microfilm.
8. Which saves much office space.
9. The contract for launching pads has been awarded to Bell & Owen.

SIMPLE AND COMPOUND SUBJECTS

A *simple subject* is the most important single word in the complete subject. For example:

The *girl* in the blue dress is a new employee. (The complete subject is *the girl in the blue dress*. The most important single word is *girl*; therefore, *girl* is the simple subject.)

Essential *elements* of the sentence are presented in this lesson. (*Essential elements of the sentence* is the complete subject. The most important single word in the complete subject is *elements*, which is the simple subject.)

A *compound subject* consists of two or more words that are equally important and are joined usually by a conjunction such as *and, or,* or *nor.*

> The *debits and credits* in the trial balance must be equal. (The
> complete subject is *The debits and credits in the trial balance.*
> *Debits* and *credits* are the most important words, equally impor-
> tant, and are joined by the conjunction *and. Debits and credits* is
> the compound subject.)

> *Boxes* containing stationery *or crates* containing spare parts are
> not to be stored in Warehouse 7. (*Boxes containing stationery or
> crates containing spare parts* is the complete subject. *Boxes* and
> *crates* are the most important words, equally important, and are
> joined by the conjunction *or.* The compound subject, therefore,
> is *boxes or crates.*)

NORMAL AND INVERTED SENTENCE ORDER

Many glaring errors in grammar are caused by the inability to identify true
subjects of sentences, especially when sentences are in inverted order. The
ability to recognize inverted sentence order and to change inverted order to
normal order is a tool that you, when writing or speaking, will use to avoid
making such errors. As given here, the presentation of normal and inverted
order promotes immediate recognition of sentence subjects.

A sentence is considered in *normal order* when the complete subject precedes the complete predicate. When the complete subject does not precede
the complete predicate, the sentence is said to be in *inverted order.* To
change inverted order to normal order, rearrange the words so that the complete subject is written first, followed by the complete predicate. You should
know that most questions are in inverted order. Here are some illustrations:

> Physical fitness plays an important part in the training of an
> astronaut. (Because the complete subject precedes the complete
> predicate, this sentence is in normal order.)

> In the training of an astronaut, physical fitness plays an impor-
> tant part. (Here the complete subject does not precede the com-
> plete predicate; therefore, this sentence is in inverted order.)

> Where did you get your information? (This question is in inverted
> order. Why? Because the subject is *you,* but *you* does not precede
> the predicate. Normal order is this: *You did get your information
> where?*)

Now consider this sentence: "Where's your shoes?" Knowledge of inverted
and normal order, plus the ability to change inverted order to normal order,
would have prevented this serious error in grammar. Changed to normal
order, the sentence is this: "Your shoes is where?" Surely, no educated person would write or say, "Shoes *is.*" He would mentally have changed the
question to normal order and would have written or said, "Where *are* your
shoes?"

A letter containing the sentence "In the following pages appear a full explanation of our reasons for not joining the Association" would lessen the
prestige of the writer and of his company. Changed to normal order, the
sentence is this: "A full explanation of our reasons for not joining the Association appear in the following pages." Obviously, the plural verb *appear* has
been incorrectly used instead of the singular *appears.*

In each of the following sentences, write the complete subject and draw a line under the simple or the compound subject. If a sentence is in inverted order, change it to normal order before making the selection.

1. To reach the top in a secretarial career, <u>you</u> must develop an extensive vocabulary.
2. Do <u>you</u> know what *Gross National Product* means?
3. <u>Action</u> on the tax bill came after weeks of bitter debate.
4. The <u>Common Market</u> is seeking lower tariffs on its exports to the United States.
5. For employment, unskilled <u>workers</u> are the least in demand.
6. What is the <u>difference</u> between the terms *recession* and *depression?*
7. Somewhere in the spacecraft is a radar <u>screen</u>.
8. <u>Efficiency</u> and <u>industry</u> are important success qualifications.
9. On the shelf behind my desk are paper <u>clips</u>, typewriter <u>ribbons</u>, and <u>staplers</u>.

COMMUNICATION PROJECTS

Practical Application

A If one of the sentences below is a fragment, make it a complete sentence. If a sentence is in inverted order, write it in normal order. Then write the complete subject for each sentence and draw a line under the simple or the compound subject.

1. <u>Bars</u> of chocolate and <u>boxes</u> of candy will be on sale today.
2. Relaxed and tanned and happy were the <u>clerks</u> returning from vacation.
3. Notwithstanding the severity of the weather.
4. In front of the desk stood two <u>callers</u> who did not have appointments.
5. An expert <u>typist</u> or a secretarial <u>assistant</u> is needed to help Mr. Ames.
6. A <u>course</u> for high-speed shorthand writers is being offered this year.
7. Is youth <u>unemployment</u> a growing problem?
8. In clerical testing programs, five-minute typing <u>tests</u> are most frequently used.
9. What is your <u>opinion</u> of sympathy strikes?
10. <u>Students</u> who are graduated from our college are well trained.
11. Because we are making a very small profit.
12. Did <u>Mr. Evans</u> buzz for his secretary?
13. <u>Time</u> and <u>tide</u> wait for no man.
14. <u>Hundreds</u> of packages of seeds were shipped today.
15. Do the type <u>bars</u> on that typewriter stick in damp weather?

B For each correct sentence, write *OK* on your paper. For each incorrect sentence, make the necessary correction.

1. At what price did <u>Missouri Motors</u> close yesterday?
2. Did <u>you</u> read carefully the fine print in the contract?
3. Has the market <u>reports</u> come in yet?
4. <u>There</u> is more <u>clerks</u> than any other classification of office employees.
5. Enclosed is the <u>names</u> that you requested in your July 10 letter.
6. In the right margin was typed the proper identification <u>initials.</u>
7. Was those <u>letters</u> duplicated for the head salesman?
8. What is your <u>reasons</u> for refusing to join the Chamber of Commerce?
9. In which of our letters was the serial <u>numbers</u> you quoted in your May 1 letter?
10. Where is the <u>point</u> of no return in this situation?

Editing Practice

Revising Telegrams Rewrite the following telegrams, and use no more than 15 words to express the message clearly.

1. Request that you stay over until after the Monday meeting. Arrangements have been made to have Bob Lyons take over your Baltimore calls.
2. Your contract approved today. Sending it to you by special delivery. Proceed according to the plan agreed upon.
3. Retail price of our Frosty refrigerator still $395. Rumored that price increase will go into effect next month.
4. Floor samples of sun lamps not yet delivered. Receiving calls for them daily. Take care of this at once.
5. Mr. Colton will arrive Thursday at one o'clock via air. Will attend directors' conference at two. Will leave at six.

Proofreading for Spelling Errors Write the correct spelling for any misspelled words in the following paragraph.

> We were glad to learn that you plan to exibit at the Housewares Show at the Hotel James on May 9. Your company has been assigned a booth on the mezzanine floor, which is easily accessable from the lobby. If there is anything we can do beforehand to help you set up your display quickly, please do not hesitate to call on us.

Case Problem

Making Introductions At the annual office picnic for employees and members of their families, George Adams would like to introduce his wife and his mother and father to his boss, John Harvey, president of the company.

1. How should George make these introductions?
2. What might be a good source of information on how to introduce people?
3. How would you make these introductions to the president and his wife and to the vice president, Robert Thompson, and his wife?

Verbs

The correct use of verbs is often a problem to speakers and writers. Guidelines for using verbs correctly are presented in this section and in Section 10 as a help for avoiding some of the more common verb errors.

DEFINITION

A verb is defined as a word that asserts or assumes action, a condition, or a state of being. You can identify a verb quickly by looking for the word that sparks the sentence into motion. Without a verb as a spark, a sentence is incomplete—an inert, lifeless group of words. For instance:

> *His secretary the letter.* (These words mean nothing.)
> *His secretary (wrote, transcribed, misfiled, retyped) the letter.* (See how each verb makes the words come to life in a different way.)

When you can quickly and unerringly identify the word that sparks a sentence into motion, you are ready to learn how to use verbs correctly.

Identify the verbs in the following sentences. If the verb is missing in any group of words, supply a verb for that group.

1. Our company manufactures space capsules.
2. We were happy to hear of your promotion.
3. Your news releases are very well written.
4. Who the mail in this office?
5. Economics is a required course at our college.
6. Who does the layout for your ads?

VERB PHRASES

To communicate accurately, a speaker or writer sometimes needs a phrase consisting of two or more verbs to spark a sentence. Verb phrases are composed of a main (principal) verb and one or more helping (auxiliary) verbs, such as *may have written, had spoken, is going, would have been lost, should have been seen.*

Study the following list of some of the more common helping verbs.

is	will	will have	might have been
was	has been	could have	will have been
has	had been	should have	could have been
had	may have	would have	should have been
shall	might have	may have been	would have been

The *main* verb in any verb phrase is always the *last* verb, and the preceding verb or verbs are the helpers. For example:

Our files *must be kept* in perfect order. (Main verb, *kept;* helping verbs, *must* and *be.*)

All communications *must be* clear and accurate. (Main verb, *be;* helping verb, *must.*)

You *should have checked* those figures. (Main verb, *checked;* helping verbs, *should* and *have.*)

Note that in the second sentence *be* is the main verb but that in the first sentence *be* is a helper. The verbs *be* and *been* will present no problem if it is remembered that the *last* verb is the *main* verb and the preceding verb or verbs are helpers.

CHECKUP 2

Select the verb phrases, main verbs, and helping verbs.

1. Mail is delivered at our office only in the morning.
2. The supervisor has already answered that question.
3. That salesman has been here twice this week.
4. The conference has been deferred until next month.
5. Who is going to the banquet?
6. Those specifications should have gone out yesterday.
7. It would be well for you to proofread more carefully.

REGULAR AND IRREGULAR VERBS

Verbs are classified as either regular or irregular according to the way their principal parts are formed. The principal parts of verbs are the present, past, and past participle. These principal parts of verbs are used to express the time of action, or tense, of a verb.

Regular Verbs

A regular verb forms the past tense and the past participle by adding *ed*, as in *walk, walked, walked* and *call, called, called.* The principal parts of regular verbs do not need special study because a mistake in the use of those verbs is rarely made.

Irregular Verbs

Irregular verbs, however, form the past tense and past participle in various ways—frequently by changing to a different word. Errors in the use of irregular verbs occur so often, particularly in speech, that facility in handling these verbs is a "must" for effective communication. Therefore, careful study of the chart of irregular verb forms on page 69 is recommended.

As you study irregular verbs, keep in mind the fact that a verb in the past tense never has a helping verb, whereas a past participle always has at least one helping verb. For example, "Has the bell rang yet?" is obviously incorrect. The past tense of *ring* is *rang,* but a verb in the past tense never has a helper. In this sentence there is a helper, *has;* therefore, the past participle should be used: "Has the bell *rung* yet?"

TWILIGHT ZONE

Lend, Loan   Although *lend* is a verb and *loan* is a noun, you will very often see or hear *loan* used as a verb, as in "The bank will surely *loan (lend)* you enough to tide you over." If you choose to join the increasing number of persons who *loan,* rather than *lend,* you will at least know that you are making a minor error.

CHECKUP 3

Find and correct all principal-part errors in the following sentences. Justify your corrections on the basis of whether or not the main verb requires a helping verb. For instance:

> The bus had went before we reached the station. (The correction is "*gone*—helper." The correct verb is *gone* because the helper *had* is used. *Went* is incorrect because the past tense is never used with a helper.)
>
> 1. We were all present when Wr. Wood come into the office.
> 2. Our personnel manager loaned me his pen.
> 3. It's so cold here that my fingers are almost froze.
> 4. We'd just began to think that you weren't coming after all.
> 5. Have you ever ate in the cafeteria across the street?

PRINCIPAL PARTS OF IRREGULAR VERBS

Present	Past	Past Participle
am	was	been
begin	began	begun
bid (to command)	bade	bidden
bid (to offer to pay)	bid	bid
bite	bit	bitten
blow	blew	blown
break	broke	broken
bring	brought	brought
burst	burst	burst
catch	caught	caught
choose	chose	chosen
come	came	come
do	did	done
draw	drew	drawn
drink	drank	drunk
drive	drove	driven
eat	ate	eaten
fall	fell	fallen
fight	fought	fought
flee	fled	fled
fly	flew	flown
forget	forgot	forgotten
freeze	froze	frozen
get	got	got
give	gave	given
go	went	gone
grow	grew	grown
hang (to put to death)	hanged	hanged
hang (to suspend)	hung	hung
hide	hid	hidden
know	knew	known
lay	laid (not layed)	laid (not layed)
leave	left	left
lend	lent	lent
lie	lay	lain
pay	paid (not payed)	paid (not payed)
ride	rode	ridden
ring	rang	rung
rise	rose	risen
run	ran	run
see	saw	seen
set	set	set
shake	shook	shaken
sit	sat	sat
speak	spoke	spoken
steal	stole	stolen
strike	struck	struck
take	took	taken
tear	tore	torn
throw	threw	thrown
wear	wore	worn
write	wrote	written

Split Infinitives   An infinitive is a verb usually preceded by *to*, such as *to run, to say, to do, to think*. When a writer places a word or words between the *to* and the verb, he "splits an infinitive"; and infinitive splitting was once considered to be a major English error. Today, however, split infinitives such as *to actually do, to emphatically state*, and *to loyally pledge* are sometimes used to make a statement more emphatic or to avoid an awkwardly constructed sentence.

But you, the beginning writer, should avoid splitting an infinitive if at all possible. In a sense, you will be on trial; and you may be criticized for Twilight Zone usages that would be accepted in communications of experienced writers.

IF, AS IF, AS THOUGH, WISH

Speakers and writers often have difficulty choosing the correct verb to follow *if, as if, as though*, and *wish*. Here is a simple rule to follow: After *if, as if, as though* and *wish*, use *were* where ordinarily *was* would be used.

> Mr. Ready looks *as if* he *were* ill. (But he is not ill.)
> Miss York acted *as though* she *were* disappointed. (But she may not be disappointed.)
> I *wish* it *were* possible to grant your request. (But it is not possible.)

A minor problem occurs with the use of *was* or *were* after *if*. *Were* is used if the expression is not true, is doubtful, or is not possible. However, *was* is used if the statement is true or could be true. Study the following examples.

> *If* I *were* you, I would ask for a transfer. (But I am not you.)
> *If* Washington *were* living, he would be amazed at the growth of our nation. (But Washington is not living.)
> *If* Mr. Leary *was* here (and he may have been), I did not see him.

CHECKUP 4

Make any needed corrections in the following sentences. If you correct a split infinitive, indicate the infinitive and the word or group of words that cause the split.

1. Mrs. Perry often wishes she was ten years younger.
2. We thought the receptionist should try to at least be courteous.
3. If Nancy was in my position, she would see things differently.
4. Everyone else's job looks as though it was easy.
5. I wish I were going to Hawaii with you.
6. Mr. Grimes always walks as if he was in a hurry to get somewhere.

Practical Application

written

A In each of the following sentences, (a) indicate the verb, (b) underline the main verb if there is a verb phrase, and (c) supply a verb for any group of words where the verb is missing.

1. Mr. Wood is supporting the plan for urban renewal.
2. Have you written reminders to all delinquent customers?
3. Ann the best file clerk we ever had.
4. Peacetime uses of atomic power have been in the process of development.
5. What has been your outstanding personnel problem?
6. A cover sheet will make your report look more professional.
7. Our candidate should have asked for equal television time.
8. The minutes of the meeting must have been mislaid.
9. Has the bulletin been read by the entire staff?
10. The foreign delegation will arrive tomorrow.
11. Our company periodic surveys.
12. Have you ever operated a key-punch machine?
13. The sales of this company have increased considerably.
14. Whom have you appointed to fill the vacancy?
15. The Williams letter should have been mailed yesterday.
16. Has there been any change in his feeling about the strike?
17. Mr. Haynes his arm.
18. How fast can you take dictation?
19. Yesterday Mr. Hill the sales record.
20. Evidence of scientific advances can be seen everywhere.

B If a sentence is correct, write *OK* on your paper. If incorrect, write the correction and your reason for making it. If you correct a split infinitive, indicate the word or words that cause the split.

1. Have the Blantons payed the balance of their account?
2. Our boss has chose the letterhead printed in red ink.
3. If I were an economist, I would be better able to answer your question.
4. The salary schedule change has fell through.
5. Some persons find it impossible to clearly reason when under pressure.
6. If the price was lower, we would place a large order.
7. Amy has drunk all the coffee in her vacuum bottle.
8. Mr. King has loaned the reference manual to his secretary.
9. If Agnes was better trained, she would make fewer mistakes.
10. Did you know that we run that advertisement last week?
11. Five-minute typing tests are most frequently used. In clerical testing programs.
12. For several years now, Mr. Mason has sang in the company chorus.
13. Does it look as though the snow were melting?
14. Have you ever spoke before a group?
15. Somewhere in the outgoing mail tray is the letters on which you forgot to make carbon-copy notations.

Editing Practice

Editing for Vocabulary Errors   Write your correction for any vocabulary errors you find in the following paragraph.

Thank you very much for sending us an advance copy of your report on consumer trends during the passed ten years. A study of your findings has given us confidence in the soundness of the planned promotion program for our new low-calorie deserts. We now know that we are in line with current public interest and demand.

Case Problem

The Straw That Broke the Camel's Back   Bob Haynes is the supervisor of one section of the office where tardiness is a serious problem. Bob's boss was so disturbed by the excessive tardiness in this section that he suggested that Bob call a meeting of his people to see what could be done about the problem. Bob called the group together, explained the situation to them, and together they set up a plan to control the tardiness. They agreed that anyone who was tardy would remain overtime twice the amount of time he was tardy. In addition, each member of the group pledged to be at his desk on time. The very next morning following this meeting, Mildred Anson, one of the clerks in Bob's section, was fifteen minutes late. When Bob talked to Mildred and reminded her that she was to remain thirty minutes after the regular time, Mildred explained that she lived beyond the bus line and had to ride with someone who worked for another company and who was on a different time schedule. Consequently, she said, she was not responsible for being late.

1. What should Bob Haynes do about this situation?
2. What should he say to Mildred?

More About Verbs

A professor of English once conducted a most illuminating, though informal, study. He was interested in finding out which elements of English grammar were stumbling blocks to his students, despite their years of grammar study. Each semester, over a period of ten years, he asked entering students to list the grammar principles that they still did not understand. When the study was completed, he found that usage of *lie* and *lay, sit* and *set,* and *rise* and *raise* ranked among the top three areas of difficulty. With the professor's findings in mind, this lesson on verbs concentrates on clearing up cloudiness about the correct usage of *lie* and *lay, sit* and *set, rise* and *raise.*

CLASSIFICATION OF VERBS

In order to use the correct forms of *lie* and *lay, sit* and *set, rise* and *raise,* it is first necessary to know how verbs are classified. Verbs may be divided into three classifications: (1) "being" verbs, (2) transitive verbs, and (3) intransitive verbs.

"Being" Verbs
The different forms of the verb *to be* are as follows:

> am, is, are, was, were
> *be* with a helper: shall be, will be, may be, can be, would be, might be, etc.
> *been* with a helper or helpers: has been, have been, had been, shall have been, will have been, could have been, might have been, etc.

These are the seven "being" verbs. Because of the need for instant recognition of "being" verbs, they should be memorized, preferably in this order: *am, is, are, was, were,* helper *be,* helper(s) *been.*

Note. A single-word "being" verb can be classified very easily. In a verb phrase, however, remember that a verb is "being" only when it is the main verb, the *last* verb in the phrase. If not the last verb, it is a helping verb.

> The folders *were* not in alphabetical order. (Since *were* is the only verb, it is readily recognized as a "being" verb.)
>
> They *should have been* here and ready for distribution. (This is a "being" verb because *been* is the last verb in the verb phrase.)
>
> The folders *were placed* correctly in the file. (*Placed* is the last verb in the phrase, and it is not a "being" verb. Therefore, *were* is a helping verb.)
>
> Mr. Betts *is going* to Chicago tomorrow. (*Going* is the main verb; *is* is a helping verb. *Is going* is not a "being" verb.)

CHECKUP 1

Select the verb or verb phrase in each of the following sentences and identify the "being" verbs.

1. The high cost of living is a perennial problem.
2. There has been much discussion of automation and the unskilled worker.
3. The national debt is running into astronomical figures.
4. Were all survey results filed yesterday?
5. Well-prepared business writers are in demand.
6. The main vault must have been locked before closing hours.

Transitive and Intransitive Verbs

A transitive verb is a verb that takes an object; an intransitive verb, a verb that does not take an object. To ensure rapid and accurate selection of transitive and intransitive verbs, study the following Memory Hook.

MEMORY HOOK

A transitive verb is a verb that is followed by an answer to the question "What?" or "Whom?" If no answer can be found, the verb is intransitive. Set up a thinking procedure like the following:

1. Say the verb.
2. Ask "What?" or "Whom?"
3. If there is an answer to either question, the verb is transitive. If not, the verb is intransitive.

See how this thought process is applied in the following illustrations.

> Mr. Eden *left* the package here this morning. (Left what? Answer —*package.* Since there is an answer, *left* in this sentence is a transitive verb.)
>
> Mr. Eden *left* sometime during the forenoon. (Left what? No answer. Left whom? No answer. In this sentence *left* is an intransitive verb.)
>
> *Do* you *know* Mary Lyons? (Do know what? No answer. Do know whom? Answer—*Mary Lyons. Do know,* then, is a transitive verb.)

Always Transitive

Whenever a past participle has one of the "being" verbs as a helper—*was done, has been broken, might be chosen, is burned*—that verb is always transitive because the subject is acted upon. For example:

> The "Top Secret" papers *should have been hidden* from public gaze. (*Hidden* is a past participle. *Should have been* is a "being" verb, but in this sentence it is used as a helper. *Should have been hidden* is automatically a transitive verb.)
>
> The wind *was blowing* with hurricane force. (Although there is a "being" verb helper here, the main verb is not a past participle. For this verb, therefore, ask the questions "What?" and "Whom?" Since neither question can be answered, *was blowing* is an intransitive verb.)

CHECKUP 2

In the following sentences, identify each verb as "being," transitive, or intransitive. Use T for "transitive," I for "intransitive," and B for "being." Watch for any past participles that have "being" verb helpers.

1. We should have received Mr. Colton's check this morning. T
2. All of us were waiting for the mail delivery. I
3. Where was the carrier at ten o'clock? B
4. Surely, the check should have been sent on Friday. T
5. Did you look at all the letters? I
6. Did you see any packages? T

LIE, LAY; SIT, SET; RISE, RAISE

The foundation for correct use of *lie, lay; sit, set;* and *rise, raise* has now been laid. In each pair, one of the verbs is transitive; the other, intransitive. To choose the correct verb form, a speaker or writer needs to determine which of the pair is transitive and which is intransitive. Use of the following Memory Hook will result in split-second recognition of the correct verb.

MEMORY HOOK

Notice that there is a letter *i* or an *i* sound in the present form of one member of each pair of verbs. These *i* verbs are *lie, sit,* and *rise.* The word *intransitive* starts with the letter *i.* Therefore, remember that the *i* verbs *lie, sit,* and *rise* are intransitive.

Present	Past	Past Participle	Present Participle	Infinitive
lie	lay	lain	lying	to lie
lay	laid	laid	laying	to lay
sit	sat	sat	sitting	to sit
set	set	set	setting	to set
rise	rose	risen	rising	to rise
raise	raised	raised	raising	to raise

Quite obviously, once the intransitive verb is identified, the other member of the pair is known to be transitive. Remember, however, that a past participle that has a "being" verb helper is always transitive.

Observe and adopt the line of reasoning set up in the following illustrations.

> Cleo said that she (lay, laid) her notebook on the desk.
> Which is needed here, a transitive or an intransitive verb? Answer—transitive.
> How do you know? Answer—because *notebook* answers the question "What?"
> Which verb is transitive? Answer—*laid*.
> Which form is correct? Answer—*laid*.
>
> Mr. Kent (lies, lays) down for an hour after lunch. (The verb has no object; therefore, an intransitive verb is needed. The intransitive verb *lies* is the correct verb.)
>
> The package was (sat, set) on the low stool. (There is no problem here. *Set* is correct because a past participle with a "being" verb helper is always transitive.)

CHECKUP 3

For each of the following sentences, determine whether a transitive or an intransitive verb is needed and tell why. Then name the correct verb.

1. Train that dog not to (lie, lay) on the rug. I
2. (Sit, Set) your marginal stops at 15 and 70. T
3. The water has (risen, raised) to the top of the pier. I
4. Those machines have (lain, laid) idle for a month. I
5. Did you know that the salary maximum has been (risen, raised)? T
6. Mr. Tarny's new house (sits, sets) on a hilltop. I
7. You left your belongings (lying, laying) on all the chairs. T
8. The engineers' reports were (lain, laid) on the bottom shelf. T

COMMUNICATION PROJECTS

Practical Application

Identify the verb in each of the following sentences and indicate whether it is transitive, intransitive, or "being." Use T for "transitive," I for "intransitive," and B for "being."

1. Manufacturers of stockings announced the development of a new fabric.
2. The word "parity" appears frequently in the newspapers.
3. We surely cannot be at our desks every minute of the day!
4. The foundry has been purchased by Allen & Brown.
5. Wheat is selling rapidly on the Exchange.
6. Do your customers like these linen napkins?
7. There were often a dozen or more callers in our small office.
8. All letters were finished before noon, despite interruptions.
9. A business correspondent writes many different kinds of communications.
10. You should have been here before 8:30.
11. Are you looking for an automatic typewriter?
12. That sentence should have been changed to normal order.
13. Opposition makes Mr. Benson more persistent.
14. A set of form letters has finally been prepared.
15. A digest of the letters should be on my desk today.

B For the rest of this chapter and throughout Chapter 4, Practical Application B will review material from earlier lessons as well as from the current lesson. If a sentence is correct, write *OK* on your paper; if incorrect, make the necessary correction.

1. Have prices rose faster than wages?
2. We invited the caller to lie down his briefcase and his umbrella.
3. Our Research Department is laying plans for using the results of the survey.
4. Does Chicago lay west or north of New York?
5. To really be convincing, you yourself must believe in what you say.
6. The work schedule was lain out just last week.
7. Your portfolio is lying in readiness for the meeting.
8. A gentleman always rises to his feet when a lady enters the room.
9. Yesterday the stencils laid on the top shelf.
10. That particular objection has been risen many times.
11. Miss Lamb has laid on my desk the folder containing laboratory data.
12. In our library is many books on the subject of nuclear fission.
13. Behind the machine is the boxes of key-punch cards.
14. When your current account is payed, we shall be glad to open a new one.
15. Loan me a few sheets of carbon paper, please.
16. In the dictionary is many synonyms for nouns.
17. Both soldiers are laying now in Flanders Field.
18. Was the flagpole set securely in cement?
19. Please let that book lay where you found it.
20. He had laid down to rest after his long trip.

Editing Practice

Wanted: An Editor Who Can Spell   If you are that editor, you will be able to find and correct any spelling errors in this paragraph.

Perhaps we should wait and see what developes as a result of our direct-mail subscription promotion before deciding to set up an inactive file. There is a possibility that many of our so-called "inactives" will renew their subscriptions and would therefore belong in the active file. I think that in this instance haste would indeed make waste.

Case Problem

The Helpful Employee   Irma Mattell recently gave notice of her intent to resign from her position as secretary in the Bell Manufacturing Company's office. Her replacement is coming in tomorrow, two days before Irma will be leaving, to be oriented to the new position. Irma has decided that a brief, typed summary of her duties would be helpful for the replacement.

1. Why would such a summary be helpful, even though Irma would be spending two days with the girl who is to replace her?
2. What should the summary contain?

Nouns—Plurals

Its inconsistencies make English a difficult language to speak and to write. One of the difficulties presented by the English language is the correct spelling of the plurals of nouns. There is no single way to form plurals. For example, consider the following sentence: "Embargoes on the importation of pianos are unknown today." The plural of *embargo* is *embargoes;* but the plural of *piano* is *pianos,* although it also ends in *o.* Here is another illustration: "Attorneys for the steel *companies* were consulted about the merger." *Attorney* ends in *y;* its plural is formed by adding *s. Company* also ends in *y,* but its plural is formed by changing the *y* to *i* and adding *es.* The plurals of nouns are formed in such a variety of ways that only a skilled writer is always correct in forming plurals. This lesson seeks to develop the high level of skill needed to form noun plurals correctly by (1) presenting solutions to the most difficult plural problems, (2) reviewing rules that may have been forgotten, (3) indicating plurals that sometimes require dictionary help, and (4) analyzing plurals that cause frequent errors in grammar.

KEYS TO CORRECT PLURALS

Analysis of the difficulties in forming plurals shows that four plural formations evidently are not understood by some business writers. These four problems and keys to their solutions will now be discussed.

Plurals of Names

Most common nouns form their plurals by adding *s* to the singular form—*book, books; letter, letters.* However, common nouns ending in *s, sh, ch, x,* and *z* form their plurals by adding *es* to the singular form. For example:

lens	lenses	tax	taxes
brush	brushes	topaz	topazes
bench	benches		

Very few writers make errors in the use of *s* or *es* to form the plurals of common nouns. If they understood that the plurals of proper nouns or *names* are formed in exactly the same way, they would make fewer errors when writing plurals of names.

farmer	farmers	Palmer	the Palmers
carton	cartons	Barton	the Bartons
brass	brasses	Ellis	the Ellises
dish	dishes	Walsh	the Walshes
branch	branches	Stritch	the Stritches
fox	foxes	Wilcox	the Wilcoxes
chintz	chintzes	Schlitz	the Schlitzes

Titles With Names

When a title accompanies a name, either the name or the title may be made plural. Never make both the name and the title plural. For instance:

Mr. Carlin	*Messrs.* Carlin, the *Messrs.* Carlin, or the two Mr. *Carlins* (*Messrs.* is the abbreviation for *Messieurs,* the French word for *Misters.*)
Mrs. Fort	The Mrs. *Forts* or *Mesdames* Fort (*Mesdames* is the French word that means more than one *Mrs.*)
Miss York	*Misses* York or the two Miss *Yorks*
Professor Weber	*Professors* Weber or the Professor *Webers*

Apostrophe Used in a Plural

Many writers are uncertain about the use of the apostrophe in plurals. Apostrophes may be used to indicate plurals of capital letters, figures, symbols, some abbreviations, and words used as words; however, many of these plurals are now commonly formed by the addition of *s* alone.

> He has not yet learned his *ABCs* (or *ABC's*).
> We have many *Ph.D.s* (or *Ph.D.'s*) on our staff.
> The temperature was in the *90s* (or *90's*) last week.

If the plural form is unclear when *s* alone is added, use the apostrophe.

> Mr. Tate uses too many *the's* in his writing.
> How many *f.o.b.'s* were recorded last month?
> He doesn't cross his *t's*.

Plurals of Compound Nouns

A compound noun is a noun consisting of two or more words. It may be either hyphenated or unhyphenated. The rule to remember is this: The plural of a compound noun is formed on the important, or main, word. For example:

chief of police	*chiefs* of police
editor in chief	*editors* in chief
major general	major *generals*
personnel manager	personnel *managers*
son-in-law	*sons*-in-law

Note. In a very few compounds, the plural is added to both parts: *gentlemen ushers, Knights Templars.*

CHECKUP 1

Correct any errors that occur in the following sentences and be able to justify your corrections.

1. We received an invitation from the Ford's.
2. We have four Samuel's in our family.
3. Mr. Fargo appointed his two son-in-laws as officers of the firm.
4. These orders apply only to lieutenants general.
5. The Harrises occupy a suite of offices.
6. Wouldn't you know that the Jones's would make the lowest bid!
7. The Misses Stewarts have won the trip to Paris.
8. Modern typewriters have +s on the top row of keys.
9. The Doctors Smiths have opened an office on Main Street.
10. No C.O.D.s will be accepted from now on.
11. How much business do the Schultzes do?
12. Bill and Jack were the runner-ups in the tournament.

PLURALS TO REVIEW

The following three rules for forming the plurals of nouns are so generally well understood that they need only to be reviewed briefly.

Plurals of Nouns Ending in Y

When a singular noun ends in *y* and the *y* is preceded by a consonant, the plural is formed by changing the *y* to *i* and adding *es;* when the *y* is preceded by a vowel, the plural is formed by adding *s.* See the following illustrations:

| supply | supplies | *but* | valley | valleys |
| facility | facilities | | foray | forays |

Note.   This rule does not apply to proper names. All names ending in *y* form the plural by adding *s*, as in *three Marys, the Averys.*

Nouns With Two Plurals With Different Meanings

A few nouns have two plurals, each of which has a different meaning. Here are some examples of such nouns:

brother	brothers (blood relatives), brethren (members of a society)
staff	staffs (personnel), staves (sticks, poles)
index	indexes (to books), indices (symbols)

Vowel Changes and En Endings

Some nouns form the plural by changing a vowel instead of adding *s.* A few other plurals end in *en.* Although these rules generally seem to be well understood, a brief refresher is needed to fill in the "plurals" picture.

Vowel Change:	man	men		woman	women
	goose	geese		mouse	mice
"en" Ending:	child	children		ox	oxen

Note.   In a very few words ending in *man,* the plural is formed by adding *s;* for example, *German, Germans; talisman, talismans; ottoman, ottomans.*

CHECKUP 2

Study the following sentences and make any needed corrections.

1. A metropolitan area is composed of several communitys.
2. Cut up this old sheet into clothes to use for dusting.
3. Prison turnkies must have knowledge of psychology.
4. The Germen are building a new and better nation.
5. Alaska and Hawaii were originally territorys of the United States.
6. We are returning this order because barrels with loose staffs are of no use to us.

DICTIONARY ALERTS

Plural forms of singular nouns ending in *o* and in *f* or *fe* vary so much that there is doubtful value in memorizing exceptions to the rules. You should be sure of the plurals of *o*- and *f*- or *fe*-ending nouns that occur frequently in your writing. You should also know that these plurals are "tricky"; therefore, if you are not absolutely sure, you should consult a dictionary.

Plurals of Nouns Ending in O

Singular nouns ending in *o* preceded by a *vowel* form the plural by adding *s*. Some nouns ending in *o* preceded by a *consonant* form the plural by adding *s;* others, by adding *es*. Do not guess at the correct spelling of the plural of a noun ending in *o* when that *o* is preceded by a consonant.

It is interesting to note that nouns that relate to music and end in *o* always form their plurals by adding *s:* for example, *piano, pianos; alto, altos; oratorio, oratorios.*

Some examples of plurals of nouns ending in *o* are given below. Make a habit of consulting a dictionary to determine the correct plurals of nouns ending in *o*.

Final *o* preceded by a vowel:

studio	studios	cameo	cameos
folio	folios	ratio	ratios

Final *o* preceded by a consonant, adding *s* for the plural:

domino	dominos	zero	zeros
dynamo	dynamos	lasso	lassos
tobacco	tobaccos	albino	albinos

Final *o* preceded by a consonant, adding *es* for the plural:

mosquito	mosquitoes	cargo	cargoes
potato	potatoes	echo	echoes
motto	mottoes	hero	heroes
volcano	volcanoes	veto	vetoes

Plurals of Nouns Ending in F or Fe

Some nouns ending in *f* or *fe* change the *f* or *fe* to *v* and add *es* to form the plural; others simply add *s*. The plural of a noun ending in *f* or *fe*, therefore, should be recognized as a spelling hazard. Study the following illustrations and observe that there is neither a rule nor a pattern for these plurals.

Final *f* or *fe*, changing to *v* and adding *es:*

shelf	shelves	self	selves
life	lives	knife	knives
half	halves	leaf	leaves
loaf	loaves	thief	thieves

Final *f* or *fe*, adding *s:*

handkerchief	handkerchiefs	safe	safes
plaintiff	plaintiffs	gulf	gulfs
roof	roofs	grief	griefs
belief	beliefs	chef	chefs
proof	proofs	strife	strifes
bailiff	bailiffs	chief	chiefs

CHECKUP 3

Make the needed corrections in the following sentences.

1. Exposure to light will ruin the prooves of your pictures.
2. Did you know that veal is the meat of calfs?

3. The scores of piano concertos can be obtained from the library.
4. The upstairs closet has three empty shelfs.
5. Tomatos from Florida are now in the market.
6. The newer motels have radioes in all rooms.

PLURALS FOR CORRECT GRAMMAR

One reason for learning how to form the plurals of nouns is that such knowledge improves spelling. A mastery of the four rules presented here, however, also can help a speaker or a writer to avoid making errors in grammar. For instance, when he knows that *news* is always singular, he says or writes "News *is*," not "News *are*." If he knows that *headquarters* is always plural, he says "Headquarters *are*," not "Headquarters *is*."

To be correct in grammar usage, a writer or speaker needs to know (1) the nouns that have the same form in both the singular and the plural, (2) the nouns that are always singular, (3) the nouns that are always plural, and (4) the foreign nouns that follow the foreign spelling in the plural.

Same Form Singular and Plural

The following are illustrations of nouns that have the same form regardless of whether their meaning is singular or plural.

Chinese	deer	odds	sheep
cod	Japanese	politics	vermin
corps (pronounced *kōrz* in the plural)	moose	salmon	wheat

When used with numbers, the following nouns usually have the same form with either a singular or plural number.

three *thousand* (orders)	four *score* (years)
two *yoke* (of oxen)	two *dozen* (apples)
six *hundred* (chairs)	

Always Singular

Here are some illustrations of nouns that are always singular and with which a singular verb must be used.

statistics (science)	molasses
mathematics	civics
economics (science)	milk
news	music

Always Plural

The following nouns are always plural and must therefore always take a plural verb.

statistics (facts)	auspices	tidings
scales (for weighing)	trousers	thanks
headquarters	proceeds	riches
credentials	winnings	antics
belongings	premises	goods
hysterics	scissors	tongs

Foreign Nouns

Some nouns of foreign origin, mainly from Latin and Greek, have been given English plurals; some have only foreign plurals; and still others have two plurals, English and foreign. Where there is a choice, the foreign forms are used mainly in formal, scientific, and technical writing. Usually, the endings of foreign nouns show them to be singular or plural. Some common endings for Latin nouns are as follows:

Singular Ending	Plural Ending
um (candelabrum)	a (candelabra)
is (thesis)	es (theses)
us (stylus)	i (styli)
a (alumna)	ae (alumnae)

Words of Greek origin like *criterion* and *phenomenon* take an *a* plural ending—*criteria, phenomena*.

Keeping singular and plural endings in mind, study the following illustrations of plurals of foreign nouns.

Singular	Foreign Plural	English Plural
addendum	addenda	
alumna (fem.)	alumnae	
alumnus	alumni	
analysis	analyses	
axis	axes	
basis	bases	
crisis	crises	
criterion	criteria	criterions
curriculum	curricula	curriculums
datum	data	
formula	formulae	formulas
hypothesis	hypotheses	
index	indices	indexes
medium	media	mediums
memorandum	memoranda	memorandums
nucleus	nuclei	nucleuses
oasis	oases	
parenthesis	parentheses	
stadium	stadia	stadiums
stimulus	stimuli	
terminus	termini	terminuses
vertebra	vertebrae	vertebras

TWILIGHT ZONE

Data   Among some modern writers there is a tendency to use *data* in most cases as a collective noun with a singular idea. These writers, therefore, use a singular verb with *data*.

CHECKUP 4

Find and correct any errors in the following sentences.

1. Mr. Gray bagged two mooses while on vacation.
2. Parentheses is to be used to enclose references.
3. Has the goods been stored in the bin?
4. Measles have caused a number of absences.
5. The alumni is interested in a winning football team.

COMMUNICATION PROJECTS

Practical Application

For each correct sentence in the following group, write *OK* on your paper. For each incorrect sentence, write the correction.

1. How many varietys of seeds were in today's shipment?
2. We have decided not to stock banjoes at this time.
3. The president and the general manager are grandsons of the Adams's.
4. We have a fine selection of handkerchieves for the Christmas trade.
5. The Misses Wagner are retired schoolteachers.
6. Did you receive congratulations from the Cole's?
7. Why do some saleswoman wear such homely shoes?
8. Mr. York's letters are full of *ands*.
9. The Vargas's are relocating their factory.
10. Chief Murphy is attending the state convention of chief of polices.
11. In your ten years of hunting, how many deers have you shot?
12. Since we have three Ann's in our office, we have resorted to nicknames.
13. Privates think that brigadiers general have easy lives.
14. There are three sixes in my license number.
15. Mr. Kelly says that all Kellies are intelligent.
16. File De Beaumont's correspondence with the Ds.
17. Here are the news emanating from WNBI.
18. The Fitchs will have no trouble floating the loan.
19. Young attornies spend much of their time preparing briefs.
20. Verbs are the dynamoes of sentences.

If a sentence is correct, write *OK* on your paper. If incorrect, write the correction.

1. Remember that there are two *is* in privilege.
2. The alumnae has sponsored the drive for a new library.
3. Here is the paper clips you requisitioned.
4. Where are the portfolios that Mr. Bunker sent us?
5. Mr. Geer acts as if he was discouraged with the sales reports.
6. We have no facilitys for duplicating more than a thousand copies.
7. You should be lying your plans now for your summer vacation.
8. Have we payed all operating costs for this month?
9. In some states, civics are required for graduation.
10. On the card was printed, "Christmas Greetings from the Davis's."
11. At the last regular meeting, your proposal was lain on the table.
12. We all wished that Mr. Allen were present at the meeting.
13. Sit the vase on the table in the living room.
14. At the head table was seated the senior section managers.
15. The combinations on all the saves have been changed.

Editing Practice

Editing for Context   Rewrite each sentence that contains a word that is contextually incorrect. Write *OK* for any contextually correct sentence.

1. Please do not let another two-week period elevate before sending in your monthly payment.
2. We have no covenant with the other manufacturers.
3. This service is given as a gesture of friendship, not with any thought of financial removal.
4. Our federal government continually operates at a deficit.
5. Rationing was necessary during the war years because of the scarcity of many commodities.

Homonyms, Anybody?   Write your correction of any homonym error you may find in the following paragraph. Before you start, be sure that you know the meaning of the word *homonym*.

> Members of the bridle procession will assemble at the church for rehearsal at 7:30 p.m. on Friday, June 2. Immediately afterward there will be a stag party at the Hotel Ritz. A stag party, as you know, is attended only by mails. We have reserved a room for you at the Ritz for the night of June 2, and by now you should have received a confirmation.

Case Problem

The Correspondence Consultant   You have been hired by Blanton, Inc., to study its correspondence and to make recommendations for improving letters written by its personnel. List the details of the preliminary planning that would be necessary to do a top job.

12	# Nouns and Pronouns— Possessive Forms

The possessive case of a noun or a pronoun is used to show ownership. If understanding this statement were all that was needed for correct use of the possessive case, writers would have no difficulty indicating who owns what. Many writers, even some experienced correspondents, however, do not understand the use of the apostrophe, which is the sign of the possessive. The purpose of this lesson is to make the use of the apostrophe so clear that any writer will be able instantly to place apostrophes where they belong. Immediate, correct application of the possessive case is the result of understanding the most common use of the apostrophe, of knowing how to use apostrophes in three special ownership situations, and of being skilled in the use of personal-pronoun possessives. The acquisition of skill in the use of the possessive case, therefore, will result from mastery of the topics covered in this section.

MOST COMMON USE OF THE APOSTROPHE

The apostrophe is used most often to show possession as applied to a noun; for example, *secretary's duties, men's clothing, ladies' dresses.* Here is a simple two-part rule for writing the possessive case of nouns correctly.

1. If the word denoting ownership *does not* end in *s*, add an apostrophe and an *s*. For example:

> The *child's* request was granted. (*Child* does not end in *s*; therefore, use an apostrophe and an *s*.)
>
> The *children's* requests were granted. (*Children* does not end in *s*; therefore, use an apostrophe and an *s*.)

2. If the word denoting ownership *does* end in *s*, add only an apostrophe. For example:

> *Ladies'* clothing is sold by all department stores. (*Ladies* ends in *s*; therefore, only an apostrophe is added.)
>
> Policemen often sponsor *boys'* clubs. (*Boys* ends in *s*; therefore, only an apostrophe is added.)

Note. Some authorities present the following exception: An apostrophe and *s* are added to a noun ending in *s* if an added syllable is heard when pronouncing the possessive; for example, *actress's behavior.*

Sometimes students need help in determining which word is the ownership word. Use of the following Memory Hook will immediately bring into focus the word that takes the apostrophe.

MEMORY HOOK

Remember that the ownership word precedes whatever is owned by that word. For instance: "The man's hats were lost in the fire." The meaning is *the hats belonging to the man. Man,* then, is the ownership word; and, since it does not end in *s*, an apostrophe and *s* are added. Consider this sentence: "Children's toys should be durable." The meaning is *toys belonging to children. Children,* then, is the word that takes the apostrophe.

To isolate the ownership word, say the word that represents what is owned. Next say "belonging to" or "of the," and then say the word that you think is the ownership word. This procedure will result in immediate identification of the ownership word and will prevent using the apostrophe with the incorrect word. Study the Memory Hook procedures used in the following illustrations.

> The *secretaries'* desks are all grouped together. (*Desks belonging to secretaries. Secretaries* is the ownership word; and, since it ends in *s*, only the apostrophe is added.)
>
> The *hero's* role is usually played by a famous star. (*Role of the hero. Hero* is the ownership word and does not end in *s*; therefore, an apostrophe and *s* are added.)

Note. The trend is to omit the apostrophe in names of organizations and institutions, except when the name ends in *men,* such as *Lions Club, Teachers College,* but *Businessmen's Club.*

CHECKUP 1

Use the rule and the Memory Hook to determine how the possessive case of each noun should be written in the sentences below and on page 86.

1. The meeting will be held in Mr. Ashbys office.
2. A number of executives attended the employees picnic.

3. The judge listened to the prosecuting attorneys arguments.
4. Womens jobs are sometimes highly specialized.
5. We must give prompt attention to all creditors claims.
6. Our typists desks are 34 inches wide.

ADDITIONAL USES OF THE APOSTROPHE WITH NOUNS

In addition to the basic possessive-case rule, three special rules cover the formation of certain types of possessives.

Possessive of a Compound Noun

The *last word* of a compound is the word that takes the apostrophe. Therefore, if the last word does not end in *s*, use an apostrophe and *s*. If the last word does end in *s*, use only an apostrophe. For example:

> My sisters-in-law's families have many advantages. (*Families belonging to my sisters-in-law. Law,* the last word, does not end in *s*.)
>
> You are using somebody else's stapler. (*Stapler belonging to somebody else. Else,* the last word, does not end in *s*.)
>
> The two vice-presidents' reports were confidential. (The last word, *presidents,* ends in *s*.)

Joint or Separate Ownership

Joint ownership is shown by using the apostrophe with the *last* member of the combination, such as:

> Jane and Sue's mother is a college professor. (*The mother of Jane and Sue.* Note the singular noun *mother* and the singular verb *is*.)
>
> There are no chairs for visitors in Bob and Mark's office. (*Office belonging to Bob and Mark.* Note the singular noun *office*.)

Separate ownership is indicated by placing an apostrophe with each member of the combination. Always remember that separate apostrophes must be used to show separate ownership. For example:

> Jane's and Sue's mothers are very good friends. (*The mother of Jane* and *the mother of Sue.* Note the plural noun *mothers* and the plural verb *are*.)
>
> There are no chairs for visitors in Bob's and Mark's offices. (*Office belonging to Bob* and *office belonging to Mark.* Note the plural noun *offices*.)

Possessive Case Before a Gerund

A gerund is a verb form ending in *ing* that is used as a noun; for example, "*Walking* to work would be beneficial," "*Dancing* is a form of poetry." A noun or a pronoun that precedes a gerund must be in the possessive case. For instance:

> Did you find *Ray's* checking of your returns a real help? (Possessive *Ray's* before the gerund *checking*.)
>
> We should appreciate *your* sending a check immediately. (Possessive *your* before the gerund *sending*.)

Appositive Showing Possession

Sometimes a noun that ordinarily would be in the possessive is followed by an appositive—a word or a group of words used to explain, or to give additional information about, a preceding word or phrase. In such cases, the apostrophe is used *only* with the appositive.

> That is Miss Forbes, the file clerk's, responsibility. (The appositive, *clerk*, takes the apostrophe. Note that there is no apostrophe following *Miss Forbes*.)

CHECKUP 2

Make any necessary possessive-case corrections in the following sentences.

1. His father-in-laws business is flourishing.
2. Alice's and Bonnie's town was flooded by the spring rains.
3. Bill's watching the clock is beginning to annoy Mr. Dunham.
4. Checking the time cards is someone's else job.
5. Jack's and Fred's desk is usually cluttered with papers.
6. A runners-up cup was awarded to Mr. Clark.
7. Mr. Barr disapproves of you using a worn-out typewriter ribbon.
8. Have you the key to David and Mike's lockers?

PERSONAL PRONOUN POSSESSIVES

The following rule has no exceptions: Personal pronoun possessives *never* take an apostrophe. Using an apostrophe in a personal pronoun possessive (*my, your, his, their*, etc.) or in the pronoun *whose* is a somewhat frequent error in business correspondence; this error is avoided by any writer who knows the foregoing rule. Study the following examples.

> The river was slowly meandering on *its* way. *(Way belonging to it.)*
> Are you sure that these identification initials are *hers?* (Never *her's*.)

Confusions in Use of Personal Pronoun Possessives

Several of the pronoun possessives are pronounced exactly like other words that have entirely different meanings. Such words are known as homonyms. Mastery of the following explanations will clear up such confusions.

Its   The personal pronoun possessive *its*, meaning "belonging to it," is often misused for *it's*, meaning "it is"—or vice versa. If the difference in meaning is understood, the error will not be made. For instance:

> *It's* a good idea to put an apostrophe in *its* proper place. (*It is* a good idea . . . place *belonging to it*.)

Their   There are three words with this sound: *their, they're,* and *there. Their* means "belonging to them." *They're* is the contraction of *they are*. If the meaning is neither of these, *there* is the correct word to use.

> *They're* having trouble finding *their* places over *there*. (*They are* having trouble finding places *belonging to them* over there. *There* is correct because the meaning is neither *they are* nor *belonging to them*.)

Your *Your* and *you're* sound alike, but their meanings are different. *Your* means "belonging to you"; *you're* means "you are."

> When *you're* well trained, *your* job will go well. (When *you are* well trained, the job *belonging to you* will go well.)

Our Clearly enunciated, *our* and *are* do not have precisely the same sound; but, because of careless enunciation, they are often confused. *Our* means "belonging to us." *Are* should be remembered as one of the "being" verbs.

> The executives are conferring about *our* salary increments. (The executives *are* (the verb) conferring about salary increments *belonging to us*.)

Whose *Whose* is a possessive pronoun meaning "belonging to whom." This possessive must not be confused with *who's*, which is the contraction of *who is*.

> *Who's* the applicant *whose* recommendations are unsigned? (*Who is* the applicant . . . recommendations *belonging to whom*.)

CHECKUP 3

Make the necessary corrections in the following sentences, and explain your changes in terms of the meaning of the sentence.

1. Do not separate a letter from it's envelope if an enclosure is missing.
2. Our typists have ordered there new office furniture.
3. If your interested, call and make an appointment.
4. Mr. Decker expects are help in assembling the papers.
5. Who's telephone was reported to be out of order?
6. You know full well that its worth more than you paid for it.
7. Mr. Gurney is the man whose going to be our next president.
8. The stationery lay right there on his desk.
9. Who's property has been condemned because of the turnpike?
10. When there ready, the printers will ask for the rest of the copy.

| **COMMUNICATION PROJECTS** |

Practical Application

Ⓐ Make the necessary corrections in the following sentences. If a sentence is correct, write *OK* on your paper.

1. The court-martials' verdict was received in silence. *martial's*
2. Brady and Cole's firms will merge soon. *Brady's*
3. The company is publishing its annual report to stockholders. *OK*
4. Lumbermens shoes' are heavy and clumsy. *Lumbermen's*
5. You will find no cameos on there jewelry counter. *their*
6. Where shall we store the shipment of stenographers notebooks'? *stenographers'*
7. When your writing an office communication, always make a carbon copy. *you're*
8. Have you bought your ticket for the policemens' ball? *'s*
9. There is a good reason for their cutting down overhead. *OK*
10. At Christmas the Lewis' windows are beautifully trimmed. *Lewises'*
11. Please send are regrets to the Bindlosses. *our*
12. Their is no reason for you to be discouraged. *There*
13. Julia is forever criticizing somebody's else English. *else's*

---

14. On which floor of this store is the lady's department? *ladies'*
15. Cleo's and Maureen's hair is always well groomed. *OK*
16. Mr. Abbot commented on you taking too long a coffee break. *your*
17. Every job has it's advantages and disadvantages. *its*
18. A new porch is being built on the Ellis' house. *Ellises'*
19. Mr. Ford appreciated you sending a salesman to call on him. *your*
20. Do you know who's going to operate the computer? *OK*

B Correct the following sentences wherever necessary. If a sentence is correct, write *OK* on your paper.

1. Lily of the valley's are my favorite flower. *Lilies of the valley*
2. The concert featured soloes by members of our staff. *solos*
3. Have you taken somebody else's place in the line? *OK*
4. The firemens' parade was the big event of the past year. *firemen's*
5. Mr. Ward is worried about Ann undertaking the administrative assistantship. *Ann's*
6. Peter and Gene were chosen to be the villain's in the play. *villains*
7. Did you see the polish on Amy and Cynthia's fingernails? *Amy's*
8. My stapler was loaned without my permission. *lent*
9. Some supervisors do not give there directions clearly. *their*
10. The cornerstone for our new factory was lain last Monday. *laid*
11. Students complaints' are often based on faulty premises. *Students'*
12. Consult the Davises whenever you have any question about etiquette. *OK*
13. Mr. North's son is living in a boys dormitory. *boys'*
14. Was the message lying on Mr. Gregg's desk when he returned? *laying*
15. We will give you our answer in three weeks time. *weeks'*
16. The *ws* on that stencil were not struck hard enough. *w's*
17. There are many doctors offices' in our building. *doctors' offices*
18. Did the Black's attend the Christmas party? *Blacks*
19. From the lobby could be heard the shrill sound of lady's voices. *ladies'*
20. Your data regarding income tax reductions is incorrect. *are*

Editing Practice

Call an Editor! Rewrite the following letter, editing it to make the necessary corrections.

Dear Howard:

It looks as though Fred was right about the Kelly's. They have admitted that their assets are froze.

Do you think that we should call for a meeting of chief of staffs of all the other industrys affected by the Kelly's misfortune? Do you know of any procedural plans that were lain in anticipation of such a happening?

I expect to be in Boston on Monday of next week, and may be we should meet for lunch and pool our information. As presidents of vitally concerned firms, you and I must corporate if we are to protect our company's interests.

Sincerely yours,

The Pool Supervisor Check to see if there are any spelling errors in the following paragraph, which was transcribed by one of your pool stenographers. If so, write the correct spelling or spellings.

We are not satisfied with the prooves of the pictures for our new housing development and ask that you retake them. The fact that each house has a fireplace is a strong selling point; therefore, all pictures for our brochure should be taken from an angle that shows fireplace chimnies. We should very much appreciate your getting the new pictures to us by May 9.

Case Problem

The Correspondence Consultant   In Section II, you outlined your preliminary plan for improving letters written by the personnel of Blanton, Inc. One phase of that plan was to study samples of letters currently being written. What are some of the weaknesses you expect to find?

13 — Pronouns—Nominative and Objective Case

"Your inquiry of June 5 has been referred to Mr. Corey and myself." "Membership in the Association benefits we manufacturers in a multitude of ways." "Call on Burr or I whenever you need information about market trends." Any business communication that contains the type of error occurring in the foregoing sentences makes a poor impression. Why? Because the incorrect case forms of pronouns that are used are especially offensive to persons who know their grammar. Using pronouns correctly is not a matter of guesswork; it is the result of study and practice. To be proficient in pronoun usage, the communicator must understand the term "case" and must be able almost automatically to use the correct case form. The discussion of case in this and the following part is a streamlined treatment of this phase of grammar. Only the pronouns that are subject to error are studied.

CASE

Case refers to the form of a noun or a pronoun that indicates the relation of that word to other words in the sentence. The subject of this study is limited to the correct use of pronouns.

There are three cases: nominative, objective, and possessive. You have already studied pronoun possessives. To reduce learning time, emphasis is placed here on nominative-case principles.

A speaker or a writer, when using pronouns, has to choose between two cases, nominative and objective. As soon as he is thoroughly grounded in nominative-case usage, he knows immediately that a pronoun not conforming to a nominative-case rule must be in the objective case. There is, then, no real need to memorize the rules for the use of the objective case.

NOMINATIVE- AND OBJECTIVE-CASE FORMS OF PRONOUNS

The pronouns that have different forms in the nominative and in the objective cases are *I, he, she, we, they,* and *who.* Accurate selection of correct pronouns is based upon knowing which is the nominative and which is the objective form of each pronoun. The forms are as follows:

Nominative	I	he	she	we	they	who
Objective	me	him	her	us	them	whom

NOMINATIVE CASE

Among the many rules for the use of the nominative case, only three are really needed for correct use of the nominative case of pronouns.

Subject of a Verb

Any pronoun that is the subject of a verb, either the simple subject or part of a compound subject, is in the nominative case.

> *I* will go to the bank. (Why not *Me will go to the bank*? Because *I*, the nominative form, must be used as the subject of a verb. *Me* is the objective form.)

Predicate Nominative

A predicate nominative is a noun or a pronoun that completes the meaning of a "being" verb. The "being" verbs, as you know, are *am, is, are, was, were*, helper *be*, and helper(s) *been*. Any pronoun that follows and completes the meaning of any one of these "being" verbs must always be in the nominative case.

> If I were (he? him?), I would correct the error. (*Were* is a "being" verb. A pronoun that completes the meaning of a "being" verb is in the nominative case. Therefore, the nominative *he* is correct.)
>
> It must have been (they? them?) whom we saw. (Do you see *must have been*? Then you know at once that *they*, the nominative case, is correct.)

Complement of the Infinitive To Be When To Be Has No Subject

Any pronoun that follows and completes the meaning of the infinitive *to be* when *to be* has no subject of its own is in the nominative case. To be sure that this rule will be applied correctly, you must understand that (1) the rule applies *only* to the infinitive *to be* and must not be used in any other situation, and (2) the infinitive *to be* will have a subject of its own only if a noun or a pronoun immediately precedes it.

Study the thinking process used in the following illustrations.

> Who would ever wish to be (I? me?)? (Do you see *to be*? Is there a noun or a pronoun directly before it? No. Then this *to be* has no subject of its own, and the nominative *I* is correct.)
>
> The receptionist mistakenly thought the visitors to be (we? us?). (Do you see *to be*? Is there a noun or a pronoun directly before it? Yes, *visitors*. This *to be*, then, does have a subject of its own, *visitors*; and the nominative-case form after it would be incorrect. Obviously, the objective *us* is correct in this sentence.)

MEMORY HOOK

For a Memory Hook on which to hang the *to be* rule, make this connection:

NO subject—NOminative case

NO is the word to remember, and *NO* starts the word *NOminative*. Hooking up the two "No's" makes for immediate, correct application of the rule.

Correct the pronoun forms in these sentences. If the correction is a nominative-case form, give your reason. Do not attempt to give a reason for choosing an objective-case form. Your only reason would be that, as the pronoun could not be the nominative form, the objective form must be correct.

1. Whom is planning to go to Chicago?
2. The most trustworthy workers are them who accept responsibility.
3. Mr. Resnik thought Joseph to be me.
4. Because his face was shaded, Joseph was thought to be me.
5. "Yes," she said, "this is her."
6. Who made the last touchdown?
7. Why did you say that it must be me who was ill?
8. The telephone operator is often taken to be her.
9. If you were me, would you look for another position?
10. Callers often take the receptionist to be she.

OBJECTIVE-CASE FORMS OF PRONOUNS

The efficient way to select objective-case forms of pronouns is to know that the objective case is correct whenever a pronoun does not conform to one of the nominative-case principles. Some writers, however, might like to be able to quote the rules for use of the objective-case forms. For that reason, principles governing use of the objective case are given here.

The objective-case forms of personal pronouns and of *who* are used when the pronoun is:

- The object of a verb, a preposition, or an infinitive.
- The subject of an infinitive.
- The complement of the infinitive *to be* when *to be* does have a subject of its own.

PRONOUN USAGE PROBLEMS

There are five instances where correct pronoun usage frequently poses a problem. Solutions to three of these problem situations are given in this section, and the remaining two will be discussed in Section 14. Follow closely the presentation and the explanations given here.

Ross and I *or* Ross and Me?

A compound subject or object is composed of two like elements connected by a coordinate conjunction, such as *Tom or David, Mr. Dunn and I, Bob or me, you and him.* When a pronoun is part of a compound subject or object, an all-too-frequent error is the use of the incorrect form of that pronoun. For instance: "Sue and (she? her?) tabulated the data." "Mr. Gray sat in front of Ruth and (I? me?)." You will be able to select instantly the correct case form of a pronoun occurring in a compound subject or object if you learn the following Memory Hook.

Whenever a compound subject or object contains a pronoun—*Ann and she, Frank or him*—mentally omit everything in the compound except the pronoun. Then read or say the sentence, and the correct form stands out like a beacon light. For example:

> Mr. Ryan and (I? me?) will find the discrepancy. (Omit *Mr. Ryan and,* and you must say: "*I* will find the discrepancy.")
>
> I should like to sit in front of Frank or (he? him?). (Omit *Frank or,* and you must say: "I should like to sit in front of *him.*")

We Men *or* Us Men?

The correct pronoun is seldom used in such expressions (called "restrictive appositives") as *we girls, us fellows, we writers, us teachers.* For this situation, too, there is a Memory Hook that will solve the problem—and solve it fast!

MEMORY HOOK

When you are about to use a pronoun in a restrictive appositive, mentally omit the noun and retain only the pronoun. Read or say the sentence and use only the pronoun. The correct form will become immediately apparent.

> (We? Us?) writers must use imagination. (Omit the noun *writers,* read the sentence, and you come up with this: "*We* must use imagination." *We* is correct because it is the subject of the verb *must use.*)
>
> Mr. Sibley told (we? us?) writers to use imagination. (Omitting *writers* and rereading the sentence forces out the correct pronoun form: "Mr. Sibley told *us* to use imagination.")

CHECKUP 2

Use the Memory Hooks just learned to determine whether the correct pronoun forms are used in the following sentences. If a nominative-case form is used to correct a sentence, be sure to quote the rule that justifies this choice.

1. Us fellows should stick together.
2. Give the papers to Mr. Wilbur or he.
3. Pete and me will carry out the extensions.
4. Would you like we girls to type the tabs?
5. Was that David or him in the elevator?
6. It must have been us accountants who mixed up the assignments.

Which Case Form After *Than* or *As?*

A pronoun that follows *than* or *as* in a statement of comparison frequently appears in an incomplete clause, such as "You are more skilled than (I? me?)." "Proofreading bores Miss Riley as much as (I? me?)." The correct pronoun form can be determined by mentally supplying the words that are not expressed; for example, "You are more skilled than *I am.*" *I* stands out as the subject of the understood verb. "Proofreading bores Miss Riley as much as *it bores me.*"

With the solution to the problem in mind, study the following examples:

> Ann says that she has higher speed than (I? me?). (Supply the un-expressed words, as follows: "Ann says that she has higher speed than *I have.*" *I* is correct because it is the subject of the under-stood verb.)
>
> Unnecessary waste distresses Mr. Reed as much as (I? me?). (The complete meaning is this: "Unnecessary waste distresses Mr. Reed as much as *it distresses me.*")

Sometimes the pronoun form depends on the meaning given by voice em-phasis. Italics are used for written emphasis, and italics are used in the prac-tice sentences where voice emphasis shows the meaning that determines the selection of the correct pronoun. For example, see Sentence 2 below.

CHECKUP 3

The following sentences provide practice in applying solutions to the three problem situations just presented. If you choose a nominative-case form, give the reason for your choice.

1. It should be Jane or me who gets the next call.
2. I do hope they give *you* better treatment than we.
3. Surely the next caller ought to be Mr. Shelby or him.
4. I do hope *they* give you better treatment than us.
5. You students sometimes give we teachers food for thought.
6. Do you think you have been as faithful as him?
7. Every one of we clerks is interested in his work.
8. Our office force works much harder than them.

COMMUNICATION PROJECTS

Practical Application

A

Make any needed corrections in the following sentences. Use these short forms to indi-cate your reasons for selecting nominative-case forms: *s.o.v.* (for "subject of the verb"), *p.n.* (for "predicate nominative"), or *to be, no subject* (for "this *to be* has no subject of its own").

1. Did you believe the victims to be Sue and I?
2. Both the manager and us girls missed the five o'clock bus.
3. Eugene can do that job just as well as him.
4. Whom has the answer to this problem?
5. Anna and I agree on most political issues.
6. It must have been her whom you saw in the foyer.
7. A fighting team makes it easier for we coaches to win games.
8. Did you say that Sandra was older than I?
9. Ask Pete or he to stop at my office soon.
10. Mr. Rowe asked we girls to arrange the display.
11. Sam is often taken to be me.
12. The telephone call was for Mr. Sheedy or I.
13. Was it him who released the information?
14. On closer acquaintance, I find that I like *Roy* better than he.

her 15. Mr. Sims took the movie star to be she. *to be with subj*

16. I should like to have you and her retype these papers. *OK*

we 17. Do you think that us men have a chance to win the tournament? *subj of 'that' clause*

I 18. It would be me who would make such a silly mistake!

her 19. Would you trust *Ellen* rather than she? *obo.*

20. Please let us bookkeepers check our own figures. *OK*

B Correct the following sentences wherever necessary. If a sentence is correct, write *OK* on your paper.

1. They're expecting to call in all their outstanding notes now. *Their*
2. All bidders specifications' have been mailed. *bidders' specs.*
3. We think that Kay is a better operator than her. *she (subj.)*
4. Now that the painters are here, our office is all tore up. *torn*
5. Who did you take me to be? *Whom — to be with subj.*
6. Between you and I, this news will upset Mr. Bowen. *me — prep*
7. The accident victim was lying in the road. *laying — past*
8. Could it be him who placed the call? *he — p.n.*
9. Nobody has to tell we typists how to set up a tabulation. *us — ind.o.*
10. Find out about the Rosses' credit rating before you answer their letter. *OK*
11. Please give these schedules to Bob and he. *him — prep.*
12. Are *you* as friendly with Simon as him? *OK*
13. Have the Ellises answered our letter? *OK*
14. Would you like to be her, even with her great wealth? *she — to be — no subj*
15. Did you know that us operators are in line for a bonus? *we — subj of that clause*
16. Our linen handkerchieves are imported from Ireland. *handkerchiefs*
17. If he were I, he would surely say the same thing. *OK*
18. Mr. Bolton plans to take his secretary and I to the meeting. *me — indirect object*
19. The sopranos' voices were sweet, but they showed lack of training. *OK*
20. Mr. Cotter and us other executives will work next Saturday. *we — subj*

Editing Practice

Plurals and Possessives   Indicate any errors in plurals or in possessive case. Write *OK* for any correct sentence.

1. There are two fife and drum corpses in our city.
2. Boys shoes' cost as much as grown men's.
3. The famous Davis' sisters are among our best customers.
4. They're so sure that their billfolds will stay there untouched.
5. I dislike his voice, but I like her's.
6. The firm is composed of Mr. Scott and his two brother-in-law's.
7. Deliver this package to the Schwartzes' front door.
8. The cafeteria sandwiches' are a little stale.
9. The sixes in this copy must have been struck with a light touch.
10. There are no George's in our office.

Only One Word   The polish of a letter can sometimes be dimmed by just one word, as is the case in this paragraph. Can you find the word and make the correction?

> Your analysis of the buying habits of our charge-account customers is very well done and will be of help to all of us here at Blanton's. The only suggestion I have to make is that you delete pages 5 and 6. These pages list details that are irrevelant, minutiae that serve only to obscure the points brought out in the first four pages. If I can be of further help, just let me know.

Case Problem

The Correspondence Consultant   Now that you have completed your study of the letters written by the staff of Blanton, Inc., you should be ready to make recommendations for improvement. What would be your recommendations?

Pronouns—Additional Usage Problems

In Section 10 mention was made of the informal study of grammar stumbling blocks conducted by an English professor. Tabulation of his data showed that uncertainty about the use of *lie* and *lay*, *sit* and *set*, and *rise* and *raise* ranked among the three top areas of difficulty. The data also showed that the inability to use *who* and *whom* correctly shared top honors, if confusion be an honor. After presenting the remaining pronoun usage problems and their solutions, the pronoun instruction in this section concentrates on taking the mystery out of *who, whom* usage.

SELF-ENDING PRONOUNS

Myself, yourself, himself, herself, itself, ourselves, yourselves, and *themselves* are the *self*-ending pronouns. These pronouns are often incorrectly and mistakenly used in place of the nominative- or objective-case form of a personal pronoun. For instance, in the sentence "Mrs. Cole and myself will be happy to accept your invitation," the writer, unsure about *I* or *me*, uses the *self*-ending pronoun as an escape hatch. Actually, he made just as serious an error as if he had written "Mrs. Cole and *me* will be happy . . . ." *Self*-ending pronouns are correctly used only to intensify or reflect back to another noun or pronoun.

Intensive Use

A *self*-ending pronoun is used to intensify—that is, to emphasize—the meaning of a statement. To illustrate:

> Mr. Myers told me the news. (This is an unemphatic statement.)
> Mr. Myers *himself* told me the news. (The word *himself* intensifies the meaning.)

A word of caution is needed here. Take care to place a *self*-ending pronoun where it will perform its emphasizing function. Careless placement might result in something like the following:

> She said that the home economics teacher cannot sew herself. (Written correctly and with a less painful implication, the sentence reads: "She said that the home economics teacher *herself* cannot sew.")

Reflexive Use

A *self*-ending pronoun may also be used to reflect back to some noun or pronoun that has already been named. For example:

> How often have you had occasion to pat yourself on the back? (*Yourself* refers to *you*.)
> Legislators should not vote themselves increases in salary. (*Themselves* refers to *legislators*.)

CASE OF PRONOUN APPOSITIVES

An appositive is a word or a group of words used to explain, or to give additional information about, a preceding word or phrase. For example:

> Our secretaries, Miss Howe and Miss Shea, will make the appointments. (*Miss Howe and Miss Shea* gives additional information about *secretaries*; therefore, *Miss Howe and Miss Shea* is an appositive.)

Note the comma before and the comma after the appositive. An important punctuation rule is this: *A nonrestrictive appositive is set off by commas.*

The case rule for appositives is the following: *An appositive is in the same case as the word with which it is in apposition.* The case form of an appositive is a problem only when that appositive is a compound containing a pronoun, such as "Our secretaries, Miss Howe and (she? her?), will make the appointments." To solve this problem, use the following Memory Hook.

MEMORY HOOK

Using the Memory Hook for compounds, which was presented in Section 13, omit the noun in the compound. In addition, omit also the word or words with which the compound is in apposition, like this:

> Our secretaries, Miss Howe and (she? her?), will make the appointments. (*Miss Howe and* would be omitted because there is a pronoun in the compound. Now omit *our secretaries,* the words with which the compound is in apposition. The result is this: She *will make the appointments.*)
>
> Mr. Baker commended our junior executives, Bill and (he? him?). (Use of the Memory Hook results in the following: *Mr. Baker commended* him.)

CHECKUP 1

Which sentences are incorrect? Why?

1. Those writers, Andy and him, are making real progress.
2. We are not ready to ship ourselves.
3. The shirkers are known to be those typists, Alma and her.
4. Would you like Ann and myself to get those papers in order?
5. Our good neighbors, Mrs. Brooks and she, invited us to tea.
6. Jim and I will treat ourselves to a good lunch.
7. Both Mr. Senay and myself have been working steadily all day.
8. The successful candidates were the first two, Selden and him.
9. The machine is operated by Paul and myself.
10. Mr. Myers put us, Brian and myself, in charge.

WHO, WHOM; WHOEVER, WHOMEVER

The pronouns *who* and *whoever* are nominative-case forms; *whom* and *whomever* are objective-case forms. If the pronoun is the subject of a verb, a predicate nominative, or the complement of a *to be* that has no subject of its own, use the nominative form. If the pronoun is none of these, use the objective form. The selection process, however, can be considerably speeded up by using the following Memory Hook.

MEMORY HOOK

When faced with a choice between *who* and *whom* or *whoever* and *whomever,* do this: Mentally substitute *he* or *him.* If *he* could be used, the correct pronoun is *who* or *whoever.* If *him* could be used, the correct pronoun is *whom* or *whomever.* For example:

> (Who? Whom?) did Mr. King mention just now? (Change the sentence to normal order and make the substitution: *Mr. King did mention (him).* The correct pronoun is *whom* because *him* can be substituted.)
>
> (Who? Whom?) was John thought to be? (Normal order: *John was thought to be (he). Who* is correct because it is the complement of a *to be* that has no subject of its own.)

Who, Whom *in an Interrogative Sentence*

In almost all instances, a question containing *who* or *whom* will be in inverted order. First, change the order from inverted to normal order. Then apply the Memory Hook above. Here are some additional illustrations.

> (Who? Whom?) is the man wearing tennis shoes? (Normal order: *The man wearing tennis shoes is (he). Who* is correct because it is a predicate nominative.)
>
> (Who? Whom?) do you take me for? (Normal order: *You do take me for (him). Whom* is correct because *him* can be substituted.)

A few *who, whom* questions are not in inverted order because there is no way that the order can be changed. In such questions, use of the Memory Hook will pinpoint the correct pronoun. For instance:

> (Who? Whom?) is supposed to revise the filing system? (Make the substitution: *(He) is supposed . . . . Who* is correct because it is the subject of the verb.)
>
> (Whoever? Whomever?) would believe your fantastic story? (*(He) would believe . . . . Whoever* is correct because it is the subject of the verb.)

CHECKUP 2

Use the Memory Hook to decide whether or not the pronouns are correct. If you use *who,* quote the nominative-case rule that applies.

1. Whom will Mr. Tudor send to Boston?
2. Who did you bring with you?
3. Whom is assigned to inspect the missiles?
4. Who did Mr. Tyler have to help him?
5. Who did you meet at the convention?

Who, Whom; Whoever, Whomever *in a Dependent Clause*

Most *who, whom* errors are made when that pronoun is used in a dependent clause. The selection procedure given here has been carefully thought out and tested. If it is followed exactly as presented, the error count will be zero. There are two steps to the procedure.

Step 1   Isolate, or take out, the clause. The pronoun is part of the dependent clause to which it belongs, and the case form is determined by the function of that pronoun in the dependent clause. When isolating a clause, start with the word *who, whom, whoever,* or *whomever.* For example:

> Edgar talks to (whoever, whomever) he meets on the bus. (Isolate the clause: *(whoever, whomever) he meets on the bus.)*
>
> I do not know (who, whom) the caller could have been. (Isolate the clause: *(who, whom) the caller could have been.)*
>
> Be gracious to (whoever, whomever) calls on the telephone. (Isolate the clause: *(whoever, whomever) calls on the telephone.)*

Step 2   If the isolated clause is in inverted order, change it to normal order. The order of the clause can be seen at a quick glance. If only the *who* pronoun appears before the verb, the clause is in normal order. If a *who* pronoun *plus* a noun or another pronoun appear before the verb, the clause is in inverted order. To make Step 2 absolutely clear, consider the clauses that were isolated in the Step 1 illustrations.

> (whoever, whomever) he meets on the bus. (The *who* pronoun plus the pronoun *he* appear before the verb. This clause, therefore, is out of order. The normal order is this: *he meets (him) on the bus.* Whomever is correct because *him* can be substituted.)
>
> (who, whom) the caller could have been. (The *who* pronoun plus the noun *caller* appear before the verb; therefore, the clause is in inverted order. The normal order is this: *the caller could have been (he).* Who is correct because it is a predicate nominative.)
>
> (whoever, whomever) calls on the telephone. (Since only the *who* pronoun appears before the verb, the clause is in normal order. Using the Memory Hook, make the substitution: *(he) calls on the telephone.* Whoever is correct because it is the subject of the verb.)

CHECKUP 3

When studying these sentences, be sure to follow the Step 1 and Step 2 procedure. Select the correct pronouns and justify your selections.

1. Our boss is a man (who, whom) everyone admires.
2. This question is for (whoever, whomever) has the correct data.
3. John Crowley, (who, whom) you met yesterday, is a missiles expert.
4. John Crowley, (who, whom) was introduced to you yesterday, is a missiles expert.
5. Do you know (who, whom) will be awarded the honorary title?
6. (Whoever, Whomever) draws the short straw will have to clean the machines.
7. Have you heard (who, whom) will be chosen to help Mr. Adams?

Clause Within a **Who, Whom** *Clause*   Sometimes confusion is caused by a parenthetical clause—*I think, he says, we believe*—that occurs within a *who, whom* clause. Whenever you see a clause like this, mentally omit it. Omitting the parenthetical clause will enable you to select the correct pronoun more quickly. For example:

> Is that the man (who, whom) you said I should introduce to Mr. Abbot? (Step 1—Isolate the clause: *(who, whom) you said I should introduce to Mr. Abbot.* Omit the parenthetical clause *you said.* The normal order of the resulting clause is this: *I should introduce (him) to Mr. Abbot. Whom* is correct because *him* can be substituted.)

However, the process of selecting the correct pronoun is the same even if the parenthetical clause is retained. Consider the clause discussed above.

> (who, whom) you said I should introduce to Mr. Abbot. (The normal order of the clause is this: *you said I should introduce (him) to Mr. Abbot.* Again, *whom* is correct because *him* can be substituted.)

CHECKUP 4

Make any necessary corrections, and explain your reasons for making them. If a nominative form is selected, give the rule that governs its use.

1. Do you know who they will select?
2. We invited Tom, whom everyone knows is so popular.
3. Do you know who will be selected?
4. You are one of the young men whom I saw at the party.
5. Please send whoever Mr. Parks says to send.
6. You may give these records to whoever you choose.
7. You may give the records to whomever asks for them.
8. Todd is a man whom I believe will do fine work.

COMMUNICATION PROJECTS

Practical Application

Ⓐ Make the necessary corrections in the following sentences. Give reasons for nominative-case choices.

1. Whom do you think will win the prize?
2. Miss Abel is one stenographer who I am sure can take Mr. Lark's dictation.
3. Mr. Weir asked Janet and myself to share the switchboard duty.
4. Otto has a disgusting habit of flattering persons whom he thinks might be useful to him. *who*
5. The calls might have been from them, Mr. Buck and he.
6. The guide explained to Bill and myself the reason for the delay.
7. We, Vincent and myself, are science majors.
8. Whom shall I ask to sit at this desk?
9. Wait a minute. I'm just going to leave myself.
10. The cochairmen, Mr. Card and him, have called a meeting for Friday.
11. I have listed the names of all who she said had the best recommendations.
12. Who is the better typist, Barbara or she?
13. Tell whomever is first to arrive to unlock all the doors.
14. Our very best friends are they, Amy and her.
15. The promotion will be given to whoever we think deserves it.
16. Mr. Kain asked Fred and myself to sell tickets for the game.
17. Who does Mr. Tubbs outrank in seniority?

18. Where are the old plumbers, Mr. Tate and him?
19. Was that assignment supposed to be for us, Dennis and myself?
20. Whom do you think you are?

Correct the following sentences wherever necessary. If a sentence is correct, write *OK* on your paper.

1. Who do you believe to be the better typist?
2. Because of the population explosion, teacher's positions are plentiful.
3. Submit your proposal to Mr. Clay or me.
4. Whom do you consider is the best scientist in our plant?
5. Who did they take Joseph to be?
6. Whose the new stenographer in the pool?
7. Mr. Gray says that there is always work for Frank and he to do.
8. Give Tony and myself a chance to develop our plan.
9. Mr. Welch is no friend of her's.
10. If it were possible, who would you wish to be?
11. Surely you do not expect us drivers to take another test!
12. Whom did you think him to be, Bob or he?
13. The election is a question of whom conducts the best campaign.
14. I left the pen with the girl whom I thought had charge of lost articles.
15. The fastest operators are Andy and him.
16. Cynthia wears as much jewelry as me.
17. The visitor who you saw in the office this morning came to see Mr. Byrne and me.
18. You should select whoever you think will work well with our group.
19. Our favorite researchers, Mr. Carr and he, have found the answer to our problem.
20. A good receptionist does not become too friendly with a caller who she does not know.

Editing Practice

Spelling and Possessives Indicate any errors in spelling or errors in the use of possessive case. Write *OK* for any correct sentence.

1. "A full day's work for a full day's pay" is a slogan that is worth adopting.
2. Since we pay by check, we do not need a reciept.
3. Their will be no sales meeting this week.
4. We have the only original copy in existance.
5. Please tell us what its all about.
6. We are sending a remittance with this order.
7. Did you know that there receiving an additional week's wages?
8. Be sure to send a letter of transmital with each contract.
9. The wives' of overseas soldiers are eagerly waiting for the mail.
10. The extra bonus was a surprise to all of us.

The Sour Note Somewhere in this paragraph is a sour note that destroys the effect of a smoothly flowing writing performance. Find the error and correct it.

      Thank you for telling us so soon that you are unable to accept an appointment as trustee for the Community Center. We realise that you give your services to many civic and religious organizations, and we can understand that there must be a cut-off place somewhere; but we did hope that you might be able to take on just one more—the Community Center. Do you think you could find time to be a "consultant-at-large," a person upon whom we could call for advice on some particularly knotty problem?

Case Problem

The Wrong Impression Fred Clay was being interviewed by William Dalton, general manager, for a position as office supervisor with the Economy Printing Company. During the interview two important points were brought out: (1) the formal training in supervision that Fred had and (2) Fred's experience as a supervisor. Fred proudly mentioned his ten years of work experience and emphasized the value of this phase of his background for the office supervisor's job. He casually told Mr. Dalton that he had no formal training in supervision but that his work experience taught him all he needed to know.

Later on, Mr. Dalton asked Fred for his philosophy of supervision. Fred replied tartly: "I believe a supervisor's job is to keep close tabs on everybody so that they get their work done and don't get out of line. It is certainly not necessary to let them in on everything. What they don't know doesn't hurt them."

A few days after the personal interview with Mr. Dalton, Fred received a letter from the Economy Printing Company thanking him for making application with them, but indicating that someone else had been hired for the position. Naturally, Fred was disappointed and tried to determine whether something had gone wrong in the interview, since his experience was exactly what the company wanted.

1. What went wrong in the interview that cost Fred this job?
2. What might Fred have said regarding training in supervision that might have helped him get this job?

Predicate Agreement— With Simple Subject

When a man writes or dictates "One of us *are*," instead of "One of us *is*," he makes a major grammatical error called "lack of predicate agreement." In conversation, this serious error in grammar might pass unnoticed or might be quickly forgotten. Listeners are concentrating on getting the message of a sentence and tying it in with other thoughts. That same error in a written sentence, however, would not escape a reader. He could see it, read it, and reread it. Any sentence error made by a business correspondent, therefore, will show—and will remain showing for a long time. Errors in subject-predicate agreement are so frequent and so noticeable that a detailed treatment of predicate agreement must be given in this section and in Sections 16 and 17. Each agreement rule applies only to one particular type of subject. Each rule should be thoroughly understood before advancing to the next.

In this part, the basic agreement rule and the rules for predicate agreement with two different types of simple subjects are presented for study and practice. The rules for predicate agreement with the four remaining types of simple subjects are presented in Section 16.

BASIC AGREEMENT PRINCIPLE

The basic agreement rule for all sentences that have a simple subject is this: *A predicate must agree in number and person with the simple subject.* The following examples illustrate subject-verb agreement.

> The executives who work in our building (is? are?) assigned special parking spaces. (The simple subject is *executives*, which is plural; therefore, the plural verb *are* agrees with the plural subject.)
>
> A man of many accomplishments (is? are?) likely to succeed. (The simple subject is *man*, which is singular; therefore, the singular verb *is* agrees with the singular subject.)

Agreement Preliminaries

Four preliminary and contributing elements must be understood before agreement rules can be applied correctly. These are the topics discussed here.

Predicate Verb and Pronoun(s) The basic principle states that "a predicate must agree." The meaning is that the *predicate verb* and any *predicate pronoun* or *pronouns* referring to the simple subject must agree with that subject. For instance:

> The office, together with the furnishings (has? have?) been cleaned for (his? her? its? their?) new occupants. (The simple subject is *office,* which is singular in number and neuter in gender. Therefore, to agree with *office,* the correct predicate verb and predicate pronoun are *has* and *its.*)
>
> Our sister (likes? like?) to have (his? her? their?) breakfast early. (The simple subject is *sister,* which is singular in number and feminine in gender. The predicate verb and predicate pronoun are *likes* and *her,* to agree with *sister.*)

Correct Pronoun Choice Whenever the gender of a simple subject is clearly masculine or feminine, the correct pronoun choice presents no problem. Some simple subjects, such as *citizen* and *employee,* could be either masculine or feminine. Whenever there is doubt as to the gender of the simple subject, use a masculine pronoun to refer to that subject. For example:

> Nobody knows what the future has in store for (him? her?) or for (his? her?) children. (The gender of the singular subject *nobody* could be masculine or feminine. Therefore, the correct pronouns are *him* and *his,* to agree with *nobody.*)
>
> Every citizen is entitled to take (his? her?) convictions to the polls with (him? her?). (The gender of the singular subject *citizen* cannot be determined. Therefore, the correct pronoun choices are *his* and *him,* to agree with *citizen.*)

Singular or Plural Verb Sometimes agreement errors are made because writers forget that a verb that ends in *s* or *es* is singular. They are confused by the fact that, whereas a *plural noun* usually ends in *s* or *es,* it is the *singular verb* form that often ends in *s* or *es.* Remember that *s* or *es* is a signal that the verb is singular. Say or write:

> The men *go;* but the man *goes.*
> Children *have talked;* but the child *has talked* or the child *talks.*
> Contestants *guess;* but the contestant *guesses* or *has guessed.*

Inverted Order To find the subject more easily, change sentences that are in inverted order to normal order. This principle, taught in Section 8 and practiced in succeeding lessons, is repeated here because failure to make the change is often the cause of errors in predicate agreement, as shown by the following examples.

> Behind the tables (was? were?) the package we mislaid yesterday. (The careless person sees *tables* and uses the plural verb *were.* *Package,* however, is the simple subject; therefore, the correct verb is *was.*)
>
> In the file (is? are?) the folders containing news clippings. (Mentally changing this sentence to normal order shows *folders* to be the simple subject. *Are,* therefore, is the correct verb.)

CHECKUP 1

Make the necessary corrections in the following sentences, using the answer form shown below.

> Sentence: If a poorly dressed stranger call, treat them courteously.
> Answer: *calls* and *him,* to agree with *stranger.*

1. A large selection of costume accessories are available in the basement store.
2. The entire plant, with all their buildings, are for sale.
3. A customer must exchange their purchases before January 5.
4. Behind the microphones is our general manager.
5. A shipment of automobile parts are on their way to us now.
6. Among those elected as directors are Mr. E.A. Holmes.
7. Each of us have our own desk.
8. Mr. Foley, as well as you, are being asked to test the machine.

THERE AT THE BEGINNING OF A SENTENCE OR CLAUSE

A sentence or clause that begins with *there*—*there is, there are, there has been, there have been,* and like expressions—is in inverted order. The subject, therefore, follows the verb. In accordance with the basic principle, the predicate must agree with the simple subject. For example:

> Miss Rowe says that there (is? are?) two callers waiting to see you. (The simple subject of the clause is the plural noun *callers.* Your selection is *are,* to agree with *callers.*)
>
> There (is? are?) several persons who have difficulty with (his? her? their?) spelling. (Changing to normal order shows the plural noun *persons* to be the simple subject. Therefore, your selection is *are* and *their,* to agree with *persons.*)

CHECKUP 2

Make the necessary corrections in these sentences, giving your answers in the form set up in Checkup 1.

1. There is not very many executives who have returned the questionnaires.
2. Did you know that there is ten questions still to be answered?
3. We realize that there is grave danger of a crisis.
4. Mrs. Gurney said that there is no more appointments today.
5. We think that there is more goods coming in tomorrow.

COLLECTIVE-NOUN SIMPLE SUBJECT

A collective noun is a word that refers to a group or collection of persons or things, such as *class, faculty, herd, jury, committee, audience,* and *company.* The correct number, singular or plural, of a collective noun is not always easily recognized. If the group or collection is considered as acting as a whole, the subject is singular; if considered as acting separately, the subject is plural.

To be interpreted as acting separately, the sentence context must be such that only a plural predicate could be used. For instance:

> A jury (does? do?) not give (his? its? their?) verdict carelessly. (*Jury* is a collective noun and in this sentence is acting as a whole, as one unit. Your selection would be *does* and *its*, to agree with *jury*.)
>
> The jury (is? are?) arguing vehemently. (To argue, more than one person is needed. The plural verb *are* is correct because the jury members are acting separately.)

CHECKUP 3

These sentences provide practice in all the agreement principles studied thus far. Make the necessary corrections, giving your answers in the form used in Checkups 1 and 2.

1. The principal announced that the faculty was excused from attendance at the assembly.
2. Did you find that there was three enclosures in that letter?
3. A lawyer, as well as many teachers, have to carry a briefcase with them.
4. One of you seem to be doubtful about your investments.
5. Every nation looks to their leaders for guidance.
6. The committee was consulting with their individual attorneys.
7. Do you believe that an employee is obligated to do some of their work at home?
8. Our company have completed their twentieth year in business.
9. On my desk are staplers that do not belong to me.
10. The audience were preparing to leave the theater.

COMMUNICATION PROJECTS

Practical Application

Ⓐ Correct the following sentences, following the answer form shown below.

Sentence: All employees of the institution does not take its vacation during the summer.
Answer: *Do* and *their*, to agree with *employees*.

1. Physics, in addition to chemistry and physical science, are being offered in evening school.
2. There is various ways of setting up a letter.
3. The Rotary Club hold their social events at the Elm Tree Inn.
4. No administrative assistant will leave until they finish their work.
5. The complete list of desks, tables, and chairs shows a need for additional equipment.
6. There is always two sides to every question.
7. The council was evidently quarreling among themselves.
8. Have even one of those girls eaten their lunch?
9. The wealthy alumnus, as well as the Trustees, appear to favor the plan.
10. There are various types of form letters that come in every day.
11. After the introductory remarks come the prepared speech.
12. You, as well as I, are eligible for the appointment.
13. Four carbons, as well as the original, is to be typed for all letters to Barr & Company.
14. The public has widely differing opinions about secondary-school education.
15. The agency reported that there was several openings for file clerks.

16. The chairman said that each group must make its own rules.
17. Every officer of the League of Women Voters have paid their dues.
18. For how long a time has those sisters been married?
19. Has there been many salesmen in the machine shop today?
20. The news about Social Security increases have just reached us.

B Correct the following sentences. If a sentence is correct, write *OK* on your paper.

1. Doesn't his balance check with your's?
2. The committee has signed their names to all vouchers.
3. Is there ten reams in that package?
4. Has the lieutenant's general daughter arrived yet?
5. Why do you suppose Mr. Knott took Sue to be me?
6. Is the president's whereabouts a deep secret?
7. Mr. Canty, as well as the other bosses, have their lunch without leaving their desk.
8. Where have the Bindloss's decided to build their factory?
9. Every one of we girls has her own correspondence routine.
10. No body of men have ever rendered finer service to the country.
11. Every man in the locker rooms have their special complaints about the service.
12. The duplicator lay on it's side in the machines room.
13. When your looking for advancement, be sure that you are qualified for a promotion.
14. The survey showed that there is plenty of jobs for everyone.
15. A worker in any of the occupations gets enjoyment from outstanding achievement.

Editing Practice

Editor Needed!   Rewrite this letter, making the necessary corrections.

Gentlemen:

Mr. Dunn and myself have carefully considered your application for further credit. In our company, however, many policies designed to cover every aspect of the business is in effect. According to one company policy, the credit officers may not extend credit beyond a $1,000 limit.

Mr. Dunn, as well as me, wishes he was able to grant your request. Until such time as your account is reduced, we shall be more then happy to do business with you on a cash basis.

Very sincerely yours,

Pseudohomonyms   As you know, pseudohomonyms are words that sound somewhat alike but have different meanings. Correct any pseudohomonym errors you find in the following paragraph.

In the name of all the personal connected with the Community Center, I thank you for accepting our invitation to act in an advisory capacity whenever legal problems arise. Your willingness to help has effected the morale of the entire staff, for we are now relieved of all worry about conforming to the numerous local ordinances. You are filling a real need, Mr. Marr, and we are very glad to have your services available to us.

Case Problem

The Perplexed Secretary   Mary Lou Jones is private secretary to an executive. One day her boss, Mr. Merriwether, indicated that he had to work all day on a speech he had to give the following day. "Do not disturb me under any circumstances," Mr. Merriwether cautioned Mary Lou. Just one hour later the telephone rang and a voice asked to speak to Mr. Merriwether. "May I ask who is calling?" Mary Lou inquired. In a slightly angered tone, the voice indicated that it was Mr. Sells, Mr. Merriwether's boss, and that he wanted to speak to Mr. Merriwether immediately.

In view of Mr. Merriwether's instructions, what should Mary Lou say to Mr. Sells? Give a reason for your answer.

Predicate Agreement—Other Types of Simple Subjects

16

The basic agreement principle, which states that the predicate must agree in number and person with the simple subject, holds true for all cases of simple-subject agreement. However, a specific rule for each of the six types of simple subjects must be learned and applied to that one type only. Keep this fact in mind when studying the following separate rules for the remaining four types of simple subjects.

FOREIGN-NOUN SUBJECT

You learned in Section 11, where the formation of plurals was discussed, that the number of a foreign noun is shown by its *ending;* for example, *datum, data; crisis, crises; stylus, styli; alumna, alumnae.* Therefore, when the simple subject of a sentence is a foreign noun, the singular or plural ending of that noun will govern predicate agreement. For example:

> The basis for his statements *was* unsound. (The predicate must be singular to agree with the singular subject *basis.*)
>
> The bases for his statements *were* unsound. (The predicate must be plural to agree with the plural subject *bases.*)

CHECKUP 1

Select the simple subject in each of these sentences and identify the rule applying to it such as *basic* (for subjects that are obviously singular or plural), *sentence or clause beginning with "there,"* *collective noun,* or *foreign noun.* Then make any corrections that may be needed.

1. There was no reasons given for his dismissal.
2. The medical staff is evidently not in agreement on this one policy.
3. Candelabra was placed on the altar before the wedding ceremony began.
4. The space ship, with its social and economic implications, are more than a figment of the imagination.
5. The faculty are to take their usual places on the dais before the Convocation.
6. Fred, as well as the other correspondents, are invited to express their opinions freely.
7. Fungi in profusion are found in the tropics.
8. There seems to be some differences of opinion about the worth of the proposal.
9. Has the analyses of distribution costs been assigned to Mr. Storrs?
10. The class has varying ideas about study procedures.

PART, PORTION, OR AMOUNT SUBJECT

Sometimes a simple subject is a word that means a part, a portion, or an amount of something, such as *all, half, some, two-thirds.* With a subject of this type, the number of the predicate cannot be determined until the following questions are answered: Part of what? Portion of what? Amount of what? For instance:

> Some (is? are?) missing. (Which is correct, *is* or *are?* Without additional information, you cannot select either verb as correct.)
>
> Some of the report (is? are?) missing. (*Is* is correct, because the subject is *some* of *one thing.*)
>
> Some of the reports (is? are?) missing. (*Are* is correct in this sentence, because the subject is *some* of *more than one thing.*)

Here is the rule that governs this type of subject: When the simple subject of a sentence is a word that means part, portion, or amount, the number of the predicate is determined by the meaning of the complete subject, not the simple subject alone.

CHECKUP 2

Make your selection of the correct word or words and indicate the word that influenced your choice. Follow this example:

> Sentence: Three-fifths of the space (is? are?) occupied by desks.
> Answer: *Is—space.*
>
> 1. Half the shipment (is? are?) damaged.
> 2. All the typewriters (needs? need?) to have (its? their?) (ribbon? ribbons?) changed.
> 3. Half the shipments (has? have?) been rerouted.
> 4. Some of the guided missiles (fails? fail?) on (its? their?) initial test.
> 5. Nine-tenths of our office (was? were?) formerly poorly lighted.
> 6. Part of the beams (was? were?) rotted by long exposure to the elements.

A NUMBER, THE NUMBER SUBJECT

A number has a plural meaning, and the predicate must be plural; *the number* has a singular meaning, and the predicate must be singular. An adjective between the *a* or *the* and *number* does not affect this principle. Here are some illustrations.

> A number of applicants (was? were?) interviewed today. (*Were,* because *a number* is plural.)
>
> The number of clerks in business offices (outnumbers? outnumber?) all other employees. (*Outnumbers,* because *the number* is singular.)
>
> A great number of inquiries about our new product (comes? come?) into the office each week. (*Come,* because *a number* is plural.)

A business writer must be able to apply the correct principles of grammar instantly. He has no time to sit and ponder. Trying to remember whether *a number* or *the number* is singular could waste thinking time; but understanding the following Memory Hook can make correct *a number, the number* application quick and easy.

MEMORY HOOK

When confronted with the choice of the correct predicate for *a number* or *the number,* picture the following:

Plural   a
Singular   the

Which is the shorter word, *plural* or *singular?* Which is the shorter word, *a* or *the?* The shorter word *a* goes with the shorter word *plural;* the longer word *the* goes with the longer word *singular.* Therefore, *a number* is *plural; the number* is *singular.*

INDEFINITE-WORD SUBJECT

The indefinite words *each, either, neither, everyone, everybody, someone, somebody, anyone, anybody, no one, nobody,* and *a person* are singular in meaning. Therefore, whenever one of these indefinite words is the subject of a sentence, the predicate will be singular. For example:

Each of us (has? have?) (his? their?) own private beliefs. (*Has* and *his,* to agree with the singular subject *each.*)
Everybody (is? are?) to take (his? their?) (place? places?) on the platform. (*Is, his, place,* to agree with *everybody.*)
A person (resents? resent?) having (his? their?) legal rights challenged. (*Resents* and *his,* to agree with *a person.*)

CHECKUP 3

These sentences provide comprehensive practice for the rules studied in Sections 15 and 16. Follow these directions: (1) name the subject; (2) identify that subject according to type; (3) make corrections where needed; and (4) give reasons for making corrections.

1. A number of persons has been asking for you, Mr. Paul.
2. Nobody is to take their confidential reports home with them.
3. Mr. Elton said that his family show their individuality by buying different makes of cars.
4. All the money have not yet been accounted for.
5. There is four state-operated hospitals in the newly admitted state.
6. Crises between labor and management makes headline news.
7. The number of available stenographers is fewer than the government needs.
8. Neither of the proposed solutions are acceptable.
9. The group announced that they were ready to report.

10. Part, but not all, of the papers was in the safe.
11. Everyone is not always able to have what they desire.
12. Miss Dean, together with the pool typists, have posted their first win in the bowling match.

COMMUNICATION PROJECTS

Practical Application

Correct each incorrect sentence in the following group, and indicate your reason for making the correction. The following example shows you how to write your answers.

Sentence: Nobody are to have their lunch hour curtailed.
Answer: *Is, his,* to agree with *nobody.*

1. Because of the delay, some of the fruit in the refrigerator cars were spoiled.
2. A number of mysterious accidents has occurred in our factory.
3. Was the alumni supposed to receive its cards this month?
4. Someone has left his notebooks on my desk.
5. Three-fourths of the time were spent in research.
6. After the victory, all the team members was in high spirits.
7. The large number of absences has held up production.
8. Put the parentheses in its proper places.
9. Neither of the applicants were chosen for the position.
10. Some bacteria is found in all liquids.
11. Only half the people in this country speaks English correctly.
12. A number of citizens is prone to criticize without knowing its facts.
13. Is the sanatorium open for inspection?
14. Neither of the women admits that she lost her receipt.
15. The number of staff members are known only by the personnel department.
16. None of the books has been returned to its special section.
17. The number of men who idle away their time are amazing.
18. Incorrect analysis of contributing causes are the reason for the protest.
19. Everyone will please tidy their own desk each night.
20. If anybody from the main office calls, be sure to get their number.

Correct the following sentences wherever necessary.

1. Some of the clerks have left their respective offices.
2. Every one of the cars you see in the showrooms are to be sold this week.
3. Everybody is judged by the quality of their performance.
4. The Board of Education recognize the need for increased school facilities.
5. A number of sets of dishes is included in the sale.
6. The Schultzes' option is to be renewed.
7. Has the data been checked by your chief accountant?
8. The audience are so large that they must be transferred to the ballroom.
9. The football heroes, Carl and he, are very popular.
10. All these facts make us realize the value of education.
11. Bill said that there were present at the meeting only Jack, Walt, and he.
12. Mr. Jacobs, as well as his assistants, are trying to beat a deadline.
13. Neither of you are receiving a duplicate income tax withholding statement.
14. Us industrialists must protest the added excise tax.
15. The number of mediocre workers are greater than one would think.
16. We found the other fellows laying on the beach.
17. Neither of the secretaries are good at computations.
18. Why don't the plant manager hire his own workers?
19. The focus of our thoughts have been on the strong points in the program.
20. In the locker rooms were stored all the missing umbrellas.

Editing Practice

Editing for Triteness   Rewrite these sentences, using more direct statements for the italicized trite expressions.

1. Your check for $686, due on August 15, is *conspicuous by its absence.*
2. It *goes without saying* that we must collect from customers in order to meet our own obligations.
3. In the past year our sales have increased *by leaps and bounds.*
4. Any plan that involves increased overhead must be *nipped in the bud.*
5. The quality and style of our coats will appeal to customers in all *walks of life.*

The Spelling-Conscious Proofreader   Find and correct any spelling errors there may be in this paragraph.

> We should like very much to accommodate your group at our hotel for your banquet on June 2, but all our dining rooms are taken for that night. However, the thought has occurred to us that you might try the Meadow Inn, where there are rooms large enough to be adequate for your purpose. Please continue to keep us in mind whenever you need banquet facilities.

Case Problem

The Beginning Dictator   Ronald G. Moore has been recently promoted to a supervisory job where, for the first time, he is responsible for writing letters to customers. He has been assigned a part-time stenographer. Rather than dictate letters to the stenographer, Ronald writes them out in longhand and asks the stenographer to type them in letter form.

1. Do you think this is an efficient procedure? Why or why not?
2. What would you suggest?

Predicate Agreement— With Compound Subject

As we saw in Section 8, the subject of a sentence may be either simple or compound. Predicate agreement with simple subjects was discussed in Sections 15 and 16. Agreement with compound subjects is presented in this section. Only two types of compound subjects are considered here—those joined by *and* and those joined by *or* or *nor.* Despite the fact that there are only two rules to be learned, many writers are confused about the correct predicate to use with a compound subject. Perhaps they do not realize that a *separate rule* covers each kind of compound subject and that there is no relationship, or carryover, between the rules. They do not understand that when they see a compound subject joined by *and,* they should use the rule that applies *only* to a compound subject joined by *and.* By the same token, when they see a compound subject joined by *or* or *nor,* they should use the *or, nor* rule.

A third topic presented later in this section, the relative-pronoun rule, might be called the "orphan" rule. The rule for agreement of the predicate in a relative-pronoun clause makes no mention of a simple or a compound subject. Your mastery of agreement rules, however, would not be complete without an understanding of this topic.

SUBJECTS JOINED BY *AND*

A compound subject joined by *and* takes a plural predicate. For example:

>Eileen *and* I *are* going. (Not *is going.*)
>Jack *and* Bill *have* made their plans.

Applying this rule is almost automatic. However, there are two instances when a compound subject joined by *and* takes a singular predicate. Watch for these exceptions.

Exception 1

When a subject consisting of two nouns joined by *and* refers to the same person or thing, a singular predicate is used. For example:

>The end *and* aim of my existence *is* a happy old age. (*End* and *aim* refers to the same thing; therefore, the predicate is singular.)
>Pie *and* ice cream *is* my favorite dessert. (This is one dessert, consisting of a piece of pie with a scoop of ice cream on top of it.)

Mastery of this agreement principle enables a writer to make his meaning clear to his readers. Look at the following illustration.

>Pie *and* ice cream *are* my favorite desserts. (Note the plural verb *are* and the plural noun *desserts*. The meaning here is that there are two kinds of desserts that the writer favors: pie is one, ice cream is the other.)

Exception 2

When two subjects joined by *and* are modified by *each, every,* or *many a,* a singular predicate is used. For instance:

>*Every* clerk, typist, *and* stenographer *is* expected to have thorough training as part of *her* educational background. (The singular verb *is* and the singular pronoun *her* are correct because the compound subject joined by *and* is modified by the word *every.*)
>*Many a* young man *and* young woman *has risen* in the business world. (The singular verb *has risen* is correct because the compound subject joined by *and* is modified by *many a.*)

CHECKUP 1

Make any needed corrections in these sentences. Give an explanation for each correction you make.

1. The letter and the envelope has been separated.
2. Bread and water is the traditional diet for incorrigibles.
3. Each man, woman, and child in the city were on the street today.
4. Accuracy and speed is both important to a typist.
5. Both Joe and Tom avails himself of all his opportunities.
6. Many an experienced worker and many a beginner have been eager to advance themselves.
7. In the early days of this nation, the bow and arrow were a formidable weapon.

SUBJECTS JOINED BY *OR* OR *NOR*

The rules for predicate agreement when a compound subject consists of words joined by *or* or *nor* can be boiled down to this: Match the predicate with that part of the subject nearer (or nearest) the verb. The following Memory Hook provides an even quicker way of applying this rule.

MEMORY HOOK

When the words in a subject are joined by *or* or *nor*, start with the part of the subject before the verb and read the rest of the sentence. For example:

> Neither the *parents nor* the *child* (was? were?) watching traffic signals. (Do you see a compound subject joined by *nor?* The part of the subject next to the verb is *child*. Say "child" and read the rest of the sentence. *Was* stands out instantly as the correct verb.)
>
> Neither the *child nor* the *parents* (was? were?) watching traffic signals. (*Parents* is the part of the subject next to the verb. Say "parents" and read the rest of the sentence. *Were* is immediately seen as the correct verb.)
>
> Either *Bill or* his *brothers* (is? are?) to be asked to exhibit (his? their?) workshop products. (*Brothers* is next to the verb. Starting with *brothers*, the sentence reads as follows: *brothers* are . . . *to show* their *workshop products*. The selection is *are* and *their*, to agree with *brothers*.)

CHECKUP 2

For practice in applying the Memory Hook for compound subjects joined by *or* or *nor*, select the correct words in the following sentences and give the reasons for your selections.

1. Neither Mark nor his helpers (has? have?) (his? their?) (mind? minds?) on (his? their?) work.
2. Neither his helpers nor Mark (has? have?) (his? their?) (mind? minds?) on (his? their?) work.
3. Either you or he (is? are?) to be transferred to the main office.
4. Either he or you (is? are?) to be transferred to the main office.
5. Neither Leo nor the twins (does? do?) good work after (his? their?) lunch hour.
6. Neither the twins nor Leo (does? do?) good work after (his? their?) lunch hour.

CHECKUP 3

Test yourself to see whether you have the two compound-subject rules under control. Make any needed corrections in these sentences and tell why you make them.

1. Neither Ann nor I are ready to start filing.
2. Each pencil, paper, and pen are to be returned to their box.
3. Neither Joe nor Tom avail themselves of all their benefits.
4. What are the sum and substance of her remarks?
5. Mercury or alcohol are used in most thermometers.

RELATIVE-PRONOUN CLAUSE

Before you learn and apply the important "orphan" rule for predicate agreement in a relative-pronoun clause, the following facts must be established.

- The relative pronouns are *who, which,* and *that.*
- A relative pronoun is called "relative" because it relates back to a word that is called an "antecedent."
- The antecedent is usually the noun or the pronoun appearing immediately before the relative pronoun.

Recognizing Relative Pronouns and Antecedents

The following illustrations are to be used as an aid to recognizing relative pronouns and their antecedents.

> Mr. Berry is one of those administrators *who* think their methods are the most efficient. (Do you see a relative pronoun? Name it. How do you know that it is a relative pronoun? Answer: "*Who* is a relative pronoun because it relates back to its antecedent *administrators.*")
>
> Where can I buy one of those erasers *that* have brushes attached to them? (What is the relative pronoun and why is it a relative pronoun? Answer: "*That* is a relative pronoun because it relates back to its antecedent *erasers.*")

In the following examples, can you see that *who, which,* and *that* are not relative pronouns? They cannot be, because they do not relate to anything. They have no antecedents.

> Who is that man carrying the brown briefcase?
> Do you know which word is correct?
> Mr. Ryan said that the man has much in his favor.

Relative-Pronoun Rule

The rule that governs predicate agreement in clauses introduced by relative pronouns is this: The predicate of a clause introduced by a relative pronoun agrees with the antecedent of that pronoun, *not* with the relative pronoun itself. Study the following Memory Hook for help in remembering this rule.

MEMORY HOOK

When you see a relative pronoun introducing a clause, omit the pronoun and use the antecedent as the subject of the clause; for example:

> Ralph is one of those employees who (thinks? think?) (he? they?) can earn much while doing little. (Omit *who.* Start with the antecedent *employees* and read on. Your selection must be *think* and *they,* to agree with *employees.*)
>
> Mr. Berry is one of those administrators who (likes? like?) to have (his? their?) work attended to at once. (Omit *who* and start with the antecedent *administrators.* Your selection is *like* and *their,* to agree with *administrators.*)
>
> Where can I buy one of those erasers that (has? have?) (a brush? brushes?) attached to (it? them?). Omit *that,* start with the antecedent *erasers,* and read on. The selection is *have, brushes, them,* to agree with *erasers.*)

In the following sentences, make corrections wherever necessary. Explain why you make your corrections.

1. A tie clasp or cuff links seems to be an appropriate gift for Mr. Kent.
2. Mr. Bender is the one who is to take the message.
3. Crackers and milk is the television snack that Bill prefers.
4. My brother is one of those reckless drivers who is always taking chances.
5. Neither you nor she are in danger of being transferred.
6. Please check the bills of lading that is in the "urgent" basket.
7. Not every writer and editor enjoy rewriting assignments.
8. The boss called my attention to some raised capitals, which is found in many typewritten communications.

COMMUNICATION PROJECTS

Practical Application

Ⓐ Write *OK* on your paper for any correct sentence. For any incorrect sentence, write the correction and your reason for making it.

1. Ham and eggs makes a substantial breakfast dish.
2. The comma or the semicolon is usually required between the parts of a compound sentence.
3. Neither he nor you are supposed to be experienced writers.
4. Every desk and chair in all the offices have been dusted today.
5. Mr. Bates bought one of those lawn mowers that does not cut up the turf with its sharp knives.
6. Jane and I am ready to type the lists now.
7. Either Mr. Cone or Mr. Blinn must give their full time to the sales campaign.
8. Each chair, desk, and cabinet in this office are in need of repair.
9. Neither Peter nor the other bookkeepers is to assemble material to be duplicated.
10. Your job is to paint the fence posts, which are being delivered today.
11. On Main Street are the best drugstore and the best department store in the city.
12. A block and tackle are of great help to construction workers.
13. Mr. Kenyon is one of those persons who is always late in keeping his appointments.
14. The tiger is one animal that is noted for pacing restlessly in its cage.
15. Many a man, woman, and child were frightened when the plane broke the sound barrier.
16. Each man and woman in this office are obligated to do their best.
17. Our sales manager is one of those men who makes friends wherever he goes.
18. Both the recorder and the treasurer submits his reports to the president.
19. Either you or Mr. Oats are to write the news release.
20. Both the editors and Mr. Kain has his wits about him today.

Ⓑ Correct the following sentences wherever necessary.

1. English is said to be the most important of the subjects that is included in the curriculum of a school.
2. There is an income statement and a trial balance still to be made out.
3. Every capital letter and punctuation mark are correctly written in Paul's letters.
4. The Mesdames Bessette is doing a thriving business.
5. There are the briefcase and the papers that I must take with me.

6. Neither Jim nor his colleagues work well with their coats on.
7. We women take just as much pride in our work as they.
8. The group have been debating among themselves as to whether they should go to the open meeting.
9. Mr. McCue is one of the few businessmen who know how to audit books.
10. Two-thirds of the consignment were lost in the railroad wreck.
11. Admittance slips or other identification are required by the guard at the main entrance gate.
12. The vallies in the graph show up very clearly.
13. Each typing error and poor erasure are noticed by Mr. Dole.
14. Who said that nobody is to eat their lunch in the office?
15. Mr. Marsh bought one of those houses that was built last spring.
16. Do you know that neither Earl nor Henry attend classes?
17. Bananas and orange juice are the reducing diet recommended in the magazine advertisement.
18. The number of delinquent accounts is scarcely surprising.
19. Did either John or Martin hand in their resignation?
20. Have the Duggan's been notified about the change of date?

Editing Practice

Editing for Correct Grammar Indicate any grammatical errors in these sentences. Write *OK* for any correct sentence.

1. The number of customers who call for your products are increasing steadily.
2. Neither the customers nor I am in favor of your discontinuing the king-sized package at present.
3. Everybody likes to take their choice of the various package sizes offered for sale.
4. Surely, there has been many such comments to reach your ears!
5. We do realize that you know more than us about the public's buying habits.
6. Every one of our shoppers, however, are disappointed whenever our stock of king-sized packages is low.
7. We think that the time has come for we consumers to express our opinions.
8. You might be interested to know that my friend and business competitor concurs in this opinion.
9. Undoubtedly, ours is only one of many like reports that has come to you since you made your announcement.
10. In our last consignment was only two cartons of the size for which we receive so many requests.

The Proofreader's Vocabulary You are proofreading this paragraph for vocabulary errors. Write your correction for any such error you find.

> The starting point of the mail promotion plan for our new shampoo is the envelope we use. If our envelope does not have some devise that will capture the interest or pique the curiosity of the person receiving the promotional material, it will not be opened. Please work up some ideas for an effective envelope; then you and I can get together and chose the one that we think will best suit our purpose.

Case Problem

The Emergency Ellen Burton and Irene Day are stenographers in the office of Baxter and Allen, Certified Public Accountants. In addition to their regular stenographic duties, Ellen is responsible for monthly billings to clients, and Irene is responsible for maintaining the correspondence files. All billings to customers are supposed to be mailed by the second day of each month. Ellen was absent from work for a week in late April because of illness and returned to the office April 29. Today is May 1, and the bills are far from ready to be mailed. The supervisor is away, and the problem must be resolved by Ellen.

1. Should Ellen ask Irene for help with the billing? Why or why not?
2. If she asks Irene for help, what should Ellen say to her?
3. What might be done by the department supervisor to avoid such bottlenecks?

Adjectives

An adjective is a word that modifies a noun or a pronoun. Generally speaking, adjectives are thought of as picture-painting words. For example, an opening sentence such as "In your letter of May 1 you ask about. . ." is an ordinary, run-of-the-mill sentence. Placing an adjective before *letter*, however, as in *your thoughtful letter, interesting letter, helpful letter, gracious letter*, makes the sentence come alive—it paints a picture. Selection of the adjective needed to paint the picture intended by a speaker or a writer is essentially a vocabulary problem—the better the vocabulary, the better the selection, the better the picture. However, this picture-making function of adjectives, while important, is not all that must be appreciated and learned about adjectives. Adjectives must be studied also to ensure their correct grammatical usage. A man may have an extensive vocabulary that would enable him to paint whatever picture he wishes; yet if he writes or says, "them reports," "these kind," or any other adjective illiteracies, these expressions will cast a dark shadow on his picture.

For effective communication, then, the following rules governing the correct use of adjectives must be mastered.

COMPARISON OF ADJECTIVES

Most adjectives change their forms to express different degrees of quality. This modification is called *comparison.* There are three forms or degrees of adjective comparison: (1) *positive*, used when the adjective is not compared with anything else; (2) *comparative*, used to express a higher or a lower degree than is expressed by the positive degree; and (3) *superlative*, used to denote either the highest or the lowest degree.

Forms of Adjective Comparison

Adjectives may be compared in any one of the three following ways:

1. By adding *er* to the positive to form the comparative degree and *est* to the positive to form the superlative degree, such as:

Positive	Comparative	Superlative
large	larger	largest
pretty	prettier	prettiest
simple	simpler	simplest

2. By adding the words *more* or *less* to the positive to form the comparative degree and *most* or *least* to the positive to form the superlative degree, such as:

Positive	Comparative	Superlative
faithful	more (or less) faithful	most (or least) faithful
amiable	more (or less) amiable	most (or least) amiable
sensible	more (or less) sensible	most (or least) sensible

3. By changing the form of the word completely, such as:

Positive	Comparative	Superlative
much, many	more	most
little	less	least
good	better	best
bad	worse	worst

Selection of Correct Forms of Comparison

Adjectives of *one* syllable are compared by adding *er, est;* adjectives of *three* or *more* syllables, by adding *more, less* or *most, least.* Some adjectives of *two* syllables are compared by adding *er, est* and others by adding *more, less* or *most, least.* Selection of the correct form of comparison for adjectives of two syllables presents no problem because the incorrect form offends the ear. For instance:

> The electric typewriter is *more useful* than the manual machine. (*Usefuler* would offend the ear.)
> Jane is the *prettiest* girl in the office. (Not *most pretty.*)

Double Comparison

Note that adjectives may be compared in any one of three ways. A common error, double comparison, occurs when two forms of comparison are used at the same time. For example:

> This box has *smoother* edges. (Not *more smoother.*)
> Mr. Eads says that this is the *worst* recession in ten years. (Not *most worstest.*)

CHECKUP 1

Test your understanding of the rules for comparing adjectives by making any needed corrections in the following sentences.

1. Miss York is the most friendliest secretary in the building.
2. Yours is the valuablest contribution that we have ever received.
3. Bill's command of English is more better than mine.
4. The busiest worker is often the happiest person.
5. I think you will find that this pen has a more fine point.
6. Receiving the promotion was the furtherest thing from my mind.

Choice of Comparative or Superlative Degree

When referring to *two* persons, places, or things, use the comparative degree; but when referring to *more than two* persons, places, or things, use the superlative degree. For instance:

> Both ideas are good, but I think this is the *better.* (Referring to two in number.)
> All the ideas are good, but I think this is the *best.* (Referring to more than two in number.)

Absolute Adjectives Absolute adjectives are adjectives that cannot be compared because in the positive degree they are already tops. For instance, if you have a *full* glass of water, nobody else could have one that is *fuller;* nor could someone have the *fullest* glass of all. Here are some examples of absolute adjectives.

complete	empty	perfect	supreme
correct	full	perpendicular	unanimous
dead	immaculate	round	unique

To express the degree to which a person or thing approaches the top, or positive degree, use *more nearly* or *most nearly.* If, for example, three persons were drawing circles, John's could be *more nearly* round than Bob's; or Tom's could be the *most nearly* round.

Many modern writers, however, do not use the *more nearly* and *most nearly* degrees of comparison for absolute adjectives. They feel that such usage makes their writing stilted and weakens the effectiveness of a message. For instance, they would write, "Ours is the *most complete* reference book on the market." And, in all fairness, we must concede that the "punch" would be lost by writing this: "Ours is the *most nearly complete* reference book on the market."

CHECKUP 2

Make any needed corrections and be prepared to give reasons for all corrections you make.

1. Which correspondent is the more efficient, Ames or Todd? OK
2. Which picture is the largest, his or mine? *larger*
3. The most immaculate desk in the office is Mr. Crowley's. *nearly*
4. Jack was told to order the type of chair he liked better. *best*

ADJECTIVE PITFALLS

Anyone who aims to use adjectives correctly must be on the watch lest he be trapped by the following five adjective pitfalls.

Other, Else, *and* All *in Comparisons*

When comparing a particular person or thing with other members of the group to which it belongs, use the words *other* or *else* with the comparative degree.

> Jack is *more* dependable than *any other* correspondent on our staff. (Without the word *other*, the sentence suggests that Jack is not a correspondent on our staff.)
>
> Burr is *more* industrious than *anyone else* on our staff. (The word *else* is needed here to set Burr off from his group.)

With the superlative degree, however, use the word *all*, not *any*.

> Jack is the *most* dependable of *all* the correspondents on our staff.

Omission of the Modifier

When a modifier such as *a, the,* or *my* is repeated before each noun in a series, two or more persons or things are clearly indicated. If the modifier is not repeated, only one person or thing is meant. For example:

> My friend and neighbor (is? are?) moving to Boston. (Since the adjective *my* is not repeated, *friend and neighbor* is one person. *Is* is the correct verb.)

> My friend and my neighbor (is? are?) moving to Boston. (Since the adjective is repeated, there are two different persons here. *Are* is the correct verb.)

Compound Adjectives

When two or more words are combined before a noun to form one adjectival idea—to make a compound adjective—they should be joined by a hyphen or hyphens.

air-conditioned bank	middle-aged man	duty-free goods
first-class typist	800-meter race	up-to-date methods
high-grade goods	coast-to-coast broadcast	well-known person

One exception to this rule involves certain well-known compounds that, through usage, have lost the hyphen. For example:

> real estate broker   social security benefits   high school teacher

These terms are usually not hyphenated when they follow a noun because they no longer function as one-idea adjectives.

> His book is *well known*. (Known is simply a predicate adjective modified by the adverb well.)

However, if the words still combine to form one idea, they are hyphenated even after the noun.

> He looks *middle-aged.*
> The bank is *air-conditioned.*

CHECKUP 3

These sentences call for application of the three rules just presented. Can you find the errors?

1. A center is usually taller than any player on the team.
2. Mr. Coe's friend and neighbor borrow the tools they need.
3. Elton does more work than anyone in this office.
4. Because the business district is moving uptown, your building is now in an out-of-the-way location.
5. A center is usually the tallest of all the players on the team.
6. Mr. Coe's brother and his neighbor borrow whatever tools they need.
7. George is a better machine operator than any man we have.
8. That last order was for 63-inch curtains.
9. Your suggestion is the best of any that we have yet seen.
10. Our first caller this morning was a middle-aged woman.

This (These), That (Those)

The adjectives *this* and *these* indicate nearness to the speaker; *that* and *those* indicate distance from the speaker. Never use the pronoun *them* as an adjective to replace *these* or *those*.

> Did you deposit *those* checks for Mr. Barr? (Not *them checks*.)
> Are you finished working with *these* files? (Not *them files*.)

This (These), That (Those) *With* Kind(s) *or* Sort(s)

Kind and *sort* are singular nouns; *kinds* and *sorts*, plural nouns. A singular noun is modified by a singular adjective; a plural noun, by a plural adjective. Study the following illustrations.

> You ought not to associate with (this? these?) kinds of persons. (The plural adjective *these* should modify the plural noun *kinds*.)
> Mr. Kent has little patience with (that? those?) sort of caller. (The singular adjective *that* should modify the singular noun *sort*.)

The expressions *kind of* and *sort of* should not be followed by the article *a(n)*. For instance:

> What kind of pen are you using? (Not *what kind of a pen*.)
> What sort of education do you think she has had? (Not *what sort of an education*.)

CHECKUP 4

Find and correct the errors in these sentences.

1. I shall attend to them as soon as I possibly can.
2. These sort of questions are rather infantile.
3. Please ask them callers to make appointments to see Mr. McKenna.
4. These kinds of machines are a complete puzzle to me.
5. Has Mr. Lord signed them letters yet?
6. Mr. Hewitt is not in favor of those kind of discussions.
7. That clerk always has a sort of a smile on his face.

FOR ADDED POLISH

Two more rules govern the choice of words when referring to two or to more than two in number. These rules, while not directly related to a study of adjectives, are fine points that a writer and speaker needs to know.

Each Other, One Another

Use *each other* when referring to two in number; use *one another* when referring to more than two in number. For example:

> Fred and Jim enjoy working with *each other*. (Two in number.)
> All the accountants must be ready to check *one another's* figures. (More than two in number.)

Either, Neither; Any One, No One, Not Any

Either and *neither* refer to one of two persons or things. *Any* or *any one, no one,* and *not any* should be used to refer to one of three or more persons or things, such as:

> *Either* of the girls will take your dictation. (Since *either* is used, there must be only two girls.)
>
> *Any one* of the girls will take your dictation. (Since *any one* is used, there must be more than two girls.)

CHECKUP 5

Make any needed corrections and justify any correction you make.

1. Not one of our two operators is on duty. *[handwritten: neither]*
2. Bill and Tom always check one another's totals. *[handwritten: each other's]*
3. Neither of the three executives has personnel problems. *[handwritten: not one]*
4. Fred, Don, and Ken are very good about sharing one another's supplies. *[handwritten: OK]*
5. Either of those four girls will type your rough draft. *[handwritten: Any one]*
6. All our secretaries are forever borrowing each other's dictionaries. *[handwritten: one another's]*

COMMUNICATION PROJECTS

Practical Application

A In the following sentences, write the corrections for all incorrect sentences, and write *OK* for all correct sentences.

1. We are of the opinion that these kind of machines will not do the work in our office. *[handwritten: kinds]*
2. Inez, despite her recent arrival in this country, speaks more better English than I. *[handwritten: Db comp]*
3. After examining both machines, I think that we should purchase the smallest one. *[handwritten: smaller, omit "a"]*
4. What kind of a format would you like to use? *[handwritten: omit "a"]*
5. Which of them three kinds of type cleaners do you like best? *[handwritten: those]*
6. Our store is the most up-to-date establishment in the city. *[handwritten: OK]*
7. Atlanta, the capital, is larger than any city in Georgia. *[handwritten: any other]*
8. Bill and Ken enjoy trying to exceed one another's production. *[handwritten: each other's]*
9. Ours is the building nearest the subway entrance. *[handwritten: OK]*
10. Which member of the Board of Directors is the oldest? *[handwritten: OK]*
11. Can you make that skirt more circular? *[handwritten: more nearly, absolute]*
12. All the advertised computers are good, but neither is exactly suited to our needs. *[handwritten: not one]*
13. Napoleon is the greatest of any general in the history of France. *[handwritten: all]*
14. You will be allowed full credit for them books you returned Monday. *[handwritten: those]*
15. Are these kinds of appliances going to be on sale? *[handwritten: OK]*

B Correct the following sentences wherever necessary.

1. Which has the better ribbon, this machine or that one? *[handwritten: OK]*
2. The memoranda on the desk was from Mr. Lamb. *[handwritten: um(s)]*
3. We have never before used these sort of form letters. *[handwritten: sorts]*
4. The main contributors to the bulletin were Ashby and I. *[handwritten: OK, k Pred nom.]*
5. Our three junior executives help each other whenever they can. *[handwritten: one another]*
6. Check these figures with whomever has time to help you. *[handwritten: whoever]*
7. Mr. Kent is taller than any man in the office. *[handwritten: any other]*
8. One-half the books on the shelf have not been cataloged. *[handwritten: OK]*

OK   9. That author and lecturer is visiting the Brookses.
like 10. Neither Mr. Rogers nor we typists likes the new fluorescent lighting.
bl comp 11. Your argument is much more stronger than Jerry's.
's 12. Secretary's voices should be low and well modulated.
best 13. Which do you think is better—high wages, security, or happiness?
me 14. The manager has placed you and I in charge of new accounts. *object of job.*
re near 15. Why doesn't the highway department make those corners rounder? *absolute*
OK 16. Everyone who knows the personnel in our offices is impressed with our willingness
to work.
ly-free 17. Do you know the price limit for duty-free goods?
anyone's 18. The plan can be put into effect without anyone objecting to it.
those 19. Do not take them remarks of his so seriously.
lies 20. The instructor lays down to rest every afternoon.

Editing Practice

Plurals and Possessives   Edit the following sentences, correcting all errors and writing *OK* for any correct sentence.

1. My brother-in-law's car is a special model. *OK*
2. The Flaherties are experts in human relations. *Flahertys*
3. Bob and Jack's fathers are scientists. *Bob's + Jack's*
4. It's a good idea, but it needs further study. *OK*
5. I think that there very much pleased with the outcome of the research. *they're*
6. We appreciate Mr. Curtin taking the time to answer our question. *Curtin's*
7. Do you know who's car is in front of the hydrant? *whose*
8. Are you in favor of an office employee's union? *employees'*
9. All the engineers have made there reports. *their*
10. Industries' main worry now is foreign competition. *OK*

Executives Also Proofread   You have dictated the following memo and are now proofreading it. Identify and correct any errors you find.

categories

For mailing purposes, file categorys are to be set up according to ZIP Codes. The Post Office requires that all bulk mailing be seperated into *separated* bundles, each of which contains mail that goes to one particular ZIP Code number. In this office, then, address files must be kept in ZIP Code numerical order, not alphabetical order.

Case Problem

A Tactful Correction   When Robert Whiting, a salesman, filled out a cash sales slip for a customer, he entered the total as $7 instead of $9. The customer took the slip to the cashier, Edith Lake, for payment; and Edith discovered the error.

1. What should Edith say to the customer so that his goodwill will be retained?
2. What should Edith say, if anything, to Robert about his error?

19   Adverbs

Everyone who has studied English grammar knows the definition of an adverb: An adverb is a word that describes, explains, or limits a verb, an adjective, or another adverb. The business correspondent needs more than the definition, however, to use adverbs correctly. He needs to study and to master the rules for correct usage of adverbs. As a preliminary to studying the adverb rules that are presented in this lesson, review the following generally known facts about adverbs: (1) Adverbs, like adjectives, have three degrees: the positive, the comparative, and the superlative. (2) Most words ending in *ly* are adverbs, but not all adverbs end in *ly*. A few adjectives also end in *ly;* for example, *oily*. (3) An adverb usually answers one of the following questions: When? Where? How? Why? How much or how little? To what extent?

TYPES OF ADVERBS

According to the way they are used, adverbs are classified as *simple* or *conjunctive*. These two classifications will be discussed in the following paragraphs. A third topic, adverbial clauses, will also be discussed.

Simple Adverbs

A simple adverb is used as a modifier only. Here is a list of some of the most common simple adverbs.

always	immediately	now	then
clearly	nearly	quite	too
here	never	soon	very

The correct route is indicated *clearly* on this map. (The simple adverb *clearly* modifies the verb *is indicated* and answers the question "How?")

Conjunctive Adverbs

A conjunctive adverb connects two independent clauses in one sentence and acts as a regular adverb in the second clause. The following adverbs are often used as conjunctive adverbs. You will need to recognize them in order to punctuate properly.

accordingly	however	nevertheless	therefore
consequently	likewise	otherwise	thus
furthermore	moreover	then	yet

The report is inconclusive; *therefore,* I cannot make a decision at this time. (The conjunctive adverb *therefore* connects the two independent clauses.)

Adverbial Clauses

An adverbial clause is a dependent clause that functions as an adverb in a sentence. An adverbial clause modifies a verb, an adjective, or an adverb in the main clause. The words in the following list introduce dependent clauses that usually function as adverbs.

after	because	if	until
although	before	since	when
as	for	unless	while

We will proceed at full speed *when* we receive the word from you. (The adverbial clause *when we receive the word from you* modifies the verb *will proceed.*)

Your speech will be more effective *if* you include a slide presentation. (The adverbial clause *if you include a slide presentation* modifies the adjective *more effective.*)

Make the needed adverb corrections in the following sentences. Identify the conjunctive adverbs and adverbial clauses.

1. These new stockings do not snag easy. *easily*
2. Please complete that job before you leave work today.
3. I enjoy swimming; however, I tire easily.
4. Time passes quick while I am on vacation. *quickly*
5. Jet planes fly swifter than the propeller models. *more swiftly*
6. From her position in the lobby, our receptionist can see plainly anyone who uses the elevators.

ADVERB OR ADJECTIVE AFTER VERB

The informal survey conducted by an English professor has been mentioned earlier in this book. His results showed that the majority of students could not use *lie* and *lay* or *who* and *whom* correctly. The results also showed that most students never had understood whether to use an adverb or an adjective after some kinds of verbs. For instance, they were puzzled as to whether a man would feel *badly* or *bad* about making an error. The instruction in this section concentrates on clearing up this widespread confusion.

Linking Verb or Not a Linking Verb?

Linking verbs such as *seem, appear, look, sound, feel, taste,* and *smell* are properly linking verbs only when they do not express action. When these same verbs do express action, they are not linking verbs. Linking verbs, then, could be classified as "no action" verbs. For example:

> Don said that the coffee *tasted* strong. (In this sentence, *tasted* is a linking verb, a no-action verb. After all, the coffee has no tongue with which to taste.)
>
> Bob *felt* bad when his suggestion was rejected. (*Felt* here is a linking verb, a no-action verb. Bob is not feeling anything with his hands; he is not acting.)

Now study the following examples and note that these same verbs can also be "action" verbs.

> Don *tasted* the coffee gingerly before drinking it. (Here *tasted* is an action verb. Don has a tongue and is using it. Action is taking place.)
>
> Bob *felt* stealthily in his pocket for the memorandum. (*Felt* here is an action verb. Bob is acting; he is feeling with his fingers.)

The Rule

An adverb is used after an "action" verb; an adjective, after a "no action" verb. In the previous illustrations, note that when *tasted* was a "no action" verb, the adjective *strong* was used. In the second set of illustrations, when *tasted* was an "action" verb, the adverb *gingerly* was used. The following Memory Hook is helpful for remembering the rule.

Hook up *action—adverb* and *no action—adjective* by retaining a mental picture of the following pairs.

Action	No Action
Adverb	Adjective

Action and *adverb* have the same number of letters, and *no action* and *adjective* match in number of letter spaces.

CHECKUP 2

Keeping in mind *action—adverb* and *no action—adjective*, make any necessary corrections in these sentences.

1. The top of my desk feels ~~roughly~~ *rough*, although it has been sanded.
2. From this distance, the skyline looks ~~beautifully~~ *beautiful*.
3. The police car appeared suddenly around the corner. *OK*
4. Although the juice smelled ~~sweetly~~ *sweet*, we could not drink it.
5. Did your secretary look carefully through the incoming correspondence? *OK*
6. Bill said that he could smell escaping gas ~~distinct~~ *distinctly*.

ADVERB PITFALLS

Five rules governing the correct use of adverbs are frequently violated in speech and in writing. Knowledge of the correct application of these rules, therefore, is necessary for anyone who wishes to give a finished grammar performance.

Position of the Adverb

An adverb should be placed as close as possible to the word it modifies. Failure to do so may cause the meaning of a sentence to be clouded—or even changed entirely. For instance:

Only I changed the ribbon on that typewriter. (No one else changed it.)

I changed *only* the ribbon on that typewriter. (I didn't change anything else on that typewriter.)

I changed the ribbon *only* on that typewriter. (I didn't change the ribbon on any other typewriter.)

Double Negative

Scarcely, only, hardly, but, and *never* are negative in meaning; no other negative should be used with them. For example:

Ken *has scarcely* time to do his own work. (Not *Ken hasn't.*)

Mr. Todd *could hardly* wait for his secretary to answer the buzzer. (Not *Mr. Todd couldn't.*)

We *couldn't help smiling* at his astonishment. (Not *couldn't help but smile.*)

Correct whatever errors there may be in the following sentences.

1. Mr. Lloyd hadn't but one request to make.
2. Before payday, Bill has a dime hardly to his name.
3. Did you know that Lucy hasn't never before done this kind of work?
4. Today only was the first time I had met the new personnel manager.
5. The lines were so busy that we couldn't get scarcely one call through.
6. I couldn't help thinking that his arguments were not consistent.
7. I thought that the applicants for the job had only been interviewed yesterday, not three days ago.
8. There wasn't but one shipping clerk in the stockroom on Wednesday morning.

Never *or* Not

Both *never* and *not* are adverbs, but their meanings are quite different. *Never* means "not ever; at no time; not in any degree, way, or condition." It is a strong word. *Not* is simply a word that expresses negation. *Never* is used all too frequently and incorrectly instead of *not*. Study the following examples:

> Mr. Lyons said that he did *not* receive your letter. (Not *that he never received.*)
>
> We have *never* been late with an interest payment. (*Never*, meaning "not ever," is correct in this sentence.)

Where *for* That

The subordinate conjunction *that,* not the conjunctive adverb *where,* should be used after such expressions as "I saw in the paper," "We read in the magazine," "The announcement notes," and so on. For example:

> Did you read in the paper *that* our company is expanding? (Not *read in the paper where.*)
>
> The notice states *that* Tom is to have an assistant. (Not *states where.*)

Badly *or* Worst Way *for* Very Much

All too often, *badly* and *worst way* are used when the meaning really is *very much.* Study the following illustrations.

> Bob's reason for taking extra lunch time was that he wanted a haircut (very much? badly?). (Who would ever want a haircut *badly?* The correct meaning, of course, is that he *very much* wanted a haircut.)
>
> David wanted to learn shorthand (in the worst way? very much?). (David would never be able to take shorthand if he learned it *in the worst way.* The correct answer, therefore, is *very much.*)

Find and correct any errors in these sentences.

1. Do you think that the redecorating job was done badly? *O K*
2. I never heard you say that you were taking your vacation in June. *did not hear you say*
3. I saw in the daily bulletin where we are going to have an extra holiday next week. *that*
4. Sue needed money in the worst way. *very much*
5. Did you see by the pamphlet where our dividend is to be increased? *that*

ADVERB AND ADJECTIVE CONFUSIONS

The word pairs to be studied here are sources of frequent errors, possibly because one member of the pair is an adjective; the other, an adverb. In each pair, the first word is an adjective; the second, an adverb.

Sure, Surely; Real, Really

When an adjective is needed, use *sure* or *real*. When an adverb is indicated, use *surely* or *really*. The following Memory Hook will help you in selecting the correct word.

MEMORY HOOK

If the word *very* or *certainly* can be substituted for the word in question, use *surely* or *really*. Hook up the final *y* in *very* or *certainly* with the final *y* in *surely* or *really*. For instance:

> The boss was (real? really?) angry this morning. (*The boss was very angry. Very ends in y; really ends in y. Really is correct.*)
>
> You (sure? surely?) have been a success as an executive. (*You certainly have been a success. Certainly ends in y; surely ends in y. Surely, then, is correct.*)

Good, Well

Good is the adjective and *well* is the adverb, except when referring to health. If the question "How?" can be answered, use *well*; if not, use *good*. Remember, though, that *well* is always used when speaking of health. For example:

> The new correspondent does *good* work. (*Good is an adjective modifying the noun work. It does not answer the question "How?"*)
>
> The new correspondent does his work *well*. (*Does his work how? The adverb well answers the question and is, therefore, correct.*)
>
> The new correspondent went home because he did not feel *well*. (*When speaking of health, always use well.*)

Some, Somewhat

Some is an adjective; *somewhat,* an adverb. For rapid selection of the correct word, learn the following Memory Hook.

MEMORY HOOK

Use *somewhat* if you can substitute the words *a little bit;* otherwise, use *some*.

> Mr. King was (some? somewhat?) doubtful about approving the plan. (Mr. King was *a little bit* doubtful; therefore, *somewhat* is correct.)
> We gave Mr. King (some? somewhat?) plans for his approval. (*Some* is correct because *a little bit* cannot be substituted.)

Most, Almost

Most is an adjective, the superlative of *much* or *many,* as: *much, more, most.*
Almost is an adverb meaning "not quite" or "very nearly." For example:

> We have (most? almost?) enough data for our statistical report. (*We have* not quite *or* very nearly *enough. Almost* is correct.)
> (Most? Almost?) secretaries have transcribed (most? almost?) all their letters by three o'clock. (Many, more, *most secretaries have transcribed* very nearly *all. Most* is correct for the first choice; *almost,* for the second.)

CHECKUP 5

Correct any errors you find in the following sentences.

1. Mr. Lyle's lack of confidence in us is real shocking. *really*
2. Most everyone likes interesting work. *Almost*
3. The mechanic said that the machine is now working well. *OK*
4. Wasn't the salesman somewhat hesitant about asking for an appointment? *OK*
5. My, but it's sure hot in this office! *surely*
6. A few of our typists are some careless about proofreading. *somewhat*
7. Why don't you see the nurse if you don't feel good? *well*
8. After hearing your story, I felt that you were sure justified in protesting. *surely*

COMMUNICATION PROJECTS

Practical Application

A Write the corrections for any adverb errors in the following sentences. Write *OK* for any correct sentence.

1. The economic situation surely looks badly for us. *OK*
2. We were surprised at Peter's doing that job so good. *well*
3. Prices dropped some during the past month. *somewhat*
4. Clem felt miserably about forgetting to deliver the message. *miserable*
5. Mr. Lester never asked us to file those names geographically. *did not ask*
6. The new secretary's letters scarcely contain a single erasure. *OK*
7. Todd appeared voluntarily before the investigating committee.
8. Are you almost ready to receive the next caller, Mr. Foley?
9. The man badly needed the services of a psychiatrist.
10. The letter was typed so poorly that Mr. Forbes refused to sign it.
11. Do not serve us the syrup that tastes so bitter.

12. Our ad man does his best work in a real quiet office.
13. Prospects for increased sales during the next month surely look well.
14. Mr. Kent didn't hardly notice the stacks of outgoing mail.
15. We would have shipped the order C.O.D., but you never told us to do so.
16. Did you see by today's paper where tariffs are to be lowered?
17. Church bells sound clear on a frosty day.
18. Dick would like to work for our firm in the worst way.
19. Mr. Jeffers cannot breathe good unless the windows are open.
20. For as long as I have worked for him, Mr. Barr hasn't never lost his temper.

Correct the following sentences wherever necessary.

1. On which floor are lady's suits sold?
2. Since the lighting has been changed, our reception room looks beautifully.
3. This set is the least expensive of any practice set on the market.
4. Bill will surely receive a fine recommendation, for he has always performed his duties faithful.
5. Which is the friendliest dog, a collie or a Pekingese?
6. Only we sell to the wholesale trade.
7. My assistant can answer your questions just as well as me.
8. The president hadn't only one suggestion to make.
9. Our chief accountant is a self educated man.
10. We have never had a better report, Mr. Douville.
11. Please see that all them stencils are cut today.
12. Elsa read in the paper where Mr. Ryan is to be the new plant manager.
13. May I have one of those pens that have retractable points?
14. That correspondent badly needs a refresher course in grammar.
15. We owe our success to the fact that our employees cooperate so well with one another.
16. Experience is sure a good teacher.
17. Your carbons would look better if you used a more sharper typing stroke.
18. Is Ronald doing good in his new position?
19. Every business needs those kind of word-of-mouth advertising.
20. All the applicants were somewhat nervous and ill at ease.

Editing Practice

Editor, Editor!   Rewrite the following letter, correcting whatever errors it contains.

Dear Mrs. Gibson:

UPSI-NOLA is a most refreshing drink. It tastes deliciously and has all those kind of nutrients dietitians recommend.

NOLA contains less sugar than any soft drink on the market. It is tested regular for caloric content by our up to date research department. Your diet is safe with NOLA.

If you have not yet tried UPSI-NOLA, your first sip will make you wish you had tried it sooner. Act quick and buy the drink that is absolutely the best of any beverage of it's kind!

Cordially yours,

Did I Say That?   As your boss proofreads this paragraph, he questions a word you have used. Actually, you transcribed exactly as he dictated; but you should have made the correction. What is this word?

You will be able to work in comfort this summer if you install a Kool Air Conditioner now. And you will also be able to maintain your production record, for you will not be hampered by the stickiness caused by undue prespiration. Shortly after you have read the enclosed "Kool" literature, you may expect a visit from our air-conditioner expert, Mr. Ray T. Hyde.

Case Problem

Introducing Yourself You have just arrived at a reception given for new students by the college president. You meet the members of the faculty who are in the receiving line and then help yourself to some refreshments. The students and various faculty members who arrived earlier are clustered in many small groups around the room, and you do not know whether to stand by yourself until someone comes over to you or whether to approach one of the groups.

1. What do you think you should do? Why?
2. If you decided to approach one of the groups, what would you say?
3. If you were responsible for arranging this reception, what would you do to make it easier for a newcomer to mix with others?

Prepositions

All the rules for grammar presented in Chapter 3 govern correct usage. The correct usage of prepositions is the objective for this section. As background for a better understanding of how to use prepositions, two definitions should be reviewed.

DEFINITIONS

A preposition is a connecting word that shows the relation between a noun or a pronoun and some other word in the sentence. Here is a list of some of the more commonly used prepositions.

about	but (meaning *except*)	off
above	by	on
after	except	over
among	for	to
at	from	under
before	in	up
below	into	upon
beside	like	until
between	of	with

A preposition always occurs in a *prepositional phrase—in the office, at our bank, around the next corner, with him,* and so on. A prepositional phrase consists of a preposition with its noun or pronoun object, together with any modifiers.

Keeping in mind the definitions and the fact that a preposition never stands alone, give close attention to the following rules of correct usage.

WORDS REQUIRING SPECIFIC PREPOSITIONS

Some words must be followed by specific prepositions. Other words require one preposition for one meaning and an entirely different preposition for another meaning. Failure to use the correct preposition with the correct word or failure to use the preposition that applies to the context of a particular sentence is a common error that spoils the effect of a finished performance.

The words that require specific prepositions, together with those prepositions and examples of their use, are listed below.

abhorrence *of*
abhorrent *to*
abide *by* a decision
abide *with* a person
abounds *in* or *with*
accompanied *by* (attended by a person)
accompanied *with* (attended by something)
acquit *of*
adapted *to* (adjusted to)
adapted *for* (made over for)
adapted *from* a work
affinity *between*
agree *to* a proposal
agree *with* someone
agreeable *to* (*with* is permissible)
angry *at* a thing or condition
angry *with* a person
attend *to* (listen)
attend *upon* (wait)
beneficial *to*
bestow *upon*
buy *from*
compliance *with*
comply *with*
confer *on* or *upon* (give to)
confer *with* (talk to)
confide *in* (place confidence in)
confide *to* (entrust to)
conform *to* (in conformity *to* or *with*)
convenient *for* (suitable for, easy for)
convenient *to* (near)
conversant *with*
correspond *to* or *with* (match; agree with)

correspond *with* (exchange letters)
credit *for*
deal *in* goods or services
deal *with* someone
depend or dependent *on* (but independent *of*)
derogatory *to*
different *from* (not *than* or *to*)
disappointed *in* or *with*
discrepancy *between* two things
discrepancy *in* one thing
dispense *with*
employ *for* a purpose
employed *at* a stipulated salary
employed *in*, *on*, or *upon* a work or business
enter *into* (become a party to)
enter *into* or *upon* (start)
enter *in* a record
enter *at* a given point
exception *to* a statement
familiarize *with*
foreign *to* (preferred to *from*)
identical *with*
inferior or superior *to*
need *of* or *for*
part *from* (take leave of)
part *with* (relinquish)
plan or planning *to* (not *on*)
profit *by*
in regard *to* ⎫
with regard *to* ⎬
as regards ⎭
retroactive *to* (not *from*)
thirst *for* or *after* knowledge
vary *from*
wait *for* a person, a train, an event
wait *on* a customer, a guest

CHECKUP 1

Supply the missing preposition in each of the following sentences.

1. Mr. Beck is always agreeable (?) any plan that will result in increased goodwill. *to*
2. Our receptionist bestows her smile impartially (?) all callers. *upon*
3. We are glad to comply (?) your request for our current price list. *with*
4. Knowledge of data processing is foreign (?) all of us except Dick. *to*
5. We entered Yellowstone (?) Cody, Wyoming. *at*
6. You need not wait (?) me this noon. *for*

SPECIFIC PREPOSITIONS MOST USED IN BUSINESS

Because of their frequent occurrence in business communications, nine of the words requiring specific prepositions have been selected for special study. They are as follows:

Agree With, Agree To

Use *agree with* when the object of the preposition is a person; use *agree to* when the object is not a person, such as:

> Don thinks it good policy to *agree with* the boss. (The object of the preposition is a person; therefore, *with* is correct.)
>
> Don will not *agree to* any proposal made by Todd. (Since *proposal*, the object of the preposition, is not a person, *to* is correct.)

Angry With, Angry At

Use *angry with* when the object of the preposition is a person; use *angry at* when the object is not a person, such as:

> Mr. Pierce was *angry with* Tom this morning. (*With* is correct because the object of the preposition is a person.)
>
> Mr. Pierce was *angry at* the manner in which Tom answered the question. (*At* is correct because *manner*, the object of the preposition, is not a person.)

Part From, Part With

Part from means "to take leave of"; *part with* means "to relinquish," "to give up." *Part from* is generally used when the object of the preposition is a person, and *part with*, when the object is not a person.

> At what time last night did you and Kent *part from* each other? (*From* is correct. The meaning is "take leave of" *each other*.)
>
> Jack seemed loath to *part with* the picture. (*With* is correct. *Picture*, the object of the preposition, is not a person.)

Discrepancy In, Discrepancy Between

Use *discrepancy in* when the object of the preposition is singular; use *discrepancy between* when the object denotes exactly *two* in number. For instance:

> There were several *discrepancies in* the analysis. (*Analysis* is singular; therefore, *in* is correct.)
>
> Did you notice any *discrepancy between* Bill's story and Fred's? (There are exactly two stories; therefore, *between* is correct.)

In Regard To, With Regard To, As Regards

These three phrases are equally correct, but a common error is the use of *regards* with *in* or *with*. Whenever *regards*, the word ending in *s*, is used, it must be paired with *as*, the word that also ends in *s*. For example:

> We have written to you before (in? with? as?) regard to your delay in making shipment. (*Regard* does not end in *s*; therefore, *with* or *in* is correct.)
>
> *As regards* insurance, we recommend that you talk with Mr. Wahl. (Since *regards* ends in *s*, the *s*-ending word *as* is correct.)

Different From, Identical With, Plan To, Retroactive To

The correct prepositions to be used after *different, identical, plan,* and *retroactive* should be memorized. These expressions are used so frequently that production would be slowed by continually checking a reference manual. Study the following illustrations.

> Do you have any carbons that are *different from* these? (Not *different than.*)
>
> Check to see whether your total is *identical with* Peter's. (Not *identical to.*)
>
> Is Mr. West *planning to* have a general meeting on Friday? (Not *planning on having.*)
>
> Can a law be made *retroactive to* some previous date? (Not *retroactive from.*)

CHECKUP 2

Make whatever corrections are necessary.

1. We have no plans as regards future expansion. OK
2. Mr. Adams agreed with the other members of the committee. OK
3. Your ideas about proper attire are very different than mine. *from*
4. Were there any discrepancies in the Polaris report? OK
5. Dick's problem is identical to mine. *with*
6. Are you angry at me or at the other girls? *with*
7. This directive is retroactive from May 1. *to*
8. We should like to talk with you in regards to your proposal. *in regard to*
9. Do you plan on having an office of your own? *to have*
10. Mr. Hess parted with David at the subway entrance. *from*

PREPOSITION PITFALLS

Preposition pitfalls trap the person who cannot choose correctly between two different prepositions that might be used or who does not know when a preposition should be used and when it should be omitted. To avoid these snares, study the following seven guides to correct preposition usage.

Between, Among

Between is commonly used when referring to two persons, places, or things; *among* when referring to more than two. For instance:

> We are finding it difficult to choose *between* Jack and Harry. (Since there are two persons, *between* is correct.)
>
> Were the notices distributed *among* all members of the staff? (*All* connotes "more than two"; therefore, *among* is correct.)

Between may also express the relation of one thing to each and all of several related things, such as:

> The security pact was *between* England and all the other countries of western Europe.

Beside, Besides

Beside means "by the side of"; *besides* means "in addition to." Study the following illustrations.

> I was privileged to sit *beside* Mr. Harris at the banquet. (Meaning "by the side of" Mr. Harris.)
>
> Were any officers *besides* Mr. Harris at the banquet? (Meaning "in addition to" Mr. Harris.)

Inside, Outside

The preposition *of* is not used after *inside* or *outside*. When referring to time, use *within*, not *inside of*. For example:

> The receptionist's desk is just *inside* the main entrance. (Not *inside of*.)
>
> We have a thermometer *outside* the east window. (Not *outside of*.)
>
> Our reports must be finished *within* a week. (Not *inside of*.)

All, Both

Use *of* after *all* or *both* only when *all* or *both* is followed by a pronoun. Omit *of* if either word is followed by a noun. For instance:

> *All of* them have saved *all* their stamps. (*All of* is followed by the pronoun *them*, and *all* precedes the noun *stamps*.)
>
> *Both of* us knew that *both* the packages should have been mailed yesterday. (*Both of us*, but *both the packages*.)

At, To; In, Into

At and *in* denote position; *to* and *into* signify motion. For example:

> After I arrived *at* your office, I found that I had come *to* the wrong place. (*At* for position; *to* for motion.)
>
> As he went *into* the park, he saw an oriole sitting *in* a tree. (*Into* for motion; *in* for position.)

Note. When either *at* or *in* refers to a place, use *in* for larger places and *at* for smaller. For instance:

> Mark lives *in* Chicago and works *at* the Marshall Bond store. (*In* Chicago, the larger place; *at* the store, the smaller place.)

Behind, In Back Of

Use *behind*, not *in back of*. *In front of*, however, is correct.

> This folder should be filed *behind*, not *in front of*, the guide. (*Behind*, not *in back of*.)

From, Off

From is generally used with persons; *off* is used with things. *Off* can be used with persons only when something that is physically resting on them is being lifted away. Never use *of* or *from* after *off*.

> You may borrow a coat *from* Bill.
>
> Take your books *off* the desk.
>
> Please take your foot *off* me. (Your foot is resting on mine; please lift it away.)

CHECKUP 3

Correct the preposition errors in the sentences below.

1. The work was divided between the three clerks. *among*
2. When I went in the office, I saw Mr. King at his desk. *into*
3. Do you do much work outside of office hours? *omit "of"*
4. Stack the letters besides the tray marked "Outgoing Mail." *beside*
5. A conference is going on in back of those locked doors. *behind*
6. Have you hidden all the money? *OK*

PREPOSITION ILLITERACIES

Some preposition errors are so serious that they mark a person as uneducated or as extremely careless. The educated person avoids illiteracies such as the following:

Of, Have

Of is a preposition; *have* is a verb. Writing *of* for *have* is a very serious error that may be charged to poor diction. For instance, all too many persons say "shuduv" for "should have" and, consequently, write the "should of" that they hear. Study these illustrations.

> Knowing that you were in a hurry, we should have replied sooner. (Not *should of.*)
>
> You ought not to have paid the bill before May 2. (Not *ought not to of.*)

Where . . . At; Where . . . To

The use of *at* or *to* with *where* is illiterate. To illustrate:

> Do you know where Mr. Kidd is? (Not *where Mr. Kidd is at.*)
>
> Where did she go? (Not *Where did she go to?*)

Help, Help From

Another illiteracy is the use of *from* after the word *help*.

> I could not help complimenting Bob on his sales record. (Not *help from.*)
>
> Don couldn't help expressing his pleasure at the news. (Not *help from.*)

Opposite, Opposite To

The use of *to* after *opposite* is incorrect. For example:

> Your locker is the one opposite mine. (Not *opposite to.*)

CHECKUP 4

See whether you can find the illiteracies in the following sentences.

1. Mr. Page would of seen you, even without an appointment. *have*
2. Have you heard where Frank is at this year? *omit "at"*
3. Amy cannot help asking all those questions. *OK*

4. In the main office, Ken's desk is opposite Mr. Horn's. *OK*
5. Do you think that we hadn't ought to of mentioned the incident to the boss? *have*
6. That error should of been corrected immediately. *have*
7. Where have all the supplies gone to? *omit "to"*

COMMUNICATION PROJECTS

Practical Application

A Correct the sentences in which prepositions are used incorrectly. Write *OK* for any correct sentence.

1. The correspondents should plan on joining some of the office activities. *to*
2. Your plan is not much different than mine. *from*
3. Mr. Dyer's office is in back of the main office. *behind*
4. We agreed to the plan favored by the majority of the committee. *OK*
5. Have you noticed that Tom's writing style is almost identical with Mr. Taber's? *OK*
6. Remember that the increase is retroactive to June 1. *OK*
7. We surely should of checked those figures. *have*
8. When he makes an error, Bill becomes angry with his machine. *at*
9. The assignment was divided between Jerry and Mr. Hardy. *OK*
10. We must insist that you return the goods inside of three days. *within*
11. Where in the world did that caller go to? *omit "to"*
12. Ann dislikes parting with any of her possessions. *OK*
13. Who, beside Bob, is being promoted? *besides*
14. Sam reported that both of the machines were in need of repair. *OK*
15. The Herald Building is opposite ours. *OK*
16. There seems to be some discrepancy in your total and mine. *between*
17. Our jewelry display is just inside of the entrance to the store. *omit "of"*
18. Please throw this advertisement in the wastebasket. *into "from"*
19. Peter could not help from stating his position on the question. *omit "from"*
20. Mr. Taylor has no statement to make in regards to the merger. *regard*

B Find the errors in the following sentences. Write *OK* for any correct sentence.

1. Do you think Bill is planning on applying for the managerial position? *to apply*
2. Just between you and I, all staff members will be upgraded in April. *OK*
3. Mr. Collins was not to the office yesterday. *in*
4. Most of us have almost reached retirement age. *OK*
5. The defendant was acquitted from the charge. *of*
6. Mr. Frye is looking very good, despite his long illness. *well*
7. Your mind works differently to Mr. Porter's. *from*
8. Which of the twins is the more dependable? *OK*
9. Do not take the dictionary off from the first shelf. *omit "from"*
10. We very much appreciate your loaning us a copy of your sales manual. *lending*
11. You sure like to operate that machine, don't you? *surely*
12. Because every man and boy did their best, the affair was a success. *his*
13. We can always get a salary advance off the cashier. *from*
14. If I were he, I would delegate some of the minor jobs. *OK*
15. We shall expect your decision inside of two weeks. *within*
16. You should of studied the layout before starting to write the copy. *have*
17. We should like to confer with you in regards to your credit rating. *regard*
18. The Harrises' order has priority for tomorrow. *OK*
19. The staff should attend upon every instruction Mr. Dunn gives. *to*
20. Whom have you chosen to head the steering committee? *Who*

Editing Practice

Make the Blanks Make Sense   Indicate a word that would make sense if inserted in the blank space within the sentence.

1. To help us determine your credit rating, please see that we get a copy of your current . . . statement.
2. We feel that we can recommend your new cleaner without . . . .
3. Next week the . . . are coming to examine our books; and you, of course, would prefer them to see that your account is paid in full.
4. We think that your machine is far . . . to all others now on the market.
5. It is almost impossible to dye two hides . . . the same shade.
6. Have you in imagination ever . . . passage on some fast ocean liner and traveled to far-off lands?
7. We know that you must have been prevented from settling your account by some . . . over which you had no control.
8. There has been a great deal of illness at home, resulting in many . . . expenses.
9. Because of the difference in price, shipping and billing from Erie would . . . the displeasure of our customers.
10. Our firm no longer operates under the name listed in the present . . . of the Red Book.

Oops!   You have typed the following paragraph and are now proofreading it. Did you make any spelling errors?

> Your copy for advanced advertising of our new complexion soap is somewhat agressive and should be toned down a little. As I read what you had written, I got the feeling that you were trying to *make* me buy. Please rewrite it, presenting your material from the viewpoint of what our soap will do for the reader—give health and beauty reasons, for instance.

Case Problem

A Case of Ethics   There is a rule at the Burns Office Equipment Company that personal mail may not be sent through the company's postage meter machine. Jack Thompson, who is in charge of the mail room, receives a batch of mail from Mary Weston, secretary to the vice-president, that contains some obviously personal letters written by Mary. Jack is not sure whether Mary inadvertently placed her personal mail among the company correspondence or whether Mary was trying deliberately to slip her personal letters in with the other letters.

1. What should Jack do about the situation? Why?
2. What should Jack say to Mary?

21   Conjunctions

A conjunction is a word used to *connect*—to connect words, phrases, or clauses. For instance:

> The original *and* the carbon are lying on your desk. (In this sentence, the conjunction *and* connects the words *original* and *carbon*.)
>
> You will find them on your blotter *or* in the tray. (The conjunction *or* connects the phrases *on your blotter* and *in the tray*.)
>
> Bill usually attends to the outgoing mail, *but* he is not in the office today. (The conjunction *but* connects the two main clauses.)

As with the other parts of speech, conjunctions must be studied for correct usage. This lesson on conjunctions will also serve as a solid preparation for Chapters 4 and 5. A thorough knowledge of conjunctions will facilitate the learning of punctuation rules and will take some of the mystery out of the various aspects of language structure. This study of conjunction usage considers first the classification of conjunctions, then the pitfalls in usage, and, finally, parallel structure.

CLASSIFICATION OF CONJUNCTIONS

Conjunctions are classified as coordinate, correlative, and subordinate conjunctions.

Coordinate Conjunctions

The coordinate conjunctions are *and, but, or,* and *nor.* The function of coordinate conjunctions is to connect *like* grammar elements, such as two or more *words,* two or more *phrases,* or two or more *clauses.* These conjunctions must not be used to connect unlike elements. The illustrations given in the first paragraph of this section show how to use coordinate conjunctions.

Correlative Conjunctions

Correlative conjunctions are conjunctions used in pairs. As with coordinate conjunctions, the function of correlatives is to connect like grammar elements. The most common correlative conjunctions are the following:

both . . . . . . and   not only . . . . . but also
either . . . . . or   whether . . . . . or
neither . . . . nor

Note that *or* is paired with *either* and *nor* with *neither.*

> *Either* a pencil *or* a pen may be used for the examination.
> *Neither* Jim *nor* his sister knew we were coming.

Subordinate Conjunctions

A subordinate conjunction introduces a dependent clause and connects it with an independent clause. Clauses joined by subordinate conjunctions are of *unequal* rank.

> *Because* we are overstocked on umbrellas, we are unable to take advantage of your offer. (The subordinate conjunction *because* introduces the dependent clause *because we are overstocked on umbrellas* and connects that dependent clause with the main clause.)
>
> Let us know at once *if* you think the idea has value. (The subordinate conjunction *if* introduces the dependent clause *if you think the idea has value* and connects that dependent clause with the main clause.)

Study the following list of commonly used subordinate conjunctions. You will need to recognize them in order to punctuate accurately.

after	before	provided that	when
although	even if	since	whenever
as	for	so that	where
as if	how	than	wherever
as soon as	if	that	whether
as though	in case that	unless	while
because	in order that	until	why

Identify the conjunctions in these sentences, and classify them as coordinate, correlative, or subordinate.

1. We know that you will be pleased with your choice. *Sub*
2. Neither Tom nor the other correspondents have any time to waste. *corrl*
3. Write at once if you wish to take the special discount. *sub*
4. All of us typists can tabulate, but not one of us likes to do so. *coord.*
5. When you arrive in Seattle, call immediately for an appointment. *sub*
6. A correspondent cannot afford to be weak in spelling and in grammar. *coord*
7. Are you satisfied with both the job and the salary? *corrl*

CONJUNCTION PITFALLS

Errors in the use of conjunctions occur when a writer or a speaker, faced with a choice, is unable to select the conjunction that correctly conveys his meaning. Another problem is uncertainty as to whether a preposition or a conjunction is correct. Study the following rules in order to avoid these pitfalls.

The Correct Conjunction

In the following discussion, the emphasis is on learning to select the correct conjunction when you are faced with a choice.

But, And   Whenever there is a contrasting or opposing idea, no matter how faint, use the conjunction *but*—not *and.*

> Ann is our fastest operator, *but* Sue is more accurate. (*But,* for contrast.)

Who, Which, *or* That?   The relative pronouns *who, which,* and *that* are correctly used as follows: *who,* to refer to persons; *which,* to refer to objects; *that,* to refer to persons, animals, or objects. Never use *and who* or *and which.*

> Barr is the man who knows how to operate the machine. (*Who,* referring to a person.)
> Learn to use the Teletype, which is a quick way of sending messages. (*Which,* referring to an object.)
> Mr. Rowe has a dog that wages war with the postman. (*That,* referring to an animal.)
> The company is made up of three very highly successful divisions, which (not *and which*) are all located in Chicago.

Since, Because *or* Being That   The use of *being that* when *since* or *because* is meant is an illiteracy. There is no such conjunction as *being that.*

> Because the bill was not paid within the discount period, we shall expect your check for $14.10. (Obviously, *because* is correct.)

That *or* **Because** *or* **Like**   Use *reason is that*, not *reason is because*. Use *pretend that*, not *pretend like*. See the following illustrations.

> The *reason* I was late *is that* our bus was stalled. (Not *reason is because.*)
>
> When David arrives, *pretend that* you do not see him. (Not *pretend like.*)

TWILIGHT ZONE

As . . . As; So . . . As   The rule concerning the use of the correlatives *as . . . as* and *so . . . as* is often not observed; this rule, therefore, belongs in the Twilight Zone. To be precise and correct, however, use *as . . . as* when making a *positive* statement and *so . . . as* when making a *negative* statement. For example:

> Bill writes just *as* well *as* I do. (*As . . . as* for positive statement.)
>
> Bill does not write *so* well *as* Jerry. (*So . . . as* for negative statement.)

CHECKUP 2

Make any needed corrections.

1. I shall always remember the advice that you gave me yesterday. *ok*
2. Your job is difficult, and you are not pressed for time. *but*
3. Does Bob ski so well as you do? *as*
4. The reason for my failure to check the enclosures is because *that* the letter contained no enclosure notation.
5. Being that the winter has been so mild, we have sold very *Since* few ski suits.
6. Can you pretend like you do not understand English? *that*
7. Mimeographed letters have never been so effective as type-written letters. *as*

Conjunction and Preposition Confusions

You learned in Section 20 that a preposition always occurs in a prepositional phrase, which consists of the preposition and its noun or pronoun object, together with any modifiers. A subordinate conjunction, however, is used to introduce a clause, which is a group of words containing a subject and a predicate. With this review as background, the following discussion points out how to avoid common confusions between conjunctions and prepositions.

Without *or* **Except** *for* **Unless**   *Without* and *except* are prepositions that are frequently used incorrectly for the conjunction *unless*. For instance:

> Mr. Burr said that you are not to leave the office *unless* you get permission. (Not *without you get permission. You get permission* is a clause and must be introduced by a conjunction.)
>
> Mr. Burr said that you are not to leave the office *without* getting permission. (*Without* is correct in this sentence because it is part of the prepositional phrase *without getting permission*.)

TWILIGHT ZONE

Like *for* As, As If, *or* As Though   *Like* is a preposition, and a preposition should not introduce a clause. However, so many persons use *like* as a conjunction that such usage is now in the Twilight Zone. If you want to be technically correct, you should not use *like* for *as, as if,* or *as though.*

> You looked *as if* you were angry. (Not *like you were angry.* The clause *you were angry* should be introduced by a conjunction.)
> Do you wish you had talent *like* his? (Here the preposition *like* is correct. *Like* introduces the prepositional phrase *like his.*)

CHECKUP 3

Correct any errors that occur in these sentences.

1. Never change any wording without you consult me. *unless*
2. Bill never opens the safe except I tell him to do so. *unless*
3. The children look like their mother and me. *OK*
4. Mr. Doan does not feel well except the sun is shining. *unless*

PARALLEL STRUCTURE

Observance of parallel structure is one of the earmarks of a well-educated correspondent. Ideas of equal importance should be expressed in parallel structure; for instance, a noun should be paralleled with a noun, an adjective with an adjective, a phrase with a phrase, and so on.

> Mr. Betts works quietly and quickly. (The word before the conjunction *and* is an adverb, and the word after the conjunction *and* is an adverb. This is parallel structure.)
> Mr. Betts works quietly and with speed. (Parallel structure is violated here because the conjunction connects an adverb and a prepositional phrase—unlike elements.)
> Did you place the letter on top of the desk or in the drawer? (The coordinate conjunction *or* connects two prepositional phrases.)

Coordinate and correlative conjunctions are the pivots for application of the principle of parallel structure, and the presentation here is divided into a discussion of the pivotal uses of each type of conjunction.

With Coordinate Conjunctions

Coordinate conjunctions must connect *like* elements. For instance, if an adjective is used before a coordinate conjunction, an adjective must also follow that conjunction. The elements that are written *before* and *after* a coordinate conjunction must match. Study these illustrations.

> The executives seem alert and (to be ready? ready?) to adopt new ideas. (An adjective occurs before *and,* the pivot; the principle of parallel structure demands that an adjective follow the *and. Ready* is therefore correct.)
> Which job do you prefer—typing, filing, or (to take? taking?) dictation? (Before the conjunction *or* there are two gerunds, *typing* and *filing.* Therefore, a gerund must follow the conjunction *or. Taking* is correct.)

Can you balance the following sentences?

1. Fast typing is one thing, but to cut a stencil is quite another. *cutting*
2. The Bensons are noted for their integrity and because they treat their employees fairly. *fair treatment of their emp*
3. Dick is pleasant, considerate, and is willing to work hard. *omit "is"*
4. Mr. Kent likes to fish, swim, and hunting deer. *hunt*
5. You may cash your check at the cashier's window, at the main office, or go to the bank. *at the bank*

With Correlative Conjunctions

Earlier in this lesson, it was stated that correlative conjunctions are conjunctions used in pairs. Parallel structure demands that whatever kind of element is written *after* the *first* member of the pair must match the element written *after* the *second* member of the pair.

> Mr. Olsen wishes *either* Tom *or* me to take the message. (After *either*, the first member of the pair, is the noun *Tom*. After *or*, the second member, is the pronoun *me*. Nouns and pronouns are considered to be like elements; therefore, the structure is parallel.)

> *Not only* had the office been cleaned, *but* it had *also* been freshly painted. (The structure is parallel because the correlative conjunctions *not only* and *but also* join two independent clauses.)

Correcting these sentences should result in correct matching of elements used with correlative conjunctions.

1. For help, you should either go to Mr. Roe or to his aide.
2. I both like to read and to play golf. *like both*
3. Jack was undecided whether he should take the test now or to wait until next week. *to*
4. A correspondent not only must be courteous but also tactful. *must be*
5. During office hours, we neither allow smoking nor to waste time. *wasting*

COMMUNICATION PROJECTS

Practical Application

A Correct each incorrect sentence. Write *OK* for any correct sentence.

1. Do you think it looks like Bob will get the promotion? *as though*
2. Mr. Cole maintains that the reason sales have fallen off is because the weather has been so inclement. *that*
3. Dick does good work, and Henry has the better personality. *but*
4. John was not able to attend the meeting because he had to go to the dentist. *OK*
5. Without you show improvement, you will be looking for another job. *Unless*
6. Finding an opening is easy, but to get the job is sometimes not so easy. *getting*
7. We are going on vacation tomorrow, and today we have work to do. *but*

8. Roger always pretends ~~like~~ he is very, very busy. *that*
9. Expert writers like them are hard to find. *OK*
10. Our firm has a fine reputation for ethical conduct and ~~as a quality manufacturer.~~ *quality manufact*
11. The reason I came early is ~~because~~ my appointment has been changed. *that*
12. Tom's report is not ~~as~~ concise as it should be. *so*
13. We cannot grant the request without your signed approval. *OK*
14. The salesroom is 50 feet wide, 80 feet ~~in length~~, and 18 feet high. *long*
15. Miss Dodson ~~neither wants~~ your help nor your pity. *wants neither*
16. We wish we could grant your request, ~~being that~~ you are such a good customer. *because*
17. There must be not only a standard credit term, but we must also hold to that term. *OK*
18. This year's edition of the manual is just as accurate as last year's edition. *OK*
19. We shall not be able to show a profit unless there is a sharp upturn in the market. *OK*
20. Such extensions of credit are neither allowed to the large customer nor to the small customer.

B List the changes needed to correct each sentence that contains errors.

1. Mr. Crowe talks ~~like~~ he is unsure of himself. *as though*
2. We wrote to you on May 1, but we never received a reply. *OK*
3. The work will be done quickly if you divide the assignment among the three correspondents. *OK*
4. There are five brothers in that family, ~~and~~ David is the oldest. *but*
5. You ought to ~~of~~ known that the prices had been changed. *have*
6. I can ~~neither find~~ the guide nor Mr. Berry's folder. *find neither*
7. Did you know that there is a chefs' union? *OK*
8. ~~Without~~ you use a backing sheet, your stencil will probably have to be retyped. *Unless*
9. You would do well not to trust ~~them kind~~ of proposals. *those kinds*
10. In our business, typewritten letters produce no more sales than ~~using~~ printed ones. *omit*
11. Have you paid the doormen, Pierre and ~~he~~? *him*
12. ~~Being that~~ Mr. Park made up the payroll, he can answer your questions. *Since*
13. Are you ~~most~~ ready to check these statements? *almost*
14. I expected Mr. Hakes to be angry and ~~that he would shout at us~~. *to shout at us*
15. Did you see in the paper ~~where~~ Gold Company has applied for a receiver? *that*
16. Mr. Pierce has never before had so much time as he has had this summer. *OK*
17. We have neither the time ~~or~~ the money to do much experimentation. *nor*
18. Bert seemed tired, ~~and~~ I could see no reason for his weariness. *but*
19. The applicant agreed to accept the position and ~~that he would~~ start Monday. *to*
20. Don't you wish that you had an extra income like Bob and me? *OK*

Editing Practice

Editing for Correct Grammar   Indicate the grammar errors in these sentences and write *OK* for any correct sentence.

1. We will write you within a week in regards to the change in store layout.
2. Your job is to edit, write headings, and the assembling of graphs for these reports.
3. Your correspondence manual is much different from ours.
4. I received the notice, and I have not yet had time to study the agenda.
5. An intelligent, industrious young man will do good in a business office.
6. Our best ad writer is Barber, and whom I would recommend that you consult.
7. We can readily see that your opinions are identical with ours.
8. It looks like we shall have to revise our form letters.
9. Between the three of us, I think we can push the project to completion.
10. Of course, we should of followed the suggestions of the management consultant.

Case Problem

The Pool Supervisor   Executives of the Hammett Company who use stenographers from the pool are complaining that their letters frequently have to be retyped because of errors in spelling. What steps would you take to remedy the situation?

The Mechanics of Style

<table>
<tr><td>22</td><td><h1>Period, Question Mark,
Exclamation Point</h1></td></tr>
</table>

Punctuation marks are devices used by the writer to help the reader toward better understanding of a message. Where the speaker interprets for his audience by pauses, changes in voice pitch, asides, and gestures, the writer uses punctuation marks to guide readers into correct interpretation of written words. The period, the question mark, and the exclamation point have many functions; their main function, however, is to tell the reader that one thought is completed and that another is about to begin. This main function and some auxiliary ones are discussed in this section.

PERIOD

To promote quicker learning and longer retention of the guides for using the period, the following discussion is divided into three main topics—when to use a period, when not to use a period, and pitfalls in the use of the period.

Use a Period

Periods are used (1) to end declarative and imperative sentences and (2) to end requests that are phrased as questions simply for the sake of courtesy.

To End Declarative and Imperative Sentences A declarative sentence makes a statement; an imperative sentence orders or entreats. For example:

> Your order will be shipped tomorrow. (Declarative sentence.)
> Ship our order on or before June 1. (Imperative sentence.)

To End Requests Phrased as Questions Because such wording as "Send us your check immediately" is abrupt and peremptory, requests or suggestions are often phrased as questions, just to be polite; for instance: "Will you please send us your check immediately." This sentence requests the reader to act rather than to answer a question and is followed by a period, not by a question mark. Compare the following sentences:

> Will you be able to give us your decision by May 1? (Here the writer wants a "Yes" or "No" answer.)
> May we have your decision by May 1. (No question is intended here. The writer actually means: "Get busy and see to it that we have your decision by May 1."

CHECKUP 1

Decide whether or not to use periods to end these sentences.

1. Please send this telegram immediately.
2. Have you had your report duplicated?
3. Will you please send us your check before March 1.
4. We had a hectic day yesterday.
5. May we have your revised bid by Monday, June 5.

Do Not Use a Period

In five specific instances, periods are not used.

After a Sentence Ending in an Abbreviation Only one period is used to indicate the end of a sentence; therefore, <u>if a sentence ends with an abbreviation, do not use a second period</u>.

> We are shipping your future orders C.O.D. (Not *C.O.D..*)

After Headings or Titles; After Roman Numerals Written With Names <u>A period should not follow any centered heading or any roman numeral used with a name or a title.</u> For instance:

> Chapter Four: The Mechanics of Style (Chapter heading.)
>
> *Huckleberry Finn* (Centered title.)
>
> Henry VIII was a much-married man. (Not *Henry VIII. was,* etc.)

After Numbers or Letters Enclosed in Parentheses <u>In paragraphs or in outlines, do not use periods with numbers or letters enclosed in parentheses.</u>

> My reasons for declining your offer are these: (a) . . ., (b) . . ., and (c) . . . . (No period with letters enclosed in parentheses.)
>
> *Fourth and fifth steps in an outline:*
>> a. The dictating machine
>> b. The telephone
>>> (1) Placing calls
>>> (2) Answering calls

After Items in Tabulated Lists or in Outlines <u>Do not use a period after short phrases unless the phrases are essential to the grammatical completeness of the statement introducing the list.</u> *Do* use a period after independent clauses, dependent clauses, or long phrases appearing on separate lines in a list. If the list includes both short and long phrases, use periods. For instance:

> Section 1 is organized as follows:
>> 1. Use of period
>> 2. Period pitfalls

(No period after short phrases.)

> Section 1 demonstrates:
>> 1. The use of the period.
>> 2. Period pitfalls.

(Period following short phrases that complete the statement introducing the list.)

> Keep in mind the following:
>> 1. A well-written letter increases prestige.
>> 2. A well-written letter promotes goodwill.

(Period following independent clauses.)

After Even Amounts of Dollars Except in tabulations, <u>do not use periods or zeros after even amounts of dollars</u>. For example:

> We have your check for $50, which is the final payment on your refrigerator. (Note *$50,* not *$50.,* not *$50.00.*)

CHECKUP 2

Find the errors and make the needed corrections in these sentences.

1. The salesman is a representative of Bland, Inc.. *one period*
2. Elizabeth I. was known as "Good Queen Bess." *no period after "I"*

3. We are enclosing our check for $10, which is the difference between the $80 due on your account and the $90 check you sent us. *OK*

4. We must refuse to (1.) accept the shipment, (2.) pay the *(1) (2) (3)* drayage, or (3.) place a duplicate order.

5. The following are headings or titles. How would you punctuate them?

   Business Communications and On-the-Job Requirements *OK*
   The World Around Us *OK*
   Chapter VI *OK*

6. For only $1.00 you will know the convenience of instant hot *# 1* water.

7. Verbs may be divided into three classifications:
   1. "Being" verbs. *no period*
   2. Transitive verbs. *" "*
   3. Intransitive verbs. *" "*

Period Pitfalls

Even some experienced writers fall into one or both of the following pitfalls: (1) using a period to end an incomplete thought or (2) using a comma when the correct punctuation is a period. These serious errors can be avoided by mastering the following guides to punctuation.

The Period Fault   The period fault is the use of a period after words that do not express a complete thought and therefore are not sentences. They are the "no sense" groups discussed in Chapter 3, Section 8. For example:

> We are not quoting prices just now. As our costs have not been computed. (The second group of words illustrates the period fault. Correctly written, the sentence is as follows: *We are not quoting prices just now, as our costs have not been computed.*)

The use of a period after condensed expressions—such as answers to questions or phrases that lead into another thought—is *not* a period fault. These expressions do not rightly belong in another sentence. If a condensed expression is declarative or imperative, it is followed by a period.

> Do we have a reference manual for secretaries? Not at present. (*Not at present* is the answer to a question and is not part of a preceding or a following sentence. It is correctly followed by a period and can stand alone.)

The Comma-for-Period Fault   The comma-for-period fault is the use of a comma to join two separate, distinct, and different thoughts. The correct punctuation in such a case is a period, because two different thoughts should be expressed as two separate sentences.

> Our correspondents are attending a workshop, they are being sent at company expense. (These separate and different thoughts must be written as separate sentences.)
>
> For years we have ordered supplies from you, we have never had cause to complain about quality or about your service. (Here, too, there are two separate thoughts joined by a comma. They should be written as two separate sentences.)

Are there any period or comma-for-period faults in these sentences?

1. Our business necessitates the keeping of many small accounts, much trouble is saved when they are paid promptly.
2. We call your attention to your overdue account. No doubt, in the rush of business, you have overlooked payment.
3. While we are awaiting word from you. We will continue with the listing.
4. Our machines are built to last a lifetime, many satisfied customers have commented on their superior wearing qualities.
5. Please join us for lunch on Monday, we are leaving at one o'clock.
6. Our new salesman made ten calls yesterday. Receiving six orders.

QUESTION MARK

A question mark is properly used after a *direct* question, after a short direct question following a statement, and in a series of questions.

After a Direct Question

A question mark ends any sentence that asks a direct question. Some examples of direct questions are as follows:

> Why has our note been discounted?
> When do you plan to make the change?
> The customer asked, "Is my coat on order?"

After a Short Direct Question Following a Statement

When a sentence begins as a statement and closes with a short direct question, a question mark is required as the end punctuation.

> You are expecting Mr. Young on Monday, are you not?
> He has been invited to lunch with you, hasn't he?

In a Series of Questions

If a sentence contains a series of questions, a question mark should be used after each member of the series. Do not capitalize the separate items.

> Do you plan to vacation in Boston? in New York? in Chicago?
> Who is to accept the plaque—the president? the editor in chief? the personnel manager?

Question Mark Pitfall

Some writers, upon seeing the word *ask* or *why* or *how* in a sentence, automatically end that sentence with a question mark. Not recognizing the so-called "indirect question" that such words signify is the question mark pitfall. An indirect question is a statement and should end with a period.

> We are frequently asked whether we give green or blue stamps. (This is a statement, not a question.)
> Mr. Syme asks how soon we intend to join the association. (This, too, is a statement and properly ends with a period.)

In which of the following sentences is the question mark used incorrectly? In which is the period used incorrectly?

1. Mr. Frisch asked Bill where he was going?
2. A busy workday seems short, doesn't it.
3. The editor asks when we plan to release the copy?
4. Are you acquainted with the president of the company? the comptroller? the plant manager?
5. When will you have your report ready, Fred?

THE EXCLAMATION POINT

The exclamation point is popularly thought of as a mark indicating strong feeling. This is true, of course, but the writer himself must decide whether he wishes to give greater emphasis to a statement or question by using an exclamation point. For instance:

Who would ever interpret my request in such a way? (This is a question, as the writer indicates by using the question mark.)

Who would ever interpret my request in such a way! (Now the writer is somewhat irked, which he shows by using the exclamation point.)

Where in the world is our Order No. 876 (Without an end punctuation mark, the reader cannot tell whether this is a question or an exclamation. If a question mark is used, the writer is just seeking information; but if an exclamation point is used, quite likely he is "hopping mad.")

Although the use of the exclamation point depends on the emotion the writer wishes to express, all writers should be familiar with the following two correct usages of the exclamation point.

After a Single Word or a Short Phrase

The exclamation point may be correctly used after a single word or a short phrase. The sentence that follows the exclamation, however, is punctuated in the usual way. For instance:

Fine! You have our authorization to proceed. (The exclamation is followed by a declarative sentence.)

Well! Did you see what happened? (The exclamation is followed by a question.)

Great Scott! What a relief that was! (The first exclamation is followed by a second exclamation.)

After the Word Oh

The exclamation point is used directly after *oh* when *oh* is the exclamation. If an entire group of words containing *oh* is the exclamation, *oh* is followed by a comma. Capitalize *oh* only at the beginning of a sentence.

Oh! What have I done?

The play was good—but, oh, how sad! (Note, also, that a comma precedes the *oh* occurring within the sentence.)

CHECKUP 5

What exclamation point corrections are needed in these sentences?

1. Well. We finally got the go-ahead on that project! *Well !*
2. Yours is an unusual story, and, oh, so interesting. *— !*
3. What a thrill you get when you sit at the wheel of our new sports car! *OK*
4. How glad I am that you are joining our staff. *, ! !*
5. What. Have you been idle all morning? *✓ !*
6. Oh! What wonderful news this is! *OK*
7. I am eager to know what firm in this state does the most business!

COMMUNICATION PROJECTS

Practical Application

A For the following sentences, make any needed period, question mark, or exclamation point corrections. Write *OK* for any correct sentence.

1. The thermometer outside the east window of our office registered 88° F.. *F.*
2. You will be interested to learn that our $75 topcoats have been reduced to $65. *OK*
3. May we have your final payment by August 15? *15.*
4. What are the two largest cities in Ohio, in Indiana, in Illinois? *Ohio? Ind? in Ill?*
5. The applicant asked whether there would be an opening for a junior executive? *).*
6. We thought that Chapter V. was poorly written. *Chap. V was*
7. Not me! I am trying to get away early every day this week. *OK*
8. The rug sells for $150, this price was clearly stated in the advertisement. *$150. P, le*
9. Please send us a credit memo at once, we need it for our records.
10. This ribbon is very faint. Although it was changed only last week. *faint, although*
11. I do not have the authority to make this decision, I wish that Mr. Watts were here.
12. You will be sure to enclose a check, will you not? *OK*
13. Well done! We are all happy about your promotion. *OK*
14. Our president is expected to return Tuesday. On the evening plane. *Tuesday on the*
15. The customer asked if we would wrap her purchase for mailing. *OK*
16. Sweaters are selling very well. So well that we can hardly meet the demand. *OK*
17. May we expect a reply by Monday of next week? *week.*
18. Peter has superior writing skill—but, oh, what a drab personality! *OK*
19. Your subscription has expired, there is still time, however, to renew it.
20. Some suggestions for good study habits are as follows:
    1. Read the entire assignment to get an overview of the task ahead of you
    2. Take each phase separately, study it, and think about it
    3. Once more, read the assignment as a whole

B Correct the following sentences wherever necessary.

1. Elizabeth II. is beloved by all her subjects. *II is*
2. Do not ship our order before May 1, our inventory will hold us until then.
3. The tickets are for a concert sponsored by the D.A.R.. *R.*
4. My plan is much more simpler than it sounds.
5. We went to the banquet, and we did not stay there long. *but*
6. Congratulations! In our opinion, the committee was eminently fair.
7. The new turnpike is wider than any road in the country. *other*
8. You surely have heard of the Desert Water Bottle. Which is the name of a cactus. *Bottle, which*

9. Whom shall I say is calling, please? OK
10. The craftsmen chose to resign rather than ~~accepting~~ lower wages. *accept*
11. May we ask you to report immediately on these claims for damages. OK
12. I do not mind anyone criticizing my writing. OK
13. The officer asked who owned the car with the flat tire?
14. We were late because the storm disrupted the schedules of commuter's trains.
15. Our maintenance crew is exceptionally efficient. OK
16. The price of $55.00 is net, not list. *$55*
17. Labor Day is one of those holidays that has meaning for all workers. OK
18. Dick was asked whether the blueprints had been filed. OK
19. How many ~~copys~~ of the bulletin are to be duplicated? *copies*
20. Our company makes silverware that is of outstanding beauty, of unusual design, and ~~is sterling~~ of the best quality.

Editing Practice

The Ad Writer   The following sentences are taken from ads written to promote the sale of "Smoothee," a new hair preparation. Rewrite any sentences that need revision.

1. SMOOTHEE *forces* your hair to lay flat!
2. SMOOTHEE—like it's name—smooths away hair problems!
3. No hair preparation does the job that SMOOTHEE does!
4. SMOOTHEE develops resistance to dandruff!
5. Buy one bottle of SMOOTHEE, and you'll never buy another!

Any Spelling Corrections Needed?   If there are spelling errors in the following paragraph, write the correct spelling.

> Your long and outstanding record of interest in civic affairs prompts us to invite you to become a promoter or a sponser of the Bellville Choral Club concert scheduled for June 9. As you probably know, the procedes will be used to help finance the Head Start project planned for this summer. We shall be happy to list you on the program as a sponser (contribution of $50 or more) or as a promoter (contribution of $25).

Case Problem

Retaining Goodwill   Fred James is supervisor of the adjustment department of a large department store. In reviewing the carbons of letters sent to customers by some of his office correspondents, Fred found the following two statements: (1) "Really, Mrs. Whitehouse, you can't blame us if you don't follow the instructions included with each mixer." (2) "You should know that we can't allow a refund unless you return the merchandise within a reasonable time."

1. Do you find anything wrong with either of these statements?
2. If so, what would you have written?

Semicolon, Colon, Dash

The semicolon, the colon, and the dash are tools that the writer uses to "hold" the reader at some point within the sentence. Using these tools, the writer guides his reader into pausing for a short rest before going on to complete the sentence. Although all three punctuation marks discussed here "hold" the reader, each one has its own particular holding function. For that reason, each "hold" punctuation mark will be discussed separately in this section.

SEMICOLON

By "holding" a reader, a semicolon guides him into quick and correct understanding of a message. Study the following discussion to learn when a semicolon is properly used.

To Indicate Omission of a Conjunction

A compound sentence is a sentence that contains two or more independent clauses. In such a sentence the clauses are usually connected by a comma and a conjunction.

> Some of our junior executives do routine work, but others perform more complex duties. (In this compound sentence, the clauses are connected by a comma and the conjunction *but*.)

Whenever a conjunction in a compound sentence is omitted, a semicolon is used to indicate the omission. For example:

> Some of our junior executives do routine work; others perform more complex duties.

Before a Second Clause Starting With an Introductory Word

In some compound sentences, the second clause starts with an introductory word such as:

accordingly	consequently	moreover
again	furthermore	nevertheless
also	however	otherwise
besides	indeed	therefore

In a sentence of this kind, the reader must hold briefly. He needs to assimilate the meaning of the first clause of the sentence and to get ready to hook up with it the meaning of the rest of the sentence. That is why a semicolon is used before a second independent clause that starts with an introductory word instead of with a coordinating conjunction.

> I thought the report much too long; nevertheless, I read until I finished it. (A semicolon and an introductory word are used in place of a comma and a coordinating conjunction to separate the two independent clauses.)

Before Explanatory or Enumerating Words

A semicolon is used before such expressions as *for example, for instance, that is,* and *that is to say* when these expressions introduce an enumeration or explanation that is incidental to the rest of the sentence.

> When I was in college, my father was my greatest handicap; that is to say, he was too free with his checkbook. (*That is to say* introduces an explanation that is incidental to the rest of the sentence.)

As Exceptions to Comma Rules

Three additional uses of the semicolon may be considered exceptions to comma uses. These rules are presented with those for commas in Section 24.

Make any necessary corrections of semicolon usage in the following sentences.

1. We Americans absorb a great many of our own products, ; however, we still have plenty for export.
2. One brother sold stationery; the other became a technical ✓ draftsman.
3. Your work shows an uneven typing touch; for instance, all carbon copies are difficult to read.
4. Changes in policy do not disturb Jack; in fact, he finds them ✓ exciting.
5. Reading broadens the mind; therefore, the person who continues to read continues to be educated.
6. On cold days, Jim's hands are too cold to write; on warm days, they are too hot.
7. We have a staff of five correspondents; nevertheless, bottlenecks are frequent.

COLON

A colon holds the reader for the express purpose of warning him that something important is coming. The function of the colon, therefore, is to give a reader time to get ready for something that merits his special consideration. To use the colon effectively, a writer must know the rules that govern its application.

Colon Before Listed Items

A colon is used before listed items in both sentence and outline form. Expressions such as *the following, as follows, this, these,* and *thus* are the words most often used to introduce a list.

The four methods of filing are as follows: alphabetic, numeric, geographic, and subject. (This is a listing in sentence form.)

The proper procedure is this:
1. Read the entire lesson first.
2. Study each item intensively.   (This is a listing
3. Study the lesson as a whole.   in outline form.)

Colon Instead of Semicolon

You have learned that a semicolon is used before such expressions as *for example* and *that is* when these expressions introduce an enumeration or explanation that is incidental to the rest of the sentence. However, when the sentence leads up to and emphasizes the enumeration, a colon is used instead of a semicolon.

A good conversationalist must remember two things: that is, when to speak and when to keep silent.

Our school offers a wide variety of subjects: for example, anthropology, ceramics, music, philosophy, sculpture, creative writing, and textile design.

Colon to Emphasize

Probably the most important reason for holding a reader by using a colon is to emphasize, to point up, a thought that the writer considers important. Study the following illustrations.

> You should always remember that punctuation is the tool of the writer. (There is no particular "punch" in this sentence.)
>
> Remember this: Punctuation is the tool of the writer. (Do you see how the revision makes the message emphatic?)

Capitalization After Colon

The rule for capitalizing after a colon is this: The first word of a *complete* sentence following a colon should be capitalized if the writer wishes to emphasize the statement or if the sentence states a formal rule.

> The three "hold buttons" are these: the semicolon, the colon, and the dash. (Not a complete sentence, not capitalized.)
>
> Remember this: Punctuation is the tool of the writer. (Complete sentence capitalized because the writer wishes to emphasize it.)
>
> Learn the following rule: Use a colon before listed items. (Complete sentence capitalized because it states a formal rule.)

Colon or Period?

If the last words in a sentence do not directly lead into a listing or a statement, use a period after those words, not a colon. A period, not a colon, is also used if an "interrupting" sentence appears between the lead-in sentence and the listing.

> The following sentences will help you to recognize independent clauses when you see them. (Period, not a colon, because the sentence does not lead directly into a listing.)
>
> Sentences that test your understanding of usage of colons are as follows: (Colon, because the last words lead into a listing.)
>
> Please send me the following items. You will, of course, ship by parcel post. (Correct, because the lead-in sentence and the listing are interrupted by another sentence.)

CHECKUP 2

Apply your knowledge of the "hold" uses of colons by making any needed corrections in the following sentences.

1. Here is a good procedure to follow: always give a little more to the job than is expected of you.
2. Mr. Howe must have the following; the Fane folder, the No. 46 blueprint, and the Link report.
3. Words frequently misspelled are these: *Accommodate, definite, separate, embarrass.*
4. The following are my reasons for resigning. Please note that there is no dissatisfaction with the company or with working conditions.
5. We are offering the following fringe benefits paid vacations, paid life and health insurance, and a discount on purchases.
6. Our inventory includes several types of office machines; for example typewriters, duplicators, and calculators.

DASH

The dash has its own specific "hold" purpose—to break the thought abruptly, thus calling special attention to the following words. Because the dash is the most forceful of the three "hold" punctuation marks, it should be reserved for writing situations where extra force is needed.

Dash or Semicolon or Colon?

Only the writer can decide whether to use a semicolon, a colon, or a dash. Only he knows what effect he wishes his words to have. If he wishes to hold the reader long enough for him to assimilate the first part of a message before going on to the second part, he will use a semicolon. If he wishes to build up the second part by warning the reader that something important is coming, he will use a colon. If, however, his purpose is to snap off the message so that the following words will have special impact, he will use a dash.

> For your advertising campaign, the most popular television channel should be used; that is, use the channel that statistics prove is tuned in by the greatest number of viewers. (A good sentence, but not a forceful one.)
>
> For your advertising campaign, my best advice is this: Use the television channel that statistics prove is tuned in by the greatest number of viewers. (This is a good sentence and a forceful one.)
>
> To make sure your advertising dollar is well spent—use the television channel tuned in by the greatest number of viewers. (The dash snaps off the main thought and thereby adds power to the rest of the message. This is the most forceful sentence.)

Forceful Summarizing, Forceful Repetition

Does the writer believe that a summation of what he has already said will make his statement stick in the mind of the reader? If so, he uses a dash before the summary. Does he hope that repeating a message will make a deeper impression? If so, he uses a dash before the repetition.

> Road maps, hotel reservations, credit cards—these must be ready before Saturday. (The dash in this sentence is used for forceful summarizing.)
>
> Your train leaves from the lower level of Grand Central Station— from the lower level, notice. (Forceful repetition. The writer wishes *lower level* to stick in the reader's mind.)

The Dash With an Afterthought

A good writer may *plan* afterthoughts in order to add variety to his writing, to soften a statement that might give offense, or to arouse his reader's curiosity. The dash is the mark used with a planned afterthought.

> Each of the words omitted—and there are several—is very important. (For variety in style.)
>
> We are unable to take advantage of your fine offer—at least, not for a few months. (To soften a refusal.)
>
> The merger seems to be shaping up—but more about this later. (This will keep the reader "in suspense.")

Correct whatever "dash" errors there may be in the following sentences.

1. Yes, I think we should give some consideration to the idea *O K* of a suggestion box—in fact, I know we should.
2. To Eileen, her father was a successful failure—a hero in de- *OK* feat.
3. How long before we may expect your bid—the bid on the *OK* First Avenue property?
4. Every morning during vacation, the Perrys climbed the hill, *OK* played tennis, and went swimming—all before breakfast.
5. I wish I had time to tell you about—but I must stop dictating *OK* now.

Punctuating Words Set Off by Dashes

No punctuation is used before an opening dash, with the exception of quotation marks or a period following an abbreviation. If words set off by dashes come at the end of a sentence, the closing dash should be replaced by the punctuation needed to end the sentence.

> Our offices are air-conditioned—a necessity in this climate. (No punctuation before dash; period used to end declarative sentence.)
> This artifact dates back to 400 B.C.—an exciting discovery indeed! (Period following the abbreviation *B.C.* precedes opening dash; exclamation point follows exclamatory expression.)

The question mark and the exclamation point may be used before a closing dash when such punctuation is needed. However, if a declarative sentence is set off by dashes, a period does not precede the closing dash.

> Your customer—what is his name?—must have kept you waiting a long time.
> Our football team—and what a team!—won the championship.
> Mr. Williams—he's the gentleman you met yesterday—will call again next week. (No period before the closing dash.)

Commas Within Groups of Words Set Off by Dashes Use commas where needed within groups of words set off by dashes. The point to remember is that the commas may be used within the group of words—not at the beginning, not at the end. For example:

> Most of our writers—and Bill, of course, will bear me out—have had excellent training.

Correct the punctuation errors in the sentences below and on page 158.

1. Very often there are callers—canvassers, applicants for non- *O K* existent positions—who waste the time of our receptionist.
2. Innate curiosity and a longing to express beauty,—these were *omit* the primary forces in Leonardo's genius.

3. Fred typed the report—and what a long one it was, too—in less than an hour.
4. Have you visited any foreign cities—London, Paris, Rome, to mention a few.
5. It is the love of learning—or is it the love of good grades— that marks the real student.

COMMUNICATION PROJECTS

Practical Application

A Correct all the incorrect sentences in this group.

1. The favorable aspects are these: Low prices, low inventories, and increasing customer demands.
2. They uttered no cry; not a sound escaped them.
3. The following suggestions are made to help you study more efficiently. If you adopt them, you will be well repaid.
4. Would you like to know more about your camera—how to take better pictures, what's new in equipment and techniques?
5. Your quotations have been mislaid; however, we hope to find them soon.
6. The Constitution makes provision for the following governmental departments; the executive, the legislative, and the judicial.
7. The dash—do you remember?—is used effectively by few writers.
8. Some persons do their best work early in the day; others do not awake fully until noon.
9. Mr. Irwin ordered the following books, cigarettes, and jigsaw puzzles.
10. We grabbed our hats,—somebody had mixed them up on the hooks,—and rushed for the train.
11. Sometimes money is made by saving money; for instance, payment of bills within the discount period saves the amount of the discount.
12. A receptionist should not be too friendly; actually, most employers prefer a little reserve.
13. The best thing for you to do is this: wait until after lunch before asking for a conference.
14. All the advanced styles for fall; the new sleeve, the latest drape, the correct skirt length are combined in one model.
15. The chairman arrived at the meeting quite unprepared; that is to say, he had forgotten to bring his notes.
16. Would you be interested in: seeing a play or hearing a concert?
17. I know that you will find her a charming girl,—charming and very pretty, too.
18. A writer must know the uses of his punctuation tools; for instance, the semicolon "holds" the reader at some point within the sentence.
19. Your service is poor in the following areas: acknowledging orders, making satisfactory adjustments, shipping promptly.
20. Which type of money order do you mean—postal, express, or telegraph.

B Correct the following sentences wherever necessary.

1. Most of your order is ready for shipment; a few items still must pass inspection.
2. Some men have writing ability; others have not.
3. You should of written us sooner.
4. Mr. Thoms always enjoys—reading, watching television, or talking with callers.
5. It's there right to vote the way they wish to vote.
6. In our office we can choose our vacation time; furthermore, we are paid in advance at vacation time.
7. In this you are exactly right: no dishonest businessman can succeed for long.

8. It is often said—I am not sure how true the statement is—that the real music lovers prefer to sit in the upper balcony. *OK*
9. The customer appears to entirely lack the rudiments of courtesy. *to lack entirely*
10. I have not attended any bowling matches;therefore, I do not know any expert bowlers.
11. For his tardiness, Harry offered the following excuses: The rain, the traffic, the scarcity of taxis. *no cap.*
12. May we have your reply before the market closes on Friday. *OK*
13. We are sure of this one thing: we will grant him no further credit. *We*
14. I wish I was rich enough to buy a new car. *were*
15. Correct the errors in the following sentences: Some of the sentences are correct. *use period*
16. We have many calls for steam irons;in fact, we sold 75 last week.
17. Why does Mr. Lang wear those kind of ties? *Deindas*
18. Bert feels that he cannot spare time to study science, literature, history—all the fascinating topics that make for good conversation. *OK*
19. In our opinion, your fields should lay fallow for an entire year. *no comma*
20. Learn to avoid the common grammar pitfalls; for instance, do not confuse plurals and possessives.

Editing Practice

The Editorial Supervisor   One of your writers overuses the italicized words in the following sentences. Supply him with two synonyms for each word.

1. We are fully *cognizant* of your sales promotion difficulties.
2. This statement is not intended to be *dogmatic*.
3. Evans was never known to *shirk* his responsibilities.
4. The increased fringe benefits will have a *terrific* effect on morale.
5. Please let me know how you feel about the *matter*.
6. A salesman's card should indicate his *line*.

Robot Secretary   Your new secretary has been with you only a week, but already you are beginning to think she is a robot. She does your work fast and efficiently—but she doesn't use her head! What support for your opinion can you find in this paragraph?

> The day after your visit to the Gift Shoppe, we received a shipment of very beautiful glassware. In that shipment was a handsome reproduction of an old Irish bowel that can be used for flowers or fruit; and the price is within the range you specified. This item is being set aside until you have a chance to see it. Won't you pay us another visit—soon?

Case Problem

Addressing Your Boss   John Teller was recently hired as junior accountant in the office of the Boswell Manufacturing Company. There is an air of informality in the office, and John notes that his co-workers refer to the president, James J. Castle, as Jim. John has been saying "Mr. Castle" whenever speaking to him or referring to him in any way.

1. Should John call the president by his first name or continue to use "Mr. Castle"?
2. Under what circumstances do you think employees should call their co-workers by their first names and under what circumstances by a courtesy title, such as *Mr.* or *Miss*?

The Comma

As do other marks of punctuation, the comma has a special function to perform; that function is to slow a reader, to give him a pause before he reads on. Frequently, sentences are composed of separate, but contributing, thought units. Using the comma to slow the reader keeps the thought units distinct and thereby prevents misinterpretation of the message.

> Underneath the desk was all rotted away. (What was rotted away? This sentence is ambiguous.)
>
> Underneath, the desk was all rotted away. (By slowing the reader, the writer shows plainly that the desk, not the floor, was rotted away.)
>
> If Tom comes to work late, once more he will be discharged. (Is this correct? How many times has Tom already been discharged?)
>
> If Tom comes to work late once more, he will be discharged. (Slowing the reader after *more* makes clear the correct thought unit.)

The comma is used so often and in such a variety of situations that lack of facility in using it can spoil the effectiveness of written communications. Therefore, the next three lessons will be devoted to discussing the many diversified uses of the comma.

IN A COMPOUND SENTENCE

A compound sentence is a sentence that contains two or more independent clauses. The comma rule for punctuating a compound sentence is this: Use a comma to separate the clauses of a compound sentence. For a better understanding of the rule, study the line of reasoning developed in the following Memory Hook.

MEMORY HOOK

Concentrate on four words—*and, but, or, nor*. Whenever you see one of these words following an independent clause, look immediately to see whether there is a stated subject of another independent clause after it. If so, use a comma before the *and, but, or,* or *nor*.

In slogan style, the rule can be remembered as *No Subject, No Comma*. For example:

> Your order was received today, and shipment will be made tomorrow. (Here we have *and*, and the noun *shipment* is the expressed subject of the following clause. The comma, therefore, is correctly used.)
>
> Your order has been received and will be shipped tomorrow. (Do not use a comma in this sentence. There is no expressed subject after the *and—No Subject, No Comma*.)

Although the comma is usually required to separate the parts of a compound sentence, there are the following minor variations in the rule.

Very Short Clauses

If the clauses of a compound sentence are very short, the comma may be omitted.

> We sent the check but we received no acknowledgment.
> Tim writes the copy and Dick edits it.

Semicolon Instead of Comma

When the "hold" function of the semicolon is kept in mind, its use to separate the parts of a compound sentence is easily understood. A semicolon is used:

When the Sentence Has a Comma in Either Clause *[use a semicolon]* If a compound sentence contains a comma or commas in either clause, the reader might become confused if a comma were also used to separate the two clauses. In this case, use a semicolon between the clauses so that the reader will be held long enough to assimilate the separate parts of the message. If no misreading is likely, however, a comma may be used to separate the clauses. For instance:

> The discount, of course, should not have been taken; and we shall be expecting your check for $18.10, the amount you deducted. (For better and quicker understanding, the reader can be held after *taken;* therefore, a semicolon has been used.)

> In the winter we sell clothing in the darker shades; but with the coming of spring with its brighter outlook, there is a demand for brighter colors. (The semicolon after *shades* makes clear the point at which the parts of the message are separated.)

> I was in Washington, D. C., last Tuesday, and thinking that I might catch a glimpse of the President, I visited the White House. (The two parts of the sentence are so closely related that a comma is sufficient to make the break between clauses.)

When Clauses Are Unusually Long When the clauses of a compound sentence are unusually long, merely slowing the reader may not be enough for rapid understanding. In this situation, a semicolon may be used if the writer wants a stronger break than the comma creates. Note, however, that the clauses are still linked by a coordinating conjunction.

> Punctuation is important to the person who uses it in his work; and complete mastery of the use of punctuation tools will advance that person in his job.

CHECKUP 1

What are the errors in these sentences?

1. If you pay within ten days, you may take the discount but if you wait a month, you must pay the full amount.
2. You may wait but time will not.
3. We will concede that your argument is sound but it does not affect our decision.
4. We have your inquiry about the part for your machine but we must send a repairman to see the washer before we can intelligently answer your question.
5. Do you ever stop for a moment to think of the advancement opportunities in this company?
6. The paper is not durable enough for our documents nor is it of the right size.
7. Although our product is new, it is giving satisfaction and the two-year testing period is paying off.

IN A SERIES

A series consists of a minimum of three items in sequence. The items may be words, phrases, or clauses. Commas are used to separate the parts of a series, and a comma is also used before the conjunction that precedes the last item in a series.

> English, shorthand, and typewriting are the foundation courses for a stenographer. (Series of words.)
> Will the new branch be located in Buffalo, in Cleveland, or in Gary? (Series of phrases.)

Use of the comma to separate the parts of a series is the most frequently used, but not the only, series rule. The following discussion completes the "series" picture.

Etc. *Ending a Series*

When *etc.* (meaning "and so forth") ends a series, it must be set off by commas—a comma before and a comma after. If *etc.* ends a sentence, the period denoting the abbreviation is the ending punctuation mark. Do not use *and etc.* The word *and* is superfluous before *and so forth.*

> An employer considers grooming, manners, work habits, etc., when promoting a man to an executive position.
> Every typist should be able to type manuscripts, outlines, statements, etc.

Semicolon Instead of Comma in a Series

A comma slows; a semicolon "holds." Logically, then, if the items in a series are long independent clauses or if they contain commas, a semicolon should be used to separate these items. For example:

> We should like you to do the following: arrange our goods into shipping units; transport them to the place where they are to be consumed; store them there if storage is necessary; and obtain a signed receipt showing the time of delivery and the condition of the goods. (Can you see that a "hold" between the items must be used?)
> During our vacation trip last year, we stopped at the following places: Oil City, Pennsylvania; Ann Arbor, Michigan; Gary, Indiana; Kansas City, Missouri; and Santa Fe, New Mexico. (A semicolon to separate the parts of the series holds the reader long enough to grasp the meaning immediately.)

Do Not Use a Comma

Commas must not be used, however, in certain series situations.

End of Series No comma is used at the end of a series (except after *etc.* as discussed above) unless the sentence structure demands a comma at that point. Such instances are rare.

> Water, heat, and electricity are services for which payment must be made promptly. (A comma after *electricity* would be incorrect.)

Repeated Conjunction If the conjunction is repeated before each item in a series, no commas are used to separate the items.

> You can get the information from Bill or Tom or Ray.

In a Firm Name When a series of three or more names connected by an ampersand (&) constitutes a firm name, no comma is used before the ampersand.

> Our investments are handled by Mell, Lyons, Pierce & Dunn.

CHECKUP 2

Keeping the word *series* in mind, find the errors in the following sentences.

1. You can find our ad in the newspaper, in current magazines, or in the various trade journals.
2. Maps, price lists, and illustrated pamphlets, will be given free to all who attend the meeting. *omit (")*
3. Do this immediately: prepare a data sheet, write a covering letter of application, and write me when they have been mailed. *; ;*
4. Mr. Burr has holdings in bonds, and in stocks, and in savings accounts. *omit " , " ,*
5. Hats, shoes, handbags, etc., will be on sale Saturday. *OK*
6. The name Veal, Chop, & Eaton belongs in the "odd-name" category. *omit (")*
7. Advancement is more likely if you are careful about grammar, punctuation, enunciation, and etc. *omit " and "*

FOLLOWING AN INTRODUCTORY WORD, CLAUSE, OR PHRASE

A comma is used after an introductory word, clause, or phrase as a signal to the reader to slow down, thereby preventing confusion and misinterpretation of messages.

Introductory Word

At the beginning of a sentence or of a clause, any word used to introduce the meaning is called an *introductory word*. An introductory word is followed by a comma. Some of the most commonly used introductory words are the following:

accordingly	fortunately	naturally	otherwise
actually	further	next	perhaps
also	however	nevertheless	personally
besides	indeed	no	say
consequently	meanwhile	now	theoretically
finally	moreover	obviously	therefore
first	namely	originally	yes

> Fortunately, the assignment is an easy one. (Here the introductory word falls at the beginning of the sentence.)
>
> I did not enjoy the play; nevertheless, I stayed for the entire performance. (The introductory word introduces a clause within the sentence.)
>
> However high the price, we feel that the purchase is justified. (In this sentence *however* is not introductory. It is essential to the message *however high the price* and, therefore, is not followed by a comma.)

Introductory Clause

An introductory clause is a subordinate clause that precedes the main thought. To slow the reader, a comma is placed after an introductory clause.

> When I give the signal, start the presses rolling. (Without the comma to slow him, the reader's eye might embrace as a thought unit the words *When I give the signal start*.)

Ability to recognize on sight the words or phrases that begin introductory clauses will enable the writer to apply this comma rule correctly. Study the following list carefully.

after	if	though
although	inasmuch as	unless
as	in case that	until
as if	in order that	when
as soon as	otherwise	whenever
as though	provided	where
because	since	whereas
before	so that	wherever
even if	supposing	whether
for	then	while
how	till	

Introductory Phrase

An infinitive phrase at the beginning of a sentence is followed by a comma unless the phrase stands as the subject of the sentence.

> To do a good editing job, one must have a fine English background. (Introductory infinitive phrase.)
>
> To do a good editing job is imperative. (Here the infinitive phrase is the subject of the sentence.)

An introductory participial phrase is always followed by a comma. However, don't confuse an introductory participial phrase with a gerund phrase that serves as subject.

> Standing on the platform, Mr. Kain could check the attendance of his staff members. (Introductory participial phrase.)
>
> Checking the time cards is someone else's job. (Here the gerund phrase is the subject of the sentence.)

Whether or not to use a comma after an initial prepositional phrase presents a problem. If the phrase is very short or if it flows into the main thought, do not use a comma. Use a comma, however, if the phrase is very long, if it is clearly introductory, or if it contains a verbal (participle, infinitive, or gerund) or a dependent clause.

> In winter our store does not close on Wednesday afternoons. (No comma because the phrase is very short and flows into the main thought.)
>
> In the third drawer of the desk near the window, you will find the letter. (Long introductory phrase.)
>
> After seeing Jane, I took a short walk in the park. (Prepositional phrase containing a gerund.)

Find the errors in "introductions" in these sentences.

1. Yes, we do sell electrical appliances. O/C
2. Holding the sample in his hand, Mr. Lunt proceeded to give a sales talk.
3. When your warehouse is finished, we should like to rent floor space. OK
4. Costs are mounting steadily; consequently, our prices must be raised.
5. To find the percentage rate, divide the smaller number by the larger number. OK
6. If you prefer the bill can be sent weekly, instead of monthly. omit ","
7. Moreover, our personal shopper will select accessories for your suit.
8. With customer satisfaction always in mind, Tom writes excellent letters.

NEVER, NEVER

There are five comma pitfalls that the writer must avoid if his messages are to be clear to his readers. You will avoid these pitfalls if you observe the "never, nevers" presented here and in the following two sections. The first is this: Never, never separate the parts of a compound by a *single* comma. A compound subject, a compound object, or a compound verb must contain at least *two* commas—or none at all. For example:

Carter or Barton can supply the special paper you need. (No single comma separates the parts of the compound subject.)

You have my permission to experiment with Plan A and Plan B. (No single comma separates the parts of the compound object of the preposition.)

Simply sign and mail the renewal card. (No single comma separates the parts of the compound verb.)

Our special services and, of course, full credit privileges are yours for the asking. (This sentence does not violate the "never, never" rule because *two* commas separate the parts of the compound subject.)

COMMUNICATION PROJECTS

Practical Application

A   Correct each incorrect sentence in the following group.

1. Naturally, the decision must be made very soon.
2. We asked for it and we got it. OK
3. Do you know the difference between a certified check and a cashier's check and a bank check?   OK
4. Speaking as a consultant, Mr. Greer made clear the advantages inherent in the plan.

5. The price you quoted is within reason, but, before placing an order, we must see some samples.
6. Our bank will be open this afternoon, this evening and tomorrow morning.
7. Tom's suggestion was very good; therefore, we are placing his name on the bonus list.
8. We can ship your order by freight, or we can send it by one of our trucks.
9. Please send me the following: at least six copies of your city directory, paper covered; the list of merchants in the city; an analysis of types of businesses; and a bill covering the cost of your services.
10. While we are considering improvements, we should be planning to redecorate the waiting room.
11. The chairman of the committee for Mr. Albin's testimonial dinner is unable to attend the Friday meeting, and he has requested that you act as substitute for him.
12. Corn, wheat, and soybeans, are important crops in our country.
13. In addition to the introduction, how much of the report has Don written?
14. Our store is now open on Friday nights, and will continue to be so open for the rest of the summer.
15. Johnson, Johnson & Barr are management consultants.

B Correct the following sentences wherever necessary.

1. We are enclosing your credit card, and should like you to acknowledge its receipt.
2. The manager asked how soon we expected to put the plan into operation?
3. Fortunately, we have your size in stock.
4. Jim will not mind correcting the rough draft, will he?
5. You may call at the store for your coat, or we will send it to you on the Tuesday delivery.
6. Because the offer expired two weeks ago, we cannot fill your order at the price quoted in the offer.
7. David's work is always very well done, that is the reason for his promotion.
8. We shall be unable to return the first chapter this week; meanwhile, proceed with the next one.
9. Unit VI. of the report must be rewritten.
10. You should receive your goods on Thursday; but in the event of a strike, of course, there will be a delay.
11. What a relief! You were most kind to let us know so soon.
12. Will you please send us the requested information immediately.
13. The supplies needed for painting a room are brushes, paint, turpentine, etc.
14. To make up for lost time, we must work evenings all next week.
15. These pills are not recommended for general use; that is, they should be taken only on the advice of a doctor.
16. On our May 2 order, we did not receive the bath towels, color green; the face cloths, rose; or the hand towels, blue.
17. You will enjoy the books we have listed below: They are instructive, and entertaining, as well.
18. Mr. Crowley insists that all of us are divided into two general classes,—those who do and those who don't.
19. On the other hand, our supply of refrigerators is low.
20. Our office is an ideal place to work quite different from the average office.

Editing Practice

The Rewrite Desk   Edit and rewrite the following paragraph to correct all mistakes.

Of all the skirts we placed on sale last week the azure ones were in greatest demand. Your order was recieved on the forth day of the sale which was after our stock of azure skirts were sold out. The quality of these garments is so good so unusual that we wanted you to have one of them at the low, sale price. Therefore we are sending you a skirt in your size in the new popular ice-blue color. If you are not pleased with the choice we have made for you please do not hesitate to return the skirt.

The Blue-Ribbon Speller   If you are a blue-ribbon speller, you will be able to find and correct any spelling errors in this paragraph.

Although we know that the use of *loan* as a verb is considered permissable, we are reluctant to sanction such usage in the letters sent by our executives. As bankers, we should project an image of conservatism and stability; therefore, we cannot afford to go along with any Twilight Zone changes. And bankers, of all people, should most certainly know the difference between *lend* and *loan.*

Case Problem

Telephone Technique   Criticize the following telephone conversation. Then rewrite it to avoid the types of errors you criticized.

Person answering.   Hello.
Caller.   Who is this?
Person answering.   Who do you want?
Caller.   I was trying to get the credit department.
Person answering.   This is the credit department.
Caller.   Is George Becker there?
Person answering.   Yes, he is.
Caller.   May I speak with him, please?

The Comma (Continued)

In some sentences a writer makes his meaning clear by using the comma; in others, he makes it clear by not using a comma. A knowledge of when and when not to use a comma enables a writer to express himself more clearly. The first step in discriminating between the circumstances that require using commas and those that do not is an understanding of the traditional terms *restrictive* and *nonrestrictive. Restrictive* means "essential to the meaning"; *nonrestrictive* means "not essential to the meaning."

The comma rule that governs such situations is this: *Use commas to set off any word or words that are not essential to the clarity of the message.* Quite obviously, then, commas are not used if the words *are* essential to message clarity.

Practically speaking, you will learn in this lesson to set off by commas any word or words that give additional information or that are, if you will excuse the expression, "excess baggage." To determine whether or not commas should be used, just ask yourself: "Are these words necessary to the meaning? Can they be omitted without affecting the clarity of the message?" If the words can be omitted, they are set off by commas; otherwise, no commas are used.

Our new policy, as we wrote you two weeks ago, goes into effect June 1. (Why are the words *as we wrote you two weeks ago* set off by commas? Because they are not essential to the message.)

The report is to be set up as we outlined in our June 1 letter. (Why are no commas used with the clause starting with *as?* Because the clause is a necessary part of the message.)

SUBORDINATE CLAUSE FOLLOWING MAIN CLAUSE

We learned in Section 24 that a subordinate clause that precedes a main thought is always set off by a comma. Use of the comma with an introductory clause, therefore, presents no problem. When a subordinate clause follows a main clause, however, there is a question about use of a comma. The problem is solved by determining whether or not the subordinate clause is necessary to the meaning. If it is necessary, no commas are used; if it is not necessary, commas are used. For example:

> He will draw up the contract after we have confirmed the details. (Are the words *after the details have been confirmed* necessary to the meaning? Yes, they are. Therefore, they should not be set off by commas.)
>
> He will draw up the contract tomorrow, after we have confirmed the details. (Is the clause starting with *after* necessary to the meaning? No? Then it is correctly set off by a comma.)

INTERRUPTING, PARENTHETIC, EXPLANATORY ELEMENTS

Interrupting

An interrupting element does exactly what its name indicates—it interrupts a message. Since an interruption is not essential to the meaning of a sentence, such interruption is set off by commas.

> Our service, moreover, includes gift wrapping of all purchases made in the gift department. (*Moreover* can be omitted without affecting the clarity of the message.)
>
> The additional discount, however, can be taken only on lots of five hundred or more. (*However* is set off by commas because it is not essential to the meaning of the sentence.)

Parenthetic

A parenthetic element is any expression that is inserted by way of comment. Such words may be used to qualify or to amend the message. The writer may wish to take away any sting that his words may cause. He may wish to point up a contrast. Whatever the reason, the words are not essential to the meaning and are, therefore, set off by commas.

> The most controversial item, as I see it, should be placed at the end of the agenda. (The qualifying parenthetic expression, *as I see it*, is set off by commas.)
>
> The gift, but not the bill, is to be sent to Mrs. Carr. (The parenthetic expression, *but not the bill*, is used to emphasize a contrast.)

Explanatory

An explanatory element is not essential to the meaning, but it does give additional information. When a writer wishes an expression to be construed as additional information, he sets it off by commas. If he wishes such words to be interpreted as an important part of the message, he does not use commas. An explanatory element need not be a clause; rather it may be any group of words giving additional information.

> Mr. Coe, who is the senior member of the staff, has been promoted to the chief executive position. (Can *who is the senior member of*

the staff be omitted without affecting the main message? Does the clause constitute additional information? "Yes" is the answer to both questions; therefore, the clause has been set off by commas.)

The man who will be promoted to the chief executive position is the senior member of the staff. (Use of the question procedure shows that this "who" clause is necessary to the meaning. Commas, therefore, are not used.)

The manager, sensing the tension, stepped in and averted a dispute. (The group of words giving additional information is a participial phrase.)

CHECKUP 1

Is the comma used correctly in these sentences?

1. Your orders will not be carried out correctly, unless you give explicit directions. *omit ","*
2. Mr. Reid attempting to finish the letters before closing time made many errors. *OK*
3. A business transaction, if mutual satisfaction is your object, should benefit both the seller and the buyer. *OK*
4. Tom's latest report is as brief as though much more satisfactory than his earlier reports. *?*
5. The best thing to do, therefore, is to wait for the auditor's report.
6. We are accepting your application, although we do think that you should have been sponsored by a club member. *omit ","*

APPOSITIVES AND RELATED CONSTRUCTIONS

The rules for using commas with appositives and with three closely related constructions will now be discussed. Grouping the latter rules with the appositive rule will aid in learning, in retaining, and in using them correctly.

Appositives

An appositive is a group of words or a single word that gives more information about a preceding word or phrase. If appositives are not essential to the meaning, they are set off by commas.

The new correspondent, Mr. John Crowley, shows much promise. (The appositive, *Mr. John Crowley*, is additional information and is correctly set off by commas.)

Our first caller, a middle-aged lady, had a real problem. (The appositive, *a middle-aged lady*, is set off by commas.)

There are some instances where the appositive is very closely connected with the noun that precedes it. In such cases, commas are not used because the closely connected term cannot be omitted without clouding the message.

His brother Tom is an accomplished writer. (If *Tom* is omitted, the message is not complete. Therefore, *Tom* is a closely connected word and is not set off by commas.)

The year 1066 will always stand out in my memory. (Omission of *1066* would obscure the meaning of the sentence. An expression that is essential to the meaning is not set off by commas.)

Degrees, Titles, and Other Explanatory Terms

When *M.D.* is written after a name, additional information is given about a person, the information that he is a doctor of medicine. *Inc.* after a firm name gives the added information that the firm has been incorporated. *Jr.* after a man's name informs everybody that this man is the son, not the father by the same name. Degrees, titles, *Inc., Ltd.,* and other explanatory terms are like appositives in that they give additional information. For this reason, they are set off by commas.

> The Reverend James Kenny, D.D., conducted the services.
> Otto Gross, Sr., is one of our best customers.
> Make the check out to Benton & Company, Inc., and send it by registered mail.

Calendar Dates

A year included in a date is explanatory, telling, for example, which May 1 is meant or which May, if the day is not given. Because it gives additional information, the year included in a date is set off by commas.

> August 14, 1945, is a date frequently mentioned in history books.
> In August, 1945, the electrifying news was flashed to the world.

States, Cities

The name of a state written after the name of a city gives additional information; for example, it tells which Springfield or which Columbus is meant. Because it serves an additional-information function, the name of the state is set off by commas.

> Mr. Davis calls Springfield, Ohio, his native city.
> Which is the larger town—Forest, Iowa, or Forest, Idaho?

CHECKUP 2

What comma errors are there in these sentences?

1. Barr & King, Inc., will send you literature upon request. *OK*
2. Our experienced writers, Bob and Paul, carry a heavy work load. *OK*
3. Professor Edward Leary, Ph.D. is the head of our department.
4. Would you rather live in Tampa, Florida, than in Tempe, Arizona? *OK*
5. When did Ivan the Terrible rule in Russia? *OK*
6. "John B. Watts, Manager" is the correct typed signature.
7. In April, 1917, the United States entered World War I.
8. You may expect our salesman, Mr. Mark Bessette, on Monday, July 16. *OK*

TWILIGHT ZONE

That, Which   When a majority of so-called "authorities" no longer adhere to what was formerly an English rule, that principle can surely be said to be in the Twilight Zone. One such principle is that of distinguishing between the use of *that* and *which*.

The meticulous writer, however, knows and observes the following rule: Clauses that are not necessary to the meaning are introduced by *which*. Clauses that are necessary are introduced by *that*. Commas are used with "which" clauses; commas are not used with "that" clauses.

MEMORY HOOK

Which is the longer word, *which* or *that?* Does it take longer to type a comma or not to type a comma? Hook up the longer word *which* with the longer time it takes to type commas. Obviously, commas are not used with the shorter word *that.*

> The handbags on the first counter, which are real bargains, should make a fine sale leader. (Additional-information "which" clause is correctly set off by commas.)
> The handbags that are on the first counter should make a fine sale leader. ("That" clauses cannot be omitted without clouding the meaning, and no commas are used with them.)

NEVER, NEVER

The second and third "never, nevers" are these:

Subject from Predicate

Never, never separate a subject from its predicate by a single comma.

> The missile experiments conducted by Dr. Grove, were described in a special bulletin. (Here the subject is separated from its predicate by a single comma, thus violating a "never, never" rule. No comma should have been used.)
> Experiments with missiles, including those conducted by Dr. Grove, were described in a special bulletin. (This sentence is correct. Note that there are two commas in the subject and that they are used to set off words that give additional information.)

Verb or Infinitive from Object or Complement

Never, never separate a verb or an infinitive from its object or complement by a *single* comma.

> All members of the staff know full well that Mr. Watts has always been, the "idea man" for our organization. (Because a single comma separates the verb *has been* from its complement, a "never, never" rule is violated.)
> We are very glad to hear, that you are interested in purchasing our patio furniture. (This sentence is incorrect because a *single* comma separates the infinitive *to hear* from its object.)

CHECKUP 3

Find and correct the errors in the sentences below and on page 172.

1. That his record is above reproach, is taken for granted.
2. The rule that I consider most valuable is on page 8.
3. Any report, which is to be sent to the president, must be approved and signed by Mr. Ladd.

4. Commas are used to indicate, that the words they enclose are not essential to the meaning. *omit ", "*
5. Paul learned at an early age, the necessity for budgeting. *omit ", "*
6. Results of the survey definitely show, that the morale of our staff is high. *omit*
7. Our organizational plan, which you are free to use, was prepared by the office manager. *OK*

COMMUNICATION PROJECTS

Practical Application

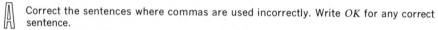

Correct the sentences where commas are used incorrectly. Write *OK* for any correct sentence.

1. The services of Rose York, R.N., are much in demand. *OK*
2. Please retype this article whenever you have some spare time. *OK*
3. The booklet, that we are sending you, was run off on our own machine. *omit*
4. We are sending you our new book, *Electronics*, by special delivery. *OK*
5. I should accept such a fine offer, if it were made to me. *OK*
6. A great fortune in the hands of an inexperienced person, may turn out to be a great misfortune. *omit ,*
7. John's brother, Peter, is graduating at the head of his class. *omit commas*
8. This policy enhances, rather than reflects on, your reputation. *OK*
9. My thesaurus which always helps with word problems has been mislaid.
10. No, we do not have a Henry J. Dean Sr. on our list.
11. Mr. Lunt's decision is closely connected with but in no way dependent on that of his competitor. *OK*
12. Please return to us for our files, the personal data on Mark Hagen. *omit comma*
13. On March 15, 1972, we shall be able to evaluate our efforts. *OK*
14. The sales tax, moreover, was increased in January.
15. Mr. Knott, who is our good friend, has invented a new method of data processing. *OK*
16. Write to Sterling, Ltd., for a list of British investment possibilities. *OK*
17. Bill's attitude on the other hand is refreshingly optimistic.
18. Mr. Daniels carefully explained, that the accident was unavoidable. *omit comma*
19. Pittsburgh, Pennsylvania, is spelled differently from other cities by that name. *OK*
20. Mr. Hunter exhausted by the pressures of the day canceled the afternoon meeting. *OK*

Correct the following sentences wherever necessary.

1. However hard we work, we cannot keep abreast of the orders. *OK*
2. Mr. Quinn is an excellent accountant; he qualified as a CPA.
3. Bella Vista is a housing development; with the nearest subway less than two miles away. *omit ;*
4. We shall be glad to ship your order if you will send us a check for $134. *OK*
5. Many inventors have been laughed at during their lives of intense application, but their inventiveness and their genius often have been recognized and appreciated years later. *OK*
6. Our visitor may be engaged in the financial, in the investment, or in the banking, *omit* business.
7. The court upheld us, and the weight of public opinion was on our side. *OK*
8. What is the correct salutation for a governor? a judge? a clergyman?
9. *Its* is possessive; *it's* is a contraction of *it* and *is*. *OK*
10. The company in question is, I think, solvent.
11. You, too, will be pleased with our quality and service.
12. The customer asked who the salesman for the Chicago territory was?.
13. May we have our statement within three days. *OK*

14. We regret that the parcel was missent; moreover, we regret the inconvenience caused you.
15. Mr. Booth, a man of vision, fostered the plan, and all of us stood by to help him.
16. The lawyer, whose office is on the first floor, is trying a very important case.
17. Our aims at all times are these: to please our customers, to satisfy our bankers, and to treat our employees fairly. *colon*
18. Names must be checked carefully, not just casually inspected, if the directory is to be of any value. *OK*
19. Skill, courage, daring all of these qualities are required of Olympic athletes. *dash*
20. Mr. Daniels, the man responsible for the idea, will present his project to the board of directors. *Omit comma*

Editing Practice

The Editing Desk   Your job is to edit this paragraph, correcting all the errors.

Miss Ayres and myself are very happy to give you additional information about our training program for secretaries. Miss Ayres as you probably allready know is our correspondence consultant, and she carries on the training program. She analyzes carbons of outgoing letters for such errors as punctuation, spelling, case forms of pronouns, etc. and discusses her findings with the secretaries concerned. In order to make the corrections stick the secretaries are scheduled for meetings about once a month. The purpose of the meetings are to clear up questions about the errors, that are most frequently made by most of the secretaries.

Mispronunciation   Because of your extensive vocabulary, you would transcribe correctly any word mispronounced by a dictator. Is any such correction needed in the following paragraph?

May I take a rain check on your invitation to speak to the Blanton sales staff on March 18? Right now I am under medical care for a bronical condition that has affected my voice, and the doctor has ordered that I curtail all speaking engagements for at least a month. But please keep me in mind for future assignments, for I particularly enjoy talking to Blanton employees.

Case Problem

Correcting the Boss   Ethel Nelson, secretary to Joseph Foster, has just placed a set of letters on her employer's desk for signature. In glancing over the letters, Mr. Foster reads the following sentence in one of the letters: "We will mail the package before January 6, 19—, so that you will have it in time."
   Mr. Foster takes his pen and draws a line through the comma following "19—" and tells Ethel that the comma does not belong there.

1. Who is correct? Why?
2. What should Ethel do about the situation?
3. How should Mr. Foster make corrections so that the entire letter does not have to be retyped?

The Comma (Concluded)

The value of the comma in making written communication effective is shown by the fact that three sections of this textbook are devoted to a discussion of its use. Because the comma is used so frequently and in so many different situations, lack of facility in handling it results in a high error score for a correspondent. The confusion and misinterpretation caused by inept use of commas may destroy customer and vendor goodwill. Additional letters may have to be written to clarify a message that should have been stated clearly in the original letter. When additional, unnecessary letters have to be written, a company loses money. The skilled writer, therefore, builds goodwill and makes money for his employer because he knows all the mechanics of written communication.

In this section, the remaining six rules that govern the use of the comma will be presented. Mastery of these rules and of those rules already presented in Sections 24 and 25 can help a writer achieve proficiency in comma usage.

WITH MODIFYING ADJECTIVES

When two or more adjectives separately modify a noun, a comma is used to separate the adjectives. For instance:

> Our boss is a fair, conscientious, brilliant man. (Our boss is a *fair man*, a *conscientious man*, a *brilliant man*. Commas are used because each adjective separately modifies the noun.)

Many writers who know this rule are unable to apply it correctly. The difficulty is in determining whether or not each adjective *separately* modifies the noun. Here is a Memory Hook useful in learning to apply correctly the rule for commas with modifying adjectives.

MEMORY HOOK

If the word *and* can be correctly used between the adjectives, a comma will separate those adjectives. If *and* cannot be correctly inserted, no comma is used. Study the following illustrations and explanations.

> Dick is a diligent, conscientious, accurate accountant. (The commas are correct because you can say "diligent *and* conscientious *and* accurate." A comma after *accurate* would obviously be incorrect because you would not say "accurate *and* accountant.")
>
> Our boss is acquainted with the latest scientific discoveries. (No comma is used here. You would not say "latest *and* scientific discoveries." *Latest*, the first adjective, modifies a unit that consists of the second adjective plus the noun.)

CHECKUP 1

Use the "and" Memory Hook and see how quickly you can insert the correct punctuation in the following sentences.

1. Our duplicator produces sharp clean-cut impressions.
2. We now manufacture light translucent coin discs.
3. Come in to see our attractive nylon curtains.
4. After we reach Chicago, we shall make arrangements for some lengthy personal interviews.
5. We are enclosing a list of bonds suitable for conservative private investment.

WITH OMISSIONS, REPEATED EXPRESSIONS, DIRECT ADDRESS

The comma is also used to save time and words, to emphasize an important thought, and to set off names and terms of direct address. These are the uses discussed in this section.

Omissions

Whenever he can do so without confusing the message, a trained writer saves writing and reading time. Sometimes he accomplishes his purpose by omitting words that are clearly understood by the context of the sentence. However, in case of such an omission, he uses a comma to slow the reader long enough for that reader to supply mentally the omitted words.

> Call loans must be paid on demand; time loans, at the end of a stated period. (The comma after *time loans* slows the reader long enough for him to supply the omitted words *must be paid*.)

Repeated Expressions

In some writing situations, repetition will emphasize an important point, will add power to the statement. Such repetition, however, must be planned; and the writer adds strength by using a comma to set off the repetition.

> Never, never use a single comma to separate a subject from its predicate. (This is repetition planned to emphasize a very important rule. The comma, by slowing the reader, adds power to the statement.)

Direct Address

Names or terms used in speaking directly to a particular person or group of persons should be set off by commas.

> Mr. Bennett, we are asking you to give us the benefit of your experience.

CHECKUP 2

The following sentences illustrate use of commas for omissions, for planned repetition, and for direct address. Make whatever corrections are needed.

1. The first part of the shipment was made on June 1; the second on July 1.
2. Our supervisor maintains that the primary requisite for success is enthusiasm keen enthusiasm.
3. No Mr. Carey we are not now in the market for awnings.
4. Harvard was founded in 1636; Yale in 1701.
5. Paul writes that he is happy in his new job very happy.
6. You will surely understand, gentlemen, why this information is confidential.
7. King & King sold our apartment house; Dell Company, our store.
8. To prevent errors, Don should set up a routine, a work routine.

IN NUMBERS AND BETWEEN UNRELATED NUMBERS

Use a comma to separate thousands, hundred thousands, millions, and so on, in numbers of four or more digits. This function of the comma prevents misreading of numbers.

> Our municipal debt of $1,500,000 is relatively small. (When the number is written correctly, there is little excuse for misreading it.)

When two unrelated numbers are written together, a comma must be used to separate them. Without some means of slowing the reader, the numbers would run together.

> By January 30, 450 stockholders had returned their proxy notices. (A comma between *January 30* and *450* slows the reader and prevents confusion.)

NEVER, NEVER

The "never, never" discussion ends with the following two principles. As study of the use of commas would be incomplete without a knowledge of the situations where a comma must *not* be used, this "never, never" series in Sections 24, 25, and 26 is important.

In Numbers

Never, never use a comma in years, page numbers, house and telephone numbers, ZIP Code numbers, serial numbers, and decimals, even if such numbers consist of four or more digits. These items are written as follows:

in 1967	1402 Main Street	Ames, Iowa 50010	2.3874
page 1212	847-3562	RA 11167099	

In Weights, Capacities, Measurements

Never, never use a comma to separate the parts of *one* weight, *one* capacity, or *one* measurement. Nonuse of the comma ensures that the numbers will be comprehended as a unit.

> The jet record for cross-country flight is said to be 2 hours 13 minutes 7 seconds. (Since no comma slows the reader, he understands that this is *one* time unit.)

CHECKUP 3

Apply the rules for using or for not using commas in numbers by making the needed corrections in these sentences.

1. Our indebtedness has been reduced to $4500.
2. All beams on my order must be 12 feet 6 inches in length.
3. We are sending you Policy 16,389.
4. For Job Order 27, 14 different styles need to be produced.
5. Please change my address to 7,481 Southern Boulevard.
6. The quotation we used appears on page 1,623.
7. We made the trip in exactly 3 hours, 50 minutes, 4 seconds.
8. In 1961 898 new accounts were added.

COMMUNICATION PROJECTS

Practical Application

 Write the correction for each incorrect sentence in this group. Write *OK* for each correct sentence.

1. To cut the cost of overhead, we must examine our numerous administrative expenses.
2. Please let me know, Mr. Marsh, when we may expect shipment.
3. Is the new manager a tall, heavily built man?
4. Please fill in the blanks on the enclosed form, all the blanks.
5. Irving was born in 1783; Longfellow in 1807; and Holmes in 1809.
6. All trivets are to be packed in large, wooden cases.
7. For further information, please call 672-3421.
8. We have reserved for you a large, comfortable, inexpensive room.
9. Memory Hooks promote instant, accurate, application of rules.
10. For the barbecue we had 48 pounds, 12 ounces of meat.
11. We are now only $3000 short of our quota.
12. Yours was a good report an excellent report.
13. The words of the Gettysburg Address may be forgotten; the spirit, never.
14. We like Mr. York's calm unemotional approach to problem solving.
15. You, Mrs. Carson, are one of our most valued customers.

Correct each incorrect sentence in the following exercise.

1. Just a month before the same sharp reminder was necessary.
2. On pages 34-35 12 graphs compared methods of production.
3. The doll's big-brimmed, flaring bonnet makes a frame for its face.
4. This toaster for example cannot be purchased at a retail store.
5. Transfer the call to Mr. Hayes not to Mr. Hakes.
6. Yes our offer was most attractive, but that offer is no longer open.
7. Many functions such as orientation and training are assigned to our department.
8. Always remember, young man, that a person makes his own "breaks."
9. The lobby was equipped with colorful, well-designed, furniture.
10. In fact our interest rate is the lowest in the city.
11. November, 1918, was an important month in our history.
12. The salesman who represents us in your territory will call on you within a week.
13. After all fellow workers unreasonable demands will defeat our purpose.
14. Please telephone us when you get to the hotel.
15. The first lot of returned goods was sold in the basement store; the second in the housewares department.
16. However, much we are opposed, we will abide by the majority vote.
17. In the first month of 1964, 2,642 jeeps rolled off the assembly lines.
18. We do not have the candlestick in brass; however, we do have the same design in pewter.
19. Genius is not so much intellect as it is the capacity for hard work perseveringly hard work.
20. The package, lying on the table, belongs to Mr. Ames.

Editing Practice

Proofreading for Spelling Errors Because of your reputation as a good speller, you are often asked to proofread for spelling errors. Make the necessary corrections in this paragraph.

Yes, it is true that Mr. Kane has definitely committed himself to helping with this year's United Fund drive—but in an advisory capacity only. He will be an *ex officio* member of the steering committee and will act as a resource person for the initial-gifts phase of the program.

The Mumbling Dictator   Jean Walker recently has been hired as a secretary in the law firm of Beatty and Barnes. Mr. Barnes does most of his dictating to a voice-writing machine, and Jean transcribes the dictation as soon as possible. Although Mr. Barnes' voice is loud enough, she has difficulty understanding him; many of his words are garbled. Jean suspects that Mr. Barnes dictates with a cigar or pipe in his mouth, but she is not really sure.

1. How should Jean handle this situation?
2. If you were Mr. Barnes, would you object to Jean's criticizing your dictation technique?

Quotation Marks, Parentheses, Apostrophes

The Stars and Stripes that fly outside American embassies signal that business of the United States Government is carried on in those buildings. Red flags placed in front of and behind a parked truck signal that the truck is out of commission. Flags in the hands of men stationed before and after the crew working on a highway signal motorists that traffic in that stretch of road is being regulated. Such flags are used to indicate that something special or different is going on. A writer, too, must have some way of signaling. He needs flags that will indicate that some expressions are special, are different from other words ordinarily used in a message. His signal flags are quotation marks, parentheses, and apostrophes. Without expert knowledge of the use of these flags, his communications will be ineffective—or actually misleading.

QUOTATION MARKS

Quotation marks are used mainly to signal the reader thus: "The speaker or the writer used these exact words." Although this flag is most frequently used for direct quotations, a writer must also be familiar with several other uses for quotation marks.

Direct Quotations

A direct quotation is the word-for-word record of something that has been said or written, and quotation marks are the flags that signal a direct quotation. In most instances, a comma precedes a direct quotation that comes at the end of the sentence.

> Mr. Smith said, "I am leaving for Chicago tonight." (Note comma following *said*.)
>
> The letter read, "Your order of May 16 has been received." (Quotation marks signal that these are the exact words appearing in the letter. Note comma following *read*.)

If the quotation is introduced by an independent clause, a colon should be used in place of a comma.

> The letter read as follows: "Your order of May 16 has been received and will be shipped before May 20."

A colon should also be used if the quotation is extremely long or consists of several sentences.

> Mr. Smith said: "I am leaving for Chicago tonight, and tomorrow morning I will meet with Mr. Brown to discuss the signing of the contract. If he signs it immediately, I will spend the rest of the day sightseeing."

When a direct quotation falls at the beginning of a sentence, the punctuation that ends the quotation depends on whether the quotation is a declaration, a question, or an exclamation.

> "I am so glad to meet you," said Mr. Howe. (In a declaration, a comma, rather than a period, is placed before the closing quotation marks.)
> "When may I see you again?" he asked. (In a question, retain the question mark before the closing quotation marks.)
> "What a remarkable play!" he exclaimed. (In an exclamation, retain the exclamation point before the closing quotation marks.)

Interrupted Quotations

When a direct quotation is interrupted, only the quoted words are enclosed in quotation marks.

> "Whenever possible," read the directive, "file all carbon copies before closing time." (The commas set off the interruption.)

Any semicolon or period that would be used if the quotation were not interrupted is placed after the interrupting words.

> "Bob will be the manager," said Mr. Scott; "Fred, the assistant."
> "I am resigning my position," wrote Mr. King. "It is time for a younger man to take over."

Quotation Within a Quotation

When quotation marks are needed within a quotation, use single quotation marks.

> Frank asked, "Did you say '16' or '60'?"

Note. All quoted material must be copied exactly as it is written. If any change is made, the material is not a direct quotation. Never enclose indirectly quoted words (usually introduced by *that*) in quotation marks.

CHECKUP 1

Find and correct all errors in the following sentences.

1. Mr. Ash said "that he would state his position very soon."
2. "Are these the only styles of shoes you have," the customer inquired.
3. "I think so, said the salesman, but we can place a special order for you."
4. Richard explained, "I said 'I do agree,' not 'I disagree.'"
5. "Your order can be filled," we wrote, "however, delivery may be delayed."

Quoting Terms and Expressions

Whenever a writer wishes to show his reader that certain expressions or terms are particularly significant, he encloses the significant words in quotation marks. He capitalizes the first word of the quote only if the expression is a complete sentence. The following are some of the ways quotation marks are used to denote expressions and terms having special significance.

For Explanations, Definitions, and Unusual Terms   Words and phrases accompanied by their definitions or introduced by such expressions as *so-called, known as, termed, marked, signed, the word,* and similar expressions are enclosed in quotation marks.

> The words "principle" and "principal" are often confused.
> Working regularly at a second job is known as "moonlighting."

Any terms that may be unfamiliar to a reader or that should be signaled as unusual are flagged thus:

> The photo-offset printer will have to make an entirely new "flat." (Technical term that may be unfamiliar to the reader.)
> Each letter in the series will be "tailor-made" to your needs. (Unusual term when referring to letters.)

Note.   This rule applies to material that is to appear in typewritten form, as in letters or reports. If the material is to be set in type, however, expressions of this kind should be underscored and the quotation marks omitted. Underscoring indicates to a printer that the expressions are to be set in *italic* type.

For Translations of Foreign Words   The translation of any foreign word or expression is enclosed in quotation marks.

> "Noninterference" is one meaning of *laissez faire.*

For Slang, Humor, or Poor Grammar   A writer who wishes to "perk up" his message occasionally uses slang, poor grammar, or an expression that is intended to be funny. In such cases, enclosing the words in quotation marks signals the reader that their use is intentional.

> We are so glad to hear "them things" about your progress.
> An "authority" is any person who is a hundred miles from home.

Note.   When *etc.* is used at the end of a quotation, that *etc.* should not be placed within the quotation marks.

> "We, the people of the United States," etc., is the beginning of the Preamble to the Constitution of the United States.

CHECKUP 2

Is the use or nonuse of quotation flags correct in these sentences?

1. The words "which" and "that" are not used interchangeably. OK
2. Notice that company is to be capitalized whenever the word "company" refers to our company.
3. The part of the upper deck of a ship forward of the foremast is known as the forecastle. ^"forecastle"

4. We engineers do not use "pushers" for the westbound grade. *OK*

5. Such white lies are rather common and are considered horn-tooting. *"horn tooting"*

Quoting Titles

The rules for quoting titles are as follows:

Quote titles of the following: parts and chapters of books (but *not* titles of books), lectures, articles, essays, sermons, toasts, mottoes, paintings, poems, sculptures, and names of ships.

> Part Seven, "Writing Craft," contains three sections.
> "There's always room at the top" is my motto.
> We are sailing on the "Queen Anne."

Titles of complete works published and bound separately, such as books, booklets, long poems, magazines, and newspapers, should be underscored. The titles of plays, operas, and movies are also underscored. Underscoring in typewritten copy is the counterpart of *italics* in printed publications.

> The title of this book is College English and Communication.
> I read the story in The New York Times.
> *The Sound of Music* delighted audiences for years.

When such words as *preface, introduction, contents, appendix,* or *index* refer to respective parts of a specific book, they are capitalized, not quoted.

Punctuating at End of Quoted Material

Are punctuation marks occurring at the end of quotations placed inside or outside the flag? To answer this question, study the following three rules.

Periods and commas are *always* placed *inside* the closing flag.

> Charging interest at a higher rate than is allowed by law is called "usury."
> A.D., meaning "in the year of our Lord," precedes the year.

Colons and semicolons are always placed *outside* the closing flag.

> Please "rush": 1 dozen packages mixed flower seeds, 4 lawn mowers, and 6 garden rakes.
> The friendly feeling of the public for a firm is known as "goodwill"; without it, no business can long endure.

Question marks and exclamation points may be placed *inside* or *outside* the closing flag, depending on whether the quoted material or the entire sentence is the question or the exclamation. If only the *quoted words* are the question or the exclamation, the punctuation is placed *inside* the ending flag.

> The personnel manager asked, "What qualifications does the applicant have?" (The quote is the question; therefore, the question mark is placed with the question, inside the closing quotation marks.)
> A voice boomed over the loudspeaker, "Attention, please!" (The quote is the exclamation.)
> Mr. Cook's directive, "Cut down overhead!" must not be disregarded. (The quote is the exclamation. Note also that the exclamation point following *overhead* takes the place of a comma.)

If the *entire sentence* is a question or an exclamation, the question mark or the exclamation point is placed at the very end, *outside* the flag.

> Is this stock one of the "blue chips"? (The entire sentence, not the quote, is the question.)
>
> What a horrible example of "featherbedding"! (The entire group of words, not just *"featherbedding,"* is the exclamation.)

CHECKUP 3

In the following sentences, make any needed corrections in the use of quotation marks.

1. Enter my one-year subscription to your magazine "Business Trends." *Business Trends.*
2. Do you know what is meant by the expression "under the counter?" *counter."?*
3. The Normandie had a tragic history. *" Normandie".*
4. Our favorite painting is Da Vinci's "Mona Lisa". *"Mona Lisa."*
5. Kipling's "If" merits many a rereading. *OK*

PARENTHESES

An expert writer uses parentheses only when a situation demands that these flags—and no other signal—be used. The expert, therefore, knows the principles of parentheses usage presented in this section. He also knows how to punctuate parenthetical words. The following principles must be learned.

Enclosing Words That Give Additional Information

Although commas and dashes are also used to enclose "additional information" words, parentheses so used have a different and special function. Words that are set off by commas or dashes *may* be omitted, but these words are of some help in supplementing the main thought of a message. Words in parentheses, on the other hand, are merely "excess baggage." For instance:

> Mr. Bell, one of Mr. Main's most efficient auditors, will be in charge of the audit. (Although the words enclosed in commas may be omitted, they do add something to the main thought.)
>
> Each of the words omitted—and there are several—is most important. (The words set off by dashes may be omitted, but without them the sentence lacks emphasis.)
>
> The executor named in a will by the testator (the person who made the will) is to carry out the provisions of the will. (The words in parentheses make no contribution to the main thought.)

Indicating References

The greatest value of parentheses is their use in enclosing a reference, a direction, or the name of an authority for a statement.

> Use of parentheses in enumerated items has already been discussed (see Part 1). (Enclosing a reference.)
>
> Insert the carbon pack (be sure that sides and top of pack are straightened), and start typing on line 15. (Enclosing directions.)
>
> Business communication involves reading, writing, speaking, and listening. (Kenneth Steele) (Enclosing the name of the authority.)

Punctuating Words in Parentheses

No mark of punctuation is used *before* an opening parenthesis mark, whether the parenthetical words are within a sentence or whether they stand alone.

> Call me tomorrow (Thursday) for confirmation of these figures.
> (No mark of punctuation before *Thursday*.)

Words in Parentheses Within a Sentence   Any regular sentence punctuation—comma, period, colon, and so on—is placed *after* the closing parenthesis mark.

> Call me tomorrow (Thursday), and I will give you the figures. (The sentence calls for a comma to separate the independent clauses, and that comma is placed after the closing parenthesis.)
> We sent our check (as promised); however, we have heard nothing from him. (The semicolon is placed after the closing parenthesis.)

The only punctuation marks that are placed *before* the closing parenthesis are question marks, exclamation points, or abbreviation periods that belong with the words enclosed in parentheses.

> All reports must be finished this week (can you beat it!), and we thought the deadline was next week.
> The newest fabrics made of synthetic fibers (Dacron, Acrilan, etc.) are our specialties.

The first word of an expression in parentheses within a sentence is capitalized only when that first word is a proper noun. This is true even when the expression is a complete sentence. For example:

> Use the enclosed envelope (it is all ready to go), and send us your check by return mail.

Words in Parentheses Standing Alone   When words enclosed in parentheses are not part of a sentence, but are entirely independent, the first word is capitalized and the end punctuation is placed before the closing parenthesis.

> Corporate sales have advanced rapidly in the past year. (See our annual report for details.)
> Please return the entry blank as soon as possible. (You might win a big prize!)

CHECKUP 4

Edit the following sentences for correct parentheses usage.

1. The stock certificate, (common) was issued to B. J. Dodd.
2. Business largely fulfills its primary function (sales) through salesmen.
3. If Hicks accepts the offer (It looks as if he will), he will have to leave within the next four weeks.
4. Would you be interested in our introductory offer of twelve treatments for $35 (regularly $3.50 a treatment?)
5. All bids must be in by Friday of this week (whew), not a week from Friday.
6. A foreclosure bars or extinguishes a mortgagor's right of redeeming a mortgaged estate. (Bailey.)

APOSTROPHES

Apostrophes, as discussed earlier, are used to show possession. They are also used as an alternate method of forming the plurals of letters, numbers, signs, symbols, and words used as words. Three additional usages are discussed here.

In Contractions

An apostrophe is used to indicate a shortened form of one or more words, such as: *nat'l* for *national; don't* for *do not;* and *o'clock* for *of the clock.* Some words formerly considered contractions are now accepted as complete words: for example, *phone* and *cello.*

For Omission of Figures

Use an apostrophe to signal the omission of the first figures of a date: *'50* for *1950.*

For Invented Words

A verb form that is made up from a letter or an abbreviation must be signaled as being an invention. To do this, add an apostrophe and *d* or *ing* to the coined verb.

> The manager *OK'd* the shipment.

CHECKUP 5

Can you find the errors in apostrophe usage?

1. Life in the 20s must have been very hectic.   *'20s*
2. We just cant meet your deadline.   *can't*
3. Names of departments of our company are to be capd in interoffice memos.   *cap'd*
4. He was born during the hurricane of 33.   *'33*
5. Has Mr. Banks OKd your proposal?   *OK'd*

COMMUNICATION PROJECTS

Practical Application

Make any needed corrections in the use of quotation marks, parentheses, or apostrophes.

1. "Heaven knows," he exclaimed. "We need the business just as much as you."   *knows!"*
2. We do not get much of the "carriage trade."   *OK*
3. Turning from the telephone, Mr. Hill declared "that somebody had given him the wrong information."   *omit quotes*
4. Mr. Barr did not mention moving (a great many things required his attention yesterday) but, of course, we can be ready on short notice.   *yesterday);*
5. "Theoretically, you are right," said Bob; "practically, you are wrong."   *OK*
6. If Mr. Page wishes to take advantage of this offer, hed better do so soon.   *he'd*
7. "Every owner of a Roamer car is a satisfied owner," stated the ad, "There can be no disappointment with a Roamer."   *period*
8. A thrifty person estimates his income and expenses for a given period. (This is known as "budgeting").   *this;*
9. One slogan for your product is this, "We know they're the best. Don't you?"   *period (This*
10. The latest directive (and its a beauty!) will shake up the entire staff.   *it's*

11. "Call for Mr. Ward" rang through the lobby! *Ward!"* *lobby.*
12. Yours for only $10 (tax included)! OK
13. *Modus operandi* means manner of operating. OK
14. Nothing worthwhile was ever achieved without hard work. (Frank Lord) OK
15. David asked, "Shall I mark this cablegram 'Deferred Rate'?" OK
16. After receiving news of the disaster (or was it a catastrophe?), the Red Cross rushed help to the area. OK
17. Do you agree with those who say, "We must let down the tariff barrier?" *"?*
18. For the latest news, listen to WNAD (890 on your dial) every hour on the hour. OK
19. The information you seek appears in the section, "Judging Cottons". *Cottons."*
20. The truth of the matter is (Haven't you guessed it?) that there are no flying saucers. *Haven't*

B. Correct all errors in the following sentences.

1. Shea and Companys employees are all carefully selected. *'s*
2. The discussion will cover the following topics: (1.) the population, (2.) the political party in control, and (3.) the recent bond issue. *omit period*
3. Has your secretary typed the "Preface" for the book? *omit quotes*
4. We have read the following poets: (contemporary poets) Frost, Sandburg, Guest, and Nash. *colon*
5. Have you seen that stirring painting, "The Spirit of 76"? *omit comma*
6. We think that $50.00 is an exorbitant price. *$50*
7. "For growth, buy stocks," said the consultant; "for safety, bonds." OK
8. OKing requests for funds is always a difficult task. OK *'ing*
9. Mr. Marsh asked whether his dictation was too fast? *substitute period for question mark*
10. All our supplies are bought by the "conference" method. OK
11. The steps in the selling process have already been discussed (see page 5). OK
12. "Halt" was the greeting we received. *"Halt!"*
13. The new stenographer asked, "What does 'open' punctuation mean?" OK
14. Do you know the difference between the use of "advise" and "advice?" *advice"?*
15. The storm ravaged the entire Atlantic coast—from Eastport, Maine, to Key West, Florida,—at hurricane force. *no comma*
16. The bank may refuse to honor (pay) the check when it is presented. OK
17. J.P. Lunt, editor of "Fashion Magazine," will address the convention. *underline mag.*
18. Because of the delay, (they claim it was unavoidable) we are embarrassed. *)*
19. This is what Mr. King said: "The estimates must be ready by Monday." OK *;*
20. *Nom de plume* is translated as pen name. *"pen name."*

Editing Practice

The Editing Desk   Another assignment has come in. Edit the following paragraph.

Yes we do give continuing communication training to our secretaries. As most of our staff members have been out of school for many years they have forgotten much of the fundamental training that is for them essential absolutely essential. We find too that some of the recent graduates are not as well prepared as they might be. We firmly believe that the letters that go out from our office advertise the quality of our company, therefore, we insist that those letters be technically correct.

Word Confusions   Word confusions are hazards for the writer who doesn't know the difference in meaning between words that sound alike. Can you straighten out any word confusions in this paragraph?

Your good friend and mine, Professor Link, suggested that I write and ask you about the advisability of taking a journalism course during my senior year at the University. In preparation for a career as a business writer, I am taking all the prescribed courses. Journalism, however, is not included in this list of courses. I know that your correspondence write news releases, but is this part of their work important enough to warrant specialized training in journalism? I should be very grateful for any advice you can give me.

correspondents

Case Problem

Solving Problems by Discussion The small-group discussion technique is often used to solve problems. Shared ideas and experiences of a group often provide better solutions to problems than the limited ideas and experiences of an individual. Here is the way this technique works. (1) Divide the group into small sections of four, five, or six. (2) Make certain everyone in each group is acquainted. (3) Elect a chairman and a recorder for each group. The recorder will take notes and will later report the major points of the discussion to the entire class. (4) Make certain that everyone understands the problem to be discussed. (5) Be sure that everyone enters into the discussion.

Here is the problem: What are the most important subjects (besides those "majored in") for business students?

---

28 | Capitalization

A speaker has various ways of indicating that he means a particular person, place, or thing. For instance, he can open a map and point to a city about which he is talking. When showing a visitor the sights of his community, he can point to buildings, rivers, parks, and so on. Rarely will he be misunderstood. A business writer, on the other hand, has only one way of indicating that he means a particular person, place, or thing. He has only capitalization. To be sure that he will be understood, a writer must know how to capitalize correctly the names of persons, places, and things. Acquiring this skill is only part of developing the necessary ability to apply correctly the principles of capitalization. The ability to know and use the fundamental, arbitrary capitalization rules and to avoid the capitalization pitfalls that trap the untrained writer must also be acquired.

ARBITRARY RULES

Arbitrary rules govern the mechanical aspects of capitalization, those situations where a writer always capitalizes or never capitalizes. The rules are those explained below.

First Words

Capitalize the first word of (1) a sentence or a group of words used as a sentence; (2) each line of poetry; (3) each item in an outline; (4) a sentence in a direct quotation; (5) a complete sentence after a colon, in order to emphasize a statement or to state a formal rule; and (6) a complimentary closing. For example:

> Correct capitalization is the mark of a polished writer. (Complete sentence.)
>
> No, not now. (Group of words used as a sentence.)
>
> Be sure to remember that:
>   a. Proper nouns are always capitalized.
>   b. A business may have its own rules for capitalization. (First word of items in an outline.)
>
> Mark Twain once said, "Everybody talks about the weather." (First word of a quoted sentence.)

The idea is this: Meaningful repetitive practice builds skill. (Capitalization after a colon in order to emphasize a statement.)

Very sincerely yours, (First word of a complimentary closing.)

Loveliest of trees, the cherry now
Is hung with bloom along the bough.—A. E. Housman (Each line of poetry.)

CHECKUP 1

Check your understanding of the rule for capitalizing first words by making any needed corrections in these sentences.

1. He asked, "Where did I put my pencil?" *OK*
2. Have we a definite discount policy? yes, indeed. *Yes*
3. The letter began, "Please forgive us for being dilatory." *OK*
4. A good closing for this letter is "yours sincerely." *Yours*
5. Two types of responses to be expected are these:
   a. The reflex response
   b. The reason response *OK*

Headings and Titles of Publications

The arbitrary rule for the capitalization of headings and titles of publications is this: *Capitalize all main words; but do not capitalize articles, conjunctions, or short prepositions.* A "short preposition" consists of three or fewer letters. Obviously, if the preposition has four or more letters, it will be capitalized. This rule applies also to the words in any hyphenated expression in a title or heading. The first and last words of a title should be capitalized, even if they are articles or short prepositions.

Their experiences are related in an article called "Two Men and an Army." (*And* is a conjunction; *an* is an article.)

The Nebraska state motto is "Equality Before the Law." (*Before* is a preposition containing six letters.)

The title of the book is *Use the Most Up-to-Date Methods.* (The hyphenated compound follows the capitalization rule.)

Have you read the essay entitled "The World We Live In"? (Here both the article and the short preposition are capitalized because they are the first and last words of the title.)

Proper Adjectives

A proper adjective is an adjective formed from a proper noun; for example, *Mexican, South American, Lenten, Victorian.* Proper adjectives are capitalized.

Note. Through long use, certain adjectives are no longer capitalized because they have lost their association with the proper nouns from which they were derived; for example, *venetian* blind, *turkish* towel, *india* ink, *panama* hat. Always check a dictionary to decide whether or not to capitalize such adjectives.

Seasons of the Year

Seasons of the year are not capitalized; for example, the *spring* styles, our *fall* opening, sales during the *winter* months.

What are the errors in the following sentences?

1. Our club play, called *A Time-Honored Custom,* is a comedy. OK
2. David's mother is French; his father, Irish. OK
3. In May we begin to plan for our winter business. OK
4. Mr. Shea's slogan is "Now Is the Time to Advertise." OK
5. North America is composed of all the North American coun- OK
   tries.

NAMES OF PERSONS, PLACES, THINGS

A capital letter is used by the writer to say: "This is a specific person, place, or thing; and this name is exclusively the property of this particular person, place, or thing." For instance:

> Bob attends the First Methodist Church. (Capitalization shows that this is the official name of a specific church.)
>
> Bob attends the first church that was built in our city. (Here there is no name that is exclusively the property of any specific person, place, or thing; therefore, no capitalization.)

Names of Persons

To every person, the sound of his own name is sweet music; therefore, a mistake in spelling or in capitalizing may endanger goodwill. Names should be written *as the owners wish them to be written,* regardless of the rules. Only when there is no way of finding out how a person prefers that his name be written are the following rules to be used.

O', Mc, Mac   The prefixes *O'* and *Mc* are followed by a capital letter without spacing; for example, *O'Brien, McCaffrey.* The prefix *Mac* may or may not be followed by a capital, as: *MacMillan, Macmillan.*

D, Da, De, Della, Di, Du, La, Le, Lo, Van, Von   These prefixes are capitalized when only the surname is written, as in *De Frias, Van Hoven, Du Mont.* When a first name, an initial, or a title appears with the surname, the prefix is not capitalized unless the individual person prefers a capital letter.

> We enjoyed La Follette's speech. (*La* is capitalized because only the surname is written.)
>
> Did you enjoy Senator la Follette's speech? (*La* is not capitalized because a title is written with the surname.)

Names of Places

Capitalize names of geographical localities, streets, parks, rivers, buildings, and so on, such as *South America, Main Street, Bryant Park, Delaware River, Medical Arts Building.*

Capitalize the word *city* only when it is part of the corporate name of a city; *Dodge City,* but *the city of Boston.*

Capitalize the word *state* only when it follows the name of a state; *Iowa State,* but the *state of Iowa.*

Capitalize the word *the* in names of places only when *the* is part of the official name; *The Hague,* but *the Maritime Provinces.*

Names of Things

Capital letters designate an official name that is the exclusive property of specific companies, associations, committees, bureaus, schools, clubs, governmental bodies, and so on. For example:

> Our children have all been graduated from Wilson Junior High School. (*Wilson Junior High School* is the official name of a specific junior high school.)
>
> Our children have all been graduated from a junior high school in Wilson. (In this sentence there is no name that is the official name of a specific junior high school.)
>
> Are you a member of the National Education Association? (Capitalizing the official title of a specific organization.)
>
> We have had no word from the State Department of Education. (Capitalizing the official title of a specific department.)
>
> Please cancel our subscription to *The Evening Sun*. (Because *The* is capitalized, it must be part of the official name of the paper. Otherwise, the sentence would be written as follows: "Please cancel our subscription to the *Evening Sun*.")

Capitalize names of historical events and documents, of holidays and religious days. For instance:

> Mr. Bell was wounded in the Battle of the Bulge. (Historical event is capitalized.)
>
> Hitler bitterly resented the provisions of the Treaty of Versailles. (Historical document is capitalized.)
>
> Manufacturing as we know it today started with the Industrial Revolution. (Period in history is capitalized.)
>
> Did you know that Easter and Passover occur at the same time of year? (Religious days are capitalized.)

CHECKUP 3

Are the names of persons, places, and things capitalized correctly in these sentences?

1. We do not have an application from a Ralph Della Porte.
2. The Democratic National Convention will be held in Chicago.
3. What cultural contributions were made during the stone age?
4. Do you prefer the Green mountains to the White mountains?
5. Real Estate Enterprises owns the Herald Building.
6. Is Pike's Peak in the state of Colorado?
7. The security council of the United Nations influences international relations.

CAPITALIZATION PITFALLS

Capitalization pitfalls result from uncertainty about the use of capitals in certain given situations. For instance, in the sentence "Chicago is west of New York," the problem is whether or not to capitalize *west*. The problem also arises with a sentence like this: "The Governor (governor?) has made his appointments." Logical and explicit solutions to the most frequently occurring problems are presented in this section.

Points of the Compass

Capitalize points of the compass—*North, West, Southeast,* etc.—when those names denote a *specific section* of the country. When compass points refer simply to direction, they are not capitalized.

> That candidate is very popular in the East and in the South. (Points of the compass capitalized because they are names of specific sections of the country.)
>
> Is Seattle north, west, or northwest of Chicago? (Points of the compass are not capitalized because they indicate direction.)

Substitutions

Substitutions are terms used in place of official names, much like nicknames. These terms may be used for both persons and places, and they are capitalized if (1) they are generally known and recognized and (2) they can be lifted out of the sentence and replaced by a complete, official name.

> Germany was very proud of the brilliance of the Desert Fox. (General Rommel was known by the descriptive term *Desert Fox.* The term *Desert Fox* can be lifted out of the sentence and replaced by the name *General Rommel.*)
>
> Mr. Martin has gone to the Windy City for a few days. (*Windy City,* describing *Chicago,* is a term that is generally known.)

Shortened Forms

Instead of writing out a complete name for some particular person, place, or thing, a writer will sometimes use a shortened form of that name. A shortened form of a name is capitalized when it is used to indicate that a *particular, specific* person, place, or thing is meant.

> Make an appointment for Mr. Owen to see the Admiral. (A *specific* admiral is meant, and his complete name can be supplied.)
>
> Among our customers we number an admiral and a general. (These are not meant to be shortened forms for a specific admiral and a specific general; therefore, they are not capitalized.)
>
> We are going to California by way of the Canal. (Here *Canal* is a shortened form of *Panama Canal.*)

Terms such as *company, college, association, club,* etc., are not usually capitalized when they stand alone, even though they are specifically used in place of the full official name of an organization.

> Our company offers a training program for new employees.

However, if one is a member of the organization and is writing formally or officially about the organization, it is customary to capitalize the shortened form.

> The Company will not submit a bid for this contract. (An official statement; therefore, *Company* is capitalized.)

Capitalize the word *federal* only when it occurs in official names of federal agencies, as in *Federal Communications Commission.* The terms *government* and *federal government* (referring specifically to the United States government) are not usually capitalized except in formal writing.

Test your understanding of the preceding three principles by making the necessary corrections in the following sentences.

1. The Mississippi River extends North and South. *north*   *South*
2. Our chief executive has asked Congress for an additional appropriation. *OK*
3. Mr. Fiddes is now living in the East. *OK*
4. The spoils system was introduced by old hickory. *Old Hickory*
5. You will save time by using the Skyway. *OK*
6. Our vacationers have just returned from the Sunshine City. *OK*

Commercial Products

Some writers have difficulty recognizing the difference between the proper nouns that are part of the official name of a commercial product and the common nouns that name the general class of the product. For instance, which capitalization is correct—*Arch Saver Shoes* or *Arch Saver shoes?* Ordinarily, *Arch Saver shoes* would be correct, because *Arch Saver* is the official name of that brand. Whenever there is doubt, the official name of the product should be checked.

> Most of our calls are for International Electric appliances. (For *appliances* made by *International Electric*.)
>
> Everywhere one turns, there seems to be an advertisement for Lightning Television. (Capitalization shows that the official name of this product is *Lightning Television*.)

Personal and Official Titles

A title written *before* a name is always capitalized; for example:

> Invitations were extended to Dr. Carlin, Admiral Shafer, and Captain McCaffrey.

Except in addresses, a title written *after* a name is capitalized only when it belongs to a person who holds a nationally or universally recognized high position—a congressman, a high government official, a reigning monarch.

> Edward D. White, Chief Justice of the Supreme Court, has resigned because of ill health. (*Chief Justice* is capitalized because the title is that of a high government official.)
>
> The rise of Peter Blake, president of Commercial Enterprises, has been almost phenomenal. (*President* is not capitalized because, while Mr. Blake might be "top brass" to the employees of Commercial Enterprises, his title has no significance to the nation at large.)

When *ex-* and *-elect* are joined to titles, they are not capitalized. *Former* and *late* used with titles are also not capitalized.

> We have not yet heard from Mayor-elect Walsh.
>
> Woodrow Wilson, former President of the United States, was at one time a college professor.

CHECKUP 5

Can you find and correct the capitalization errors in these sentences?

1. Mr. Canty, Superintendent of Schools, attended a national meeting of educators. *superintendent school*
2. The Dunbar Vacuum Cleaner has given us good service. *OK*
3. Not long after World War II, general Eisenhower became President. *General*
4. All advertising material for Bragg electric fans will be supplied without charge. *OK*
5. Elizabeth II is the queen of Great Britain. *Queen*
6. Nabisco Wafers have been on the market for several years. *OK*
7. Harry S. Truman, Ex-President of the United States, is to be one of the speakers. *ex*

COMMUNICATION PROJECTS

Practical Application

A Write the corrections for the capitalization errors in these sentences. Write *OK* for any correct sentence.

1. Have you seen Mcdermott lately?
2. Political preferences of the west were polled just before the election. *West*
3. Mr. Ward has an interest in some Wisconsin dairy farms. *OK*
4. Our new consultant was formerly a Professor of Economics. *professor*
5. The Autumn styles reflect the brilliant colors of the changing leaves. *autumn*
6. The Turnpike is one of America's best superhighways. *OK*
7. Before he joined our staff, Bates worked for the Wright Aeronautical corporation. *Corp.*
8. During the Victorian age the British Empire knew its greatest expansion. *age*
9. You really should read Anderson's play, *The Eve Of St. Mark.*
10. Mr. Dunn has a new Byrd convertible. *OK*
11. We always have an extra day's vacation after Labor day. *Day*
12. The plane was chartered for the vice-president of the United States. *Vice-President*
13. *Very Sincerely yours* is frequently used to close a letter. *sincerely*
14. Will the Senator be at City Hall on Tuesday? *OK*
15. The country around Garden city is rather flat. *City*
16. All alterations are in the charge of a parisian seamstress. *Parisian*
17. The message is this: "your sales approach was commented on favorably." *Your*
18. Did you know that the constitution state is noted for its scenery? *Con State*
19. You should write to Fred Watkins, president of the Chamber of Commerce. *Pres.*
20. Burr is to report to the Colonel immediately upon termination of his leave. *OK*

B Correct all errors in the following sentences.

1. Have you received a reply from President Kyte of the Grocers Association? *OK*
2. The staff members have been working in a wasteful, chaotic, unorganized, manner. *omit ,*
3. Chapter V is headed "Effect of unkind words." *Unkind Words*
4. In the East, Mr. Ames, you will see many places that have historical significance. *OK*
5. The State of Oklahoma supports many educational institutions. *state*
6. A writer must have a knowledge of punctuation rules a thorough knowledge. *rules,*
7. The Late President Coolidge was noted for his frugality with words. *late*
8. Ida is a receptionist; Beth, a stenographer; and Sue, a secretary. *OK*
9. Who discovered the North pole? *Pole*
10. Your assignment was to revise page 1,006, not 1,009.

11. Fire Prevention Week starts on Monday, October 8. *OK*
12. I found valuable, the first and tenth chapters of this secretarial handbook. *omit ,*
13. How well acquainted are you with the Federal Insurance Contributions act? *Act*
14. However angry he might have been, he concealed it well. *OK*
15. You can obtain this information from The Treasury Department. *the*
16. There is as you are well aware, a good reason for this decision. *is,*
17. Some persons want the government to support the new proposal. *government*
18. Although our product is new, it is giving satisfaction, and it is paying off. *satisfaction;*
19. Have you read the latest biography of the Great Emancipator? *OK*
20. Please give me your inventory of stamps, envelopes, form postcards, etc. *,*

Editing Practice

The Editorial Supervisor   The italicized words in the following sentences are words that your writers are overusing. Suggest two synonyms for each of the words.

1. Your *patronage* is important to us. *support   concern*
2. We shall be interested to hear what your *reaction* is. *feeling ; attitude*
3. Yours is indeed an attractive *proposition*. *proposal   offer*
4. Maybe we can make a *deal*. *agreement   arrangement*
5. Personality is definitely an *asset* to a businessman. *benefit   advantage*
6. Martin *runs* his business very efficiently. *operates   manages*

Spelling and Pronunciation   Many words are misspelled because the writer mispronounces them and therefore writes what he hears, rather than the correct spelling. Study this paragraph and indicate any misspellings that might have been caused by mispronunciation.

> Thank you very much for sending us a notice of your special sale on piston rings. For the past six months, however, our stock of piston rings has been accumalating to the extent that we are grieviously concerned about *accumulating* storage space. Although we are not interested in your June 2 sale, we would appreciate your letting us know whenever you have any other good buys.

Case Problem

Making It Clear and Simple   You have been asked to revise and simplify a memorandum that contains the following paragraph. Rewrite the paragraph in everyday, clear language.

> Subsequent to April 10, Mr. Lawrence terminated his contract with this organization after completing a considerable number of years of continuous and exemplary service. Apropos to his decision to sever relations, Mr. Lawrence stated that he had procured an infinitely superior contract that was the quintessence of betterment. We must employ perseverance in endeavoring to replace this lost contract with one of comparable caliber.

---

29   Abbreviations

Why must the business writer have specialized training? Several reasons can be stated, but "to be able to make his messages clear" stands out as being the primary purpose underlying the training of a business writer. In business, time and goodwill are tied in closely with profits. A cloudy message wastes time and causes ill feeling because it can necessitate additional letters to clear up ambiguities. Mastery of the abbreviating techniques discussed in this section helps the correspondent to achieve his message-clarity aim. Generally speaking, abbreviating in the body of any written communication is considered incorrect and in poor taste. The trained business writer, however, knows the situations where abbreviating would be correct. For instance, in the sentence "David works for the FBI," the abbreviation is entirely in order. A business correspondent, then, must study and apply the following principles for the use of correct and modern abbreviations.

ABBREVIATING PERSONAL TITLES AND FIRM NAMES

For reasons of courtesy, a title usually accompanies a person's name, be that title just *Mr., Mrs.,* or *Miss.* Because there are so many different titles in use today, it is important for you to know the rules for abbreviating, or not abbreviating, those personal titles.

Titles After Names

The following titles written *after* names are always abbreviated: *Esq.; Jr.; Sr.;* and academic, professional, and religious titles—*B.A.* (Bachelor of Arts); *M.D.* (Doctor of Medicine); *D.D.* (Doctor of Divinity).

Titles Before Names

The spelling out or abbreviation of titles varies, depending on whether they precede full names or surnames only. However, the following titles are exceptions and are always abbreviated: *Mr., Messrs., Mrs., Dr.,* and *St.* for "Saint." Note that *Miss* is not included in the list. *Miss* is not an abbreviation.

Mr. James Adonizio	Dr. George Howard
Mr. Adonizio	Dr. Howard

Titles Before Surnames Only A title written before just the *last name* of a person is written in full.

Governor Reed	Professor Green	Superintendent Adams

Titles Before Full Names A *full name* is a surname with a first name or an initial. When a title precedes a full name, practice differs. In formal usage, such titles should be spelled out. In business correspondence, technical writing, tabulations, or wherever brevity is desirable, abbreviated forms are commonly used.

Supt. T. Alan Crowe	Prof. S. David Rowe

Titles of Respect and Dignity *Reverend* and *Honorable* are titles of respect and dignity used in addressing clergymen and government officials of any rank. Spell out such titles, except in addresses, lists, and notices. *The* precedes the titles in formal usage. Note that a given name or a title must follow either *Reverend* or *Honorable.*

The Reverend Doctor Wharton	The Honorable Ray T. Wright

Note. You can also refer to the *Forms of Address* section at the back of many dictionaries or to the listing on pages 511-513 of this book.

Firm Names

The name of a firm is not abbreviated unless that company prefers the abbreviation. In case of doubt, the name should be checked.

Correct any abbreviation errors in these sentences.

1. Miss. Alice Linton will report for duty on Monday. *omit period*
2. We have asked Prof. Leary to conduct the experiment. *Professor*
3. The only dissenting vote was that of Sen. Hugh Alcott. *OK*
4. There are now two drs. working in the factory dispensary. *doctors*
5. The Rev. Mr. Wood has been transferred. *Reverend*
6. Send the statement to Frank J. Lyons, Junior. *Jr.*

PUNCTUATING ABBREVIATIONS

This section discusses the use or the omission of periods in abbreviations.

Names of Associations and Government Agencies

Abbreviations for names of associations and for various agencies are in increasing use and are considered correct. A marked modern trend is to write lettered abbreviations "solid"—with no periods and no spacing. Call letters for radio and TV stations have always been written solid. This timesaving practice may be used for almost all lettered abbreviations, provided the writer is sure that the reader will know what the abbreviations mean. For instance:

AAA	American Automobile Association
AFL-CIO	American Federation of Labor and Congress of Industrial Organizations
AT&T	American Telephone and Telegraph
FBI	Federal Bureau of Investigation
NEA	National Education Association
TVA	Tennessee Valley Authority
UAW	United Auto Workers

Chemical Symbols

Chemical symbols and formulas, which today are used frequently in business communications, are not followed by periods.

$$O \text{ (oxygen)} \qquad Fe \text{ (iron)} \qquad H_2O \text{ (water)}$$

IOU and SOS

Contrary to popular belief, *IOU* and *SOS* are not abbreviations. They do not "stand for" anything; therefore, no periods are used with them.

Letters Substituted for Names

Sometimes letters are used to designate persons and things, as in *Mr. A, Exhibit D, Madame X,* and so on. In such cases no periods follow the letters.

Shortened Forms

Because of long and frequent use, some shortened forms have become accepted as complete words. For instance, *ad* is now used for *advertisement; gym* for *gymnasium; phone* for *telephone; lab* for *laboratory;* and *percent* for *percentum.* Such shortened forms are regarded as complete words; therefore, they are not followed by periods.

Check your understanding of the use of periods in abbreviations by correcting the following sentences.

1. WXVB—TV has been added to the C.B.S. network. *CBS*
2. Mr. Ash calls his assistants "Miss A." and "Miss B.," because he can never remember names. *A" B"*
3. Doctor Savage is working with the H. atom. *H atom*
4. The Red Cross will receive 35 percent of the campaign fund. *OK*
5. If his credit is sound, his IOU. is likely to be accepted. *omit period*
6. The school gym. is the best place for the football rally. *omit period*
7. Does the VA provide counseling services for all veterans? *OK*
8. Mr. Gray prefers to fly by T.W.A. *TWA*
9. The AFL-CIO is the parent organization of our factory union. *OK*

TO ABBREVIATE OR NOT TO ABBREVIATE

Every business writer should know when to abbreviate and when not to abbreviate. The following rules are to be used as guidelines.

Always Abbreviate

A.D. *and* B.C. *in Year Dates*   Important historical dates are often accompanied by the abbreviations *A.D.* (for *anno Domini,* "the year of our Lord") or *B.C.* ("before Christ). *A.D.* is written before the year, but *B.C.* is written after the year; for example, *A.D. 500, 500 B.C.*

a.m. *and* p.m. *in Statements of Time*   These abbreviations for *before noon* and *after noon* should be written in small letters with no spacing. Always use figures with these abbreviations; do not use the word *o'clock* with them.

I have an appointment at 10 a.m. (Not *10 o'clock a.m.* or *ten a.m.*)
I have an appointment for Tuesday morning. (Not *Tuesday a.m.*)

Note.   The abbreviation for *noon* is *n.* However, *noon* is usually spelled out, as *12 noon.*

Number *as* No. *Before Numerals*   Before numerals, *number* is abbreviated as *No.,* except when it occurs at the beginning of a sentence. Spell out the word *number* at the beginning of a sentence to avoid misreading.

Your Order No. 623 will be shipped on Friday.
Number 46323 is the policy on which premiums lapsed.

Correct the following sentences.

1. I simply cannot remember my Social Security No. *number*
2. All appointments for Tuesday p.m. have been canceled. *afternoon*
3. No. 789 was the prize-winning ticket. *number*
4. We close at 4:30 o'clock p.m. *omit "o'clock"*
5. Columbus discovered America in 1492 A.D. *A.D. 1492*

Never Abbreviate

Names of Cities, Certain States, Certain Months   Never abbreviate names of cities no matter how long the names may be. Never abbreviate the names of the following states: *Alaska, Hawaii, Idaho, Iowa, Maine, Ohio,* and *Utah.* Never abbreviate these months: *May, June, July.*

Note.   For use with ZIP Codes, the U.S. Post Office Department has introduced two-letter abbreviations for all states, as: *Alaska, AK; Hawaii, HI; Idaho ID.* Note that these abbreviations, which are listed on pages 514-515, consist of two capital letters, with no periods or spaces.

Fort, Mount, Point *and* **Port** *in Names of Places*   Never abbreviate *Fort, Mount, Point,* and *Port* in place names. They are written as follows: *Fort Knox, Mount Desert, Point Pleasant,* and *Port Royal.*

Compass Points   In business communications, a compass point used in a sentence should not be abbreviated; for example, "The new building is at the *northeast* corner of Elm and Cutler Streets" is correct. However, compass directions used in a specialized business, such as real estate, would be written as *N, NE, SSE,* and so on.

Terms of Measure   Except in technical work and on invoices, do not abbreviate names of the common units of weight, length, capacity, area, volume, temperature, and time. In ordinary business writing, they are written as follows: *50 pounds, 7 yards, 4 square miles, 8 dozen, 50 degrees, 16 gallons,* and so on.

CHECKUP 4

Now correct these "never abbreviate" sentences.

1. This shipment contains an extra 5 lbs. of salt.   *pounds*
2. You must mean the NW, not the NE, section of the city he lives in.   *northwest   northeast*
3. Jul. 30 was the date on which you promised payment of the Jn. invoice.   *July   June*
4. We will call at your N. Y. office on Monday.   *New York*
5. The market for our product in the Port Jefferson area is growing steadily.   *OK*
6. Where in Ida. is the new atomic power plant?   *Idaho*

Avoid Abbreviating

Names of Streets   In the message part of communications, do not abbreviate names of streets, roads, avenues, and so on. However, these names may be abbreviated in lists, in inside addresses, and on envelopes.

Geographical Names   It is preferable to spell out names of counties, states and possessions, provinces, and countries.

Days and Months   Names of days of the week and months of the year are preferably spelled out. Because of lack of space, as in a table or a list, abbreviating may be necessary.

CHECKUP 5

Correcting these sentences will check your understanding of the "always," "never," and "avoid" rules for abbreviating.

1. Is the state of Wash. included in Mr. Fry's itinerary? *Washington*
2. What is the No. of your office building? *number*
3. Fred is several years my jr., although he does not look it. *junior*
4. We asked for a price on 25 sq. ft. of floor tiles. *square feet*
5. Our factory will shut down for a week on Friday at 6 p.m. *OK*
6. The beaches in South Co. are well patronized. *County*
7. Enclosed is Policy Number 96754, which covers fire insur- *no.* ance on your office equipment.
8. I know that Mr. Dodd lives on Euclid Blvd., but I am not sure *Boulevard* of the number.

COMMUNICATION PROJECTS

Practical Application

A In the following sentences, correct any incorrectly written abbreviations. Write *OK* for any correct sentence.

1. You named Phila. as the capital of Pennsylvania and Saint Paul as the capital of Minnesota. *Philadelphia* *St.*
2. Do you think that 50 gals. of the new brand of lubricating oil would be sufficient for our needs? *gallons*
3. Station W.N.L.C. has many local sponsors. *WNLC*
4. Was the Battle of Hastings in A.D. 1066? *OK*
5. Our trucks are not allowed on the Rose Blvd. route or on any main thoroughfare through the town. *Boulevard*
6. There is a painting of Saint Edmund on display at the exhibition that opened today at the Civic Center. *St.*
7. No. 46899 is missing from our files. *number*
8. Persons living in the TVA area pay relatively little for electricity. *OK*
9. Mark is the rewrite man for the lab scientists. *OK*
10. We always call on Mister Barber when we need legal advice. *Mr.*
11. Make your appointment for the p.m., if at all possible. *afternoon*
12. Mr. Hunt is secretary & treasurer of Blair Company. *and*
13. We expect to ship your order Tuesday a.m. *morning*
14. Our most thorough researcher is Dr. Pierre. *OK*
15. We have yet to hear from the Reverend Doctor J. B. Greeley. *The*
16. Mixing Na. and Cl. will produce salt. *Na + Cl*
17. Exhibit H is powerful evidence for the prosecution. *OK*
18. Is Pt. Arthur on the coast of Texas? *Port*
19. Were the V.I. ceded to us, or did we buy them?
20. An office on Main Street has been opened by Eugene Ferry, Doctor of Dental Surgery. *D.D.S.*

B Correct all errors in the following sentences.

1. We are interested in the prospects for heavy industry in the Prov. of Quebec. *province*
2. While the Spring sale is still on, they would like to buy some furniture for their new home in the country. *spring*

3. You understand, of course, that the price quoted is f.o.b. Milwaukee. *OK*
4. Our new junior executive is James P. Hale, CPA. *OK*
5. Arnold's employees are screened (carefully selected.) *selected).*
6. We must have our ads ready by May 4. *OK*
7. Yes, Mr. Barr plans to visit Kansas city while on his inspection tour. *City*
8. There are a no. of reasons for refusing to cut prices at this time of year. *number*
9. Where else can you get such a "steal?" *"steal"?*
10. From this date on, all C.O.D.'s will be refused. *OK*
11. The words "embarrass" and "accommodate" are often misspelled. *OK*
12. Everybody knows whose home was at Mt. Vernon. *Mount*
13. Did you know that the president of this company is the possessor of the Navy cross? *Cross*
14. This statue dates back to 200 B.C. *OK*
15. Although the book is called *All about Insurance*, it gives little practical information. *About*
16. Since World War II, West Ger. has made a remarkable recovery. *Germany*
17. The weather in the south is sometimes cold. *South*
18. A mysterious Madame X called this morning. *OK*
19. The inscription read "Obedience to Law Is Liberty". *Liberty."*
20. We should like to know the name of the largest mfg. concern in your city. *manufacturing*

Editing Practice

Plurals and Possessives   Rewrite any sentences that contain errors. Write *OK* for any correct sentence.

1. Do you think that Janet keeping cosmetics in her desk is good business practice? *Janet's*
2. The paper cutter is not in it's usual place. *its*
3. Orders for banjoes increase just before Christmas. *banjos*
4. Mr. Ames said that your progressing very rapidly. *you're*
5. The German's economic recovery is a tribute to that nation. *Germans'*
6. They realize that their is still more planning to be done. *there*
7. There is no precedent for are system of billing. *our*
8. The Davises' financial standing is very sound. *OK*
9. Because highly specialized knowledge is needed, editors in chief's positions are not easily filled. *chiefs'*
10. Whose going to manage the new branch office? *Who's*

The Evaluator   Would you OK this paragraph? If not, why not?

You may expect a visit from our electrical expert on Monday morning, June 4. As you know, we guarantee our washing machines for three months after purchase; and we are only too glad to give you prompt service. That is why you really should of reported immediately that the rinsing cycle on your washer is not working satisfactorily. If your experience parallels that of other Launderquik users, your machine will need no further adjustment; but please remember that we are standing by and will be happy to help in any way we can. *have*

Case Problem

A Ticklish Situation   Mr. Nobel is one of the best customers of the Paterson Electrical Supply Company. On March 15, he sent payment for an invoice dated March 1, with terms of 2/10, n/30. Mr. Noble deducted the cash discount to which he was not entitled. When the credit manager at the Paterson Electrical Supply Company called the matter to his attention, Mr. Noble indicated that he always makes payment within the discount period but that someone in his office slipped up and forgot to mail this month's payment on time.

1. What should the credit manager for the Paterson Electrical Supply Company do about this situation?
2. Suppose Mr. Noble made a habit of deducting the cash discount whenever he paid after the expiration of the discount period. What might you, as credit manager, write Mr. Noble in your letter refusing to accept the deduction?

Numbers

A business communication that did not contain a number, be it only "May 14," would be most unusual. Numbers are used for indicating sums of money, for ordering goods, for selling goods, for adjusting claims, for making appointments, and for a host of other business operations. Because the potential for error in any given situation increases in direct proportion to the multiplicity of usage, the errors in writing numbers could be many. The business correspondent, therefore, needs to know the rules that govern the writing of numbers and how to apply those rules.

NUMBERS WRITTEN AS WORDS

Numbers That Begin Sentences

Always write in words any number that begins a sentence. If it is awkward to spell out the number, the sentence may be rephrased. For example:

> Seventy-five percent of the students passed the examination.
> One dollar opens your savings account at our bank.
> With only $1, you can open a savings account at our bank. (The sentence has been rephrased to make the amount stand out.)

Numbers One Through Ten

Numbers one through ten should be written in words when those numbers are used in isolated instances—either singly or with one other number.

> Mr. Penn has been our accountant for ten years.
> Mr. Penn has been our accountant for eight or ten years.

The "one through ten" rule also applies to names of numbered streets. They, too, are written as words.

> Many bargains are available at the Third Avenue stores.
> The Tenth Street station is being enlarged.

Fractions Standing Alone; Mixed Numbers

When a fraction stands alone (is not used with a whole number), that fraction is written in words: *one-half, three-fourths*. When a mixed number (a whole number and a fraction) is spelled out, the word *and* should separate the whole number from the fraction: *two and one-half, three and one-third*. A mixed number is only spelled out at the beginning of a sentence; otherwise, it is expressed in figures.

Time of Day

You learned in Section 29 to use figures with the abbreviations *a.m.* and *p.m.* With the term *o'clock*, use words for the time. When expressing time on the hour without *a.m.*, *p.m.*, or *o'clock*, spell out the hour.

> We arrived at three o'clock.
> They always have dinner at eight. (Not *at* 8.)

Round Numbers

Round numbers can be either spelled out or expressed as figures. Where the writing is of a formal or literary nature, spell out round numbers that require no more than two words (a hyphenated compound number such as *twenty-six million* counts as two words). In business correspondence, however, round numbers are often expressed as figures.

> We have received two hundred requests for samples. (In business correspondence, the figure *200* could be used.)
>
> More than 750 students attended the rally. (Figures are used here because more than two words would be required to spell out the number.)

When spelling out even numbers over one thousand, express the numbers in the fewest possible words.

> fifteen hundred (Not *one thousand five hundred.*)
>
> twenty-five hundred (Not *two thousand five hundred.*)

Ages

When expressed in years only, ages of persons are most often written as words. However, when the age of a person is given as a significant statistic—for example, in news releases or in matters pertaining to employment—figures are used.

> Surely Jane is more than twenty-five years old!
>
> Dr. Boggs, who is 56 years old, is a leading authority on conservation. (Item in a news release.)

Centuries and Decades

In formal writing, numbers referring to centuries and decades are written as words. However, there are instances where the use of figures is acceptable. For example:

> This antique dates back to the seventeenth century. (Do not use *17th century.*)
>
> This antique dates back to the sixteen hundreds. (Here *1600s* or *1600's* would also be acceptable.)
>
> The unemployment rate in the United States was high in the nineteen-thirties. (Here *1930s* or *1930's* would also be acceptable; however, do not use *'30s.*)

CHECKUP 1

Find and correct any errors in the following sentences.

1. The survey shows that 35 is the average age of our employees. OK
2. Mr. Clark will be glad to see you on Thursday at 9. nine
3. He is an authority on the England of the eighteenth century. OK
4. Would you like us to send you an additional 10 copies of the folder? ten
5. Please run off two thousand two hundred copies of the form. twenty-two hundred
6. Brian said that he is able to save 1/5 of his income. one-fifth
7. 12 items in the shipment were damaged. Twelve

NUMBERS WRITTEN AS FIGURES

Numbers are usually written as figures in the instances mentioned below.

Numbers Higher than Ten

In business correspondence, numbers 11 to 99 and numbers over one hundred are usually written in figures. However, numbers 11 to 99 may be written as words when the writing is of a formal nature.

> We have had 11 transfers during the past year. (This is correct.)
> We have had eleven transfers during the past year. (The writer wishes to use a more formal style.)

When writing a series of numbers, use *all* figures or *all* words so that the form will be consistent.

> The shipment consists of 18 chairs, 6 desks, and 12 tables. (Note *6 desks*, not *six*.)
> Please order five pens, eleven erasers, and eight tablets. (Note *eleven erasers*, not *11*.)

Sums of Money

In business communications, sums of money are written in figures. Only in specialized writing, as in legal documents, is money written both in words and in figures. Remember that the period and the two zeros are not used with even amounts of dollars: *$25*, not *$25.* or *$25.00*. In tabulations, of course, the period and zeros are used to even the columns.

When writing sums of money in a series, the dollar sign must be used with each member of the series.

> Our new handbags are priced at $5, $7, and $10.

Age in Years, Months, Days

Age expressed in years, months, and days or in years and months is written in figures.

> On June 1, Fred's age will be 25 years 7 months and 5 days. (Because the age is considered as a single unit, no commas are used in the series.)

Time Connected with Discount or Interest Rates

For clarity and emphasis, periods of time mentioned with terms of discount or interest rates are written in figures.

> If you pay within 10 days, you will receive the usual discount. (The figure *10* makes the discount term stand out.)

House, Street, ZIP Code Numbers

In business correspondence, house numbers are written in figures, with the exception of the number *one*. The abbreviation *No.* or the sign # should not be used with house numbers or with RFD numbers.

> The package was addressed to One Park Place, not 14 Park Place.
> Please change my address to RFD 2.

Spell out numbered street names from one through ten. Use figures for numbered street names over ten. When figures are used, the ordinal ending *st, th,* or *d* may be omitted so long as a word such as *East* or *West* separates the street number from the house number. If no such word intervenes, use the ordinal ending for clarity.

505 Fifth Avenue	340 East 72 Street
155 Eighth Street	1205 34th Street

The postal ZIP Code number follows the name of the state, and no punctuation precedes or follows this code. In running text, such as the body of a letter, a single space separates the state and the ZIP Code: *Chicago, Illinois 60604.* In other uses—envelope or inside address, for instance—three spaces separate the state and the code. For example:

Fowler Products
231 Stanton Street
Chicago, Illinois   60604

Decimals

Decimals are always expressed in figures, without commas: *4.5; 1.3456.* In technical writing, where exactness is imperative, a cipher is written before the decimal point when there is no whole number: *0.2546.*

CHECKUP 2

Check your understanding of the rules for writing numbers in figures by correcting these sentences.

1. Our price of $26.00 a gross is our lowest possible quotation. *$26*
2. We seldom receive fewer than one hundred twenty mail orders each week. *120*
3. Try as I will, I can get no answer but 0.4368. *OK*
4. Is ninety days the maximum length of term for a trade acceptance? *90*
5. We ordered 90 tulip bulbs, ten rose bushes, and 20 dahlias. *ninety twenty*
6. Depending on quality and workmanship, we can offer you bedspreads at 8, 10, 15, and $20. *$8, $10, $15, and $20.*
7. The house at 1 Main Street is for sale. *one*

Numbers Used With Words

Percentages   Percentages that appear in isolated instances in sentences are written in figures followed by *percent: the 6 percent method.* In technical writing, fractional percentages are expressed as decimals: *at 4.5%.* In business correspondence, they are written as fractions or as decimals: *at 4½ percent* or *at 4.5 percent.*

When percentages occur in pairs, they are written in figures with *percent* following the second figure: *from 2 to 10 percent.*

Note.   The percent symbol (%) is used only in technical and statistical matter and in tables, invoices, and interoffice memorandums. When the percent symbol is used in a series, repeat the symbol with each figure of the series.

Money Expressed in Cents   Isolated amounts of cents that appear in a sentence are written in figures followed by the word *cents: only 50 cents.* In a series, to be consistent, the dollar sign and the decimal point are used for cents: "I spent $4 for stamps, $2 for envelopes, and $.60 for cards." The symbol ¢ for cents is used only in price quotations and in technical communications: *250 blocks at 75¢ and 4 bags of cement at 98¢.*

Million, Billion   Present practice in writing extremely large numbers is to spell out *million, billion,* and so on. Such sums can be written as follows: *more than 2 billion dollars* or *more than $2 billion.* Note that the number of millions or billions is expressed in figures.

Consecutive Numbers

When two numbers form one item, those numbers must be written together. In such cases, one number is written as a word; the other, as a figure. As a rule, spell out the first number unless the second number would make a significantly shorter word.

> Our order called for ten 30-inch strips. (Note that this is shorter than *10 thirty-inch strips.*)
>
> Get me 75 six-cent stamps. (Contrast this with *seventy-five 6-cent stamps.*)

CHECKUP 3

Make any necessary corrections in these sentences.

1. Congress has appropriated $3 billion for research. OK
2. Flight time was 4 hours 30 minutes and 10 seconds. OK
3. Our discounts range from 5 to 8 percent. OK
4. The price of milk is now 32 cents in this city and its suburbs. OK
5. To fill a special order, we need 210 five-pound boxes. OK
6. The quotation was taken from page 1010. OK

WRITING DATES

The *ordinal endings* mentioned in this section are the *st, d,* and *th* that follow figures: *1st, 2d, 3d, 15th,* and so on. Note particularly *2d* and *3d.* Writing these endings as *nd* and *rd* is out of style. Correct writing of dates is a question of using or not using ordinal endings; and the following rules represent the latest and best business practice.

Day Following Month

When the day follows the month, that day is written in figures, *without ordinal endings: April 15, January 2, July 17,* and so on.

Day Preceding Month

When the day precedes the month, the day may be written either in figures or in words. When figures are used, they must be used *with ordinal endings: the 15th of April, 2d of January,* and so on.

COMMUNICATION PROJECTS

Practical Application

 Correct any figure errors you can find in the following sentences. Write *OK* for any correct sentence.

1. Blake Company now has about 300 charge-account customers.
2. Does the 3d Avenue bus go to the city limits?
3. We will meet you for lunch at one o'clock.
4. If life begins at 40, Mr. Page is a relatively young man.
5. The Norman Conquest took place early in the eleventh century.
6. Fully 1/2 the strikers were ignorant of the issues involved.
7. After sending you 5 reminders, we must conclude that you do not intend to pay your bill.
8. There are no 11 o'clock appointments open for next week.
9. Yours was the sixty-eighth entry received by the contest committee.
10. Would you like me to arrange a meeting at 2 on Friday?
11. There were 315 salesmen present at the meeting.
12. Remember to order 100 seven-cent stamps.
13. All schedule changes must be made before the 5 of June.
14. Mortgage rates have increased to 5½ percent.
15. We asked for ten quires of stencils, 15 reams of paper, and three styli.
16. The cost of the submarine exceeded $5,000,000.
17. These manila envelopes sell for 7 cents each.
18. We have a wonderful selection of dresses at 25, 35, and $50.
19. 111 clerks are employed in our shipping department.
20. Profit on the sale of groceries is said to range from 13% to 15%.

Correct all errors in the following sentences.

1. About one thousand five hundred persons visited the atomic submarines during Navy Day.
2. Persons who were young during the 20's know the meaning of the term "Jazz Age."
3. Did you know that President Elston is an honorary member of the company's Thirty-Year Club?
4. Send the gift to #46 Avery Street.
5. The editorial began, "What about the National Debt"?
6. The Company gave a party to celebrate Mr. Kain's sixty-eighth birthday.
7. The typist at the first desk (the one who shared her lunch with us,) is our most skilled operator.
8. There will be a slight delay on your order for twenty-five 4-foot poles.
9. We are prepared to allow a 3% discount for payment within 10 days.
10. Roger was 16 years 3 months and 6 days old on the opening day of school.
11. The atomic weight of platinum is one hundred ninety-five and nine-hundredths.
12. Your letter of August 3rd was most welcome.
13. The cost of living is expected to rise 3% to 5% in the next year.
14. We must revise page 555.
15. Issue vouchers for all sums of money, even for as little as five cents.
16. We shall be glad to discount your note in thirty days.
17. His doctor recommends that Mr. Ross walk 5 miles each day.
18. We must make provision for an audience of 375 persons, exclusive of our staff members.
19. The Governor has set the 12th. of May as the opening day for the centennial celebration.
20. Do you think that the cashier is good for a "touch"?

Editing Practice

The Rewrite Editor   Edit and rewrite the following paragraph.

As promised in our letter of May 10th we are sending you a list of panelists for our W.B.S.B.—T.V. program. From the nominations received from you and from other authorities we have selected the following: Sen. Coulter, Gen. Alton B. Burrows, Professor Ely, and Mr. John C. Stock, who is the proprietor of a chain of laundrys. We hope you can attend the organizational meeting to be held next Friday at eight p.m.

Spelling Notebook   As a means of self-improvement, your secretary keeps a notebook in which she writes correctly any words she misspells. What entries would you suggest as a result of proofreading this paragraph taken from one of her transcripts?

We were very much impressed with your written application for the position of junior bookkeeper with our firm; and, as we do have an opening, I should like to talk with you and learn more about you. How about droping in to see me on Monday morning, May 1, at 10:45? My office is on the second floor, directly in front of the elevator.

Case Problem

The Difficult Caller   Marie Gallagher, secretary to Gorden Howell of the Lakeland Insurance Company, receives a telephone call for Mr. Howell from William Best, a customer who is a representative of a business machine firm. Mr. Howell often purchases equipment from Mr. Best. Marie tells Mr. Best that Mr. Howell is out of the office for the day. Mr. Best insists on telling Marie his troubles. He is irate because the Lakeland Insurance Company purchased three new adding machines from a competing firm. He wonders why, since he is both a policyholder and a supplier of the company, he was not given the opportunity to make the sale. He even threatens to cancel his insurance.

1. What should Marie say to Mr. Best?
2. What should Mr. Howell do about the situation when he returns?

Writing
Craft

31   Structuring the Thought Unit

A child learns to read by recognizing and saying individual words. For instance, he looks at a picture and says the words underneath: "I . . . see . . . Jack." As he learns to identify more and more words, he begins to see words in combination, not in isolation. His reading speed and comprehension increase in proportion to the number of word combinations that have meaning for him.

An adult, however, reads in thought units and makes his own pictures. His eye spans several words at once; his mind registers the meaning of the words within the eye span. He reads this sentence: "Because of the unseasonably warm weather, our stock of men's overcoats is moving very slowly." When he has read the word *weather,* the reason for the message is assimilated. After *overcoats,* he records added meaning; and after *slowly,* the message is clear and complete. Of course, the adult reading process is so rapid that the meaning of the entire sentence seems to be encompassed in one glance, the picture formed in a flash. However, the picture understood by the reader can be clear only when the writer has correctly structured the thought units within the sentence.

In order to structure thought units correctly, you must write as a unit the words that belong with that unit. For example, in the sentence "Our machines are sold by courteous and obliging salesmen—attractive in appearance and needing oil only once a month," the picture formed by the words is ridiculous. Analysis shows that the thought unit *attractive in appearance and needing oil only once a month* goes with *machines,* not with *salesmen.* A writer who is a good craftsman would have written, "Our machines, attractive in appearance and needing oil only once a month, are sold by courteous and obliging salesmen."

Writing is an art. The purpose of the three sections in Chapter 5 is to provide training that can lead to good writing craftsmanship. The rewards for mastering the craft are great, and employment opportunities for those trained to write well are plentiful.

Writing can even become a specialized career. The first step on the road to proficiency in writing is to develop the ability to structure sentences according to proper thought units.

WORDS IN THOUGHT UNITS

Sometimes a confusing, a laughable, or even an incorrect picture is formed because a single word is not connected with its proper thought unit. For example, read the following newspaper advertisement.

LONG LADIES' GLOVES ON SALE SATURDAY

Short ladies would not be able to take advantage of this sale, would they? The thought unit *long ladies* is incorrect. The proper thought unit is *long gloves,* and the copywriter should have written the advertisement as shown below:

> Ladies' long gloves on sale Saturday.

Failure to place an adverb correctly in a sentence is a frequent error. Note the placement of *only* in the following sentence.

> Ray only has one more payment to make on his car.

The thought unit *only has* is incorrect; the correct thought unit is *only one more payment.* The sentence should read as follows:

> Ray has only one more payment to make on his car.

PHRASES IN THOUGHT UNITS

Incorrectly placed phrases, as well as incorrectly placed words, can change the meaning of a message completely. This fact is known to expert writers, who edit their work carefully to see that phrases are correctly placed. For instance, an expert would not write this sentence:

> Most guests came to call on President and Mrs. Taft in taxis.

Placing *in taxis* with *President and Mrs. Taft* indicates that the President and his wife were in taxis. Actually, the writer meant that most guests used taxis as their means of transportation, and he should have written the sentence like this:

> Most guests came in taxis to call on President and Mrs. Taft.

Now read the following classified advertisement and see what happens because of the incorrectly written thought units.

> For Rent: Large furnished room only for gentleman with attached bath.

Surely, a *gentleman with attached bath* would be unique! A *furnished room with attached bath,* however, would present a familiar picture. The revised advertisement should read:

> For Rent: For gentleman only, large furnished room with attached bath.

CLAUSES IN THOUGHT UNITS

Rather surprisingly, some writers who have little difficulty in applying the thought-unit rule to the placement of words and phrases do not transfer that knowledge to the placement of clauses. A master writer must be trained to avoid writing a sentence like this:

> We will release the financial report when the time comes to the newspapers.

When the time comes to the newspapers is confusing. Application of the thought-unit rule to the placement of clauses results in the correction shown below:

> When the time comes, we will release the financial report to the newspapers.

The main danger of a misplaced clause is that it may mean something entirely different from what is intended, as in this sentence:

> Mr. Burr placed the vase on the desk that was given to him by his wife.

Desk that was given to him by his wife means just that—the *desk* was given to him by his wife. However, suppose it is the *vase*—not the desk—that was given to Mr. Burr. In that case, the sentence should have been written as follows:

> Mr. Burr placed on the desk the vase that was given to him by his wife.

AMBIGUOUS *WHICH* CLAUSES

Which clauses merit separate and special treatment because their specific function is understood only by expert writers. Part of the expertness of these writers is due to the fact that they have been trained to place a *which* clause with the word it modifies, explains, or amplifies.

A less adept writer sometimes places a *which* clause with a wrong word, but more often he uses such a clause to modify an entire idea. Too, some correspondents think that the solution to many of their writing problems lies in using a comma followed by a *which* clause; this solution, however, is often an incorrect one. The following paragraphs illustrate and explain correct *which* clause usage.

> We have a pamphlet dealing with government bonds, which we will send you on request.

Placing the *which* clause with *government bonds* means that the *bonds* will be sent on request. The exact meaning is that the *pamphlet* will be sent, and the sentence should read:

> On request, we shall be glad to send you our pamphlet dealing with government bonds.

Note that the revision gains added writing polish because a *which* clause is not used.

Another misuse of *which* clauses is shown below:

> Further delay in payment will impair your credit, which neither of us wants.

In this sentence the *which* clause modifies a complete idea, *further delay in payment will impair your credit*. In terms of thought-unit reading, however, the ambiguous, if not insulting, meaning is *your credit, which neither of us wants. Which* clauses must not be used to refer to a complete idea;

therefore, the sentence should read, "Further delay in payment will impair your credit, and both of us are interested in maintaining your good standing."

The assumption that *which* clauses should be avoided altogether would be false. When correctly used, they are an aid to polished and effective writing. A *which* clause may be essential to message clarity, as in the sentence shown below:

> Read page 5, which contains the complete information about your department.

CHECKUP 1

Keeping thought units in mind, revise the following sentences to make the meaning clear.

1. Barton's tea is accurately measured and packed by machines in small gauze bags.
2. We will all ride to the airport when the time comes in a limousine hired by the company.
3. Sale on Summer Girls' Slacks!
4. Persons often borrow money from banks which they do not need.
5. Inflation and economic unrest are conditions that will continue in all probability.

WHO DID WHAT?

In business communications, absolute clarity as to who has done or who is to do a specific thing helps prevent costly errors. Sometimes, however, a reader does not get the meaning intended because the writer confuses the thought by having the wrong person or thing connected with an action. In such cases, the thought-unit principle is violated, and confusion is caused by doubt or uncertainty as to *who* did *what*. For example:

> If not satisfied, we will return your money.

Consider the thought unit *If not satisfied, we*. The meaning here is that *we* are the ones who might not be satisfied. If a customer returned the goods and asked for his money back, the manufacturer could refuse on the grounds that he, the manufacturer, was very well satisfied with the customer's money. This revision makes the correct meaning of the sentence immediately apparent to the reader:

> If you are not satisfied, we will return your money.

Occasionally, the who-did-what violation reaches the height of the ridiculous, as in sentences where an object, not a person, seems to be performing an action. For example:

> Entering the room, the typewriter was seen teetering on the edge of the table.

The thought unit *entering the room, the typewriter* pictures the typewriter as entering the room. This kind of phrasing shows a serious lack of communication know-how. A person should be performing the action of entering the room, as in this revision:

> Entering the room, Mr. Blair saw the typewriter teetering on the edge of the table.

Here is another illustration of this type of error.

> After climbing to the top of the tower, the whole city lay spread before us.

What does the thought unit *after climbing to the top of the tower, the whole city* mean? How could a city climb to the top of the tower? Revised, the sentence would read:

> After climbing to the top of the tower, we saw the whole city spread before us.

A who-did-what violation, sometimes called a *dangler*, does not necessarily occur at the beginning of a sentence. For example, note the error in the following sentence:

> Mr. Paine saw the expected caller glancing up from his desk.

As written, the thought unit is *caller glancing up from his desk*. Was the caller at his own desk, and did he glance up from that desk? Was the caller glancing up from Mr. Paine's desk; and if so, what physical contortions were necessary to perform the act? Most likely, it was Mr. Paine who glanced up from his own desk. In order to eliminate the confusion, the sentence should be written like this:

> Glancing up from his desk, Mr. Paine saw the expected caller.

INDEFINITE, CONFUSING PRONOUN REFERENCE

As everyone knows, pronouns are words used in place of nouns. Unless the nouns for which they substitute are clearly indicated, however, messages will not present clear and correct thought units. Part of the know-how of the craftsman is his ability to make all pronoun references definite and unmistakably clear.

Confusing He or She

When you use the pronouns *he* or *she,* you must be certain that the reader knows who *he* or *she* is. The antecedent of the *he* or *she* must be clear. Consider the confusion that could arise from a statement like the example given below:

> Mr. Culver made the sale to Mr. York just before he left.

Who left, Mr. Culver or Mr. York? The *he* in this sentence is indefinite and, consequently, confusing. If it is Mr. Culver who left, the sentence should read, "Just before Mr. Culver left, he made the sale to Mr. York." If it is Mr. York who left, the effective writer would revise the wording of the sentence like this:

> Just before Mr. York left, Mr. Culver made the sale to him.

Indefinite It

The use of the pronoun *it* to refer to something that is not immediately clear is a common offense against the rules of polished writing. For example, read the following sentence:

> I will place the pigskin in punt position; and when I nod my head, kick it.

Kick what? This indefinite *it* could result in a painful injury, wouldn't you say? The indefinite *it* must be replaced by the noun to which it should refer; and the revised sentence reads:

> I will place the pigskin in punt position; and when I nod my head, kick the ball.

Inept writers tend to use the pronoun *it* as a catchall word. Too often there is no antecedent to which the *it* can refer. Consider the use of *it* in this sentence:

> It is the positive sales approach that is the effective element in these letters.

The use of *it* in this example not only is vague but also makes the sentence wordy. Consider how much more effective the sentence would be if it were written like this:

> The positive sales approach is the effective element in these letters.

Other Indefinite Pronoun References

In oral communication "they say" is commonly used by speakers who are uncertain of the source of their statement. Such vagueness in written communication is amateurish, because references must be definite and exact. For example, read the following sentence:

> They say that sales will decrease during the next six months.

Who is meant by *they* in this sentence? Lack of definiteness is an earmark of a poorly trained writer. A precise writer would present the information this way:

> *Market News* reports that sales will decrease during the next six months.

Another type of indefinite reference that is puzzling and annoying to a reader is illustrated in this sentence.

> Although I dictated all morning on Tuesday, my secretary typed only two of them.

The slipshod *two of them* is vagueness carried to an extreme. Two of what? stories? letters? reports? news releases? A clear and explicit thought could be communicated by writing:

> Although I dictated all morning on Tuesday, my secretary typed only two of the letters.

CHECKUP 2

Test your understanding of the who-did-what and the pronoun-reference rules by revising the following sentences.

1. Will the owner of the car with License AX3083 please remove it. *his car*
2. There is always a mob jammed around the booth selling tickets. *ticket-selling booth*
3. They wear plain, dark suits in our office. *The men by Asche caught Joe Burns*
4. Joe Burns was caught by Professor Asche while he was using a crib sheet during an examination.
5. Even after consulting five reference books, the problem remains unsolved. *I could not solve the problem.*

COMMUNICATION PROJECTS

Practical Application

Ⓐ All these sentences contain violations of thought-unit rules. Revise them.

1. When worn out, you can have the part replaced without charge. *the part is it*
2. We bought a case of paper cups, which proved to be a wise move.
3. Nancy Wills, 20, was charged with failure to carry a license on Route 6. *was picked up on Route 6 & charged*
4. To make a hole in the dough, use a thimble rather than your thumb. Of course, you should boil it first. *the dough*
5. Drag racing is a favorite pastime in this city, but not very many of them result in serious accidents. *races (was pleased that his)*
6. Fred Hewitt's suggestion was accepted by the Board, which pleased him very much.
7. On the radio, it gives baseball scores every day. *the broadcast*
8. It almost seems impossible to sell this stock. *your skills*
9. If you are a good bowler, teach it to the new members of the League.
10. When our boss talked with the caller, he told him that he would be invited to speak at the meeting. *our boss caller to expect an invitation*
11. Ten percent discount on flannel boys' trousers!
12. To develop typing speed, time must be spent in intelligent practice. ✓
13. The electrician installed a light over Mr. Lord's head that was recessed.
14. To reserve rooms at a hotel, a telegram should be sent at least three days in advance.
15. The group watched the elephants file by on our narrow balcony.
16. While climbing the stairs, the clock struck two. *while (I) was climbing*
17. With errors clearly marked, Mr. Whipple returned the letter to his secretary.
18. The president spoke to the old man praising his work.
19. To make the sale, the car should be polished brightly.
20. When explained calmly, Mr. Salazar was concerned about Jim's problem. *after it was explained calmly*

B

Revise any sentences that do not conform to thought-unit rules. Write *OK* for any correct sentences.

1. Mr. Forbes selected a young man for the promotion who was trained in machine operation.
2. I could see the old office building where I used to work in the distance.
3. Ann was startled by a mouse uncovering her machine.
4. Our list of customers now numbers almost 50,210.
5. David is always pleasant, which makes him very popular.
6. While walking through the foyer, many customers were seen.
7. Did you see Barr's advertisement of pure men's silk hosiery?
8. Being in perfect running condition, the trainer was sure that his horse would win.
9. They have many fringe benefits in that company.
10. In stepping from the elevator, Mr. King's ankle was turned.
11. We only have the repairman call once a month.
12. Only the Board of Directors can nominate the three new officers.
13. In your reference manual, it says to use open punctuation.
14. Our sales manager is satisfied with only first-class service.
15. Don's boss will give him the assignment when he returns from Chicago.
16. I only have been to Vermont once before.
17. The men sailed out to meet the great liner in the small boat.
18. When October comes, we often take long walks in the woods.
19. Maurice will go if an emergency arises for the medicine.
20. After traveling all day, our destination was still miles away.

Editing Practice

Editing for Context   Edit these sentences and rewrite any sentences containing words that do not fit the context.

1. This sale was dated in accordion with the instructions in your letter.
2. As far as we know, the firm you inquire about is solvent.
3. Are you buying this stock for speculative purposes?
4. The York Hotel offers a prodigy of social events.
5. The securities you mention are not listed on the Board.
6. Our golf course is considered idly constructed for beginning players.
7. You should receive your rights on May 1, one right for every share of stock.
8. Please have a redcap meet Mr. Ward at the airport.
9. There is a thrill to a game played on a coarse overlooking the ocean.
10. Our grill provides food for the hunky golfer.

Proofreading a Memo   Even though memos are sent to fellow employees rather than to customers, the messages should be correctly written. What, if any, corrections would you make in this memo?

> Installation of esculators in our store will be completed on May 15. In preparation for this Blanton innovation, I am asking Merchandise Managers for the different floors to give some thought to rearranging departments and displays. For instance, I think we can increase sales by featuring our "leaders" in the arrear at the top of the moving stairs. As they are riding from floor to floor, customers have time to look; and an eye-catching display could motivate them to stop off—and buy! Please feel free to call on me if you think I can be of help.

Case Problem

The Annoyed Customer   Judy Lawrence is temporarily employed in the curtain and drapery section at Robeson's Department Store. An angry customer comes into the department with a pair of curtains that she purchased from another salesclerk, who said that the curtains would not fade or shrink when they were washed. Apparently, this information was not correct. The customer proceeds to vent her anger on Judy.

1. What should Judy say to the customer?
2. What can the store do to retain the customer's business?

---

32 Advanced Writing Techniques

What constitutes a flawless performance in any activity—music, art, dancing, athletics, science, writing? The performance often looks easy enough, so easy that the observer or the reader feels that he himself, with a little practice, could do just as well. Part of the secret of stardom in any career or sphere is the perfection of techniques to such a degree that a production is so beautiful, so smooth, and so polished that it appears to be effortless. Every written communication is a production put on by the writer. A career writer, therefore, is more than a scribbler of messages; actually, he is a music maker. His sentences, paragraphs, and entire communications can be made to sing just as truly as a violin and a bow can be made to sing. A poor writer is poor because he continually sounds "sour" notes and makes glaring errors like this: "The arguments presented in this case *is* most convincing."

An average writer is average because he occasionally "flats" a note by writing this kind of sentence: "To become *familiar* with our system, you must *familiarize* yourself with departmental functions." He does not know, or does not use, those added refinements that are the mark of a polished performance.

The highest accolade goes to the writer who is an artist, the communicator whose words make flawless music. To become a star on the writing stage, a performer must perfect his command of advanced writing techniques.

WORD USAGE

To perform acceptably as a writer, a person must have facility in the use of synonyms, antonyms, and homonyms. He must avoid trite expressions, repetitious wording, and negative words. He must communicate in a precise manner. These techniques of good written communication were discussed in Chapter 1.

To perform professionally, however, a writer must have at his fingertips the advanced techniques that make the difference between a good production and a polished one. What are some of these advanced techniques?

Positive Words

Positive words are pleasant to hear and to read. They are words that create a receptive, pleasant glow in the mind of a reader. Consequently, the master writer knowingly uses words that produce this desirable psychological effect. The words in the following list evoke a positive response.

advancement	courage	genuine	satisfaction
agreeable	eager	gratify	success
attractive	earnest	happy	trustworthy
cheerful	easy	integrity	valued
comfortable	encourage	liberal	victory
compensation	enjoy	pleasure	warmth
confident	fortunate	profit	welcome
cordial	generosity	progress	willingness

Planned Repetition of Words

Although careless repetition of words is considered a mark of the poor writer, *planned* word repetition is a technique of the master writer. Planned repetition is sometimes used to emphasize by painting a vivid picture; for example, the repeated *same* in the following sentence shows Stuart to be in an abysmal rut.

> Stuart does the same things every day, at the same time, in the same way, and with the same lack of enthusiasm.

Repetition is one of the cardinal principles of advertising; therefore, an ad writer must be adept in planned repetition of words. The following ad is repetitious, but the repetition is clever and purposeful.

> HEALTHTONE will add years to your life, and HEALTHTONE will add life to your years.

Words and the Sound of Music

A sentence sings when the words in that sentence create a flow of pleasant sounds. To compose sentences that flow smoothly, a writer should avoid the following:

Using Too Many Harsh Sounds   In our language there are many unpleasant-sounding consonants: *j, dj, ks, qu, nk, sh, s.* Listen to the sound of these words: *gesture, satchel, tragic, illegible, church, cabbage, virtue, anxious, bushel.* Listen to the harsh music produced by too lavish a use of the unpleasant *s* and *sh* sounds in the tongue-twister "She sells seashells by the seashore." Now listen to the following sentence and "feel" the effect of too many harsh, unpleasant sounds.

> Be assured that there will be no change in our existing policy with regard to future orders, charges, and exchanges.

Using Too Many Similar Sounds   Many words, although different in meaning and in spelling, have similar sounds. An expert watches for these sounds and does not use too many like sounds in any one sentence. Listen to the following sentence, which contains too many *ee* sounds, and note its lack of musical quality.

> When you steer your weary feet here to our restaurant, you have a treat awaiting you.

Correcting the This or Thus Fault

A rather common writing fault is the use of *this* or *thus* to refer to an entire preceding thought. This lack of definiteness sometimes forces a reader to reread, or to recast, a sentence in order to comprehend the writer's meaning. The slipshod, inexact use of *this* and *thus* can spoil an otherwise fine writing performance. For example:

> Our stockroom is overcrowded. This has existed since we moved
> to the new building on Juniper Street.

To what does the *this* refer? To the overcrowded *condition* of the stockroom. An accomplished writer would have stated the point specifically, as in the following:

> This condition has existed since we moved to the new building
> on Juniper Street.

Now read the following sentence, which shows another example of unclear word reference:

> Mr. Burr has passed the C.P.A. examination, thus proving that
> he is competent to open a set of books for you.

Thus, as used here, is ambiguous. The thought could have been expressed more clearly and more directly as follows:

> The fact that Mr. Burr has passed the C.P.A. examination is proof
> of his ability to open a set of books for you.
> Mr. Burr has passed the C.P.A. examination and therefore is
> competent to open a set of books for you.

Correcting the So and the And So Faults

Another technique of the polished writer is to avoid the writing of sentences in which *so* or *and so* is used to introduce a clause. For instance, note how awkwardly *so* is used in this sentence:

> Ronald Clark has been in our employ for only one month, so we
> are unable to tell you much about him.

So in this sentence is used to connect a result-giving clause with the reason-giving main clause. Although *so* is an accepted conjunction, hack writers work it to death. *Because* is a better choice for relating cause- and result-giving clauses. The following sentence shows how the same thought may be expressed with polish:

> We are unable to tell you much about Ronald Clark because he
> has been in our employ for only one month.

The following sentence shows the *and so* fault.

> Mr. Flynn has had much experience in personnel work, and so
> we recommend that you talk with him.

In this sentence, *and so* introduces a clause, but *and so* does not appear in any list of conjunctions. The sentence could have been written correctly in either of the following ways:

> Mr. Flynn has had much experience in personnel work; therefore, we recommend that you talk with him.
> We recommend that you talk with Mr. Flynn, who has had much experience in personnel work.

ADVANCED BALANCE TECHNIQUES

In Chapter 3, Section 21, much of the presentation was focused on the balancing of elements used with coordinate and correlative conjunctions; for example, not *Our portables are light, smooth-running, and won't stain,* but *Our portables are light, smooth-running, and stainless.* Ability to use like elements with conjunctions is an important balancing technique.

The advanced techniques of balance are concerned with the preservation of the flow and the rhythm of writing. Ideas of equal value must be expressed in parallel constructions. In the following writing situations, ideas and thoughts are thrown out of balance because essential words are omitted. Note how these imbalances are corrected.

Balancing Comparisons

Comparisons are balanced only if they are complete, and they can be complete only if all necessary words are included in them. The omission of only one necessary word can throw a comparison out of balance, as in the example below.

> Research shows that men spend more time looking at window displays than women.

As written, the sentence could mean that men spend more time looking at window displays than they do looking at women—a somewhat doubtful statement. The comparison lacks balance, as well as sense, because an essential word is omitted. One word can solve the problem and make the meaning of the sentence clear.

> Research shows that men spend more time looking at window displays than women *do* (or *spend*).

Here is another imbalanced comparison:

> Mr. Boyd's standing in the Elko-Haber Corporation is more than a clerk.

Lack of sense in this sentence results from omission of essential words. An expert would write:

> Mr. Boyd's standing in the Elko-Haber Corporation is more than *that of* a clerk.

An imbalanced comparison like the one below provides a chance for expert revision.

> Owen can write just as well, if not better, than Allen.

Disregarding the words set off by commas, the sentence reads as follows: *Owen can write just as well than Allen.* In the following revisions, the first is acceptable, but the expert will write the second and more polished sentence.

> Owen can write just as well as, if not better than, Allen.
> Owen can write just as well as Allen, if not better.

Balancing Modifiers

There are many ways in which the omission of single-word modifiers can destroy balance. Such omission can result in an illogical message, such as the following.

> We need a traveling salesman and stenographer.

Failure to write *a* before *stenographer* makes *traveling salesman* and *stenographer* the same person. Dim, indeed, is the prospect of hiring a person who can serve in the dual capacity of traveling salesman and of stenographer.

> Please requisition a pen, bottle of ink, and envelope.

Since the modifier is not repeated with each member of this series, *a* is the modifier for all three members of the series. However, *a envelope* would never be considered polished writing. The series should be *a pen, a bottle of ink, and an envelope.*

> Mr. Taylor speaks often of his parents, wife, and children.

The modifier *his* is the correct modifier for all three members of this series and is technically correct; however, a writer with a "feel" for language would repeat the modifier in order to achieve fullness and roundness of tone.

> Mr. Taylor speaks often of *his* parents, *his* wife, and *his* children.

Balancing Verbs

In some sentences, verbs appear in compound constructions; for example:

> We have been to the exhibit but will go again if you think we should.

In this sentence *but* connects the verb phrases *have been* and *will go.* Structural balance demands that whenever the parts of verbs in compound constructions are not exactly alike in form, no verb part should be omitted. In the following sentence this rule has been broken.

> I never have, and never will, make a dishonest tax return.

Failure to write the past participle *made* with the auxiliary *have* causes the meaning to be *I never have make and never will make.* Since the verbs in this compound construction are not exactly alike in form, no verb part should be omitted. Therefore, the sentence must read:

> I never have *made*, and never will make, a dishonest tax return.

The following sentence shows the same kind of error.

> Your check was received yesterday and the garden sets shipped by express.

The omission of the auxiliary verb after *garden sets* structures the sentence like this: *Your check was received, and the garden sets was shipped.* The plural noun *garden sets* requires a plural verb; therefore, the sentence must read:

> Your check was received yesterday, and the garden sets *were* shipped by express.

Balancing Prepositions

The omission of a preposition can also throw a sentence off balance. You learned in Section 20 that some words must be followed by specific prepositions. When two prepositional constructions have the same object, you must use, in each construction, the preposition that is idiomatically correct. Failure to supply the correct preposition results in a mismatch; for example:

> Office workers should have confidence and respect for their supervisors.

In this illustration, *confidence and respect* is a compound, both parts of which are modified by the prepositional phrase *for their supervisors. For,* then, is the preposition used with both *confidence* and *respect.* But would anyone ever say or write "confidence *for* their supervisors"? The correct preposition to use with *confidence* is *in.* To be balanced, the sentence should read:

> Office workers should have confidence *in* and respect for their supervisors.

Balancing Conjunctions

In oral communication, subordinate conjunctions, particularly *that* and *when,* can often be omitted without causing any confusion. In written communications, however, such omissions can destroy the balance of the thought units of a sentence and thus can confuse the reader.

> Mr. Williams frequently talks about the time he had neither money nor position.

If this were an oral communication, the speaker could make his meaning clear by pausing slightly after the word *time.* The reader, however, might see the thought unit *Mr. Williams frequently talks about the time he had,* with the result that the following words would not make sense. Therefore, the sentence should be written like this:

> Mr. Williams frequently talks about the time when he had neither money nor position.

The following sentence may also be misread:

> We investigated and found the furniture was shipped on May 2.

The omission of a subordinate conjunction confuses the reader. Consider the thought unit *We investigated and found the furniture,* and think how the remaining words can throw a reader off balance. Rewritten for clarity and for smooth comprehension, the sentence reads:

> We investigated and found that the furniture was shipped on May 2.

In informal writing, however, subordinate conjunctions may be omitted if their omission will not confuse the reader.

> Yes, we do have the book you mentioned.

The omission of *that* in this sentence does not confuse the reader; therefore, the writer was quite correct in omitting the word.

Balancing Clauses

Another mark of writing distinction is the avoidance of incomplete (elliptical) clauses whenever failure to write the complete clause would confuse the reader. In the sentence "You are a better man than I," the meaning *than I am* is clear. But listen to this:

> Did Mr. Wilson pay the bill or his wife?

This sentence could be interpreted as follows: *Did Mr. Wilson pay the bill, or did he pay his wife?* Both of the following revised sentences make the meaning clear; the second sentence, however, is more polished.

> Did Mr. Wilson pay the bill, or did his wife pay it?
> Who paid the bill, Mr. Wilson or his wife?

COMMUNICATION PROJECTS

Practical Application

Some of these sentences contain too many harsh sounds; others, too many similar sounds. Rewrite them.

1. The proofreader missed the error; so, "Mr." remained misspelled.
2. Much to our chagrin, we must acknowledge that we should have made more judicious use of your excellent suggestions.
3. The "Landers" sets we have on hand are handsomely bound.
4. Of course, the coarse mesh can stand more force and pressure.
5. Research shows that hodgepodge word usage produces messages that dissolve into unintelligible gibberish.

B Rewrite any sentence that violates an advanced writing technique. Write *OK* for any correct sentence.

1. We all must work on this vital problem—and work, and work, and work!
2. The crates were not properly marked. This caused much confusion.
3. Did Mr. Shea fill out the requisition or Bob?
4. The order was for a box and carton.
5. Jack never has and never will understand the finer techniques of writing.
6. The goods left our shipping department in perfect condition, so the carrier must be at fault.
7. Mr. Gates likes Tom's work better than the other accountants'.
8. Our high school burned down my last term.
9. The staff has great admiration and faith in Mr. Lewis.
10. We could see the author had little talent.
11. Now that a sane Fourth has become a tradition, we must think about planning for a sane Christmas.
12. We need help with the typing, the checking, and the assembling.
13. After the suit was altered, the customer would not take it nor pay for the alterations.
14. The contract was satisfactory to the signer. This was reflected in his attitude.
15. Our product is better, not equivalent, to the best.
16. Luke seldom went into town, thus trying to show his complete indifference to the whole situation.
17. Hugh asked everyone he met along the way to bring a record and sheet of music to the party.
18. Miss Clifford never has, and never will, be able to understand the procedure that must be followed.
19. Shall I report for duty next week?
20. The manufacturer was concerned about the high cost of the raw materials that went into his product, so he raised the price of the goods he sold.

C In these sentences, correct any violations in thought-unit construction or in advanced writing techniques. Write *OK* for any correct sentence.

1. Bill realized the mistake he had made too late.
2. Replying to your June 4 letter, the consignment of machine tools was shipped on June 1.
3. Our supervisor thinks more of Edson's work than he does Barry's.
4. Any man who works for that company is trained for just one job.
5. Fred was pleased, but all the others dissatisfied.
6. Having a broken arm and nose, we returned the statue.
7. The cost of buying the machine would be less than renting it.
8. We sat for hours watching the game, shivering.
9. The report on the new sales methods contained many thought-unit violations, thus making it confusing to read.
10. We prefer to shop in that store because they keep everything in plain sight.
11. You wish to become an executive, so you need an exceptionally fine English background.
12. Mr. Bond told Fred that he would need help to meet the six o'clock deadline.
13. Did Mr. Eliot buy the house or his wife?
14. Adam lives in Bronxville, which is a suburb of New York.
15. It stresses in your July 8 letter that check marks must be placed on forms that have been proofread.
16. Did Bob win the game or Steve?
17. Having put the car in the garage for repairs, walking or taking the bus was the only way to get there.
18. Joan was hurt in the accident, but all the others uninjured.
19. George and Harry learned the value of setting goals and working toward them at an early age.
20. That's the good news that I was speaking about.

Editing Practice

Editing the News   Edit and rewrite the following excerpts from news items to be published in a local paper.

1. Some scouts came upon an unknown lake hiking through the woods.
2. The high school drum corps is on its way to the exhibition in a bus.
3. The following article is one in a series written by Peter Bessette, a Mohawk Indian priest for the Evening Standard.
4. The Academy band will give its last concert before taking its annual leave at Jones Field.
5. Mr. Lane became owner of the farm on which young Abe Lincoln helped his father in 1922.

Spelling and Pronunciation   Can you find any spelling errors that were probably caused by mispronunciation?

> The pulleys on our Order 675 of May 9 are being returned to you today. Our maintainance supervisor reports that he cannot use these pulleys because they are 4½ inches in width, instead of the 4⅝ size specified on our order. When you bill us for this order, please credit us with $5.68, the shipping charges we paid to return the goods.

Case Problem

A Better Plan   Bill Carpenter keeps the payroll records at the Barrett warehouse. Previously he had performed the same work for the Moore Transfer Company. Bill thought the records at Moore's were set up much better and that the system of keeping records at Barrett's, therefore, should be changed.

1. Should Bill present these ideas to his present employer?
2. How can he do so without being offensive?

Writing Power

A powerful speaker establishes rapport with his audience and speaks so convincingly that he influences the thinking of his listeners. The power of any political figure can be measured by his effectiveness in motivating voters to rally around his standard. The power of a salesman is reflected in his persuasiveness as a user of words. Much of the success of an executive hinges on his ability to inspire the members of his staff to work with and for him. Power, then, results from the ability to influence the thinking and the actions of other persons.

Many aids to power are available for the speaker to use. A warm and friendly tone, sincere facial expressions, vivid gestures—all these devices can be used by the speaker to induce a favorable reception. A writer, on the contrary, cannot use such devices to evoke the desired response. A writer must depend entirely on his writing skill.

Of course, writing skill is a special kind of know-how. A master of the writing craft must know how to bring out the important points in his message. His communications must be smooth, interesting, logical, potent. He must be master of all the writing techniques that produce results in the form of increased profits and increased goodwill. The power of the written word, the influence exercised by a writer, will be as great as the communicator's ability to use the guides for developing writing power.

STRENGTH VERSUS WEAKNESS

One of the factors that contribute to strength is the absence of weakness. This statement infers that a writer shows strength by avoiding the specific pitfalls that weaken his communications. Study the examples in the following paragraphs.

Active Versus Passive Voice

Voice is the modification of a transitive verb that shows whether the subject acts or is acted upon. Any verb phrase composed of a past participle with a "being" verb helper is in the passive voice: *will be shipped, has been sent, was done, is frozen.* In the active voice, the subject is the doer of an action; in the passive voice, the subject is acted upon.

> Gibson sent us a message. (Active voice.)
> A message was sent to us by Gibson. (Passive voice.)

The active voice is a stronger, livelier means of expressing thoughts than is the passive voice. The passive voice, however, may be used when strength is not a factor. For example, "Your order will be shipped on Monday, July 9" and "We will ship your order on Monday, July 9" are equally effective sentences. In some specific situations, though, the active voice must be used because the use of the passive voice would weaken the message or the point that is being made. For example:

> Last year our machines were sold to 75 out of every 100 business firms in Omaha.

This sentence is intended to make a selling point, but see how much stronger the statement is when it is rewritten in the active voice.

> Last year, 75 out of every 100 business firms in Omaha bought our machines.

Shifts in Voice, Tense, Person, Number

Whenever a sentence contains two or more clauses or whenever a paragraph contains closely related sentences, the expert writer is careful to see that there is no shift, no variation, in voice, tense, person, or number. As an expert, he is concerned because the shift is technically incorrect; but he is perhaps more concerned because the shift weakens his communication.

Shift in Voice When one verb in a compound or a complex sentence is in the active voice, the other verb or verbs must also be in the active voice. Using the active voice in one clause and then shifting to the passive voice in another clause, or vice versa, is a communication weakness.

> In winter the file clerks freeze with the cold, and in summer they are stifled with the heat.

The shift from the active voice in the first clause to the passive voice in the second clause reduces the strength of the statement. Both verbs should be in the active voice, or both verbs should be in the passive voice. Active voice is the stronger; therefore, the sentence should read:

> In winter the file clerks freeze with the cold, and in summer they stifle with the heat.

Shift in Tense   A verb has six principal tenses—present, past, future, and the three "perfects"—each tense showing the time of an action. A writer strengthens his communications by avoiding a shift in tense unless an actual difference in time must be indicated.

> Baker uses such simple language that any reader will easily understand his meaning.

This sentence shows a shift in tense, from present tense in the first clause to future tense in the second clause. The statement can be strengthened by avoiding the shift as follows: "Baker uses such simple language that any reader easily understands his meaning."

Shift in Person   A shift in person within a sentence is such a glaring weakness that any reader notices it immediately. For example:

> I should like to know the name of a branch store where you can get service within twenty-four hours.

The first person *I* is the subject of the first clause; the second person *you* is the subject of the second clause. The shift is weak because it is illogical. Why should *I* want to know where *you* can get fast service? The sentence should read:

> I should like to know the name of a branch store where I can get service within twenty-four hours.

Shift in Number   A shift in number from singular to plural, or vice versa, weakens a message because this type of shift, like the shift in person, conveys an irrational message.

> A communicator must be well trained, or they will not be able to build goodwill.

Communicator in the first clause is singular in number, but *they*, which refers to *communicator*, is plural in number. You can gain strength by avoiding this shift; therefore, you should write:

> A communicator must be well trained, or he will not be able to build goodwill.

SENTENCE AND PARAGRAPH CONTROL

The copybook adage "A chain is as strong as its weakest link" might be paraphrased as follows: "A communication is as strong as its weakest component." The components of a business communication are sentences and paragraphs; consequently, for writing power, a writer must have sentence and paragraph control.

Sentence Control

For the purpose of developing writing power through sentence control, a writer must know that (1) each sentence must contain only one main thought, and (2) each sentence must be the proper length, neither too long nor too short.

One Main Thought In Chapter 4, Section 22, you learned not to use a comma to join two separate and distinct thoughts. From the viewpoint of writing power, the comma-for-period fault weakens a message because more than one main thought is expressed in a single sentence, such as the following example:

> We are interested in your views on merchandising, we need to do some more research before we can present our own opinions.

The correct punctuation, of course, is a period. However, other alternatives for correcting the comma-for-period fault include (1) using a coordinate conjunction, (2) using a semicolon or a semicolon and a transitional expression, and (3) using a subordinate conjunction to make one of the thoughts dependent on the other. These methods are more advanced techniques than the one of simply writing two separate sentences, and expert use of them produces more effective communications. For example, compare the following revisions of the example given above, and note how the relationship between the two thoughts is clarified in the last three revisions.

> We are interested in your views on merchandising. We need to do some more research before we can present our own opinions.
>
> We are interested in your views on merchandising, but we need to do some more research before we can present our own opinions.
>
> We are interested in your views on merchandising; however, we need to do some more research before we can present our own opinions.
>
> Although we are interested in your views on merchandising, we need to do some more research before we can present our own opinions.

More about the use of transitional expressions is given on page 228, and how to subordinate thoughts properly is explained on page 229.

Proper Length An overlong sentence is ineffective and weak because it buries any message it contains. The reader gets lost in the maze of words; his attention span is overtaxed. For example:

> We were sorry to learn from your letter of March 4 that you failed to receive the February and March issues of THE BANNER; and since it is apparent that the magazines, which were forwarded in the regular course of mailing, bearing your correct name and address, were lost en route, we are glad to supply duplicates.

Whew! Such a spate of words to say that he is sorry and will send duplicates. The writer was correct in making the point that the fault was not the publisher's; but this point should have been written as a separate sentence. Study the revision at the top of page 228.

> We were sorry to hear that you did not receive the February and March issues of THE BANNER, and we are glad to supply duplicate copies. The magazines, bearing your correct name and address, evidently were lost en route.

A succession of short sentences lessens writing power because the reader is jerked along from thought to thought. For example:

> We received your letter. It arrived this morning and was most welcome. All the salesmen read it; they liked your suggestions. Your letters are always friendly. We enjoy hearing from you.

No expert would ever write such a stop-and-go, stop-and-go communication. He would write something like this:

> Your welcome letter arrived this morning, and all the salesmen liked your suggestions. Your letters are always so friendly that we enjoy hearing from you.

There are situations, however, that call for the planned use of short sentences. Short sentences are often useful in bringing out a series of important facts. The following excerpt from a sales letter illustrates the planned use of short sentences.

> Gently press the door latch, and the door swings gently open. There goes the light. Do you see how convenient it is? Now look inside. That pristine white will never stain, and the shelves are so well made that even small containers will not upset.

Paragraph Control

Paragraph control is achieved by presenting only one main thought in a paragraph, by avoiding overlong paragraphs, and by gliding smoothly from one paragraph to another.

Proper Length   In general, a paragraph should not be longer than six to eight lines. If the development of one thought requires more than six to eight lines, the writer should carry that thought over to another paragraph. To bridge the gap between paragraphs, the writer can use transitional expressions such as the following:

again	equally important	in addition
also	further	likewise
besides	furthermore	moreover

Smooth Transitions   When a reader has finished reading any polished business communication, he is left with the feeling of having moved smoothly from beginning to end. The knowledgeable writer ensures the smooth flow of ideas by using carefully chosen transitional expressions to carry the reader along. Here is a partial list of such expressions:

accordingly	hence	on the contrary
after all	however	on the other hand
at the same time	meanwhile	similarly
consequently	nevertheless	still
for this purpose	notwithstanding	therefore

STRUCTURING FOR EMPHASIS

Written communications are effective when the writer gives force to the important phases of any message. Once he himself has determined the salient points, his problem is that of structuring sentences in such a way that the reader, too, recognizes the important part or parts of the communication. The power principles that enable a business writer to write forceful and effective messages are the principles of emphasis.

Proper Subordination of Ideas

Proper subordination of ideas depends on the ability to determine the difference between an important idea and a lesser idea. The important thought is expressed as a main clause, and the lesser idea is properly written as a subordinate clause. The principle can be remembered as follows: "Main idea—main clause; subordinate idea—subordinate clause." Consider the following sentence:

> I had just started to write up our bids when your revised specifications arrived.

Which idea is more important, the fact that I had just started to write up the bids or the fact that your revised specifications arrived? The arrival of the revised specifications is the more important idea; therefore, it should have been expressed as the main clause. The sentence should read:

> Your revised specifications arrived just as I started to write up our bids.

Coordination Versus Subordination   When a sentence contains two ideas of equal importance, it should be divided into two main clauses. For example, consider the following:

> The work is difficult, but the rewards are great.

On the other hand, writing power is considerably diminished when the writer fails to see that the thoughts he expresses belong, not in two main clauses, but in a main clause and a subordinate clause. Note the following example:

> There were other candidates, and Bruce received the promotion.

This sentence places equal stress on what the writer considers to be two main ideas. The emphasis should properly be placed on Bruce's receiving the promotion, even though there was competition. For force, as well as for clarity, the sentence should be written:

> Although there were other candidates, Bruce received the promotion.

Interrupting Expressions   Unwittingly, some writers destroy the forcefulness of proper subordination by writing the lesser idea as an interrupting expression. For instance, read the sentence at the top of page 230.

> You are, considering the risks involved in such an investment, very fortunate.

The main thought, *you are very fortunate,* is interrupted by the lesser idea, *considering the risks involved.* This interference with the flow of the main thought is so distracting that the force of the statement is completely lost. Properly written, the sentence reads:

> Considering the risks involved in such an investment, you are very fortunate.

Variety in Sentence Structure

Communications that lack variety lack emphasis. The expert writer varies the structure of his sentences. Some of his sentences are simple, some compound, some complex. He varies his connectives and his transitional expressions. His writing is interesting, sparkling; consequently, his communications have force. Study this sentence:

> Your car was brought to our repair shop and has been here for two days. We looked it over carefully and found that the trouble was dirt in the carburetor, and we gave it a good cleaning. The car is now ready for you to pick up when you return from your vacation, and we shall be waiting to see you smile when you press the accelerator and hear the smooth hum of the motor.

This communication has no force because the writer uses too many compound sentences and too many *ands.* An expert would write something like this:

> Your car has been in our repair shop for two days. After looking it over carefully, we found that the trouble was caused by dirt in the carburetor. Naturally, we cleaned the carburetor thoroughly; and now the engine is as good as new. We shall be waiting for you to pick up the car when you return from your vacation. Also, we shall be waiting to see you smile when you press the accelerator and hear the smooth hum of the motor.

Emphasis by Climax

In any series—of words, of phrases, of clauses, or of complete thoughts—you can emphasize the most important member of the series by building the series from the least to the most important member. Study the following illustration.

> The successful businessman is industrious, wide-awake, and honorable.

The word sequence is carefully planned. To be successful, the businessman first of all must be industrious, then wide-awake, and then—most important of all—honorable.

Emphasis by Mechanical Aids

When communicating orally, some people emphasize important points by shouting or by pounding on a desk. These means of emphasizing points are effective only when seldom used. When used too often, they make so much noise that the listener cannot hear the words; thus overemphasis can cause the message to be lost.

A writer, too, has mechanical ways of emphasizing points. He can:

- Underline.
- Tabulate.
- Use dashes or a series of dots.
- Use exclamation points.
- Set words or expressions in all capital letters.
- Use the red half of the typewriter ribbon for typing important words.

Mechanical means of emphasizing have a function; but when they are over-used, they make such a din that the reader cannot hear the message. An expert writer does not need to use them often. His writing power is so great that he can make his choice of words accomplish almost any purpose that he has in mind.

POWER FAILURE

Now that you have studied the various aspects of writing power, a word of warning is needed to prevent power failure. That warning is this: Mastery of craftsmanship techniques will not make your writing effective unless you use language that is simple, direct, and clear. Communication has for its purpose the conveying of a message of some kind, not the parading of an extensive vocabulary.

Although the writing of individual correspondents is sometimes dressed up to the point of utter confusion, government letters and publications are generally considered to be tops in "way out" communications. An illustration of government gobbledegook at its best appeared in the July-August 1964 issue of THINK magazine and goes as follows:

"The records are crowded with speeches made and letters written as if they had no other purpose than to be incomprehensible . . . . In fact, (one) could do worse than study two communiques about air raid precautions, the first written by an aide to President Franklin D. Roosevelt, and the second written by Roosevelt himself.

"The aide's memorandum read: 'Such preparations shall be made as will completely obscure all Federal buildings occupied by the Federal Government during an air raid for any period of time from visibility by reason of internal or external illumination. Such obscuration may be obtained either by blackout construction or by termination of illumination. This will, of course, require that in building areas in which production must continue during the blackout, construction must be provided that internal illumination may continue. Other areas may be obscured by terminating the illumination.'

"A mildly exasperated Roosevelt suggested this revision: 'Tell them that in buildings where they have to keep the work going, they should put something across the windows. In buildings where they can afford to let the work stop for a while, they should turn out the lights.'"

COMMUNICATION PROJECTS

Practical Application

A

Rewrite the following items according to the directions given in parentheses.

1. Automation will actually benefit business employees; it will create new jobs. (Give major importance to the first clause.)
2. A modern typewriter is truly a product of evolution. Originally, they were crude machines; but today they are marvels of perfection. (Correct any shift in voice, tense, person, or number.)
3. Our store is on State Street and is the largest in the city. (Give major importance to the fact that our store is the largest in the city.)
4. It has been a busy day. We had many customers. We had to omit our coffee break. (Combine into one sentence and use proper subordination.)
5. When conferring with the caller, the Dean told him that college students should take some courses they did not like; but study them faithfully, and you will get increased knowledge. (Correct any shift in voice, etc.)
6. One night we were working late, and we saw a light in the president's office. (Subordinate the less important idea.)
7. Is your car out of commission, and does it need some small repairs? Send it to us, and we will give it special attention. We are most thorough, and our prices are reasonable. (Rewrite and vary sentence structure.)
8. Mr. McCue occupies a commodious office. It is on the seventh floor of our building. This office is very quiet. (Combine into one forceful sentence.)
9. Bill had been warned by Mr. Foley that the excuse would not be accepted again. (Change to active voice.)
10. My plane was late, and I missed my first appointment. (Subordinate the less important idea.)

B

Rewrite the following sentences, rewording them to make them more powerful.

1. We very often hear that history repeated itself.
2. Our expert mechanic removed pieces of rust from the radiator, and your car is now as good as new.
3. The customer comes into the store and orders his suit. Afterward, he spent an hour discussing our credit regulations.
4. Since the error was made by Carter, he should correct it.
5. The broker saw before him disaster, ruin, defeat, and broken health.
6. I am now, having studied the situation carefully, ready with my report.
7. Our electronic air conditioner will be found to be of much pleasure and comfort to you.
8. My work has been very satisfactory to Mr. Miller, and he will be glad to recommend me.
9. You asked for immediate delivery of the signed contract; nevertheless, we are sending it today by special messenger.
10. Important communications must first be outlined, or it will be ineffective.

C

These sentences review the writing techniques presented in Sections 31 and 32. Rewrite all the sentences.

1. In our business, typed letters bring in no more sales than using mimeographed ones.
2. We are neither interested nor concerned with Arnold's project.
3. Solid-color flannels will be popular this fall, which is the prediction of the fashion experts.
4. Before buying a dishwasher, the dealer should give a demonstration.

5. We learned the truth would never be told.
6. Carpeting has and will continue to be the mark of luxury.
7. Mr. Eads told us that his father died before he was born.
8. Our firm has built a beautiful building on Main Street that is so light and airy.
9. We went trout fishing, but caught only one of them.
10. Office conversation is enjoyed by Jim as much, if not more, than by the other clerks.

Editing Practice

The Correspondence Supervisor   Edit and rewrite the following paragraph.

Just this morning I returned from a vacation in the far west and your letter is receiving priority first to be answered. Yes, we do publish Mr. Haltons book *Have You A Problem Situation?* We are sending you the requested information about this book as well as prices for all other books written for foremen in factories (see the enclosed brochure.) You must be very proud of your in-service training program.

Power Failure   The following sentence is an illustration of power failure. How would you have written this message?

Your anticipatory behavior at the first flash of St. Elmo's fire will be changed when Safety lightning rods are installed on the roof of your domicile.

Case Problem

Remembering Names   How well do you remember names after an introduction? Six of your classmates will select assumed names and introduce themselves to you. You may ask one question of each as you try to fix the name in your memory. Then introduce each one to another student.

Creative
Business Writing

The Psychology of Business Writing

"What's in it for me?" is the automatic response that is to be expected of a normal person when he is presented with a proposal of any kind. And, psychologically, this conscious or subconscious response is "automatic" and "is to be expected" because part of our standard equipment at birth is a drive (some psychologists prefer "instinct") for self-preservation, for food, for shelter, and for clothing. To put it bluntly, we're just made that way.

The normal person we speak of may be reading a letter written for the purpose of selling a product or a service. Maybe it is an adjustment letter, telling him what is being done about a claim he has made. Or perhaps the letter is an invitation to serve on a committee, to contribute to a worthy cause, to give a talk, or to exhibit goods at an exposition. Regardless of the subject of the letter, however, our knowledge of psychology tells us that any letter calling for action on the part of the reader will get the desired result only if it has a built-in answer to the question every reader is sure to ask: "What's in it for me?"

Understanding this one psychological principle will enable a correspondent to write better letters in terms of results; but to write the best letters, he needs more knowledge of human behavior and of what makes us "tick." For instance, he must know that although the particular purpose of his letters may be to motivate readers to buy his goods or to use his services, the all-pervasive general purpose is to make friends who will prefer to trade with his firm, rather than with his competitors.

In the remaining sections of this textbook, you will study the various types of business writing. In this section, you will learn bedrock principles, the application of which will lend a master touch to every bit of writing you will ever do. Your success as a writer, then, will be promoted by your study of the following topics.

"WHAT'S IN IT FOR ME?"

You will be able to supply built-in answers to this question if you know and understand the areas of self-interest discussed below.

Financial Gain

With very few exceptions, those of us who work for a living are interested in earning more money. Therefore, if a reader can increase his income by acting on your proposal, you should send him a letter that emphasizes his opportunity for financial gain. For example, if your purpose is to sell stocks or mutual funds, a sentence like the one that follows on page 237 might be a powerful prod to action.

If in 1960 you had invested $5,000 in Probity Capital, your investment would today be worth $10,230—more than double your money! (These figures, of course, must actually be a matter of record.)

Making Money by Saving Money   Increased profits for businessmen often result from cutting expenditures. In some cases, such as by taking advantage of special discounts, the businessman is aware that he can make money by saving money. Seeing this point in writing, however, will impress upon him the fact that the special discount *you* are offering will make money for him. For example:

> Take advantage of our special discount terms, and you will realize savings that will boost your profit.

In other instances, a businessman might not realize how much he could save by acting favorably on the subject of your letter. Therefore, you should tell him in simple, direct, and forceful terms. For instance, if you want to interest him in purchasing an office machine, the financial-gain incentive might be:

> The Rapidsorter will take the place of four employees—a truly significant cut in your payroll expense.

Quoting Dollars and Cents   A little bit of psychology must also be used whenever you quote amounts of money. If those figures represent income, quote them in the largest possible amount; if they involve paying out money, quote them in the smallest amount. Everybody is eager to get as much money as he can but is willing to part with as little as possible. For instance, suppose that you write for a real estate firm and that one of your listings is a six-apartment building, each apartment renting at $150 a month. The income figures you quote in promotional pamphlets, newspaper ads, or letters should be presented like this:

> Your yearly income from this property will be a comfortable $10,800. (Not *Each apartment will bring you an income of $150 a month.*)

However, when you quote figures on mortgage *payments* for this building, you should quote the lowest terms possible.

> The amount remaining after the down payment can be financed by a 30-year conventional mortgage that will cost you only $88.73 a month.

Health and Security

Health and security are major concerns of most people, and buying incentives that are based on these concerns appeal to people's instincts for self-preservation.

Advertisements for many products—in particular, for medicines—appeal to your desire to preserve and to promote your own good health. Therefore, you should be alert for opportunities to use this incentive. If, for instance, you are promoting the sale of an electric dishwasher, you should stress facts that relate to good health, such as:

> And your dishes, glasses, and silverware will be germ-free, because, as laboratory tests have proved, the final cycle makes them hospital-sterile.

Satisfaction of the desire for security is the main selling point for a variety of products—insurance, lightning rods, burglar alarms, office safes, and so on. An appeal to people's desire for security can, however, be a part of any promotion effort you undertake. Suppose, for example, you are promoting a new car, the Puma, and you can emphasize any one of several buying incentives. Knowing the importance of the security motivation, however, you would emphasize that factor in your promotional material. For example, you might say something like this:

> You and your family will be safe in a Puma. Merely press a button on the dash, and all doors will immediately lock. You need not fear that a child will fall out, nor need you fear that anyone from the outside can reach the occupants of your car.

Personal Comfort

Another facet of human behavior is the innate and universal desire for comfort and beauty in daily living, both at home and at work. For some letters, then, the built-in answer to "What's in it for me?" will be "more comfort, more beauty, or more relaxation." The action spark of this type of letter is a deliberate appeal to the senses, the emotions.

You can undoubtedly think of many, many goods or services that can be sold by using this approach. For example, the following sentence could be used to promote the sale of mattresses.

> Each morning you will wake up rested and refreshed, ready for a productive and happy day.

Here is an illustration of the appeal to the comfort incentive, as applied to a business situation.

> The comfort of this Executive Chair will carry you pleasantly through the entire working day—no aches, no pains, no three-o'clock fatigue.

We must also take into account the fact that added comfort sometimes results from making the work load easier and quicker. For instance, see what this picture-making sentence could do to motivate a housewife to buy an automatic washer.

> Load the machine, flip the switch—then go out on the patio and relax in the sun.

Quite possibly, of course, the housewife's reaction might be, "Oh yeah? Relax in the sun, indeed." However, the spark is there; and her very next thought could well be, "But I *could* get the upstairs work done, and I could play bridge or go shopping every afternoon."

THE DRIVE FOR PERSONAL RECOGNITION

Like the instinct for self-preservation, the drive for personal recognition is universal. This drive may be partially satisfied by acquiring possessions that society recognizes as status symbols, such as a luxury car, a beautiful home, or expensive clothes.

Within each of us, then, there is a little "me"—call it ego, soul, dignity of man, or whatever you will. This knowledge is essential to the business writer, for writing success is largely dependent on how well the writer can sustain the reader's sense of self-importance. Study the guidelines presented in the following paragraphs.

Focusing on the Reader

You inflate the reader's ego when you emphasize the fact that he comes first, that he is the important part of any message. Always assume that the reader is interested primarily in himself and in his own advancement. Therefore, you can increase the effectiveness of your communications if you word them so that they will have a *you* flavor, not an *I* or a *we* approach. Compare the following illustrations of *we* and *you* approaches.

> *We:* Please send us your check for $16.89, so that we may balance our books.
>
> *You:* Your check for $16.89 will balance your account and will maintain your fine credit standing.
>
> *We:* We know from experience that our Airflo oil burner is not only a great timesaver, but a moneysaver as well.
>
> *You:* You will be delighted with the saving afforded by the Airflo —a saving in time and in money as well.
>
> *We:* We are firmly of the belief that . . . .
>
> *You:* You will undoubtedly agree that . . . .
>
> *We:* The timely articles that we print in *Tomorrow* are chosen to attract intelligent, interested readers.
>
> *You:* Research shows that you are the kind of intelligent, interested reader who will be attracted by the timely articles in *Tomorrow*.

Using the Reader's Name

A person's name is extremely important to him because it marks him as an individual, sets him apart from the rest of humanity, and gains for him the personal recognition he seeks. To avoid detracting from the importance of a reader's little "me," the knowledgeable writer will be sure that the reader's name is spelled correctly.

Using the addressee's name in the body of a letter is a "Me" builder. Because it is *his* name, *his* claim to personal recognition, the sight of that name gives a reader satisfaction and pleasure. In the following illustration, note how the use of direct address warms up and personalizes the message of the letter.

> Answering your inquiry has been a pleasure, Mrs. Roberts, and we hope you will always feel free to call on us whenever you think we can be of help.

Do not, though, use the reader's name more than once in the body of any letter. If you fail to heed this warning, your letters will give the impression of fawning on the reader. And who wants to be a bootlicker?

Being Courteous

Writing courteous letters is a "must" for the business communicator. Although a reader may not notice how polite you are, he will most surely be miffed by your failure to say "please" and "thank you." Your courtesy should make each reader feel that he is your most important customer.

Answering Letters Promptly

We all resent having to wait because being made to wait makes us feel that we are considered unimportant. Therefore, you risk arousing resentment when you do not answer correspondence promptly. You should make every effort to answer letters in not more than twenty-four hours after you receive them.

Of course, there are some letters that cannot be answered immediately. You might need time to look up the facts upon which your reply will be based; you might have been away from the office when the letter arrived. In such cases, be sure to let the correspondent know that the delay was unavoidable. For example, you might write an explanation like the following sentence:

> The price list requested in your May 9 letter came off the press this morning, and you will find it enclosed with this letter.

However, the best thing to do when you receive an angry letter from a customer is to delay answering the letter until you no longer feel like writing an angry reply. Or write the letter and get the bile out of your system; then tear up the blast. Suppose, for example, you had written a letter questioning a customer's deduction of shipping charges. You then receive a caustic, rude reply telling you that you had already agreed to this deduction. In the heat of anger, you might reply as follows:

> All right, so we made a mistake; but you don't have to get nasty about it.

But if you give yourself a cooling-off period, your letter might read:

> Thank you very much for your letter of June 17, in which you explain the deduction of $13.87 from our May 31 statement. Your account now shows no balance due.
>
> We are sorry that we did not record the fact that the May 15 shipment was to be sent prepaid, but you may rest assured that we will make every effort to prevent any such future incident.

Using Status Symbols

You have learned that the drive for personal recognition can sometimes be satisfied by attaining status—by owning something or doing something that the general public will notice and will perhaps admire or envy. The appeal to people's desire for status is a standard sales procedure; this appeal may be either the main selling point or a strong supporting one. Whenever you see a sentence like the following, you will know that the writer is appealing to your desire for status.

> Be the first in your neighborhood to enclose your property with an artistic Colonial picket fence.

You, however, will be writing letters on a variety of topics and for a number of different purposes; you will not be writing sales letters only. Now that you know the strength of an appeal to the desire for status, you will use that appeal whenever it lends itself to any type of writing you do. Suppose, for example, that you are writing an announcement of the reopening of the Mayfair restaurant. You would naturally stress the delicious food, the comfort and luxury of the new furnishings, and possibly the reasonable prices. You could also incorporate in your copy a sentence like this:

> The new Mayfair will cater exclusively to persons of refinement and good taste.

MAKING AND KEEPING FRIENDS

To be successful, a business must have customers; the greater the number of customers, the greater the success. Building a large following of customers, however, involves an intangible that may be called goodwill, good public relations, or simply making and keeping friends. This intangible is the psychological factor that motivates customers to trade with one particular company, rather than with its competitors.

Generally a writer can make friends for his firm if he writes communications that would give *him* pleasure and satisfaction if he were to receive them. The actual writing of such communications, however, depends on his knowledge and his use of the specific guidelines explained in the following paragraphs.

Using a Conversational Tone

Suppose you went to a store to make a purchase and suppose that the clerk, who was waiting on another customer, looked at you and said, "Your entrance has been duly noted, and careful attention will be given you within a few minutes." Wouldn't you wonder how that salesman ever got a job? Yet many businessmen make the mistake of writing their letters in just such a stilted manner.

The result-getting writer uses a conversational tone that makes the reader feel that he is being talked *to*, not *at*. In the illustrations below and at the top of page 242, note the difference between the *talking at* and the *talking to* approaches.

> *At:* Please reply at your earliest convenience.
> *To:* You will be doing us a real favor by sending this information soon.

At: Please mark your reply for the attention of the writer.

To: If you mark your reply for my attention, we'll be able to give you quicker service.

Being Cordial and Pleasant

Stop for a moment and think—are you drawn to the person who is pleasant, who meets you more than half way, who *shows* that he is happy to be with you? Of course, you say "Yes." Logically, then, your letters will have friend-making possibilities if their wording draws readers to you and your firm.

For an example of what can be done to make a message pleasant and cordial, study the following alternate illustrations.

> Your application for charge-account privileges has been cleared, and your charge plate is enclosed.

Here the message is perfectly clear and is slanted toward the reader. However, it lacks a cordial tone. Compare the following revision of the same message.

> Welcome to the ranks of Blanton charge-account friends! Your charge plate is enclosed, and we are looking forward to your visiting with us often.

Showing Concern for the Customer

Since the business communicator may write to hundreds of customers, he needs special skill in conveying the impression that any one reader is of particular importance to him. Only in this way can he excel in the competition for customers.

Business communications of a social nature—letters of appreciation, of congratulation, of sympathy—can show an interest in persons as individuals. Therefore, the wide-awake correspondent never misses an opportunity to write such friend-making letters.

Even when writing letters that are strictly for business, an expert recognizes possibilities of wording them in a way that evidences interest in affairs that are important to the reader. Study the following pairs of sentences and note how each second illustration turns an ordinary communication into a message that shows interest in and concern for the reader.

1. In answer to your letter of May 4, the sale of children's socks can be increased by displaying them in the shoe department as well as in the children's department.
2. When we read your May 4 letter, we could see that you do indeed have a problem; but we think we can help you solve it. (The letter goes on with the suggestion made in the first example.)

1. We are sending you a list of the special discounts we are prepared to offer you on goods purchased for your August sale.
2. Knowing that your August sale is the big event of your business year, we are sending you well ahead of time a list of special discounts on goods that can be purchased for that sale.

Being Helpful

A writer who is quick to extend a helping hand, whether or not any profit is involved, will make friends for his firm. If in some subtle way he can make the point that being helpful caused him extra work, he will make steadfast, permanent friends. The following illustration shows how a request for information might be handled by an untrained writer, by an average writer, and by a master writer.

> *Untrained:* We are sorry to inform you that we do not carry tile flooring.
>
> *Average:* Our company does not sell tile flooring, but the information you request can be furnished by Pratt & White.
>
> *Master:* Our company does not sell tile flooring; but we have made inquiries and have learned that you can obtain the information you need by writing to Pratt & White, 75 Broad Street, Dart, Ohio 05725.

Keeping Friends

All business writers know that their letters must have the overall purpose of making friends. However, a fact not so generally recognized is that keeping old friends is just as important as making new ones. For what will it profit a businessman to gain a new customer if, at the same time, he loses a faithful, steady customer?

While all the psychological factors discussed previously will apply to letters written to customers already on our books, the real secret of keeping a friend is to *tell* him frequently how much we appreciate him and how important he is to us. And we will keep our customers, not by "buttering them up," but by using some such sincere expressions as these:

> Doing business with you, Mr. Flahive, is always a pleasure.
> Our long-time friendship is a source of great satisfaction.
> We very much appreciate your friendship, and we are glad that you feel free to call on us for help.
> Without good friends like you, Mr. Frome, our business could not prosper.

COMMUNICATION PROJECTS

Practical Application

 Read this letter and list the sales principles applied by the writer.

> Dear Mrs. Campbell:
>
> You will be pleased to learn that we are filling your July 14 order by sending you a Sterling coffee maker.
>
> The Moonbeam coffeepot you ordered is out of stock, and we have discontinued that line of electrical appliances. But rather than disappoint you, we have selected and are shipping to you today the more expensive Sterling model—at no extra cost to you!
>
> May your pleasure and pride in entertaining be heightened by serving your guests with the aid of your beautiful, new Sterling coffee maker!
>
> Cordially yours,

B. Rewrite the following sentences and give them a *you* flavor.

1. We believe very firmly that you can sell our Perma shirts at a good profit.
2. We need this information right away.
3. We think you can cut your price on china and still make a fair profit.
4. We wish to announce that for the month of May we are offering a 10 percent discount on all our dining room furniture.
5. We take pleasure in informing you that you have an invitation to preview our fall fashions.
6. We believe that our used cars are reasonably priced.
7. We think that our beautiful city is an ideal vacation spot.
8. Quickwit products are superior to the products of our competitors.
9. We shall notify you by mail as soon as your radio is repaired.
10. The sale next Tuesday will offer special bargains to our charge-account customers.

C. Reword the following messages to give them a conversational tone.

1. Further information will be furnished upon request.
2. We do not know how to thank you for your thoughtfulness.
3. Information about parcel post charges is printed on page 213 of our summer catalog.
4. Charge-account privileges are extended only after credit references have been reviewed.
5. Keep in mind the fact that our advertising rates will be increased starting January 1.
6. Please be assured that your complaint will receive a thorough investigation.
7. Assembly instructions can be obtained by sending your request to the manufacturer.
8. This is to inform you that your order will be processed at an early date.
9. Interest in our endeavors is always appreciated.
10. We will be pleased to reserve accommodations for any delegate to the convention.

D. Here is an opening paragraph of a form letter written to customers who have stopped buying. How would you write it?

Upon examining our books, we find that you have not recently used your charge-account privileges with us.

Editing Practice

Plurals and Possessives Indicate the correct plural or possessive forms of the words enclosed in parentheses.

1. The (alto) voices were too loud for good musical balance.
2. All (ellipsis) in these sentences must be listed on your paper.
3. The (Stewart) office building was sold last week.
4. Have the (Perry) decided to move their factory equipment to Idaho?
5. The principal item of exchange after Christmas is (men) ties.
6. Do you think that the (Fritz) should be accorded credit privileges?
7. We are so proud of our drum (corps) performance in the competition.
8. How many (cupful) of coffee do you drink at lunch?
9. We are sorry that we cannot give you a three (month) extension of credit.
10. Mr. McKenna shot two (moose) while on his hunting trip.
11. The sale will be held at (Harvey & Manning) store.
12. We went for a ride in the (Jones) new sports car.
13. Mr. Williams gave his three (son-in-law) stocks for Christmas.
14. Several (passerby) stopped to look in the window.
15. The store manager spent the day listening to (customer) complaints.

Spelling Pitfalls   This paragraph contains some of the words most frequently misspelled in business writing. Test your own spelling ability by making any needed corrections.

> We consider it a privilege to recommend William Keogh for the position of administrator of your hospital. Mr. Keogh has just completed his ninth year with us, and we believe that our growth and development during those years are due largely to his brilliance and hard work. Although we will find him difficult to replace, we realize that our operation is too small to challenge a man of his capabilities. Any institution or firm lucky enough to obtain William Keogh's services is to be congratulated.

Case Problem

A Compounded Error   Dorothy Cary typed a stencil, proofread it quickly, and ran off a thousand copies. Then Dorothy spotted it—a misspelled word on each of the thousand copies. This material should not be mailed, should it? But what about all the paper and time lost?

1. Should Dorothy say anything about the error or let the material be sent without mentioning it?
2. If she decides to say something, what should she say to her boss?

Planning for Effective Writing

If you were a member of a business administration seminar on the principles of successful business operation, you would expect that planning and organizing would certainly be discussed. You would be right, because the success of any venture, business or personal, depends in large measure on planning and organizing know-how.

Written communications are a large and very important phase of business operations. Every year, business correspondents write the equivalent of 300 letters for every man, woman, and child in the United States and Canada. This figure does not include the millions of direct-mail advertising pieces, nor does it include the millions of internal memorandums and reports that are written daily.

Logically, then, in your role as a business writer, you can expect to promote the success of your employer's operations—and your own personal advancement, too—by acquiring the planning and organizing skills upon which success is greatly predicated. The purpose of this section of your textbook is to equip you with these skills.

THE MECHANICS OF PLANNING

Writing business communications is not a "soft" job that involves merely sitting down and dashing off a few words. Before the expert does any writing at all, he gets organized. He knows *why* he is writing, *what* he is going to say, and *how* he can make his writing most effective.

Determining Your Purpose

If you didn't have a reason for writing, you wouldn't write. Therefore, every letter you write must have a purpose; and before you consider anything else, you must ask yourself, "Why am I writing this letter?" The experienced writer can mentally identify his purpose, but the beginner should jot it down so that he can keep it before him as he develops his course of action. For instance, he might make notations such as the following:

> Get credit information from Dunn about Dart, Inc.
> Ask for bid on 500 reams of duplicating paper.
> Allow 30 days' credit, instead of the 90 requested.
> Answer inquiry about our Executive line of office furniture.
> Refuse Grossman extra credit.
> Request quote on 2,000 tons of ¾-inch tubular stock.

Assembling the Information

Once you have defined the purpose of your letter, the next step is to assemble the facts and information that will enable you to write a letter that is clear, correct, and complete. Omitting this step in the letter-planning process will necessitate exchanging additional letters for clarification, an unnecessary expense that will cost your company money and that will dim your prestige as a writer.

As an illustration, suppose you are writing to ask for a bid on 500 reams of duplicating paper. This type of communication is generally considered routine and would probably be assigned to a beginning writer. You write the following:

> Please quote us your best price on 500 reams of duplicating paper.

Can you see that the manufacturer needs much more information before he can quote a price? And can you also see that there is no business letter that can be called "simple" or "routine"?

Therefore, to be sure that your letter will be clear, correct, and complete, you should jot down the points you wish to make, possibly like this:

> Request bid   (1)
> Ask for prompt reply   (6)
> Delivery to be staggered—100 reams each month for 5 months (5)
> Specify that paper is for *ink* duplicator (Ink duplicators take rough-finish, absorbent paper; liquid duplicators use paper with a high gloss.)   (2)
> 20-lb. weight   (4)
> 8½"x11" size   (3)

Orderly Presentation The above notations cover the information you need, but you jotted them down as they occurred to you. If you were to write the letter in the order in which you made the notes, you would have a mishmash of a message.

Consequently, the final step in the assembling-information procedure is to number the notes to indicate the order in which the information is to be presented. This step is illustrated by the numbers 1 to 6 placed after the items listed on page 246.

The expert letter writer needs only to jot down key words: "request bid, ink duplicator, 8½"x11", 20 lb., staggered delivery, prompt reply." This expert, however, was once a beginner; and he became "expert" by his careful, thorough performance at the start of his career.

Visiting by Mail

You now know *why* you are writing and *what* you will say, but *how* you say it depends on planning and organizing the material so that the communication flows smoothly from start to finish. To insure a smooth flow, a writer must work from an outline.

There is, however, no need to outline separately every letter you write, because you can form a broad, ready-made outline by comparing a letter to a visit by mail. If you were to call on your reader in person, your procedure would be as follows:

1. Greeting ("Good morning, Mr. Gray.")
2. Purpose of the call ("Mr. Robie asked me to drop in and talk with you about . . . .")
3. Business of the call (whatever you are there to talk about)
4. Leave-taking ("Good-bye, Mr. Gray, and thank you for giving me your time.")

This procedure is the outline for a personal call. Let's see how it could also be the outline for a call by mail.

Greeting   The salutation is the greeting part of a letter. If the letter is written to an individual, the salutation should be *Dear Mr. (or Mrs.) Baker,* not the cold *Dear Sir* (or *Madam*). *Gentlemen* is the salutation used in a letter to a company.

Purpose of the Call   In a personal visit, the greeting is followed by a statement of the purpose of the call. Similarly, the opening paragraph of a letter tells the reader what will be discussed in the body of the letter. Here are three examples of opening paragraphs that state the purpose of the call.

> We were pleased to learn from your letter of June 18 that you are interested in knowing more about our Executive line of office furniture.
>
> We think there must be some misunderstanding about terms quoted for our Order 867, placed on July 6.
>
> We are considering the purchase of a building that could be used as a warehouse, and we would like information about your listings.

Business of the Call   This is the "meat" of your call, the place for your message. For instance, if you were writing that letter ordering 500 reams of duplicating paper, here is where you would make the orderly presentation of the notes you jotted down.

Leave-Taking   A letter may sometimes have a final paragraph that is a part of the leave-taking. Consider the examples on page 248.

We know that, as usual, you will ship promptly.

Thank you for giving us an opportunity to explain the apparent discrepancy in your May 31 statement.

We are looking forward to filling many more of your orders.

If you plan to use such a final paragraph, there are two pitfalls that you must avoid. First, never use a participial closing, an *ing* expression, such as *Wishing you the best of luck in your new venture, we are* or *Looking forward to seeing you at the conference, I am*. This construction went out with high-button shoes, and today we write *We wish you the best of luck in your new venture* or *I am looking forward to seeing you at the conference*. Second, never "thank in advance." Offering thanks before a person has assisted you is silly and presumptuous. Express gratitude in a final paragraph only when the reader has already rendered a service.

In all letters, the complimentary closing is the real leave-taking and is the writer's last chance to set the tone of his communication. The choice ranges from the cold closing *Very truly yours* to the warm closing *Yours cordially*. An incongruous closing can create the wrong impression, as shown in the following examples:

Unless we receive your check by March 15, we will turn your account over to a collection agency.

Cordially yours,

We are looking forward with much pleasure to having you and Mrs. Cole with us at our anniversary banquet.

Very truly yours,

IMPLEMENTING THE MECHANICS

Mastery of the mechanics of planning is necessary for effective business writing; however, if we stopped there, our letters would be routine, dull, and ineffective. Additional training is needed to implement these mechanics; consequently, you must learn the special skills presented in the following discussion.

Atmosphere Effect

All of us have met someone for the first time and have immediately thought, "I'll bet he's smart" or, on the other hand, "What a dope!" If asked to state the reasons for our judgment, we probably wouldn't be able to come up with anything that made much sense. Further acquaintance might change or confirm our first thought, but once again we'd be hard put to it to explain why. In such cases we are unable to explain our reaction because, in a sense, our opinions come out of the air; that is, from the air surrounding the person. This aura that projects impressions is sometimes called the "atmosphere effect."

Now let's see how we can apply our knowledge of atmosphere effect to business writing, so that our readers will think, "I'd like to do business (or I like doing business) with this company."

First Impression The first wavelength that reaches a reader as he opens a letter is "a quality firm," "a very ordinary company," or even "a shoddy operation." To create a desirable atmosphere effect, the stationery must be of good quality, the letterhead design attractive, the typing imprint uniform, the right-hand margin even, and the erasures not discernible.

Further Acquaintance   Additional wavelengths that will affect reader opinion arrive as the recipient reads the letter. Therefore, correct and polished grammar, spelling, punctuation, word usage—all these are needed to solidify the "quality firm" impression flashed at first glance. Outdated wording like *attached hereto, the writer, under separate cover* must be avoided; otherwise, the atmosphere effect would be that of a fuddy-duddy and unprogressive business operation.

Paragraph Length   Paragraph length is a key factor in creating the first impression. However, the length of paragraphs in a letter is so important to atmosphere effect that it merits special treatment.

A fact that must be kept in mind as you plan your letter is that reading is *hard work* and, human nature being what it is, almost everyone fights shy of hard work. When a reader opens your letter and sees a densely packed page, he will probably say to himself, "What a job to wade through this!"

But if you are a trained writer, your readers won't have to wade through the communications you write. Your paragraphs should not exceed eight lines. Writing more than eight lines will not be necessary if, after you have written five or six lines, you are alert to a shift in thought that would justify starting a new paragraph.

An added advantage you have is a command of the transitional words and phrases presented in Section 33. These expressions enable you to carry your reader smoothly from sentence to sentence and from paragraph to paragraph. For instance, where would you "break" the following overlong paragraph and how would you edit it for smoothness?

> We are sorry to hear that you have had some difficulty with the heating system we installed for you in July. We are glad that you took the time to tell us your story. You know that we guarantee our work for one year; but you may not know how eager we are to see that you get maximum comfort and satisfaction from your new heating system. You may not know that sometimes a newly installed heating system needs a minor adjustment. Our heating engineer, Mr. John J. Nolan, will call at your house at 9 a.m. on Monday, October 3. He will very quickly make the minor adjustment your heating system evidently needs.

Although there are various editing possibilities for this paragraph, your revision might very well go like this:

> We are sorry to hear that you have had some difficulty with the heating system we installed for you in July. However, we are glad that you took the time to tell us your story.
>
> You know, of course, that we guarantee our work for one year; but you may not know how eager we are to see that you get maximum comfort and satisfaction from your new heating system. Also, you may not know that sometimes a newly installed heating system requires a minor adjustment.
>
> Our heating engineer, Mr. John J. Nolan, will call at your house at 9 a.m. on Monday, October 3. He will very quickly make the minor adjustment your new heater evidently needs.

Now that you know why you should not write long paragraphs, be careful lest the pendulum swing so far over that your letters are full of short, choppy paragraphs, like the following:

> We'd like your best price on 500 reams of paper for ink duplicating.
>
> The size is 8½"x11". The weight is 20 lb.
>
> Delivery is to be staggered as follows: 100 reams on the first of each month for five consecutive months.
>
> We must have your bid by Friday, July 9.

Unquestionably, this writer kept his paragraphs short; in fact, they are so short that he gave his reader quite a bumpy ride. With minor changes, he could have written the letter as follows:

> Please quote us your best price on 500 reams of paper for *ink* duplicating—size, 8½"x11"; weight, 20 lb.
>
> Because of a storage problem, delivery must be staggered as follows: 100 reams on the first of each month for five consecutive months.
>
> We would appreciate receiving your bid by Friday, July 9.

Facilitating Action

Would you agree that most of us have a tendency to do immediately the tasks that are easy and to put off those that will take time and effort? Undoubtedly you would answer "Yes." And you would also agree that making it easy for a person to act will increase your chances of getting a favorable and prompt response. Here are some devices for facilitating action that will enable you to get better and quicker results from your letters.

Courtesy Carbon A courtesy carbon is a duplicate that is sent with the original copy of a letter. This device is effective when the subject of a letter is such that the reader can reply by writing his answers in the margin of the carbon. The reason for its effectiveness is that the reader is relieved of the chore of planning and composing a reply.

For example, suppose you are president of the Chamber of Commerce and are writing to give one of your colleagues a choice of dates for the annual meeting and to ask him to recommend a speaker for that meeting. If you send him a courtesy carbon, he can answer your letter by writing in the margin *January 21* and *Dr. Crouch, superintendent of schools.* What do you think are the odds that you will get a quick answer?

When you assemble information for a letter that will be accompanied by a courtesy carbon, one of your notes should be *Call attention to courtesy carbon.* When you are composing that letter, be sure that you convey to the reader the no-work-involved idea. For example, say something like this:

> Just jot your comments in the margin of the enclosed carbon and drop it into the mail.

Enclosed Card or Return Slip Another method of obtaining a favorable and quick response is to enclose a card or return slip with the letter. Suppose your firm, Universal Products, is planning a drive for new customers. A mailing list has been purchased; all high-level decisions have been made; and you are writing the promotional material that offers each reader a free copy of the latest edition of your special-discount catalog. You know that a self-addressed return card will be enclosed and that the company will pay for the postage.

The psychological motivation for your letter will be financial gain—making money by saving money—and the spur to action will be a final paragraph such as this:

> You will start to save money just as soon as you fill out and return the enclosed card. No postage is necessary.

Preparing copy for the return card is also part of your job, and even here you can promote action by your choice of words; for example, *money-saving,* rather than *special discount.*

Universal Products
147 State Street
Bath, Maine   04530

Gentlemen:

Please send the latest edition of your money-saving catalog to:

Name _____

Street _____

City   State   Zip

Attached Perforated Form   Still another means of facilitating action is to use a perforated return form that can be detached from the letter. For some letters, this method will be just as effective as a separately enclosed slip.

When you write this type of letter, be sure to include a paragraph that calls attention to the form; for instance:

> To renew your subscription—and to receive a bonus of six free issues!—fill in the form at the bottom of this page, tear it off, and and mail it *today.*

Watch That If!   Whenever a person is given a choice of doing or not doing, he will very probably choose not to do. Therefore, never give your reader a choice of acting or not acting. Always assume confidently that he will act—and act favorably.

If is the word that indicates a choice; and *if* is the word to watch. Perhaps we can best illustrate this bit of psychology by rewording the last two examples.

> If you would like to receive the latest edition of our money-saving catalog, just fill out and return the enclosed card. No postage is necessary.
>
> If you wish to renew your subscription—and win the bonus of six free issues!—fill in the form at the bottom of this page, tear it off, and mail it *today.*

The *if* in each of these examples hinted that the reader might *not* like to receive or wish to renew—and the chances are that he will go along with the *not*.

Rereading Your Letters

Many employees remain at the bottom of the salary heap because they do not put an extra lick of polish on the work they do. There is no future for a person whose philosophy is, "Aw, that's good enough."

A business writer's extra lick of polish is the final check of his communications. After he finishes his letter-writing stint for the day, he should reread the letters as if they were communications he has received, not letters he has written. From this fresh and different viewpoint, he should be able to spot any errors he has made or any poor psychology he may have used. And, although he may regret the additional time and effort involved in making a final check, his intelligence tells him that only by so doing can he turn out a top-notch job.

COMMUNICATION PROJECTS

Practical Application

A You are replying to a letter that asks whether your store carries Thirsty towels in the 24-by-26-inch size, and you have made the following notes. Number them to indicate the order in which the information should be presented to the customer.

> Price—$1.49 each, two for $2.75, six for $7.92
> Mention color choice
> Yes, we do sell the 24"-x-26" Thirsty
> Will give fast delivery
> Facilitating action: Tell her to write her order on reverse side of this letter.

B Using notes you have just arranged, write the letter.

C You have been assigned to write a form letter to be sent to cash customers to induce them to open charge accounts. Using the following properly arranged notes, write the letter.

> Invitation to open charge account
> List advantages:
>   a. Need not carry large sums of money
>   b. Merchandise needed now can be purchased now—no waiting
>   c. No red tape or delay on exchanges or adjustments
>   d. Will get personal attention
> Friend-making final paragraph

D Choose two business situations in which the use of a courtesy carbon would be an effective device for facilitating action on a letter. Give reasons for your choices. Also, discuss two situations in which an enclosed card would promote action.

Editing Practice

Editing for Redundancies   Edit and rewrite the sentences on page 253, and eliminate all unnecessary repetitions.

1. Perishables depreciate in value very quickly.
2. We are glad to hear of the final completion of Order 845.
3. Payment of bills within ten days is the customary practice of our firm.
4. My boss rarely ever travels by air.
5. I do not remember of telling Bill to file the letter under *state of.*
6. Please bring with you notebook, pen, eraser, and etc.
7. Before it can be cashed, every check must be endorsed on the back.
8. Bruce may perhaps be able to solve your communication problem.

Making the Headlines   You work for the editor of a daily newspaper, and you are responsible for writing and revising headlines. How would you rewrite the following?

STUDENTS REEK HAVOC AT GAME

OPERATION ON TRAIN SAVES MAN'S LIFE

Case Problem

A Personal Matter   Roberta Greene is busy typing a report for her supervisor when she receives a telephone call from her friend, Ruth Evans. Ruth wishes to find out about a dance that is being planned by their sorority. Roberta knows that Ruth is on her first job and may not realize that personal calls during office hours are not looked on with favor by management.

1. What should Roberta say to Ruth?
2. Why are personal calls usually taboo during office hours?

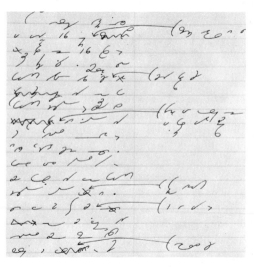

Writing
Business Letters

Business Letter Style

If you were a secretary and if you heard that your boss said you had style, would you be pleased? Yes, you would. And you would think he meant that you were always fashionably and tastefully dressed for work in an office. But he may have been paying you a bigger compliment; he may have meant that he was impressed with the way you do your job, as well as with your excellent appearance.

In other words, *style* can refer to performance, as well as to appearance. For instance, think of driving style. Think of the driver who operates in such a manner that his riders are constantly pushing their feet against non-existent brakes, a behind-the-wheel style that causes his friends to avoid riding with him. On the other hand, consider the topnotch receptionist who makes many friends for her company because she has cultivated a friendly, considerate, and gracious style of greeting customers. A person's style, both appearance- and performance-wise, can mark him for success or failure. In the same way, a business writer is successful to the degree to which he has mastered—and to the degree to which he applies—the principles of polished and effective business letter style.

Dean Swift, author of *Gulliver's Travels*, once said, "Proper words in proper places make the true definition of style." Today, more than two hundred years later, his words continue to stand as a general guide to effective writing style.

The business writer, however, must be concerned with style as it relates both to appearance and to performance. He must study mechanics and format so that the setting for his letters will have the stamp of "class" that will favorably dispose a reader to the message of the letter and to the company that sends the letter. These principles, as well as those of good writing style, are presented in this section of your textbook. To make the most of your ability, study these principles well.

PROPER WORDS

Words are the tools of a writer's trade, the implements with which he fashions the letters he writes. To become a master craftsman, a writer must have the right tools for each job he does and must be sure that they are the best in quality and the latest in design.

Your vocabulary study has prepared you for selecting correct words, as well as for distinguishing between words whose meanings are frequently confused. But the use of word tools that are proper for business writing requires special training if those tools are to be the best in quality and the latest in design. You must learn to use modern words, to eliminate unnecessary words, to express yourself simply and plainly, and to avoid business jargon. These steps are essential to effective writing.

Use Modern Expressions

Expressions, like fashions, change. Few men today would wear a celluloid collar; few women, high-buttoned shoes. In letter writing, fashions change, too. Some expressions are just as old-fashioned as celluloid collars and high-buttoned shoes, but many people continue to use them in business letters. Make sure that you know the expressions that are out of date so that you can avoid them; but also make sure that you know and use modern expressions in your letters.

this is to acknowledge
thanking you in advance
hereby insist

Use	*Do Not Use*
say, tell, let us know	advise
now, at present	at this time, at the present time, at the present writing
as, because, since	due to the fact that
letter	favor
regarding, concerning	in re
if, in case	in the event that
please	kindly
a specific word	same

contents duly noted
concerning yours
of....

according to our records
anticipating your reply
at your convenience
no "beg to's"

Eliminate Redundancy

Redundancy in writing or in speech results from using words that are unnecessarily repetitious; for instance, using *free gratis* for *gratis.* Since *gratis* means "free," *free gratis* means "free free." The following list includes some common redundancies that should be avoided.

Use	*Do Not Use*	*Use*	*Do Not Use*
about	*at* about	converted	converted *over*
above	*up* above	enter	enter *into*
alike	*both* alike	experience	*past* experience
beginner	*new* beginner	identical	*same* identical
check	check *into*	practice	*customary* practice
cooperate	cooperate *together*	otherwise	*as* otherwise
connect	connect *up*	repeat	repeat *again*
continue	continue *on*	together	*both* together

Use Plain, Simple Words

The purpose of a business letter is to convey a clear, easily understood message; but this purpose cannot be achieved by a writer who insists on parading his extensive vocabulary. The proper words for business writing are plain, simple words that will be intelligible to any reader, regardless of his educational background.

As an illustration, suppose that John Keane has applied for a position with your company and has given you several employment references. One of Mr. Keane's references says the following:

> In all fairness, we think we should tell you that Mr. Keane is a cunctator.

Would you know what was meant, particularly if you didn't have a dictionary handy? A writer who was less of a vocabulary "show off" might write the sentence thus:

> In all fairness, we think we should tell you that Mr. Keane is a procrastinator.

The chances are that you would understand this statement. But why take chances when plain, simple words would insure the clarity of the message? You wouldn't need a dictionary or any other help to understand the following sentence:

> In all fairness, we think we should tell you that Mr. Keane habitually fails to get his work done on time.

Avoid Jargon

Most trades develop a technical vocabulary that is likely to be unintelligible to anyone outside the trade. This vocabulary is called *jargon*. You should learn and use the special words of your trade, but remember that jargon is COIK (Clear Only If Known). For example, if you are writing to a shoe store manager about *findings*, he'll know that you mean the merchandise other than shoes in his store, such as polish, shoelaces, hosiery, and accessories. This jargon is understandable to him. However, the same manager could talk all day to his customers about their buying *findings* without selling any. Why? The term is COIK—Clear Only If Known.

Related to jargon are the numerous words coined by writers and speakers. These invented terms often creep into the letter writer's vocabulary and, like any habit, are repeated monotonously. For instance, the accountant afflicted with this habit may write the following:

> *Accountingwise*, Xceedo sales have not strengthened our position *profitwise*. If you will finalize a price increase, favorable advances will be realized *marketwise*.

Use jargon and self-coined expressions with caution, for they are COIK. Select a mode of expression that is fresh and simple—words and phrases that will be understood by your reader, the plain words discussed earlier in this section.

WRITING SKILL

Every writer must use proper words, but the business writer must combine those proper words in such a way that he will make friends and, at the same time, will facilitate action. The effective business letter should be concise, clear, cohesive, and complete.

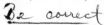

Be Concise

A concise style of writing implies brevity—but do not confuse brevity with curtness or abruptness! Compactness suggests brevity, the use of enough words to say what you wish to say without being rude. Concise wording is always appreciated in business because it saves time; and in business, time is money.

The main enemy of conciseness is repetition. For instance, note how needlessly wordy these sentences are:

> In your letter of November 12, you ask for an extension of 30 days to pay your account. In compliance with this request, we are happy to announce that your request to extend the due date 30 days has been granted.

Do not repeat anything that reader already knows.

The reader already knows the nature of his request. If he doesn't, he'll remember it from what is said in the sentence that follows the repeated information. However, the sentence that follows is too wordy. The following examples eliminate the repetition and express the same thought much more effectively.

> The due date of your balance has been extended 30 days. Or: We have extended your due date 30 days.

Another enemy of conciseness is irrelevancy. For instance, note how much of the following is irrelevant to the subject of the letter.

> One of our best customers got pretty annoyed today because we didn't have any water chestnuts in stock. Usually we do, but my partner thought I had ordered them, and I thought that he had.
> Now I would like to order two cases of water chestnuts. And from now on, I will do the ordering . . .

At times, whole paragraphs can be eliminated without destroying any pertinent information. Be sure that whatever you include in your letters is relevant to your purpose.

Be Clear

A clear style is a vivid, unambiguous manner of writing. Tell the reader what he wants to know in specific, not general, terms. A skilled business letter writer would never be guilty of making an obscure statement like the following example:

> We have many satisfied customers of our tools, and they have found that they seldom need repairs but when they do they service them quickly.

Equally as bad as the ambiguity in the example above is the running together of ideas. *Avoid* Short sentences tend to be clearer than long, involved ones. See how much clearer the message is when it is written as two precise sentences.

> Thousands of satisfied customers use Exmore tools. These customers are satisfied because seldom, if ever, do Exmore tools need repair.

The revised statement is not vague, as the first is. Instead of dealing in vague generalities, a clear style deals in specifics. For example, *Your order will be shipped in the very near future* is too general a statement to be clear. *Your order will be shipped on September 12* is specific and therefore quite clear.

Be Cohesive

Cohesiveness in style refers to the way a letter holds together. In the cohesive letter, there is unity of thought—each sentence and paragraph flows smoothly into the next. The business writer should use connecting or linking words to lead his reader from one idea to another. Here are some examples of linking words.

naturally	on the other hand
however	nevertheless
thus	therefore
for instance	of course

These linking words help to hold the message together. Keep in mind, though, that clear, orderly thinking in organizing a letter, as discussed in Section 35, is the most important factor in writing a cohesive letter. Linking words simply make the logic of the letter more quickly apparent to the reader.

Be Complete

Suppose you received the following letter and nothing more.

Gentlemen:

Send us our order.

Sincerely yours,

Such a letter is almost rude in its curtness. At least, the writer could have said "please"! However, the letter is rude for another reason also: it is not complete.

A complete letter gives all pertinent information: whose order? what order? when to ship it? where to ship it? why? how? Revised to answer these questions, the complete letter would look like this:

Gentlemen:

Please refer to our Purchase Order 2515, dated June 15. Your salesman, Mr. Jackson, promised delivery of this order by July 15. If the chairs do not arrive before July 30, they will not be available for our Midsummer Bargain Day Sale.

Have the chairs been shipped? If not, could they be sent by truck instead of by freight? Please let us know immediately by wire.

Sincerely yours,

APPEARANCE

In Section 35 you learned about atmosphere, the appearance factor that influences opinions. You should apply your knowledge of the atmosphere effect to the format of business letters in order to create and solidify the impression that your company is a fine firm with which to do business. Correct business-letter mechanics and format are presented in the discussion below and on pages 262-272.

The physical appearance of a letter is determined by the mechanics of placing the letter on the page. The picture that results from looking at the format, or form, should be designed to create a pleasing impression. Often the format of the letter is the first image that a reader receives of your company.

Thus, an attractive letterhead that is printed on good quality paper, a message that is proportioned to provide balanced margins, and a form that is pleasing to the eye cause the reader to anticipate your letter with pleasure. Sloppy letters, like sloppy people, cause the reader to draw away.

White Space The symmetry of a well-placed letter is inviting to the reader. A letter placed too high, too low, or too far to either side upsets the balance of white space that frames the picture, or message. All letters, however long they are, should have a generous margin of white space on all sides.

Typewriting Quality Whatever the choice of letterhead, letter format, or punctuation style, a letter can please the eye only if it has been attractively typed. The quality of the typescript is governed by three factors: the evenness of touch, the typewriter ribbon, and the neatness of erasures. An even touch will produce typescript of even density—not a sprinkling of light and dark letters across the page. A well-adjusted electric typewriter guarantees consistent density of typescript, since each key strikes the paper with the same force, regardless of how much or how little pressure is used by the typist. The type keys should be cleaned regularly to prevent dust-and-ink-clogged letters from marring the appearance of the typescript.

A good-quality ribbon should be used, one that is suited to the kind of typewriter—standard or portable, manual or electric. When the ribbon has been used so frequently that there is not sufficient ink to produce clear typescript, the ribbon should be replaced. Ribbons come in a variety of colors, but black is the color most frequently used. With tinted stationery, however, a colored ribbon of the same hue might be more attractive. For example, a florist who uses light-green stationery might prefer to use a dark-green ribbon.

Of course, erasures should be kept to a minimum, and if there are noticeable erasures, the letter should be retyped. Some erasures are usually necessary, but these should be made so neatly that they are not noticeable. Good erasing tools are as essential to the typist as a good set of carpentry or plumbing tools is to the carpenter or the plumber. A good typing eraser and a typing shield that will prevent the smudging of adjacent letters help to make the erasing process easier.

The Letterhead

Most letterheads are printed. Some examples of well-designed, printed letter-heads are shown on the next page. The selection of size, shape, and quality of paper as well as the selection of the letterhead design should be made with the advice of stationers, printers, or advertising agencies. In seeking this advice, consider the following points:

- Quality stationery gives the impression that the firm attaches importance to its letters; inferior stationery endangers prestige.
- While the usual size of letterheads is 8½ by 11 inches, special sizes are used to create special impressions. For example, physicians, lawyers, and other professional people often select the smaller, baronial (5½ by 8½ inches) stationery because it is more prestigious than the larger size.
- Tinted paper is sometimes selected for special effects. A garden shop may, for instance, select green paper.
- Businessmen believe in the power of a picture—"a picture is worth ten thousand words." Increasingly, art work and photography are used in let-terheads, especially in promotional letters. Of course, second pages of letters should be of the same quality, size, and color as the letterhead, but they should be blank, without any printing. Information copies or file copies are usually typed on onionskin paper.

The Envelope

Business envelopes are usually printed with a return address designed to echo the letterhead being used. <u>It is essential that the information contained in the envelope address be identical with that in the inside address.</u> The fol-lowing guidelines, illustrated in the envelope below, should always be ob-served:

- As a general guide, begin the mailing address approximately halfway across the envelope (about 4 inches from the left edge for a regular-size—No. 10 —business envelope). The blocked style, single-spaced, is preferred by the Post Office Department.
- Always include the ZIP Code number. Leave three spaces between the state and the ZIP Code number. In two cases, however, the number may

```
BUSINESS EDUCATION WORLD
330 West 42 Street, New York, N.Y. 10036



Please Forward
                                                                AIRMAIL



                        Mr. Henry Schubarton
                        1300 Remington Boulevard
                        Indianapolis, Indiana    46227
```

Massachusetts General Hospital
32 FRUIT STREET
BOSTON, MASSACHUSETTS 02114
895-3240

GENERAL ELECTRIC
COMPANY

570 LEXINGTON AVENUE, NEW YORK, N. Y. 10022 · · · TELEPHONE Plaza 1-1311

MARKETING and

PUBLIC AFFAIRS

8/teen
COSMETICS, INC.   510 Avenue of the Americas · New York, N.Y. 10011 · Telephone 255-2212

Cecilia PRODUCTS LTD. · 510 AVENUE of the AMERICAS · NEW YORK, N.Y. 10011 · TELEPHONE 255-2860

EXECUTIVE OFFICES

Olde Carriage Inn
TELEPHONE
753-3410

450 Post Road, James, Maine 15919, 617-984-0303

Elizabeth Arden
SALES CORPORATION
3 EAST 54TH STREET · NEW YORK 10022

CABLE ADDRESS: ELIZARDEN
CODES: A.B.C. 6TH BENTLEY'S

EASTERN AIR LINES INCORPORATED / 10 ROCKEFELLER PLAZA / NEW YORK, NEW YORK 10020 / 212-986-4500

 **EASTERN**

joseph reiss marketing inc.   510 avenue of the americas • new york 10011 • tel. 255-2212

Children's Hospital
3700 CALIFORNIA STREET
SAN FRANCISCO, CALIFORNIA   94118
441-8200

**Cincinnati
General
Hospital**
3231 Burnett Avenue
Cincinnati, Ohio   45229
NORMANDY 9-8000

BUNKER HILL HOSPITAL
300 Rutherford Avenue
Charlestown, Massachusetts 01339

 CUTLER • HAMMER
CONTROL
MILWAUKEE, WISCONSIN

EXECUTIVE OFFICES
4201 N. 27TH STREET
MILWAUKEE, WIS. 53216
PHONE: 414-442-7800

Courtesy of the organizations above

PARTS OF A TYPICAL BUSINESS LETTER

□ UNITED PRODUCTS CORPORATION

(1)
500 Madison Avenue   New York, New York   10022

(2)
March 16, 19--

(3)
Advertising Displays, Inc.
154 West 57th Street
New York, New York   10019

(4) ATTENTION MR. JAMES CARPENTER

(5) Gentlemen

(6) Subject: Filing Cabinets

Thank you for your inquiry regarding metal filing cabinets for your new offices. We have recently added several new models to our extensive line, so that you have a wide choice of styles available to fill your needs.

(7)
Our latest catalog in color is enclosed. To help you in selecting the models best suited to your business, we have checked several designs that have proved most popular with other display firms. Complete details regarding sizes, colors, and various individual features accompany each photograph. You will note that we also carry large stocks of office furniture, equipment, and supplies.

We look forward to hearing from you and hope you won't hesitate to call on us for any further information you may need. A reply card is enclosed for your convenience.

(8)
Cordially yours

(9)
UNITED PRODUCTS CORPORATION

Joseph Pellegrini
(10)
Joseph Pellegrini
General Manager

(11) JP/br
Enclosures
(12)   Catalog
Reply card
(13) cc Mr. Walter Grimes

1 Printed Letterhead	8 Complimentary Closing
2 Date Line	9 Company Signature
3 Inside Address	10 Signer's Identification
4 Attention Line	11 Reference Symbols
5 Salutation	12 Enclosure Reminder
6 Subject Line	13 "cc" Notation
7 Body	

a

Zip Code be typed on a separate line—to avoid a two-line address or to avoid an over-long final line in the address.

Mr. William Anson
Beaver, Idaho
83803

Miss Ann Rey
14 First Street
New York, New York
10009

- On-arrival directions (*Please Forward, Confidential,* and so on) should be typed about four lines below the return address.
- If special mailing services are required, such as *Special Delivery* or *Air Mail,* indicate the service below the stamp.
- The Post Office Department prefers that no information be placed below the ZIP Code number.

Punctuation Styles

There are three commonly used punctuation styles for business letters, as listed below:

1. Open
2. Standard (also called "Mixed")
3. Closed

It is important to remember that the punctuation of the *message* is the same, regardless of which style is used for the other letter parts.

Open Punctuation Style   This style, shown on page 266, requires that no punctuation be used after any part of the letter except the message. Open punctuation is frequently used with full-blocked arrangements, as both styles are considered time-savers for the typist.

Standard Punctuation Style   In the standard punctuation style, only the salutation and the complimentary closing are followed by a mark of punctuation. The salutation is followed by a colon, and the complimentary closing is followed by a comma. The standard style, which is the most commonly used one, is shown on page 268.

Closed Punctuation Style   The closed punctuation style requires that a punctuation mark appear at the end of every line of every part of the letter —except the message. This style is perhaps the least used of the three.

Letter Arrangement Styles

You may select from among six commonly used styles of letter arrangement. There is no standard by which the appropriateness or inappropriateness of a specific style can be firmly established. However, some companies adopt one particular arrangement, and in such instances, as an employee, you would be expected to conform. In all other situations—as in selecting clothing, for example—it is up to the writer to make an appropriate choice from the letter styles discussed and illustrated in the following pages.

Full-Blocked

VIGOROUS, AGGRESSIVE

Letter Style   **With a subject line and open punctuation**

March 6, 19--

Mr. Roger S. Patterson
Western Life Company
2867 East Fourth Street
Cincinnati, Ohio   45202

Dear Mr. Patterson

Subject: Form of a Full-Blocked Letter

This letter is set up in the full-blocked style, in
which every line begins at the left margin. A few
companies modify it by moving the date to the right,
but most firms use it as shown here. Because this
style is the fastest to type, it is considered very
modern. It is natural, although not necessary, to
use "open" punctuation with this style of letter.

This letter also illustrates one arrangement of the
subject line, which may be used with any style of
letter. Like an attention line, a subject line may
be typed with underscores or capitals. In a full-
blocked letter, it must be blocked; in other letter
styles, it may be blocked or centered. It always
appears after the salutation and before the body,
for it is considered a part of the body.

Legal firms and the legal departments of companies
sometimes prefer to use the Latin terms Re or In Re
instead of the English word Subject.

Yours very sincerely

Mary Ellen Smith
Mary Ellen Smith
Reference Department

urs

The arrangement of a letter depends upon the horizontal placement of the various letter parts. The vertical sequence in which the parts are positioned, as illustrated on page 264, is fixed in a logical pattern that is normally not altered to suit individual tastes.

Full-Blocked Letters   In the full-blocked arrangement style, letters are written with all the parts beginning at the left margin. This style, which is illustrated above, saves typing time because the typist does not have to use the tabulator in setting up the letter. Frequently, open punctuation (see page 265) is used with the full-blocked style.

Simplified
THE EFFICIENCY EXPERT'S
Letter Style **With open punctuation and full-blocked design**

March 6, 19--

Mr. Richard W. Parker, Jr.
Humphrey Lumber Company
520 Southwest Park Avenue
Portland, Oregon 97208

THE SIMPLIFIED LETTER

You will be interested to know, Mr. Parker, that several
years ago the Administrative Management Society (formerly
NOMA) designed a new letter form called the "Simplified
Letter." This is a sample.

1 It uses the full-blocked form and "open" punctuation.

2 It contains no salutation or closing. (AMS believes
such expressions to be meaningless.)

3 It displays a subject line in all capitals, both preceded and followed by two blank lines. Note that the
word "Subject" is omitted.

4 It identifies the signer by an all-capitals line that is
preceded by at least four blank lines and followed by
one--if further notations are used.

5 It seeks to maintain a brisk but friendly tone, partly
by using the addressee's name at least in the first
sentence.

Perhaps, Mr. Parker, as some say, this form does not really
look like a business letter; but its efficiency suggests
that this style is worth a trial, especially where output
must be increased.

Ralph E. Jones
RALPH E. JONES, TRAINING CONSULTANT

Simplified Letters The Administrative Management Society has developed and advocates the use of the simplified letter style shown above. The arrangement of the simplified letter is the same as the full-blocked style. However, the simplified letter is different in the following ways:

1. The salutation and the complimentary closing are eliminated.
2. The subject line, which is standard in the simplified style, and the writer's identification line are always typed entirely in capital letters.
3. Listings in the message are indented five spaces, except when the items in the listing are numbered or lettered. When the items are identified by

Blocked

THE MOST FLEXIBLE

Letter Style   **With foreign address, quotation, and postscript**

March 10, 19—

REGISTERED

Mr. Philippe Vargos, Gerente
El Aguila, S. A.
1242 Avenida Insurgentes
Mexico D. F.
MEXICO

Dear Mr. Vargos:

It is current practice in American business letters
to display price quotations and similar special data
in a special paragraph, like this:

> The paragraph is indented five spaces on
> both sides and is preceded and followed
> by one ordinary blank linespace.
>
> If it is necessary to use more paragraphs
> for the quotation, then a standard single
> blank line is left between paragraphs.

We indicate the mail service (a double space below
the date) only if we are sending the correspondence
by some special service, such as "special delivery"
or "registered"; and we do so only to get the fact
indicated on our file copy of the correspondence.

Yours very sincerely,

David J. Collins

Assistant Director
Bureau of Information
and Public Relations

DIC/urs

P. S.   We treat postscripts in the same way that we
treat other paragraphs, except that we precede each
postscript by "PS:" or "PS—" or "P. S."

---

letters or numbers, they are blocked. However, no periods are used after the numbers or letters.

The chief purpose of the simplified letter is to save time. The claim is made that the use of this style saves 10.7 percent of the time required to type a 96-word letter in some other style. However, efficiency is not the sole criterion for selecting a letter style. Many writers consider the simplified style cold and impersonal, and as a result, they prefer to use one of the traditional styles.

Semiblocked
CONSERVATIVE, EXECUTIVE
Letter Style

With attention line and cc notation

March 7, 19--

Savard, Foster & Company
171 Westminster Street
Providence, Rhode Island   02904

ATTENTION TRAINING DIRECTOR

Gentlemen:

For a letter design that is both standard
and distinctive, try this style: semiblocked (one
of the two most popular styles) with the paragraphs
indented <u>ten</u> spaces (instead of the usual five).

This letter also shows you an alternative
arrangement for the attention line: centered, in
all capitals (instead of being blocked at the left
margin and underscored). In two regards, however,
the use of the attention line here is standard: It
is accompanied, as it should be, by the salutation
"Gentlemen"; and it is typed <u>above</u> the salutation.

Worth noting also in this letter are the
following: (1) positioning the date at the margin,
as an alternative to starting it at the center; (2)
the use of "standard" punctuation, which calls for
a colon after the salutation and a comma after the
complimentary closing; and (3) the use of the "cc"
notations at the bottom to indicate to whom carbon
copies of the letter are being sent.

Yours very truly,

Elsie D. Frost
Elsie D. Frost, Director

URS
cc Miss Filene
cc Dr. Young

Blocked Letters   A letter in blocked style, as illustrated on page 268, <u>follows</u>
the format of a full-blocked letter except in the position of the dateline, complimentary closing, company signature, and writer's identification. <u>All these
parts usually</u> start at the horizontal center of the page. However, the date
may be aligned to end at the right margin, and the subject and attention
lines may be either centered or indented five or ten spaces.

Semiblocked Letters   <u>A semiblocked letter</u>, as shown above, <u>follows blocked</u>
style. However, first lines of paragraphs are indented five or ten spaces.

Indented
SPECIAL SPACE EATER
Letter Style   **With double spacing and standard punctuation**

March 8, 19--

Miss June R. Zane
    2831 Browning Avenue
        Knoxville, Tennessee   27901
Dear Miss Zane:

    The indented style is one of the few that may be typed in either single or double spacing. The double-spaced form, therefore, is convenient when you have a short letter that must be stretched.

    When you plan the placement of a double-spaced letter, you must remember that it will stretch out to twice its single-spaced length. This letter of 83 words, double spaced, occupies as much space as would a single-spaced letter of 166 words.

           Cordially yours,

           Henry L. Sullivan
           District Manager

HIS/urs
cc Chicago Office

Indented Letters   The indented letter style is perhaps the oldest letter arrangement, for it was the style principally used when all letters were handwritten. The first line of each paragraph and the second and succeeding lines of each part of the letter are indented, usually in a series of 5-space steps. As in most other letter styles, the date may be started at the center, may be centered, or may be positioned to end at the right-hand margin. This, of course, is the most time-consuming style to type because of the many paragraph and other indentions required. A letter in indented style is illustrated above.

Hanging-Indented
FOR SUPER-DISPLAY SALESMANSHIP
Letter Style   **With paragraphs and signer's name displayed**

                                        March 9, 19--

            To All the Typists Who
            Need a Way to Display
            A Special Sales Letter
            So It Looks Special

            Dear Ready-for-Rescue:

            Yes, this is a hanging-indented letter, with a key
                 word "hanging" in the margin at the start of
                 each paragraph and with other lines indented.

            Yes, this letter style takes attentive production.
                 You set a tab stop some appropriate number of
                 spaces in from the margin and indent all lines
                 except the first one in each paragraph.

            Yes, the hanging-indented style is designed solely
                 for sales promotion--this form is too cumber-
                 some for ordinary correspondence. Since the
                 whole point of the display is to feature those
                 paragraph starters, the letter has to be pre-
                 pared especially to fit this arrangement.

            Yes, indicating the signer's name in the reference
                 position, as below, instead of below the space
                 where he signs the letter, is a procedure that
                 may be used with any form of letter. It is a
                 good device to use when a signer has a signa-
                 ture he likes but which is illegible!

                      Yours very truly,

                      LETTER DISPLAY, INC.

                      Louis J. Leslie
                      Vice-President, Sales

        LTLeslie/urs

Hanging-Indented Letters   The hanging-indented style is not widely used except in advertising or sales letters, where it serves to attract the reader's attention. This style, which is illustrated above, is similar to the blocked style with this exception: the second and all other paragraph lines are indented five or ten spaces, but the first line is *not* indented.

Note: There is still another arrangement style—the "formal" or "personal" style—in which the inside address is placed at the bottom of the letter, as shown by the illustration on page 272. The inside address is typed from two to five spaces below the signature, at the left margin. No reference initials are used in this style.

Respectfully yours,

Joseph P. Warner

Dr. Leo K. Purdy
Institute of Commerce
1900 Eighth Street
Des Moines, Iowa   50308

COMMUNICATION PROJECTS

Practical Application

A Which of the letter formats on pages 266-271 would you prefer to use? Why? Write a letter to your instructor and state your preference and the reasons for your choice.

B Do you like the format of the letter on page 267? What advantages and disadvantages do you see? Would you use this form in your own business writing? Why or why not? Write a letter in the simplified letter style and answer these questions. Address the letter to your instructor.

C Modernize the following expressions.

1. Due to a change in accounting procedures . . .
2. Please advise as to what disposition you wish . . .
3. We are replacing the broken gasket and will rush same to you.
4. Thank you for your favor of April 2.
5. In re your letter of May 2, the discount . . .

D Eliminate any redundancies in these sentences.

1. I will not repeat these instructions again.
2. We will meet Mr. Stone at about three o'clock.
3. Those two new typewriters are both alike.
4. Our stock clerk stores the pencils up above the paper.
5. We are now in the process of converting over our factory to a warehouse.

E Revise these sentences, using plain, simple words.

1. No salesman should make pejorative remarks about his competitors.
2. You will undoubtedly agree that ours is a viable group.
3. Silence is tantamount to consent and agreement.
4. Your comment was perspicacious, to say the least.
5. Colloquies during working hours are to be confined to business topics.

Updating the Correspondence   Rewrite these letter excerpts, and eliminate all passé words and expressions.

1. Your favor of July 16th has crossed my desk.
2. Hoping that this meets with your approval, I am,
3. We should be grateful if you would kindly call at our office in the near future.
4. Please let us know your decision at your earliest convenience.
5. Thank you in advance for your cooperation.
6. Please advise by return mail.
7. We would suggest that you take advantage of the cash-with-order saving.
8. Enclosed please find our check for $24.
9. We received your order for two dozen hammers and are sending you the same.
10. At the present writing the merchandise you ordered is not in stock.

Analysis of Spelling Errors   Correct the spelling errors in this paragraph and, in one sentence, tell why they were made.

Because of limited storage space, we keep our inventory of office supplys to a minimum. We have only one storeroom, where boxes are stacked to the ceiling; and passageways are narrow allies barely wide enough to permit a person to slip in and out. However, please continue to send us notices of any special sales that you think would interest us.

Case Problem

Carbon Copies   In some firms it is a practice to make a carbon copy of a reply to a routine letter on the back of the letter being answered. Suggest some possible advantages and disadvantages of this procedure.

Request Letters

In order to operate efficiently, businessmen need all kinds of information and services—price lists, catalogs, specifications for raw materials and finished products, repair and maintenance services, samples of products, bids and price quotations, and so on.

Businessmen often obtain the information or services they need by writing letters of request. Typical reasons for request letters are these: (1) to reserve a hotel room or a conference room, (2) to obtain an appointment, (3) to obtain printed materials, such as catalogs, price lists, magazines, books, and reports, (4) to ask for special favors—permission to quote from copyrighted publications, permission to use a company's library or special book collection, (5) to order merchandise, (6) to ask for information missing from a letter, (7) to seek technical information about products or services.

In business, time is money, and the need to get accurate information in the least amount of time is also money. Hence millions of dollars are spent annually to find new and faster ways of producing the information needed by businesses. For example, less than a hundred years ago, requests for money owed were handled by writing letters. Today even small offices request payment by means of a printed monthly statement—either typewritten or prepared by other manual means. Increasingly, billing has become a completely mechanized procedure; high-speed computers now calculate and print each hour thousands of requests for money owed. Without new technological methods of handling information, business as we know it today could not function effectively.

In spite of great labor-saving advances, the writing of request letters is still an important business function. Why? Some businesses are less mechanized than others, and some forms of request are too infrequent to mechanize. More important, however, is the fact that mechanized requests lack the personal touch that can build good human relations and goodwill for a company.

GUIDES FOR WRITING REQUEST LETTERS

Letters of request are usually considered routine. More often than not, request letters ask for something that the reader is happy to give because he might have an opportunity to sell a product or service. As a result, some businessmen feel that they do not have to expend much effort in writing request letters. However, request letters require much planning and thought if the business writer is to accomplish his objectives. The following guidelines should be observed:

- Give complete information.
- Give accurate information.
- Be sure the request is reasonable.
- Be courteous.
- Be brief.

Note how these guidelines are followed in the request letter illustrated on page 275.

Give Complete Information

A letter of request should give the reader all the facts he will need in order to answer the writer. In general, the letter should answer the following questions: Who? What? How many? When? Where? Why? Note how the following letter answers these questions.

Gentlemen:

Please send me 50 reprints of the article "Is Automation the Big Bad Wolf?" which appeared in the February issue of Management Weekly. My check for $12.50 is enclosed.

May I have these reprints by March 14? On that date we are having the annual meeting of our branch office supervisors, and I am counting on having this material available for distribution.

Cordially yours,

```
                                        5550 Dorchester Avenue
                                        Chicago, Illinois   60613
                                        October 14, 19--


        Desert Aire Company
        333 East Superior Avenue
        Detroit, Michigan   48215

        Gentlemen:

            I am interested in the Desert Aire dehumidifier
        that you advertised in the May issue of Home Circle
        magazine.  To help me decide whether this is the
        dehumidifier I want, would you please answer the
        following questions:

            1.  What is the capacity?  That is, how much
        moisture can be removed from the air daily?  What
        is the maximum area of coverage?

            2.  What is the price?

            3.  Is the Desert Aire available locally?  If
        so, where may I obtain it?

            I would appreciate your help with these questions.

                                        Very truly yours,

                                        Claudia Gaxton
                                        Mrs. James Gaxton
```

Since letters of this type are nearly always on company letterheads, it is not necessary to include the address of the writer inside the letter. However, if the letterhead contains the addresses of several offices, or if the writer wishes the reply to be sent to a different address, he should indicate where the reply is to be sent.

The writer, of course, should allow the supplier sufficient time to handle the request by writing well in advance of his needs; it is unfair to ask for the impossible. If the writer of the above example is not sure that he has allowed enough time, he might include something like this:

> Please rush these copies to me by airmail special delivery, and bill me for the extra cost.

In the preceding example, the writer has given the reason for his request. Although it is not always necessary to do so, giving the reason will sometimes aid the reader in serving you more satisfactorily. For example, if the supplier knows that the branch office supervisors are having their annual meeting, he might recall other printed materials that would be of interest to the group. Knowing why in this case also gives the reader an incentive for rushing the materials. In the example below, the writer gives the reason why special hotel accommodations are needed, so that the hotel manager can use good judgment in selecting an appropriate room or suite. A request for a hotel reservation is normally quite routine, but the details must be clearly stated if, as in this case, special requirements must be met.

Gentlemen:

Please reserve a room for Mr. Kenneth Falcone for December 4-7. Mr. Falcone, executive vice-president of Rheinhold Products Corporation, will arrive at the hotel about 6:30 p.m. on the 4th; therefore, please hold the reservation until he arrives.

During his stay, Mr. Falcone will be conferring with five Memphis executives. He would like to have a room large enough to accommodate a conference table and six chairs. Perhaps a small suite—a living room with an adjoining bedroom and bath—would be satisfactory. If a suite is not available, a large double bedroom would probably be adequate.

Will you please confirm this reservation, giving details on the type of accommodations that you are holding.

Very truly yours,

Not all request letters require as much detail as the preceding example. Note how the following letter, though brief, supplies all necessary information.

Gentlemen:

My check for $4.50 is enclosed for a one-year subscription to Golfing News. Please send the magazine to the following address:

Mr. Howard C. Bartlett, Jr.
14 Old Mill Road
Princeton, New Jersey 08540

Very truly yours,

A letter requesting an appointment must also carefully spell out all necessary information. The reason why an appointment is requested is usually stated in order to convince the executive that the appointment should be accepted. In addition, giving the reason for the appointment also enables the executive to make any necessary preparations for talking with his visitor. All other necessary information—who, when, where—must, of course, be included also. Note how the information is given in the following example.

Dear Mr. Mitchell:

I expect to be in Wichita the week of August 12. May I see you sometime during that week to show you our new training film on safety in the aircraft industry? This film, with sound and in full color, was made with the assistance of the country's foremost aircraft safety engineers. I think you and your inspectors will find the film worthwhile.

An hour is all that is needed to show the film and to describe some of the other training films we have recently released. Any day of the week will be satisfactory to me. Please let me know your preference so that I may complete my itinerary. Incidentally, will your projection room be available? If not, I'll bring my projector and screen.

Sincerely yours,

Give Accurate Information

Before it is mailed, each letter of request should be checked for accuracy of information. It is easy to give a wrong date, an incorrect amount, or an incorrect title or address. Accuracy is particularly important in letters ordering goods or services.

Although larger companies use a special purchase order form for most purchases, they sometimes order merchandise by letter, and smaller companies may place all orders by letter. Complete and accurate information is doubly important in these cases.

Gentlemen:

Please ship by air express the following:

Quantity	Catalog Number	Description	Price	Amount
2	C230	Transcontinental TV Antennas	$22.90	$45.80
3	M63	Alvin 7-Transistor Portable Radios	26.56	79.68

Please rush this shipment so that I will have it for a customer by April 17. Bill me at the usual terms of 2/10, n/30.

Very truly yours,

Be Reasonable

Although most people would not knowingly make an unreasonable request, a surprising number of writers are guilty of this kind of thoughtless action.

What would you think if you, as a correspondent for an oil company, received the following request from a college student who was preparing a report about the oil industry.

> Please tell me all you know about oil.

You would surely think that such a request is unreasonable! First, the student could have obtained a great deal of information from the college or public library, but he obviously had not investigated either source. Second, he didn't have enough knowledge of his subject to know what he didn't know; he therefore could not ask for specific information. Third, "all" that a specialist in the petroleum industry knows about oil could fill at least several volumes.

Before you request information, ask yourself these questions: "Do I know what I want to find out? Is there some place where I can find the information without imposing on someone else? Am I making a reasonable request—one that the reader will have the time to fulfill? Am I allowing the reader enough time to give my request adequate attention?" The answers to these questions will make some letters unnecessary to write; those that are written will be specific, pertinent, and reasonable.

Be Courteous

Closely related to the unreasonable request is the discourteous one. The writer of a discourteous request often has a mistaken notion of his reader's obligations; for example, he might think, "The reader owes me this; he must comply with my request whether or not I say 'please' or 'thank you.'"

The discourteous request writer is likely to make a request like the one shown below:

Paul Forbes
Metal Art Products Company
225 San Jacinto St.
Austin, Texas 78704

Dear Sir:

Send your catalog and latest price list of sheet metal products.

Yours truly,

Mr. Forbes will, of course, send the catalog and price list regardless of whether he is given the courtesy of *Mr.* in the inside address; whether the title of Sales Manager is included; whether the formal *Dear Sir* is used instead of the friendlier salutation *Dear Mr. Forbes;* or whether the writer says *please.* Yet Mr. Forbes would have been more favorably impressed (and more inclined to be helpful) if the letter had been written in a courteous manner, as the letter at the top of page 279 was.

Mr. Paul Forbes, Sales Manager
Metal Arts Products Company
225 San Jacinto Street
Austin, Texas   78704

Dear Mr. Forbes:

Will you please send us a copy of your complete catalog, including prices, on the Weld-Craft line of sheet metal products.

We are in the process of developing a new line of automatic washers and want to be sure we have available the latest information on your sheet metal.

Sincerely yours,

Making it easy for the reader to act is another form of courtesy. One method is to use courtesy carbons (described in Section 35). Another is to number the questions or requests when there are several. For example, read the following letter:

Dear Mrs. Colfax:

Thank you for the samples of Dura-Flex and Sheenglow drapery materials. I am delighted with the wide range of colors and textures. To help me in making a selection for the executive offices, would you please answer the following questions:

1. Is the Dura-Flex material fire-resistant?
2. Does the Dura-Flex line come in a darker gray than the samples supplied?
3. The nubby texture of the Sheenglow fabric is ideal for the conference room. Is Sheenglow also available in a smooth finish for the adjoining library?
4. Do you have local representatives who might be available to counsel us on color harmony?
5. What local firm do you think would give us the best job (and price) on making draperies from your materials?

As soon as I have the answers to these questions, I shall be able to make a decision. Your help will be appreciated.

Sincerely yours,

Be Brief

Another aspect of courtesy is brevity. It is discourteous to waste the reader's time by asking him to read rambling thoughts and irrelevant detail. Providing too much information is a common fault of letters of request. Suppose the letter to Mr. Forbes (page 278) had been written as shown at the top of page 280.

Dear Mr. Forbes:

Our Research and Development staff have, for the past several months, been engaged in the process of developing a new line of automatic washing machines. From the results of their study and research, we are attempting to project our requirements for materials and to determine costs of production. As you may well imagine, one of the raw materials we will need is sheet metal. This brings us to the purpose of our letter.

Yesterday afternoon I had my secretary check our catalog file. I find that for some reason we do not have your catalog on file, although we did have one as late as last week. Someone must have taken it. The price list is gone, too. Well, when we do assemble our costs and source of suppliers of raw materials, we believe your company should be represented, etc., etc.

Most of the details given above are unimportant to the basic purpose of the request—to obtain a catalog and price list of sheet metal products. If Mr. Forbes received many of these long-winded letters, he would be too busy reading his mail to answer requests. A letter of request should be complete enough to give the reader all the information he needs in order to serve you properly—but brief enough to enable him to serve you quickly.

COMMUNICATION PROJECTS

Practical Application

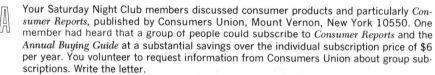 Your Saturday Night Club members discussed consumer products and particularly *Consumer Reports*, published by Consumers Union, Mount Vernon, New York 10550. One member had heard that a group of people could subscribe to *Consumer Reports* and the *Annual Buying Guide* at a substantial savings over the individual subscription price of $6 per year. You volunteer to request information from Consumers Union about group subscriptions. Write the letter.

B Select four newspaper or magazine advertisements that invite you to write for additional information about products or services. Write a letter to each of the four companies and ask for a catalog, sample, brochure, or other descriptive information.

C Write a letter to Cansler's Department Store, 3215 Main Street, Burlington, Wyoming 82411, to order an Irish linen tablecloth with lace edging. You make the following notations to guide you in organizing and in writing the letter.

Why? To order a linen tablecloth
What? Stock No. 457, 48 by 96 inches, Bedford Brand Irish linen tablecloth, at $39.95
How? Send by airmail, charge to my account
When? At once
Where? Address of the writer
Who? The writer

D Write to the Circulation Department of Item Business Letters, 65 Southwestern Avenue, Chicago, Illinois 60632, to inform them of a change of address. You have moved from 2251 Boardman Avenue in Ann Arbor, Michigan 48104, to 43 Market Place, Cleveland, Ohio 44106, and you would like to have your subscription sent to your new address.

E Write a letter to the Better Credit Bureau of 925 Hester Street, Chicago, Illinois 60632, and ask for a copy of their pamphlet *The Selling Side of Credit Correspondence*. Mr. Edwin B. Moran and Mr. Robert L. Roper are the editors. Enclose your check for $1.50 in payment.

F Request a reservation at the Palm House, Madison at Jefferson Street, St. Louis, Missouri 63107. You plan to attend the Executive Board Meeting of the National Cost Accountants Association on February 23, to be held at the Palm House. You need a single room with bath at a moderate rate.

G Write a letter to Dictaphone Corporation, 730 Third Avenue, New York, New York 10017, asking for a free copy of the pamphlet *How Much Do You Know About Business Letter Writing?*

H Make a list of a number of different ways to say "please" and "thank you." Five different ways and you score "par"; eight, you score a "birdie"; ten, an "eagle."

Editing Practice

The Correspondence Supervisor   Edit and rewrite the following paragraph, correcting all errors.

We wish we could grant your request for a five percent discount on the purchase of 125 of our DEEPSLEEP mattresses. The price we quote allows you to retail DEEPSLEEPS at $40.00 which is a very low price for this quality of merchandise. Comparable mattresses sell for 3, 5, or 10 percent more than our's. When we tell you that our profit on each mattress is only 90¢, we are sure that you will understand why we are unable to allow any special discounts.

Rewrite Desk   Improve the following first lines taken from request letters.

1. Please find enclosed my check for $8.25 for a Hawthorne Exerciser.
2. This is to notify you that we have not received the merchandise requested on our Purchase Order N 3271 sent to you over a month ago.
3. Referring to your quotation for bid on 8½ x 11 paper stock which you mailed on October 7 and was received on October 10, you failed to indicate paper weight.
4. We wish to call attention to the fact that your check which you said was enclosed was not enclosed.
5. We want to notify you that our subscription which you say expires in December does not expire until February.

Case Problem

Short and Sweet   Simplify the following involved sentence taken from a rough draft of a report.

There are no more misplaced papers in small offices, in proportion to the volume handled, than in large organizations and at first this is difficult to understand when you consider that the chances for error are greater in a large organization where more papers are handled and more people are involved, however, the realization of this error possibility causes large organizations to give adequate attention to the important aspects of filing routine, with a resulting increase in speed and accuracy of filing.

Response Letters

Among the most important letters written in business are response letters. They are usually written for the following reasons: (1) to acknowledge an order received and to give the date and method of shipment and the terms of payment; (2) to transmit printed materials, such as a catalog, a price list, or a booklet; (3) to agree to or to confirm a meeting or an appointment; (4) to express regret that an appointment cannot be made or kept, and perhaps to suggest another date; (5) to answer questions about the company's product or service; (6) to explain a delay in shipping or an accounting error; (7) to acknowledge receipt of information, materials, money, or merchandise; (8) to follow up on decisions reached at meetings and during conversations.

THE IMPORTANCE OF RESPONSE LETTERS

Generally speaking, letters of response are sales letters. In most cases, they represent an opportunity for the company's correspondents to give service, develop goodwill, and build sales. In no other type of business letter are the positive outlook and the *you* attitude more important. Response letters should be looked upon as opportunities to gain new friends (or to keep old ones); they should never be written grudgingly or matter-of-factly.

Five basic rules should guide the writer of response letters.

- Be prompt.
- Be helpful.
- Be sales-minded.
- Be complete.
- Be specific.

Be Prompt

Every inquiry, every request, and every favor should be acknowledged promptly. Many companies require that every letter be answered within forty-eight hours of its receipt; some organizations allow only twenty-four hours for a response.

Even when an inquiry cannot be answered in detail, a reply should be sent promptly. You should at least acknowledge the letter and give the inquirer a date on which he may expect to receive the information he seeks. For example:

Dear Mr. Cottrell:

   The contract you asked about is being studied this week by the members of our Operations Committee. I am quite sure that they will have a decision by March 19. At any rate, we will write you as soon as we have something to report.

                         Sincerely yours,

AUTO-TYPIST

AMERICAN AUTOMATIC TYPEWRITER COMPANY

2323 N. PULASKI ROAD · CHICAGO, ILLINOIS 60639 · (AREA CODE 312) 384-5151

January 8, 19--

Mr. Frank K. Judson
Judson Insurance Agency
6235 Eight Mile Road
Detroit, Michigan   48233

Dear Mr. Judson:

Thank you sincerely for your recent letter.

It is always a pleasure to send information about the Auto-typist. The
enclosed folder tells how and why the Auto-typist speeds the handling of
letters and transforms ordinary form letters into sparkling, attention-
getting, individually typed personal letters at a cost of only a few
cents each.

Keep in mind also, Mr. Judson, that Auto-typist Selector models normally
handle more than 60 percent of all routine dictated business correspondence
simply at the touch of buttons.

Sound interesting?

Chances are that you will have many questions, which cannot be answered
by printed literature alone, about the specific application of the Auto-
typist to your particular work. For example, the model best suited to
your work, expected production, prices, service and delivery are but a few
of the questions the Auto-typist dealer in your area will be happy to
answer without the slightest obligation.

May we suggest that you phone or write today to Mr. Paul E. Becking, Dura
Business Machines, Inc., 19326 Woodward Avenue, Detroit, Michigan 48233;
telephone 883-4670.

Cordially yours,

Richard F. Drake
Sales Promotion Manager

Enclosure

PS: This letter was Auto-typed, of course.

Courtesy American Automatic Typewriter Company

The writer in the example on page 282 has acknowledged an inquiry and
has promised a reply about March 19. The file copy of this letter would be
placed in a tickler file for March 19 so that the writer will remember to let
Mr. Cottrell know the decision of the Operations Committee.

If a correspondent receives many similar requests, he can write one letter
to be used as a guide in answering all the requests. Such a letter is shown
above. Sometimes the same letter may be used to answer all or nearly all
the requests; in this case, the letter could even be duplicated, with space left
for the typist to fill in the inside address, the salutation, and any other variables. In other cases, the letter may need to be modified to suit each inquiry.

For example, the following form letter could be used whenever an item is out of stock. The words in boldface type would vary from letter to letter, depending on the inquiry.

Dear **Mrs. Raymond:**

Requests for our booklet, **"101 Tested Recipes,"** have been much heavier than we expected; and we are temporarily out of stock. Another printing has been ordered, however, and we expect a new supply on **February 2.** Your copy will be mailed to you as soon as the shipment arrives.

We certainly appreciate your interest in Gourmet products. You will get much enjoyment from your use of the recipes in this excellent, colorful booklet. We have already had many enthusiastic letters from those who have tried them out.

Very sincerely yours,

Promptness is particularly important when you need to acknowledge a gift. A delayed response implies lack of appreciation, whereas a prompt thank-you assures the donor that you truly do appreciate his gift. The acknowledgment, like the one below, need not be long, but it should, of course, be sincere and cordial.

Dear Mr. Silverman:

Thank you for the beautiful volume of wildlife prints I received today. The book promises to be a fascinating one, and I can hardly wait to examine it more closely.

I appreciate your thoughtfulness very much. I'll give you my "review" at the first opportunity.

Cordially yours,

Since customers and potential customers are pleased and impressed by prompt responses, you should always capitalize on your promptness by mentioning how quickly you have acted. Usually you need only to indicate when you received the letter you are answering, as shown by the following illustration:

When I received your letter this morning, I checked immediately into the availability of a charter plane for your Iowa meeting, and I am pleased to report that . . .

When you "go the extra mile" to give prompt service, you should let the reader know what you have done. The reason for telling the reader about it is simply that no one can be impressed by special effort unless he knows about it. Note how the following letter capitalizes on the special service given to the customer.

Dear Miss Dwyer:

Generally, our shop needs about a week to make up an order as large and as varied as the one you placed with us yesterday. However, because your need for these picture prints and frames is urgent, we have given your order top priority. The materials will be shipped tomorrow, and you should have them by Thursday of this week. I hope this will be early enough to fill your requirements before you depart for Europe.

Yours sincerely,

Be Helpful

The thoughtful letter writer gives more than a bare minimum of help when he responds to an inquiry or a request. For example, in the letter on page 283, the writer has responded by enclosing a folder, by describing the usefulness of the automatic typewriter in answering routine correspondence, and by telling the reader where he can obtain additional information.

Going beyond the minimum to help does not mean verbosity in responding, but it does mean being aware of a customer's total needs and designing a letter to satisfy those needs. For example, the writer of the letter below not only fills the request made of him but also anticipates the inquirer's interest in a closely related item. Yet, to go beyond the minimum, the writer did not have to write a long, long response.

Dear Mr. Trotter:

The booklet you requested, How to Train Your Dog, is enclosed. Please accept it with our compliments.

You mentioned in your letter that you are an avid hunter. I suspect that, for that reason, you are especially interested in the training of hunting dogs. Have you seen the Berhune Training Series for Hunting Dogs? I am enclosing a tear sheet from a recent issue of Sporting News in which this series is described. Our magazine has received several letters praising these materials.

Cordially yours,

A correspondent can't always give the reader what he wants, of course. Even so, he should be as courteous and as helpful as possible. For example, the letter on page 286 probably won a friend for the writer's company, even though the correspondent could not give the customer what she wanted.

Dear Mrs. Darnell:

I wish it were possible to send you the Tufftex wallpaper catalog you requested. Unfortunately, our supply of this catalog is completely exhausted; and a reprint is not planned.

Blocker's Paint Store in Danville carries the catalogs of most of the leading wallpaper manufacturers. In this store you will very likely find just what you need. Good luck!

Sincerely yours,

Be Sales-Minded

Everyone employed in business—the salesman, the receptionist, the manager, the messenger, the president, the deliveryman, the switchboard operator, the correspondent—is expected to do his part in making friends for his company. Employees should demonstrate an interest in and a helpful attitude toward the buying public and thereby create an image of friendliness, reliability, and efficiency.

The sales-minded person conveys the idea that he is more interested in having satisfied customers than he is in merely making a sale. He does not allow his letters to sound routine. Each letter is as individualized as time permits, and each sounds special.

One way of making response letters seem special is by varying the expressions used. If each day you must respond to many requests, you may be inclined to make them all sound alike; for example:

This is to acknowledge receipt of your request for . . .

The danger does not lie in the fact that two customers may find out that they have received exactly the same letters. The danger is that the writer becomes bored, and his boredom results in a mechanical indifference that shows in his responses. On the other hand, if the writer tries to write his letters in different ways, he adds to his own interest, as well as to the interest of his readers. In how many different ways can you express *This will acknowledge receipt of your request for . . . ?* Here are a few:

Thank you for your order for . . .
Your order for Etko is appreciated and . . .
We are grateful for your interest in Etko, and . . .
Your request for Etko arrived this morning, and I . . .
The Etko you asked for is being . . .
Many thanks for your confidence in Etko . . .
This morning I had the pleasure of sending you . . .
I know you will be pleased with the new Etko that . . .
You made a wise choice when you . . .

You, of course, can add to this list. The point is that you shouldn't allow your letters to sound like a broken record. By varying your wording of the same ideas, you will make your letters sound fresh, and you will give the reader the feeling that you are writing especially to him.

The ultimate mission of every business activity is a sale. Most letters of response give the writer an opportunity to drive directly toward a sale. Unlike the usual sales letter, however, the letter of response is an answer to a direct request. In other words, the reader is inviting you to sell him something!

The following letter is an example of an effective response written by a sales-minded correspondent.

Dear Mr. Houston:

Thank you for your inquiry about EMIT, the weekly letter prepared especially for businessmen.

As a subscriber to EMIT, you'll get, in each Monday morning's mail, valuable information about significant business changes and national trends . . . and the enclosed form will bring you four months of this helpful service on a special introductory basis. The fee? A low $4 for the next four months.

The EMIT BUSINESS LETTER not only keeps you informed of present trends and developments, but also gives you advance notice of new government policies . . . political moves and their meanings . . . economic policy . . . foreign affairs . . . the stock market . . . union plans and tactics . . . employment . . . wages . . . anything that will have an effect on you, your business, your personal finances, your family.

To take advantage of this special introductory offer and to benefit from EMIT's keen judgments and helpful advice, fill in and return the enclosed form. Your $4 payment, for four months of service, is a tax-deductible business expense. It is a 50 percent saving over the regular annual rate of $24 . . . at which more than 8 out of 10 regular EMIT readers renew their service year after year. You may send your payment along with your order or ask to be billed later.

Either way, I'll start your service as soon as I hear from you; and you'll have each weekly issue on your desk every Monday morning thereafter.

Sincerely yours,

Note the chatty narrative style of the letter. Adding ellipses (. . .) in this instance contributes to the easy flow of the letter. This device is not recommended for all response letters, but in some letters it can be used effectively.

Remember that the good response letter offers an excellent opportunity to be of service as well as to make a sale. You can see these points in action in the following printed response letter.

Dear Friend:

Here is the Continental Music Library brochure you requested. It describes the unusual new home music library which you may own and enjoy for no more than you might spend on stereo records each month if you already owned a stereo phonograph. To broaden its market for stereophonic records, Continental has made it possible for you and your family to enter the fascinating world of stereo. And you needn't make any of the time-consuming and costly mistakes that many people do when they buy equipment and records.

We have taken care of all details for you in this superb Continental high-fidelity stereo system, assembled by expert engineers. We have created and assembled for you a finely engineered and matched set of stereophonic components; a complete 50-record library of the world's best music; a remarkable 10-record audiovisual encyclopedia of music, the first of its kind; a full set of beautiful library cases; and a custom-designed, hand-rubbed hardwood cabinet for displaying the entire library.

Yes, simply because Continental wants to broaden the market for stereo records, you can now have the Music Library installed in your home for only $25 down and $18.05 a month until the low price of $675 is paid. This is just about what it would cost for the few records that you would buy each month if you already owned stereo equipment. Look how much more you get for the same amount of money!

To order your Music Library, simply fill out the enclosed postage-paid card and mail it today. It will bring you a selection of records to choose from and samples of wood finishes to match the type of cabinetry that will best suit the decor of your home.

Sincerely yours,

Even though Continental's letter is a printed form letter, it has been written with the personal touch that combines all the essential qualities of the well-written response. Note the effective use of the *you* attitude, the use of word-picture images, and the logical presentation of benefits that the product has for the reader. This letter of response, therefore, provides an excellent opportunity to persuade a customer to buy.

Be Specific

In all letters of response, the writer should specifically identify the subject of the letter he is answering. In the examples given here, notice how the writer has taken pains to be specific.

In acknowledging the receipt of money, you should refer to the amount and to the purpose for which the money was paid. For example:

> Thank you for your check for $77.80, which we will apply to your account.

> We appreciate receiving your check for $188.96 in payment of Invoice A-9701.

In confirming appointments, repeat the time and place of the meeting so that there will be no misunderstanding. For example:

> We are pleased to accept your invitation to attend the press conference on September 14 in the Cornell Room of the Mayfair Building.

> I enjoyed our telephone chat this morning. As agreed, I shall meet you in Tulsa at ten o'clock Friday morning, March 3, in the Mayo Hotel lobby. Harold Ronson will be coming with me.

When the receipt of important business papers, such as contracts, policies, stocks, and bonds is acknowledged—and their receipt should always be acknowledged—the papers should be specifically named or described. For example:

> The contract for the installation of new flooring in our Muncie plant has arrived. Thank you for your prompt action.
>
> The Watson Corporation stock certificates, totaling 500 shares, arrived safely yesterday afternoon. They were delivered this morning to the Bayside Trust Company.

Frequently orders for merchandise are acknowledged by letter. These acknowledgments should specify the date of the order and the purchase order number. The acknowledgment should also refer to the date and method of shipment, as well as to any special instructions concerning the order. For example:

> We are pleased that you are taking advantage of our special autumn sale on office equipment. Your Order 637, dated September 24, will be shipped express this afternoon. As you requested, we will arrange delivery to your Seventh Street warehouse.

Follow-up letters, another form of response, should always be written to confirm decisions reached and agreements made at important meetings and conferences or over the telephone. These letters should specifically enumerate the major points of the agreement or decision, as shown by the following letter:

Dear Bob:

As agreed at our meeting in Battle Creek, I am summarizing for you the results of our discussion about the plans for the national sales conference to be held in Los Angeles in August.

1. By January 25, Ray will prepare a rough-draft agenda and circulate it to all district sales managers for comments and suggestions.
2. Ed will investigate accommodations, prices, and facilities available and prepare a tentative report to be sent to each of us on the planning committee by February 15.
3. We will meet again on March 3 in St. Louis, the time and place to be arranged by you.

From our discussion so far, I think we're going to have a lively conference!

Sincerely yours,

Be Complete

An important quality of every business letter is completeness, and the letter of response is no exception. "Have I given the reader everything he needs?" is the question every writer must ask before he mails a response letter. If the writer is not able to answer all the questions asked, he should direct the inquirer to a source where the answers can be found.

5550 Dorchester Avenue
Chicago, Illinois   60613
October 14, 19--

Desert Aire Company
333 East Superior Avenue
Detroit, Michigan   48215

Gentlemen:

I am interested in the Desert Aire dehumidifier
that you advertised in the May issue of Home Circle
magazine. To help me decide whether this is the
dehumidifier I want, would you please answer the
following questions:

4 gal (9,000 cu. ft.)
6 gal (13,500 cu. ft.)
8 gal (18,000 cu. ft.)

    1. What is the capacity? That is, how much
moisture can be removed from the air daily? What
is the maximum area of coverage?

    2. What is the price? *A-72, B-93, C-101*

    3. Is the Desert Aire available locally? If
so, where may I obtain it?

I would appreciate your help with these questions.

                             Very truly yours,

Yes —
Stern-Livermore
Russon's-Larkspur
              Claudia Gaxton
              Mrs. James Gaxton

To make sure that they write complete answers, some writers underline
the important points in the letter of inquiry. Other writers also jot comments
in the margins of the letter. The underscored words and the marginal notes
then serve as an outline to help the writer be complete.

This technique is illustrated by the letter of inquiry shown above and the
response to the letter, shown on page 291. Note how the writer, in responding to the inquiry, answers the questions in the order they were asked. Note
also that he answers *every* question, even though the enclosure will answer
the same question. By personalizing the letter in this way, the writer has
made it more effective.

Desert aire Company

October 16, 19--

Mrs. James Gaxton
5550 Dorchester Avenue
Chicago, Illinois   60613

Dear Mrs. Gaxton:

Thank you for your interest in the Desert Aire dehumidifier.
I am delighted to answer your questions.

1. The Desert Aire is available in three capacities:

    Model A removes 4 gallons of moisture in 24 hours
    from a space as large as 9,000 cubic feet.

    Model B removes 6 gallons of moisture in 24 hours
    from a space as large as 13,500 cubic feet.

    Model C removes 8 gallons of moisture in 24 hours
    from a space as large as 18,000 cubic feet.

2. Model A is priced at $72; Model B, at $93; and Model C,
    at $101.

3. Stern Appliances in Livermore and Russon's in Larkspur
    handle the Desert Aire. Either store would be very
    happy to arrange for a demonstation. — *error!*

The enclosed booklet describes the Desert Aire in detail.
There is no finer dehumidifier on the market; you'll always be
glad you chose Desert Aire.

I hope you will find this information helpful.

Sincerely yours,

John A. Hobson

John A. Hobson
Sales Manager

JAH:thb
Enclosure

333 East Superior Avenue   Detroit, Michigan 48215

PRINTED RESPONSES

Many letters of response are the result of advertising. For example, an advertisement placed in a national magazine may offer a free booklet or sample and thus may draw hundreds of thousands of requests. Obviously, so many requests cannot be answered by writing individual letters; such letters would be much too costly and time-consuming. Therefore, a printed card or letter is prepared before the appearance of the advertisement. Note the printed response card shown on page 292.

Of course, a printed response must be carefully planned. If it is too specific, its use will be limited. If it is too vague, it will not be useful in any situation.

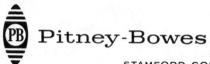

Pitney-Bowes

STAMFORD, CONNECTICUT
06904

Here's the Material You requested

And we hope you'll find some ideas in it that you can use to profit . . . If you would like to know how our products might be used in your business, you'll find a handy postpaid card enclosed in the booklet. Mailing it will bring a prompt response. Thank you for your interest.

Sincerely yours,

E. M. Davis

Executive Vice President

Courtesy Pitney-Bowes Inc.

The hotel reservation card shown on page 293 works because it fits a highly standardized situation. In less highly standardized situations, printed responses may not always work so well.

For example, if a company plans a magazine advertisement to which a heavy response is expected, the correspondent tries to anticipate in advance every question that will be asked by those making inquiries. To meet the anticipated inquiries, he usually prepares a form letter or a combination of form letter and explanatory booklet. However, no matter how careful he is in preparing his answers, he will have to write some individual letters of response to customers whose questions he did not anticipate.

A word of caution about printed responses: make sure that the letter sent really answers the request. In the rush to respond to a large number of requests, you can easily make errors, either because you read the request carelessly or because you are not thoroughly acquainted with the contents of the form letter. For example, suppose that a dealer who is not now a customer requests information about costs of factory repair service from Etko and that he receives the following form letter.

To Repairmen of Etko:

The Etko service and parts manual that you requested is enclosed. Normal repair procedures are described opposite each subassembly. However, should you have any difficulty, you can either write or telephone our Engineering Department (956-2100, Extension 4051).

Please note that factory repair service is also available—and at low cost. For information about factory service, please request Factory Engineering Manual 521.

Sincerely yours,
ETKO MANUFACTURING COMPANY

John T. Pratt, Service Department

JTP:jk
Enclosure

First of all, the dealer is not a repairman, and he did not ask for a manual of service and parts. Second, had the correspondent read the request carefully, he would have known that the information wanted was contained in Factory Engineering Manual 521 and would have sent this manual or at least have referred the request to someone else who could have sent it. Lost: One potential customer because of an inappropriate form letter.

WE ARE PLEASED TO CONFIRM YOUR RESERVATION AS FOLLOWS:	THE *Statler* **Hilton**
single with bath Rate $20	DETROIT, MICHIGAN 48231
Accommodations Requested	Phone 313-965-7800
Arrival Day Monday Date 3/1/-- Time 6 p.m.	PLEASE PRESENT THIS CARD TO ROOM CLERK
Departing On Wednesday	ON ARRIVAL
Special Instructions	

NOTICE TO GUESTS

Reservations held only until 6:00 P.M. unless a later arrival time is confirmed. Rates subject to 4% Michigan use tax.

Name Mr. J. A. Hobbins

Firm   Meade and Company

Street & No. 767 Park Avenue

City & State East Orange, New Jersey   Zip Code 07017

If a room is not available at rate requested, reservation will be made at next available rate.

Credit Card No. 0601203

Courtesy The Statler Hilton

Practical Application

Mr. Kenneth Lapner, who is controller of Appleby Manufacturing Company, 1330 West Fourth Avenue, Appleby, Iowa 51430, and a personal friend of yours, has mailed to you his firm's annual report. You know that Ken was largely responsible for preparing the report. Furthermore, you think that he did an excellent job. Acknowledge the receipt of this report.

As an assistant in the personnel department of the Exceedo Corporation, you are asked to answer the following letter of inquiry. Include this information: (a) there is not now (June 12, 19—) an opening in your accounting department; (b) you would like to know more about the applicant's qualifications (before asking him to come for an interview); (c) because the company is expanding, the accounting department may need an additional certified public accountant before January 15 of next year; and (d) you believe that your firm provides excellent opportunities for advancement.

> 1625 Market Street
> Springfield, Illinois   62701
> June 10, 19--

Mr. Henry Johnstone
Personnel Director
Exceedo Corporation
4237 Riverside Drive
Peoria, Illinois   61601

Dear Mr. Johnstone:

I am interested in obtaining an accounting position at Exceedo.

My background includes one year of public accounting experience. I have my certificate of examination and will become a certified public accountant in Illinois by the end of June.

My educational background includes a well-rounded program in economics and, of course, liberal arts. Specifically, I completed the program for the Master of Business Administration degree at Denver University last January. My baccalaureate was awarded by the University of Illinois in the field of economics.

In the event that there is an opening in the Accounting Department of Exceedo, I should like to submit my complete résumé for your consideration. Please let me know what steps I should take.

> Sincerely yours,
>
> William E. Fargo

You receive the following message from Bards on January 2. You have seldom purchased from Bards. Criticize the message from the standpoint of sincerity.

A sincere thank-you . . .

As we look forward to the New Year, we are especially grateful to those customers who, year after year, contribute so much to the success of our company. You are one of our loyal, regular customers; and we deeply appreciate the business you have given us. We hope our service to you has been satisfactory in every way and that we will have many more opportunities to serve you in the future.

Best wishes for a happy, healthy, prosperous New Year.

> *Better Buy Bards*

Write an acknowledgment, in Dr. Hunter's name, to the following letter. A subscription charge was not made—the service is complimentary.

BUSINESS TOPICS
429 West Fourth Street
New Albany, Pennsylvania   18833

February 5, 19–

Dr. Ralph Hunter
School of Education
Northern Illinois University
DeKalb, Illinois   60115

Dear Dr. Hunter:

We are happy to place your name on our mailing list to receive BUSINESS TOPICS.

Feel free to use the materials in your classes. Incidentally, your library also subscribes to BUSINESS TOPICS, should you wish to refer your students to our columns.

We believe you will find our publications both interesting and useful to you and to your students.

Please let us know whether we can be of further service to you.

Sincerely yours,

E. J. Cook
Managing Editor

Confirm the following reservation made by Dr. E. J. Thornton, 6321 Grand Avenue, Hammond, Indiana 46326. You have reserved the accommodations Dr. Thornton wants, and the rate will be $17.50 a day. You hold reservations until 6 p.m. on the day of arrival unless you are notified of late arrival.

Dundee Hotel
Hazelton at Parkway Drive
Minneapolis, Minnesota   55406

Attention: Reservation Clerk

Gentlemen:

Please reserve a double room with twin beds and bath for three days beginning June 26. Mrs. Thornton and I prefer a quiet room facing an inner court. The rate should not exceed $18 a day.

Please confirm.

Sincerely yours,

Editing Practice

Updating the Correspondence   Rewrite these letter excerpts to improve the wording.

1. We hand you herewith the price list you requested.
2. In the event that you will be unable to ship our merchandise on May 1, please advise.
3. We are enclosing our check in the amount of $580.
4. Under separate cover, the brochure is going out to you today.
5. Up to the present writing, we have had no letter from Bailey.
6. We wish to thank you for taking the time to analyze our sales appeals.
7. I have before me your letter of April 3.
8. The change in the building specifications has been noted.

Case Problem

Right Meeting—Wrong Report   Jim Halloran is employed in the purchasing department of the Evans Tool Company. His supervisor telephoned him and asked him to attend an important meeting of the sales department staff and to explain how the purchasing department and the sales staff can work together more effectively in obtaining the most marketable goods. Jim misunderstood the subject he was to discuss and, instead, prepared a talk on how suppliers are chosen. During the chairman's introduction of Jim, it became apparent to him that he had misunderstood the topic.

1. What should Jim do when he is called upon?
   a. Give the report he prepared?
   b. Admit his mistake and ask for more time?
   c. Blame his supervisor for giving him the wrong information?
   d. Bluff his way, hoping no one will notice?
2. How could this situation have been prevented?

Claim and Adjustment Letters

When a customer feels that he has something due him—perhaps an apology, an exchange of merchandise, or better service—he writes a letter to explain his case. This letter is called a claim letter. Eventually, the business will have to answer the claim letter in a manner that is fair both to the customer and to itself. The reply to the customer's claim letter is called an adjustment letter. The saying *An ounce of prevention is worth a pound of cure* applies especially to claims and adjustments. The best policy, of course, is to conduct such an efficient business operation that no adjustments are necessary.

However, since mistakes will happen, claims will continue to be made against business firms. You, as a writer of business letters, must be able to write effective claim letters, and you must also be skilled in writing effective adjustment letters to satisfy claims against the company for which you work.

THE NATURE OF CLAIMS

If you order and are billed for merchandise that you fail to receive, you have a just claim against the company from which you bought the merchandise. You might write the following claim letter to the company.

April 3, 19—

Mr. A. J. Rath, Accounting Department
Hadden and Company
Terre Haute, Indiana   47804

Dear Mr. Rath:

   Please refer to your Invoice X-2321, dated March 21. We were billed for six gross of paper towels at $14.40 per gross, but we received and signed for only one gross.

Have the other five gross been shipped? Are the undelivered towels on a back order? Is the invoice in error? We should be happy to have you send us the additional five gross if they can be shipped within the next week. Please let us know whether this additional shipment is possible.

Of course, we shall send our payment as soon as we understand what has happened to our order and what the payment should be.

Sincerely yours,

There are, of course, many additional situations from which claims arise. A product you receive may be defective or may not fulfill specifications. A piece of merchandise that was not ordered may be delivered. Goods may be damaged in transit. A customer may claim the right to an adjustment under a warranty or guarantee. A person may be billed incorrectly for goods purchased, or perhaps he may misunderstand the price, the terms of payment, or the date of delivery. Policyholders may write letters to their insurance companies in order to present claims for damages sustained by fire, smoke, or windstorm.

Whether a mistake, a misunderstanding, or a claim growing out of a contractual relationship has been made, you, as a business correspondent, will find it necessary from time to time to send claim letters. You may be annoyed, angry, or hurt by the mistake, oversight, or misunderstanding that has occurred. But, although you can be thought of legally as the "injured party," it is a mistake to show in your claim just how "injured," annoyed, or angry you are. The causes of approximately 98 percent of all claims are completely accidental. Furthermore, most businesses recognize just claims and want to settle them fairly, because they are basically honest and believe in fair business dealings.

For example, suppose that a claimant (a person who makes a claim) who did not understand the foregoing facts had written the following claim letter instead of the one you just read.

Dear Sir:

I don't see why you can't get things straight.

I ordered six gross of paper towels last week. But when the shipment arrived, it contained only one gross, and I signed for only one gross. Such carelessness on your part is inexcusable.

Now, to add insult to injury, you're trying to collect for the five gross that you didn't ship. You'll have to sue me for that. Furthermore, unless I hear from you within five days, I'm not going to pay you anything.

Yours truly,

The example above illustrates the writer's lack of sympathetic understanding. And what effect does such a letter have on the reader? It certainly does not endear the writer to him. An angry letter causes the reader to want to fight, rather than settle, a claim.

The point should be clear. When you write a claim letter, recognize that the person who will receive your claim is a human being too. You should adopt a positive attitude toward the reader—assume that your reader will want to know about your claim and will want to make any necessary adjustment. In most instances you will find that this assumption will be the correct one.

WRITING CLAIM LETTERS

In addition to maintaining a positive attitude toward the business or person to whom a claim letter is sent, you should observe the following rules:

- Be sure of your facts.
- Describe completely and concisely what is claimed.
- Suggest reasonable solutions.
- Avoid threats and demands.
- Avoid accusations.

Be Sure of Your Facts

The successful claim must state clearly all the facts about the claim. If, for example, part of an order is missing, it is important to establish that the portion of the order was missing on arrival. You must be certain that every item has been weighed, counted, checked, and rechecked so that you know exactly what was received and what was not received. Many other slipups can happen on the claimant's side—errors he makes in his own order, misplacement of a shipping or acknowledgment copy, errors in calculating extensions on bills, misunderstanding of verbal instructions on an order—even errors made at the receiving dock or in the storeroom. How embarrassing it is if the claimant later finds that the error is his! Be doubly sure of your facts before writing a claim letter.

Describe Completely and Concisely What Is Claimed

Give the details necessary to establish your claim, such as dates, styles, catalog order numbers, and purchase order, invoice, or check numbers. Only in this way can the receiving business determine how the error occurred. More important, only in this way can the receiving business determine the source of the error and fix responsibility in its own company so that the mistake cannot occur again.

Suppose, for example, that you had not received the January and February issues of *Travel World*. You remember that you wrote the company a note on an expiration notice received in December and explained that your Check 345 for $6.97 had been sent on October 3, 19—, for a one-year renewal. This note had not been acknowledged. On February 10, the claim letter you write could look like the one at the top of page 299.

Dear Mrs. Roberts:

   Will you please check our subscription record to Travel World?
We have not received the January or the February issue.

   Early in December, we received an expiration notice indicating that
the December issue was our last. We returned that notice to you
with the following message written across it: "On October 3, 19—, our
Check 345 for $6.97 was sent to you for a one-year renewal. Your
acknowledgment advice (No. 60585Z 2877697) was received on
October 13, 19—." The December note was not acknowledged, but
our check has cleared the bank.

   Could our check of October 3 have been credited to the wrong
account? Will you please investigate and let us know.

                                        Sincerely yours,

Note that the letter gives *all* details, completely but concisely, so that Mrs.
Roberts can check your subscription account.

Suggest Reasonable Solutions

The claim letter that suggests a reasonable solution strengthens your chances
of gaining a just settlement. For example, if you placed an order and received
only part of it, one solution might be to indicate that you will accept the
missing portion if it arrives by a specific date, as shown by the following
statement:

> We shall be happy to accept the missing goods if they reach us
> before April 15, the first day of our Carnival of Values sale.

Or suppose that you were overbilled $100 on an order. In this case you
could say:

> Through an oversight, we were billed $450 for the merchandise
> on our Purchase Order 4927; the figure should have been $350.
> Please credit our account for $100, or send us a new statement
> for the correct amount.

Avoid Threats and Demands

Give the receiver of your claim the benefit of the doubt. Of course, no
courteous person would use such phrases as *you must, I want you to, I demand, unless you,* or *I must insist.* Furthermore, a claimant who makes
threats and demands will only alienate his reader. Rather than use such
strong language, a good writer will use a positive approach and will give the
reader sound reasons to support the claim. The chances are that this approach
will result in a faster settlement of the claim.

   Suppose that the letter you wrote to Mrs. Roberts in the Circulation Department is not answered within a reasonable length of time. From the
masthead of an earlier issue of the magazine, you find that Mr. A. A. Gordon
is listed as director of the Circulation Department. A persistent individual

will want to send his follow-up claim about March 10 to Mr. Gordon, who presumably is Mrs. Roberts' superior officer. Here's the letter that could be written.

March 10, 19—

Dear Mr. Gordon:

On February 10, 19—, we wrote to Mrs. Roberts in your Circulation Department. A photocopy of that letter is enclosed.

Our letter has not been acknowledged, and we still are not receiving monthly issues of Travel World.

Will you please give our letter to the appropriate person in your department for reply. We miss reading Travel World.

Sincerely yours,

Selecting and addressing the follow-up claim to a higher official indicates adequate concern for wanting a reply; yet the letter still doesn't threaten or blame or accuse.

Threats should be left to a lawyer to make after the claimant has exhausted his letter-writing resources. In the letter to Mr. Gordon, the possible solution suggested is that of giving the letter to the appropriate person for a reply. This solution suggests two subtle points to Mr. Gordon: (1) as the director, Mr. Gordon delegates rather than answers each letter received in his department; and (2) perhaps the first letter should not have been directed to Mrs. Roberts.

Avoid Accusations

You should also be sure to avoid accusing tones when you write claim letters. Suppose that a customer, Mr. Marquandt, owed you $550, less a cash discount of 2 percent ($11) if paid within 10 days after receipt of the invoice. His check for $539 was not received, however, until 20 days after the invoice date—a full 10 days after the discount period. Should you claim the $11 due you or let it go? This is a judgment decision that each company will have to make. Usually, most companies are willing to allow three to four extra days for the mails to clear, but not an extra ten days! Obviously, a claim letter is necessary. Here is one that might be written:

Dear Mr. Marquandt:

Thank you for your Order 1789, amounting to $550, for Babbitt's micrometers. This shipment left our plant on May 4, and our bill with our usual terms of 2/10, n/30 went out that same day. I'm sure both the shipment and the accompanying statement reached you by May 8.

I know you can appreciate the importance of good records, Mr. Marquandt. They are as essential to you, in retailing, as they are to us. With so many records to process, we both know very well how easy it is to overlook—or perhaps even misread—a statement when it is approved for payment.

Your check for $539 arrived yesterday, May 28. We can credit your account for this amount and carry over to your next order the $11 still remaining. Or, if you wish, you can send us the $11 to complete your payment.

By the way, we are planning to introduce a new and competing line—Schwarting Precision Tools—manufactured in Switzerland. The Swiss have always been famous for fine craftsmanship, and I think you will want to investigate these reliable tools for your own store. I'm enclosing the Schwarting catalog; all checked items are now in stock.

Sincerely yours,

This letter meets the test of an effective claim letter. It is positive in tone, and the facts are clearly and concisely presented. Two acceptable solutions are suggested to the customer. Instead of accusing, the writer courteously shows the reader his appreciation; in addition, the writer tries to develop goodwill.

In writing claim letters, remember that you're writing to people—people who are just as human and just as reasonable as you are. Calmly explain your facts; suggest reasonable alternatives; and avoid any discourteous threats, demands, or accusations. A claim letter written in this manner is likely to produce a favorable and prompt adjustment.

MAKING SATISFACTORY ADJUSTMENTS

Suppose a customer is involved in each of these everyday business situations: (1) He ordered personal stationery by mail, but upon receiving his order, discovered that his address was printed incorrectly; (2) he made a claim against an out-of-town retailer for overbilling him, forgetting that he had a previous unpaid balance on his account; (3) he sought damages from an appliance manufacturer for a defect that he discovered in an electric mixer he purchased. In each of these cases, the customer would probably sit down and write to the appropriate party a claim letter asking for an adjustment.

To handle adjustment letters satisfactorily, the writer must use language skillfully and have a sound understanding of the psychology involved in claims work. Because all claims are somewhat distasteful and irritating to the claimant, the adjustment-letter writer should soothe the claimant's feelings. As much as possible, too, he should try to retain or rebuild the claimant's goodwill as a future customer. Finally, within the limits of company policy, he must provide an adjustment that is equitable.

Any person responsible for making adjustments must be familiar with his company's policies. Policies, of course, are the guide rules for the actions of a business. Such rules ensure that a business will act in a consistent manner in its transactions. These rules provide guidelines for arriving at adjustments that are fair both to the customer and to the company.

Equitable Adjustments

Equitable adjustments mean reasonable, right, fair, honest, or impartial decisions in dealing with claims. The writer of the adjustment letter must act as a judge. He must collect all the facts for and against the claim, weigh the evidence, and arrive at a decision that is right both for his business and for the customer. Therefore, before the adjuster replies to a claim letter, he must consider all aspects of the situation and be satisfied in his own mind that his decision is equitable.

Making the Right Decision

Even the most clever writer of adjustments will be unable to write a letter to retain goodwill and future sales if the basic adjustment decision is unfair or unjust to the customer. The writer of adjustment letters must evaluate each claim individually before making a decision. However, some guides are available for weighing the evidence and for arriving at wise decisions. Three sources of evidence that the adjuster should tap are the company, the claimant, and the transaction itself.

The Company You may assume that your company is ethical in its dealings, as most businesses are. (You would not want to be associated with any other kind of business.) Ask yourself the following questions to determine the extent of your company's blame in causing the claim. Do you know, without a shadow of doubt, that the company is not at fault? Could anyone in the company have made a misleading statement? Could the advertising have been misunderstood? Could your records be at fault? Is it possible that someone in the company made a mistake? If, through such questioning, an element of blame on the part of the company is revealed, the adjuster will probably decide to honor the claim, at least in part.

The Claimant To help you evaluate the claimant and his share in the cause of the claim, ask questions like these: Could the claimant be mistaken? Is his claim, if true, the kind that a reasonable person would make? Has he provided all the information you need to check his claim and fix responsibility for it? In his association with your company, does he have a record of fair dealings?

The Transaction The answers to the following questions will help you arrive at an equitable decision about the transaction. Were there any implied contractual obligations peculiar to the nature of your business that were not carried out? For example, does your company guarantee "Double your money back if you are not satisfied"? Could there have been faulty parts in or faulty assembly of the product? Was the use of the product explained fully at the time of sale? at the time of delivery? during the tryout? If you find a defect either in the product or in the transaction, you should arrive at a decision favorable to the claimant. Most businessmen want to please their customers.

The facts from such a study of the claim, in relation to your company, the claimant, and the transaction, provide the evidence you need to arrive at an equitable decision. At times you may have to write inquiries to your claimant to determine some of the facts. For example, read the letter shown at the top of the following page.

Dear Mr. Potter:

Thank you for your letter about our Model 927 Alaskan Pride refrigerator on which you request an adjustment. In checking our files, we do not find a certificate of purchase to validate the period of guarantee. Would you please let us know the name of the dealer from whom you purchased Model 927 and the approximate date.

With this information, we can validate your guarantee and arrive, we believe, at a satisfactory adjustment. Please send us this information as soon as you can.

Sincerely yours,

Armed with the needed additional information, the adjuster will be able to arrive at an equitable decision on the claim.

WRITING ADJUSTMENT LETTERS

Arriving at a just decision is one matter; communicating this decision to the claimant in a way that will satisfy him is another. The least difficult adjustment letter to write is one for a case where the claim can be allowed as requested. The most difficult is a letter for the claim that must be disallowed. The letter for the claim in which some compromise is found equitable is between these extremes.

three types of claims: allowable, disallowed, & compromise

① An Allowable Claim

Mistakes occur even in the best-regulated businesses. When the fault is your company's or your own, admit the error freely. The claimant will respect the person who is big enough to admit a mistake, especially if he has erred for the first time. The writer should accept the responsibility of correcting his error without quibbling over the added cost or effort caused by his mistake. Remember that the aim of the writer is to keep the claimant as a customer. Note how the writer of the following letter attempts to retain the customer's goodwill.

Dear Mr. Zender:

A shipment of the parts you ordered for your Model 619 Jonathan Drill was sent to you by air freight this morning. These parts will replace the Model 623 parts you received in error.

Our order department has a wonderful record for efficiency and accuracy, but in this case I must admit that they were asleep. Such things, unfortunately, do happen, but we'll do everything possible to see that you aren't the victim a second time.

At your convenience, please return the Model 623 parts COD. With its new parts, your Model 619 Jonathan Drill will work like new again. Let me know, Mr. Zender, how we can be of further service to you.

Sincerely yours,

Some companies will allow a customer's claim, even on flimsy evidence, if the cost of doing so is not too great and if, by so doing, a customer will be kept. In such a case, future sales will compensate for the present loss.

A Partially Allowable Claim

A more difficult letter to write is the one in which a compromise solution is necessary. If the negotiation is concerned with an item of high value, the company may want to send an adjuster in person to the claimant in order to seek a compromise.

For example, suppose that you have determined that the customer in the example on page 303 does have a potential claim. A bit of enamel has chipped from the liner of his refrigerator. The spot does not affect performance and is not apparent. To return the refrigerator to the factory in order to replace the liner will cost $400. You believe that a compromise, something less drastic than returning the refrigerator, is in order.

The amount of the suggested adjustment, of course, might vary from one company to another because of differences in company policy.

Weighing the evidence in light of company policies, you determine that a $50 adjustment is equitable and is likely to keep your claimant as a satisfied customer. Your letter describing your proposed adjustment might say the following:

Dear Mr. Potter:

We are unable to tell whether the small enamel chip in the liner of your refrigerator was caused during shipping, in the retail store, or during installation. Our inspection report shows that the refrigerator appeared to be in perfect condition when it left our factory. Still, Mr. Potter, we want you to be satisfied.

Since the chip does not show and will not affect the performance of the refrigerator, we question the advisability of replacing the liner. In fairness to you, though, we are prepared to make an adjustment of $50, to show our sincerity and good faith.

If this adjustment is satisfactory, please call your dealer, Mr. Hoppick, to let him know. Our check will be sent to you through him.

We believe you can look forward to many years of service from your new Alaskan Pride.

Sincerely yours,

A Nonallowable Claim

Perhaps the most difficult letter to write is the one in which you must refuse to grant an adjustment. Sometimes the refusal is necessary just to avoid setting a precedent for allowing unjustified claims. The cost of settling one such claim might be small, but a business cannot afford the cost of settling many unjustified claims.

For example, assume that you are a fabric manufacturer. Unless you handle fabrics on consignment, you cannot permit every retail outlet to return yard goods just because the goods don't sell. Suppose, however, that you receive a request from Mr. Colter to return unsold goods. Of course, you must disallow the claim. However, you should do so in such a way that you will retain Mr. Colter as a customer. Your letter to Mr. Colter should protect your company's position and, at the same time, should show interest in the customer's point of view. For example:

Dear Mr. Colter:

Thank you for writing us about the spring suiting materials you wish to return for credit.

We have checked our records and find that you received the goods on February 25, in plenty of time for your pre-Easter sales.

Of course, you can see why fashion prints of the kind you bought must be sold during a particular season. We wish we were in a position to absorb your materials into our stock; unfortunately, though, we would have no outlet for them.

May we recommend that you cut your price almost to cost and include them in your summer clearance sale. Most stores do this successfully when a fashion item fails to move. Jenkins Departmnt Store used a novel way of disposing of similar materials last year—they featured the fabrics as drapery materials rather than as suiting.

Our Mr. Bowman will be in your store on May 15 to show you our new fall and winter patterns. If you have not sold the material by that time, Mr. Colter, he may have some additional suggestions for you.

Sincerely yours,

Note that this letter offers suggestions for selling the merchandise and also seeks to retain Mr. Colter's goodwill.

COMMUNICATION PROJECTS

Practical Application

A Mr. Will Baxter, owner of Baxter's Implement Company, 416 South Main Street, Warsaw, Ohio 43844, has returned to your plant a defective Knee-High Power Lawn Mower. He says in his letter that his customer wants a new mower to replace it. Your service department found and replaced a defective valve—hardly a good reason to replace the whole mower. Your service department also carefully inspected and adjusted the mower and declared it to be in perfect working order. The mower will be returned to Mr. Baxter by truck on Thursday. Write to Mr. Baxter and explain the adjustment.

B Review the letter of adjustment addressed to Mr. Potter (page 304). Suppose that in your judgment of the problem, you consider it wise to let Mr. Hoppick, the dealer who sold the refrigerator to Mr. Potter, call to make the compromise offer. Assume further that your claims adjuster, Mr. Harold Markham, has called at the home of Mr. Potter to inspect the damage. Write to Mr. Hoppick and give him the information he needs in order to talk with Mr. Potter.

Mr. A. J. Hoppick's address is Hoppick's Appliances, 6243 Outland Drive, Lexington, Kentucky 40506.

C Suppose you are working in the office of Stern's Furniture Company, a retail furniture store. In checking a purchase order and receiving report against a sales invoice of June 10, you find a $50 discrepancy. You ordered a living-room suite, No. LR6715, at $273.33

net. The sales invoice shows a charge of $323.33 for this item. The net invoice amounts to $758.18. You prepare a check for the $708.18 you owe. Write a letter to Rathburn Furniture, 6725 Canal Street, Chicago, Illinois 60607, and explain the deduction of $50 in your check. In shipping you the order, Rathburn's was a full ten days ahead of schedule. Be sure to thank the store for this quick delivery service.

D Assume that you work in the office of the Rathburn Furniture Company. You receive a check for $708.18 and a letter of explanation from Stern's Furniture Company, Owosso, Michigan 48867 (described in Practical Application C). In checking with the shipping department, you find that No. LR6715D, the deluxe model living-room suite, and not No. LR6715, the regular suite, had been shipped to Stern's. The error is your company's, but you think that Stern's should know (if they haven't sold the suite yet) that they have the deluxe suite on their sales floor. It would cost you more than $50 to ship the correct suite and return the one shipped in error. Write a letter to Stern's and explain the error. Try to phrase your letter so that Stern's, if they have not suffered a loss, will be willing to send you the additional $50.

E You receive the invoice shown below from The Center for New Media, Inc., for publications ordered. You received the two pamphlets listed; but the third item ordered, a book titled *Opportunities for Programmers*, costing $5, was not received. Although the invoice showed that $5 was to be refunded, you did not receive a check or an explanation of why *Opportunities for Programmers* was omitted from the order. Two weeks have now passed, but no check has arrived. Outline a reply and write a claim letter for the $5 you have not yet received.

THE CENTER FOR NEW MEDIA, INC.
A Nonprofit, Educational Organization
575 West Avenue
Chicago, Illinois   60606
233-7684

To: Mr. Jonathan Wells		No. 13742
2615 East Fifth Avenue		Date: March 2, 19—
Springfield, Illinois 62702		Order No. 2151

1 each	Electronic Data Processing	$ .30
	Teaching Programmers	.35
		$ .65
	Your remittance	$5.65
	Amount to be refunded	$5.00

F The complaint shown below has been forwarded to you in the Claims and Adjustment Department. You are authorized to send a check for twice the retail price of $1.59 to any dissatisfied customer and, at your discretion, to send a new can of Billy's Lather to replace a faulty one. You talk with Mr. Hanson in the product-quality control department. He is unable to explain what caused the situation described in the letter. The research and product development department would like to have the can in question returned. Answer the claimant's letter, making an effort to retain his goodwill.

Dear Sirs:

For ten years I was a satisfied customer. Billy's Barber Shop Soap has provided me with several thousand clean shaves.

Just last week I bought a can of Billy's New Aerosol Barber Lather. Quite frankly, I don't like it. Three shaves and the fizz is gone. There's still plenty of lather in the can, but I can't get it out.

What shall I do?

Sincerely yours,

H. Albert Smith

Editing Practice

Applied Psychology   As written, these sentences would create ill will. Rewrite them from the viewpoint of good public relations.

1. We have already sent you one copy of our catalog.
2. You made a mistake of $2 on our invoice of May 1.
3. You neglected to indicate the number of your policy.
4. You complain that Order 469 did not arrive on time.
5. Your failure to reply has added to our difficulties.
6. Your recent communication fails to express satisfactorily your delay in sending the check.
7. We were surprised to learn that you found Order 467 unsatisfactory.
8. We will replace the chair that you claim was broken in transit.
9. We are returning your check for $253 because of your carelessness in neglecting to sign it.
10. There is very little possibility that we will be able to deliver your order by December, because a number of bright customers got their orders in weeks ahead of you.

Case Problem

Attending to Customers   Bill Sommers is a salesman in the men's furnishings department of Reed and Allen's Department Store. Early on Saturday morning his supervisor came by and said, "Bill, see if you can get your new merchandise marked and put on the shelves as quickly as possible. It's going to be a busy day, and I have several special things for you to do." While Bill was rushing to complete the job, a customer, Mr. Hutchins, entered the department. Even though Bill was the only available salesman, he continued marking the merchandise and let the customer wait. Just as Bill finished his marking and went to wait on his customer, Mr. Hutchins left the department.

1. Was Bill justified in ignoring Mr. Hutchins in order to finish marking the new merchandise? Why or why not?
2. What should Bill have said to Mr. Hutchins as soon as he saw him?

Credit and Collection Letters

Doing business on credit is a fundamental characteristic of our system of private enterprise. In a competitive system, the buyer is king. He asks for and gets many services from the seller. One of the services he receives is the privilege of buying on credit. The seller invites the use of credit because he knows that charge customers buy more and are more loyal customers. Today, the use of credit is widely encouraged by business firms and retail stores. Rare is the adult who does not have at least one credit card in order to charge such purchases as gasoline, hotel accommodations, airline tickets, car rentals, restaurant bills, and merchandise of all kinds.

The most common type of credit is open-account credit, which allows the customer 30 days to pay. Consumers buy on open account from milkmen, paper boys, utility companies, and retail stores. Business firms also buy on open account from their suppliers. To encourage prompt payment, suppliers often allow retail stores and other large customers a cash discount if an invoice is paid within a certain period. Typical terms are *2/10, n/30*, which means that the customer may deduct 2 percent from the total of his bill if he pays for the goods or service within 10 days and that the entire amount is due in 30 days.

THE THREE C'S OF CREDIT

Credit privileges for both the consumer and the businessman are granted or refused on the basis of character, capacity, and capital—the three C's of credit.

Character

Character refers to the honesty and integrity of a person or a business. The person with good character is ethical and trustworthy. He has a strong desire to meet his obligations and is not satisfied until his debts are paid.

Capacity

Capacity is the ability of a person or business to meet obligations. A person may desire to pay a $1,000 debt; but unless he has sufficient income, he will not be able to meet his bills. Questions such as the following help to determine capacity: Is aggressiveness a characteristic of the individual or of the business? Is good judgment exercised by the individual or by the management of the business? Is the individual intelligent? healthy? well trained? Is the business stable?

Capital

Capital refers to personal or business assets—cash, securities, real estate, and personal property. Creditors consider capital assets the most important of the three C's because these assets determine whether the business has the ability to pay if legal action to obtain payment should be required.

INVESTIGATING CREDIT APPLICATIONS

The credit manager of a business firm or store has the responsibility for determining the character, capacity, and capital of applicants for credit. Obviously, he can't trust everyone; he can grant credit only to those who give him reasonable assurance that they will pay their bills when due. To do otherwise is business suicide. At the same time, the credit manager has learned through experience that he can trust most people. He wants to offer credit to those who are eligible, because such practice means more sales for the company. The successful credit man is both discerning and sales-minded. These two qualities must be kept in balance.

Each applicant for credit must be investigated. Usually the applicant must fill out a written application, which includes information regarding his assets,

Electrical Wholesalers

1200 West Street
Grand Rapids, Michigan   49502

January 12, 19--

Great Lakes National Bank
1500 Morrison Avenue
Detroit, Michigan   48234

Attention Credit Manager

Gentlemen:

Mr. J. L. Stegner, owner of Excell Electrical Distributors,
621 Fulton Street, Grand Rapids, Michigan 49503, has applied
to us for credit. He has given your bank as a reference.

We shall appreciate your answering the following questions
about Mr. Stegner and his business. Any information you
give us will be held in confidence.

1. What is the average monthly balance in his checking
    account(s)?
    What balances, if any, are there in his savings account(s)?

2. On what basis (secured or unsecured) have you extended
    credit?
    Is any amount outstanding?
    On what basis?

3. Has your lending experience been satisfactory?
    Have there been any overdrafts?
    Have there been any drawings against uncollected funds?
    What has been the maximum amount of loans made by your
    bank to him?

4. We are considering extending credit up to $2,000 on terms
    of 2/10, n/30. In your judgment, is such a limit one
    that this company can reasonably be expected to pay without
    difficulty?

                              Yours very truly,

                              Dominick Verazzia

DV:lp   Dominick Verazzia
Enclosure   Credit Manager

his debts, his income, and his character references. Retail stores usually require an interview with the applicant.

Credit investigators use various sources—firms and stores with which the applicant has done business, banks, and credit rating bureaus—to obtain information about an applicant. For example, the letter above was written by a wholesaler to a bank to ask for information about a credit applicant. On page 310 the bank's reply to the credit inquiry is illustrated. Note that the bank provides accurate answers to the questions asked without divulging the specific account or loan balances.

GREAT LAKES NATIONAL BANK

1500 Morrison Avenue, Detroit, Michigan 48234

January 18, 19--

Mr. Dominick Verazzia
Credit Manager
Electrical Wholesalers
1200 West Street
Grand Rapids, Michigan 49502

Dear Mr. Verazzia:

This letter is in reply to your inquiry of January 12, 19--,
regarding Mr. J. L. Stegner, owner of Excell Electrical
Distributors, 621 Fulton Street, Grand Rapids, Michigan 49503.

Mr. Stegner maintains both a regular checking account and a
savings account. Balances average in medium four figures and
in low four figures, respectively.

Unsecured loans reached a yearly high of low five figures during
May. Nothing is outstanding, and our experience has been
entirely satisfactory. Seasonal credit was extended in March,
19--, on a secured basis up to a high of low five figures. Payments have been made according to terms.

In our opinion, Mr. Stegner, who is well known to us and favorably regarded by us, is responsible for $2,000 on the terms
mentioned.

Very truly yours,

Leon Cort

Leon Cort
Assistant Cashier
Customer Relations

LC:df

Letters sent to the other business references supplied by the credit applicant would be similar to the one illustrated; only the questions asked would
vary. For example:

1. Approximately how many years has the credit
   applicant had an account with you? _____
2. What is the maximum amount owed you at any
   one time? _____
3. What is the maximum amount of credit you
   would be willing to grant the applicant? _____
4. How would you consider the applicant as a credit
   risk? (Please check) Excellent __ Average __ Questionable __

Electrical Wholesalers

1200 West Street
Grand Rapids, Michigan 49502

January 20, 19--

Mr. J. L. Stegner
Excell Electrical Distributors
621 Fulton Street
Grand Rapids, Michigan 49503

Dear Mr. Stegner:

We are pleased to extend you credit in any amount up to $2,000.
Our sales terms are 2/10, n/30.

We look forward to a long and pleasant business association,
Mr. Stegner. Our representative in Grand Rapids, Mr. Frank
Obstler, will call on you each month to make sure that you
are getting the merchandise you want when you want it. Please
feel free to review with him your stock of parts and supplies
to make sure that you have an adequate inventory to meet your
needs at all times. Mr. Obstler will also keep you up to date
on new products as they come from our factory.

Please let us know when we can be of service to you.

Yours very truly,

Dominick Verazzia

Dominick Verazzia
Credit Manager

DV:lp

GRANTING CREDIT

A majority of those who apply for credit are granted this privilege. When an investigation reveals that an applicant is a good risk, the business firm or store writes him a letter of welcome. In this letter the seller should explain the terms of credit and should encourage the customer to use his new charge privileges. Because the granting of credit signals a new source of business, the welcoming letter is frequently signed by an officer of the company. The letter granting credit provides an excellent opportunity to establish a good business relationship with a new customer. For this reason, many large businesses resist the temptation to send form letters to new charge customers.

Mayfield and Company

1500 Central Avenue, Toledo, Ohio   43505

March 16, 19--

Mrs. Russell Taylor
5312 Reno Road, N. W.
Toledo, Ohio   43505

Dear Mrs. Taylor:

We at Mayfield and Company take great pleasure in opening a charge account in your name. We feel sure that this will be the beginning of a long and mutually pleasant association.

As a charge customer, you will enjoy many privileges at Mayfield's. For instance, our charge customers receive advance notice of special sales, so that they may take advantage of wonderful bargains before they are offered to the general public. Charge customers, too, are entitled to free gift wrapping on any purchase of $1.50 or more. Your account plate is good in our Terrace Restaurant, in our Calorie-Watcher's Bar, and in our Book Rental Department. Use your plate for anything and everything!

On the first of each month, you will receive an itemized statement of your purchases made through the 25th day of the preceding month; purchases made after the 25th appear on the following month's bill. Remittances are expected by the 10th.

We hope you will make regular use of your charge account. Mayfield's looks forward to serving you.

Sincerely yours,

David C. Harson

David C. Harson
President

DCH:ar
Enclosure:
   Account plate

Businessmen recognize that an individually typed letter, even one that is prepared by automatic typewriter, provides a desired personal touch that will lead to good customer relations.

The letter illustrated on page 311 grants credit to Excell Electrical Distributors and is addressed to the owner, Mr. Stegner. Note how the letter spells out both the credit terms and the personal services Mr. Stegner can expect to receive.

In recent years, businesses have developed many new types of retail credit, such as revolving accounts and a wide variety of installment plans. The retail customer should, therefore, receive a specific description of the credit terms of his account. The letter illustrated on page 312 grants credit to a customer of a retail store.

REFUSING CREDIT

Perhaps the most difficult letter to write is the one in which the writer refuses credit. Some credit managers believe this matter is so delicate that it should be handled in person rather than by mail. Others believe that a delaying tactic should be used; that is, the customer should not be told directly that he is being refused. They prefer to say something like this:

> On the basis of the information we have received regarding your credit standing, we feel that we cannot give you a definite decision at this time.

Still other credit men believe that the refusal can be handled effectively by letter without serious injury to the customer's pride. For example, the following letter of refusal was written by a credit man who believes in "leveling" with the customer. To avoid a negative response on the part of the rejected customer, however, the writer has presented the factual, nonemotional information that caused the credit application to be rejected. In addition, the writer has counterbalanced the refusal by adding positive statements.

Dear Mr. Peterson:

You have complimented us by requesting credit privileges at Young's.

As in the case of all those who apply for credit, Mr. Peterson, we have made a careful investigation of your ability to handle additional credit. However, your present credit obligations are substantial, and we feel that you should not endanger your credit reputation by taking on additional credit obligations.

Please continue to allow Young's to serve you on a cash basis until such time as you are able to reduce your present obligations. When the circumstances are more favorable, you may be sure that we shall welcome the opportunity of considering your application again.

Cordially yours,

The credit man who refuses credit to an applicant, whether in person or by letter, has one objective—to convince the customer that he should buy on a cash basis. This effort calls for the highest form of communication skill. Note how this is done in the example above and in the letter on page 314.

COLLECTION LETTERS

The more thorough the credit investigation, the fewer the losses from bad accounts. However, even the best regulated credit department will grant credit to some customers who will not pay their bills. Charge customers who do not meet their obligations must be reminded to make payment.

Airwork
CORPORATION

CITY AIRPORT • DETROIT 13, MICHIGAN • AREA CODE 313-LA 1-2300

November 20, 19--

Mr. William Barker
Aviation Services Inc.
Cleveland Hopkins Airport
Cleveland, Ohio   44109

Dear Mr. Barker:

We would very much like to establish Aviation Services on an
open account basis. Unfortunately, the credit investigation
concerning Aviation Services has indicated to us that we will
be unable to do so, at least at the present time.

While we realize that practically all of us in the aviation
industry are faced with the problem of high receivables and
operating costs, we still cannot increase our open accounts
if there is an indication that our terms of 30-day payments
could not be met.

For the present time, we would like to handle Aviation Services
on a C.O.D. basis. This, of course, is by no means a reflection
on your own integrity or the integrity of your associates. At
some future time, whenever you suggest, we will be glad to re-
check credit references in the hope that your account can then
be put on an open basis.

We are geared to make prompt shipments to many companies on a
C.O.D. basis, and we do hope that you will keep us in mind
whenever you have requirements that we can fill. We will do
our best to give you top-notch service.

Regards from Airwork,

Donald Mc Murry
Credit Department

DM:bsw

Courtesy The Dartnell Corporation—Gold Medal Award Letter

Collecting an overdue account is not an easy task. No one likes to ask for money. Yet businesses must ask—or lose money. The trick is to get the customer to pay without losing his goodwill. The collection of overdue accounts will be greatly simplified if the following rules are observed.

Be Sure Customers Understand Your Credit Terms

The terms of credit should always be explained to the customer at the time credit is granted. In commercial credit (between wholesaler and retailer), it is also advisable to review credit terms pleasantly, but firmly, when you acknowledge a new customer's first order. If your terms are 30 days net, you expect your money in 30 days. Do not hedge with weak statements like *We hope you will send your check in 30 days.* You should instead say, *Our terms are 2 percent discount if you pay within 10 days; the net amount is due in 30 days.*

Assume That Customers Will Pay

When a customer fails to pay a bill on the date the payment is due, you should assume that this failure is an oversight. Most of your customers are honest, but they may tend to forget or to procrastinate. And psychologically, a distasteful task such as separating oneself from money tends to be delayed to the last moment. If the usual monthly statement does not produce results, send the customer a second statement a week or ten days later. You can write or stamp *Second reminder* or *Please remit* on the statement. Some credit departments use a rubber stamp with a humorous reminder, such as a drawing of a finger with a string tied around it or a cartoon face drawn with a very sad expression. Some companies use printed forms, usually impersonal, sometimes humorous, like those illustrated on page 316. Most customers will respond to gentle hints that their accounts are overdue and that you want your money. Remember, the first follow-up is not an attack; it's a gentle nudge and is highly impersonal.

Send Additional Reminders Frequently

If a customer does not respond to the second statement, it's time to go into action. An account that is 120 days overdue is usually much more difficult to collect than one that is only 40 days overdue. Therefore, if you haven't received payment within ten days after sending a second statement, you should write a letter to the customer. Thereafter, send frequent reminders until the account has been paid.

THE COLLECTION SERIES

Suppose you have sent E. L. Tourmey, a charge customer of the department store where you work, a monthly statement and a reminder. Ten days have elapsed since the reminder was sent, but you have received no response. Your first follow-up letter, though written in unequivocal terms, should still give Mr. Tourmey the benefit of the doubt.

First Follow-up Letter

Dear Mr. Tourmey:

  The balance due us on your account is $113.52. To date you have not responded to two statements mailed to you.
  Does the balance shown agree with your own records? If not, please let us know at once. If our records and yours agree, please send us your check for $113.52 to clear your account.

Sincerely yours,

Courtesy of the organizations above

Suppose Mr. Tourmey does not respond to the first follow-up letter. When should the next letter be sent? Practice will vary from company to company. In general, the second letter should be sent not later than 15 days after the first. The tone of the second letter, though friendly and courteous, should be firmer and more insistent than the first.

Second Follow-up Letter

Dear Mr. Tourmey:

We do not understand why we still have not received the $113.52 balance you owe us.

Let's review the facts. The net amount was due on June 10. We did not hear from you. A second statement was sent to you on July 1. We did not receive your check. We wrote you on July 11 asking you if there was an error. As of this date, July 26, you have not replied. In all fairness to us—and to yourself, Mr. Tourmey—will you please send us your check immediately.

Sincerely yours,

How many letters will be sent to Mr. Tourmey before legal action is taken? Practice will vary, of course; but most companies will send from three to five letters before turning the account over to a lawyer or employing the services of a collection agency.

In a five-letter follow-up series, the third letter to Mr. Tourmey will be more insistent than the second. The fourth letter will demand payment; the fifth letter will indicate legal action. No matter how good your collection letters are, legal action will be necessary to collect a few accounts. It is, of course, only fair to warn the person of this impending action and to give him one last chance to pay his account. Note the increasingly stern tones in the following letters.

Third Follow-up Letter

Dear Mr. Tourmey:

Help us save your reputation.

Your account is now 75 days overdue. Two statements and two previous letters have been ignored. You still owe us $113.52.

You received the merchandise. You knew our credit terms. Still you have not sent your check for $113.52. At this point, your credit standing is in doubt; your reputation is in jeopardy.

Help save your credit rating and your reputation. Send us your check for $113.52 now.

Sincerely yours,

Fourth Follow-up Letter

The tone of the fourth letter in the collection series is still more severe. Note, however, that the writer is still trying to appeal to the delinquent customer's self-interest.

Dear Mr. Tourmey:

This letter is the sixth reminder that you owe us $113.52—two statements and four letters. Your account is now fully 90 days overdue!

We believe that these six reminders represent a maximum of patience on our part. But patience grows thin—especially when you have failed either to answer our previous letters or to send us your check.

Please help us, Mr. Tourmey, to maintain your credit standing. To do so, we must insist that you send us your check for $113.52 within the next seven days.

Sincerely yours,

Fifth Follow-up Letter

Before Mr. Tourmey's account is turned over to a lawyer or a collection agency, the following letter might be sent:

Dear Mr. Tourmey:

Unless we receive your check for $113.52 within ten days, we shall have to turn your account over to our attorney for collection.

We regret the need for this action. Yet, in all good conscience, what more can we do? This letter is the seventh reminder of your overdue balance. The $113.52 is now 100 days overdue.

Of course, we want our money; we do not want to embarrass you with a legal action. We do not want to add legal fees to what you now owe us. All we want is a check for $113.52.

Please help us avoid this action and help yourself maintain your credit standing.

Sincerely yours,

Each of these collection letters had two objectives: (1) to collect the money due and (2) to retain the goodwill of the delinquent customer. As it becomes clearer and clearer that the customer is not "playing fair" with his creditor, however, the tone of each succeeding letter becomes more and more insistent and, finally, demanding. By the time the last collection letter in the series is sent, it is obvious that the customer is not going to pay. The principal function of this final letter is to scare the reader into paying his bill in order to avoid legal action.

COMMUNICATION PROJECTS

Practical Application

A   As a credit investigator, you must determine the character, capacity, and capital of each credit applicant. What are some of the questions you would want answered about (1) the character of an applicant? (2) the capacity of an applicant? (3) the capital of an applicant? Remember, the answers to your questions should help you decide whether to grant or to refuse credit.

B   Assume that you work as an assistant in the credit office of a large retail mail-order business. Make the necessary assumptions needed to write (1) a letter granting credit to a new customer and (2) a letter refusing credit to a new customer.

C   Assume that you work in the credit department of Lathrop's, a large department store. J. L. Stonehouse has been a charge customer of the store for three years. Although he is usually slow in paying his bills, he has settled within 45-60 days of purchase. This month, however, Mr. Stonehouse has not paid the balance of $132.19, in spite of the fact that you have sent him two statements and two letters. Write the next letter that should be sent to Mr. Stonehouse. Appeal to his sense of fair play. The account is now 90 days overdue.

D   The first reminder of an overdue account is usually a gentle nudge. Prepare three such reminders to be included with the second monthly statement. Make the first one a humorous reminder. In the second reminder, inquire whether or not there has been a mistake. Use your imagination for the third reminder—assume that the customer has forgotten; show the customer that you have confidence in him, or develop other similar ideas.

E   Write a series of three collection letters that can be used as form letters by Bards Department Store. The first letter will be mailed 15 days after the second statement. The remaining letters will be mailed at 15-day intervals. The third letter should warn of legal action.

Editing Practice

Editing the News   Edit and rewrite the following excerpts from copy submitted by the police court reporter.

1. Police found the man who had been hit by an automobile in a rooming house on Front Street.
2. State troopers captured the bandits who tried to rob the National Savings Bank within three hours.
3. Two officers hastened to the house where the robber was last seen in a radio car.
4. The defendant entered a plea of *nolo contendere* to the reduced charge through his attorney.
5. A car reported stolen this morning by Henry Martin was found later in the Shore Road district.

Case Problem

The Social Graces   What would you say to each of the following people under the circumstances indicated?

1. Clark Miller has just been promoted to the position of supervisor of your department.
2. Marilyn Thompson has just returned to the office after a three-week absence because of illness.
3. Tim Livingston asks you to go to lunch with him, but you have promised to have lunch with someone else, a person who does not like Tim.

Letters That Say No

Almost every business decision involves either a yes or a no. When a purchasing agent decides to buy a particular brand of typewriter, he has in effect rejected all other brands. When five contractors bid on a construction job, the awarding of the contract to one contractor constitutes a refusal of the other four. When a consumer buys a new car, he is in effect saying no to every other make he might have bought.

Choosing a product and choosing a course of action are comparable. When one salesman is selected from ten who apply for a position, the other nine must be turned down. In addition, many customer claims and requests for credit must be refused by businesses. In fact, some businesses annually receive thousands of requests; and when a favorable decision is not in the best interests of the business, the request must be refused. Every business writer, therefore, must know how to say no and yet retain the goodwill of the person whose request he is denying.

REQUESTS THAT MUST BE REFUSED

To understand the reasons for "No" letters, consider some of the typical requests that a business receives and must refuse. Requests that are opposed to a basic company policy are frequently received. Wholesalers, for instance, receive numerous requests from consumers who wish to buy their products at the wholesale price. Book publishers receive requests for unauthorized discounts on their products. Manufacturers often are asked to sell their product direct to the consumer or to unauthorized retailers. Sometimes requests ask for information that may actually be a company secret, such as a product plan, formula, or trade secret. Other requests for information may be unreasonable because of the time and cost of collecting and sending the facts asked for. Endorsements of political figures or controversial ideas are often requested and usually must be refused. Some requests for speeches or requests to attend meetings may also have to be refused because of lack of time or conflicts in schedules. Requests for confidential information about company personnel are nearly always refused.

In addition, every business receives more requests than it can honor for donations to welfare agencies, to educational institutions, to religious groups, to medical research organizations, to service clubs, and to civic and professional groups of all kinds. As good citizens, most businessmen do contribute generously to various worthy causes. Yet there is a limit to the amount that can be budgeted for such contributions, no matter how much the assistance is needed and warranted. Such requests often must be refused.

In short, businessmen must say no to many requests; however, they must say no for good reasons. To do otherwise would not be in the best interests of the company.

WRITING "NO" LETTERS

"No" letters are necessary, but learning to say no gracefully and yet in a way that retains goodwill requires an understanding of these five basic guidelines for writing refusal letters:

- Be positive.
- Show appreciation.
- Don't slam the door.
- Don't recall past sins.
- Give reasons.

Be Positive

People tend to reflect toward others the attitudes displayed toward them. If you are negative in your approach to others, they are likely to be negative toward you. If you are positive in your approach, they are likely to react toward you in a positive manner. For example, if you frown when you meet a person, the chances are that he will not react with a smile. On the other hand, put a pleasant smile on your face, and the odds are that he *will* respond with a smile. Psychologically, then, if you want your reader to respond in a positive manner, you must write in a positive manner—even when you are saying "No." Consider the contrast between the following examples of negative and positive statements:

Negative	*Positive*
Your product does not meet our specifications.	Our engineers believe that the brand we selected is closest to our specifications.
You do not meet our standards for this particular job.	Although your qualifications are excellent, we feel that we must continue to search for someone who meets all the unique qualifications for this job.
In view of your poor payment record, we are unable to grant you credit.	We shall be glad to evaluate your credit record after you have settled some of your obligations.
We must say "No."	Unfortunately, we cannot give you a "Yes" at this time.
Your prices are too high.	Perhaps, when you have adjusted your prices to make them more competitive, we shall be able to do business with you.
We cannot give you the information you want.	We should like to send you the information you request, but we know you will understand why this is not possible.

The letter on page 322 illustrates how positive words and a positive attitude can soften a refusal and retain goodwill.

September 24, 19--

Miss Mary Smith
YZR Association
Program Committee
300 Madison Avenue
New York, New York   10017

Dear Miss Smith:

Thank you for your nice letter of August 30 regarding the YZR Annual Charity Ball.

As a matter of policy, our corporate operations do
not advertise in souvenir programs. The number of
proposals we receive in this area is, as you might
imagine, very substantial.

We do appreciate your thinking of General Electric,
however. Please accept our best wishes for this
very worthy project.

Sincerely,

R. O. Stratton

R. O. Stratton, Manager
Institutional Advertising

ROS:cr

Courtesy General Electric Company

Show Appreciation

When the answer to a request must be no, another way that the writer can soften disappointment and pave the way for future friendly relations is to show appreciation. A "No" letter that shows appreciation will help to retain goodwill that might otherwise be lost. The writer never knows when he may call for help from someone whose request he once refused!

Assume, for example, that each of five contractors has presented a detailed bid for a new factory building. When a contractor is selected, it is courteous to write to the unsuccessful bidders because these bidders have spent time, effort, and money in preparing their bids. See how the following letter shows appreciation and softens the negative response.

Dear Mr. Guerro:

The contract for our new factory building has been let to Alco Construction Company. Their bid was the best for the type of construction required and for the materials specified.

We want you to know, though, how much we do appreciate the time and effort that you and your engineers spent in preparing your bid for this project. Although this contract has been let to Alco, we sincerely hope you will bid for us again when future contracts are offered.

Thank you for working with us on our building plans.

Sincerely yours,

Don't Slam the Door

There is little reason for slamming a door when it can be gently closed or even left ajar. Too firm or too final a refusal in a letter is like slamming a door in someone's face—such an act merely angers him. Even though you feel strongly that you do not want the services or products offered by a particular person, nothing can be gained by snubbing him. A gentle refusal as illustrated by these examples does not anger. Instead, it holds out hope and keeps open the lines of communication.

Perhaps at some future time we shall . . .
Maybe, when our needs expand . . .
We are keeping your application on file for . . .
We wish that we were able to consider your request, but . . .
It is possible that next year . . .
We shall certainly keep your proposition in mind when . . .

The following letters illustrate the impact of slamming the door versus that of saying no in a gentle manner. Suppose that you were a job applicant and that you received the following refusal:

Dear Mr. McKay:

Only a few applicants for our junior executive training program can be accepted. Those we accept must have the highest aptitudes for, and interest in, our kind of business.

We do not see in your application the qualities we need. Frankly, therefore, we believe it would be a waste of your time and ours, too, to interview you.

Because we have so many qualified applicants, we are returning your application and data sheet. We can't consider you.

Sincerely yours,

Slam! Even if you were not qualified, you would certainly be angry at having the door slammed in your face. Consider, in contrast, the tactfulness of the following letter:

Dear Mr. McKay:

Thank you for your interest in the Marlboro Corporation. We appreciate your application for a position in our management-trainee program. Unfortunately, at the present time there are no vacancies in this program for a person with your qualifications.

We shall be pleased to keep your application and data sheet on file. Perhaps at some future time an opening for someone with your qualifications will be available.

Sincerely yours,

As the applicant, you would not be disgruntled by this gentle refusal, nor would you blame the company for it. The gentle refusal maintains goodwill and friendship for the future.

Don't Recall Past Sins

Closely related to slamming the door is blaming the reader for the "No" decision you must make. Little can be gained by recalling past sins of your reader, sins that cause you to refuse him. Out of kindness, you should not rub salt into a wound of another. Thus, only the naïve writer would say the following:

> We wouldn't buy from you on a bet. The last order we gave you was received two weeks late, even though you promised faithfully to have it here on time.

You will help your reader save face when you avoid statements that suggest fault or blame. Here are additional examples of sins that should not be recalled when you write "No" letters:

> Because of your mistake, we cannot . . .
> Since we were dissatisfied with your previous service . . .
> You neglected to let us know that . . .
> Because of your unsatisfactory repair of . . .
> Since you failed to . . .

Suppose that bidders for a contract had been notified that the bids would be opened at 12 noon on March 3. Suppose that one contractor did not submit his bid until the following morning. You have heard from business associates that this contractor has in the past submitted bids after the deadline so that he could undercut the lowest bidder. For ethical reasons, you cannot accept the late bid. However, you should certainly not write a letter like the one illustrated at the top of page 325.

Dear Mr. Azin:

You failed to submit your bid at or before 12 noon on March 3.
You have been known in the past to use such a practice in order
to undercut the bids of your competitors. Submitting bids after the
deadline is unfair to other bidders. We cannot condone such an
unethical procedure.

We must, therefore, reject your bid.

Sincerely yours,

On the contrary, your letter to the unsuccessful bidder should be written
as follows:

Dear Mr. Azin:

Your bid was received at 9 a.m. on March 4.
Since bids were opened at 12 noon on March 3, we are returning
your bid unopened.

We know you will understand why the bid must be returned.

Sincerely yours,

Such a letter should cause this contractor to submit future bids on time.

Give Reasons

In refusal letters, it is important to avoid emotional outbursts that cause the
reader to seethe or boil over in anger. Refusals should be based on factual
and objective reasons. Obviously, the reasons should be true, as well as convincing. Consider the following illustrations of logical reasons for a refusal.

Because our profit margin is so small, a further reduction in
price would result in a loss to us.

Our budget for charitable donations for this year is exhausted.

Our dealer agreement gives Johnson's the exclusive right to sell
our products.

To collect the information you request would require several
weeks, and we simply cannot afford to devote this time to the job.

The Evin-Glade line we are now carrying is a very good item for
us, and we do not think a change is wise at this time.

If you must refuse a specific request, you can often propose another course
of action that will bring a favorable response. See how this can be done in a
straightforward fashion.

Although I cannot speak at your June meeting, I would be happy
to speak at your July meeting. Please give me at least six weeks'
advance notice.

Why not put your ideas in writing and send them to us? After we
have carefully considered your written proposal, we can get together to discuss the matter.

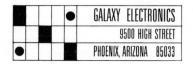

GALAXY ELECTRONICS
9500 HIGH STREET
PHOENIX, ARIZONA 85033

May 15, 19--

Mrs. Gladys Murphy
Director of Development
Ashby College
8000 Adams Street
Tucson, Arizona   85715

Dear Mrs. Murphy:

I appreciate your request for a contribution to the Ashby College Development Fund.

For many years we have made donations to worthy institutions like yours through our Mutual Participation College Donation Plan. Under this plan, our company matches dollar for dollar the cash gifts made by its employees to support the institutions in which they have personal interest. We feel that alumni have an obligation, as do business enterprises, to support education.

Since we have such a plan, Mrs. Murphy, we are sure that you can understand why we are unable to support by direct contribution the numerous requests we receive from colleges. I do hope that the employees in our organization who are friends and alumni of Ashby will choose to give your Development Fund their support. In that way we can contribute, too.

Thank you for writing to us. Best wishes to you in your drive for funds. Ashby is a fine school, and it deserves support for its program.

Sincerely yours,

Albert Chimos

Albert Chimos
Director
Public Relations

AC:mc

Note how the writer of the letter illustrated above has carefully explained why the request must be refused. Note also that the policy of the company has a built-in alternative—if the employees contribute, the company will match their contributions.

Now assume that you work for a wholesaler who sells only to retail outlets. A consumer (not a retailer) has sent you a rather large order. You must refuse because it would not be fair to your retail-store customers for you to sell directly to consumers at wholesale prices. Note how the reasons given in the letter on page 327 soften the refusal because they show that the writer's decision is factual and objective.

Dear Mr. Thompson:

We are forwarding your order, with a copy of this letter, to Mayo's Department Store, 221 South Main Street in Bloomsdale. Mayo's is the nearest retail outlet in your community for Power Plus products. We refer you to Mayo's for three excellent reasons.

1. Mayo's has an exclusive franchise to sell Power Plus products to consumers in Bloomsdale.
2. Mayo's is the only dealer in Bloomsdale with a complete service and repair department for all Power Plus appliances.
3. Mayo's carries a complete line of Power Plus appliances. You can see them all and ask for a demonstration.

Since we are unable to handle your order, we hope that you will visit Mayo's soon.

Sincerely yours,

COMMUNICATION PROJECTS

Practical Application

Rewrite the following refusal letter to improve both the craftsmanship and the tone.

Rev. Elias J. Atkinson
6215 Broadway
Rockford, Illinois   61106

Dear Reverend Atkinson:

We have received your order for an electric Atlas Pencil Sharpener. As manufacturers, we do not sell direct to consumers. We cannot fill your order. We looked up your nearest supplier of Atlas Pencil Sharpeners. The American Office Supply Company, of 310 Amsterdam Street, Rockford, Illinois 61106, carries a complete stock of our products. We hope you will write us again if we can be of further service to you.

Yours very truly,

The following letter was written by a clothing wholesaler to a consumer who had asked for wholesale prices. Criticize the letter, and rewrite it as you think it should be written.

Dear Sir:

As a consumer, you are not entitled to know the wholesale price of Alexander Suits. Wholesale prices are the personal business of our firm and of our authorized dealers. Obviously, if we told you our wholesale price, you'd know the retail markup of Alexander Suits when you go to buy them. Frankly, we are surprised that you'd make such a request!

Yours truly,

Your company has been asked to contribute $50 to help pay the cost of a banquet honoring the local high school's champion football team. As an individual you are willing to contribute $10. Your company, however, has a policy against contributions for such occasions. Write a refusal letter to Miss Jane Fry, chairman of the banquet committee.

D You have been asked to speak at the Young Economists Club of Jordan College. The request came one week before the scheduled meeting. Although you are free on the Tuesday evening of the meeting, you do not believe that you have sufficient time to prepare your speech. Write a note of refusal to Howard Smith, the president.

E You are the purchasing agent of a printing company, and Harold Johnson, a salesman, writes to you for an appointment. Although his letter is somewhat vague about the topics he wants to discuss, he emphasizes a "sure-fire" product, *Ezyrase*, which he says will save you thousands of dollars. You do not have time to see Mr. Johnson; furthermore, you have been warned, on good authority, to beware of this product. However, Mr. Johnson has been of considerable help to you in the past, and you do not want to alienate him. Write a letter and tactfully decline the appointment.

Editing Practice

The Editing Desk   Edit and rewrite the following paragraph; correct all errors.

> The carbon copy of your statement of April 1, shows that you were quite right to question the price of the coat you bought on March 15. The correct amount is $80.00 as you note not the $90.00 charged on the statement. A directive has been issued to all our typists forbidding the xing out of any typed material words or figures. In the name of the company I thank you for telling us about the incorrect amount on your statement, and for calling our attention to the xd-out figures.

Case Problem

The Complainer   Gary Randall works in the accounting department of the Rolfe Corporation. Seated at the desk to the right of Gary is George Andrews, a chronic complainer. George constantly gripes to Gary about the poor lighting, the bad ventilation in the office, the unfairness of their supervisor, the shortcomings of other employees, and his personal troubles. Gary tries to overlook George's incessant complaining, but the constant interruptions are beginning to affect Gary's work.

1. What should Gary do about the situation?
2. What, if anything, should he say to George?

---

42 Sales Letters

Communication specialists agree that practically all letters written by businessmen are sales letters. A response letter sells goodwill and, indirectly, a product or a service. A claim letter sells a point of view—that is, reasons why a claim should be granted to the writer. An adjustment letter may try to sell the idea that a settlement favorable to the claimant is not warranted. One type of business letter, however, is written *primarily* to sell a product or a service or to pave the way for a salesman to call. Everyone receives such letters—invitations to subscribe to a magazine, to buy insurance, to join a book club or a record club, or to buy a set of encyclopedias. The money spent on sales letters of this type amounts to millions of dollars yearly.

Writing sales letters is a highly specialized area of communication. The writer must know how to select the right audience, how to obtain up-to-date mailing lists, and how to use letters to find prospects. He must also know why people buy and how to appeal to these buying motives. For these reasons most sales letters are prepared by advertising specialists. Although you may not have occasion to write sales letters, you should understand the guidelines that govern the writing of effective sales messages.

SELECTING AND ANALYZING THE AUDIENCE

Next to the face-to-face visit of a salesman, the sales letter is perhaps the most effective direct contact with the customer. Whereas radio, television, and newspaper advertisements are necessarily broad appeals to a mass audience, the sales letter is selective—it can be beamed directly at a handpicked group of prospects. For example, a letter announcing new drugs or surgical instruments is sent to a selected list of physicians; a publisher of encyclopedias directs his message to families with young children; a plumbing supply house sends letters to contractors. The writer of sales letters can pinpoint those who are likely to be interested in the product or service he is selling and can direct his message to that group only.

Obtaining Mailing Lists

No matter how expertly the sales letter is written, it will not produce results unless those who receive it are susceptible to buying the specific product or service offered. Before writing a sales letter, you should make sure that you have a carefully selected, up-to-date mailing list of prospects.

If a selective mailing list is not available, a sales letter may be used to identify interested prospects. Anyone who responds to the first letter is presumed to be a prospective buyer, and the lead should be followed up by a call from a salesman, by a letter, or by both. The letter below and the one on page 330 are both intended to develop a list of sales prospects. Note the action-getting reply card (page 331) that accompanies the Eastern letter.

Wouldn't You Like To Say
"I Made That"?

You can! Perhaps you have admired and envied the skill of your friends who are expert craftsmen, but you have always felt that you had no gift for such a hobby. We can make you an "expert" in just a few days. The man who made the beautiful chair pictured in the enclosed pamphlet confessed that, at the beginning, he was "all thumbs"; he had never worked with power tools before. Using a Shaarf home workshop, he merely followed the life-size patterns and the E-Zee instruction book supplied by us (patterns and instruction books are available for over 60 different pieces of indoor and outdoor furniture). It was all done in one weekend.

The Shaarf home workshop is so easy to own that you wouldn't believe it possible. How? For full details, just fill out the enclosed card and drop it in the mail. This simple act can save you hundreds of dollars and bring hours of pleasure to you in your home. Do it today.

Cordially yours,

September 20, 19--

Mr. Michael Angura
District Sales Manager
National Imports, Inc.
200 Concord Street
Brooklyn, New York   11201

Dear Mr. Angura:

We have a great executive pick-me-up for you when you travel
for business this fall from New York. It's called Triangle
Travel, and it works like this.

Take your wife along on a business trip. When your work is
finished, fly to a vacation resort. Then, after you've
thoroughly relaxed, fly directly home. That's a Triangle
Travel trip.

Now, resorts in the Bahamas, Florida, Puerto Rico and Mexico
become easy extensions of your business trips. You combine
hard work with relaxation, return home physically and mentally
refreshed.

The cost? Far less than two separate trips. On a business
trip to Atlanta, for instance, you can take your wife, fly on
to a vacation in the Bahamas and return to New York--all for
just $324 total fare for two (tax not included).

We've mapped out some trips from New York, including fares
and hotel accommodation costs, in a full-color Triange Travel
booklet. We'll send you a copy if you'll mail us the enclosed
reply card.

Cordially,

K. A. Fraser
District Sales Manager

KAF:jb
Enclosure

Courtesy Eastern Air Lines Incorporated

In mass mailings the name and address are omitted because this personal
touch is too costly. In the illustration on page 329, a two-line catch opening
is used; some advertisers consider this technique more effective than a general salutation, such as *Dear Homeowner* or *Dear Friend*.

Mailing lists are obtained from various sources. The most valuable sources
for any firm are its own customer files, prospects reported by salesmen, inquiries that have come in by mail, and other correspondence. Printed materials, such as telephone directories, credit-rating books, and legal and public
notices published in newspapers, are also good sources. Membership lists of

Triangle Travel

☐ I would like to receive a copy of Eastern's Triangle Travel booklet.

Mr.
Mrs.
Miss
_____
Name

_____
Address

_____
City   State   Zip

Courtesy Eastern Air Lines Incorporated

fraternities, business associations, civic clubs, alumni groups, and social clubs are excellent sources of mailing lists.

Many business firms rent mailing lists from list brokers, list compilers, or list owners. The rental fee usually ranges from $20 to $30 per thousand names. Such lists are normally rented for a single mailing; the envelopes, supplied by the purchaser, are addressed by the broker and returned to the purchaser for mailing. Available lists include such specialized groups as former subscribers to magazines, buyers of mail-order merchandise, licensed pilots, and purchasing agents.

Some large companies rent mailing lists containing hundreds of thousands of names. Before renting the entire list, however, they usually test the list by sending letters to a selected sample of names. If the response is satisfactory, they rent the entire list. Before sending letters to the entire list, the firm may test two or three different letters to determine which one has the greatest pulling power.

Determining Buying Motives

Why do people buy? People buy products and services to satisfy needs or wants. Although the people's needs are relatively simple—food, housing, clothing, and transportation—their wants are endless. They want not just food but delicious food; they want smarter clothing, a newer car, a nicer house than the people next door have. They want security, status in the community, approval from their friends and loved ones. They want modern conveniences that help them avoid exertion; they want more fun out of life.

In some cases, people may not be aware that they want or need something. This lack of awareness is where salesmanship enters the scene—the job of the salesman, the advertiser, and the sales-letter writer is to satisfy wants and to stimulate the sale of a product.

A number of years ago, outdoor cooking for the average family was limited almost exclusively to roasting hot dogs and hamburgers over a wood fire. Today nearly every kind of food is cooked outdoors on home grills and barbecue spits. All kinds of special equipment—asbestos gloves, turning forks, long-handled salt and pepper shakers, automatic barbecue spits—have been developed to meet the needs of America's outdoor chefs. Enterprising salesmen and persuasive advertisers created these new sales opportunities by appealing to an interest in leisure activities, to the need for outdoor activity, and to the idea of families doing things together.

Inducements to buy, as described above, are called sales appeals. Advertisers spend hundreds of millions of dollars every year searching for the answer to this question: What sales appeal will have the greatest pulling power on the consumer?

See how the following excerpts tempt the reader by appealing to his buying motives. What different kinds of wants are the advertisers seeking to satisfy?

Product or Service	Want-Creating Appeals
Trading stamps	You're so *smart* to *save* America's most valuable stamps.
Living-room furniture	Enjoy the dramatic beauty of Borge's Danish Modern, the symbol of *true elegance.*
Record club	Let music take you on a world tour of *beauty, romance,* and *adventure.*
Fences	Frame your home and grounds in *intimate privacy* and *safety.*
Telephone service	Isn't there *someone somewhere* who would *love to hear your voice* tonight?
Gift shop	*Thrilled* is the bride who receives a *distinctive* gift from Corby's.

Product or Service	Want-Creating Appeals
Packaged spaghetti dinner	*Your family* will give *you rave notices* when you serve Napoli Spaghetti. All the *color* and *vigor* of the Italian Riviera are captured in this *zesty* dish.
Dog food	*Be good to your dog.* SAVOR is now *flavor-primed.* Makes your dog an *eager eater.*
Soft drink	Now it's *Fresh-ade* for those who *think young.*
Postage meter	*Thousands of small businesses* have replaced *old-fashioned* stamp sticking with this *compact, low-cost, desk model* postage meter.
Newspaper	The *Gazette* is much more *interesting* and *you* will be, too.

WRITING A SALES LETTER

Sales letters vary in length (some occupy less than a single page; others are six to eight pages long), in organization, and in the appeals used. There is no such thing as a standard sales letter, just as there is no standard advertisement. Many letters that would not meet the experts' requisites of a good sales message have been highly successful; others, written by professional advertising specialists, have not produced results.

The test of a good sales letter is its *pulling* power; that is, the number of responses it receives. The response may be a returned coupon, a request for a free sample, or an actual order. If a perfectly written letter employing the most subtle sales strategy does not cause the reader to respond, it is a poor letter.

Generally speaking, an effective sales letter has these three qualities:

- It attracts the reader's attention.
- It arouses the reader's interest and creates a desire to buy.
- It convinces the reader that he should act on his desire.

Although achieving these qualities might sound easy, no sure-fire formula for writing a successful sales letter has been found. The wastebaskets that are filled daily with thousands of unread sales messages attest to that fact. Yet sales letters are used successfully and extensively by thousands of business organizations. Probably no two sales letters written about a product are alike; business is always experimenting with different approaches, different appeals, different want-satisfying devices.

Attracting the Reader's Attention

A sales letter is like a door-to-door salesman—it is seldom invited to call. As a caller without an invitation, the sales letter must attract favorable attention immediately. As in door-to-door selling, a favorable appearance and approach can create the proper sales atmosphere.

The appearance of a sales letter can make the difference between whether the letter is read or whether it is deposited in the nearest wastebasket. Al-

Mr. John J. Jones
Jones Company
134 Jones Street
Jonesville, Massachusetts

Dear Mr. Jones:

Oliver Winchester once said, "A gun is a machine for throwing balls."
He was right, of course. But it also extends the user's personal power
and the radius of his influence.

Much the same can be said of paper. You, as an experienced graphic arts
executive, know that while the primary purpose of paper is functional,
the right paper multiplies a favorable corporate image many times.

A current example of excellence in modern papermaking is Oxford Paper
Company's new North Star grade, Star Sapphire Enamel. Because Star
Sapphire Enamel is noticeably brighter and glossier than similar sheets,
and Star Sapphire Enamel Dull has a unique richness and softness not
found in comparable grades, this new paper rightfully deserves its
place at the top of Oxford's well-known North Star line.

Moreover, because Star Sapphire Enamel prints equally well by either
letterpress or offset, inventory problems are greatly simplified. You
can count on prompt delivery because there are ample mill stocks of
this new sheet.

Today, Mr. Jones, you can depend on Oxford North Star papers, and new
Star Sapphire Enamel in particular, to give you the finest in repro-
duction quality and to extend your company's image and prestige far
beyond your corporate doors.

Next week's mailing to you...Oxford's "surprise package"...will help
emphasize this point.

                                          Sincerely yours,

                                          OXFORD PAPER COMPANY

                                          William T. Rich
                                          Advertising Manager

LASTING IMPRESSIONS BEGIN WITH OXFORD PAPERS
OXFORD PAPER COMPANY, 277 PARK AVENUE, NEW YORK, N.Y. 10017

Courtesy Oxford Paper Company

though there is no single format guaranteed to make a sales letter appear
interesting to a prospective reader, certain qualities have proved interest-
provoking when applied carefully to particular audiences. Superior-quality
stationery and an engraved letterhead give an appearance of dignity and
importance; a newsletter format looks informative; an attached free sample
appeals to the desire to receive something for nothing; a short, spaced-out
letter is easy to read.

The salesman knows that he must keep the prospect's door open if he is to
complete his sales presentation; the sales-letter writer knows that he must

keep the prospect reading in order to create a desire to buy. The lead phrase, sentence, or paragraph may pique the reader's curiosity, pay him a compliment, or "shake" him; it may dangle a promise to save his time, to give him something for nothing, to improve his status. The device used to attract the reader's attention must convince him that he will benefit by finishing the letter. Such a device is used in the letter shown on page 334. Other examples of attention-getting openings are these:

Opening	*Product or Service*
Is your child getting the school grades of which he is capable?	Encyclopedia
WANTED— FOR SPEEDING	Office machine
Up-to-the-minute enjoyment at an old-fashioned price. That's what you get . . .	Magazine
You have been selected to try at our expense the most beautiful . . .	Neckties
Will your family sleep safely tonight?	Insurance
2 OUT OF 5 FARM ACCIDENTS LAST YEAR COULD HAVE BEEN PREVENTED	Safety guards
Brahms? Berlioz? Bartok? Sinatra? Como? Bellafonte? Who is your favorite?	Record club
Who *wouldn't* love you?	Perfume
FREE-FREE-FREE!	Household cleanser
Now you can look ten years younger!	Reducing machine

Fresh approaches to attract attention must constantly be sought. However, a writer must be careful not to use tricks. The salesman who puts his foot in the door to keep the door from being closed in his face is not likely to have much luck selling his product. Marking a sales letter "Personal" or making scare statements is like putting a foot in the door. These devices will fool no one and are certain to land a letter in the wastebasket.

Arousing Interest and Creating Desire

Once you have captured the reader's attention, you should aim to create a desire for the product or service. To do this, you must first arouse the reader's interest in what is being sold. A person becomes interested in and desires a product only when he recognizes that the product is capable of satisfying a want or a need. The letter may hint that if the reader uses the product or service, he will attain a longer life, beauty, economy, security, romance, a youthful appearance, enlightenment, smart appearance, wealth, or freedom from drudgery.

International Business Machines Corporation

590 Madison Avenue
New York, New York 10022
212/PLaza 3–1900

October 10, 19--

Miss Sally Jones
Secretary to
  Mr. Albert Chang
XYZ Corporation
110 Main Street
Tenafly, New Jersey   07670

Dear Miss Jones:

Close your eyes just a moment and picture working eight hours a day by
candlelight. Flickering shadows. Sputtering flames. Definitely harder
on the eyes than modern lighting.

Aren't you glad we have all the modern inventions of today--including
those that smooth and speed your work. But there is still another
important office convenience that could help both you and your boss.

IBM "Executary" Dictation Equipment is so advanced that, using it, he
can pause...review...change his mind...and re-record, instantly erasing
unwanted material. He can hand you error-free dictation.

For you, this makes draft copies as old-fashioned as gaslight. You can
transcribe faster from precorrected material, too. You'll type his
work once and be proud to have him sign the neat results.

Altogether, it sounds good because it is good...for you and the boss.
And bringing it to his attention will be further evidence of your
helpfulness.

If you'd like to know more about IBM "Executary" Dictation Equipment
before discussing it with him, I'll be glad to send you literature
describing the many special features...including IBM error-free dictation
and transcription.

Sincerely,

J. N. Smith

J. N. Smith
Sales Representative

mcw

Courtesy IBM Office Products Division

In creating desire to buy, the writer selects each word, each phrase, for its
power to appeal to a want. Note in the letter above and in the following examples how desire-creating words and phrases are used.

> Joslin is the *latest* in *high-speed, moderately priced* copiers. *Fully
> automated,* it delivers 850 to 1,000 *sharp* black-on-white prints
> per hour and *handles copies up to 18 inches wide.*

> Examine the swatches carefully; note the *close weave,* the *subtle
> pattern* that *complements your finest sport jacket.* The fabric not
> only *sheds wrinkles* but also has the *look of costly imported worsted.*

Note how the following excerpt from an actual sales letter seeks first to arouse the reader's interest and then to create a desire for the product.

Dear Mr. Rayford:

Borrow a brainchild!

We'll lend you the remarkable Afton Whisk calculator at no charge.

After using it for only a few days, you won't be able to do without it. But don't worry. It costs only $125. That's right—only $125, which is one-third the cost of other calculators. The Afton Whisk calculator adds, subtracts, multiplies, and divides; it's faster than electric machines and weighs less than six pounds; it's portable; and it costs only $125.

You need the Afton Whisk calculator because you are wasting valuable time—your own or your employees'—working with figures the slow, old-fashioned way. Just about everyone in your office who works with figures can use an Afton: engineers, salesmen, accountants, executives, secretaries, clerks, and statisticians. And in fifteen minutes anyone can learn to operate this compact machine. Let's see. If Afton saves you a half hour a week, before long it pays its way, and the time saved becomes pure profit.

Sincerely,

Driving for Action

In a baseball game, it's the runs scored that count—not the number of times the batter gets on first, second, or third base. Many a sales letter is stranded on base because the writer does not understand the strategy of scoring—how to make the customer say, "Yes, I'll accept your offer."

The strategy for scoring with sales letters starts with the first attention-getting question and infiltrates every sentence of the letter. Throughout the letter, the writer must develop a "Yes" attitude in his reader.

Developing a "Yes" Attitude From the opening sentence, the sales letter should try to put the prospect in a "Yes" frame of mind and to keep him there to the final "Yes" decision. Only a very inexpert salesman would put a customer into a "No" frame of mind by asking, "You don't want to buy my lawn mower, do you? (The natural answer: "No, I don't.")

Throughout the sales letter, sentences and questions should be phrased so that the reader has to agree with what is said. Many sales letters begin with an obvious "Yes" question, such as: "Do you want to save 15 minutes a day?" Questions that demand "Yes" answers put and keep the reader in a positive frame of mind and make the big "Yes" easier to get. Read these examples and see how easy it is to answer "Yes!"

Do you want your child to enter college?
Wouldn't you like to save $200 a year on your fuel bill?

Making It Easy to Act A good shoe salesman will not show a person more than two or three pairs of shoes at one time. If he must show more, he will usually put the first pairs away before bringing others to the customer. Why?

Courtesy The Mutual Benefit Life Insurance Company

The more pairs of shoes a customer sees, the more confusing and difficult it is for him to make the all-important decision: "This is the pair of shoes I want." The fewer the decisions, the easier it is to say "Yes."

In sales letters, keep to a minimum the decisions that must be made. This is done by making it as easy as possible for the reader to act. See how easy it is to say "Yes" in the examples below and also in the letter shown above.

Just initial the enclosed postpaid reply card and drop it in the mail now.

The enclosed card requires only your signature. SEND NO MONEY NOW.

Practical Application

A. You are the manager of an exclusive dress shop in the suburb of a large city. List sources of mailing lists of prospective customers.

B. Read at least ten advertisements from a magazine, a newspaper, or a sales catalog. Make a list of the sales appeals you find.

C. Select some product you would like very much to buy: a stereophonic record player, a sailboat, a sports car, or a portable typewriter. Write a sales promotion letter as though you were the dealer for this product. Try to get prospects to come to your place of business for a free demonstration. *or Service*   *Typed ; any style*

D. Write three eye-catching openings for each of the following: (a) a power lawn mower that can be ridden, (b) an electric blanket, (c) a fly-now-pay-later trip to a foreign country, (d) a hobby magazine, and (e) an outboard motor.

Editing Practice

Applied Psychology   Change the following letter excerpts into sentences that will maintain good public relations.

1. Your error of 10 cents in the check of May 26 can be corrected by sending us that amount in stamps.
2. Your failure to send us your check on the 15th has forced us to carry your account beyond the time limit set in our contract.
3. Your delay in paying your bills is poor business policy.
4. You claim that the table was not inspected before shipment.
5. We do not see how you can expect us to do any more for you.
6. Your salesman pulled a boner by failing to get the correct street address.

Case Problem

Etiquette for Social Situations   Analyze the following statements to determine whether they are correct or incorrect. If you need help, consult a book of etiquette.

1. When a man and a woman are together, the man should always walk on the side nearer the street.
2. A woman should never extend her hand when being introduced to a man.
3. At the formal dinner table, one should never begin eating until his host begins.

43 | Public Relations Letters

Public relations letters seek to mold favorable public opinion, to influence thinking about a particular company's policies, products, or actions, or simply to make friends. To a large extent, every business letter is a public relations (PR) letter. Every time an employee writes to people outside his own company, he influences people's opinions of the company. The writer of an adjustment letter attempts to make a settlement that will be fair to his company but that will also leave the customer satisfied. The correspondent who replies to a letter of inquiry tries to cultivate a friend. Every business letter affects the image of the company.

The difference between public relations letters and other business letters is that PR letters are written *primarily* to sway public opinion. Indirectly, public relations letters are sales letters. Instead of seeking to sell a specific product, however, public relations letters seek to promote a favorable company image. This image may be one of friendliness, fair play, reliability, prestige, or efficiency—or any combination of these qualities.

CREATING A FAVORABLE COMPANY IMAGE

Many companies spend millions of dollars each year to influence public attitudes toward their enterprises and toward the people who work for them. Some companies sponsor special television shows, on which the only advertising shown is a mention of the company's name. Some firms run newspaper and magazine ads that are intended primarily for public enjoyment or enlightenment. Large grants for research are given to medical and educational groups by some companies. Others make large endowments to universities and colleges and offer scholarships to worthy students. Although nearly all companies feel an obligation to offer such services for the benefit of society, they are at the same time very much aware of the public relations value of such actions.

In an effort to create a favorable company image, many large organizations employ public relations specialists whose function is to see that the company has its "best foot forward" at all times. PR specialists are trained to use all communication media—letters, newspapers, radio, television, magazines, films—to influence public opinion. They prepare countless news releases, radio announcements, and articles; they arrange for press conferences, speaking engagements for top executives of the company, public receptions, and so on. They seize every opportunity to develop a favorable feeling toward the organization for which they work. For example, when a downtown building is being remodeled or expanded, causing some inconvenience to shoppers and pedestrians, the alert PR man arranges to install a colorful sign, which may read something like this:

PARDON OUR GROWING PAINS!

We will finish our work on August 17. In the meantime, please excuse our noise and dust!

Merton's—GROWING TO SERVE YOU BETTER

The public relations man is also likely to see that peepholes are installed at strategic points so that "sidewalk superintendents" may observe the progress of the construction.

Every business is daily judged in the courts of public opinion. And public opinion is powerful! If opinions are favorable, the way is usually smooth; if they are unfavorable, the going can be rocky indeed. Following are typical situations in which public relations specialists seek to influence public opinion.

- A manufacturer in a small city finds it necessary to build a new power plant to handle expanded production. After careful study, management has come to the conclusion that the best location for the new plant is on the river near the city park. For obvious reasons, the company expects that there will be some objection from the public to locating the new plant near the park—a few trees must be cut down, the view of the river from the park will be obstructed, the typical power plant is not a thing of architectural beauty, and so on. Even though the company has permission from the City Council to go ahead with its plans, management knows that it must also have support from the public—from customers, friends, employees, and neighbors. The PR department uses every available communication medium to persuade the public that the company's proposed action is justified.
- A commuter railroad is operating at a deficit. In spite of the fact that fares have increased 200 percent in the past five years, the company is still losing money and must ask for another increase. Of course, the railroad is sensitive to the opinions of its customers; it needs their understanding and their support. The PR department of the railroad may place advertisements in newspapers, purchase radio time, issue circulars to riders, and write letters to leading citizens in order to explain why the railroad has found it necessary to seek authority to raise fares.
- During the past year, an automobile company has fallen from its position as one of the top three producers, and profits are down. Management knows how important it is for the stockholders to understand the situation. They know that faith is easily shaken when the facts are not clear. The PR department is given the responsibility of preparing a letter to stockholders, to explain the company's position and plans and to assure stockholders of the bright future ahead.
- An airline writes to homeowners who live near the airport, to apologize for noise created by jet engines and to assure people that improvements are being made.
- A college has changed its name from Midwest Teachers College to Midwest University. The PR department writes a special letter to the alumni of the institution in order to inform them of the change.
- A large public school system has recently started a foreign-language program in the elementary schools. A news release is issued to newspapers and a letter is written to parents and to various civic organizations in order to inform the public of this new development.

A local dairy that was forced to reduce home deliveries from three to two a week handled the situation by sending customers a letter of explanation like the one illustrated on the following page.

Dear Mrs. Alcott:

For twenty years Harrick's has been delivering milk and dairy products to the homes of Ashton three days a week. Even though the cost of delivery has increased substantially during the past two years, we have continued to offer the same service at no additional charge to our customers.

Unfortunately, the expense has now become so great that we are forced to make the decision either to cut the frequency of delivery or increase the prices of our products. We think you will approve our decision to cut deliveries to two days a week and to maintain prices at their present level.

Therefore, beginning November 1, Harrick's will deliver your dairy products on _____ only. No doubt, you will want to increase your order on those days so that you will have an adequate supply for the week. We'll telephone you in the next week to find out what changes you wish to make in your order.

We appreciate your business, Mrs. Alcott, and we pledge to continue supplying you with the highest-quality dairy products at reasonable costs.

Sincerely yours,

PROMOTING A NEW BUSINESS

Promoting a new business requires a combination of public relations and sales techniques. Suppose you work in the sales-promotion department of the Acme Oil Company, which owns a chain of service stations. Acme has recently opened a new service station in the town of Manchester and has employed a local man, Jerry Calkins, as manager. Your job is to help Jerry off to a good start—to help create an atmosphere that will gain customers for him. Besides running a number of newspaper ads and distributing thousands of circulars, you write the following letter, which is to be duplicated and mailed to a list of 1,500 telephone subscribers in Manchester. The image that is being created for this new business is built mainly around Jerry Calkins—hometown businessman, family man, civic worker, friend.

May We Introduce
To You—

Jerry Calkins, manager of Manchester's newest and most modern service station—the Diamond 77 Station—located at Maryland and Division Streets.

Maybe you already know Jerry and his family. Jerry grew up in Manchester. He attended local grade schools, Northeastern High School, and Riverside Technical College, where for two years he specialized in auto mechanics. Perhaps you are acquainted with his wife Judy, too. She was born and raised in nearby Fairview. For the past five years she has been very active in local music circles and in the Parent-Teachers Club of Green Mountain School. Sylvia (age 7) and Tom (age 11) are in the second and sixth grades at Green Mountain.

For the past seven years, Jerry has been associated with Venus Motors in Manchester. He brings to his new job the experience and mechanical know-how that will help keep your automobile in tip-top condition. Also, Jerry has surrounded himself with a staff of eager and able young men to service your car with everything from gasoline to seat covers.

On two or three nights a week, you may not see Jerry at the station. As a civic-minded neighbor, he will be at Green Mountain School, working with the boys in Scout Troop 62 or working with the new Bantam League basketball team. During the rest of the week, though, he'll be on the job to greet you.

Do drop by to say hello to Manchester's newest businessman. Jerry Calkins and his staff will welcome you warmly.

Cordially yours,

Of course, the PR image you are trying to create will not emerge unless Jerry and his staff give customers excellent service. Customers must find at the Diamond 77 Station the friendly, reliable, efficient service that the letter promises.

Building an Image

The first months for Jerry Calkins are crucial. Once the image has started to emerge, he must keep building it. Acme wants to help Jerry get firmly established, because Jerry's success will, of course, benefit both himself and the company. In your campaign to build an image, you prepare the following form letter for Jerry to mail to every customer who visits the station.

Dear _____:

Thank you for stopping at the Diamond 77 Service Station this week. We are proud to welcome you as a new customer, for it gives us an opportunity to show you the friendly, courteous, and complete service that you and your car will receive—service that we try to make superior to the best you have ever had.

Let me make you a personal promise: Whether it is Gordon Jackson, Butch Wheeler, Raymond Almont, or I who service your car, it will get that stem-to-stern, personal attention you have the right to expect. You do not have to remind us to wash the windshield or check the oil, battery, water, and tires. This service is automatic. We'll keep a record of your oil changes and lubrication jobs so that you will always know when it's time to give your car the Diamond 77 care. We'll also look after minor repairs that your car may need from time to time.

Do we appreciate your business? You bet we do! If we're ever too busy to say "Thank you," the gasoline, oil, or services you've purchased will be on the house. You won't pay a cent for that visit to Diamond 77.

We appreciate every opportunity to serve you. Do drop in as often as you can.

Sincerely yours,

Recognizing a PR Moment

Timing the PR letter is important; the precise time when the public will listen to and accept an idea is a *PR moment*. Obviously, the PR moment for creating a business image occurs when the business first opens. Another PR moment to impress a new customer is immediately after his first visit. The two letters just illustrated are examples of good timing.

A new piece of equipment can also provide a PR moment. Suppose that Jerry Calkins has just installed an additional lift. Jerry takes advantage of this PR moment to announce the change. The opening paragraph of his announcement might start like this:

> We have a new addition! The new automatic safety lift that we have just installed will "baby" your car and will let us give you faster and better service.

In a similar way, anniversaries and special dates in the life of the business often provide appropriate PR moments. For example, at the end of three months of operation, Jerry Calkins might capitalize on the occasion by writing an "anniversary" letter that begins like this:

> From zero to 2,000 gallons of gasoline per day. That's the sales story of the Diamond 77 Service Station during the past three months.
>
> We opened our service pumps on February 1. Now, just three months later, more than 500 friends like you stop regularly for gasoline and service. In the months ahead, we pledge ourselves to continue the complete automobile services that you want and that your car deserves . . .

PUBLIC RELATIONS—OTHER PROMOTION OPPORTUNITIES

The opportunities for writing letters to friends and customers of a business are limited only by the imagination. Of course, many such letters have a definite sales objective. Yet they also enhance the image of the firm. The following examples are typical:

- An invitation to open a charge account
- An announcement of a special privilege or service to preferred customers
- A plea to charge customers to use their accounts more frequently
- A welcome to new residents and visitors
- A congratulatory message
- An invitation to a demonstration, lecture, or reception
- A reminder of a holiday or special occasion
- A thank-you for business patronage

Inviting Charge Accounts

A cash customer of a store or a firm is often invited to open a charge account. The following charge-account invitation includes an application form. All the

SHOP THE EASY WAY . . . SAY CHARGE IT!

Neiman-Marcus offers the following credit services —

- 30 Day Account: You are billed once a month and payment is due upon receipt.
- Pivot Account: A convenience for budgeting everyday needs. Pay as little as 1/6 of your statement balance — or more if you like. A nominal service charge is added monthly.
- Special Account: Take as long as 6 months to pay for special "investment" purchases such as coats, suits, luggage, and jewelry. Even longer for china, silver, and antiques.
- Trousseau Account: Assemble all of your needs on one account and divide your payments over 6 to 12 months. A nominal service charge is added after the sixth month.
- Furs — Jewelry: Choose a beautiful Neiman-Marcus fur or fine jewelry and divide your payments over 6 to 12 months.

Please Print

Neiman-Marcus

application for charge account

Name Mrs. Henry Moran

Address 546 Ridge Dr. City Dallas Zone 75214

Name of Firm Moran & Son   State Texas

Title or Position architect

Business Address 4641 Greenview Avenue, Dallas 75214

Name of Bank First National   Branch

Have Accounts at Sanger-Harris, Fitches, Dreyfuss

Signature X *Mrs. Henry Moran*

Preference: ☑ Regular 30 Day   Date August 8, 19--
☐ { Pivot (6 mos. Plan)
   { Credit limit desired $ _____   Form D51-4-66

Courtesy Neiman-Marcus

customer needs to do, as indicated by the statement at the top of the application, is fill in the form, fold and seal it, and drop it into the mail.

Giving Charge Customers Special Privileges

Giving special attention to charge customers is good business. Generally speaking, these customers are loyal patrons; they buy more than cash customers, and they return to the store again and again. Most stores make a point of creating occasions when charge customers are given special privileges or attention. Such a PR letter is shown at the top of page 346.

Dear Mrs. Smith:

Bullock's invites you, as one of its select customers, to an advance showing of Gabrielle D'Orsay furs. Please mark this date on your personal calendar right now: Tuesday, September 17, at three o'clock in the afternoon. Your admission ticket is your Bullock's Charge-Mat or a copy of this letter.

The showing will be held in the Cascade Room on the third floor. The latest in luxury fur capes, jackets, coats, and stoles will be modeled by our "Sophisticated Six." Tea and other refreshments will be served to all our guests during and following the showing.

The furs you will see will not be placed in stock for sale to the general public until October 1. We want you, a preferred Bullock's customer, to have first choice.

Sincerely,

Encouraging Charge Customers to Use Their Accounts

Charge customers who have not made frequent use of their accounts can be encouraged by letter to use their charge privileges more often. Here is a clever letter that may prove irresistible to the "delinquent" charge customer.

Dear Customer:

You've
Earned

10¢	Is it worth 10 cents a line to you to read this
20¢	letter?
30¢	We'll gladly pay you that amount—but only if
40¢	you read the entire letter.
50¢	Now, we reason this way: You really are a valued
60¢	customer. But lately you haven't been in even
70¢	to say "Howdy." We would like you to come back;
80¢	we would like to see you often; we would like
90¢	you to reopen your account. We think that it is
$1.00	better for us to have a long-time customer like
$1.10	you on our books than a new customer whom we
$1.20	don't know. And since it would cost us at least
$1.30	$2.50 to open a new account, we would rather pass
$1.40	this amount to you.
$1.50	So we say, "Here is a $2.50 check on the house."
$1.60	Come in and select anything you wish, to the value
$1.70	of $25 or more, from our extensive stock of nation-
$1.80	ally advertised clothing and shoes for the entire
$1.90	family. Invest in that household appliance—pop-
$2.00	up toaster, steam iron—you have been dreaming
$2.10	about. Or do your gift shopping early for such
$2.20	items as diamonds, watches, radios.
$2.30	The enclosed check, worth $2.50, is your down
$2.40	payment.
$2.50	Why not come in tomorrow.

Cordially yours,

DALLAS. TEXAS 75201

WELCOME TO DALLAS . . . . .

for the meeting of the Association of School Business
Officials on October 14 through October 20. We hope
you are planning to attend this meeting and will bring
your family. We know that you will have a delightful
visit in our city.

Please plan to make Neiman-Marcus your unofficial headquarters and, if your busy schedule permits, plan to
have lunch in our famous Zodiac Restaurant - informal
modeling from 11:30 A.M. to 2:00 P.M.

A warm welcome awaits you at Neiman-Marcus and you are
invited to see our collection of Winter fashions.

If you do not already have an account with us, please
fill in and return the convenient application card.
As a charge customer you will receive our fashion brochures, notices of coming events, and our world famous
Christmas Booklet.

Sincerely yours,

Stanley Marcus

Courtesy Neiman-Marcus

Welcoming New Residents and Visitors

Hotels, department stores, and various businesses often obtain lists of the
visitors who are expected to attend conventions in their city and write them
letters of welcome. The letter illustrated above is an example of such a welcome.

When a new family moves into a community, many alert business firms
write a letter of welcome. Naturally, the purpose of the letter is to win friends
and customers. Note the technique employed in the letter illustrated at the
top of page 348.

Hello Neighbor:

Kreck's—Muncie's favorite bookstore—welcomes you to the community. We hope you will like our friendly people, our modern stores, our lovely city parks and playgrounds, and our exciting cultural and amusement centers. We're a proud, growing, bustling community.

Kreck's has grown up with Muncie. We were the first bookstore in the city, opening our doors back in 1927. Since that time we have supplied the reading needs of the community—from detective story paperbacks to the latest fiction to art encyclopedias. The top ten best sellers are featured in our window every week; yet we have a complete stock of the classics, too—books that are always best sellers. Come and browse with us. Enclosed is a certificate that entitles you to any paperback in our store (or you may use it as a credit of $1.50 toward any other book of your choice). We'd like to show you why Kreck's is known as Muncie's favorite bookstore. There is a reason.

Sincerely,

Writing Congratulatory Letters

Any occasion for congratulations is a PR moment. For example, some businesses write letters to congratulate parents on the arrival of a new baby. The list of names is usually obtained from hospital notices in the local newspaper.

Enclosed with the following letter is a pair of miniature long trousers.

Dear David:

You're a mighty discerning young man to have chosen the parents you did, and that's why I'm writing you this letter instead of them. Congratulations!

Here's your first pair of long pants. A little early, perhaps, but I want you to get used early to coming to Clarke's for all your clothing needs. Your dad has been a friend of ours for some time now. We like to think he is well satisfied with his purchases, and we hope you'll bring him in to see us often.

Tell you what: If you'll come in with your dad one year from now (I'll remind you), I'll have a present for you that you can really use.

Sincerely,

Sending Special Invitations

The following letter is typical of those that are used to invite customers to special demonstrations or receptions. Note that such a letter may also serve a sales function.

Dear Mrs. Layton:

Rachel Lindsay, author of the best seller Parched Domain, will be at Babcock's all day on Friday, March 15. You're invited to meet her. Copies of Parched Domain (called "the most captivating

novel of the year'' by the <u>Charleston Gazette</u>) will be on sale,
and each book sold will be personally autographed by the author.

Get your personally autographed copy of <u>Parched Domain</u> and
stay to become acquainted with Miss Lindsay. While you're here,
take a look at some of our exciting new books on Japanese crafts.

We will expect to see you on Friday the 15th.

Cordially,

Writing Letters for Special Occasions

Holidays and other special occasions provide opportunities to build goodwill
and to promote sales. Study the techniques employed in the following
examples:

Dear Dad:

Mind if we sneak a small string around that middle finger of your
left hand?

Not that we think you're absentminded. Far from that. But just in
case the press of business has caused you to suffer a temporary
lapse of memory, we thought it would be helpful to remind you that
May 12 is Mother's Day. You hadn't forgotten? Good!

What we don't want you to forget is that Loman's is the store from
which <u>she</u> would purchase her gift if she were doing the shopping.
Leather-crafted desk sets, luggage, luxurious handbags, manicure
sets, boudoir sets, oil paints, and crafts—everything and anything
she could possibly want.

Why not drop in this week? Ask for Mrs. Hampton; she will be
pleased to help you choose just the right gift for the occasion.

Cordially yours,

Dear Mrs. Tibbets:

Let's talk about golf. Yes, I know that there's snow on the ground
and nary a leaf on the trees. The fairways aren't fair, and the cups
runneth over on the greens.

But even December is golden weather at Princeton Sports Shop. If
you could see our fantastic selection of golf balls, clubs, bags, shoes,
carts, jackets, caps—everything you can imagine—you'd know what
I mean. No, we aren't stuck with an overambitious order placed
last summer. We intentionally stocked up because just about this
time of year every golfer longs to hike out to the club and smack
a few. That's why nothing would please your golfer more this
Christmas than a new set of clubs, a new bag, a couple of dozen
new golf balls, or a good-looking pair of golf slacks. Sam Snead
Championship clubs? Wilson's K-77? We've got 'em!

The best part of the story is that all golf equipment is on sale at
30 percent off. Why not come in to the Princeton Sports Shop and
take care of that special man of yours now?

Sincerely yours,

LILY-TULIP CUP CORPORATION
PACKAGING, VENDING, SERVICE PRODUCTS IN PAPER AND PLASTIC

1100 North Glenstone Avenue, Springfield, Missouri 65801   UNIVERSITY 2-2744

June 29, 19--

Dallas Paper Company
1876 Water Street
Dallas, Texas   75205

Gentlemen:

THANK YOU!

Yes, we most certainly owe you a special word of thanks. Normally
we are so busy with our problems we seldom take time to express
our appreciation to customers such as you who pay their accounts,
month after month, year after year, quietly and regularly, with no
effort on our part.

It has been said, and it is true, a credit man is so busy saying
"Please remit" he overlooks the opportunity to say "Thank you." So
we are forgetting the problems for the moment to express our gratitude
to you and your entire organization for your acceptance of our product
and the fine manner in which you have consistently maintained your
account.

The success of our efforts depends entirely upon the cooperation of
our accounts; so it is to you we feel most indebted. Our appreciation
is great--our thanks sincere.

Cordially yours,

LILY-TULIP CUP CORPORATION

J. A. Patterson

J. A. Patterson
Regional Credit Manager

JAP:wh

Courtesy The Dartnell Corporation—Gold Medal Award Letter

Thanking Customers for Business Patronage

Someone has made the statement that only troublemakers get personal attention from a business firm; the loyal customer who never squawks and who quietly and promptly pays his bills receives no attention at all. An increasing number of business firms, however, are trying to remedy this situation. The letter of the Lily-Tulip Cup Corporation, illustrated above, is an excellent example of one company's effort to thank and show appreciation to good customers.

Another example of such effort is shown by the following letter, a thank-you for prompt payment.

Dear Mr. Porter:

Enclosed is your canceled note covering the purchase of your automobile. It is paid in full.

We appreciate the manner in which you have met your payments on this purchase, Mr. Porter. It is a pleasure to do business with you.

I am enclosing a certificate that entitles you to preferred credit privileges. Just present it to any of our branch banks for quick service on loans of any kind. We shall be pleased to help you.

Cordially yours,

Note that in addition to thanking the customer, the writer also uses the letter to serve a sales function and encourage future business.

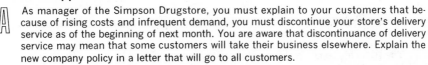

COMMUNICATION PROJECTS

Practical Application

A As manager of the Simpson Drugstore, you must explain to your customers that because of rising costs and infrequent demand, you must discontinue your store's delivery service as of the beginning of next month. You are aware that discontinuance of delivery service may mean that some customers will take their business elsewhere. Explain the new company policy in a letter that will go to all customers.

B Assume that you have graduated from college and have worked for five years as a tax accountant in a public accounting firm. You have now decided to set up your own tax accounting business, and you plan to use your home as an office. In promoting the new business, you choose to announce your venture by writing a letter that will be sent to 50 small-business owners in the community. The fact that you have had experience in tax work, plus your excellent training, should be emphasized. Write the letter. Supply any details that will improve your chances of selling your services.

C Develop a letter that encourages charge customers of a retail store to use their charge accounts. Use your ingenuity in making the letter different from others you have seen.

D In most American cities, a service called the *Welcome Wagon* greets new residents of the city and relays to them greetings from each of the businesses interested in making contact with potential customers. Assume that you are employed by a lumber firm, McCauley Lumber Company. This company offers a complete selection of builders' supplies, including lumber, hardwoods, windows, doors, and screens. As a service to the home handyman, free advice is given on building furniture, closets, home workshops, recreation rooms, and so on. Write a welcome letter (to be distributed by the Welcome Wagon) to newcomers to the city. Assume that the letter will be accompanied by a five-dollar coupon to be used on any purchase of twenty dollars or more at the McCauley Lumber Company.

E Jackson Motors, a foreign car dealer in your city, is about to introduce for the first time in your state a new Italian sports car, the Milano. A special preview showing, including refreshments, is planned for all good friends of Jackson's. The showing will be held at the dealer's showrooms, 1426 South Fourth Street, on Friday afternoon at four o'clock. Write a letter inviting customers to this special showing of the Milano.

Editing Practice

Editing to Improve Writing Techniques Edit the following sentences to remove all evidence of poor writing techniques.

1. I learned the answer would depend on an intensive study of the problem.
2. Benson is one of the best if not the best accountants in the state.
3. Dean always has and always will write factual reports.
4. In his writing, Dodd consistently uses monotonous wording, thus making his communications ineffective.
5. We must complete the research, assembling of facts, and writing the report.
6. We have received some startlingly new designs from Paris, and so we shall be able to help you serve even your most fastidious customers.
7. The reports would lie on his desk for hours and sometimes days.
8. There is no future for the business communicator who is careless or indifferent to the techniques of writing.
9. Within five minutes after I gave Mr. Sparks the message from the advisory committee, a reply was dictated.
10. To properly prepare this special report, you will need to engage a private research consultant.
11. You may use either of these four machines for your typewriting practice.
12. Jim said that he couldn't find any paper for the duplicating machine after looking through all the shelves in the stockroom.
13. The company issued a new personnel policies manual, and it spelled out the changes that had been made in vacation schedules.
14. Did you find out why our stockholders are concerned about their proxy?
15. Ted moved that we adjourn the meeting until tomorrow to cut off further discussion about the new constitution.

Plurals and Possessives Indicate the correct plural or possessive forms of the words enclosed in parentheses.

1. The (Lynch) are not building up their inventory.
2. We think that (chintz) will be high fashion this spring.
3. The company posts all important notices on (it) bulletin board.
4. Mr. Lane is a man (who) integrity is well known.
5. (Children) energy seems almost inexhaustible.
6. For income purposes, invest in public (utility).
7. The (senator-elect) expenses were taken from the campaign fund.
8. Mr. Trent's part in the program was the singing of three (solo).
9. Have you seen the (Brooks) full-page advertisement?
10. (Handkerchief) move slowly, except at Christmas time.
11. Mr. (Wilcox) office was just remodeled.
12. The two (general manager) reports were combined into one proposal.
13. All the (secretary) in our department are fluent in Spanish or French.
14. The traffic department has added a hundred new cars to (it) fleet.
15. The public relations department of the school sent a letter to the (alumnus) to ask them for contributions to the new building fund.

Case Problem

Making Statistics Meaningful As an employee of the public relations department, Paul Edison is responsible for taking visitors through the company plant and for telling them facts and figures about the company. Here is part of the talk he uses on his tours: "Five years ago, we had only 127 production workers. Today, we have 1,270. Five years ago, we produced 19,550 clocks each year. Today, the workers produce 247,000 clocks annually. Five years ago, we were losing $1,000 a week. This year, our profits will be about $250,000." These facts are an important part of Paul's presentation, but they are difficult for visitors to grasp because of the way in which Paul presents them.

Can you present the facts in such a way that visitors will grasp them more readily?

Social-Business Letters

Many letters written by business people serve a social-business purpose. They are not strictly business letters; that is, they do not involve the day-to-day commercial operations of the business. They are more personal—even semi-social in nature. The business executive does not lose his personal identity simply because he holds a responsible position in an organization. In fact, he often participates in even more activities than the average individual, and these activities may be only indirectly related to his job.

The typical executive is a member of professional organizations in his field, such as the National Sales Executives Association, the American Institute of Certified Public Accountants, or the Administrative Management Society. He may continue to be active in his college fraternity; he may hold office in his college alumni association; and he may belong to several civic or church groups. The company for which the executive works considers these activities desirable, even though they are not strictly related to business, because active, outgoing employees make an important contribution to the company image, described in Section 43.

As a result of his professional and personal associations, the executive is obligated to write letters of a semisocial nature. He writes congratulatory letters to friends and business associates who have received promotions; thank-you letters for favors, gifts, hospitality, and special services; condolence letters to those who have suffered misfortunes; letters involving the affairs of professional, social, and civic organizations to which he belongs; and formal social communications. These are social-business letters—in effect, the public relations letters of an individual employed in a business organization.

FORMAT OF SOCIAL-BUSINESS LETTERS

For social-business letters, a smaller size of stationery—baronial or monarch —is preferred by most executives. Of course, the regular company stationery also may be used.

Basically, the format of a social-business letter is the same as the format of a regular business letter. However, the salutation in a social-business letter is often followed by a comma, rather than by a colon. In addition, the inside address is usually written at the foot of the letter, like this:

Cordially yours,

Mr. Harold Sampson, Registrar
Davenport College of Business
12 South Division Avenue
Grand Rapids, Michigan   49502

LETTERS OF CONGRATULATION

Job promotions, honors bestowed by groups or organizations, appointments or elections to office, and other achievements of a business or of its employees are all appropriate occasions for writing congratulatory messages. In fact, such occasions are excellent PR opportunities. Since everyone wants to be respected and admired, a cordial letter of congratulations on such important occasions will always build the reader's goodwill toward the writer, and such goodwill, of course, is a valuable asset to the businessman.

Congratulating Individuals

Most social-business letters written by businessmen are to congratulate individuals on some important occasion in their careers. For example, suppose that you are a business executive and that you read in the local paper that a fellow member of the Office Executives Club has just been promoted to a new position in his company. As a thoughtful person, you might write a letter of congratulation like the following:

Dear Phil,

 It was a pleasure to read in last night's Star-Ledger of your promotion to manager of administrative services at Sperry-Wilcox. You've certainly merited this promotion, Phil, and I am delighted at this recognition of your ability. Congratulations! I hope that you will like your new assignment and that it will be a stepping-stone to even greater things.

Sincerely yours,

The businessman should never neglect the opportunity to build goodwill on any occasion on which a friend, a business associate, or an acquaintance has been honored by a group or an organization. Of course, the warmer and more friendly the letter, the more effective it will be. For example, the following letter clearly expresses the writer's pleasure in the honor bestowed on his friend.

Dear Ann,

 The Administrative Management Society made a wise choice in naming you "Business Teacher of the Year." As you know, you have always been at the top of my list, but I'm delighted to have this fine organization agree with me. The recognition is well deserved, and my congratulations are sent with a warm feeling of friendship.

 This occasion is also an opportunity to thank you for your many hours of committee work for AMS. We know a committee's work will be done efficiently, thoughtfully, and on time when you are a member. It has always been a pleasure to serve with you.

Cordially,

Sometimes, however, the businessman wishes to congratulate a person he does not know or whom he does not know very well. Such a letter will necessarily be somewhat more formal in tone than one written to a friend, but it should be cordial nevertheless. Often such letters are used to build valuable business contacts; hence they must be carefully, skillfully written, as shown by the following example.

Dear Mr. Favershaw:

Please add my congratulations to the many you have already received on your being awarded the Distinguished Service Medal by the Junior Chamber of Commerce. This high honor is one in which you can take great pride.

The Junior Chamber has done much to stimulate good business—and good business practice—in Stanbury, and I know you have been very instrumental in this work.

My best wishes to you for continued success.

Cordially yours,

Some occasions calling for letters of congratulation are more personal in nature. For example, a social honor, an important anniversary, or some personal achievement would all call for congratulatory letters. Another occasion would be the appointment or election of a friend or business associate to office in a civic organization. Here is a letter that could be written on such an occasion.

Dear Don:

I heartily endorse the judgment of the Youth Club of Yorkville in electing you its president for the coming year.

You have made many fine contributions over the years to the youth development program of Yorkville. No one has given more time, energy, and talent to this fine work; no one deserves more than you to be recognized for the achievements of the Youth Club.

I know that one of your big concerns for the coming year will be your drive for funds for a new Youth Club building. Let me know whether I can be of help. I, too, think that such a building is long overdue in Yorkville.

Sincerely yours,

Another excellent opportunity for a personal letter of congratulations is any important achievement by the children of friends or business associates. Such a letter may be written to the parents or, especially if the writer knows the family, directly to the youngster. Note the example shown at the top of page 356.

Dear Michael,

It was indeed a pleasure to read last night in the <u>Westwood Advocate</u> that you have won the junior oratorical contest of the Dad's Club for the Greater Westwood area. Congratulations!

The competition is tough in these contests. Many years before you were born, I participated in a similar contest. Lacking your gift, though, I placed ninth!

I know that you and your parents take pride in this accomplishment, Michael. Good luck!

Sincerely yours,

Not only are letters of congratulation written to customers and friends outside the organization, but they are also frequently sent to fellow employees in the company. In fact, some executives consider these letters among the most important they write. Of course, an obvious occasion for such letters is a job promotion. Here is an example:

Dear Miss Livingston:

I was pleased and proud to learn of your promotion to administrative assistant to the executive vice-president. It is a very important position in the company, and I am sure that no one is better qualified to fill it than you.

How long has it been since you and I first became acquainted as fellow employees? My best recollection is that you preceded me in joining the company by about two months. Do you realize that this makes us almost five-year "veterans"?

At any rate, it has been great fun to be associated with you, and I look forward to an even closer relationship in the future. If I can give you any help (and I'll do better than I did on those reports I "helped" you with a couple of years ago!), just call on me.

Sincerely,

An important anniversary with the company is another occasion for writing a congratulatory letter, as shown here:

Dear Charlie,

Congratulations on your tenth anniversary with Temple Insurance. I know how you feel—"Has it really been that long?" In view of your accomplishments, though, you might ask, "Hasn't it been longer than that?" You have made remarkable progress in such a short time, and all of us who have worked with you marvel at your ability to handle difficult jobs so smoothly. We've learned much from you, my friend!

I hope to be around on your twentieth to congratulate you again. Of course, by that time you'll be so high up in the company that I'll have to get permission to write you. But it'll be worth it.

Warmest wishes for continued success.

Sincerely,

A letter of congratulations may also be appropriate when an employee retires. The tone of such a letter, however, depends primarily on the attitude of the person retiring. Some look forward to retirement; others do not. If you don't know the feelings of the retiree, use a style similar to that used in the following example:

Dear Mrs. Lobdell:

It does not seem possible that the company could be having a retirement party for you at the end of this month. I don't see how we can operate successfully without you!

You have been told many times of the fine contribution you have made to the growth of Winchester's, but I should like to add my own tribute. The promotion program you have established for Winchester Fabrics has made us the envy of the industry. Many of your promotion pieces have been classics in beauty, in simplicity, in design—and in results. It must be a source of pride to you to have seen your creative ideas successfully implemented.

I'm grateful to you—as is everyone else in the company— for helping us to reach our present stature in the bookcloth industry. All good wishes to you in your retirement. I hope you will enjoy many, many years of happiness with your friends and family.

Sincerely,

A slightly different kind of letter of congratulation is that written by one business firm to another. Of course, such a letter very often has sales overtones.

Dear Mr. Beck,

How pleased I was to have had the opportunity of attending your open house last Saturday. The new branch store in Fernwood is a beauty! I was very much impressed with the brilliant architectural design of the building as well as with the magnificent furnishings. Surely Marshall's of Fernwood is a fine addition to the community, and I predict a long and successful "run."

Please let me know how my company or I may serve you in your new location. We want to be good neighbors, and we welcome the opportunity to prove it. Congratulations!

Cordially yours,

THANK-YOU LETTERS

Occasions that call for thank-you letters often arise; for example, to acknowledge receiving a gift, to express appreciation for thoughtfulness, for special favors, and so on. Thank-you letters in business are just as necessary as the "bread and butter" notes sent to friends who have entertained you in their homes or who have done something especially nice for you. In fact, failure to write a thank-you when it is called for can lose goodwill, because people expect their gifts and special efforts to be appreciated and are displeased when appreciation is not shown.

Promptness in sending a thank-you note is equally as important as what is said, because any delay in sending the letter may be taken to imply a lack of sincere appreciation.

Writing Thanks for a Gift

The typical business executive often receives gifts from suppliers and from others with whom he does business. Although some business firms deplore this practice, it nevertheless exists. Some companies prohibit the acceptance of gifts by individuals, as indicated tactfully in the following example:

Dear Mr. Ranier:

The handsome twelve-volume Encyclopedia of World Art arrived this morning. It is magnificent. I don't think I have ever seen more beautiful color reproductions anywhere. I am amazed at how well you have captured the brilliance and detail of the original paintings.

You may be sure, Mr. Ranier, that we shall make very good use of this encyclopedia in our company library. Each copy will bear this inscription on the inside front cover: "Presented to the Rowlinson Company library by the Rand Donnelly Corporation."

In behalf of all the employees at Rowlinson, may I express our deepest appreciation to you. Your gesture was a very thoughtful one.

Sincerely yours,

Writing Thanks for Hospitality

When hospitality has been extended to you, common courtesy calls for a thank-you. For example, suppose that you visit a supplier's factory in another city to discuss the purchase of his product. He makes reservations for you at a hotel, takes you to dinner, and in other ways looks after your physical comfort—he even entertains you in his home. Of course, a "bread and butter" note is a must.

Dear Mr. Borden:

Thank you for the many courtesies extended to me on my visit to Calgrin. My stay was certainly more pleasant because of your personal thoughtfulness in arranging for my comfort.

The high spot of the whole visit was the evening spent in your beautiful home. You and Mrs. Borden are gracious hosts. The food was excellent; the conversation, stimulating; the people, delightful. The time passed so quickly that I was embarrassed to find that I stayed so long—so engrossed and comfortable was I in being a part of such company.

I have mailed a small package to Mrs. Borden. It represents but a token of my appreciation for the many kindnesses shown me. I shall not soon forget my visit to Calgrin.

Sincerely yours,

Writing Thanks for Courtesies

When a person receives a letter of congratulation upon a promotion, a special recognition, or an achievement, he should acknowledge it with a thank-you letter. For example:

Dear Stan:

It was thoughtful of you to write me about my recent promotion. One of the most satisfying things about being promoted is that one gets such pleasant letters from the nicest people! I do like my new job, and I will enjoy it even more after I have really gotten the hang of it.

Thank you, Stan, for your good wishes. About that offer to help—I may call on you sooner than you think, so be prepared!

Sincerely,

Writing Thanks for Special Favors

Often a friend or business acquaintance goes out of his way to do a favor for another. He may, for example, have recommended a friend for membership in a club, may have recommended a particular firm to a customer, or may have been of special service in a business situation. A special favor of this kind deserves a thank-you; for example:

Dear Mr. Breakstone,

Yesterday we had a visit from Mr. J. P. Gillette of Vacation Inns, Inc. He placed a very large order for furniture for his new motel installation in Jacksonville—one of the largest orders we have received this year. Mr. Gillette told us that you recommended us highly to him.

We are extremely grateful to you, Mr. Breakstone, for this very great favor. While we appreciate the order immensely, we appreciate even more your confidence in us. It is a compliment of the highest order.

I hope that we may be able to return the favor in some way before long. We'd like that chance.

Cordially yours,

FORMAL INVITATIONS AND REPLIES

From time to time, businessmen receive formal invitations to such events as an open house, a special reception to honor a distinguished person, a special anniversary, or a formal social gathering. Such invitations are usually engraved or printed and are written in the third person.

The examples below and on page 361 show the formal printed invitation, the formal handwritten invitation, the handwritten acceptance, and the handwritten refusal. An acceptance or a refusal is occasionally typewritten; how-

Printed Invitation

The Advertising Club
requests the pleasure of your company
at a formal showing
of its new film
"America at the Crossroads"
Saturday, the eleventh of July
at two o'clock
Rendezvous Room of the Gladstone Building
R.S.V.P.

Handwritten Invitation

Mr. and Mrs. Arthur Cramden
request the pleasure of
Mr. and Mrs. Peter Marlin's
company at dinner
on Tuesday, the ninth of August
at eight o'clock
4112 Juniper Drive
R.S.V.P.

ever, this practice is not recommended. Handwritten invitations and replies are written on plain white notepaper.

LETTERS OF CONDOLENCE

Just as you would send a sympathy card to one who has suffered the loss of a close relative or friend, business executives write letters to friends and associates upon learning of misfortunes and tragedies in their lives. Naturally,

Acceptance

Miss Gail O'Connell
accepts with pleasure
the kind invitation of
The Advertising Club
for Saturday, the eleventh of July

Refusal

Mr. & Mrs. Peter Marlin
regret that a previous engagement
prevents their accepting
Mr. & Mrs. Cramden's
kind invitation
for the ninth of August

letters of condolence should be genuinely sympathetic. It is not easy to comfort those who have suffered losses; letters of condolence, therefore, are among the most difficult letters to write. Although hand-written condolence letters are preferable, typed letters are acceptable. If you are unable to write a really personal note of sympathy, you may send a printed sympathy card. Following is a letter of condolence.

Dear Tracy:

I was saddened to learn of the death of your mother last week. Please accept my sincere sympathy.

When my mother passed away two years ago, a friend sent me a copy of the enclosed poem by Franklin Rivera. I have received much consolation from reading these words, and I thought they might also be a comfort to you.

My thoughts are with you and your family in this time of grief.

                                        Sincerely yours,

COMMUNICATION PROJECTS

Practical Application

A When you were in school, one of your closest fraternity friends was Walter "Whizzer" Pinkston. On graduation Whizzer took a position with the production control department of Consoldiated Chemicals, Louisville, Kentucky 40204. Recently you noticed in *Chemical Comments* that Whizzer was promoted to the newly created post of Director of Management Training. The creation of this post is a pioneering venture for the chemical industry. Write a short letter to your old friend to congratulate him on his promotion.

B Assume that you are assistant personnel director of a small company, the Blazek Heating Company, Inc., Hannibal, Missouri 63401. It is your responsibility to write letters (for the signature of your company president, Carl A. Gillette) to thank retiring employees for their service to BHC and to wish them well. A token gift (a $50 check) accompanies each letter. A retirement letter must now be written to Philip A. LeSeuer, a 40-year employee, recently head of the Accounts Payable section of the company. Mr. LeSeuer is still in excellent physical condition and resents very deeply that, merely because of his age, he must leave a full-time position to which he can still contribute a great deal. Write the letter to Mr. LeSeuer for the President's signature and thank Mr. LeSeuer for his faithful service to the company.

C Last week you returned from a business trip to Minneapolis, Minnesota. During your three-day stay in Minnesota, you were the house guest of Mr. and Mrs. August Swenson, long-time friends of your family. Mrs. Swenson (Olga) even met you at the airport and insisted on personally driving you to your business appointments, rather than have you experience the inconvenience of traveling by bus (Minneapolis was in the midst of a month-long taxicab drivers' strike at the time). Write a note of thanks to the Swensons, who live at 1817 East Fairmont Drive, Minneapolis 55404. (A gift might accompany this letter and be mentioned in a postscript.)

D Prepare a formal invitation inviting prospective customers to attend a preview showing of a new line of Danish furniture, "Svenska Royale," which your store will introduce soon. The program will include a filmstrip describing the complete line. This filmstrip will be narrated by Mr. Ingmar Bjorndahl, decorating consultant from the Svenska firm, Copenhagen, Denmark. The showing will be held at 5 p.m., Monday, December 4, in the Contemporary Corner of your Fineline Furniture Store, with a coffee hour to begin at 4:15. An RSVP should be requested.

E Recently you purchased life insurance policies for each of your three children from Frank Gavin, an agent of the Columbia Life Insurance Company, Denver, Colorado 80203. As appreciation for your business, Frank has sent you and your family a gift carton of citrus fruit from Phoenix, Arizona, where he vacations each winter. Write to Frank to thank him for the gift.

F You have only recently learned of the illness and death of Mrs. Mark Davidson, the wife of one of your best customers and long-time friend. Mrs. Davidson (Jan) leaves, in addition to her husband, two small sons, Bill and Bob. Write a letter to Mark, who is Purchasing Agent for Allied Industries, Bennington, Vermont 05201, to extend your sympathy.

Editing Practice

Editing for Redundancies   Correct these sentences by eliminating all unnecessary repetitions.

1. Clean this machine each day, as otherwise you will not get the best performance.
2. The sink would fit just inside of the doorway.
3. Mr. Miller will not repeat his instructions again.
4. The rush was over with long before five o'clock.
5. Past experience has taught us that we must collect bills promptly.
6. Ray expects to get advice free gratis.
7. Bob's and David's reports are both alike.
8. Before we accept the missile work, our machinery must be converted over.

Case Problem

Listening for Essential Ideas   Your instructor will read an article to you. Listen carefully; then summarize the article in as few words as possible.

CHAPTER

8

Other Written Communications

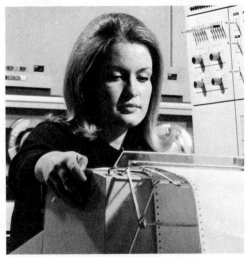

Memorandums

Memorandums, usually shortened to *memos*, are the primary means by which the employees of an organization correspond with each other whenever the situation calls for fulfilling the business rule of "put it in writing" (PIIW). Although memos are never directed to persons outside the organization and are usually sent through special interoffice mail channels instead of through the regular mails, they serve purposes similar to those of ordinary business letters: to request or to give information, to transmit documents, to announce company policies, to recommend promotions, to request job transfers, and so on. Often, as discussed in Section 46, memos are used to make informal reports.

FORM OF THE MEMO

To promote efficiency and economy in the preparation and processing of in-house correspondence, most companies use interoffice memo forms printed on stationery 8½ by 11 or 8½ by 5½ inches. Like invoices, purchase orders, and other commonly used business forms, memos often are packaged as "snap-out" forms; that is, the forms are in preassembled carbon packs, which provide an original copy for the addressee, one or more "cc" or information copies, and a file copy. Ordinarily only very small offices use completely type-written memos, such as the one illustrated on page 367.

The heading of a printed memo form, such as the one on page 369, usually includes (1) the name of the company, (2) the title *Interoffice Memorandum*, and (3) the guide words *To, From, Subject,* and *Date.* If the company is large and has several divisions or has offices in several locations, the heading may include such additional guide words as *Department, Location,* and *Telephone Extension.*

The To Line

The *To* line usually includes the full name of the addressee with an appropriate courtesy title, such as *Mr., Miss,* or *Dr.*

> TO: Mr. Lloyd T. Anderson
> TO: Dr. A. H. Jones
> TO: Miss Alice Johnson

As illustrated below, it is particularly appropriate to include the addressee's job title when:

1. The writer wishes to show deference to the addressee.

> TO: Mr. George T. Warren, Chairman of the Board

```
                    INTEROFFICE MEMORANDUM

    TO:      Mr. Charles P. Gilbert      FROM:  Ronald N. Forsythe

    SUBJECT: National Sales Conference   DATE:  August 15, 19--


    As requested in your August 12 memo, here are my suggestions
    concerning the forthcoming national sales conference:

    1.  I recommend that we hold our meeting in the Midwest this
        year.  My own choice is Springfield, Illinois, because of
        its central location.

    2.  Most of the men prefer to hold meetings away from the
        city.  Several motels with excellent room, meeting, and
        other necessary accommodations are located on the out-
        skirts of Springfield.  I believe that any one of the
        motels listed on the enclosed sheet would be a good con-
        ference site.

    3.  Since a number of men have joined the staff since the
        last national sales conference, I recommend that all rep-
        resentatives with less than one year's service be asked
        to attend a special one-day indoctrination session to be
        held in advance of the arrival of the other salesmen.

    4.  A number of our salesmen are not so familiar with our
        advertising and general sales-support policies and pro-
        cedures as they would like to be.  Therefore, I suggest
        that this year's agenda include a panel discussion of
        these topics.

    Please let me know whether you would like to discuss these few
    suggestions or any other aspect of the conference.

                                      R. N. F.


    urs
    Enclosure
```

2. **The name of the addressee is the same as, or could easily be confused with, that of another employee.**

> TO: Miss Patricia Lindberg, Sales Correspondent
> (Mrs. Pat Lundberg is administrative assistant to the
> sales manager.)

3. **The addressee has several job titles, and the message pertains to the duties associated with only one of those titles.**

> TO: Mr. John T. Allen, Chairman, Employee Benefits Committee
> (Mr. Allen is also the director of marketing.)

To assure prompt and accurate delivery of interoffice mail such as memos, particularly in large offices, many writers include appropriate address information, for example:

TO: Mr. Jacob Toppen, Room 1610, Accounting Department
TO: Mrs. Julia Perez, Personnel Department, 5th Floor

Distribution* and CC *Notations When a memo is being sent to a number of people, it is appropriate to type "See below" in the *To* line and include a *Distribution* notation at the bottom of the memo.

TO: See below.
DISTRIBUTION:
Mr. David Bernstein, Accounting Department
Miss Anne Davis, Purchasing Department
Mr. Frank C. Green, Manager, Accounting Department
Mrs. Louise Garofalo, Personnel Department
Mr. George Harris, Vice-President, Personnel
Dr. R. S. Vincent, General Manager

If space permits, the *cc* notation is placed below the name of the addressee, as illustrated below; otherwise, the notation is positioned below the typist's initials, just as in a business letter.

TO: Mrs. Phyllis Dunbar
cc: Mr. K. T. Raymond
      Mr. L. A. Kirsch

The From *Line*

The writer of a memo does not use a courtesy title with his name. For identification purposes, he may include his job title or his departmental affiliation. He may also indicate the location of his office and his telephone extension.

FROM: Barbara Fisher, Secretary, Legal Department,
      Room 1660, Ext. 3204

The Date *Line*

Just as in letters, the date should be written in full, not abbreviated or expressed in figures.

DATE: February 4, 19— (*or* 4 February 19—)

The Subject *Line*

The subject of the memo should be stated as briefly as possible, preferably so as to fit on one line; for example:

SUBJECT: Request for additional clerk-typist

The style of capitalization in the subject line varies. For the sake of speed, some writers capitalize only the first word and, of course, words that are always capitalized; for example:

SUBJECT: Meeting with Dayton office personnel

MITCHELL HOME PRODUCTS, INC.
INTEROFFICE MEMO

TO: All Salesmen in Territory 4

FROM: Howard L. Chester, Sales Supervisor

DATE: June 10, 19--

SUBJECT: Ratio of Customer Calls to Completed Sales for May, 19--

I know you are always interested in comparing your sales efforts with those of the other salesmen in Territory 4. Consequently, I've compiled the following data from your daily reports. (To read these columns, notice, for instance, that Salesman A, during May, 19--, called on an average of 2.3 customers for every sale he realized.)

CUSTOMER CALLS PER SALE MADE

Territory 4 Averages

Salesman	Month of May, 19--	May, Last Year	Year to Date
A	2.3	3.8	4.2
B	3.6	3.9	3.5
C	6.8	8.5	6.7
D	8.9	9.6	8.3
E	4.7	5.7	4.3

Territories 4, 5, and 6 Averages

Territory	Month of May, 19--	May, Last Year	Year to Date
4	5.3	6.3	5.4
5	3.7	4.2	4.3
6	5.8	6.9	7.1

You will notice from the averages by territories that the ratio of customer calls to sales in our territory for May of this year is better than a year ago and than the year to date. Although our ratio is improving, we have not yet reached the low average ratio reported from Territory 5. It may be that all of us will need to study the methods used by Salesmen A and B to see how they are able to produce the high ratio of sales to customer calls.

H. L. C.

bt

The Body or Message

Unlike a business letter, a memo ordinarily does not include a salutation. Therefore, the body or message of the memo begins three or four lines below the subject line. Unless the message is very short, the body should be single-spaced. Paragraphs may be indented, but frequently they are blocked.

The Signature

Many writers prefer to have their initials—or their full name— typed below the message, to align with the fill-ins at the top right of the memo (see the illustration on page 367). Some feel that it is unnecessary to repeat information that already appears in the *From* line; therefore, they simply initial the memo near their typewritten name or below the message.

Reference Initials and Enclosure Notation

The initials of the typist and, when appropriate, the enclosure notation are typed just as they are in a regular business letter.

TONE OF THE MEMORANDUM

The tone of the memorandum depends on (1) the relationship between the writer and the recipient, (2) the nature of the subject, and (3) company policy. A few companies insist that memos be written in the third person only ("It is believed" rather than "I believe") so that facts are not mixed with opinions. Most companies, however, leave the tone of the memo to the discretion of the writer.

The tone of a memo is determined largely by the position and the personal preference of the individual to whom it is addressed. Generally, communications addressed to top management are more formal than those addressed to persons of equal or lesser rank than the writer. However, there is no hard-and-fast rule for determining tone. Some top executives may insist on formality. In the absence of specific instructions, the new employee should take the middle ground—not too informal (such as using contractions like *you'll* and *here's*) and not too deferential. For example:

> Here is the report you asked me to prepare on staff reaction to our new company magazine, *Direction Finder*. The following points deserve special mention . . .

ORGANIZATION OF THE MEMORANDUM

Regardless of the form and tone of the memorandum, its main purpose is to convey a message. It should be as brief and to the point as possible without being curt or skimpy. Like a letter, a memorandum attempts to sell a point of view; for example, selling a superior on the need for more personnel or new office equipment. A memo, however, is usually more economical in its use of words.

The organization of a memorandum can vary; a typical memo, however, contains three elements: (1) a statement of purpose, (2) a message, and (3) a statement of future action to be taken.

Statement of Purpose

Always explain your reason for writing the memo. You may refer to a memo written or received previously, to a meeting attended, to a telephone conversation, and so on. Never assume that the subject line alone is enough to define the purpose of a memo. The purpose of a memo may be stated as follows:

As you requested in your memorandum of August 17, I am sending you a report of employee turnover during July.

You will recall that at our last meeting of the Advertising Committee I was asked to investigate the cost of special shipping tickets for our new Diamond line. Here is what I found . . .

I am attaching a photocopy of a letter that I received this morning from Claude Jenkins. I believe Claude's comments give further evidence of the need for improving our billing procedures.

On December 9, Mary Hertz will have been on the Carlson staff for ten years. I recommend that we arrange a special anniversary luncheon in her honor on that date.

Message

The main points of the message should be stated so that they can be read easily and quickly. One way to make a message clear immediately is to enumerate the important points. For example:

After making a careful study of the situation, I recommend the following:

1. That the work hours for the Circulation Department staff might be staggered. Half the group could report for work at 8:30 and leave at 4:30; the other half could report at 9 and leave at 5.

2. That the elevators be reserved for passengers only, from 8 to 9 each morning. The use of elevators for mail and freight during the morning rush hour delays employees going to their offices.

If the memorandum pertains to several major topics, side headings can be used. For example:

The need for additional shipping-room personnel varies by branch office. Some offices appear to be overstaffed, while others are seriously short of personnel.

Rochester. In the Rochester plant, two additional people are needed at once. Business in that area of New York State is growing very rapidly, and in recent months serious bottlenecks have developed in getting out customers' orders.

Scranton. The staff in Scranton is adequate at present. The problem here is not one of quantity but one of quality. With the new training program, however, this problem should soon be overcome.

Boston. In this office, the shipping room is overstaffed. This overstaffing is the result of the decline of shipping from the Boston plant since the Springfield warehouses were completed.

Statement of Future Action

Usually the memorandum should end with a statement of future action to be taken or with a request for further instructions, as illustrated in the examples below and in the memo on page 367.

Do you wish me to follow up on these suggestions?

Our committee will meet again on June 21, and at that time I will report on the decisions reached.

Please let me know whether the solution I have recommended is satisfactory to you.

I shall be glad to give you more details on my meeting with Mr. Frankheimer if you wish to have them.

The memo on page 369 illustrates effective organization. Note that the purpose is stated in the first two sentences and that the detailed information is carefully explained and is displayed in tabular form. The implications of the table are summarized in the first part of the last paragraph, and a suggestion for future action is made in the last sentence.

COMMUNICATION PROJECTS

Practical Application

A Your employer, Carl H. Felderman, is considering the purchase of a portable typewriter for his daughter, who is now in college. He asks you to check the prices of the models carried by local stores. You obtain the following information: (1) Speedster Portable, pica and elite types, $125.75; (2) The Streak, pica and elite types, $129.50; (3) the Blaze, pica ($134.50) and elite ($137.75). All carry one-year guarantees and are available in many colors—the Speedster at Dane's Supply Store; the Streak at Kenton's Office Equipment Store; and the Blaze, which has a built-in copyholder in its carrying case, at the Economy Office Store. Organize this information into a concise, easy-to-read memorandum and submit it to Mr. Felderman. Be sure to follow the memorandum style outlined in this lesson.

B Mr. Jasper T. Lane, head of the Claims Division in your company, has become concerned during the past six months over the amount of time his office staff is spending at coffee breaks. The situation appears to be getting out of hand, and he would like to call the entire division of forty people together on Thursday morning, February 15, at 10:30, in Conference Room 2, to discuss the subject. Mr. Lane asks you, his staff assistant, to write (for his signature) a memorandum to announce the thirty-minute meeting to all Claims Division personnel. All telephone lines in the division are to be "covered" during the period of the meeting.

C Every year one student from your college is chosen as its representative to the national convention of Collegiate Student Business Leaders. This year's convention will be held in Chicago on November 25 and 26, 19—. Your school chooses its representative on the basis of a competition in which the interested students present their qualifications in writing to Mr. John A. Ferdin, faculty coordinator of the event. Write a memorandum to Mr. Ferdin in which you show why you should be chosen to attend this convention. Supply all necessary details.

D Your company has announced a policy of paying one-half the tuition for courses completed in local evening schools when such courses are of direct benefit to the employee's work. In order to take advantage of this program, each employee must submit a request in writing to the personnel director, Mr. Keith J. Blount, at least one month before the anticipated registration. Assume that you are interested in taking a course called Introduction to Electronic Data Processing at a local evening school. Write a memorandum to Mr. Blount, state your reasons for taking the course, and show how your work would be benefited. Fill in all the necessary details.

E The Superior Tool Company Employees Association, of which you are secretary, has accumulated $1,000 over the past two years, to be used for charitable purposes. In order to determine what would be worthwhile causes, the Association has decided to ask each supervisor to discuss the matter with his subordinates and to submit to the Association's secretary by Monday, December 5, a list of five suggestions for using this fund.

Write a memorandum to all supervisors of the company, and ask for their help in finding a use for the money. Ask that the memorandum be posted on all departmental bulletin boards. Inasmuch as this topic might seem to lack urgency or a sense of great importance within the departments, do your best to dramatize your appeal. In short, sell the reader on the importance of a speedy response.

Editing Practice

The Correspondence Supervisor   Edit and rewrite the following paragraph.

We are very sorry to learn, that the coffee table you purchased from us did not arrive in perfect condition. A replacement table will go out on the very, first delivery scheduled for your section of the city which should be on Wednesday. It is our sincere wish to give service, quality, and to satisfy our customers, therefore, we are greatful to you for writing us about the table. You have helped in the maintainance of the reputation, that we value so high.

Case Problem

A Confidential Matter   The office is buzzing with news that the new office manager is to be appointed today. Will it be Ted Anson, Fred Marshall, or someone from outside the firm? Glenda Knox, secretary to the vice-president, Jerome Anshen, knows who has been appointed because her boss made the selection. However, Mr. Anshen has asked that she keep the matter confidential until an official announcement is made. Frances Lucas, Glenda's best friend in the company, would like to know who has been appointed and asks Glenda at lunch, "Please tell me who got the job; I won't breathe a word to a soul, I promise."

1. Should Glenda tell Frances? Why or why not?
2. What should she say to Frances?

Informal Reports

Information is the food on which a business feeds and grows, a diet that may range from a single item to a long, detailed, extensive body of information. Most interesting, though, is the fact that the person who writes a lengthy report usually has to rely on many, many other persons for all the bits of information that make up his presentation.

For example, let's think of the annual stockholders' report published by a large corporation. Although one man may have written that report, the information it contained was contributed by hundreds of other persons. Every official in every department was called upon to furnish facts related to his own segment of the operations. But to get those facts, every official had to obtain information from all the employees whose work was concerned with the specific items he needed in order to write a complete report for his department.

As to type, then, reports may be classified as follows: (1) the multiple-page formal document and (2) the brief informal report called for under other circumstances. Therefore, to promote your own success as a business writer, you will need training in the writing of formal and informal reports, the training provided in this and the next section of your textbook.

As you prepare now to study the techniques of writing informal reports, please remember that *informal* does not mean "unimportant." In business, all written material is important; otherwise, it would not have to be written. And remember, too, that although your future *may* require the writing of formal reports, it most surely *will* be studded with the writing of hundreds of informal reports.

PIIW

PIIW means "put it in writing" and is the basic principle for the informal reports that you will make.

There are several good reasons for developing the habit of putting into writing whatever information is requested. In the first place, an oral report probably will not stay with the boss; he may hear, but may not remember, what you say. On the other hand, the act of reading will help to fix the message in his mind; and if later on he is hazy about what you said, he can pick up your report and reread it. To be effective, then, reports should be made in writing.

The practice of writing informal reports is also a form of self-protection. Because your boss is a very busy man and therefore may not remember what you said yesterday, he may frequently ask some such question as, "Did you remember to . . .?" And, despite the fact that you say, "Yes, I told you yesterday that . . .," the impression he gains and retains is that you are a person who has to be "jacked up." If, however, you had written the information for him, the chances are that there would be no need to ask questions; consequently, "irresponsible" would not be one of the adjectives he would use to describe you.

And, finally, your written informal reports can be a means by which your outstanding performance will show on the record. For instance, you will get little credit for doing excellent secretarial work; such excellence is expected of you, is taken for granted, and is somewhat of an intangible. Your informal written reports, however, will be a consistent, visible, and lasting reminder that you frequently furnish your boss with information important to him. But this item for the record will work for you only if reports are skillfully written. To acquire such skill, you need the training provided by the following presentation.

MECHANICS OF WRITING INFORMAL REPORTS

The first step in the writing of any report, formal or informal, is the preparation of an outline. For informal reports, you have a ready-made preliminary outline, the memo form you learned in Section 45, which is as follows:

To:
From:
Date:
Subject:

Whether you use this exact form or whether you adapt it will depend upon the circumstances under which you are operating at any given time. *How* you use the outline will also depend on a number of variables, which can best be explained by a discussion of the separate items.

To

The way you write the addressee's name depends partly upon the degree of formality or informality of your office atmosphere. For instance, if everybody is on first-name terms with the boss, if he expects to be called by his first name, and if you know that the report is for his personal information only, you might write this:

> To: Tom Blaine

But suppose you know by the content that the report will be read by other persons, as well as by the boss, or you know that the report will be placed in the files for future reference. In such case, you would write this:

> To: Mr. Blaine
> *or*
> To: Mr. Thomas Blaine

From

The "From" line should match the tone of the "To" line. For example, the first two lines of a very informal report written only for the personal information of the boss would look like this:

> To: Tom Blaine
> From: Ann Cray

A different "From" line is needed for a report that is not for the exclusive information of the boss or for a report that will be filed. Keeping in mind the fact that all readers will know the boss but may not know who you are, your opening lines would be written as follows:

> To: Mr. Thomas Blaine
> From: Ann Cray, Secretary

Subject

The "Subject" line should be a comprehensive, yet clear and precise, statement that will prepare a reader for rapid assimilation of the information given in the report. Composing a subject line, therefore, requires a high degree of skill if its purpose is to be accomplished. Let's look at some illustrations. Here is a subject line for a salesman's report to the sales manager.

> Subject: Sales

This line would be meaningless to the sales manager. He would have to read the report in order to grasp its subject. The following line, however, would have oriented him immediately.

> Subject: Sales Report for Week of May 10, 19—

Now suppose that you are a personnel director and that you receive a report whose subject line is this:

Subject: Employee Turnover

Quite possibly you have forgotten that you asked for a report on some phase of employee turnover. If so, the above subject line does nothing to refresh your memory or to prepare you for a quick grasp of the facts presented in the report. But how about the following revision?

Subject: Employee Turnover Statistics for the 19— Fiscal Year

Date

Absolutely without exception, every report should carry the date on which it was written. Conditions change so rapidly that facts presented on one date may not be valid at another time. And frustrating indeed is the experience of finding in the files some item of information that could be valuable—provided you knew when the report was written.

Wherever dates are given in the body of a report, those dates must be specific. You would not write, "On Wednesday, we received 117 inquiries about . . . ." You would write, "On Wednesday, December 16, 19—, we received . . . ."

Adaptation of Memo Form

Although the memorandum form is your outline for writing informal reports, in many cases you would not use the exact memo format. One of the possible variations would be the following:

Ann Cray
September 8, 19—
Employee Turnover Statistics for the 19— Fiscal Year

This adaptation shows that Ann Cray wrote the report on September 8, 19—, and the subject is stated as a heading, or title. The assumption is that this report would go only to Mr. Blaine. However, if an addressee's name is necessary, the body of the report could start as it does in the following illustration.

Mr. Blaine: Statistics on employee turnover for the 19— fiscal year are as follows:

Carbon Copies

Whenever you write an informal report, no matter how minor you think it is, be sure to make a carbon copy for your own files. The boss may mislay your original; bosses sometimes do, you know. And, without a carbon, where would you be if he says you didn't turn in a report he asked for? Or if the need arose, how could you verify any point about which there is a question? But if in your files you have a folder marked "Reports" and if you have therein a carbon of every report you write, you may be able to help yourself, as well as the boss.

```
To:       Mr. Martin A. Lindberg

From:     Anne Cray

Date:     April 7, 19--

Subject:  Suggestion for Increasing Typing Production


On an average of three times a day, our typists
are assigned a job that must be typed three times
in order to obtain the necessary number of read-
able copies (usually 12).  Since each typing
requires an average of 15 minutes, each such job
presently requires a total of 45 minutes to complete.
Each day, then, we are spending a total of 2 1/4
hours to produce three complete jobs.

I suggest that each of the three jobs could be
done in one typing--15 minutes--by:

     1.  Purchasing an interchangeable metal
         platen (available from Reliable Typewriter
         Exchange, 218 Ash Street, at a cost of
         $20).

     2.  Using lightweight carbon paper (available
         from our present supplier at no extra
         cost).

     3.  Using lightweight onionskin paper (avail-
         able from our present supplier at no
         extra cost).

A. C.
```

PLANNING AND WRITING INFORMAL REPORTS

Many persons, including some correspondents, think that writing involves merely sitting down and dashing off a few words. This is a false notion that accounts largely for the fact that good business writers are scarce and therefore are very much in demand.

Actually, a topnotch writing effort of any kind represents hard work and is the result of much thought, careful planning, and excellent training. And for the know-how that will enable you to write informal reports of the very best quality (like the one illustrated above), you need to study, think about, and apply the following principles.

Being Clear, Complete, Correct, and Concise

At this point in your communication training, you know that *concise* does not mean "incomplete." To be concise, you must say everything that needs to be said; but you must say it in the fewest possible words.

You are also well aware of the fact that your writing must be clear and complete, so you would not write a "fuzzy" sentence like this:

> Mr. Wright spoke to Mr. Klein about the vacation schedule for the Accounting Department, and he said he would have it ready sometime next week.

Instead, you would write a clear, complete, definite message, such as the following:

> Mr. Klein reported to Mr. Wright that the Accounting Department vacation schedule would be set up by Thursday, March 4, 19—.

Some extra consideration must be given to correctness as applied to reports. Perhaps we should use the stronger term, "accurate," because any information important enough to be reported must be more than substantially correct; it must be completely accurate. For example, if you were asked to report the number of free-sample requests that came in on a given day, you'd better be sure that you give an exact, not an approximate, count.

Wording

The wording of reports differs from that of letters. A letter is designed to do more than convey a message. Every letter has as its accompanying purpose the winning of new customers or the retaining of present customers; therefore, the tone of a letter is warm and friendly. A report, on the other hand, is a straightforward, factual presentation—and it should be worded as such.

As an illustration, read the following opening paragraph of a letter answering a request for information about your company's in-service training courses.

> In response to your request of April 2, we are very glad to tell you that our company presently has a schedule of three in-service training courses. (The second paragraph would give the titles and other details of the courses.)

Now, note how the wording changes when the same information is given in a report.

> Our company presently conducts three in-service training courses: (1) History and Policies of the Company; (2) Report Writing; and (3) Inventory Control Methods and Procedures.

TYPES OF PRESENTATION

How brief or how detailed should your informal report be? Should you give the requested information in a single paragraph? Should you present the information in outline form? For the most effective presentation, should you tabulate the information?

No one but you, the writer of the report, can answer these questions because only you are close enough to the situation to know why the report was requested, to be able to project the probable uses of the information, and so on. To make a wise decision as to the form your report should take, though, you must know the types of presentations and the purposes that each best serves.

Paragraph

The paragraph form is used for the presentation of a simple fact. For example, if your boss has asked you to let him know how many days were lost last week because of absence—and if you know for sure that all he wants to know is the total number of days—you might write the following in a memo-style report:

> In the Sales Department during the week of March 11, 19—, absences totaled 7 days.

Or, if you wanted to give a little extra information, you might write:

> In the Sales Department during the week of March 11, 19—, 4 employees were absent for a total of 7 days.

Outline

If, however, you know that your boss takes a very personal interest in his staff, you might correctly guess that he would like to know *who* was absent. Therefore, you might write:

> Information regarding absenteeism in the Sales Department during the week of March 11, 19—, is as follows:
> 1. Total days of absence: 7
> 2. Number of employees absent: 4
>   a. John Anderson, 2 days
>   b. Vincent Lanzo, 2 days
>   c. Willard Starr, 1 day
>   d. Angela Vargas, 2 days

Tabulation

In some cases, the most effective way to present information is to tabulate it. The advantage of the tabulated form is that the reader can see everything at a glance—he does not have to wade through a river of words. Obviously, the decision to tabulate would be influenced by the amount and kind of information to be given and by the writer's projection of the uses to which the information may be put.

For example, suppose you have been asked to give an absenteeism report and you happen to remember the rumor that the "top brass" is considering hiring a company physician. The thought may occur to you that your report might be one of the several bits of information that will contribute to whatever decision management makes. Even if your guess is wrong, you could lose very little by setting up a table like the one at the top of page 380.

Sales Department Absenteeism
Week of March 11, 19—

Employee	No. Days Absent	Reasons for Absences
Anderson, John	2	Illness (cold)
Lanzo, Vincent	2	Illness (cold)
Starr, Willard	1	Illness (cold)
Vargas, Angela	2	NSA Conference

TOTAL DAYS OF ABSENCE: 7
TOTAL EMPLOYEES ABSENT: 4

UNSOLICITED REPORTS

An unsolicited report is, quite simply, one that you make on your own initiative rather than as a result of having been asked. In business, any idea that you might have for increasing efficiency, productivity, or any aspect of profit-making will be more than welcome. And, more than likely you will want to put your idea in writing in order that you may present it in the most complete, logical, and generally effective manner: in the form of an unsolicited report.

How do you go about preparing and submitting an unsolicited report? Here are some details that you should consider before you begin to write.

To

You will want to direct your suggestion or idea to the person who has the authority to put it into effect. Usually this person will be your boss; but even if it happens to be someone else, courtesy and protocol demand that the suggestion be routed *through* your boss *to* that other person. For example:

TO: Mr. John F. Blaine (your boss)
   Mr. Paul C. Booker (the "authority person")

Subject

In any report, the subject line must tell the reader what the report is about. In an unsolicited report, though, you probably will want to slant the wording of the subject so that it will appeal to the reader's particular interest. For example, if you know that your boss is greatly concerned about increasing the productivity of the typists in his department, you might select a subject line like the one used in the informal report illustrated on page 377.

COMMUNICATION PROJECTS

Practical Application

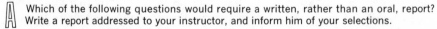

Which of the following questions would require a written, rather than an oral, report? Write a report addressed to your instructor, and inform him of your selections.

1. How do our December sales this year compare with those for December of last year?
2. What's the name of the company that services our machines?

3. Who's on the steering committee for the Housewares Show?
4. Where did you file the "Pending Projects" folder?
5. When do you think we should have the next staff conference?
6. What kind of photocopying machines do the company's secretaries prefer?
7. How many vacation days have you taken this year?
8. Do all the departments in the company have formal arrangements for noontime telephone coverage?
9. Is there an adequate number of coat hooks in the cloakroom?
10. Would a centralized stockroom or individual supply closets on each floor be more efficient?

B Write a subject line for each of the selections you made in the preceding assignment.

C Your boss is interested in the following stocks: Dow Chemical, Consolidated Edison, and American Telephone and Telegraph. He has asked you to find out the closing prices of these stocks for Monday and Friday of the previous week. Consult a newspaper for the information you need, and write an informal report to give him this information.

D Under the subject line "Employee Turnover Statistics for Fiscal Year 19—," write a report that includes the following data:

> At the beginning of the fiscal year there were 4,241 employees. During the year, 466 new appointments were made; 26 employees were transferred from other branches; 46 former employees were reinstated—making 538 additions to the staff. During the same period, 582 employees were separated: 230 by resignation; 24 by death; 25 by transfer to other branches; 7 by removal for cause (discharged); 6 by retirement; 290 for miscellaneous reasons. At the close of the fiscal year, there were 4,197 employees, a decrease of 44 for the year.

E Write an unsolicited report to present an idea that you would like to see put into effect.

Did
X

Editing Practice

Preferred Spelling   Some of the words in this paragraph do not conform to preferred spellings. Identify and respell them.

> As your counsellor and as advisor to the staff of the school yearbook, I should like to talk with you about the inadvisability of cancelling our plan for including an acknowledgement section in this year's book. Can you find time to drop in to see me sometime this week? I shall be in my office every afternoon from two to four.

Case Problem

To Ask or Not to Ask Questions   One of the most important things a new employee must learn is when to ask for help and when to use his own judgment in trying to solve a problem. The person who solves his own problems is appreciated only when his work is correct. On the other hand, a new employee who makes mistakes because he is afraid or hesitant to ask questions may very well find himself in serious trouble. What would you do in the following situations?

1. During Evelyn's first week on the job, her boss asks her to make five copies of an interoffice memorandum. On the list of those who are to receive the memo is a Mr. Allen. Evelyn knows that there are two Mr. Allens in the company—one is the vice-

president in charge of manufacturing and the other is the purchasing manager. Because the memo concerns the purchase of new equipment, Evelyn decides that the purchasing manager is the one who should receive the memo. Accordingly, without asking her boss, Evelyn addresses the memo to him.

a. Do you agree with Evelyn's decision?
b. What alternative action would you suggest?
c. Is it possible that both Mr. Allens should receive a copy of the memo?

2. Linda's boss is in a meeting in Mr. Collins' office. He has telephoned her from there and asked her to find a report in the file and to bring it to him immediately. Linda knows that Mr. Collins is the treasurer, and she knows his telephone extension; but the company occupies a very large building, and she does not know where his office is located.

a. What steps might Linda take to locate Mr. Collins' office?
b. Will Linda's boss be embarrassed if she takes too long to deliver the report?

3. Dan has just started to work as an order-editor and finds on his desk an order for an item that he has not heard of. He knows that recently many items were declared out of stock, and he assumes that this is one of them. Therefore, he notes this information on the order.

a. Do you agree with Dan's action?
b. Should he have checked further?
c. What could be the consequences of his action?

Formal Reports

Formal business reports are usually concerned with complicated problems or with questions necessitating investigation, analysis, research, and documentation. For instance, here are some typical report subjects: an analysis of the methods of marketing a company's products; a study of the various advertising media used by a business and the rate of return for each type of advertising; a plan for reorganizing a department of a business; a study of future needs for factory space for a manufacturing enterprise; an analysis of working procedures in several departments of a business, with recommendations for simplifying these procedures; an experiment to test a new product for durability.

The writing of a formal report may require weeks or even months of exhaustive study, and the completed document may contain anywhere from one or two pages to more than a hundred. Regardless of length, formal reports must be expertly written, because they are the bases upon which a company may decide to risk thousands of dollars.

Interestingly enough, there are some brilliant investigators who can do the research and can compile the facts, but who simply cannot write a report.

Therefore, some companies employ a specialist whose sole function is to take the material assembled by the researcher and put it into report form. These writers, of course, are in the top salary bracket.

In this section you will receive specialized training that will prepare you for the high-level job of writing formal reports. Fortunately, you have a head start because your knowledge of informal reports is an excellent background for writing the more complex formal reports.

PREPARING THE REPORT

Each business organization has its own style and form for reports. Style and form may also vary somewhat within a company by department and by the nature of the subject being treated. A technical report, such as one specifying requirements for manufacturing radio-tube components, may be organized in outline form with little text. Similarly, the reports of chemists, petroleum engineers, pharmacists, and other scientists and engineers are likely to include considerable tabular material, such as tables and graphs, with a relatively small amount of written interpretation. On the other hand, many business reports are mainly narrative, with a minimum of tabular matter. Though the style and form of the report may vary by business and by subject, most formal reports include these basic sections:

> Introduction
> Summary
> Body
> Conclusions and Recommendations
> Supplementary Material

Before any of these sections can be written, however, much spadework must be done. The investigator must define the purpose and determine the scope of the report; he must gather reliable facts and assemble and analyze them; he must draw conclusions from his factual analysis and make recommendations that are reasonable in view of company needs.

Defining Purpose and Scope

Why is the report being written? The answer to this question must appear in the introductory section of the report. In a study of the current letter-writing practices of the XYZ Company, for example, the purpose of the report might be stated as follows:

> 1. To determine the present letter-writing styles being used in XYZ Company.
> 2. To select a model letter style and punctuation standard for company-wide adoption.
> 3. To make recommendations for improving letter-writing practices throughout the company.

The report writer can easily undertake a topic too large to be treated effectively. The experienced report writer clearly defines the scope of his problem and sets up boundaries beyond which he cannot go. Think, for example, how difficult it would be to write a 1,000-word paper on "Correspondence Practices of Office Workers." This topic is so broad in scope that any attempt to treat it in one report would be foolhardy. Therefore, the scope of the report should be limited to one specific phase of a general topic. For example:

> Too General: Correspondence Practices of Office Workers
> More Specific: Letter and Punctuation Styles Currently Used by Stenographers in the XYZ Company

Gathering Information

The old adage "No chain is stronger than its weakest link" can be paraphrased as "No report is stronger than the facts behind it." Computer specialists, in speaking of the preparation of reports by machine, emphasize this statement vividly with their term *GIGO* (pronounced *GUY-GO*), standing for "garbage-in, garbage-out." The value of any report depends on the quality of the material going into its production. If "garbage" goes in, "garbage" is bound to come out. With reliable facts behind it, a reliable report can be written; with questionable data, only a questionable report can result.

In gathering information and documenting it, a writer should be familiar with the authoritative references in his field. There are, of course, many general references that everyone needs. Such standard sources as the *Writer's Guide to Periodical Literature*, *The Business Periodicals Index*, *Facts on File*, *The World Almanac*, and *The New York Times Annual Index* are invaluable helps to nearly any writer.

In each field of business, such as accounting, marketing, or office administration, there are basic references as well as current periodicals that should be reviewed frequently by report writers. Naturally, anyone doing research must first learn how to find and use books, periodicals, card catalogs, and various indexes. When data are to be obtained in other ways, such as through questionnaires or personal interviews, other research techniques must be mastered.

Working Bibliography   As he consults the various reference works relative to his subject, the writer should make up a list of the books, periodicals, reports, and other sources he expects to use as references for his report. This preliminary list of sources is called the *working bibliography*. If the writer makes each entry of the working bibliography on a separate card (5 by 3 or 6 by 4 inches), it will later be easy for him to assemble the final bibliography of sources he actually used. The writer will also find the bibliography cards useful when footnoting material in his report.

A book card for a working bibliography should contain all the following information:

- Author's name (last name first)
- Title (and edition, if there is more than one)
- Name and location of publisher
- Date of publication (latest copyright date)

In addition, it is helpful to include for the writer's own use the library's call number for the reference.

The following illustration shows a bibliography card that has been prepared for a book reference.

Martin, E. W. Jr.   651.26
                                                       MA

   Electronic Data Processing:
     An Introduction
   Richard Irwin, Inc.
   Homewood, Illinois, 1961

When magazines, newspapers, and other periodicals are to be consulted, a bibliography card like the one shown below should be prepared. This card should show the author, the title of the article (in quotation marks), the name of the publication (and location, if a newspaper), the date, volume, and number of the publication, and the page numbers.

Obrochta, Richard J.

   "How to Succeed in Business"
   Administrative Management,
   September, 1962, pp. 14, 15
   Vol. XXIII, no. 9

Note-taking Cards should also be used for taking notes. They are much more practical for this purpose than sheets of paper because they are sturdy and can be sorted and resorted easily.

The ease with which material can be organized and a report can be written depends to a large extent on how well notes have been made from reading. Most good writers take more notes than they need. This practice gives them a great deal of information, which they can "shake down" to the essentials before writing the report.

When taking notes from reading, be sure to identify carefully the source of the material. Use a new card each time a new source or topic is begun. Normally, summary statements or phrases with page references are sufficient for note cards. Whenever a quotation is to be used, however, be sure to copy the statement carefully, enclose it in quotation marks, and show the number of the page from which the quotation is taken. When you are organizing the material for writing later, it is helpful to include a brief subject reference at the top of each card; for example, if you are tracing the development of a product, you might identify references by such topics as "year," "developer," or "site of development."

STRUCTURING THE REPORT

After the writer has collected and studied the material relating to the topic, he can begin to organize his report. Note cards should be reviewed, sorted by topic, and tentatively organized into a logical sequence for the report.

Outline

Using organized note cards as a guide, the writer should make an outline to serve as the structure, or framework, of the report. The outline should be kept as simple as possible. While the writer is determining the outline, he should keep in mind the kinds of topic headings he will want in his report. If outline entries are carefully thought out, many of them can be incorporated into the final report as topic headings. The writer should keep in mind the following points as he makes his outline:

- The purpose of the report is to convey information efficiently.
- A good report structure gives the reader a sense of movement; one thought naturally reads into another.
- The purpose of the outline is to save the writer's time when he starts writing.
- The outline should be arranged to present material in logical units and sequence.

Headings

Most books, articles, and business reports require a generous use of headings to indicate the organization of the material. Headings of equivalent weight should be in the same style. For example, the main divisions of an article, a report, or a chapter in a book may be centered, and the subdivisions of each main heading may be typed as paragraph headings. When there are more than two divisions, however, the following arrangement of headings should be used:

CENTERED FIRST ORDER HEADING
Centered Second Order Heading

BLOCKED THIRD ORDER HEADING

Blocked Fourth Order Heading

Indented Fifth Order Heading

The report writer should be consistent in his use of headings in order to help the reader understand the report's organization and to facilitate reading and understanding of the material. In general, a topic form is better than a sentence form for headings. For example, "How to Write Reports" is preferable to "This Is How to Write Reports."

WRITING THE REPORT

There are considerable differences between the informal writing style of the business letter and memorandum and the writing style commonly found in the formal report. These differences will be pointed out in the following discussion.

Style

Long business reports are important documents upon which a businessman bases many of his high-level decisions. Consequently, such reports tend to be written in a serious, formal style, usually in the third person. Such an impersonal style is necessary to avoid interjecting a personal tone that would weaken a report by making it appear to be merely a statement of one person's opinions and beliefs, instead of a sound evaluation of the data gathered for the report. Of course, usually only one person, the writer, is evaluating the facts, but the more he can de-emphasize the *I* and cite facts to back his evaluation, the more objective and more persuasive will his report sound to others.

A poor report writer, presenting his report on letter-writing practices, might make these statements:

> It seems to *me* that we are too old-fashioned in our letter arrangement styles.
>
> *Personally, I* would *prefer* to use the modified-block letter style for all company correspondence.
>
> Even though most of the other departments prefer closed punctuation, *I* have a strong *preference* for open punctuation and think we ought to adopt it as our standard.

Even though the facts may provide a sound basis for the evaluations given in the examples above, these sentences do not seem objective because the writer has used so many personal references. In addition, the writer has not shown how his judgments are drawn from the data that he has gathered.

On the other hand, the good report writer knows that merely stating a judgment will not persuade anyone to accept it, no matter how soundly based on fact and reason the judgment may be. Therefore, the expert writer uses an impersonal style and relates his evaluations to the facts found in the study. He carefully avoids any expressions that may imply that his evaluations are based on personal opinions instead of sound reasons and facts. Instead of the sentences given on page 387, he would write the following:

> The evidence gathered in this survey shows that the letter styles used by XYZ Company are not as up to date as those of other similar organizations. (The facts would then be cited.)
>
> Use of the modified-block letter style would be appropriate for XYZ Company because the style has the modern look of simplicity and also is faster and easier to type.
>
> Five of the eight departments studied use closed punctuation; however, adoption of open punctuation would have the following advantages: (Explanation of advantages would follow.)

This same impersonal writing style should characterize all sections of the report. Remember that reasoning from facts is an important factor in the success of any business report.

Title Page

The title page usually includes the complete title of the report, the name and title of the author, the name of the person for whom the report is prepared, and the date the report is submitted. Each of these items should be attractively arranged on the page. A typical title page is illustrated on page 389.

Table of Contents

This section is prepared after the report has been completed. One commonly accepted form is shown below.

TABLE OF CONTENTS

The Introduction

The introductory section of a long report is designed to tell the reader why the report was written, how the data were gathered, and what the report does (or does not) do.

Suppose that Raymond A. Kelleher, controller of the XYZ Company, has asked his office manager, Blair Hawkins, to investigate the letter-writing practices in the company, with a view toward improving the entire correspondence function and cutting costs. In such a report, Mr. Hawkins would use the following parts in the introductory section.

```
                    March 6, 19--
                    Prepared for:  Raymond A. Kelleher
                    Prepared by:   Blair Hawkins
```

Purpose and Scope   First, the writer should explain why the report was written. He should clearly enumerate, if possible, basic objectives of the report.

> This report was prepared at the request of Mr. Kelleher, control-
> ler of XYZ Company. The purposes of the report are:
>
> 1. To determine what letter-writing styles are being used in
>   each department of the XYZ Company.
> 2. To determine what punctuation styles are being used in each
>   department of the XYZ Company.
> 3. To identify correspondence problems in each department.
> 4. To seek ways of improving correspondence practices in the
>   company.

A brief statement of scope may be included in this section, as:

> This report does not include grammatical practices, spelling problems of stenographers, tone, word-choice, or problems of writing technical articles.

Procedure   The introductory section of the report should also describe the method used to collect and analyze the data. An example follows.

> In order to collect dependable information for this report, all supervisors responsible for correspondence in each department were interviewed. The questionnaire shown in Appendix A of this report was sent out in advance and filled out by each supervisor. Later, the questionnaires were reviewed briefly and were checked during the final interview conducted by Mr. Zinkula. In addition, all current periodicals in business communications were consulted so that the results of the company survey could be compared with recommended present-day practices.

√ Summary

For the busy executive, the summary is included early in the report (following the introduction). This section gives the reader the most significant information in capsule form, so that he does not have to read the entire report. When time permits, the reader can complete the reading of the report. The length of the summary may range from one paragraph to four or five pages, depending on the material that has been gathered. The following is an opening paragraph of the summary in the XYZ letter-writing practices report.

> SUMMARY
>
> This study has shown that there is considerable variation in the correspondence practices followed in the XYZ Company. The data gathered, when analyzed, show the following significant trends:
> 1. Little use is made of the correspondence handbook.
> 2. All departments use at least two different letter styles.
> 3. Department heads do not consider standardized letter styles important.
> 4. The correspondence supervisor for the company, Mr. Enoch Malone, will require the support of top management in order to put his recommendations into practice.

Body

The body is the report proper. In this section the writer tells what he did, how he did it, and what he found. Writing this section should present no great difficulties if the writer follows a carefully prepared outline and has good notes. It is important for the writer to confine his remarks to accurate, verifiable facts and to present his ideas in a clear, concise manner. Many of the suggestions given in Chapter 5 for forceful, clear writing apply to the writing of reports.

Conclusions and Recommendations

This section can easily be the most important one in any report, for it is here that the real results of the report appear. The writer's conclusions tell the busy executive, on the basis of the most reliable data available, "Here is what the report shows."

Personal observations should be reduced to a minimum—conclusions that are drawn should spring from the facts only. In the light of the conclusions and from his knowledge of the company, the writer can make recommendations. (Note: As a guide to making worthwhile recommendations, the writer should glance back at the listed purposes of the report. As a rule, there could well be at least one recommendation for each stated purpose.)

By referring to the purposes stated in the introduction of the report on letter-writing practices, the writer might include the following conclusions and recommendations:

CONCLUSIONS AND RECOMMENDATIONS

From an analysis of the data gathered in the study, the following conclusions are drawn:

1. The authority of the correspondence supervisor is being undermined.
2. Most departments do not use the correspondence manual.
3. Old-fashioned letter styles are widely used within the company.
4. Punctuation problems are not adequately solved.
5. Correspondence is not standardized within the company.

With these conclusions in mind, the following recommendations are made:

1. Have top management give support to the correspondence supervisor in the form of a strong letter sanctioning his work.
2. Bring the correspondence manual up to date, and provide copies for each department supervisor.
3. Choose a standardized correspondence format for the entire company.
4. Call a meeting of all supervisors to explain the new correspondence policy.

Supplementary Information

Supplementary information, which is given after the conclusions and recommendations, provides substantiating data for the report. Some or all of the parts discussed below may be included.

Bibliography   This section is an alphabetic listing of all the references used in the report. Bibliographical entries are listed in alphabetical order by author. Forms for book and periodical entries are shown below and on page 392.

Books

Kenny, Harvey E., *American Business Policy*, National Book Company, New York, 1968.

Sharp, Robert A., and John J. Morgan, *Improving Written Communications in Business*, Hempstead Book Company, Boston, 1967.

Periodicals

Stone, Betty A., "Secretarial Correspondence," *Office World,* Vol. XXX, No. 14, October, 1965.

Ziska, Armand P., "Office Personnel Problems," *The Administrative Outlook,* Vol. IX, No. 5, November, 1968.

Appendix The appendix consists mainly of supporting information to back up the material in the body of the report. Long tables, charts, photographs, questionnaires, letters, and drawings are usually placed in this section. By including such material at the end of the report, the body of the report is freed from the kinds of detail that make reading difficult.

Letter of Transmittal

A short letter of transmittal (see page 393), composed after the report has been completed, accompanies the report. It is often written in the form of a memorandum and usually contains such information as:

- A reference to the person who authorized the report.
- A brief statement of the general purpose of the report.
- Appropriate statements of appreciation or acknowledgment.

MECHANICS OF REPORT WRITING

An immaculate physical appearance, expert placement, and meticulous attention to the mechanics of English, spelling, and punctuation emphasize the importance of the report and give it added meaning when it is read. For this reason, mechanics, as well as organization and writing style, are important in preparing the report.

Of course, all the mechanics of English, spelling, and punctuation discussed in earlier chapters apply to report writing. Some suggestions for setting up a report are necessary, however, and they are presented in the following paragraphs.

- Use common sense and show variety in paragraphing; take care to avoid too many long and too many short paragraphs. Keep in mind that the topic sentence, telling what the paragraph is about, very frequently appears first. Also, the closing sentence is often used to summarize the meaning of the paragraph.
- Be generous in your use of headings. Take care to leave plenty of white space around major headings, tables, and other display materials. Be sure that all headings of the same value within a section are parallel in wording. For example:

Nonparallel	*Parallel*
Writing the Introduction	Writing the Introduction
The Body	Writing the Body
How to Write the Closing	Writing the Closing

TO   Mr. Raymond A. Kelleher, Controller

FROM   Blair Hawkins, Office Manager

DATE   May 2, 19--

SUBJECT   Attached report on letter-writing practices

The study of letter-writing practices in our company, which you authorized on April 2, 19--, has now been completed. You will find the results of the study, together with my conclusions and recommendations, contained in the attached report.

These results are, I believe, significant; and I hope they will be of value to you. Much credit should be given to Frank Zinkula, my assistant, who personally contacted each department head in order to verify the data shown. I shall be glad to go over the report with you in person, if you wish.

BH

ck
Enclosure

- Use footnotes to give credit when the ideas of others are borrowed and used, either verbatim or modified, in a report. A footnote should be placed at the bottom of the page or at the end of the article or chapter. All footnotes should be numbered and should show the author, the reference, and the page number of the source. Various styles of footnotes can be found in standard reference manuals.
- Select carefully any tables, charts, diagrams, photographs, drawings, and other illustrated materials used to supplement the written word. To promote better understanding of the contents, you should choose the items that contribute the most to the report. Try to eliminate any items that are not pertinent.
- Bind the report attractively. Many types of binding, from the single staple to an elaborate sewn binding, can be used. Reports that are subject to frequent, rigorous use should be protected by being placed inside a special hardback report folder. Usually it is best not to use only a paper clip for binding, as the chances of losing part of the report, especially the appendix, are very high.
- Observe these rules of good manuscript form:

1. Type all reports on standard 8½- by 11-inch paper. Legal-size paper will not fit standard office files.

2. Use double spacing except for long quotations (usually three or more lines), in which case single spacing is advocated. Of course, you should type on only one side of the sheet. Consult a standard style manual for other spacing details.

3. Leave ample margins. Commonly accepted are these:

> Left margin: 1½ inches to allow for side binding
> Other margins: 1 inch
> First page only: When it contains the title,
> allow a 2-inch top margin.

4. Always prepare at least one carbon copy.

5. Traditionally, the first page is not numbered when it contains the title. All other pages, beginning with 2, should be numbered in the upper right corner.

6. Follow this pattern for any material presented in outline form:

> I.
>   A.
>   1.
>   a.
>   (1)
>   (a)

COMMUNICATION PROJECTS

Practical Application

Your supervisor, William J. Whitson, asked you, as his substitute, to attend an important meeting while he is out of town. The purpose of the meeting was to discuss employee turnover—a subject that is of growing concern to the company management. From the notes you took, prepare a report to Mr. Whitson in which you give him the full details of the meeting. Supply other data that you think might be appropriate. Here are your notes:

1. Annual turnover rate: Women employees, 35%; men, 15%.
2. Reasons given for leaving the company (in order of frequency): Women—Working conditions undesirable, higher salary in another company, commuting too difficult, marriage, friction with supervisor, no opportunity for advancement.
   Men—Better salary, no opportunity for advancement, working conditions disliked, friction with superior, company fringe benefits inadequate.
3. Recommended actions: Improve facilities by (1) redecorating offices and installing air conditioning and (2) replacing old furniture and equipment with modern and efficient articles; encourage frequent departmental meetings that will give employees an opportunity to express their opinions; institute training program for supervisors; initiate a salary survey of similar businesses; study promotion policies; obtain services of a management consultant to make recommendations concerning fringe benefits; consider the possibility of designating a personnel relations counselor to handle grievances.
4. Each department manager is to consider the turnover problem with reference to his experiences with employees under his supervision, is to be prepared to discuss the problem further, and is to make recommendations at a special meeting to be held on May 14. Prior to this meeting, by May 9, supervisors should submit a memorandum on morale in their departments.
5. In the discussion, it was brought out that there seems to be an atmosphere of unrest and that morale is generally low. It was also pointed out that the commuting problem may be eased shortly, when the proposed new bus route (direct from the Lackawanna Park district) goes into effect.

B In Chapter 7, Section 36, several styles of business letters were discussed. Refer to this discussion and study the characteristics of each letter style and its merits as you see them. Then write a report in which you describe each style, listing its advantages and disadvantages, and present your recommendations. Use illustrations. Refer to other sources if you wish.

C Assume that you are employed in an office. You have been asked by your department manager to study the form of long reports used by various departments in the company. You are to recommend a standard form for all reports. In your study you find that there is no consistency in the form and style now being used; everyone seems to have his individual preference. Many reports are poorly organized and contain inadequate information about purpose, bibliography, and so on. Drawing on the information in this lesson, write a memorandum to all supervisors and department heads, and discuss the form of the report that should be followed by everyone in the company. Use illustrations if you think they will help to make your report clearer.

D Write a brief memorandum to your instructor in which you describe the function of each of the following parts of a report:

1. Title page
2. Table of contents
3. Introduction
4. Summary
5. Body
6. Conclusions and recommendations
7. Supplementary material

Editing Practice

Editing for Writing Power   Edit and rewrite these sentences for the purpose of improving writing power.

1. Confident of his ability, the position was eagerly sought by Allen.
2. The opinions expressed in your letter of June 9 have been carefully studied.
3. Mr. Lane is our new supervisor, and he is a specialist in writing all kinds of business communications.
4. We revised the news release. The original was ambiguous. We needed to be more explicit.
5. One of the motors developed a knock, when all plans for a record flight had to be abandoned.
6. We specialize in quality goods; but price, too, has been considered by us.
7. Go to Edson's, and there one can find many outstanding bargains.
8. Not having been able to obtain, through banks or agencies at his disposal, any information concerning your credit rating; and as he did not know the rules governing such cases as yours, the new manager sent the goods C.O.D.
9. Although he couldn't really spare time away from the office, but wanting to visit the new plant, Jack's plans were indefinite.
10. The report to management, about the new accounting system that was started recently for the plant in Cincinnati, was very long and complicated so then the accounting manager had to call a special meeting to explain it.

Vocabulary and the Report Writer   Identify and correct the vocabulary errors that weaken the effectiveness of this report writer's opening paragraph.

This report on sight possibilities for the construction of a new warehouse was authorized by Mr. James E. Walsh on June 8, 19—. The information presented here is the result of frequent conferences with the ten leading reality agents in this city. A personal inspection trip was made to every lot offered for sale, and each parcel was evaluated in terms of its suitability for the location of a warehouse.

Case Problem

The Avid Conversationalist   Harry Walker, the mail clerk at Robins, Inc., is supposed to complete his daily delivery of mail by 11 a.m. and then return to the mail room in time to process the outgoing mail for an 11:40 a.m. pickup. However, when Harry gets to the credit department, Max Miller usually engages him in a lengthy one-sided conversation. As a result, in one or two instances Harry has not completed processing all the outgoing mail on time. Today Harry is late in getting started on his deliveries, and Max tries to engage him in another lengthy conversation.

1. What can Harry say to Max so that he will not offend him?
2. What should Harry do if Max persists in talking?

Telegrams, Minutes, and News Releases

News releases and minutes of meetings are two common types of written communications that you, as a business writer, may well be expected to prepare. In addition, you will frequently be expected to write messages that will be dispatched either by teleprinter or by another form of telegraphy. A knowledge of how to write each of these communications is essential for the business writer.

Equally important to your future in business are the rapid technological advances that are changing the ways in which much business information is produced, transmitted, processed, and reported. New electronic tools will continue in your lifetime to change the communications field. You must keep abreast of these changes if you are to adjust your writing skills to future demands of business. For example, the teleprinter and all other forms of telegraphy have been changed radically in the past decade. You must know what these changes are and how they affect message preparation and transmission. Also, electronic data communication has opened completely new fields of study in information science and in communication theory. Writing computer instructions in a language (COBOL and FORTRAN are the names of two of many of these new computer languages) that can be "read" and "understood" by a computer is a whole new area for the business writer to explore. Specialized writing and analysis skills can lead to many new exciting, well-paid business opportunities that did not exist just a few years ago.

Your future as a business writer will be bright if you learn how to keep abreast of the changes that occur and how to adapt your communication skills to new demands. To help you adjust to and attain this bright business future is the purpose of the discussion that you will find in the last part of this section.

First, though, let us consider what you need to know about writing news releases, minutes, and telegraphic messages. Let us consider news releases first.

NEWS RELEASES

Publicity, advertising, public relations, goodwill—all these terms denote the effort of a business to get its name, its reputation, and its product before the public. In fact, large companies—even schools and colleges—today employ publicity directors whose job it is to attract favorable public attention to their organizations.

An important means of getting the planned publicity of business into the hands of the public is the news release. Whenever a business plans an event that it considers newsworthy or capable of adding to its public image, its public relations personnel prepare and submit a news release to various news outlets for publication. Such a news announcement may concern the appointment of a new company president after a meeting of the board of directors; it may tell of a large local expansion in a company's plant, which will increase the work force and have a great impact on the economy of the community; it may publicize the introduction of a new line or new product; or it may concern the awarding of some honor (perhaps for long, faithful service) to a member of the organization; and so on. Any item that will interest the public and create goodwill for the organization is an appropriate subject for a news release.

Any news story emanating from a company must, of course, be approved for publication by an executive. In large companies, the director of public relations probably would have this responsibility. In small companies, individual department heads might handle their own news and distribute it in keeping with company policy, or releases might be issued from the office of the president.

In order to be published and thereby serve its purpose, the release must be newsworthy; that is, the contents of the release must be of sufficient interest to the public to justify being published. Naturally, the writing style of the news release, as well as the form in which it appears, will have a strong effect on the newspaper editor who will decide whether or not it is to be published.

Form of the News Release

With hundreds of releases coming to his desk each week, an editor will select for publication the items that require the least amount of rewriting, everything else being equal. Therefore, the news release must give complete, accurate information in a "news style" of writing that presents the facts in a clear and interesting way.

In addition, news releases may be typewritten, duplicated, or printed, but carbon copies should never be sent to an editor. A carbon copy suggests that the news story is not fresh, that the editor may not be the first or the only choice of the writer for releasing the story.

Many organizations use a special form for issuing news releases. These forms are arranged so that editors can get to the heart of the story without wasting time. Like a letterhead, a news release form usually contains the name and address of the company or organization and the name, address, and telephone number of the person responsible for issuing the release to the public.

A well-written news release is illustrated on page 399. Observe the following points about the preparation of this release:

- The news release is double-spaced and has generous margins for possible changes by the newspaper editor.
- The writer includes a tentative headline to identify his story. Editors, of course, may change this title to fit the space requirements of the publication.
- The news release indicates the time when a story may be published. In the example, note the prominence of the phrase *For Immediate Release*. At times, releases are sent to newspapers before an event occurs so that news will reach the public at almost the same time that the event takes place. For example, if a company plans to announce a million-dollar gift to a local hospital at a banquet on Saturday, June 25, the release might read *For Release after 6 p.m., Saturday, June 25.*
- In a long release, subheads may be inserted between parts of the release to relieve the reading monotony and to guide the editor as he scans the story.
- If there is more than one page to the release, the word *MORE* in parentheses should be added at the end of each unfinished page. The end of a release is indicated by *-xxx-*, which stands for "30," the telegrapher's abbreviation for "the end."

Writing the News Release

Regardless of how good the form is in any written communication, the words the writer uses to transmit his message determine whether it will be read and used. In writing a news release—just as in writing letters, memorandums, and reports—certain guides will help the writer develop an effective writing style and will improve his chances of getting the release printed.

- The opening paragraph of a news release should summarize the entire story and should present the most newsworthy information first. In this opening section, the writer should give the *who, what, why, how, when,* and *where* of the news story and give them in a form that will stand by itself. If, for example, an announcement is to be made of the appointment of Walter Dakin as Sterling's advertising director, the amateur news writer might lead off this way:

Put most important info. first

> Alex Prior, president of the Sterling Furniture Company, Westwood, Virginia, announced the appointment of Walter Dakin as advertising director.

However, Alex Prior is not the person the item is about—Walter Dakin is the subject. Therefore, he should be given the lead.

> Walter Dakin has been named the new advertising director of the Sterling Furniture Company, Westwood, Virginia, according to Alex Prior, president.

- Each succeeding paragraph should supply background facts in the order of their importance. If the editor should need to cut part of the release be-

NEWS RELEASE

Sterling Furniture Company

Westwood, Virginia   23205

Robert A. Cooper—Director of Public Relations

Donald Samson
Manager
Sterling News Bureau
Area Code 703, 986-9300

For Immediate Release   3/19/--

WALTER DAKIN NAMED ADVERTISING DIRECTOR

OF STERLING FURNITURE COMPANY

Westwood, March 19, 19--. Walter Dakin has been named the new

advertising director of the Sterling Furniture Company, Westwood,

Virginia, according to Alex Prior, president.

Dakin succeeds Ralph Rembrandt, who was promoted to vice-

president of sales a month ago.

The new advertising director joined the firm in 1963 as a

junior executive trainee. In 1964 he was assigned to the sales

division in charge of product information; and in 1966 he was

appointed assistant director of advertising. He is a graduate of

the University of Virginia.

-xxx-

cause of space limitations, he will "kill" it from the bottom up. For example,
note how the last paragraph of the news release illustrated above can be
omitted without making the first two paragraphs of the release an incomplete
news story.

> Walter Dakin has been named the new advertising director of the
> Sterling Furniture Company, Westwood, Virginia, according to
> Alex Prior, president.
> Dakin succeeds Ralph Rembrandt, who was promoted to vice-
> president of sales a month ago.

MINUTES OF MEETINGS

Nearly every business has a number of committees that meet periodically, perhaps weekly, biweekly, or monthly. In addition, special meetings are called from time to time for the purpose of settling important matters that arise. In most cases, a written record—called *minutes*—of the proceedings is submitted. The purpose of minutes is to make a permanent record of the decisions reached and the actions that are to be taken, and to inform those who were not present at the meeting about what took place. Nearly every business employee, at one time or another, serves as a secretary to a group or committee; as secretary, he is responsible for keeping an accurate set of minutes.

Recording the Minutes

The faithful recording of the proceedings of all meetings is an important function, for the minutes usually serve as the only historical record of a meeting.

There is probably no one best way to record what happens at a meeting. The secretary must use his own judgment as to what is unimportant (and hence not worth recording). If an agenda of the meeting has been prepared beforehand, the secretary should receive a copy of this plan. The agenda lists briefly the business to be transacted and acts as a guide to the person who presides at the meeting. The agenda, too, helps the secretary check to be sure that all scheduled items are accounted for in the minutes. Much of the success of good note-taking revolves around the personal efficiency of the secretary. However, any secretary preparing to record the proceedings of a meeting should find quite helpful the general guides listed below and on page 401.

- Record the time and place of the meeting.

- List the persons attending and those absent. In a small group, of course, this is possible (see the illustrations that follow); in a large group, however, it is usually sufficient to show the number of people present, such as "Forty-five members were present."

- In the opening section of the minutes, mention the fact that the minutes for the previous meeting were read and approved, amended, or not approved.

- Develop the art of recording the important points in the discussion of each item on the agenda. Why? Sufficient supporting facts are required so that those who were present can recall the discussion from hearing the minutes and so that those who were not present can be informed. Papers read during the meeting are often attached to the final typewritten minutes, because it is usually not possible for the secretary to record verbatim all such information.

- Record verbatim all resolutions and motions, as well as the names of the persons who introduced and seconded the motions. If the secretary has difficulty in getting such information when the motion is first made, he

```
          EMPLOYEES' ATHLETIC CLUB OF THE BALCOURT COMPANY

             MINUTES OF MEETING OF FEBRUARY 1, 19--


TIME, PLACE       The regular monthly meeting of the Employees' Ath-
ATTENDANCE        letic Club of the Balcourt Company was held in the
                  company cafeteria at 5:15 p.m.  The president, Elmer
                  Bradley, presided.  All members and officers present.

MINUTES           The minutes of the last meeting (January 4, 19--)
                  were read and approved.

OFFICERS'         Treasurer:  The treasurer's report showed receipts
REPORTS           of $585.15, disbursements of $432.16, and a balance
                  in cash of $309.10, as of January 31, 19--.  Frank
                  Casque moved that the treasurer's report be received
                  and placed on file for future audit.  Edwin Brandon
                  seconded the motion.  Motion carried.

                  Secretary:  The secretary indicated a 10 percent in-
                  crease, on the average, in attendance at club functions
                  during the past year.  (The secretary's report was
                  given in an informal manner; hence no motion to accept
                  it was necessary.)

COMMITTEE         Chairman Berry presented the report of the nominating
REPORTS           committee.  Nominated were:

                          President:  Edward Allen
                          Vice-President:  Sadie Green
                          Secretary:  Mary Linden
                          Treasurer:  James Alden

                  The president called for nominations from the floor.
                  No additional names were suggested.  Everett Jamison
                  moved and Thomas Hofer seconded the motion that nomi-
                  nations be closed and that a unanimous ballot be cast
                  for the committee's slate of officers.  Motion carried.

OLD               Plans for the Easter Dinner Dance, to be held at the
BUSINESS          Marshfield Inn on April 14 were discussed, but action
                  was not taken.

NEW               James Barkalow introduced a motion to increase the an-
BUSINESS          nual club dues from $5.00 to $6.50.  The motion was secon-
                  ded by Amy Ingo and passed by a majority of the members.

ADJOURNMENT       The meeting adjourned at 6:10 p.m.

                          Respectfully submitted,

                          Parker Blakiston

                          Parker Blakiston, Secretary
```

should insist on having the motion repeated or even put in writing so that
the exact motion is recorded.

- Type the minutes first in draft form so that they can be edited before being
put in finished form. Sometimes, too, the secretary may want to get another
person's approval before typing the minutes in final form. The secretary
signs the minutes, thus certifying their accuracy. Sometimes the presiding
officer countersigns them.

- Normally, make one copy of the minutes and file it in the folder, notebook,
or binder used for this purpose. Sometimes minutes are duplicated and sent

to each person present at the meeting or to designated officers who would be
interested in the business of the meeting.

Form of the Minutes

Various formats are used for presenting the minutes of a meeting. The secretary's main job, however, is to make sure that all the essential information
appears in a neat, well-arranged form. Some organizations prefer to emphasize the main points on the agenda by using a standardized format.

The minutes on page 401 illustrate an acceptable format for this type of
communication. Notice the standard pattern and topical headings that are

used for all meetings of this group and the way in which the motions and discussion are concisely summarized.

Other groups use a more traditional format in which the proceedings of the meeting are written out in rather complete detail. The example on page 402 illustrates the traditional style.

WRITING FOR THE TELEPRINTER

Telegrams are the most common form of message sent or received by teleprinter equipment. Growing out of the wireless telegraph invented by Samuel Morse, telegraphy has had a long and exciting history as the fastest method of transmitting written messages prior to the development in the past ten years of electronic data communications equipment.

Telegrams, however, continue to be important in today's business. In fact, so important is this type of message that many large companies maintain teleprinter equipment in their various divisions in order to provide for rapid transmission of messages to plants and divisions that may often be widely dispersed across the country. The best-known brand name of equipment used in this field is *Teletype*. Some telephone and telegraph companies maintain a service that connects teleprinters. With this service, customers call as they would by telephone but actually communicate through the teleprinter equipment. *TWX* (teletypewriter exchange service) is the brand name of the exchange service of the Bell System; *Telex* is the name of the exchange service sold by Western Union.

Teletypewriter Messages

For purposes of economy, teletypewriter messages should be as brief as possible. Any redundancy in the messages should, therefore, be eliminated. However, the word *redundancy* has a special meaning in reference to teletypewriter messages; it includes not only repetitiveness but also *any* part of a message that can be omitted without loss of meaning. Brevity in teletypewriter messages is important because the cost of sending a message is based on the number of words. A full-rate telegram, the fastest but most expensive Western Union telegram, is based on a minimum charge for a 15-word message, plus an additional charge for each word over 15.

It would, of course, be false economy to sacrifice completeness and clarity for brevity; that is, it would be a waste of money to write a 15-word message that risks being misunderstood when just three additional words would insure its clarity. Still, the skilled composer of teletypewriter messages can usually express his thoughts in surprisingly few words by eliminating any unnecessary words.

The composer of the teletypewriter message, unlike the letter writer, does not always need to use complete sentences; and he may dispense with some of the courtesies expected in the typical business letter. Contrast the following paragraph from a letter with a telegram that means the same thing, as they are shown side by side on the following page.

Letter	*Telegram*
We should appreciate your checking our Pur-	
chase Order 6651 for delivery date. The order	
was promised to reach our store by Monday,	Must have our Order
May 31. To date, it has not been received. We	6651 before June 7
must have the men's suits for our summer	
sale, which will begin at noon on Monday, June	
7, 19—.	

Note that the telegram writer states in 8 words what the letter writer says in 50 words.

Teletypewriter messages are frequently used in connection with changes in travel plans. The following telegram explains a change in plans because of bad weather.

> United Flight 346 grounded because of bad weather. Will arrive on B & O Pennsylvania Station 4:48 a.m. Tuesday.

The message is concisely written, but it contains 17 words, two more than the minimum charge for a full-rate telegram. However, the writer can eliminate the redundant words and convey the same message to the reader in only 13 words.

> Weather has grounded United Flight 346. Arrive B & O Pennsylvania Station 4:48 a.m., Tuesday.

Another common means of saving time and money in sending teleprinted messages is through the use of abbreviations and codes; for example, LA for Los Angeles, ATL for Atlanta, DTR for Detroit. Standard lists of such address abbreviations are used by telephone and telegraph companies, air lines, and other organizations. Some companies develop common code abbreviations that are used to exchange teleprinted messages within the company. However, the cost to encode or decode a message of nonstandard language is a deterrent to the frequent use of codes unless the code is a computer language.

From a study of teletypewriter messages, you can see that considerable difference exists in purpose—and thus writing style—between business letters and teletypewriter messages. As a rule, the well-written teletypewriter message has these features:

- Only necessary words are included. For instance, in the telegram example above, the phrase *because of*, the words *will*, *bad*, and *on* were easily eliminated without loss of meaning.
- Explanatory information is usually omitted. In the telegram about the purchase order, the date the order was promised was not mentioned and the time of day that the suits were needed was not stated. Only vital information appeared.
- Information understood by both sender and receiver is omitted. When writing the telegram expediting the order for suits, the writer did not have to say *"our Purchase* Order 6651" as this information was understood by simply saying "Order 6651."

The telegram form reads:

DOMESTIC SERVICE
Check the class of service desired; otherwise this message will be sent as a fast telegram

TELEGRAM	X
DAY LETTER	
NIGHT LETTER	

WESTERN UNION
TELEGRAM
W. P. MARSHALL, PRESIDENT

1206 (4-55)

INTERNATIONAL SERVICE
Check the class of service desired; otherwise the message will be sent at the full rate

FULL RATE	
LETTER TELEGRAM	
SHORE-SHIP	

NO. WDS.-CL. OF SVC.	PD. OR COLL.	CASH NO.	CHARGE TO THE ACCOUNT OF	TIME FILED
	PD		Dover and Company	10:25 a.m.

Send the following message, subject to the terms on back hereof, which are hereby agreed to

Newark, New Jersey, June 15, 19--

R. F. Wiston Company
100 Long Hill Road
Pittsburgh, Pennsylvania

Request immediate confirmation of price changes for your AL23, AL24, AL25 lines.

                Ed Willis
                Dover and Company

EW/am

Teletypewriter Message Format

For teletypewriter messages, details regarding the sending of the message, the word count, and the charge per word vary according to the particular service and the utility offering the service. Current costs of the different kinds of telegram services—for example, full-rate telegram, day letter, night letter, money order, or special services such as birthday or holiday greetings and overseas cable information—can be obtained from your local Western Union or cable office.

Details about format remain rather constant, however, and should be understood by anyone who is responsible for preparing a teletypewriter message.

Teletype forms may vary slightly from one company to another, but you should usually fill out the form in the following manner, as shown by the properly completed telegram above.

- Make at least one carbon copy. Additional copies may be made so that a confirmation copy can be sent to the addressee and copies can be sent to other departments as needed.
- Single-space the message and use ordinary punctuation as you would in any business writing. (For many years, typists attempted to simulate teleprinter type by typing the message all in capital letters and by spelling out punctuation; for instance, using the word *STOP* to indicate a period. Such practice is now obsolete.)
- Type the signature of the sender and the name of the company. (Note that stenographer's initials are used only for the sender's reference.)
- Follow instructions for filling in appropriate sections on the form. Thus, in the sample telegram above, since the message is to be charged, the name *Dover and Company* is typed in that box. If the telegram were to be

charged to a telephone number, that number would replace the company name. Were the telegram to be sent collect, the word *Collect* would be typed under *Pd. or Coll.* In addition, the class of service (full rate, day letter, night letter, etc.) should be checked.

YOUR FUTURE IN BUSINESS WRITING

Typewriters that don't use paper? They're here in the present. Typewriters in which the writing "output" is displayed only on a cathode-ray tube (CRT), a television-like picture tube, are now available. The "written" message can be stored in a computer that is thousands of miles away, but the message can be "retrieved" almost instantly whenever it is needed and wherever it is needed.

Paper may become obsolete in the future. Because of the tremendous information explosion, engineers estimate that sufficient wood pulp for papermaking would not be available if all the underdeveloped countries of the world were suddenly to emerge to a technological level equal to the standard now present in the United States. Just consider the amount of paper that is used every day in a business office.

The CRT for replacing paper and the computer techniques for capturing, storing, processing, and retrieving information will be a part of your future. Complete libraries can be captured, stored, and retrieved electronically. Suppose you are a student in the year 2010. From your easy chair at home, you will dial your "phonovision," a combination telephone and CRT. The number dialed is your access number to your local educational information center. Of course, you will identify yourself first with your social security number. Almost instantly, you and your educational counselor will be exchanging greetings. (With laser technology, it's possible that instead of the two-dimensional picture on the CRT, your counselor will appear in your living room as a three-dimensional vision!) What happens then? Before the greetings are completed, the computer will have searched for and found your record and will have processed your record in order to make three or four recommendations for your next course of study. From the recommendations, you and your counselor agree that you need some additional training in communication. Your agreement causes the computer to transfer to the school from your local bank account the tuition charges. You are then given the access number to communication programs, and you say farewell for the moment to your counselor.

In the meantime, your personal file of detailed information about you, which is stored in the computer "memory," is matched against what you need to know. Thus, when you dial the access number to communication programs, the proper course selection has already been made by the computer. You read and respond to the computer-selected exercises. The accuracy or inaccuracy of your responses determines the next step of learning. Thus, through computer-managed instruction, you will proceed through each step of the learning process until you have reached a predetermined level of competency.

The illustration above is just one example of the many changes in communication that you, as a business worker, can expect during your work life. The point of the illustration is this: <u>Competent as you are in your written communications today, electronic technology will rapidly change the requirements for tomorrow</u>. These changes will demand continuing study if you are to adapt to new requirements. Yet the changes will provide an exciting frontier of new business responsibilities if you are willing to adjust to them.

COMMUNICATION PROJECTS

Practical Application

A   As public relations director for Wadsworth Manufacturing Company, Oakland, California, you are responsible for writing all news releases for the company. Your president, Mr. John Yates, tells you that he will announce to the board of directors on Friday, December 9, 19—, the promotion of Harold S. Wier to advertising manager. He asks you to prepare a news release that can be published after the board meeting, which usually adjourns about 4 p.m. Wier has been with your company for ten years, first as a salesman (five years), then as sales supervisor (three years), and currently as assistant advertising manager (two years). He lives in Manchester, a suburb of Oakland, with his wife and three children. He is a graduate in business administration from Briarwood College. At Briarwood, he earned school letters in football, basketball, baseball, and swimming. In talking with you about his new position, Wier paid tribute to the fine work of his predecessor. Later, you learn that Donald H. Sheldon, former advertising manager, resigned a month ago because of a misunderstanding with the president. Wier stated, "Our basic advertising policy remains unchanged. We shall continue to stand for new media and new methods; but for the time being, we will concentrate our efforts in trade magazines and newspapers." Using an acceptable format, write a news release for this story. (Your telephone number is 628-3415.)

B   As secretary to the standing committee on office procedures, your principal responsibility is to prepare minutes of all meetings. Distribution of these minutes is to be made to committee members only; hence, a very concise form may be used. From the following information, prepare minutes of the latest meeting of this committee.

1. The meeting, held in Room 2310, Administration Building, was called to order by Reston at 2 p.m., November 25, 19—.
2. Correction made in minutes of preceding meeting (October 25) as follows: Revised procedure manual will be ready November 15, not October 1. Approved as corrected.
3. Dryerson reviewed employee suggestions for September. Awards of $50 each for two accepted suggestions were approved. Dryerson to make arrangements for presenting the awards at the next board of directors' meeting.
4. Revised written procedure for handling purchase order presented by Raydon. Accepted with editorial revision.
5. The meeting adjourned at 4:15 p.m., with the understanding that the next meeting would be held at the same time and place on December 15.
6. Amburn, Dryerson, Egan, Raydon, Reston, and Simpkins were present; Bergman was absent.

C   At yesterday's meeting of the College Business Leaders Club, you were chosen to be president for the next school year. Prepare a news release for your school newspaper and for possible publication in the "School Scene" section of the local daily paper. List other officers elected; make up the necessary names and background information.

D Assume that you had been serving as secretary to the College Business Leaders Club when you were elected to the presidency (Practical Application C) at the last meeting. Write the minutes for this meeting. Supply necessary details.

E Your employer, Mr. Jeremy Hallstead, will speak to the Young Executives Club at the Hotel Leamington in Minneapolis on July 7 at 7 p.m. He has asked you to wire the hotel for reservations for July 6 and 7 and to request a two-room suite with bath. (While in Minneapolis, he is interested in interviewing young men for sales work with your company.) Choose the most economical telegraphic service and compose the message, asking for (1) a confirmation and (2) information regarding the availability of a chalkboard, a 35mm projector, and a screen to be used for Mr. Hallstead's talk.

F Revise the following full-rate telegrams. Aim for brevity, clarity, and completeness. Limit each telegram to 15 or fewer words.

1. We are shipping by air express the parts you ordered for Machine 8462 except for Part 17F21, which will be shipped to you next Tuesday.
2. Insurance application you sent me, No. 82636415, has been tentatively approved. Final approval cannot be made until we receive the premium from your client. May we have the premium by return mail.
3. George McDonald and I are arriving for Florida sales meeting on Eastern Flight 123 and want you to make arrangements to have the company car meet us at the airport.
4. Our Purchase Order 6189 for six blue luggage sets and two dozen umbrellas has not arrived and our inventory is almost depleted. If the order has not yet been shipped, arrange shipment by express.
5. The duplicate computer print-out of the monthly sales forecast was accidentally damaged during shipment, so please airmail another copy immediately.

Editing Practice

Supply the Missing Words   Indicate a word that you think would make sense if inserted in the blank space within each sentence.

1. If this booklet does not give you the . . . you desire, please write us again.
2. Thank you for being so . . . about the delay in filling your order.
3. We are happy to tell you that your . . . has been established at the Hotel James.
4. We hope that we shall have the pleasure of serving you whenever you have . . . to use hotel facilities.
5. Once you know the . . . of a charge account, you will never shop without your charge account plate.
6. Please sign the original copy and return it to us in the enclosed envelope, retaining the . . . for your files.
7. We understand that you will probably . . . to purchase as much as $100 worth of merchandise monthly on your account.
8. We hope that your clerical staff will . . . some means of checking purchases made by persons of the same name but of different addresses.
9. We have taken steps to see that there is no . . . of this type of mistake.
10. We hope that our business dealings will be . . . pleasant and profitable.
11. The report . . . the data that had been gathered by the newly elected subcommittee.
12. The new inventory system was . . . just before the Christmas rush began.
13. An office worker's . . . is judged not only by the volume of work completed but also by the accuracy of the work.
14. All the payroll . . . were noted on the check stub.
15. Government . . . are available to many different groups in many parts of the country.

Proofreading for Homonym Errors   Identify and correct any homonym errors you find in the following paragraph.

The principal task of report writing is not the report itself; it is the assembling of facts that are the bases for statements made therein. The value of a report, then, depends upon the thoroughness with which all aspects of the situation have been studied. Any supervisor can cite numerous instances of poor reports that were due solely to a slapdash job of assembling facts.

Case Problem

Should He Bluff?   Mark Lester, a new assistant office manager, was at a personnel meeting where merit ratings were being discussed. Unfortunately, Mark knew very little about merit ratings because he had never rated anyone on the job. Soon after the meeting began, the chairman asked Mark to give his opinion about changes in the merit rating procedures and forms.

1. Should Mark bluff his way through or admit that he knows very little about merit ratings?
2. What should he say?

Communicating Orally

Effective Oral Communication

As you walk into the lobby of the large modern building occupied by the Acme Sales Corporation, you are greeted by the warm smile and friendly voice of the attractive receptionist. "May I help you?" You say, "I'm here to see Mr. Gilliam; he's expecting me." She tells you, "Mr. Gilliam's office is on the fourth floor, Room 424. May I have your name, please? I'll tell Mr. Gilliam that you're here. Take the elevator to the left." As you approach the elevator, you overhear the receptionist telephone Mr. Gilliam's secretary to say that you are on your way up. Already you are favorably impressed with the Acme Sales Corporation. As you step into the elevator, the operator inquires, "Your floor, please?" In a few seconds, the operator announces your floor. "Watch your step, please." You enter a tastefully furnished office where some forty or fifty employees are busily engaged in different kinds of activities. An attractive young lady approaches you and announces, "I'm Mr. Gilliam's secretary. He will be with you in a few minutes. Won't you be seated, please?"

While you are waiting, you glance around the office. Several workers are talking on the telephone. In one corner, a supervisor is explaining to a young man how to operate the stencil duplicator. In a conference room, a small group is gathered around a table listening to a man explaining a large chart. A young executive in a glass-enclosed office is using a dictating machine. On a bulletin board behind you is posted a notice of a sales training conference for the salesmen in District C; another notice on the bulletin board announces a meeting of the Office Employees' Association on Friday.

As you are ushered into Mr. Gilliam's office, you reflect on the importance of oral communication in the office you have just seen. Fortunately, you have had some training in oral communication. Why is it fortunate? You have come to see Mr. Gilliam to be interviewed for a position in his firm. You are about to put your training to work.

IMPORTANCE OF ORAL COMMUNICATION IN BUSINESS

From the moment you cross the threshold between the classroom and the business world, your conviction will grow stronger each day about the vital role of oral communication in all business activity. From the receptionist in the main-floor lobby to the president on the top floor, information is constantly being transmitted orally from one employee to another, from members of the organization to people on the outside, and from people on the outside to members of the organization. The success that any organization enjoys depends, to a very large degree, on the success of its members in making themselves understood and in persuading others to accept their ideas.

Though written communication is used extensively in transacting business, oral communication is used more often and by more people. Some business positions require the use of oral communication almost exclusively, and the people who fill these jobs are hired on the strength of their ability to speak well. The salesman, the office receptionist, the switchboard operator, the person who handles customer service or complaints—all these people must be highly skilled in oral communication. The office or factory supervisor, the public accountant, the personnel manager, the bank teller, the business executive, and the secretary are but a few of the other workers who make extensive use of oral communication in carrying out the responsibilities of their positions.

If you aspire to leadership in business, your ability to speak forcefully, persuasively, and convincingly will play a vital role in helping you achieve your goal. At meetings and conferences, speakers will include employees, top management people, and outside consultants. On many occasions, you will do much of the talking. You will seek to solve grievances of employees; you will conduct meetings and small group discussions; you will give talks to employees, to the public, and to business and professional groups. In your daily contacts with supervisors and co-workers, you will use oral communication for reporting, instructing, reprimanding, giving information, and asking for information.

So important to the business leader is this power to communicate orally that Clarence Randall, a business executive, said in a speech he gave at Harvard University:

> ". . . at every point to which he [the business executive] turns in his work, he senses the necessity for the adequate communication of ideas. Each hour of the day, from the humblest foreman to the chief executive of the company, the person bearing responsibility must engage in telling others what to do and how to do it. Knowledge and wisdom are wasted if unexpressed; genius is completely unharnessed if the lips are inarticulate. The business man today must be able to write and speak the English language with clarity and felicity, or stand aside and let his chair be occupied by someone who can."[1]

USES OF ORAL COMMUNICATION IN BUSINESS

Following are some of the many ways in which business workers depend on oral communication.

- *To sell goods and services.* Every retail sales person relies on oral communication to make sales. The insurance salesman who calls on you at your home makes a sale through effective oral communication; the airline ticket agent uses oral communication to assist you in arranging your proposed trip; the door-to-door canvasser must rely on oral communication to convince you of the advantages of his wares.

[1]From *A Businessman Looks at the Liberal Arts*, by Clarence B. Randall, copyright 1957. Reprinted by permission of The American Foundation for Continuing Education, Chicago, Illinois.

- *To give instruction to an individual or to a group.* The teacher, whether he performs in a school situation or in special business or industrial classes on the job, is dependent on oral communication; the sales manager who conducts special training classes for his salesmen must be an effective oral communicator; even the computer programmer who must show his new assistant how to operate the machine relies on oral communication.

- *To explain or report to supervisors, to subordinates, and to those on the same level.* The sales manager may report orally to the vice-president in charge of sales; the supervisor in the office interprets a new company policy for his group; an employee explains a grievance to his supervisor; the general manager's secretary tells the file clerk to pull all correspondence with the Lane Manufacturing Company.

- *To give information to customers and potential customers.* A customer calls a department store for information about the sizes, colors, and prices of vinyl tile; another customer telephones for advice about the best method of cleaning the blinds she recently purchased.

- *To give formal speeches before groups.* The president of a company is asked to give a speech before the members of the Rotary Club; an accountant is asked to talk to a college class in advanced accounting; the secretary to the president of a large manufacturing firm is asked to address a group of college girls on "The Advantages of Becoming a Secretary."

- *To participate in social-business conversation.* The office manager telephones the secretary of the civic club to which he belongs to report that he will not be able to attend the luncheon meeting tomorrow; a sales representative congratulates a former associate who has gone into business for himself.

- *To interview employees and prospective employees.* The personnel manager and the section supervisor interview applicants for an accounting position; the supervisor discusses with an employee his merit rating at the end of his probationary period.

- *To acquire information necessary to conduct the everyday affairs of business.* The credit manager of a department store calls the local credit bureau to determine the credit rating of a new customer; the mail clerk telephones the post office to find out which class of mail to use for a special mailing his company is planning; the accountant visits the Bureau of Internal Revenue office to discuss methods of figuring depreciation on equipment; a secretary telephones a travel agency to get information about hotel accommodations in Seattle.

- *To purchase goods and services.* A housewife asks a department store salesman many questions about a rug she would like to buy; the purchasing agent telephones a local stationer to order file folders; the manager of a truck fleet inquires about a truck-leasing plan.

- *To provide service for customers and potential customers.* The credit manager explains to a customer the procedure for opening a charge account; the floor manager assists a customer who has received a set of table linens that are the wrong size.

- *To participate in meetings.* The sales manager conducts the meeting of the Sales Executives Club of which he is president; the secretary contributes her ideas for the convention of the National Secretaries Association to the members of the planning committee.

- *To participate in informal discussion with fellow employees.* The receptionist takes up a collection to buy a gift for a fellow employee who is about to be married; the mail-room supervisor organizes a committee to plan the office Christmas party; the promotion manager gets all the employees in the office together for lunch.

These are but a few of the activities that may be witnessed daily in business—activities that rely for their success almost wholly upon effective oral communication.

FORMS OF ORAL COMMUNICATION USED IN BUSINESS

Oral communication in business takes many forms. Among the most commonly used forms are the following:

- Face-to-face conversation—interviews, sales, social-business situations, informal discussions between supervisors and employees

- Telephone conversation—with another office, with customers, with suppliers

- Conversation via interoffice communication devices—between executive and secretary-receptionist, between salesman on selling floor and clerk in stockroom

- Dictation and recording—dictating a letter to a secretary, using a dictating machine for dictating letters, recording meetings on tape

- Radio and television appearances—giving interviews or reporting information

- Formal speeches—debates, panels, addresses to employees, the public, customers, or professional groups

- Leadership of or participation in group discussions or meetings—leading employee group discussions, participating in stockholders' meetings and in meetings of business and professional organizations

- Instruction—teaching training classes for salesmen and retail store employees

Each of these forms of oral communication requires a slightly different technique. The difference may be in the amount and kind of prior preparation required, the manner in which the voice is projected, or the manner in which the participant makes his presentation. For example, speaking over the telephone requires a knowledge of how far the telephone should be held from the lips and how loudly the speaker should talk. A radio presentation may be read from copy and, therefore, requires a knowledge of how to read without sounding as though you are reading. Leading a meeting requires a knowledge of parliamentary procedure. Teaching a class requires that the teacher know how to ask questions properly. Participating in a panel or in a group discussion requires the ability to think quickly and to put thoughts into understandable language without hesitancy.

ORAL COMMUNICATION AND EMPLOYEE MORALE

Effective oral communication is essential to good employee relations. Through oral communication, a free flow of information and ideas can be maintained between management and employees and within the company's various levels of authority. It is generally found that when employees have frequent and easy means for discussion and expression of their ideas, morale is high. Personal conferences, committee meetings, group conferences, and speeches that allow for question-and-answer periods are among the means of oral communication open for improving relations between management and employees.

Where morale is high, employees generally have better communication relations with the public. Oral communication with the public is handled by every employee. Public relations is considered so important that many businesses train their employees in such areas as public speaking and proper telephone technique.

PUBLIC RELATIONS AND ORAL COMMUNICATION

The success of a business is based upon customer satisfaction. Business is greatly concerned with writing techniques. Considerable time and money are spent to word letters so that they will not offend and to develop advertising copy that will win new friends for the firm. The manner in which a customer is treated over the telephone or in person is equally important in building goodwill, if not more so. All employees—whether sales people, secretaries, receptionists, cashiers, or clerks—create a public image of the firm they represent by the way they speak to customers. One curt or rude employee can cause a business to lose many customers. To the customer, each employee he meets *is* the firm. If he is made to feel that his interests are important, the customer will be satisfied; if he is made to feel that the firm is not interested in his satisfaction, he is very likely to take his business elsewhere.

COMMUNICATION PROJECTS

Practical Application

Think of a business position that you would someday like to hold. On a separate sheet of paper, list under the following headings the oral communication activities that are likely to be exercised in this position.

1. Daily oral communication activities
2. Occasional oral communication activities

B Prepare a two- to three-minute talk on one of the following topics and be prepared to give this speech before the class.

1. Why Effective Oral Communication Is Essential to Every Business Worker
2. The Most Effective Use of Oral Communication I Have Experienced
3. How Effective Oral Communication Contributes to Effective Leadership

C Be prepared to defend or oppose the following debate topic: *Resolved: That Oral Communication Is More Important to Business Than Written Communication.*

D List as many business positions as you can that require the use of oral communication almost exclusively.

E Practice reading the following paragraph as though you were going to read it for a radio broadcast. Try not to make it sound as though you are reading the material or have memorized it.

In every line of business and in every profession, men are judged by what they say and how they say it. Speech is the most important agency through which men communicate with one another. Instructions, explanations, and reports are made to a large extent through the medium of the spoken word. Likewise, the products of industry and agriculture are sold and policies determined largely by means of both public and conference speaking. Thus, speech is an extremely important agency for influencing the conduct and thought of our fellows.[1]

F Without using any motions or diagrams, orally give directions for one of the following:

1. How to reach the nearest movie theater
2. How to reach the school library (or cafeteria) from the classroom in which this subject is taught
3. How to tie a Windsor knot in a necktie (men); how to apply lipstick properly (women)

G Be prepared to describe an object orally without telling the class what the object is. If you have described the object clearly, the class should be able to identify it from your description.

Editing Practice

Spelling and Vocabulary   Some of the following sentences contain spelling errors; some test vocabulary; some are correct. For each correct sentence, write *OK* on your paper. Correct each incorrect sentence.

1. This is indeed a happy occassion for Blanton's.
2. They're very sure that the specifications are accurate.
3. Not even a millionnaire can stand excessive overhead.
4. The intelligent young person heeds the advise of his elders.
5. The tone of Mr. Rudd's voice precludes any argument.
6. Mr. Rourke was most favorably effected by the profit-sharing plan.
7. All our customers have benefitted from the new billing procedures.
8. You must not breath a word about the latest invention.
9. We are equiping our offices with a loud-speaker system.
10. Their treasurer was formally a medical student.

[1]William Phillips Sandford and Willard Hayes Yeager, *Effective Business Speech*, McGraw-Hill Book Company, New York, 1960, p. 9.

Editing for Context Rewrite any sentences containing words that do not fit into the context. Write *OK* for any correct sentence.

1. Please come in before Friday to sign the affidavit.
2. We find it necessary to addend to a uniform discount policy.
3. To countenance serious inflation, drastic legislation is needed.
4. There is no such article listed on the manifest.
5. We are not affiliated with any other manufacturer of cable grips.
6. Our sales to you on account demented our complete confidence in your integrity.
7. Have you ever thought of taking out an annuity policy?
8. You probably feel that the small sum involved does not ward our action.
9. We bought the material at a tremulous saving in cost, which increased our profits.
10. Please do not comply us to take this disagreeable step.

Case Problem

The Rude Caller When Joan, the secretary to Mr. Niles, answered the telephone, the caller asked to speak to Mr. Niles. Joan responded, "May I ask who is calling?" The voice at the other end said, "No, you may not," and Joan heard the telephone receiver slam. "What a rude person," thought Joan, with a perplexed expression on her face.

1. Was the caller the only rude participant in that brief telephone conversation? Why not?
2. What should Joan have asked the caller in order to get the information she wanted? Why?

Guides to Effective Oral Communication

Two executives were discussing the candidates for an important supervisory position in their organization.

"Both men have had about the same amount of training and experience. How are we going to decide whether the position should go to Tom or to George?"

"This position calls for someone to represent us at meetings of many groups in the territory we serve, doesn't it?"

"Yes, it does; and a great many contacts have to be made over the telephone, too."

"Well, which of these two men do you think can do a better job in both these respects?"

"There's no doubt in my mind that Tom would be far superior in making presentations, in leading group discussions, and in talking over the telephone to our customers. He knows how to speak well; he has an effective vocabulary; and he makes a very good impression in terms of his appearance."

"Then it seems quite clear that we should offer the position to Tom, don't you agree?"

Undoubtedly you would agree with this decision, too. Every day, numerous candidates for good positions fail because they are weak in oral communication. Because obtaining a good position and succeeding in it depend so heavily on persuasive oral communication, it is important to be aware of the two major factors—physical appearance and speech—that determine one's effectiveness in communicating orally.

PHYSICAL APPEARANCE

In most situations where oral communication is used, the speaker can be seen by his audience. (Important exceptions are, of course, talking on the telephone and using recording devices.) Because the speaker is seen before he is heard, he makes an impression on his audience before he utters a word. The impression he makes is based primarily on posture, use of hands, facial expression, eye contact, body and head movement, and general personal appearance.

A speaker's physical appearance sets the stage for acceptance or nonacceptance of what he says. A speaker who creates a good physical impression quickly gains the interest of his listeners. Of course, he must have something interesting and worthwhile to say if he expects to hold the attention of his audience for any length of time; but he has overcome the first barrier to effective oral communication if he has good posture, is dressed appropriately, is well groomed, and knows how to make each listener feel that he is speaking directly to him.

Posture

Many speakers underestimate the importance of posture to good physical appearance. This is a serious mistake. Regardless of how short or tall he is, the speaker should stand up to his full height. He'll find that as he develops good posture, he will develop better breathing control. He will appear more confident and give his audience the feeling that he knows what he is talking about and that his message is important. Of course, a speaker should never appear stiff or pompous and all-knowing. He should develop a natural posture, constantly reminding himself to stand erect, with shoulders back and stomach in.

Hands

What should you do with your hands when you speak? A speaker distracts his audience by picking imaginary lint from his clothing, putting his hands to his face, or toying with some article he is holding. The listeners automatically direct their attention to his physical maneuvers and soon lose track of what he is saying. If he is standing, a speaker should place his arms and hands in a relaxed position at his sides (rather than behind his back or folded in front). From time to time he can make natural gestures. If there is a lectern in front of him, the speaker may place his hands on either side of it; but he must remember never to lean on the lectern.

When a speaker talks from a sitting position, he will be heard better if he sits slightly forward in his chair. His arms and hands may rest in his lap, on the arms of the chair in which he is sitting, or partially on the edge of the table or desk in front of him. However, he should never use the desk or table as a place to rest his head and elbows. A lazy-looking speaker encourages disinterest on the part of his audience.

Facial Expression

A speaker's facial expression influences the impression he makes on his listeners. A relaxed, pleasant, interested expression will create a better atmosphere for communicating, of course, than a wrinkled brow and turned-down mouth. As you look in a mirror from time to time, see whether you can capture your personality as others see it. Are your facial muscles relaxed? Is your smile natural, pleasant, and genuine? What characteristics in your facial expression are appealing to those around you? See if you can develop animation and show enthusiasm in your facial expression. Remember that a deadpan expression generates only boredom.

Eye Contact

Whether the audience is composed of one person or a hundred people, every person likes to feel that the speaker is talking directly to him. Therefore, the speaker's eyes should never leave his audience for any extended period of time; it's hard for a listener to stay interested when the speaker looks constantly at his notes, the wall, the ceiling, or out the window. When talking to one or two persons, the speaker should look squarely into the faces of his listeners (without, of course, staring them down) unless he is directing their attention to an object such as a chart. When speaking to a large audience, the speaker should move his eyes over the entire audience; he should look into the faces of his listeners and not over the tops of their heads.

Body Movement

Body movement also contributes a great deal to the physical effect created by a speaker. The effective speaker never paces back and forth; he knows that excessive movement will distract an audience. It is permissible for a speaker to move his body from the hips in order to turn from side to side or to move his body in a forward motion in order to emphasize a remark. Of course, if the speaker is using a chart or other illustrative material, he must move from time to time to the visual device. However, a speaker should stay in the same spot as much as possible.

Grooming and Dress

Personal appearance—grooming, cleanliness, and attire—is also an important factor in effective communication. How a speaker looks and dresses expresses personality just as surely as how he speaks or conducts himself. There are so many factors of personal appearance that they cannot be considered here in depth. But the person interested in better oral communications should be aware that he communicates best when he appears at his best. Good appearance breeds confidence. Appearing clean, being dressed neatly and conservatively, avoiding extremes in personal grooming and clothing styles, and selecting attire and accessories that are tasteful and in harmony with one another and with the speaker's personality are some of the factors of personal appearance that must be considered by the business person. A speaker who is weak in any one of these factors cannot hope to be very persuasive as an oral communicator—whether he is speaking merely to one person or to a thousand.

SPEECH QUALITIES

Although a speaker's physical appearance creates the first impression of him as a communicator, the quality of his speech may have an even greater influence on his audience. The quality of speech is determined by the following factors:

- Force or volume of voice

- Pitch or level of voice

- Rate or tempo of speech

- Enunciation

- Pronunciation

The force of a speaker's voice and the pitch and the tempo at which he speaks are greatly influenced by the way that he breathes. The amount of air that is taken into the lungs and breathing control help determine how much force a speaker's voice will have; both factors also affect the voice pitch. The rate of speaking will be determined by how frequently a speaker must breathe more air into his lungs. He should speak only when breathing air out—never when taking air into his lungs. Good posture can help a speaker breathe into his lungs the maximum amount of air and can help him control the amount of air he is expending.

Force or Volume

Force, volume, and intensity are all synonyms for an important voice quality. To communicate orally, a speaker must be heard. Sufficient volume, therefore, is necessary; and good breathing control is important for sufficient volume. If you have trouble being heard, you should practice breathing deeply and controlling your breath with diaphragm and abdominal muscles, just as a singer does. The large abdominal cavity should be used to store a supply of air that can be released evenly to produce a clear, sustained tone. How much force you must use will, of course, be determined by such factors as how good the acoustics are in the room in which you are speaking, how large your audience is, and whether or not you are using a microphone or other electronic device that will amplify your voice.

Pitch or Level

A speaker's voice will be more audible if he maintains a pleasing pitch. Pitch refers to the level of a sound on a musical scale. Practice can help correct the shrillness of a voice that is pitched too high or the excessive resonance of a voice that is pitched too low. Equally in need of correction is the even pitch that results in a monotone. An effective speaker varies his pitch. The rising and falling of voice pitch is called intonation. Intonation can indicate that a statement is being made, that a question is being asked, or that a speaker is pausing. A drop in pitch indicates finality or determination and is, therefore, used at the end of a declarative sentence. For example, in reading the following sentence you should close with a drop in pitch.

> No, I cannot go with you *under any circumstances*. (Emphasize the word *any*.)

A rise in pitch is used for a question, suspense, doubt, or hesitation. The following sentences should close with a rise in pitch.

> Is *that all there is?* (Put greater emphasis on the word *all*.)
> I'm not *sure* if I can meet you, *but I'll try*. (Emphasize the words *sure* and *try*.)

Gliding the pitch up and down or down and up usually expresses sarcasm or contempt, as in the slang expression "Oh, yeah?"

The most important aspect of pitch is variation. Variation of pitch not only helps hold the listener's attention but also helps him know the exact meaning intended. Important words can be stressed by a rise in pitch. Comparisons can be stressed by using the same pitch for each element; contrasts, on the other hand, can be made by pitching the first element high and the second low.

Notice the different shades of meaning that emerge as you read the following sentences and emphasize the italicized words.

> *She* gave him the money. (She did, not someone else.)
> She *gave* him the money. (It was a gift.)
> She gave *him* the money. (Only this one person got the money.)
> She gave him *the* money. (A particular sum of money.)
> She gave him the *money*. (Not something else.)

Rate or Tempo

Tempo, too, should be varied to avoid the extremes of speaking too rapidly so that words are not understood or speaking too slowly so that the audience does not pay close attention to what is being said. Regulate your rate of speaking so that you can enunciate each word clearly and so that the listener can hear each word without difficulty. A good rate for speaking is 125 words per minute; oral reading rates and radio speaking tend to run slightly higher—about 150 words per minute. To determine what 125 words per minute sounds like, read aloud the following paragraph in a half minute. If you read too rapidly or too slowly, read it over until you achieve the correct rate. At the end of a quarter minute, you should be at the diagonal line. Use the diagonal line as a guide for determining whether you should increase or decrease your speaking rate.

> A good speaker talks slowly enough to be understood by his audience, and he speaks in a pleasant voice, articulating and pronouncing each word correctly and distinctly. To develop a/good speaking voice, you must spend sufficient time in practice. An effective speaker is an asset to business and will find more opportunities for moving ahead than the person who cannot speak effectively. (63 words)

Changing the tempo contributes to variety, as well as to clarity. Important words may be spoken slowly; unimportant words or phrases, more rapidly.

Try to speak in thought units in order to assist the listener in interpreting the words he hears. If the sentence is short, the thought unit will be the entire sentence, as "Office custom will indicate the mode of dress." When there are several thought units within a sentence, the speaker should pause slightly after each thought group, as "It is a matter of custom / that the white shirt is generally preferred, / but some shades of colored shirts are appropriate."

Use pauses to stress major points. By pausing between major points or after important statements, you add variety and emphasis to the points you want the audience to remember.

Enunciation and Pronunciation

Because both of these elements are of particular importance in effective business speaking, they will receive special treatment in Section 51.

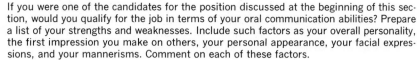

COMMUNICATION PROJECTS

Practical Application

A If you were one of the candidates for the position discussed at the beginning of this section, would you qualify for the job in terms of your oral communication abilities? Prepare a list of your strengths and weaknesses. Include such factors as your overall personality, the first impression you make on others, your personal appearance, your facial expressions, and your mannerisms. Comment on each of these factors.

B Select three prominent individuals (in politics, sports, or the arts) who frequently appear before the public in some type of speaking role. List the factors—pro and con—that affect their speaking effectiveness.

C Read each of the following sentences in three ways so that the meaning is changed by your emphasis.

1. She mailed the letter today.
2. This is the place I spoke of in my letter.
3. Is she coming to the reception, too?
4. If it is possible, please come in earlier tomorrow.
5. Please forgive me; I didn't expect to be late.

D Read the following sentences twice. Then, standing before the class, read them aloud. Try to keep your eyes on the audience as much as possible as you read the material.

1. Did you really expect him to come to work today?
2. I doubt whether I can come to the office party.
3. No, they are very capable typists.
4. What difference does it make?
5. She is never late, if she can help it.

E Read the following paragraphs twice. Then, standing before the class, read them aloud. Try to keep your eyes on the audience as much as possible as you read the material.

Every business is concerned with communication from the top down, from the bottom up, across, into, and out of the organization.

Improving communication is a problem of the greatest importance in improving the human relations and the management of an organization. Good communication down, up, and across largely determines the amount and kind of satisfactions, exclusive of their pay checks, that workers get from their jobs. Good communication plays a vital role in providing such nonfinancial incentives as (1) sense of security, (2) sense of belonging and feeling important in the life of the organization, (3) recognition for good work, and (4) continuing opportunities for service and advancement. Many morale studies have indicated that nonfinancial incentives frequently are more important to employees than higher wages or salaries.[1]

F Present a short talk to the class on some topic of your choice. Try to make each person feel as though you are talking individually to him.

Editing Practice

Synonyms or Antonyms?   In each item below two words are synonyms or antonyms. For each item, identify the pair by letter and indicate whether the words are synonyms or antonyms.

1. (a) slander   (b) reference   (c) equality   (d) disparity   (e) excellence
2. (a) opener   (b) glamor   (c) candor   (d) hypocrisy   (e) sagacity
3. (a) hunt   (b) perform   (c) discipline   (d) start   (e) chasten
4. (a) estranged   (b) reconciled   (c) old   (d) erudite   (e) odd
5. (a) affable   (b) garrulous   (c) gracious   (d) loquacious   (e) joyous
6. (a) blissful   (b) clever   (c) happy   (d) boisterous   (e) busy
7. (a) respiratory   (b) sordid   (c) involuntary   (d) stolid   (e) phlegmatic
8. (a) excusing   (b) modest   (c) faultless   (d) extraneous   (e) pretentious
9. (a) convex   (b) solid   (c) harrowing   (d) cadaverous   (e) concave
10. (a) contrive   (b) death   (c) action   (d) undershirt   (e) demise

Editors' Alert   The following sentences require thorough checking. Make any needed corrections, and if necessary, rewrite any poorly worded sentences.

1. For the present all staff members offices will be located on the third floor.
2. There's absolutely no other methods to solve so complicated a problem in so short a time.
3. We ordered 25 cases at $4.25 a case, for a total of $160.25.
4. Why don't he and Maxwell think that the ideas which you suggested at the meeting are good?
5. We must continue on to improve even this excellent record.

[1] William Phillips Sandford and Willard Hayes Yeager, *Effective Business Speech*, McGraw-Hill Book Company, 1960. p. 7.

6. Please fill out and return to us the enclosed questionaire, which will help us select for you the literature you will need.
7. We believe that the test letter should yeild at least 5,000 good prospects for follow up.
8. Our company has always in the past—and always will—be notorious for its excellent service.
9. The assignment was only given to Breslin and I on Friday, and we have hardly had time to begin it.
10. 400 trainees attended the special management classes given by the company last September.

Case Problem

The Wrong Girl   Margaret Dillon and Esther Beckett both typed for Mr. Boles, president of the company for which they worked. One day Mr. Boles came to Margaret with a typed letter in which there were several errors. He was quite disturbed over the careless proofreading and asked that the letter be retyped. Margaret noticed from the reference initials that the letter was not her work, but had been typed by Esther.

1. What should Margaret say to Mr. Boles?
2. What should Margaret say to Esther?

Enunciation and Pronunciation

Hal Edwards was called into the office of the manager of the shipping department and was reprimanded sharply for an error he had made. He had shipped forty desk lamps to the Robinson Furniture Mart in Los Angeles, California. The lamps were the style ordered, but Robinson Furniture had ordered fourteen lamps—not forty. As a result of this error, Hal's firm had to pay the return shipping charges on the twenty-six lamps from Los Angeles to Detroit, Michigan. These charges amounted to almost two days of Hal's salary. Of course, the Robinson Furniture Mart wasn't very happy about the extra bother the error caused. Why was such an error made? The order clerk who telephoned the order from the sales department enunciated the word *fourteen* so poorly that Hal thought she said *forty*. Unfortunately, Hal neglected to repeat the quantity to the order clerk. Poor enunciation can lead to costly delays and unnecessary expenses.

DISTINGUISHING BETWEEN ENUNCIATION AND PRONUNCIATION

The terms *enunciation* and *pronunciation* are closely related. However, they have slightly different meanings, and it is important that each term be understood by the person who desires to improve his speech.

Enunciation

Enunciation refers to the distinctness or clarity with which each of the sounds of a word is uttered. For instance, saying "runnin" for *running* or "gonna" for *going to* are examples of our careless enunciation. Enunciating difficulties occur in *ing* words, such as "feelin" for *feeling* and "typin" for *typing*. Also, when we speak rapidly, we often tend to run our words together, dropping some of the sounds. Saying "dijago" instead of *did you go* and "meetcha" for *meet you* are examples of this type of speech carelessness. A person who slurs too many of his words is difficult to understand, particularly over the telephone. Naturally, both the speaker and the listener will become annoyed if the listener must ask the speaker to repeat several times what he has said. Much of this kind of difficulty can be avoided if we simply speak more slowly.

Pronunciation

Pronunciation refers either to the sound that the speaker gives to the various letters or combination of letters that make up a word or to the way in which the speaker accents the word. A person who says "pro*noun*ciation" when he should say "pro*nun*ciation" is guilty of a pronunciation error. Should you say "libary" or "library," "'com·par·able" or "com·'par·able"? The dictionary indicates that the pronunciations are *library* and '*com·par·able;* and these are the pronunciations used by most people.

Of course, there are regional differences in pronunciation; and in addition, a number of words have more than one acceptable pronunciation. In the latter case, the dictionary lists first the pronunciation used most widely in the country.

A number of difficulties in pronunciation arise because some letters or combinations of letters are pronounced one way in some words and another way in others. For example, *ow* is given a long *o* sound in *know* but an *ow* sound (as in *ouch*) in *now*. Other difficulties in pronunciation arise because a letter may be sounded in some words while in other words the same letter is silent; for example, *k* is sounded in the word *kick*, but it is not sounded in such words as *know* and *knee*. Because of these inconsistencies in our language, it is essential to consult the dictionary whenever you are in doubt about the pronunciation of a word.

Though errors in pronunciation are less likely to cause misunderstandings than errors in enunciation—you would know what the speaker meant if he said "com·'par·able" instead of '*com·par·able*—such errors tend to distract the listener and may cause him to consider the speaker careless or uneducated. The business worker eager to succeed does not wish to be branded with either of these labels.

Furthermore, since most words are written as they sound, you can improve your ability to spell correctly by carefully pronouncing and enunciating each word you use. Many words are misspelled because letters that should be sounded are overlooked. People who repeatedly say "goverment" instead of *government* overlook the *n* that belongs in the middle of the word. Some words are misspelled because extra sounds are inserted where they do not belong; for example, "athaletic" instead of *athletic*. Care in pronunciation will help prevent other errors, such as "quite" for *quiet* and "praps" for *perhaps*.

Most business workers have to give and to receive information and instructions over the telephone or in face-to-face conversation. To prevent the costly misunderstandings that are often caused by improper pronunciation and enunciation, every business worker must try to develop and practice intelligible speech.

SUGGESTIONS FOR IMPROVING ENUNCIATION AND PRONUNCIATION

The following four-step plan is recommended for improving enunciation and punctuation:

1. Use the dictionary to check the preferred pronunciation of words about which you are uncertain.

2. Speak slowly enough and with sufficient care so that each letter in a word is sounded as it should be sounded and so that words are not run together.

3. Learn to use the physical organs of speech properly.

4. Practice proper enunciation and pronunciation, particularly of words that are frequently mispronounced or poorly enunciated.

In Section 1 you learned how to use the dictionary to determine the preferred pronunciation of words; in Section 50 you learned how to control your speaking rate. Now you will learn how to use effectively the speech organs over which you have control. You will also practice correct enunciation and pronunciation of words that frequently cause difficulty.

DEVELOPING A FLEXIBLE JAW

A rigid jaw leads to muffled speech. Many sounds are oral sounds and should, therefore, be made by the mouth. If they are forced through a locked jaw, they are certain to be muffled and indistinguishable. Keep your jaws locked tight and try to pronounce these words—*either, able, buy.* Can you understand yourself? Obviously you can't, and you would not expect any listener to understand the words you are saying.

An intelligible speaker moves his jaw freely between an open and a closed position. Say each of the vowels and notice the different positions of your jaw as you say *a, e, i, o, u.* Compare your jaw positions as you say first the sound *ow,* as in *how,* and then the sound *oo,* as in *room.* When you say *ow,* your jaw is dropped. However, when you say *oo,* you move your jaw only slightly, if at all.

Practice will help give you the free-moving feeling of a flexible jaw. First, stand before a mirror and practice the following words to be certain that your jaw is unlocked.

open	mine	able	around	ideal	one nine eight
buy	going	morning	arrival	ninety-nine	responsible

Now practice the phrases shown below. This exercise will help you develop a flexible jaw.

going to buy	around and around	high in the sky
down and out	up and down	up and around

Finally, practice these sentences to prove that your jaw is flexible and that it moves sufficiently.

She put the pen down on the table.
Many men have power, prestige, and ability.
Telephone 469-4589 as soon as possible.
My flexible jaw makes me a better speaker, does it not?

DEVELOPING ANIMATED LIPS

As you were practicing the words, phrases, and sentences in the preceding section, you probably noticed that in addition to your jaw moving up and down, your lips were assuming many different positions. Six consonant sounds are made by action of the lips. The lips are closed for the sounds of *m*, *b*, and *p*. The lower lip touches the edges of the upper front teeth for the sounds of *v* and *f*. The lips are rounded for the sound made by *w*, as in *woman*.

Poor enunciators do not move their lips very much; as a result, their speech is often unintelligible. The good speaker, on the other hand, uses a variety of lip positions. In addition to the lip movements for the six consonants previously mentioned, the *oo* sound in *who*, *lose*, *shoe*, and *do* requires rounded lips. The lips are widely stretched for the *e* sound in *me*, *we*, *key*, and *see*. In words like *few*, *boys*, *use*, and *how*, the speaker is required to use two different lip positions. The sound for *ow*, as in *how* and *now*, requires that the jaw be dropped and the lips be rounded to form a circle.

Using proper lip positions, practice these words. First read across and then read down the columns.

me	my	be	by	pen	pound
vase	very	voice	vest	vine	violent
first	fine	forest	fence	few	file
waste	when	why	wary	west	winter

Now practice the following phrases. Be certain that you avoid lazy lip movements.

friend in need	rapidly weighed	wintry weather
office manager	very fine work	answer the phone
mimeograph stencil	watered stock	empty the wastebasket
ditto master	economic waste	lose the shoe

Are your lips animated sufficiently, so that you can enunciate clearly each word in the sentences given below and at the top of page 429? Practice the sentences until every sound is clear.

Peter Piper picked a peck of pickled peppers.
She sells seashells by the seashore.

How now, brown cow?
The rain in Spain falls mainly on the plain.
Which witch was the wickedest witch?
Hickory dickory dock, the mouse ran up the clock.
The whistling west wind whipped the whispering trees.
Who picked up the bale of mail this morning?

DEVELOPING A LIVELY TONGUE

Repeat several times the phrase *the tip of your tongue.* As you say the words, notice the lively movement of your tongue. Try saying the same phrase with your tongue held loosely in your mouth and with a minimum of movement. Did you notice the lack of clarity? In order to speak clearly and with precise enunciation, you must move your tongue to several positions—the front of your mouth, the back of your mouth, and the roof of your mouth—and even between the top and bottom rows of teeth for the *th* sound, as in *this, either,* and *that.*

Now that you know what a lively tongue feels like, stand before a mirror and practice the following words:

feed	food	seed	sad	sod	sued
main	men	so	saw	peel	pale
twist	train	late	law	pad	port

Did you notice the movement of your tongue? Now practice these words, which require the tongue to be placed between the teeth.

thigh	thy	ether	either	loath	loathe
then	the	with	whether	wrath	through

Using an active tongue, practice the following phrases and sentences until every sound is clear.

actually colder
attempted assault and battery
health, wealth, and happiness
through thick and thin
this and that and those and them
seesaw at three-thirty
Linger a little longer, lovely lady.
The third-rate theaters appealed to the holiday crowd of shoppers.
Thirty thousand thermos bottles were sold there.
The sixth and seventh letters were so smoothly dictated.
Nothing gained, nothing lost, but nothing accomplished either.
This number is 336-3154, but Miss English is not here.

You have been given several suggestions for improving your enunciation and pronunciation. It is important for you to continue to be conscious of the way you enunciate and pronounce words, to use your dictionary to check the pronunciation of words about which you are in doubt, and to continue to practice good speech habits. If you will follow these suggestions, you will find that your speaking will improve and that the improvement will quickly become easy and natural for you.

COMMUNICATION PROJECTS

Practical Application

A The following phrases are frequently run together even though each word should be enunciated separately and distinctly. Practice saying these phrases properly, first in isolation and then in an original sentence that you create for each phrase.

give me	did you	going to	do you	got to
used to	want to	kind of	come here	will you
over and over	didn't you	don't know	going to go	have to

B From one of your textbooks, select a paragraph that you think will be of interest to the class. Read the paragraph aloud to the class, and be careful to enunciate words clearly and to pronounce them correctly. Each member of the class will list every word he hears you enunciate poorly or mispronounce.

C You wish your secretary to place a number of long-distance telephone calls for you. Dictate the following names and telephone numbers, making certain that the names and numbers are intelligible. Spell the difficult or unusual names; for example, "Setliff Furniture Company (S-e-t-l-i-f-f) of Poughkeepsie (P-o-u-g-h-k-e-e-p-s-i-e), New York. I want to talk with Mr. Setliff personally. The number is 914 435-6658."

Person to Be Called	Company and City	Telephone Number
1. Jacques Momarte	LaFrance Travel Agency New York, New York	212 443-2354
2. Will speak with anyone	Bona Fide Printing Company Los Angeles, California	Don't know
3. Miss Sally Larkin	Educational Placements Sioux City, Iowa	712 231-1478, Ext. 39
4. Randolph Gregory	Multiplex Electronics, Inc. Worcester, Massachusetts	617 465-5519
5. The office manager	Reliable Insurance Company Des Moines, Iowa	Don't know

D You wish to send the following message by telegraph to one of your customers. You telephone the message to the telegraph office. You will be called on in class to read all the information as you would read it over the telephone.

> *To be sent to:* Mr. Reginald B. Johnston, Vice-President, The Warner-Lincoln Manufacturing Company, 113-45 Hawthorne Avenue, N.W., Atlanta, Georgia 30305.
> *The message:* Returning 150 Superior desks, No. 199-A. Replace with 138 Exec-Sec desks, No. WZ-387, when available.
> *Sender:* Your name and address.

E As office manager, you find it necessary to order a number of items from a local stationer. Since you need the items in a hurry, you telephone the information to the stationer. Assume that you have dialed the number and that the person at the other end says, "Wilson Stationery Company; may I help you?" Pick up the conversation from this point, and place the order for the following items.

1. 6 boxes of medium-hard carbon paper, No. 880, 8½ by 11½, Stock No. 2-105-19
2. 4 boxes 20-lb. white typewriting paper, 8½ by 11, Stock No. 13-1276
3. 2 quire stencils, Stock No. ABD-1379
4. 1 dozen No. 2 pencils, Stock No. 54-927

Editing Practice

States, Capitals, Principal Cities In each item at the top of page 431, there are two states, capitals, or principal cities that are misspelled. Spell them correctly.

1.	Lincoln	Colombia	Cheyanne	Pierre	Jefferson City
2.	Racine	Laramie	Pittsburg (Pa.)	Bethlahem	Portsmouth
3.	Michigan	Idaho	Arizona	Montanna	New Jersy
4.	Honalulu	Allbany	Richmond	Charleston	Indianapolis
5.	Seattle	Spokane	Hoboken	Scenectady	Cincinatti
6.	Wichita	Clevland	Agusta	Duluth	Butte
7.	Olimpia	Providence	Topeka	Frankfourt	Helena
8.	Minnesota	Colorado	Pensylvania	Virginia	Rhode Island
9.	Minnapolis	Juneau	Trenton	Charleston	Jeferson City
10.	Brooklyn	Pasedena	Brockton	Levenworth	Lowell

Editors' Alert   Check the following sentences and make any improvements they need. Watch carefully every detail.

1. This amazing appliance is truly portible, weighing only two pounds, 3 ounces.
2. The number of sales we have made in the first half of the fiscal year are astounding and certainly attest to the quality of our men and women in the field.
3. Of course I realize that the mistake is our's, however, we must have the pipe in order to meet the terms of our contract.
4. Whatever you can do to expedite the shipment will be greatly appreciate, because our whole entire crew will be forced to stop without it arriving on time.
5. We considered the investment a year ago and decided against it at that time but perhaps the situation has changed and you can tell us how the venture would now be worth while for us.
6. Under any other circumstances we would be glad to have a speaker represent us at your conference, but as I explained, circumstances do not permit anyone to contribute the time right now.
7. Ten men and 12 women spent from one p.m. to three testing the experimental on the job training courses.
8. It is the method that he is proposing that bothers me, not the goals of the project, which seem quite worthwhile.
9. I think we need a system of industrial awards, presented each year by the president of the United states, as an incentive to increase industrial research in these particular areas.
10. I do not mean to accuse American Industry of lack of initiative but to recognize that there is need for encouragement, as there is in all human endeavors.
11. Really, I cannot comprahend how you can tolerate such sloppy procedures; certainly we would never under any circumstances first loose a customer's check and then claim that he sent a check for the wrong amount.
12. Most of all we would like to honor the laurence's, who have tirelessly contributed of their time to this extremely important fund raising drive.
13. On March 28 342 cartons disappeared before they could be loaded onto the trucks, which we are at a loss to explain.
14. If it was three hundred cases or even 340 cases instead of 342, I would suspect a mathematical error in our paper work; however I think we must assume they are lost somewhere within the plant.
15. Rodriguez and Carson's office is located in the south-west corner of the third floor.

Case Problem

The Helpful Co-worker   Bill Thomas had been working at the Arrow Accounting Service Bureau for about one month, under the supervision of Larry Parker. One day, while he was working on a report for which Larry had given him specific oral instructions, Bill was told by Marvin Lowery, who sat at the desk next to him, that he was doing the report incorrectly. Marvin had been with the company over twenty years and had prepared many similar reports.

1. What should Bill say to Marvin?
2. How would you feel if you were in Bill's place and had been told that you were doing the report incorrectly?

Communicating With Individuals

Near the top of the list of communications activities of business employees—if not at the top—is talking with individuals. The business worker talks with his fellow workers—with colleagues in the department in which he works, with his supervisor and various department heads, with top management, and with service employees such as messengers and custodians—many times during the day. In addition, most employees talk, either on the telephone or face-to-face, with individuals outside the company—customers, salesmen, suppliers, visitors, and various people soliciting or giving information. In fact, many business employees depend largely on their oral communication skill to earn a living—the salesman, the switchboard operator, and the receptionist are examples. Everyone who has contact with the public plays an important role in developing and furthering the company image. When the agent at the airline ticket counter speaks to a passenger, he speaks not for himself, but for the company. The same is true of a receptionist, a secretary, or a credit clerk. In one sense, those who speak for the company *are* the company to those who do business with it.

GENERAL RULES FOR INDIVIDUAL COMMUNICATION

Following are guidelines for communicating effectively with individuals.

Be a Good Listener

It may seem strange to place good listening habits at the top of the list, but listening is one of the most important skills connected with oral communication. Attentiveness and interest, attributes of the good listener, can often "communicate" better than talking. For example, if the airline ticket agent is attacked verbally by an irate passenger whose plane was delayed, the agent can go a long way toward soothing the passenger by merely listening attentively. Often, the agent doesn't have to say anything; he realizes that what the customer most wants is attention and sympathy.

Many executives listen with special concentration when they are faced by people who have grievances. They find that, more often than not, the person who feels he has been wronged will talk himself out of his complaint. Of course, good listening is not practiced only with people who have problems. Everyone is entitled to be heard, whether he is expressing a point of view, a casual comment, a complaint, or a directive.

Share Conversation Time

Don't do all the talking. Give the other person a chance. Be a good listener. Watch for signs that the other person wants to say something or is becoming bored. No matter how interesting you think you are, how well informed, or how articulate, you must give your listener a chance to speak if you are to keep his attention and respect.

Encourage Others to Talk
Remember, you are measured as a conversationalist more on your willingness to listen and appear interested than on your ability to talk. Ask frequent questions, and be sure to comment occasionally on statements the speaker has made.

Look at the Speaker
When someone speaks, he likes to have the complete attention of his listeners. Every speaker resents having to compete with outside distractions—conversations in another part of the office, something going on outside the building, papers being shuffled, or objects on which the listener's gaze may be fixed. Look at the speaker when he is talking.

Compliment When Appropriate
Many people with whom we communicate are seeking approval. Compliment when the occasion demands it. This is especially important in tense conversation situations. If a valued employee has a complaint that you cannot eliminate, put him in the right frame of mind for a "No" answer by complimenting his work or his loyalty. The same technique will work with a customer. If you find yourself in a tense situation with a customer, try to find a way to compliment him—his taste, his promptness in paying his account, and so on. In all conversations, be generous with praise when it is timely and when it is deserved. Never give a compliment, however, unless you can do so with sincerity.

Don't Drag Out Conversations
Except in social situations, it is not wise to prolong conversations unduly. If you're asked for opinions, give them quickly and clearly. Not everyone wants to hear the story of your life or every detail about your weekend or a blow-by-blow account of why you were late getting to work. This doesn't mean that you have to be brusque. Try to sense what the situation calls for and act accordingly, but when you are in doubt, the best rule to follow is to keep your conversations short.

Address a Person by Name
Be sure you understand the name of a person whom you have met for the first time. Repeat the name as you are introduced: "I'm happy to meet you, Mr. Crouzet." If you aren't absolutely sure of someone's name, ask that person to repeat his name for you; you can say "I didn't hear your name clearly" or "How do you pronounce (or spell) your name?" Then pronounce the name aloud to fix it in your mind, and when appropriate, use the name in

the course of the conversation. Finally, always be sure that you use the person's name when you say good-bye. If you follow these steps, you should have no difficulty remembering the person's name the next time you meet.

Get On the Same Level

It is said that Napoleon had his desk raised so that he could look down upon everyone who came into his office. Not long ago most executives sat behind a huge desk when they talked to visitors; at the desk, they appeared more important, more courageous, more domineering.

The trend today is toward a more relaxed atmosphere. The executive who is an effective communicator moves from behind his desk and faces his visitor without a barrier between them. This makes possible a better give-and-take atmosphere and therefore better communication.

RECEIVING VISITORS

Although in most companies the receptionist is the hostess to all visitors, nearly every employee meets the public. This is especially true in small offices and in retail stores. You should, therefore, be familiar with the basic rules for meeting the public.

Give Prompt Attention to Visitors

Recognize a visitor's presence immediately. Even if you are busy, glance up and nod at the person who is waiting. Say to the new arrival, "I'll be with you in a moment. Won't you sit down?"

Greet Visitors Pleasantly

Be pleasant and friendly when you greet visitors, and use their names in your greeting whenever possible. Add a personal touch to your greeting, such as "Good morning, Mr. Loring. How are you on this lovely day?" or "It's good to see you again, Mr. Loring." These friendly greetings make the caller feel that he is getting special treatment.

Be Courteous to Everyone

Every visitor should receive friendly and courteous treatment. Even if the visitor is upset about something or is just plain grumpy, you must overlook his discourtesy and treat him with understanding. Perhaps he is annoyed about what he thinks is unfair treatment from your company. If this is the case, he may be justified, and you have an opportunity to mend a business rift. Treating such a person discourteously will tend only to anger him further. Usually a person responds well to pleasant treatment, and your courteous attitude will help to calm the visitor and to make him willing to give your company a chance to make amends.

Apologize for Delays

If an appointment cannot be kept promptly by the person who is to receive the visitor, you should let the visitor know why ("I'm sorry, Mr. Foster has been delayed a little while in a meeting"), and you should tell him how long he must wait ("Mr. Foster can see you about 10:15"). Make the visitor comfortable (a selection of current magazines and the morning paper should be on hand). Take the opportunity to show him that you have a genuine desire to help. For example, you might ask, "Shall I telephone your office and tell your secretary that you will be delayed a half hour?"

You will have some visitors whose shabby appearance may lead you to believe they could not possibly have business of interest to one of the company executives. Don't be too sure! Sometimes the one who scorns that well-groomed look is a VIP—he may be the most important stockholder in the company. Even though he is not, he is, of course, entitled to the same courteous treatment that you extend to everyone else.

Find Out the Purpose of the Visit

Almost every caller will have an appointment with an executive or other member of the company. In this case, he will merely say to you, "I am Frank Bagley; I have an appointment with Mr. Silver"; and you will usher him to the appropriate office or telephone the host that his visitor has arrived. If you do not know, however, whether the visitor has an appointment, you must ask, "May I help you?" or "Whom do you wish to see?" If he has no appointment, take his name, the name of the company he represents (if any), and the purpose of his call. Relay this information to the person who you think can be of most help to the caller. After getting permission to show the visitor in, invite him to follow you to the appropriate office. Then present him like this: "Mr. Simpson (host), this is Mr. Bagley (visitor)."

Be Discreet and Tactful

Protect both your employer's and the company's interests by being discreet in your comments to visitors. For example, if your employer is late coming to the office in the morning or returning from lunch, it is not necessary to supply details to the visitor. Instead of saying "Mr. Lawrence is late getting in this morning," say "I expect Mr. Lawrence about 9:30." If he is late returning from lunch, you might say, "Mr. Lawrence had a very important luncheon meeting and should return shortly." Avoid conversation about company business or personnel. If the subject comes up, be noncommittal and change the topic of conversation as quickly as you can. Never engage in idle negative statements, such as "Hasn't business been poor lately?" or "We have a terrible time getting good typists."

Be discreet in giving any opinions solicited by the visitor about the business he has come to transact. The person whom he is to see may have a different opinion from your own. The visitor may want to show you his products and ask whether you think the company might be interested. If you are not responsible for company purchases, however, you should not give a personal opinion as to the company's possible interest in buying the products. Of course, you should not be rude even though you are pressured for comment. Simply say pleasantly, "I am sorry, but I really have no idea of what our company's needs might be."

MEETING THE PUBLIC BY TELEPHONE

Meeting the public by telephone requires techniques that are different from those used in meeting the public face-to-face. Persons engaged in telephone conversations are unable to see one another; they must depend entirely on their voices to communicate friendliness, interest, and desire to be of service to the caller.

Most people take telephone usage for granted—and this is one of the reasons that so many office workers are ineffective telephone communicators. Too many employees assume that a business telephone conversation is the same as a personal telephone call. Actually, the telephone is one of the most important communication media in business; and it must be used with great skill, especially when talking with outside callers and with superiors in the office.

The following tips may seem elementary to you. Nevertheless, they should be reviewed.

- Talk directly into the mouthpiece.
- Talk slowly and naturally. Exaggerate your enunciation slightly. Shouting is never necessary.
- If a caller must be transferred to someone else in the company, say, "If you will hold on just a moment, I will have your call transferred." Then depress the telephone plunger twice, very slowly, and repeat until the operator returns to the line. Then say, "Will you please transfer this call to Mr. Branch on Extension 4103."
- If, while talking, you must put down the receiver, place it on a book or magazine rather than drop it on a hard surface. In this way, you will protect the caller's ear from irritating noises.
- Place the receiver gently in the cradle when you hang up.

General Rules of Telephone Courtesy

Courtesy is the watchword of telephone effectiveness. Greet the caller pleasantly. If you know in advance who the caller is, you might say something like this: "Good morning, Mrs. Seaton," or "Hello, Frank." If you do not know the caller, identify yourself first—"Hargrove" or "Miss Corbett" or "Douglass speaking." In answering the telephone for a department, be sure to identify yourself—"Mailing Department, Miss Toelstrup" or "Shipping, Ackerman." A secretary usually answers her employer's telephone like this: "Mr. Kahn's office" or "Mr. Olson's office, Miss Ducey speaking."

Your voice should be friendly and your manner courteous, regardless of who is calling. This manner is *especially* important when talking to outside callers. Remember that the impression created by your voice should be that of a friendly smile. Show the caller that you want to be helpful; always listen attentively and don't interrupt. So that the caller will know you are listening to his comments, acknowledge them occasionally with a "Yes" or with some other simple verbal response. Use the caller's name at least once before hanging up, and conclude the call with a remark like "Thank you for calling us, Mrs. Lawrence" or "We will look into the matter for you right away, Mr. Roberts."

Originating Calls

The telephone company has made the following suggestions for originating calls:

- Plan the conversation before you call. A little forethought will save both time and money. If your conversation will be an involved one, jot down notes in advance.
- Place your own calls. Not only is it faster and easier to do so, but it is also more courteous. No busy executive likes to be greeted with "Hold on, Mr. Lacey; I have Mr. Carpenter on the line." Mr. Lacey then has to wait until Mr. Carpenter gets on the line. Since Mr. Lacey is the person being called, it is discourteous to keep him waiting.
- To avoid delays, identify yourself promptly and state the purpose of your call. For example, say, "This is Bill Farnum of Bailey and Jones. I would like to speak to the person in charge of adjustments."

Receiving Calls

To ensure efficient use of the telephone when you receive a call, observe the following suggested procedures:

- Answer promptly and identify yourself immediately. You should answer at the first ring, if possible, and never later than the second ring.
- Respond to inquiries graciously, take appropriate notes, and verify important details. "Yes, we should be glad to send you a duplicate copy of last month's statement. You want the July, 19—, statement; is that correct?"
- At the close of the conversation, take the required action. Be certain that you keep all promises you make to the caller.
- Allow the caller to hang up first.
- If you are going to be away from your telephone, let someone know; and indicate how you would like him to handle any calls that are directed to you during your absence.

Answering for Others

Two special suggestions are appropriate when you are answering calls for other people in your firm.

- If the person called is not available, offer to be of help or to transfer the call to someone who can help.
- If the caller wishes to speak only to one individual and that person is not available, obtain the caller's name and telephone number and record any message he wishes to leave.

Handling Complaints

The real test of your ability to handle calls will be revealed when you must deal with an annoyed customer who has a complaint. You must remember that you represent your firm and that little or nothing will be gained by allowing yourself to become angry. Your task will be made considerably easier if you follow these suggestions in handling telephone complaints.

- Listen carefully to the caller's complaint. Take careful notes of all important details.
- Express interest in and an understanding of the caller's problem. "Yes, I can see why you were annoyed by the mistake in your bill, Mr. King; but I am sure we can correct it right away."
- Tell the caller what action you will take. If you cannot make the adjustment yourself, refer the caller to someone who can. Don't make the caller repeat his entire story to someone else; each time he is passed to another person, he becomes angrier.

COMMUNICATION PROJECTS

Practical Application

A Assume that you are employed as administrative assistant to John H. Halloran, purchasing agent of Thermo Electronics, Inc. Mr. Halloran has informed you that he has an important conference in his office and does not wish to be disturbed under any circumstances. If the following situations occur during the conference, what would you say to each of the individuals involved?

1. Mr. Gillette, a supplier, telephones and says it is urgent that he speak to Mr. Halloran.
2. An out-of-town visitor, Mr. Haines, comes to the office at 9:30 for an appointment that is scheduled for 10:30. However, he was in the area and decided to come earlier.
3. Mr. Halloran's wife telephones.
4. The president of the company, Mr. Abbott, telephones and says it is important that he speak with Mr. Halloran at once.

B The office services manager, Mr. Howard Clayton, has asked you to prepare a one-page memorandum to all secretaries on each of the following subjects. Choose one subject and then write the memorandum.

1. How to place outgoing telephone calls
2. How to receive incoming telephone calls
3. How to handle delays in telephoning
4. How to say no gracefully to a caller
5. How to handle complaints by telephone

C List five "do's" and five "don'ts" for receiving visitors in an office.

D What essential qualities should the good listener have?

E Suggest three greetings a receptionist might use to find out the purpose of a caller's visit.

F Give examples of how a good communicator can make use of a compliment in order to gain his point.

Editing Practice

Editing to Improve Writing Techniques   Rewrite the following sentences, and correct all evidence of poor writing techniques.

1. Mr. Gunn thought that he could enter and us not hear him.
2. Our chief joined the company 1960.
3. Because I came to the meeting does not mean that I shall consent to the plan.
4. McCaffery's ability to supervise and do all the various types of writing makes him an unusual executive.
5. The basket was empty and the letters all in the mail.
6. Your competitors are outselling you because they use a less expensive and modern method of trading.
7. The operations of business generally on a larger scale than the average professional man.
8. Forbes can handle the situation as well, if not better, than I.

Case Problem

The Negligent Employee   Horace Brady, the sales department head, receives the following written report from Mike Carr, a supervisor. Accordingly, Mike must talk with Julie about the quality of her work and the reason for her failure to receive a salary increase. What should Mike say to Julie when she comes to his office?

> I cannot recommend Julie Newland, my secretary, for a salary increase at this time. During her first six months on the job, she tried very hard to do good work; but she soon lost interest. Now my work is taking second place to her long coffee breaks and her personal visits and telephone calls. Yesterday, for example, it took three hours to get three short letters typed.

Communicating With Groups

Ask any executive how many meetings he attends in the course of a week and he is likely to say "Too many!" It is true that the typical executive may attend from two to as many as twelve or more meetings every week. The frequency of meetings is decried by everyone; yet the meeting is one of the most important media of group communication in business. The responsible business employee has frequent opportunities to participate in group meetings. He may be selected as a member of a *standing* (permanent) committee that meets regularly, such as a finance committee, a publicity committee, or a recreation committee. He may also be called upon to sit in on committees formed for a temporary purpose, such as a committee appointed to study commuting problems of employees or to investigate ways of improving the service in the employee cafeteria. Committees formed for a special purpose are disbanded once that purpose is achieved are called *ad hoc* (pronounced *ad häk*) committees.

Because meetings consume so much time and talent in the typical organization, they must be organized and run efficiently. The time spent in meetings adds up to many thousands of dollars a year in the average company. In addition to attending meetings during business hours, the business worker often goes to many meetings and serves on a number of committees outside the company—for example, in professional, social, religious, political, and civic groups.

PARTICIPATING IN GROUP MEETINGS

Every person who is invited to join a group discussion has an obligation to contribute his best. Time and money are wasted because employees take meetings for granted and do not contribute their maximum efforts to the discussion. They often come to a meeting unprepared, uninterested, and uninspired. The six basic rules for participating effectively in a meeting are explained in the following discussions.

Be Prepared

The first rule for participating effectively in a meeting is to be prepared. Find out beforehand all you can about the topic to be discussed at the meeting. If there is an agenda (see page 443), study each item carefully and review topics about which you are not conversant. For example, if the subject of merit ratings is to be discussed, be sure you know what the current company policy about merit ratings is and what forms are connected with the procedure. You may have to refer to one or more books or articles on personnel administration. In addition, it is often useful to get the opinions of knowledgeable people who will not be present at the meeting. If there is to be a discussion of a revision of the merit rating form, study the form thoughtfully, try it out, and ask various people who use the form what they like most and least about it.

Being prepared means coming to a meeting with a set of well-founded opinions. Opinions that are worth listening to in a business meeting are the ones backed up by facts. People are often opposed to a new idea merely because they don't know enough about it. The old saying, "You're down on what you're not up on," applies to participation in a meeting. Make certain that this saying never applies to you.

Express Opinions Tactfully

When someone asks you for your opinion or when you volunteer an opinion, be tactful in expressing yourself. Often, opposing points of view can cause strong disagreement. No matter how strongly you may feel that you are right and that the other fellow is wrong, your chances of winning his support are no better than your tactfulness in presenting your views. For example, don't say, "You're wrong, and here's why." Instead, you might say, "Your point of view certainly has merit, but I have doubts because . . ." Never tell someone he is wrong—*wrong* is a strong term, and your right to use it requires indisputable evidence. In selling your point of view, the "Yes, but . . ." technique is effective; that is, acknowledge the other person's point of view and show your respect for it and then present your own ideas. For example, "Yes, I agree that the solution seems simple and that your idea represents one way to approach the problem, but . . ."

In expressing yourself, separate facts from opinions. Label as facts only those statements for which you have solid evidence. Opinions should be signaled by such words as "it seems to me," "as I understand it," or "in my opinion."

Be Positive

One of the most unwelcome participants in a group meeting is the person who thinks "No." His primary mission seems to be that of killing the ideas and proposals that others voice. He seldom presents a positive idea of his own, but he is always the first one to say of someone else's idea, "That won't work."

Most meetings are held for the purpose of solving problems, and problems cannot be solved in a negative atmosphere. Participants must be willing to approach a problem with the attitude that the only way to solve it is to present as many ideas as possible. No one immediately vetoes an idea someone else has presented; instead, each person tries to see the idea's merits and to enlarge upon the idea's possibilities, no matter how weak it may seem at first. To smother ideas before they are fully aired is not only rude but also extremely disheartening to those who are genuinely trying to reach intelligent decisions.

Show Courtesy to Other Participants

The ideal meeting, as mentioned previously, is one in which everyone participates freely. The overaggressive speaker who monopolizes the discussion will discourage the participation of others. Even though you may be more knowledgeable about the topic than anyone else in the group, you should never display your intelligence in an offensive, overbearing manner. You may win the skirmish and lose the battle—the too-sure, know-it-all person often does.

More victories have been won in group discussion by modesty and tact than will ever be achieved by overaggressiveness. Don't jump in while others are speaking; wait your turn patiently. Show interest in what the other fellow is saying. You will win more friends by listening and taking notes on remarks by others than by interrupting their remarks—regardless of how inane the remarks may seem to you. Acknowledge that others may have as much information as you have or perhaps even more.

The courteous group member does not (1) resort to sarcasm when he disagrees with someone, (2) interrupt the person who is talking, (3) fidget, (4) gaze into space, or (5) carry on side conversations with other members of the group while someone else has the floor.

Keep Remarks Short and Pertinent

Some participants in a meeting take a circuitous route to reach the point they want to make. They ramble endlessly and indulge in frequent side excursions. If you have something to say, get to your point quickly. Meetings become boring and unproductive mainly because some participants insist on relating personal preferences, experiences, and opinions that have little or no bearing on the discussion at hand.

Take Notes

As mentioned earlier, the habit of taking notes is a good one to develop. The act of taking careful notes (1) keeps you on your toes, (2) tells the speaker that you consider his remarks worth recording, and (3) provides a valuable reference source during and after the meeting. Take notes not only on what the speaker is saying but also on what you want to say when it is your turn to speak. Some note-takers even write out their remarks (especially if they know shorthand) so that their presentation is both well organized and complete.

LEADING A GROUP DISCUSSION

Without doubt, the most important person at a meeting is the chairman. By skillful direction, he can turn an ordinary meeting into a rich and profitable experience for everyone. Without good leadership, the most promising discussion can become worthless. The good discussion leader follows the basic rules outlined here.

Make Advance Preparation

A good leader prepares thoroughly for meetings and conferences. He knows the time and place of the meeting, the names of those who are to attend, and in general what the meeting is to accomplish. Notification of a meeting of a standing committee usually takes the form of an agenda (a list of the topics to be discussed and the names of those who are to lead the discussion). The agenda is sent as far in advance of the meeting as possible. For a monthly meeting, those who are to attend the meeting should receive the agenda at least a week ahead of the meeting date. This advance notice will give the participants an opportunity to prepare themselves for the discussion. For a weekly meeting, it is sufficient to have the agenda in the hands of the committee members a day or two before the meeting. A sample agenda is shown on page 443.

Generally, the topics for discussion should be listed on the agenda in the order of expected controversy—the first item should be the one most likely to meet unanimous approval, and so on down to the item that is likely to be the most controversial. This procedure is psychologically sound; if a group agrees on the first topic, it will naturally be likely to work harmoniously on succeeding topics.

```
                  Meeting of the Hospital Fund Drive Committee
                          June 16, 19--, 10:30 a.m.
                      Library Reading Room, Fourth Floor

                                  AGENDA



        Chairman:  M. Brady

        1.  Reports on fund drives by floors
                Arlene MacTavish - First Floor
                Sam Wong         - Second Floor
                Ruth Monett      - Third Floor

        2.  Follow-up on home mailings - Thelma Dickinson

        3.  Advising contributors about deductions on state and federal in-
            come tax - E. L. Britt

        4.  Proposed meeting of all supervisors and program planned for the
            meeting - M. Brady
```

Prepare the Meeting Room

The room in which the meeting is to be held should be made ready in advance. The responsibility for seeing that the meeting room is properly set up should not be entrusted to just anybody—too often the job just doesn't get done. The result is that there is an insufficient number of chairs, there are no ashtrays (or the ashtrays are overflowing), the room is poorly ventilated, there is no chalk for the chalkboard, and so on. A meeting should start promptly; one way to avoid delays is to have the meeting room in order beforehand. If visual aids are to be used, someone should check well in advance to make sure that the proper equipment is on hand and is in working order. If an operator is required for projection equipment, the meeting date should be confirmed with him on the morning of the day of the meeting. Many meetings with a program featuring a motion picture have been fiascoes because the film didn't arrive, the operator forgot the day and time, there was no electrical outlet, or the extension cord was too short to reach the outlet.

Arrive Early

The chairman of the meeting should plan to arrive a few minutes early at the meeting place because (1) he will need time to check the facilities, and (2) he should set an example for the others. Arriving early also gives the chairman a chance to distribute the agenda. (Even though everyone has received a copy of the agenda, not everyone will remember to bring it to the meeting.) The chairman or his secretary should also bring along a few extra pencils and pads—there will be some participants who will have neither. If reports or other papers are to be discussed, the chairman will bring a few extra copies with him, even though copies may have been distributed in advance.

Establish a Down-to-Business Atmosphere

The chairman sets the tone of the meeting. If he begins late or is apathetic about getting the proceedings under way, the participants are likely to lose whatever enthusiasm they may have had when they entered the room. Generally it is best to start a meeting precisely at the hour for which it is scheduled, even though there probably will be latecomers. If the members of a group realize that the meeting will start without them, they are likely to make an effort to be punctual.

The Discussion

The good leader talks as little as possible and draws out the opinions of the participants. Unfortunately, some people think that *leader* and *talker* are synonymous terms when it comes to running a meeting. The skillful leader brings out each participant's best thinking. The leader's function is not to show how much he knows, but to steer the discussion in the proper direction. He knows that the greater the participation—that is, the more minds at work on a problem—the better the chances are of accomplishing the objective of the meeting.

Encourage Participation

Everyone has something to contribute to a meeting. Some people, however, are shy and will say nothing unless they are encouraged. Call on these people in a manner that invites them to participate; for example, "Ann, you have had a lot of experience in publicity. What do you think of Harold's suggestion of an exhibit in the lobby of the building?" or "Mr. Rader, we would be interested in having the benefit of your experience in working with records. Do you think the proposed new form will present any problems for the file workers?"

A leader encourages participation, not by evaluating the ideas and suggestions of others as they are voiced, but by trying to find something complimentary to say to the speaker when he has finished; for example, "Thank you, George. That's certainly one way to approach the problem," or "Good idea, Mrs. Wayle. We'd like to hear more about that experiment later."

Squelch the Orators

In any group there will always be one or two individuals who want to do all the talking. Certainly they have a right to be heard, but unless they are listed on the agenda as the principal contributors, they should not be permitted to monopolize the discussion. Only a strong leader can prevent a loudmouth from taking over the meeting. The chairman should be tactful but firm. "That's very interesting, Joe, but I think we ought to hear from Miss Jennings," or "Let's get back to you a little later, Irene. I think we would all be interested in having as many points of view as we can get."

Keep the Discussion on the Track

Meetings have a tendency to get off the track, and if the chairman is not careful, the main problems to be solved at the meeting will be bypassed entirely. All too often, a subject comes up that is of genuine personal interest to all those present at the meeting but has little or no bearing on the main topic. People just naturally like to tell about their personal experiences, likes and dislikes, and amusing anecdotes. These digressions should be permitted now and then because they lighten the discussion; we can't be completely serious all the time. However, when side issues begin to waste valuable time, the chairman must cut them off. He can do so tactfully. "That must have been an unusual experience for you, John. I don't know how you managed to stay so calm and collected under the circumstances. But to get back to our discussion of the revision of the office manual. Mr. Warren, how complete do you think the discussion on report style should be?" Generally you can keep the discussion on the track without being rude, but bluntness is justified as a last resort. "Joe, time is getting away from us, and we are nowhere near a solution to our problem. Let's see if we can't bring this discussion down to specifics. Carl, what are your recommendations?"

Summarize From Time to Time

As already mentioned, it is neither necessary nor desirable for the chairman of a group discussion to evaluate everyone's remarks as soon as they are presented. He listens attentively and makes no comment except, perhaps, to stimulate further discussion. "Good, Tom. That's an interesting point of view. I gather that you are opposed to any change in the procedure at this time. Right?" Above all, the leader does not tear down ideas or argue with the speaker; doing so will only discourage other participants from expressing themselves. The chairman of the meeting is only one person, and it is usually not within his province to judge every idea expressed.

Now and then, however, the chairman should summarize the major points that have been presented up to that time. "We are agreed, then, that we should not open a branch office in Richmond at this time. You believe that for the remainder of this year, at least, the Virginia territory can be serviced adequately from Washington. Right? Well, let's move on, then, to the problem of warehouse space in Washington. Is it sufficient, or will additional space be needed? Charlie, you've had more recent contact with the situation than anyone else here. What do you think?"

Know How to End

If the chairman has prepared the agenda carefully and has run the meeting efficiently, there is no reason why the meeting cannot end at the hour scheduled. If the discussion seems likely to extend beyond the closing hour and it is important to continue, get the approval of the group; for example, "Ladies and gentlemen, it is five minutes of twelve, and it looks as though we won't get out of here by noon. Shall we continue the discussion, or would you rather schedule another meeting for this afternoon?"

After the meeting, the secretary should write up the minutes and distribute them as soon as possible. Memorandums should be written to those who

ℐnteroffice 𝓜emorandum

TO Mr. E. L. Britt   **SUBJECT** Payroll Deductions on
Contributions Made to
the Hospital Fund

FROM M. Brady   **DATE** January 8, 19--

This memorandum is a reminder that the Hospital Fund Drive
Committee agreed yesterday that you should write a policy
statement concerning payroll deductions on contributions
made to the Fund.

If possible, I would like to see your statement in rough
draft before it is duplicated.

Thank you, Ed, for your valuable help to the Fund Drive
Committee.

M. B.

MB/af

are assigned special responsibilities at the meeting. Such a memorandum is illustrated above.

Formal Meetings

Some groups run their meetings under parliamentary rules. If you are elected to office in such a group, you should have a copy of *Robert's Rules of Order,* the standard guide to parliamentary procedure.

COMMUNICATION PROJECTS

Practical Application

A Why should the chairman of a meeting not evaluate the ideas of participants as they are given?

B How might the leader of a meeting encourage the participation of those who are shy?

C What is the difference between a standing committee and an *ad hoc* committee?

D Explain what is meant by the expression *be positive* in reference to participating in a meeting.

E What are three reasons for taking notes at a meeting?

F Prepare an agenda for an *ad hoc* committee meeting for which you are to act as chairman. Select a discussion topic, such as "Improving Procedures for Receiving Callers in the Blank Company." Then develop a list of topics concerned with phases of this subject and assign them to individuals in your class.

G At a meeting of the recreation committee of XYZ Company, Charles Finch was given the responsibility of obtaining adequate facilities for the annual spring dance. Write a follow-up memorandum to Finch to remind him of the assignment. Supply any details you think appropriate.

Editing Practice

Applied Psychology   The wording of the following letter excerpts does nothing to cement good human relations. Revise the sentences.

1. The complexities and subtleties of this onerous obligation will be apparent to any institution not eleemosynary in character.
2. You must have had the goods since before the war—Revolutionary War, of course.
3. We are refusing your application for credit because investigation shows that you are dilatory in paying bills.
4. We want to know why you are not using your charge account with us.
5. Although we cannot understand why the buttons on the No. 745 coats do not match, we are sending you a full set of replacements.
6. Because of your failure to give us your house number, our driver had to bring back the parcel, thus delaying delivery for three days.
7. You made an error of $2 in the total on our March 1 statement.
8. When we asked for delivery by March 15, we meant this year—not next.

Case Problem

The Poor Chairman   As chairman of the recreation committee, Bill was very discouraged after the first meeting. He couldn't understand why so many committee members were late to the meeting. Hadn't he called all the members that very morning and asked whether they could meet at 2 p.m.? He waited until 2:20 before enough members were there to start the meeting. When he asked the group what recreation activities they wanted to discuss, he got little response. Finally, one member suggested forming a baseball team. Bill quickly discouraged that idea, and very few other ideas were presented. The meeting adjourned at 4 p.m. with nothing settled other than that another meeting would be called soon. What went wrong with Bill's meeting?

Preparing and Delivering a Speech

Nearly everyone is called upon at one time or another to "say a few words" to an audience. Since active people belong to one or more business, professional, civic, church, or social groups, they are bound to be asked to express themselves in public. The more active a person is in these organizations, the more opportunity he has to speak before groups. The responsible business executive may frequently speak before professional organizations, at company meetings, and before many different civic, religious, and educational groups.

Even people who do not participate in extra-business activities find that they must be prepared for public appearances—introducing a speaker, explaining a procedure to a group of clerical workers, extending greetings to visitors to the company offices, making a presentation at a meeting of company salesmen, and so on.

A speech is like a letter in that it reflects an image of the company that employs the speaker. An effective speech, like an effective letter, conveys a message clearly and convincingly and at the same time builds an image of goodwill.

The first step in delivering an effective speech—whether it is a two-minute introduction, a five-minute commentary, or an hour's discourse—is to plan it carefully. Planning involves previewing the speaking assignment, gathering and organizing material, outlining, and rehearsing.

PREVIEWING THE SPEAKING ASSIGNMENT

Regardless of whether the speech topic has been selected for the speaker or whether the topic is the speaker's own choice, every speaker must ask himself three basic questions before gathering and organizing his material. (1) What is the purpose of the speech? (2) To whom is the speech to be given? (3) How much time is allowed for the speech?

What Is the Purpose of the Speech?

Every speech has a purpose—to explain something, such as a company procedure; to describe something, such as the features of a new product or an experience; or to report on something, such as a market survey. The purpose may be to present a point of view, to inspire, or to win support for a proposal. Every speech must be organized to fit its purpose.

Let's assume that you have been asked to tell the company salesmen about the engineering features of a new typewriter the company has manufactured. If your talk is entitled "How the Rapidex Typewriter Is Made," you are obviously not expected to dwell on how to sell the product, how much money has been allocated to promote it, or how much it cost to transport the raw materials to the factory. The purpose of the talk is to give the salesmen product information they can use to persuade prospects that their machine is superior to the competitors'. Your remarks should center on the materials used for the various parts of the typewriter, the engineering features that permit the machine to be operated so easily, the color selection, and so on.

To Whom Is the Speech to Be Given?

The effective speaker finds out everything he can about his audience before he gathers material for his speech. If he is to discuss automation before a group of cost accountants, his emphasis will be very different from the one he would use in discussing the same topic with a group of factory foremen. If his speech is one of several that are to be given, he should inquire about the rest of the program so that he can put his topic in perspective with the others. The speaker should find out as much as he can about the interests, occupations, and age level of the audience. In addition, it is helpful to know the expected audience size and the expected ratio of men to women. The program chairman can supply this and other useful information. With his help, the speaker can find out what the audience already knows about the subject and what the audience expects to learn from the presentation. With such knowledge at hand, the speaker can avoid rehashing facts already known and can give particular emphasis to areas of most interest to the audience.

How Much Time Is Allowed for the Speech?

The speaker must know precisely how much time is allowed for the speech. Obviously, he should not try to crowd into thirty minutes a topic that requires an hour. Therefore, once the speaker knows the amount of time he has been allotted, he should plan his speech so it can be adequately presented in this time period.

The smart speaker, when given thirty minutes for a speech, takes only twenty-five. If the topic he has been assigned is a broad one, like "Automation," he should select the facet of the subject that best fits his audience. For example, the speech may deal with "Automation in Credit Records" for an audience composed of credit managers, or it may cover "How Does Automation Affect the Executive Secretary?" for an audience composed of executive secretaries.

GATHERING AND ORGANIZING DATA

There is no substitute for preparation. Even the most gifted speakers always prepare carefully beforehand, whether they are to speak for only a few minutes or for an hour. If your topic is one that you can prepare for by reading, read as widely as possible. Find a good library that has up-to-date magazines, books, and bulletins on your topic, and get as many points of view as you can. Check and double-check on facts—especially statistical information. Take notes—more than you can possibly use in your speech. Put the notes on cards and start a new card for each new subject or source. Be sure to identify on the card the source of your information in case you want to refer to it later.

The advantage of writing notes on cards is that it is easy to discard unwanted material and to arrange and rearrange the remaining material in the best order for the preparation of your speech outline. In fact, if your notes are prepared well, your final arrangement of the cards will represent an outline.

For some topics, valuable information can be obtained from talking to other people. If you are speaking on "What Salesmen Like Most About Their

Jobs," for example, talk to as many salesmen as you can. Again, take card notes on your findings.

OUTLINING AND ORGANIZING THE SPEECH

After the speaker has selected the topic and has gathered and organized his data, he is ready to begin outlining the speech. The following is a guide to preparing an outline:

1. Speech Title—   Time Allotted—
2. Purpose of Speech—
3. Introduction (arouse interest and give purpose)—
4. Body of Speech—Principal ideas to support purpose
   a. Principal idea No. 1
      Supporting information and material
   b. Principal idea No. 2
      Supporting information and material
   c. Principal idea No. 3
      Supporting information and material
5. Conclusion
   a. Summary of principal ideas
   b. Plea for action (if applicable)

The Introduction

The introductory remarks should be brief and should arouse the interest of the audience in the speaker and in his subject. Various methods of introducing the talk may be used; for example:

- A direct statement of the subject and of the importance of that subject to each member of the audience

   The title I have chosen for my remarks is "Automation in the Office—Myth or Revolution." Everyone here has a stake in automation because his future may depend upon how well he understands this important development.

- An indirect opening that is of vital interest to the audience, with a statement connecting the subject with this interest

   Tomorrow your job as cost accountant may be abolished or at least changed so that you won't recognize it. Why? Because many of the things you are now doing by hand can be done better and more cheaply by machine.

- A striking example or comparison that leads up to the purpose or subject of the speech

   In 1951 the federal government had exactly one business data processing system in operation. But only twelve years later, the government was using more than 1,248 such systems. As private enterprise begins to match this astounding pace, what impact will automation have on you, the office worker?

- A strong quotation relating to the subject

> "There is nothing in this world constant but inconstancy." So said Swift many years ago. This statement has more meaning today than ever before . . .

- Important statistics related to the subject

> In the past three months in this city, more than three hundred office workers were replaced by machines.

- A brief anecdote

> Last week my secretary handed me a clipping from her home-town paper. It was about experiments that are now being made with a "machine stenographer." The manufacturers hope to perfect it so that the dictator merely dictates into the machine, and his letter comes out all transcribed, ready for mailing. My secretary never once thought about being replaced by such a machine; she was worried only about whether it could straighten out the grammar and punctuation that I insist on mangling!

The Body of the Speech

Once audience interest is aroused, you are ready to provide the principal ideas that will support the purpose you have established for your speech. How many ideas you will present and develop will depend wholly upon the amount of time you have been allotted for the speech. It is better to develop each idea fully enough to be convincing than to present many ideas that are weakly developed and therefore not fully accepted or understood by the audience.

How is an idea communicated? First, it must be stated in a brief but clear and interesting way. Then the idea should be developed by explanation and illustration. Finally, the idea should be summarized.

Among the techniques available to the speaker for developing his ideas are those in the following list. Which techniques the speaker selects will depend upon the nature of the data he is presenting.

- Giving examples
- Making comparisons
- Quoting statistics
- Quoting testimony of a recognized authority
- Repeating the idea in different words
- Defining terms used in stating the idea
- Using descriptive language that makes the listener "see" the situation
- Using narration to relate a story connected with the idea
- Using audio and/or visual aids

Here is an example of how one idea used in a speech might be communicated, following the suggestions that have been presented. Suppose a speech was designed to try to persuade an audience of businessmen that air travel is best for business purposes.

Principal Idea: Air travel saves businessmen time and money.

Development: 1. Tell the story of two businessmen traveling from and to the same cities to conduct their business. One went by air and returned home the same day. The other went by train and had to remain overnight.

2. Show a chart of figures comparing the cost of travel between two cities by private automobile and by air transportation.

3. Give several examples of travel time between your city and another heavily visited city nearby, making comparisons in time by air, automobile, bus, and train.

4. Quote the president of a large corporation who says he uses air transportation exclusively for all business trips for himself and for other executives of the company. They find that both time and money are saved.

Audiovisual Materials   Many speakers use such audiovisual materials as slides, filmstrips, motion pictures, and charts to enrich their presentations. Whatever visual aid is used, it must be large enough so that the audience can see it without difficulty. Good visual aids make a talk more interesting by providing a change of pace. Talks dealing with figures can be clarified and brought to life by using well-prepared charts and diagrams.

Motion pictures should be previewed to determine whether they are appropriate. Above all, facilities and equipment should be checked prior to the presentation so that there will be no delays after the talk has started.

The Conclusion

The conclusion of a speech should be brief and to the point. A summary of the major points made in the speech and a plea for action, if applicable, is all that is needed. The summary may repeat key words or expressions already used or may restate the principal ideas in different words. Sometimes an example, a comparison, or an effective quotation serves as an appropriate summary. In any case, the final statement should tell the listeners very specifically what they should do, believe, or understand as a result of the presentation.

PRACTICING THE SPEECH

The inexperienced speaker should write out his entire speech from the outline he has developed, *not* for the purpose of reading the speech but so that he can refine his expressions, improve his choice of words, and time his presentation.

After the speaker has refined the speech, has read it through several times, and has timed the reading, he should prepare an outline on index cards. This outline should include phrases, quotations, and statistics. If possible, it should be prepared in large, clear handwriting or in jumbo typewriter type so that the speaker can refer to the notes casually from a distance of two or three feet. Supplementary materials should be keyed into the outline in some way (underlined, solid capitals, or in color) that will make them stand out for the speaker.

Using the final outline, the speaker should practice delivering his speech and should try to anticipate the conditions of the actual talk. A beginning speaker often finds the following practice suggestions helpful. Stand erect— before a mirror if possible—and imagine your audience before you. Watch your posture, facial expressions, and gestures as you deliver the speech. If you can practice before an audience of family or friends who will be sympathetic but frank in their analysis, so much the better. If you can record your presentation, you will be able to hear how clearly you speak and to judge the overall effectiveness of your presentation.

DELIVERING YOUR SPEECH

Though *what* you say in your speech is extremely important, *how* you say it is equally important. The best talk ever written can put an audience to sleep if it is poorly delivered. On the other hand, an average speech can bring an audience to its feet if the speaker is poised, dynamic, and persuasive. To deliver a speech effectively, a speaker must possess the following important characteristics: confidence in his ability to deliver an effective message, a pleasing personal appearance, and good stage presence and delivery.

CONFIDENCE

"I don't have a knack for public speaking." "Speakers are born, not made." "I'll make a fool of myself if I try to give a speech." "I'll get stage fright and forget everything I'm supposed to say." These are typical reactions of a novice speaker. If you believe any of these statements, then you, like so many other people, underestimate yourself. You're better than you think!

When you are talking to an audience, pretend that you are carrying on a face-to-face conversation with an individual. Remember that the audience is just as eager for you to perform well as you are. Don't be upset if you are nervous—even experienced speakers and actors are! Feeling nervous is a result of anxiety about doing a good job, and most authorities feel that a little stage fright helps to sharpen the mind. However, try not to show the audience any signs of your nervousness.

One way to develop confidence is to make sure that the conditions under which you are going to speak are as favorable as you can make them. Try to arrive fifteen or twenty minutes before you are scheduled to speak. If you speak best standing behind a lectern—and most people do—ask your host to provide one. Even an improvised lectern, such as a cardboard box covered with a cloth and set on a table, is better than no lectern at all. If possible, get the feel beforehand of the space you are going to occupy when you do address the group. Know in advance how you will approach the podium. If you think your approach will be awkward for you or for others on the stage or distracting to the audience, ask your host to change the arrangement. Check the ventilation, the lighting, the public-address system, and the seating arrangement. In short, make all the advance preparations you can to assure a feeling of familiarity with your surroundings. This is another big step in building confidence.

APPEARANCE

Nothing is more important to your confidence as a speaker than your appearance. When you are to give a speech, spend a little extra time on personal grooming and selection of clothing to assure yourself that your appearance is as good as it can be. Clothing should be freshly cleaned and pressed, and shoes should be polished and in good repair.

Advice to women:

- Choose the minimum amount of jewelry and accessories, and make sure that what you do select is tasteful. Avoid jewelry that makes a jangling noise when you gesture.
- Choose makeup shades carefully and apply makeup skillfully.
- For most out-of-the-office speaking assignments, a hat is necessary.
- Although a touch of bright color is appropriate—even desirable—be careful not to overwhelm your audience with bizarre color combinations or dazzling prints or stripes. You want the audience's attention on what you are saying—not on what you are wearing.

Advice to men:

- A colored or striped shirt is not strictly taboo, but in most cases a white shirt is preferable.
- At least one button of the suit coat should be fastened, whether or not a vest is worn.
- Socks are extremely important, because in most cases the speaker is seated before the audience while waiting to be introduced. Even if you do not ordinarily wear long socks, you should wear them at this time so that bare shins are not visible.
- Don't be too conservative with the necktie you choose—some experts recommend bright flecks of color. Make sure that your socks and tie harmonize.

Knowing that you are immaculately and tastefully groomed builds confidence in yourself and establishes the audience's confidence in you.

GOOD STAGE PRESENCE AND DELIVERY

Speak Out

You have a responsibility to make sure that you are heard by each person in the audience. Any person who can't hear will become disinterested, bored, and annoyed. If possible, before you deliver a speech, check the volume of your voice in the room where you will speak.

Keep your chin up when speaking so that your words will be directed out to the audience rather than down to the floor. Vary the pitch of your voice so that the audience is not lulled to sleep by a monotone. When you want to emphasize a point, raise your voice; when you wish to stir emotions, drop your voice so that it is barely audible to the audience. Either extreme of tone, of course, will lose its desired effect if prolonged.

Be Poised

If you have stage fright, take a deep breath before you begin to speak; this will relax your vocal cords. Stand with your weight distributed evenly on both feet, and don't shift from one foot to the other excessively. Don't stand too stiffly or too leisurely—appear alert but at ease. If your listeners think that *you* are comfortable, then they are more likely to be comfortable.

Be Aware of the Audience

The effective speaker is aware of his audience at all times, not only in selecting and preparing his topic but also in giving his speech. Audiences respond favorably only to speakers who talk directly to them and who smile occasionally. The speaker who looks at the ceiling, at his notes, or into space quickly loses rapport with the audience.

As you speak, move your eyes slowly back and forth over the entire audience, and pause here and there to "take in" a particular segment of the crowd. Smile frequently. Train yourself to watch the audience carefully and to be sensitive to its changing moods. If, as you are talking, you see blank or disinterested expressions on the faces of your listeners, you will know that your talk is dragging and that the audience has tuned you out. This situation may call for an amusing story, a personal anecdote, or merely a change in the pitch of your voice. If you are using visual aids, you might direct the audience's attention to a chart or other illustration when the talk seems to pall.

If your audience seems tired because the hour is late or too many speakers have preceded you, be quick to sense its boredom. If you aren't sure you can reawaken its interest with a sparkling performance, cut your talk to the bare essentials. Usually it is better to omit a portion of your speech than to run the risk of boring an already weary audience. The audience will be grateful to you.

Avoid Objectionable Mannerisms

A good speaker avoids objectionable mannerisms. When you talk, for example, do you toy with an object such as a paper clip, rubber band, or watch? Do you clear your throat, wet your lips, or remove your eyeglasses frequently? Do you punctuate your remarks frequently with an "uh" or "anda"? Do you have pet expressions or slang that you overuse? If you are not aware that you have any such mannerisms, ask some of your friends to listen to a rehearsal and to criticize. A speaker who has even one annoying habit cannot give a completely successful talk, for mannerisms distract an audience.

Don't Read or Recite From Memory

Familiarization not memorization

Never memorize or read your speech to the audience. Only a gifted actor can make a memorized speech sound unmemorized, and nothing is more boring to an audience than a singsong recitation. In addition, a speaker who memorizes his speech often becomes so flustered when he forgets his lines that he has difficulty in continuing. Often his speech does not follow a logical order because he omits something important or mixes up the parts.

Reading a speech so that the ideas sound convincing is also difficult. The reader tends to lose contact with his audience because his eyes are too often on his copy.

Instead of reciting or reading your speech, become sufficiently familiar with your material so that all you need is a brief outline with key words and phrases to make your speech flow in logical sequence. Use a conversational tone. Imagine that you are conversing with your audience, not giving an oration. Your voice should reflect the warm, easy tone that you would use if you were talking to a group of very good friends.

Use Notes

Most speakers—even the most experienced—rely on notes to guide them in their presentations. There is nothing wrong with using notes. It is a greater crime for a speaker to dispense with notes and to give a rambling, disorganized speech than to use notes to guide him in presenting an organized speech. Even if the notes are not actually used, having them on hand gives the speaker confidence because he knows he has something to fall back on if he should have a temporary lapse of memory.

Look at your notes only when absolutely necessary, and return your attention quickly to your audience after each glance at your notes. Keep your notes out of sight as much as possible while you are giving your talk, and turn the pages or cards as inconspicuously as you can. An audience is quickly discouraged by a large, slowly dwindling stack of notes.

Plan Distribution of Material

Often the speaker will have duplicated material to distribute to the audience. As a general rule, such material should not be distributed at the beginning of a speech. If it is, the audience will be too busy examining the "giveaway" to pay attention to the speaker. The important points of a speech should be made before any material is distributed to the audience.

Use Stories and Anecdotes Discreetly

Nearly every speech of any length is brightened considerably by touches of humor and by human-interest narratives. Of course, such stories should not dominate the speech. Observe the following rules in using humor and human-interest stories:

Make Sure They Are Relevant   Use stories and jokes that add interest to the subject or illustrate a particular point.

Make Sure They Have a Punch Line   The story should have a point. Before telling a joke to an audience, test it on friends. Many stories and jokes fall flat because they are too subtle for a mass audience, because they are not well told, or because they are completely irrelevant.

Make Sure They Are in Good Taste   Make sure that stories or jokes do not offend or embarrass the audience. Avoid risqué stories or jokes that make fun of physical handicaps, religious convictions, or racial or religious groups.

Make Sure They Are Short   A story or joke that lasts more than a few minutes is likely to pall. Only the most skillful storyteller can get by with longer accounts. Rehearse stories carefully before delivery, and time them to make sure that they are not too long.

INTRODUCING A SPEAKER

One of the most important speaking assignments is introducing a speaker. A good introduction sets the stage for the main address. If the introducer does an outstanding job, the main speaker's task is greatly simplified. In introducing a speaker, observe the following points.

Make the Introduction Brief

The audience has come to hear the speaker, not the person who is introducing him. Therefore, keep the introduction short—not more than two or three minutes in length.

Use an Anecdote

Do some research on the speaker. Find out from his friends and associates some personal traits or achievements that do not appear in the usual sources. A human-interest story about the speaker's hobby, family, or generosity will warm the audience to him. Although you should have complete details about the speaker's experience, education, and attainments, you do not need to use them all. An audience is quickly bored, and sometimes a speaker is embarrassed, by a straight biographical presentation, no matter how impressive the speaker's background is. Only the most significant dates, positions, and accomplishments should be given. You need only to convince the audience that the speaker is qualified to speak on the topic assigned, that he is worth knowing, and that he has something important to say.

Avoid Trite Openings

When introducing a speaker, avoid such trite expressions as "The speaker for the evening needs no introduction," "I give you Mr. John Jones," or "Without further ado, I present Mrs. Clementine Perkins."

Keep Your Eyes on the Audience

Don't face the speaker when you are introducing him—face the audience. Then wait until the speaker has taken his position at the lectern before seating yourself.

Save the Name until Last

Many successful toastmasters recommend that the speaker's name not be mentioned until the very end of the introduction. Reference is made to him during the introduction only as "our speaker." Then at the end of the introduction, something like this is said: "It is my pleasure to present Mr. Charles E. Stone."

CLOSING REMARKS

At the end of the main speaker's remarks, someone on the platform or at the speaker's table has the responsibility for closing the meeting. If the speech was a particularly good one, you may say, "Thank you, Mr. Burns, for your most enlightening and inspiring message. We are indeed grateful to you. Ladies and gentlemen, the meeting is adjourned." If, however, the speech has been average or even disappointing, as indicated by the reaction of the audience, you may close by merely saying, "Thank you, Mr. Aubrey, for giving us your ideas on new horizons in office procedures. Ladies and gentlemen, thank you and good night."

In any event, never prolong the closing remarks. If the speech was good, there is nothing a host may say that will add to its effectiveness. If it was poor, the audience is usually tired and wants to be dismissed.

COMMUNICATION PROJECTS

Practical Application

A   List three topics on which you feel qualified to speak. For each topic, give two reasons you feel qualified to speak on this topic. Indicate one audiovisual aid that you might use in presenting each topic before a group. For each topic, suggest one attention-getting title for a twenty-minute speech.

B   Select one of the topics you listed in Practical Application A for a five- or six-minute presentation before the class. Prepare an outline for this speech, and follow the format suggested on page 450.

C   After your outline has been approved by the instructor, write out your speech in full. Then read, refine, and time the speech. Finally, following the suggestions made in the text, make an outline of the speech on no more than four 5-by-3-inch index cards.

D   Suggest two ways that a beginning public speaker can overcome the common problems enumerated below:

1. Excessive verbalizing (using "uh," "anda," and so on)
2. Shaky knees
3. Annoying mannerisms, like scratching the head or toying with speech notes
4. Overuse of notes

E   As president of your graduating class, you are asked to serve as master of ceremonies at the Honor Awards Banquet at your school. The after-dinner speaker is the Reverend Horace A. Cedergren, an eminent orator, author, and world traveler, and presently pastor of the First Presbyterian Church of your city. Compose a unique, tailor-made message of introduction for the Reverend Mr. Cedergren. Supply any additional details about the speaker that you feel will add interest to the introduction.

F Your class will be allowed exactly five minutes to think about one of the following problems of delivering a speech (your instructor will select the problem for you). After you have given individual thought to the chosen topic, your instructor will appoint someone as the class recorder and then ask all of you to offer your oral suggestions to the class. The goal of this "brainstorming session" is to bring out a large number of ideas. Your instructor will let you evaluate them later.

1. How to keep a talk from dragging
2. How to deliver your speech in an interesting, entertaining way.
3. How to make class lectures more interesting (the student viewpoint)

G From the list of job classifications below, select one that you believe is of special interest to your class. Research this topic and make an outline for a five-minute talk. Outline your talk and be prepared to present it to your class.

bookkeeper or accountant
stenographer or secretary
receptionist
administrative assistant

retail salesclerk
salesman
punch-card tabulating machine
   operator
computer operator

Editing Practice

The Editorial Supervisor   Edit and rewrite the following paragraph.

We are indeed happy to add your name to the list of Wakeman distributors. Your's will be a large territory for you are our only outlet in the buckeye state. We are sending the booklet requested by you, "Wakeman Soap For Every Use;" and we shall of course be glad to amplify any of the topics presented therein. Good luck to you.

Case Problem

Playing Fair   A co-worker and friend confides to you, "I don't think Mr. Larkin likes me. I was late twice this week and only fifteen minutes each time, but he warned me that if I'm late just one more time, he will deduct an hour's wages from my salary check." Your experience with Mr. Larkin (who is also your supervisor) has led you to believe that he has always been fair to the employees and that he was merely carrying out his responsibility in seeing that employees report to work on time. In discussing the matter with your friend, however, you don't want to appear to be an "apple polisher."

1. Do you think Mr. Larkin played fair with your co-worker?
2. What would you say to your co-worker?

CHAPTER

10

Obtaining a Job

55 | Writing to Get the Job

One of the most important sales letters you will ever write is a letter of application. In this case, of course, the product you are selling is the most important one you'll ever sell—yourself. You can obtain many positions without a written application; however, there are many others where, to be considered for a job, you must submit a letter of application. Nearly everyone will, during his working years, write at least one letter of application. Letters of application are frequently requested in "Help Wanted" advertisements ("Write Box H-2, *Times,* giving full particulars—education, experience, and personal data"). Application letters responding to advertisements will help the employer answer this question: "Is it worth my time to invite this person to come for an interview?" If the job is an attractive one, the employer will get dozens—perhaps hundreds—of applications. Since he does not have time to interview everyone who is interested in the job, he selects for interviews only those whose application letters impress him.

Letters of application are also used (1) when you are applying "blind" (that is, you have no contacts in the company for which you would like to work), (2) when you have been recommended by someone for a position and you are advised to apply in writing, and (3) when the employer requests them. The letter of application is your representative; it determines whether or not you are given the opportunity to cross the threshold of the company to which you apply.

Most employers prefer a brief letter of application accompanied by a data sheet. A data sheet—sometimes called a résumé or personal profile—gives information about an individual's education, experience, and references. Every person seeking a job should prepare a data sheet whether he writes an application letter or not. The data sheet is often asked for at the interview; but even if it weren't needed, the experience of preparing it is extremely valuable to the job hunter. It forces him to inventory his qualifications and shows him where his strongest abilities lie.

THE IMPORTANCE OF THE WORK SAMPLE

When you write to apply for a job, you are giving the prospective employer a sample of the product you are selling. For this reason, you should take extra care in preparing the letter and the data sheet. Both should be neatly typewritten on a good grade of white bond paper, 8½ by 11 inches in size. (Never use company letterhead stationery or hotel stationery!) Leave ample margins on all sides. Before mailing the letter, double-check your spelling, grammar, and punctuation. Be prepared to rewrite your letter or data sheet several times in order to get the most nearly perfect one you can possibly develop.

THE DATA SHEET

Because the data sheet should be prepared before the letter of application is written, it will be discussed first.

Perhaps the biggest advantage of having the data sheet accompany the application letter is that most of the detail regarding the applicant is removed from the letter itself. This permits the letter to serve the functions of selling the applicant's job qualifications and of obtaining a personal interview. The data sheet, on the other hand, is helpful because it saves time for the reader by presenting the facts in summary form. A well-developed data sheet is evidence that the applicant has prepared himself by directing his qualifications specifically toward the job he seeks.

Many people send out dozens of letters of application and in such cases may prepare duplicate copies of their data sheets. However, an individually typed data sheet is always preferable to a duplicated one. If it is reproduced, however, the data sheet should look professional. Never send a carbon copy of a data sheet or one that has been reproduced by the fluid process (purple aniline dye).

Format

The organization and layout of a data sheet varies. However, the data sheet is commonly divided into these sections: (1) personal information, (2) education, (3) work experience, and (4) references. Each section should be arranged to set forth clearly the qualifications of the applicant. The typing should be clean and even; the margins should be well balanced and uncrowded; and the headings should stand out. In choosing a format, make an effort to select one that best fits your own situation. In doing so, keep in mind these points:

- Simply relate the facts; leave interpretation of these facts to the reader.
- Be sure the facts are complete. For example, say *when* you were graduated and from *where; when* you resigned from a position and *why.*
- Be neat and orderly in your presentation; there should be no obvious typographical errors, smudges, or other evidence of sloppy work. Arrange each division of your data sheet with the most important information first, the least important information last.
- Use brief phrases rather than complete sentences. For example, say "Took legal dictation" rather than "I took legal dictation each day from Mr. Mahoney, an attorney."
- Limit your data sheet to one page if possible. This forces you to organize well and to list only the important details about yourself.

An effective data sheet is illustrated on page 464. In the illustration, note the prominence of the name, address, and telephone number of the applicant.

Personal Information

Under the personal information section of the data sheet, give your date of birth, height, weight, marital status, and health. You may include other personal facts; however, information about your race and religion may not legally be requested by employers.

```
                                        Kathleen M. Marsh
                                        1420 Bellewood Drive
                                        Jackson, Michigan   49202
                                        Telephone (193) 826-2198


POSITION APPLIED FOR      Secretary, with opportunity for advancement to Executive
                          Secretary or Administrative Assistant.

EXPERIENCE

July, 1968, to            Terhune Products Company, 8740 Westwood Street, Jackson,
Present                   Michigan--Secretary

                          Duties:  General secretarial duties in marketing department,
                          including taking and transcribing dictation; filing;
                          operating adding, duplicating, and other office machines.

                          Reason for leaving:  Moving to Ames, Iowa

                          Starting salary: $85              Present salary· $95

Summer, 1967              Blumberg's Department Store, 1240 State Street, Jackson,
                          Michigan--Stenographer

                          Duties:  General stenographic duties.

                          Salary: $70

EDUCATION                 Jackson College, Jackson, Michigan--1966-1968.
                          Awarded Associate in Secretarial Science degree.

                          Jackson High School, Jackson, Michigan--1962-1966.
                          Graduated with honors upon completion of the college
                          preparatory curriculum.

PERSONAL                  Date of Birth:  March 10, 1946
                          Marital Status:  Single

REFERENCES                Mr. James L. Terhune
                          Director of Marketing
                          Terhune Products Company
                          8740 Westwood Street
                          Jackson, Michigan

                          Mrs. Alice M. Lennon
                          Office Manager
                          Blumberg's Department Store
                          1240 State Street
                          Jackson, Michigan   49201

                          Prof. Harold C. Kaplan
                          Secretarial Science Department
                          Jackson College
                          Jackson, Michigan
```

Education

Your educational background will count very heavily in job-hunting. Make the most of your presentation by including the following facts. First, name any colleges you have attended and the dates of attendance. List any degrees or diplomas you have obtained. Detail here such information as:

- Your major course of study (accounting, secretarial administration, advertising) and major subjects completed.
- Other subjects you have had that will enhance your value as an employee. For example, a course in office management or business communication

will be of interest to the prospective employer even though you are applying for a job in the accounting department. Be specific about subject titles. "Accounting IV" tells the employer nothing; "Corporation Accounting" is more specific.

Second, name the high school from which you were graduated and the date of graduation. If you took subjects that relate to your qualifications for the position, list them.

The job applicant will also want to stress leadership qualifications, extracurricular activities, and special honors. Businessmen want employees with a wide range of interests; they want people with social poise and with leadership potential. Therefore, in listing both hobbies and interests, the writer should try to show that he has many varied interests and that he has developed social graces and leadership qualities through extracurricular activities.

Work Experience

The most important job qualification of a new graduate is educational preparation. Nevertheless, the job-seeker should not underestimate the value of *any* kind of work experience, part-time or full-time. Almost everyone has held some type of job during vacation periods or on a part-time basis while attending school. Such jobs as paper carrier, soda jerk, busboy, waitress, filling-station attendant, filing clerk, gardener, or even baby-sitter are experiences that speak well for the young man or woman seeking a job in business. Such experiences, therefore, should be reported; they demonstrate that the applicant is industrious, has initiative, and is dependable. If an applicant worked to pay for his education, he should state this fact.

In organizing this section of the data sheet, list the latest work experience first; that is, list work experience in reverse chronological order. Each job should show inclusive dates, as well as the reason for leaving. For example, an applicant might write "Prior Drugstore, 1966-68, Assistant Manager; left for advancement." On the other hand, a lack of experience in the area of work for which you are applying should not be emphasized on the data sheet. Rather, it might be better to take the positive approach and say, "While attending school, I performed a number of part-time jobs, such as baby-sitting and soda-fountain clerking, to help earn my way." When you write your letter of application, you can then show how your knowledge of the job for which you are applying will more than compensate for your lack of experience.

References

Three to five names of references are recommended; at least one of these should be a character reference, such as a minister or family lawyer. If you have had little or no job experience, you might include as references instructors who know your scholastic ability and preparation. If you have had job experiences, however, list one or two former employers who know you and your work. Always include the job title of each reference. For instance, you might write "Mr. J. J. Walsh, Office Manager . . ."; "Dr. I. J. Kingston, Professor of Marketing . . ."; or, if you are listing a character reference, "Mrs. Maybelle A. Di Falla, personal friend." Include the complete address of each reference, as shown on the sample data sheet on page 464.

Of course, you should always obtain permission from each individual—either in person, by telephone, or by letter—prior to using his name as a reference. Answering inquiries for prospective employers is a time-consuming task, and references agree to this task because they have confidence in you, like you, and want you to succeed. In return, you owe them the courtesy of keeping them informed about your progress in getting a job.

THE LETTER OF APPLICATION

After you have completed your data sheet and you can see clearly how your qualifications fit the job you seek, you are then in a good position to organize your application letter. The letter of application is your sales message. Although the data sheet that usually accompanies the letter helps the employer determine whether or not you have the education and skills required for the job, the application letter gives him a better picture of you as a person. In other words, the data sheet is factual and, for this reason, rather formal; the application letter is a sales message and can be personalized. Study the letter on page 467. The following guidelines should help you in writing a letter of application.

Get to the Point Immediately

The first paragraph of the application letter should state the following:

- The source from which you learned about the vacancy (if it is not a "blind" application)
- The position for which you are applying
- Your intent to apply for the position

There is no one best opening for a letter of application. The following opening sentences have been used successfully.

Newspaper Ads
- Please consider me an applicant for the position of credit correspondent, as advertised in today's *Tribune.*
- I am applying for the cost accounting clerk position that was advertised in the *Tulsa World* on Sunday, October 5.
- The position of administrative assistant to the sales manager, which you advertised in yesterday's *Sacramento Bee,* is one for which I feel especially well qualified. Please consider me an applicant.
- I am interested in the position of systems analyst listed in the Help Wanted section of last night's *Kansas City Star.* I should like to apply for that position.

Referral
- A mutual friend, Mr. Gerald P. Gates, has suggested that I write you concerning a position as secretary in your company.

```
                                        322 North Kline Street
                                        Buffalo, New York   14209
                                        May 27, 19--


        Mr. David Jackson, Personnel Manager
        Endicott Manufacturing Corporation
        416 East Euclid Avenue
        Buffalo, New York   14220

        Dear Mr. Jackson:

            I would like to apply for the position of administrative
        assistant to the editor of your company magazine, "Endicott
        Quotes."  This vacancy was called to my attention by Professor
        H. C. Callans of Tremont College.  Professor Callans believes
        that my qualifications are suitable for this position.

            My college training, I think, provides an excellent
        foundation for the position.  I have always been interested
        in writing, and you will see from my data sheet that I have
        concentrated heavily on English and journalism.  I have held
        editorial posts in both high school and college.  During my
        sophomore year I studied shorthand and typewriting; I have
        continued to use these skills in my college work.  A summary
        of my qualifications is enclosed.

            As an administrative assistant to your editor, I would
        have the opportunity to assist in an editorial capacity as
        well as to use my secretarial skills.  I have had experience
        in proofreading and in layout.  My secretarial skills are well
        above average, and I find it very easy to work with others.
        Although I certainly don't know all the answers, you will find
        me eager to learn and to improve.  I am happiest when I am busy!

            If you wish to telephone me about an interview, you can
        reach me at Tremont College (484-8000, Extension 338) any week-
        day.  My last class is over at 3 p.m., and I could arrange to
        come to your office after that time.

                                        Sincerely yours,

                                        Jane C. Dawson

                                        Miss Jane C. Dawson


        Enclosure
```

- Your company has been recommended to me by Mrs. Flora Addington, placement director of Phillips College, as one with exceptional opportunities for a person interested in advertising. I should like to inquire about a possible opening in the art department.

- Attorney Frank E. Larsen, a friend of my father's, has told me of an opening for an assistant editor on your company magazine. May I be considered an applicant? (In this opening, it is assumed that the employer is acquainted with Mr. Larsen.)

Blind

- I believe my qualifications for a position as adjuster will interest you. May I tell you what they are?
- I have chosen your company's personnel department as one in which I would like to work. Perhaps you will be interested in my skills and abilities.
- Here are five reasons why I think you will be interested in interviewing me for the position of traffic supervisor in your company.

Tell Why You Should Be Considered

The second paragraph of your letter tries to convince the employer that you are a desirable candidate for the position referred to in the first paragraph. For example:

> Undoubtedly, Mr. Johnston, you want a secretary who can take dictation and transcribe rapidly and accurately. She should also have a thorough grasp of secretarial procedures—filing, telephone duties, letter writing, and mail routines. My training at Bryant College (detailed on the enclosed data sheet) has prepared me to handle all aspects of secretarial work competently and confidently. You will be proud to sign the letters I place on your desk.

Here is another example of a second paragraph in which you demonstrate your qualifications.

> A summary of my qualifications is enclosed. As you will see, my training at Lockyear's Business School was very comprehensive. Not only did I complete all the accounting courses offered by the college, but I also studied personnel management, economics, business psychology, office supervision and management, typewriting, and statistics. In all my courses, I consistently ranked in the upper 25 percent of the class.

Of course, the nature of the second paragraph will depend on what you have to sell. If your business experience is limited and unlikely to impress the employer, you will have to emphasize your educational background. In such a case, you might follow the above paragraph with a statement such as this:

> Of particular interest to me in the accounting course was machine accounting. In this class we learned the applications of accounting theory to automated procedures and equipment. I am especially eager to work in a large organization, such as yours, where EDP is being used on a wide scale.

Here is another example of capitalizing on achievements in school:

> You will notice from my data sheet that English and business communication were among my favorite subjects. In addition, I was a member of the debating team, was on the journalism staff, and was president of our speech club. You will find my written and oral communication skills well above average.

The following applicant admits lack of business experience; however, he compensates for this lack by means of his interest and enthusiasm.

> I must confess the lack of first-hand experience as a bank teller, Mr. Green. Compensating for this, however, has been my interest in your bank and in the work your tellers do. Several times in the past year, I have talked with Jim Yaeger, who started his teller training with you a year ago, about the interesting duties he performs. These discussions make me even more certain that banking is the kind of work I want to do. I am convinced that within a short period of time, I can learn to perform effectively as one of your tellers.

If you have had business experience that is related to the position for which you are applying, make the most of it.

> I am particularly interested in machine accounting in which automated equipment and procedures are employed. Last summer I was a temporary employee in the systems department of Jones-McComb Corporation, where I had an opportunity to become acquainted with EDP techniques. This experience was valuable, and I have decided to do further study in the field in evening school after I have obtained a position.

Show Willingness to Work and Learn

When an employer hires you, he is taking a risk—a risk that you may not be fitted for the position. One of the best assurances you can give him that you are a safe risk is your willingness to learn and your genuine interest in the job. For example:

> Obviously, there will be many routines and procedures that will be new to me. You will find me eager to learn and to improve.
>
> I shall bring to the job a willingness to work and an eagerness to improve. Let me prove that statement to you.
>
> I am not afraid of hard work; in fact, I enjoy it.
>
> I have no illusions about my lack of experience; yet I am quick to learn and I enjoy learning.
>
> I pride myself on my punctuality, accuracy, and stick-to-itiveness. I learn fast and I remember what I learn.

Make It Easy for the Employer to Ask You for an Interview

The last paragraph of your letter of application should be the action-getting paragraph—aimed at obtaining an invitation for an interview. Make it easy for the employer to contact you.

> I can come to your office for an interview between 9 a.m. and 5 p.m. on any weekday. My telephone number is 664-7613 (the home of my parents). If you would prefer to write, please use the address at the top of this letter.

Some job-hunters are more direct; they prefer to follow up on the letter rather than wait for the employer. For example:

> I can come to your office for an interview between 9 a.m. and 5 p.m. any weekday. After you have had a chance to review my qualifications, I shall call your secretary for an appointment.

Some successful applicants enclose a return postage-paid card containing information such as the following:

Dear Miss (Applicant's Name):

Please come to my office on _____
                                        (Date)

at _____ for an interview.
        (Time)

                              Very truly yours,

                              (Interviewer's Name)

If a postal card is enclosed, you might include the following statement in your letter.

> Just complete the enclosed postal card and ask your secretary to drop it in the mail. I am available at any time that is convenient for you. If you would prefer to telephone, my number is 693-2518.

Send the application letter in an envelope of the same good-quality bond paper as that on which the letter is written. Here again, the rules for neatness, good style, and placement apply. Choose a plain (unprinted) white business envelope such as a No. 10 (4⅛ by 9½ inches). Include your return address in the upper left corner of the front of the envelope.

OTHER EMPLOYMENT LETTERS

Requesting Permission to Use Someone's Name as Reference

As mentioned earlier, it is common courtesy to request permission to use someone's name as a reference. Although permission may be requested by telephone or in person, it is often requested in writing.

Dear Reverend Roberts:

   As you may know, I was recently graduated from the Topeka College of Business, and I am now making application at several firms in the Kansas City area for a position as a management trainee. May I list your name as a reference on my application forms? I should be most grateful for this privilege.

   You may jot your answer at the bottom of this letter, if you wish. I am enclosing an envelope for your reply. Thank you.

                              Sincerely,

Thanking Those Who Help You

After a position is obtained, those who have helped you in any way should be thanked in writing. For example:

Dear Reverend Roberts:

You'll be pleased, I am sure, to learn that I have accepted a position as management trainee with the A. S. Harrison Company in Kansas City. The job is exactly what I wanted. It gives me an opportunity to learn retail-store management from the ground up; some day, perhaps, I will be a manager of a branch store for the company. At least, this is my ambition.

Thank you very much for allowing me to use your name as a reference. I know that your kind words in my behalf were instrumental in my obtaining the job.

Sincerely,

Letters Following Up the Interview

After you have been interviewed, it is good strategy (as well as courtesy) to write to the interviewer, especially if you have reason to expect that a decision will not be made in a short time. Your thank-you letter gives you another opportunity to do a selling job. The letter might follow this form:

Mr. E. T. Cartright
Personnel Director
Loftin Corporation
San Francisco, California 94112

Dear Mr. Cartright:

I enjoyed very much meeting you and talking with you on Tuesday. Certainly, I came away with a much clearer picture of the work of a mail-room supervisor in the Loftin Corporation. The work sounds very exciting and challenging, and I am more convinced than ever that it is something I would like to do.

Thank you for your time and the many courtesies you showed me. I was especially glad to meet Mrs. Hamm; please convey my best wishes to her.

Cordially yours,

Accepting the Position

If you have been notified that you have been chosen for a position, it is wise to accept in writing, especially if the firm is out of town or if your reporting date is a week or two away. The style illustrated in the letter on the following page might be followed.

Dear Mrs. Ambrose:

I am pleased to accept the position as your secretary. I know that I shall enjoy working with you in the field of public relations and communications. The salary of $97.50 a week, plus benefits, is quite satisfactory to me.

As you have asked, I shall report to your office on Monday, March 9, at 8:45 a.m.

Cordially yours,

Declining a Position

Occasionally it is necessary to decline a job after it has been accepted. Naturally, a job should never be declined without solid, justifiable reasons. In such an event, give the reasons for your action. The following example illustrates a letter giving an acceptable reason for declining a job.

Dear Mr. Wilkes:

This morning I received some distressing news. My aunt, with whom I have been living and who depends on me to look after her, was told by her doctor that she would have to move from this area to a milder climate for reasons of health. She has now completed arrangements to leave Boston at the end of this month, and I must accompany her.

I am sorry that I shall have to decline the position that you offered to me. It was a wonderful opportunity, and I shall always be grateful to you for your kindness. Thank you.

Sincerely yours,

COMMUNICATION PROJECTS

Practical Application

 Scan the "Help Wanted" ads of your local Sunday newspaper, and locate a position similar to the one you aspire to upon graduation. Answer the ad and attach a data sheet that has been prepared specifically for this job.

 A friend of yours, Bill Barker, works in the sales department of the Marx Company, a textile firm that manufactures woolen suiting materials. Only last week Bill told you that his department will soon have an opening for a sales correspondent. This position requires a knowledge of sales work and the ability to write effectively, the type of work in which you are interested. However, Bill reminds you that promotions are usually made from within the company but that the man next in line for this position does not have your good qualifications. Write an uninvited letter applying for the job, and attach a data sheet that has been prepared specifically for this position.

 Write a letter to one of the people listed on your data sheet to ask permission to use his name as a reference.

Assume that you have accepted the position for which you applied in A or B above. Write a letter to one of the people who served as a reference and thank him for his help.

Two weeks ago today you accepted a position as management trainee in the transportation firm of Rapid Transit, Inc., Marlboro and Mayberry Streets, Memphis, Tennessee 38112. You are to begin work next week. Today, however, you were offered a comparable position with their chief competitor. This position has greater potential, a higher starting salary, and considerably better fringe benefits. You decide to accept the latter position. Write a letter to John H. King, Director of Training at Rapid Transit, declining the position that you originally accepted.

Editing Practice

Editors' Alert   Here are more sentences on which you can sharpen your editing skills. Try to develop an all-seeing eye that doesn't miss a detail. If necessary, rewrite the sentences.

1. As of January 28, we have accredited your account in the amount of $52.35, as shown by the enclosed reciept.
2. According to the latest bulletin, the new technical manual that has been in progress for the passed 4 years will not make its debit until June.
3. We are reluctant to acknowledge that a price raise is necessary but we can no longer postphone the decision.
4. I have asked Hagstrom to develope the leads suggested in your memo, and will personally take on the matter of discussing the matter with key executives here.
5. Having done everything possible to expedite the schedule, the laying of the cornerstone can now be moved up to the first of the month, instead of being held on the 10th.

Case Problem

Office Grooming   Norman Harper was quite concerned when Della Adams, his secretary, arrived at the office with her hair in curlers and a scarf over her head. There has always been an unwritten rule that both men and women in his office dress in a manner acceptable for business.

1. What should Norman say to Della?
2. Should Norman send Della home as a disciplinary measure? Under what conditions?

---

56   The Employment Interview

Every person who communicates orally is constantly selling himself. His response to questions, his description of experiences and situations, his explanation of procedures and methods—all contribute to the impression he makes. Perhaps no other single occasion offers a young man or woman a better opportunity to use oral communication to advantage than the job interview. Regardless of how skillful and knowledgeable the applicant is, how impressive his data sheet, or how persuasive his letter of application, all may be for naught if he fails to sell himself when he meets a prospective employer face-to-face.

A job interview can be either a frightening or an enjoyable experience, depending largely upon the amount of advance preparation and planning you give to the interview.

PLANNING FOR THE INTERVIEW

Preparation for the interview begins long before it actually takes place. Before he applied for a position, the applicant had to choose the type of work he wanted to do and train rigorously for it. Later he had to choose the type of company for which he wanted to work, compile a data sheet, obtain an interview and perhaps write a letter of application. Such long-range planning is necessary, of course. The following discussion will be helpful in preparing for a job interview.

Know What You Have to Offer

Every good salesman knows his product thoroughly—better than anyone else knows it. He has analyzed it from every conceivable angle; he knows its strengths and its weaknesses. He understands fully what features of his product are most likely to appeal to a prospective buyer; and these are the features he emphasizes in his sales presentation.

As a salesman, the job applicant must know his product, too. His product is himself. Preparing a data sheet gives the applicant an opportunity to see on paper what he has to sell—to see his strong points compared to those likely to be possessed by competitors for the position. The items emphasized on the data sheet are those every employer is interested in—education, experience, and special interests and abilities. The job applicant should know his qualifications so well that he can communicate them orally without hesitation.

The first step in planning for the interview, therefore, is to anticipate questions that may be asked about education, experience, and personal qualities. Here are examples of some of these questions:

- What subjects did you concentrate on while attending college?
- Which of these subjects did you like best? Why?
- Tell me something about your course in _____ (personnel administration, business communications, office management, or other subjects).
- I see by your application that you worked at Blank's for two summers. What kind of work did you do? What did you like most about your job? What did you like least?
- What do you most enjoy doing outside of working hours—hobbies and other activities?
- Were you active in school organizations? Which ones?
- Do you consider your skills (a) about average? (b) above average? (c) below average?
- Do you like to write? Do you consider yourself strong in English?

Answers to such probing questions will tell the interviewer a great deal about you and about how well you would fit the position, how quickly you would adjust to the job and to the people around you, and what your potential is for growth. In preparing for a job interview, then, you might ask yourself this question: What would I want to know about me if I were the interviewer?

Plan How You Will Look

On no other occasion is it more important to look your best than at an employment interview. Plan ahead, therefore, to make the most of your appearance. Knowing that you look well will help to make you feel more at ease.

Wear clothes that are becoming and that have a conservative styling. Make sure that your apparel fits properly and comfortably. Do not wear anything in which you feel ill at ease—you should be able to concentrate completely on the interview itself without being distracted by such things as shoes that are tight, a hat that slips off your head, or a suit that is too small. When dressing for an interview, give special care to the items in the following checklist.

GUIDE TO GOOD GROOMING

√ **Women**	√ **Men**
__ A tailored dress or suit, freshly cleaned and pressed (no frilly party dresses)	__ A conservatively cut suit, freshly cleaned and pressed (no sports jackets or extreme styles)
__ A simple, stylish hat that coordinates with dress or suit (optional)	__ A hat (optional)
__ Well-brushed or polished shoes in good repair that match apparel—no flats	__ Freshly shined shoes in good repair (Oxfords are preferred, but loafers are acceptable if they are not too sporty.)
__ Clean gloves	__ A conservative tie that complements suit
__ Hose	__ Socks to match tie (Long socks are preferred. If short socks are worn, be sure they are not at "half mast.")
__ A simple purse that matches apparel	__ A white shirt (Watch for frayed collar or cuffs.)
__ A fresh hairdo	__ A fresh shave and a recent haircut
__ Careful attention to nails, makeup, and general grooming (The word *conservative* should dictate appearance.)	__ Careful attention to nails and to general cleanliness
__ A clean coat, free from lint	__ A clean coat, free from lint

---

Your appearance will give the interviewer his first impression of you, and it is likely to be a lasting one. People who dress carelessly will surely give the impression that they will be careless workers. Those who are too sporty will give the impression that they do not take business seriously or that they are not capable of exercising good judgment.

If your interview is to take place in the early morning, plan to arise early enough to give yourself time to dress carefully. Always allow yourself extra time for reaching the place of interview. You can read or window-shop if you arrive too early, but you cannot erase the negative impression you will make if you are late.

Plan What You Will Say

Interviewers operate in different ways. Some will do most of the talking and will ask only a few questions about your education and experience. Others will draw you out as much as possible and say very little. Anticipate in advance such general statements from the interviewer as these:

- Tell me about yourself. (This request will give you a chance to emphasize your most salable features. He doesn't want to know about your childhood; rather, he wants you to answer such questions as these: What do you do best? What do you like best?)
- Review your college work and your experience. (Here you will emphasize the college courses that will best implement your qualifications for this particular job. The same is true of your experience.)
- What do you think your strongest points are? your weakest?
- Tell me why you think you should be hired for this position.

Anticipate also some personal questions, such as:

- What kind of person do you think you are?
- Do you like to work?
- What do you enjoy doing in your leisure time?
- Do you read a great deal?
- Where do you live?
- What salary do you expect?
- Are you punctual in your appointments?
- Do you have financial obligations?

Although you should anticipate the questions you are likely to be asked, it's a good idea also to think of questions you want the interviewer to answer. Not only will the information he supplies be valuable to you, but your asking questions will also show the interviewer that you have given careful thought to the position. Be prepared, therefore, to ask such questions as:

- What duties are required in this position?
- Does the company provide opportunities for further education?
- What are the opportunities for advancement?
- What type of insurance is available through the company?
- What about employee social and recreational facilities?

Anticipate the Salary Question

More often than not, the salary paid for a position—at least the general range—is known to the applicant before he appears for the interview. If he does not know the salary, however, and the interviewer has not mentioned it, you should say, near the end of the interview, "I understand that the beginning salary for this position is $_____ a month. Is this correct?"

Sometimes information about the salary is withheld, or the salary is listed as *open*. This means that the company has set a general salary range for the job, but the specific amount paid will depend upon the qualifications of the applicant.

If the interviewer asks you the question "What salary do you expect?" be prepared to give an honest, straightforward answer. Find out in advance what similar jobs are paying; then say something like this: "I understand that similar jobs in this area range from \$_____ to \$_____ a month. I had expected to receive about \$_____." (Mention a figure somewhere in the middle or, if you consider yourself unusually well qualified, near the top.)

Plan What You Will Take With You

Every applicant for a position should take with him the following items:

- A filled fountain pen or a good ball-point pen
- A pencil with a good eraser
- A data sheet (This may be put in a plain folder, in a large envelope, or in a special acetate folder. The data sheet should never be folded and put in a pocket or purse.)
- A small pad on which to take notes

Applicants for stenographic positions are usually given a typewriting and shorthand test. In addition to the items listed above, they should also take a clean stenographer's notebook, a good typewriter eraser, and possibly an eraser shield. Although these items are usually supplied by the company, you should be prepared in case they are not.

If you are applying for a position in which showing samples of your work would be helpful, take samples along. Put them in a folder or in a clean envelope.

On the day of the interview, give yourself plenty of time to arrive at the interviewer's office on schedule. Take no chances on delayed trains, taxis, and buses; start early. Last-minute dashes to make an appointment are likely to find you disheveled and breathless. Plan your schedule so that you can walk into the receptionist's office with calm assurance.

You'll usually be asked to fill out an official application form, and arriving ten or fifteen minutes early will give you a head start on this task. You will want to complete the application blank slowly and carefully (it will be part of your permanent record if you get the job). Try to get a copy of this application blank before arriving for the interview. In this way, you can be sure to give it the attention it deserves.

Find Out All You Can About the Company

There are two main reasons for finding out in advance all you can about the company. First, knowing something about the organization will help you to decide whether it is a place in which you would like to work. Second, you should have a strong answer to the often-asked question, "Why did you choose our company?" Too many applicants have no ready answer to that question beyond the weak "I just heard it is a nice place to work," or "It's close to my home." It is much more effective to say, "I have always been interested in investments; and I know that your company is one of the leading investment firms in the country."

How should you research facts about a company? You might talk to the person, such as your placement counselor, who referred you to the organization. You might ask this person or an instructor for the name of an acquaintance who works there; then talk to the employee. If you have an opportunity, pick up copies of employee magazines, booklets, or advertising brochures. Above all, learn the exact name (and the spelling) of the person who is to interview you. If you are not absolutely sure, contact the interviewer's secretary by telephone or the company receptionist in person.

THE INTERVIEW

When you arrive at the office, you will be greeted by a receptionist. Give your name and the purpose of your visit. "I'm (your name). I have an appointment at nine with Mr. Wilkinson." If you have to wait a few minutes, review your data sheet, check over the completed application blank, read the literature that will probably be available in the reception office, or otherwise occupy yourself. Don't engage in conversation with the receptionist unless you are invited to do so.

When you are ushered into the interviewer's office, try to be relaxed (though not casual or arrogant) and to look pleasant. Extend your hand to the interviewer only if he has extended his. It is enough to say, "How do you do, Mr. Wilkinson." You do not need to give your name; the secretary or receptionist will already have announced your arrival.

Seat yourself only when you are invited to do so. Keep with you the materials you have brought. Don't place anything on the interviewer's desk unless he invites you to do so. He may or may not ask to see the application blank and the data sheet. The occasion will come, however, when he asks you about your education and experience. This is the time to give him your data sheet if he hasn't already requested it. Say something like this: "Here is my data sheet on which that information is summarized. I also have completed the application blank." (Hand him both.)

Wait for the interviewer to make the first move. He will let you know at once how the interview will be conducted—whether he is going to ask most of the questions or whether he prefers that you take the initiative. Usually he will direct the proceedings.

Don't smoke. Even if you are a smoker, it is probably best to refuse a cigarette if it is offered to you. Say simply, "No, thank you; not just now." If you are a nonsmoker, you merely decline with "No, thank you."

Face the interviewer and speak directly to him. Don't stare at the floor or out of the window while either of you is talking. Of course, you should take your eyes from the interviewer's occasionally, but leave no doubt that you are talking and listening to him. Speak slowly and enunciate carefully. Give your answers and statements in a straightforward manner; show that you have thought them through and that you can speak with precision. Give short answers; the interviewer doesn't want your life story or your complete personal philosophy in answer to every question. At the same time, a mere "Yes" or "No" is not sufficient. For example, if you are asked this question, "I see you had one course in accounting. Did you like it?" it is not enough simply to say "Yes" (assuming that is how you actually feel). You might add "I enjoyed the course very much, and I plan to take more accounting in evening school."

Be specific about your special qualifications. If you are asked about your skills in shorthand and typewriting, give the results of your last tests. Say something like this: "I can write shorthand at 100 words a minute fairly consistently on new material. My typing speed on the last few tests was in the upper 60's." Or "My accounting courses consisted of principles, cost, intermediate, and departmental. In the latter course we were introduced to automation as it relates to accounting, and I especially enjoyed that." Or "I consistently made top grades in communications courses, and I particularly liked writing credit and collection letters." Or "One of the most interesting things I did during my summers at Blank's was to verify the cash balance each day. It wasn't easy to make everything come out when we had so many people handling the cash, but I was successful at it and learned a lot from the experience."

On the other hand, be noncommittal about controversial matters. If you are asked what you thought of Blank's as a place to work and your opinion isn't especially favorable, say something like this: "My work there gave me some valuable experience, and I enjoyed much of it." If you are asked for your opinions about people for whom you have worked and for whom you feel no special fondness, say something like this: "Miss Lodge was often helpful to me; I believe I profited from working with her."

The interviewer will usually be interested in why you left other positions, especially when you have indicated on your application blank that you left because of unsatisfactory working conditions or for other negative reasons. If you gripe to the interviewer about the people or about the company policies, however, he may get the impression that you are a chronic complainer. Try to be objective and to say something like this: "I found it difficult to adjust to some of the procedures and to the unusual hours at Blank's. Many of the people were extremely pleasant and helpful. There were some with whom I didn't seem to have much rapport, but I am sure some of the fault was mine." The interviewer will appreciate your frankness as well as your discretion.

Try to be at ease; smile occasionally. The interviewer needs someone to fill a position that is open. He is just as eager as you are to make a decision in your favor. Most interviewers are pleasant, friendly, and understanding. Try to display an air of confidence. Above all, don't fidget. Nervousness often shows up in such habits as brushing imaginary lint off clothing, straightening and restraightening a tie, fussing with hair, toying with an object such as a purse or a paper clip, and putting hands to the face. Avoid such habits; give your attention to the interviewer.

The interviewer will let you know when he has finished the interview. The usual sign he will use is to rise. As soon as he does so, you should also rise.

The exchange that takes place might be something like the following conversation.

> *Interviewer (rising):* I enjoyed meeting and talking with you.
> *You (rising):* Thank you, Mr. Wilkinson. I appreciate the time you have given me.
> *Interviewer:* We have your telephone number, and we will call you just as soon as we have reached a decision.
> *You:* Thank you. I shall look forward to hearing from you.
> *Interviewer:* Good-bye.
> *You:* Good-bye.

Leave as quickly as possible and thank the secretary and the receptionist as you leave.

FOLLOWING UP THE INTERVIEW

As soon as possible after the interview, make a written summary from notes and memory of the facts you learned in the interview and the opinions you have formed about the company and about the job for which you were interviewed. If you are being interviewed for jobs in several different companies, this written summary will prove an excellent way to refresh your memory about the interview when you are trying later to make your final job choice.

Whether or not you follow up the interview with a thank-you letter to the interviewer will depend on how much you want the job. If the position is an especially desirable one, you will want to thank the interviewer for his time and to reemphasize some of your special qualifications. For other suggestions relating to follow-up letters after interviews, refer to Section 55.

COMMUNICATION PROJECTS

Practical Application

Ⓐ Prepare written answers to each of the following questions and statements likely to come up in an employment interview.

1. Why do you wish to work for our company?
2. What kind of work do you enjoy doing most?
3. What kind of work do you enjoy doing least?
4. What salary do you expect?
5. What are your job goals for the next ten-year period?
6. Why have you selected this type of work?
7. Tell me about yourself.
8. Why did you leave your last position?
9. How do you spend your spare time?
10. What do you do in the summer?

Ⓑ List ten "Do's" and "Don'ts" for the job applicant *preparing* for an interview. Then list ten "Do's" and "Don'ts" to be observed *during* the interview.

C Assume that you are interested in an office position in the U.S. Civil Service Commission. Find out all you can about the tests that are scheduled for your region in the near future. Then prepare a three-minute talk on this subject to be given to your class.

D Your interviewer has made reference to a person for whom you worked one summer, saying: "I see that your department supervisor at Blank's was Myra Loudon. I know Myra through my work in AMS. She is a tough person to get along with. Did you find her so?" How would you answer (assume that you feel exactly the same way as your interviewer about Myra Loudon)?

E Answer the following questions:

1. Why do you think that you should thank the secretary and the receptionist when you leave the interviewer's office?
2. It is suggested that you take a small notebook along with you to the interview. What notes might you want to make?
3. Why is it important to choose carefully the company for which you would like to work?
4. In large companies, the applicant for a position is interviewed at least twice; first by a personnel specialist, and later on by the person for whom he will work. What do you think is the main purpose of the first interview? How might the two interviews differ?

F Assume that you have been interviewed for an office position in the Haynes Manufacturing Company. Your interviewer, Mr. Horace Willson, was very pleasant and seemed favorably impressed with your qualifications. However, he said that he plans to interview several other applicants before making a decision and that it will probably be two or three weeks before a decision is reached. Write a letter to Mr. Willson and thank him for the interview. (It's a job you especially want.) Emphasize special points or additional facts that may improve your chances for getting the job.

Editing Practice

The Rewrite Desk   Edit and rewrite the following paragraph.

Will you please except our sincere apology for failing to return promptly the merchandise that we were unable to use? The shipment arrived during our rush season, and our stock clerks, therefore, were concerned with goods that could be placed on the shelves rather then with those that should be returned. We assure you that a delay such as this, will not occur again.

Case Problem

Courtesy to the New Employee   Dave Dale is a new auditor assigned to the desk next to Henry Marks. When Dave first reported for work, the auditing supervisor, Mr. Ralph Wargo, had intended to introduce Dave to all the members of his staff. However, Mr. Wargo was unexpectedly called to a meeting before he could introduce Dave to Henry or to any of the other employees in the office.

1. What should Henry do?
2. What should Dave do if Henry does nothing?

**Advancing
on the Job**

57

Communication Duties on the Job

When you apply for your first position, you will be hired because the interviewer is confident that you will be able to do the required work. He has heard from your references; he has reviewed your application form; and he has talked with you to gain information that he could not obtain from other sources. He is convinced that you are well prepared.

Indeed, you *are* well prepared! As a result of your experiences in your business communications class, you should be well equipped to handle all communication problems that will confront you in your work. You will read all types of communications that cross your desk, listen to customers in face-to-face conversation and over the telephone, speak to your boss or to customers to give them information they have requested, and write all types of effective communications.

Remember, though, that everyone else in your office was hired because an interviewer considered him to possess the necessary business skills. Therefore, when a promotion is imminent, the person selected for that promotion must be more than merely competent; otherwise, a selection could be made by drawing a name out of a hat.

This section will present and discuss those "extras" that mark one person as better qualified for advancement than others in his group.

YOUR FIRST PROMOTION

Most beginners start their careers as stenographers and are promoted to secretarial positions when they have proved their ability to perform in a higher-level position. Sometimes college-trained applicants are hired initially as stenographers; but they must know, and must be able to perform, secretarial duties that involve communication.

What are the differences between the duties of the secretary and those of the stenographer? A stenographer's principal responsibilities are to take and to transcribe dictation, and to type from rough drafts or from dictating machines. Shorthand and typewriting skills, though, are not the only skills needed by the stenographer; these skills must be supported by a strong background in English. The stenographer must have a sound knowledge of spelling and the rules of grammar and punctuation, in addition to familiarity with the correct form for business letters, business reports, and other business documents. The stenographer must prove her ability in all these aspects of communication before she will be considered for a secretarial position.

The secretary, too, must be proficient in all these areas; but she must be able to accept greater responsibility for the communication activities of the office. If you are initially employed as a secretary, this increased responsibility begins on the first day of work; if you are first employed as a stenographer, you must give evidence that you are secretarial material by taking the initiative to handle additional responsibilities on your own whenever the opportunity presents itself.

THE SECRETARY'S COMMUNICATION RESPONSIBILITIES

As a secretary, you probably work with a busy executive who has many communication responsibilities. If you can relieve him of some of these duties and free him for more important tasks, you will make yourself valuable to the firm and particularly to your boss! The areas that you should be able to handle include dictation and transcription, the processing of incoming mail, the preparation of outgoing mail, the writing of letters, the signing of letters, and the preparation of messages.

Dictation and Transcription

Most secretaries enter the business world as stenographers. Although they may advance into the ranks of management, where their stenographic skills are used only occasionally, they usually must possess these skills in order to obtain their first job.

Techniques of taking and transcribing dictation are not within the province of a book on communications. The assumption must be made that the prospective secretary has acquired these skills and has perfected them. In fact, she is the authority on English for the employer and is expected to be able to edit the executive's dictation. Many executives frankly admit that they do not know the finer points of grammar, punctuation, capitalization, and spelling; they also admit that they rely on their secretaries to polish and correct their dictation. Most executives also expect secretaries to verify the facts, figures, and names used in the letters they dictate.

Editing How much editing should the secretary do on the letters the boss dictates? The amount of editing depends almost entirely on the boss. Some administrators dictate very methodically, indicating punctuation, unusual spellings, and paragraphs. Usually these executives are so sure of themselves that they want very little editing done. Others dictate only the barest outline of a letter and say to the secretary, "Fix it up." Most bosses, however, are somewhere between these two situations; and if the dictator makes errors in grammar and punctuation, the secretary usually can feel free to make the necessary changes. Obviously, the secretary must be positive that she is right before she transcribes the letter. If she is not sure about something, the secretary may say to the executive, "You mentioned April 11 as the first day of the meeting. Did you mean April 12?" or "In my notes I have 'I don't want to set any precedents in this decision.' I believe you actually said, 'I don't want to set *a precedent.*'"

Finished Letters After the letters have been transcribed, the secretary should proofread them carefully while they are still in the typewriter. In this way, errors can be corrected without running the risk of misaligning the correction. A letter that is not correct or that contains unclear sentences should not be placed on the employer's desk for signature. Never try to pass over an error or a garbled sentence.

Transcribed letters should be accompanied by the addressed envelope and the enclosures. The envelope should be inserted over the letterhead so that the flap faces the letterhead; by so doing, you won't obscure the message. If the executive is not at his desk when the letters are brought in for his signature, they should be placed face down or inside a folder. Never leave letters lying about faceup—there are too many inquisitive eyes!

Incoming Mail

The arrival of the mail is one of the most important moments of any executive's day. When he arrives at his office in the morning, his first attention usually is given to the incoming mail. The secretary should arrive sufficiently ahead of her boss so that, if possible, the processed mail will be on the executive's desk when he enters the office.

Sorting the Mail   In a small office, all incoming mail may be picked up and distributed by the secretary, the receptionist, an office assistant, the boss himself, or whoever arrives at the office first. In a large office where a great deal of mail is received, the mail is picked up and distributed by a special staff in a central mail room. In either case, letters addressed to individuals or to departments are usually delivered unopened. Letters addressed to the company without specific reference to individuals or to departments are opened, read, and then distributed to the appropriate persons.

Usually, the secretary has the responsibility for receiving and opening her employer's mail. The mail is handled in the following manner:

- Letters marked "Personal" are placed, unopened, in the executive's IN basket or on his desk.
- All other letters are opened, read carefully by the secretary, and placed on top of the executive's desk or in his IN basket. If passersby can see into the office, place the letters inside a folder so that they cannot be seen.
- The mail should be arranged in the order of its importance. A commonly accepted arrangement is as follows (in order from top to bottom):

> Telegrams
> Letters marked "Personal"
> Other first-class mail
> Circulars and advertisements
> Magazines and newspapers

- If there is a great deal of mail, it may be separated into three individual folders marked "Telegrams," "First-Class Mail," and "Other Mail." Some secretaries separate the mail according to the urgency with which it must be handled (some telegrams are not important, while a particular newspaper item or circular may be). In this case, folders are set up with such labels as "First Priority," "Second Priority," "For Reading Only—No Action," and so on. Of course, the secretary must know enough about her employer's business to know which pieces of mail are in most urgent need of attention.

Opening the Mail   Letters should be opened with a letter opener. Mail should not be ripped open or cut open with scissors, because the contents might be damaged. Each envelope should be checked carefully for enclosures.

In companies where checks or other important papers are frequently received, the envelope is slit open on three sides (so that it opens like a sheet of paper) to make sure that enclosures are not overlooked. Also, because addresses are frequently given only on the envelope, the secretary should make sure that she has a record of the address before destroying the envelope.

Outgoing Mail

The secretary's responsibility for outgoing letters does not end when she places the letters on the executive's desk for his signature. First, she should make certain that the executive is aware that letters are awaiting his signature and that he signs letters in sufficient time to get them out in that day's mail. The secretary then must check to see that every letter is signed and that any enclosure mentioned in a letter is actually with that letter. She should also double-check to see that each letter goes into its proper envelope. Nothing is more embarrassing than to have one person receive a letter that should have gone to someone else.

After she prepares the letters for mailing, the secretary should make sure that the mail goes out on that day. If the outgoing mail collection has been missed, the secretary should either deliver the mail to the mail room or drop it into a mailbox on her way home.

Writing Letters

Many letters that an executive would ordinarily have to dictate do not require careful thought, technical knowledge, or decision-making. These are the letters that a secretary could write for her employer, and these are the letters that are discussed in this section. The secretary who has been trained to write routine letters can lighten her employer's work load by politely suggesting that the job of answering such letters be turned over to her.

The types of letters most often written by the secretary include letters making reservations, letters requesting something, letters of referral, thank-you and acknowledgment letters, letters about appointments, and transmittal letters. Most of these letters were discussed in Chapter 7. Some are so important to the secretary, however, that they will receive additional emphasis here.

Reservation Letters   For letters making hotel and travel reservations, either the employer's signature or the secretary's signature may be used. Refer to Chapter 7 for additional information on writing reservation letters. The letter that follows has been written for the employer's signature.

Gentlemen:

   Please reserve a single room (outside room with shower) for me for September 15 and 16, at a rate not to exceed $19.
   I shall arrive about 3 p.m. on September 15 and expect to check out before 2 p.m. on September 17. Please send me a confirmation of this reservation.

Very truly yours,

Request Letters Request letters, too, may be written either for the employer's or for the secretary's signature. Here is an example of a request letter written for the secretary's signature.

Gentlemen:

Yesterday Mr. Kenneth Jordan, treasurer of our firm, attended the annual Controller's Institute sponsored by your organization. He brought back with him a pamphlet entitled "How to Improve Your Records," which we feel would be especially interesting to all our accounting supervisors.

We should, therefore, appreciate receiving 25 copies of this pamphlet if they are available. We would be very happy to pay for the postage necessary to send them to us, as well as to pay any charge you may make to cover the cost of printing.

If you have exhausted your supply of these pamphlets, may we have permission to reproduce a sufficient number of copies for our use? Mr. Jordan would be most grateful to receive these pamphlets or to have your permission to reproduce material from them.

Very sincerely yours,

Referral Letters Often the executive may not be able to give personal attention to letters sent to him but really meant for someone else. In such cases, the secretary usually writes an acknowledgment letter for her own signature and attends to any necessary follow-through with the other person. The following letter would be sent to the requester; at the same time, a copy of the original letter and a carbon copy of the reply would be sent to the person who can fulfill the request.

Dear Miss Anderson:

Thank you for asking us to send you 50 copies of our booklet, "Secretarial Tips," for distribution to students in your class in secretarial procedures. We are pleased that you think so highly of our pamphlet.

Unfortunately, our office supply of this pamphlet is exhausted. However, I am referring your request to our Chicago office, from which the pamphlet was originally distributed. You should receive the 50 copies within ten days.

Very sincerely yours,

Letters While the Boss Is Away Even though the secretary may not be requested to write letters while the boss is in the office, she may be expected to acknowledge important letters received while the boss is away and to explain any delays caused by his absence. Letters written for these reasons are usually brief, courteous, and noncommittal. A noncommittal letter does not reveal private company business; for instance, where the boss is or for what reason he has gone.

Sometimes the correspondence cannot await the return of the boss. Such letters are often referred to another individual in the company. Only urgent or highly important letters are routed in this way.

Dear Mr. Carrington:

Thank you for your letter of May 10 to Mr. Mattell.

Mr. Mattell will be out of the office for about three weeks, so I am referring your letter to our credit manager, Mr. Martin A. Glendening. You will be hearing from Mr. Glendening just as soon as he has an opportunity to review your application.

Very sincerely yours,

George Esterbrook
Assistant to Mr. Mattell

Following is the memo to Mr. Glendening that the assistant writes to transmit the letter to him.

TO: Mr. Martin A. Glendening   DATE: May 13, 19—

FROM: George Esterbrook
           Assistant to Mr. Mattell

SUBJECT: The attached letter from George A. Carrington

As you know, Mr. Mattell is in Philadelphia this week attending the convention of the American Psychological Association. I am attaching a letter that came today from Mr. George A. Carrington and that requires an immediate response. I am also sending you a carbon copy of my letter to Mr. Carrington.

Would you please take care of this request, Mr. Glendening? I would be grateful if you will send me a blind carbon of your letter to Mr. Carrington.

GE

Care must be taken not to express opinions that may disagree with those of the employer or that may place him in an embarrassing position. For example, if a personnel director received a job application while he was out of town, his secretary would *not* write the following reply:

Thank you for your application for a management trainee position. Your qualifications seem to be excellent, and I know Mr. Gardner will be much impressed by them.

The boss may feel otherwise about the applicant's qualifications, or the company may not be able to make use of the applicant's services at the

To: Mr. *Floyd Simpson*

HERE'S A MESSAGE FOR YOU

Mr. *Edward Nelson*

OF *Whiting's Office Supply House*

PHONE NO. *224-3987* EXT. *———*

- [ ] IS WAITING TO SEE YOU
- [ ] CAME TO SEE YOU
- [ ] WANTS TO SEE YOU
- [✓] TELEPHONED
- [ ] RETURNED YOUR CALL
- [✓] PLEASE PHONE
- [ ] WILL CALL AGAIN

Shipment #87A987 not received. Merchandise needed immediately. Please notify when they can expect to receive it.

TAKEN BY *Claine Lamkin* DATE *6/5/--* TIME *10:30 A.M.*

present time. Therefore, a noncommittal letter like the following would be more appropriate.

Dear Miss Carr:

Thank you for your application for a management trainee position. The personnel director, Mr. Wesley Gardner, is out of the office this week. When he returns, you may be sure that he will write you.

Sincerely yours,

This letter does not commit Mr. Gardner beyond getting in touch with the applicant. Note, too, that the letter does not provide any confidential information regarding Mr. Gardner's whereabouts.

Signing Letters

When the executive is away or is in a hurry to leave the office, he may ask the secretary to sign his, the executive's, name to dictated letters; or he may ask his secretary to sign all routine correspondence, even when the boss is at his desk. In such a case, the secretary customarily places her initials immediately below the signature of the executive, like this:

Cordially yours,

Paul K. Laughton
J. S.

Paul K. Laughton

Some employers, however, prefer that their signatures be faked—especially when the letter is written to people whom they do not know personally.

Messages

Every secretary quite frequently must take messages for her employer while he is out of the office or in conference. Often these messages are given to the secretary either over the telephone or in person. The efficient secretary writes these messages as they are given to her, but she should read them back to make certain that she has included all the information and that all the information is correct.

These messages should be presented to the boss in writing, because he may not be able to act upon them immediately and the written document will serve as a reminder for future reference. In addition, the written message protects the secretary so that she cannot be reprimanded later by her boss, who might say, "Why didn't you tell me about Mr. Simpson's call? He's very upset with our company for not following up on that lost shipment." For this reason, the efficient secretary makes a carbon copy of the message and also later reminds her boss if some action needs to be taken. "Have you telephoned Mr. Simpson about that lost shipment he reported this morning?" serves as a polite reminder.

The illustration on page 490 shows one type of message form used in many offices.

Notice that the fewest possible number of words is used in the message illustrated; yet the message is complete and clear.

COMMUNICATION PROJECTS

Practical Application

A Your employer, Donald Thuesen, is on vacation and will not return to the office for another ten days. As his secretary, you acknowledge all letters that are received in his absence. Write a letter that with little or no change would fit most of the correspondence requiring acknowledgment.

B A letter from Mr. Donald Bennett to your employer requests a decision within two weeks regarding Mr. Bennett's proposed schedule for redecorating your company's offices. Your employer, Mr. John Kenyon, is out of the office for a month and cannot be reached. Since you cannot give an official answer, you refer this letter to Thomas Rooney, the vice-president. Write the appropriate letter to Mr. Bennett, and inform him about what you are doing.

C Assume that you are secretary to Pierre La Roche, head of the office services department, which directs all mailing facilities in the company. For more than a year Mr. La Roche has been studying the advisability of using a centralized postage meter instead of distributing stamps to each department in the company. He has asked you to write for product information to these two companies: National Postage Meters, Inc., 3 Lantern Lane, Chicago, Illinois 60615; American Postal Machines Co., Akron, Ohio 44305. Write the two letters.

D In each of the following routine situations, the secretary, instead of the boss, would usually compose the letter. Write these four letters.

1. Your boss, Kermit Lindley, wants a three-year subscription to *Today's Executive* magazine. Write a letter placing the subscription order. Mr. Lindley's check for $12.50 will be sent with the letter.
2. Having heard of a study on office automation recently conducted by the American Executives Association, your boss asks you to write for a copy of their report, "Here's What Automation Is Doing to the Office."
3. John Searles, office manager of your company's midwestern sales office in Chicago, has just become the proud father of twin boys. Your boss asks you to draft a letter of congratulations to Mr. and Mrs. Searles. Assume that your boss is a fairly close friend of Mr. Searles and his wife, Clara.
4. While your boss, Mr. West, is in the hospital recuperating from a recent operation, a letter is received requesting that he appear on a panel with a group of businessmen at the next meeting of the Future Businessmen of America club of Orion High School. The meeting is to take place on April 10. Since Mr. West will still be recuperating at that time, you are to write a letter to the president of the FBA club, Bill Easton, explaining why Mr. West will not be able to participate.

Editing Practice

The Supervising Editor   The following sentences lack writing polish. Edit and rewrite them.

1. Our sales catalog contains many items priced far below those of any other company. This offers you a very considerable saving.
2. Nothing must go wrong. Our business is to see it doesn't.
3. We have instructed our representative in your city that he should make a satisfactory adjustment and to live up to our policy of giving customers satisfaction.
4. The reason Stuart did not finish the report on time was because he was to change some statistics at the last minute.
5. Please order at once a thesaurus, book of synonyms, and abridged dictionary.
6. Each business writer has certain style peculiarities of their own.
7. Many young business communicators hope to become supervisors because of the prestige they have.
8. Under the last line of the letterhead is to be printed our telephone number.
9. Mr. Cole's confident manner, his knowledge of men, and his friendliness—all combine to make him an unusually effective executive.
10. We do a wholesale business only; therefore, we cannot supply the vacuum cleaner you ordered, but we have three representatives in your town, any one of whom will be glad to demonstrate our vacuum cleaner, so we urge you to get in touch with one of the stores listed below.

Case Problem

Signing for the Boss   Often the boss must leave the office before he can sign outgoing letters and he instructs his secretary to finish up the letters and get them in the mail. Employer A asks his assistant to sign his name and to place her initials below the signature. Employer B tells his secretary to sign his name, but not to bother with her initials—that most people won't know the difference. Employer C instructs his secretary not to sign his name but to place below the typewritten signature the following notation: "Dictated but not read." What are the pros and cons of each of these methods?

58

Communication and Advancement

Just as "One swallow does not make a summer," a single promotion does not indicate complete success. The successful secretary is the person who reaches higher and higher positions that eventually lead to a top secretarial job. Many secretaries have advanced to the position of executive secretary or administrative assistant—and some have become officers of the company.

The duties discussed in this section will provide you with some of the training that you will need in order to advance to higher positions. In smaller companies, where there are probably no administrative assistant or executive secretary levels, secretaries are expected to assume some or all of the communication responsibilities discussed in this section. Although your job title may not change, your increased competency will be recognized in the form of higher and higher salaries.

THE ADMINISTRATIVE ASSISTANT AND THE EXECUTIVE SECRETARY

In some businesses, the highest level of secretarial position is called an *executive secretary* because the person with this title is actually an executive who has many decisions to make and who often supervises the work of typists, clerks, stenographers, and/or secretaries. In other businesses, a person with similar responsibilities may be called an *administrative assistant*. The executive secretary and the administrative assistant have similar communication responsibilities; both are, in reality, assistants to an executive. Therefore, the term *administrative assistant* will be used to refer to this level, whatever actual job title is used.

THE ADMINISTRATIVE ASSISTANT COMMUNICATES

The administrative assistant will, of course, be expected to perform the communication activities described in Section 57. In addition, there are several advanced-level responsibilities she must also assume.

Incoming Mail

Although the administrative assistant *may* perform the mailing duties discussed in Section 57, she most surely *will* take on additional responsibilities for handling the mail, such as:

Reading the Mail Usually the administrative assistant is expected to read the mail before she places it on the employer's desk. There are two important reasons for reading the mail: (1) to keep informed on matters that have a bearing on the executive's work and (2) to make the executive's job of answering the mail an easier one.

Suppose the executive receives a letter from Mr. Brown, a business acquaintance who lives in another city. Mr. Brown says he will be visiting the executive's city on a certain date and hopes to see him. The assistant reads the letter, checks the executive's calendar, and makes the following notation on Mr. Brown's letter: "You will be in Birmingham during that week."

Or suppose the executive receives a letter from Mr. Green, a supplier, in which Mr. Green makes reference to a specification sheet he received from the executive. The assistant attaches to Mr. Green's letter the specification sheet referred to so that the executive will have on hand the information he needs to reply to Mr. Green.

These are only two examples of ways in which the adminstrative assistant can take on additional responsibilities for correspondence. The assistant may also be called on to perform the following tasks:

- Underline important dates, amounts, or statements on incoming letters.
- Place notations in the margin of incoming letters, such as "I will take care of this" or "He refers to a telephone call from Mr. Chalmers" or "He means June 11 (instead of June 10)."
- Place a routing slip on letters that probably should be handled by another department. Of course, if the letter is addressed to the executive, he should be given the opportunity to read it even though someone else will reply. The routing slip, however, makes it easy for him to handle the letter if he agrees with the recommendation to route it elsewhere.
- Read and flag for the executive's attention magazine or newspaper articles in which he may have special interest. This may be done by clipping to the publication a memo slip containing a notation such as "See pages 43, 44, and 76."

Digesting the Mail If the executive is extremely busy and receives a large amount of correspondence, he may expect his assistant to prepare digests (summaries) of important messages. If the executive is planning to be out of town on an extended business trip, he may ask his assistant to send these summaries to him weekly or more often.

Digest of Important Mail Received October 3

Mr. J. W. Williams	Accepts your proposal on the refurnishing of the Monkton office. On his way there now, and will write when he returns.
Mrs. Hattie Hicks (Arlington Mills)	Can't speak at the Interior Decorators Association meeting as previously agreed. Going into hospital for major surgery.
Mr. Ronald Axelrod	Can you come to Providence on November 8? His London representative will be there. They want to discuss Liverpool situation with you. (Your calendar is clear.)
G. O. Trout (memo)	Wants you to introduce the honor guests at the president's reception on October 19.
Mr. George Gaynor (Phillips Originals)	Appreciates your help on the Calvert Memorial Room. Board bought everything you recommended. Can you have dinner at his club on November 2? (Your calendar is clear.)

Writing Letters

Many executives depend on their administrative assistants to write letters and memorandums for them and to follow up on letters that require future action. The initiative for writing letters for the executive may come from the assistant or from the employer, who might write on an incoming letter a notation such as "Tell him I'll see him." When the assistant takes the initiative, she may do one of the following:

- Write a rough-draft reply and attach it to the incoming letter when it is placed on the employer's desk.
- Make notations on the incoming letters, such as "I will answer" or "I'll tell him you will be away that week" or "Will send today."

There is no hard-and-fast rule about the duties of the administrative assistant in handling the employer's correspondence. Whether the assistant writes letters for her employer depends entirely on the executive's wishes and the assistant's ability. In any event, the assistant should never be presumptuous. Until the employer states that he does not wish to see routine letters, the assistant should turn over *all* incoming letters to him; only after the employer gives permission to originate correspondence should the assistant take this responsibility.

Communication Follow-Up   The efficient administrative assistant assumes responsibility for following up on the employer's communication activities. For example, if certain letters must be answered by a specific date, the assistant should remind her employer when an answer is due. The assistant can either maintain a tickler file or record reminder notes on a desk calendar pad.

Among the types of correspondence that may require follow-up are incoming letters with enclosures omitted, outgoing letters that have requested appointments and that have not been answered, materials requested that have not arrived, or some other action referred to in incoming or outgoing correspondence that has not materialized after a reasonable lapse of time. Here are some examples of such follow-up letters.

Dear Mr. Wallin:

    Mr. Gregory left Monday on an extended trip to our branch offices. He asked that if we did not receive a letter from you by today regarding the appointment he requested, I inquire of you whether March 11 at 1 p.m. is satisfactory. I am to let him know before he leaves Oakland on March 9, so that he can plan the remainder of his trip accordingly.

    I expect to telephone Mr. Gregory at 4 p.m., March 8. Therefore, would you wire or telephone me (274-9175) collect before that date and tell me whether you can see Mr. Gregory when he is in Minneapolis?

                        Cordially yours,

Dear Mr. Kingman:

   We received your letter of March 12 with 24 vouchers enclosed. However, the voucher made payable to Roger Lamkin for $75, dated February 16, was not included even though this voucher was on the list of vouchers being sent.

   Therefore, we would appreciate your sending this voucher to us by airmail special delivery so that we can complete our posting before March 25.

                                        Very truly yours,

   Business correspondence must be answered even while the employer is away from the office. Incoming mail must be handled; urgent mail must be acknowledged or answered; and routine mail should be answered. The assistant should, therefore, set up a procedure for taking care of correspondence while the executive is away. Here are some practical suggestions for processing the mail.

- If the boss will be away for more than two or three days, acknowledge all letters to which a correspondent might reasonably expect a prompt answer. An example of such an acknowledgment letter is given on page 490.
- Forward mail to a knowledgeable person in the company if the incoming letter indicates that some action must be taken immediately.
- If the employer is on an extended trip, send him copies of letters requiring action before he is expected to return to the office. Be certain to send him any necessary supporting materials.
- Answer all letters that your boss would expect you to handle if he were in the office.
- Place in a folder all mail received—letters awaiting the executive's attention, photocopies of letters forwarded to others for reply, carbon copies of letters that you or others have answered, advertising mail, newspapers, and so on.

Signing Letters   In Section 57 you learned how a secretary signs a letter for her employer. An administrative assistant, however, sometimes writes a letter for his or her own signature, as shown in the following examples.

Very truly yours,   Cordially yours,

(Miss) Catherine Wilson   Warren Jackson
Administrative Assistant to   Assistant to the Controller
Mr. Latimer

MEETINGS AND CONFERENCES

Many informal meetings require little preparation, but the success of most meetings depends on someone's taking the responsibility for planning and arranging them. This responsibility is usually given to the administrative assistant, who attends to these details: (1) reserves and sets up the meeting room and restores it to order after the meeting; (2) prepares an agenda—a list of topics to be discussed at the meeting; (3) makes definite assignments for each participant; and (4) takes notes on the discussion and prepares minutes of the meeting.

The Meeting Room

When the boss is the chairman of the meeting, his assistant usually is given the assignment of setting up the meeting room and returning it to order after the meeting. The details discussed here, therefore, must be taken care of by the assistant.

Seating Arrangements   Many meetings start poorly because seating arrangements are inadequate. The resultant delay, confusion, and milling around could take the sparkle out of even the most carefully planned conference. There should always be a sufficient number of chairs for participants and a few extra chairs for unexpected guests.

If possible, conference members should be seated around an oval table. Such an arrangement takes the stiffness out of a meeting and gives everybody an opportunity to see, hear, and concentrate on contributions made by a speaker or by fellow participants.

Other Details   On the table in front of each chair, place a copy of the agenda, several pencils, and a writing pad. Ashtrays, too, should be provided. When a chalkboard is to be used, make certain that it is clean and that a clean eraser and plenty of chalk are on hand. If audiovisual aids are to be used, make certain that the proper facilities are available. If an operator is needed to run the equipment, make sure that he is reminded of his obligation *well before the time of the meeting.* A smoothly run meeting depends largely on how well the advance preparations are made—nothing should be left to chance.

After-the-Meeting Details   After the meeting is over, the assistant should make certain that all equipment and unused supplies are returned and that the meeting room is restored to its original order. Any problems connected with the operation of borrowed equipment should be reported. Check all seating locations to be sure that no personal possessions have been left behind. Inspect chairs, tables, windows, drapes, and so on, to be sure that everything is left exactly as it was found.

The Agenda

The form of the agenda varies greatly. The agenda illustrated at the top of the next page is typical for an informal committee meeting. When parliamentary procedures are followed in a meeting, the agenda will be more formal and will include such information as the name of the presiding officer, the specific time at which each topic is to be presented, the resolutions to be considered, and the like.

Meeting of the Forms Control Committee
August 14, 19—
10:30 a.m. — Board Room

Mr. Crowley	Customer Service Department's proposal to redesign all its forms
Miss Caesar	Purchase of Vari-typer for use in preparing personnel forms
Mr. Oldham	New Era Blank Book Company's offer to provide free consultant on forms design
Mrs. Minor	How new data processing equipment is affecting sales of office forms
Mr. Orr	No report
Mr. Scott	No report
Mr. Levy	No report

Usually the agenda is sent to all participants before the meeting takes place. This advance notice gives the participants an opportunity to prepare their comments, suggestions, or questions. The assistant should also place in the meeting room a copy for each participant—nearly always someone mis-places his agenda or forgets to bring it to the meeting.

The Notes and Minutes

The administrative assistant is often the recorder for a meeting conducted by the boss. A stenographic notebook is best for taking notes about the meeting because the center rule on each page divides the name of the speaker from his remarks.

The assistant should transcribe the notes of the discussion as soon as possible, preferably the same day. Section 48 gives specific suggestions for preparing minutes.

RESEARCH ACTIVITIES

As mentioned earlier, the typical executive writes many letters, memorandums, and formal reports. Some of these communications involve research. The research or work may consist merely of looking up information in the department's own files, of telephoning and writing memos to gather facts and figures from other departments, and of occasionally consulting a periodical or a reference book.

On the other hand, some executives are engaged in activities that require more formal research. The marketing department of a large oil corporation will have a staff of research specialists—people who carry on dozens of studies simultaneously to determine where and how its products are being used, the need for new products, and the need for improvements in existing products. A personnel department may undertake research on wage and salary trends, employee benefits offered in various industries, and labor contracts. A construction engineer researches causes of collapse of buildings and bridges. Some executives are editors, and one type of research they must do is that of checking the accuracy of statements made by authors of the articles in their company publications. Many executives write articles for magazines and other periodicals; some even write books.

In all these cases, the administrative assistant's responsibility for research is likely to be heavy. She may be required to make frequent use of the company library and of nearby public and college libraries; in some instances, she may even maintain a small library for the executive's or department's exclusive use.

Many executives are often called upon to deliver speeches. For example, a sales manager may be extremely active in various national organizations dealing with marketing, selling, and advertising. Such an executive is always on the lookout for speech materials—he must keep completely up to date on events in his field of specialization. The responsibilities of an assistant to such an executive often encompass reading many current periodicals and keeping a speech file for the employer.

Basic References

There are a number of basic reference sources with which every administrative assistant should be familiar. Among these are the following:

A Good Dictionary   The dictionary is probably the most important reference source. For most writing purposes, a dictionary such as *Webster's Seventh New Collegiate Dictionary* (G. & C. Merriam Company) is sufficient. Executives who do a great deal of writing or editing should have available an unabridged dictionary.

A Secretarial Handbook   A secretarial handbook contains such information as the following: rules for the use of English grammar, capitalization, spelling, punctuation; guides for transcribing, mailing, and filing business correspondence; aids to proofreading; styles and formats for typing; and information relating to postal, express, and telegraphic services.

Secretarial handbooks provide references for most general types of secretarial duties. Several are available. Perhaps the most popular is *Standard Handbook for Secretaries*, by Lois Hutchinson (McGraw-Hill Book Company).

A Reliable Fact Book   Most assistants find frequent use for a fact book such as *The World Almanac* (Newspaper Enterprise Association Inc.) This fact book contains such varied information as names and addresses of colleges and universities, population figures, baseball records, names of congressmen and senators, and Academy Award winners.

An Authoritative Grammar Reference   Assistants whose bosses write a great deal should have handy a good grammar reference. One such reference is the *McGraw-Hill Handbook of English*, by Virginia Shaffer and Harry Shaw (McGraw-Hill Book Company).

Special References

Every administrative assistant will need special references that pertain to the business of the executive for whom she works. For example, if she works for a lawyer, she may need a good law dictionary, such as *Black's Law Dictionary*

(West Publishing Company), and a handbook for the legal secretary, such as *Handbook for the Legal Secretary*, by Besse M. Miller (Prentice-Hall, Inc.). Other examples of special references follow:

> Administrative Assistant to a Doctor. A medical dictionary, such as *Blakiston's New Gould Medical Dictionary*, by N. L. Hoerr and A. Osoi (McGraw-Hill Book Company); a medical secretary's handbook, such as *Handbook for the Medical Secretary*, by Miriam Bredow (McGraw-Hill Book Company).

> Administrative Assistant to a Publisher. Various style books, such as *A Manual of Style*, University of Chicago Press Staff (University of Chicago Press); *Writer's Guide and Index to English*, Porter G. Perrin (Scott, Foresman and Company); *The New York Times Style Book for Writers and Editors*, edited and revised by Lewis Jordan (McGraw-Hill Book Company); *Roget's International Thesaurus*, P. M. Roget (Thomas Y. Crowell Company).

> Administrative Assistant to a Chemist. *A Handbook of Chemistry*, compiled and edited by Norbert A. Lange (McGraw-Hill Book Company).

> Administrative Assistant to an Accountant. *Accountant's Handbook*, edited by R. Wixon (Ronald Press Company); *Office Management Handbook*, edited by H. L. Wylie (Ronald Press Company).

Use of the Library

To use library facilities efficiently, the assistant should become acquainted with the librarian and should seek her help. The librarian will be able to point out the available sources of information and special reference works as well as the library's auxiliary services, such as the interlibrary loan system. Often, too, when the assistant is not acquainted with the titles of books or articles or the names of authors, the librarian's help is a great timesaver.

Once the assistant has found all the references she is seeking, she should follow these practical suggestions for recording the information she needs.

- Be systematic and orderly in all note-taking. Most researchers use cards for this purpose.
- Always check to make sure to use the latest edition of the book.
- Be careful to record, for each reference, the author's name, the title of the book or periodical, the title of the article (if a periodical reference), the volume and number (if applicable), the publisher's name, the date and place of publication, and all relevant page numbers.
- Write on only one side of the card and limit each card to one subject. (See Section 47 for further suggestions for taking notes.)

Reading and Writing Reports

In the area of communications, the reading and writing of reports often occupies a major portion of the working day of today's business executive. A valuable administrative assistant should be prepared to read some of the reports normally read by her boss and be able to write a brief summary of the highlights of each report. This summarizing must be done skillfully so that no important aspects of the report are omitted and so that no facts are misrepresented. To avoid misinterpretation, the assistant might include in her summary the exact page references of important items. For example:

> Sims gives five reasons for requesting the new equipment in the accounting section. (See page 10.)

The administrative assistant may also be called upon to write reports. For example, your boss might ask you to request that all office supervisors submit information regarding absence and tardiness of the employees under their supervision. The boss might want you to tabulate the information and to summarize it so that he will know how many absences and tardinesses there have been in each department, the reasons for them, which members of the staff are the most frequent offenders, what steps are being taken to reduce absenteeism, and so on. Because of the training provided in Sections 46 and 47, you are fully prepared to write any type of report assigned to you.

Contributing Ideas

Business is hungry for good ideas that will reduce overhead, increase sales, promote new products, and make and keep friends. Many companies have suggestion boxes for employee ideas and at the end of the month, may award cash bonuses for the best ideas contributed.

To reach the level of top management, you must be someone with imagination, someone who can make constructive suggestions. In Section 46 you learned to put your ideas in writing and to present them effectively. Therefore, you will be interested in the illustration, shown on page 502, of an administrative assistant's proposal for saving time and materials.

HUMAN RELATIONS

The administrative assistant is the "voice, mind, and personality" of the employer; that is to say, many employees look upon the assistant as a representative of the employer's point of view. The administrative assistant sets the tone of the office; her attitudes, moods, and actions affect the morale of the entire office staff. If she is disagreeable to a certain individual, that individual can easily get the impression that the assistant is merely reflecting the boss's attitude toward him.

Because she does represent her employer to the office staff and to the general public, the administrative assistant must try to promote good human relations at all times. A good assistant knows and observes the following guides to good human relations.

Be Discreet

An assistant to an executive is in a position to learn about matters of the utmost secrecy. Her employer may discuss with her such confidential matters as salaries, his personal feelings about employees, plans for reorganizing the department (which may involve releasing certain employees), and his personal family matters. If an employer can't trust his assistant, he needs a new one! Even the slightest leak by the assistant assumes greater proportions than

HYATT and RANDALL PUBLISHERS
Interoffice Memorandum

TO   Mr. William Bray, Office Manager   FROM Howard Stephenson,
                                                  Administrative Assistant
                                                  to the President

SUBJECT Suggestion Regarding Carbon Copies   DATE June 8, 19--
        of Correspondence

My suggestion is that carbon copies of replies to incoming letters be placed on the backs of those letters instead of on a separate sheet of paper. Advantages of using this procedure are as follows:

1. The reply cannot be lost or become separated from the letter to which it belongs.

2. Paper will be saved because a second sheet of paper will not be needed for the carbon copy. The back of the incoming letter carries the carbon copy.

3. Filing cabinet space will be saved because only one sheet of paper needs to be filed.

If you think this suggestion is workable, I should be happy to discuss it with you at your convenience. My extension is 3886.

                                         H. S.

---

it may actually deserve. The best rule to follow is this: Reveal nothing about the employer's feelings, attitudes, and habits; if he wants these things known, he will reveal them himself.

It is especially difficult to be discreet when dealing with other company executives or with VIP's from outside the company. Because of their position, these men and women may feel that they are entitled to know everything that transpires in the office. Usually the only way for the assistant to satisfy these people is to say that she knows nothing about the matters in question. For example, suppose a young department head says, "I hear the company is setting up a new branch office in Portland and that Watkins is to be the manager. What do you know about it?" Even though you may know perfectly well that the rumor is correct, you have no authority to confirm it. You merely say something like this: "I wasn't aware that any announcement had been made; I haven't seen anything on it." If the department head persists, you may have to say, "Would you like to ask Mr. Blair (your boss)? I don't have the information."

Be Impartial

We are all human, and we all have our pet likes and dislikes regarding people. There are all kinds of people in an office—some are easy to like; some are not. As an administrative assistant, however, you can't afford to show partiality. Although one cannot be "all things to all people," this course is a wise one to follow in the office. An assistant can't afford to choose sides. She must try to weigh her actions and attitudes on the basis of facts rather than emotions. The employer has the authority to hire, promote, and fire; and this power can cause anxiety on the part of employees. Because the boss is an important figure to everyone who works for him and because the administrative assistant is his confidante, the assistant must be objective, noncommittal, fair, and impartial.

The assistant should avoid being too friendly with anyone in the department. If the assistant joins office cliques, she is suspect by employees outside the clique. Being too friendly with certain individuals puts the assistant on the spot insofar as gossip and tale-bearing are concerned. The assistant must rise above the petty pastime of gossip.

Be Loyal

One way of demonstrating loyalty is by keeping confidences. There are other ways, too. Because he represents authority, the boss is a target for criticism. It always was this way, and it always will be! When the assistant hears the boss criticized justly or unjustly, she either rises to the executive's defense or says nothing. The assistant should never agree openly with such criticism. Nothing shakes the faith of loyal employees more than an assistant who confirms unfavorable rumors about the boss.

Loyalty to the employer is mandatory. But just as important is loyalty to the employees. Employees often share many confidences with the assistant—matters pertaining to their health, their pet dislikes, their love affairs, their feeling toward the company, their family squabbles, and so on. When things are told in confidence, they should be kept from everyone else—even the employer. One of the surest ways to jeopardize morale in an office is to carry everything to the boss. If employees can't trust the administrative assistant, they will have nothing to do with her. Under such conditions, a spirit of teamwork is difficult to obtain.

Be Businesslike

Human relations in an office are affected by the amount of work that is accomplished. Unless employees can contribute something worthwhile to an organization, they are not likely to be satisfied, productive workers. Many people have the mistaken notion that if a country club atmosphere prevails in the office, everyone is happy and more productive. Such is not the case! Certainly everyone likes a little sociability, some fun, and some periods of relaxation. If this atmosphere predominates, however, the purpose of work is lost.

The assistant should be businesslike in her attitude toward the job and toward her fellow workers. This does not mean that she is a sourpuss. It means simply that she is aware that there is a job to be done and that the job demands hard work and efficient methods.

Here are a few "don'ts" for the administrative assistant seeking a businesslike attitude:

- Don't visit among employees for social purposes. Stay at your desk unless you have business to attend to elsewhere.
- Remember that the telephone is a business instrument—not a social one. If friends persist in calling you at the office, tell them that you are too busy to talk and that you will telephone them in the evening.
- Don't joke frequently about business matters or about office "characters." It is easy to take business matters—and some employees—lightly, to make everything a game. Joking about company matters destroys purpose and takes away the genuine satisfaction that employees receive from doing their jobs well.
- Don't let employees monopolize your time. Some employees like to visit and are constantly finding excuses to come to the assistant's desk (they may really want to see what the boss is doing). Show by your businesslike attitude that employee visits should be completed quickly.
- Dress for business. Avoid extremes in clothing and accessories.

But Be Pleasant

The foregoing suggestions might give the impression that the assistant should be a piece of furniture—cold, hard, and indifferent. Nothing could be further from the truth. The assistant should smile easily and should be friendly to everyone. She should never let her bad moods show, even though she, like everyone else, has them. She is cool, calm, and collected in all situations. Remember, the assistant often sets the tone for office conduct and performance, and being pleasant and friendly is just as important to good human relations as being businesslike is important to productivity.

COMMUNICATION PROJECTS

Practical Application

You are administrative assistant to Donald McNulty, office services manager of the Clarkston Office Equipment Company. Mr. McNulty is scheduled to make a speech to a local chamber of commerce on the subject "Effects of Automation in the Office," and he has asked you to compile some specific information on these topics:
1. How automation will affect the secretary-stenographer
2. How automation will affect the general clerical worker
3. How automation will affect the records manager and the file clerks

Mr. McNulty has told you that there are three sources from which reliable information may be obtained: for the secretary-stenographer, the National Secretaries Association, Kansas City; for the general clerical worker, the Life Insurance Association of America, New York; for the records manager and the file clerks, the National Records Management Institute, Cleveland. Supplying necessary details, draft a letter to each of the respective groups.

B As administrative assistant to Jeffrey Cantor, industrial relations manager for the Carson Textile Company, you are asked to handle routine communications for your employer. Recently the company purchased an excellent film, "The Development of a Happy, Contented Worker," for use within the company. Write a memorandum to all department heads, and suggest the use of this film as a means of achieving more productivity from the workers; mention a preview showing of the 30-minute film for all department heads. The showing will be held at 4 p.m. on Tuesday, May 4, in the employees' cafeteria. You are to coordinate the use of the film.

C Your employer, Lee Davis, is the public relations director of the Union Light and Power Company. Mr. Davis and the advertising staff have written a colorful brochure, "What's New in Home Appliances," the first in a series of publications that have been made available in limited quantities to the general public. During the last week, you have received the following requests, and Mr. Davis has asked you to send a personal letter (for his signature) and a copy of the brochure to each inquirer.

1. Dear Sirs: Please send me information on appliances. Yours truly,
2. Gentlemen: Do you have any free information you can give me on the new uses of electricity in the home? Sincerely yours,
3. Gentlemen: I have heard about your fine booklet on new electrical appliances in the home. Please send me 250 copies, which I intend to use in a mailing to all my electrical appliance customers. Connors Electrical Appliances Store (The request must be refused.)
4. Sirs: Would you permit me to duplicate certain sections of your fine brochure on new electrical appliances for the home? I am interested in making this information available to my customers and will be sure to give you credit for the authorship. Sincerely yours, (The request is granted.)

D Occasionally, your employer, Mr. Kenneth A. Jameson, must leave rather suddenly on an out-of-town trip for several days. When this happens, you as his assistant must compose many letters canceling all appointments for those days. Such letters must be definite, referring to the time and place of the original appointment. Often, they must express regret for the inconvenience caused and suggest another time for the appointment. Write a form letter that generally may be used for canceling Mr. Jameson's appointments.

Editing Practice

The Rewrite Desk Edit and rewrite the following paragraph.

In your letter of August 17th, you ask for a reference for Chas. Wood. We have never employed a Chas. Wood; but a Thomas Wood worked here as receiving clerk from the third of April, 1958 to the first of January 1960. If this is the Mr. Wood about who you inquire we can save the writing of 2 or 3 letters by telling you that Thomas Wood's work was most satisfactory and that we found him industrious and cooperative.

Case Problem

Supervising Others You supervise the work of ten stenographers at the Holman Company. Judy Ames, one of the stenographers, has made an error on an important letter that must be mailed today. It is now ten of five, and five o'clock is quitting time. When you ask Judy to please make the correction before she leaves so that you can get the letter in the last mail, she says, "But if I'm late, I'll miss my ride." What would you do in this situation?

Appendix

A Spelling 400

A

absence
accessible
accidentally
accommodate
accrual
accumulate
accurate
acquire
acquisitive
across
adaptability
adequate
adhere
adjacent
adjoining
adjourn
adjunct
admissible
advisory
affiliate
aggressive
agreeable
allege
allocated
altogether
amateur
amortize
analogous
analysis
anonymous
anxious
apostrophe
apparatus
apparel
appraisal
appreciable
approximate
aptitude
around
arrears
ascend
ascertain
assistance
assumption

attorneys
authoritative
authorize
auxiliary

B

bankruptcy
becoming
beginning
believing
benefited
bookkeeper
boundary
brilliant
brochure
bulletin

C

calendar
campaign
canceling
cancellation
capacity
carburetor
career
careful
carried
carrying
centralized
chargeable
charging
choose
chose
chronological
cipher
coincidence
collapsible
collectible
column
commensurate
committee
comparable
comparative
comparison

compel
compelling
competent
competitive
compilation
comptroller
concise
concurred
conferred
conscientious
consensus
conspicuous
contingency
continuous
controlled
convenient
coolly
corroborate
courtesy
credentials
criticism
criticize
crystallize
cycle
cylinder

D

dealt
deceased
defensible
deficit
delinquent
demurrage
depreciation
dilemma
director
disappear
disappoint
disapprove
discipline
discretion
diseased
disillusion
dissatisfied

dissension
dissolution
distributor
dividend
dripping
dropping
durable
dutiable

E

economical
efficiency
electrical
elementary
eligible
eliminate
embarrass
eminent
emphasize
endeavor
enforceable
enumerate
envelop (v.)
envelope (n.)
environment
equaled
equalize
equally
equipping
equivalent
erroneous
especially
essence
exaggerate
excellent
excessive
excusable
exercise
exorbitant
expeditiously
expendable
explanation
extension

extraordinary
extravagance

F

facilitate
facilities
facsimile
familiarize
fascinate
feasible
February
finally
financier
flourishing
forcibly
foreign
forfeit
forty
fragile
fraudulent
freight
friend
fulfill

G

gasoline
gauge
generalize
genuine
gorgeous
governor
grammar
grievance
grieve
grievous
guarantee

H

handicapped
harass
heretofore
hesitant
hindrance
hyphen

I

illegible
imaginary
imminent

imperative
implement
impossible
impromptu
inadvertent
incapable
incessantly
incidentally
inconceivable
incredible
incredulous
indispensable
inexhaustible
inferred
insurable
intelligence
intelligible
intercede
interrupt
intricate
invalidate
investigator
invoicing
irrelevant
irreparable
irresistible
itemize
itinerary

J

janitor
jeopardize

K

knowledge

L

laboratory
lavatory
legible
leisure
liaison
likable
likelihood
linoleum
liquefy
loose
lose

lucrative
luxurious

M

machinery
mahogany
manageable
mandatory
marital
mathematics
measurable
measurement
mechanical
mediocre
mileage
millionaire
misapprehension
miscellaneous
monopolize
mortgage
mutually

N

naïve
necessarily
necessitate
negligible
negotiate
neutralize
nickel
nonsense
notarize
noticeable
nucleus
numerical

O

objectionable
obligatory
obsolete
obtainable
occasional
occupant
occurrence
omission
operator
ordinarily
original
overrated
oxidize

P

pamphlet
panicky
parallel
pardonable
parity
participant
pasteboard
pastime
peaceable
perceptible
permissible
personnel
persuasive
pertinent
phenomenal
Pittsburgh (Pa.)
politician
possession
potential
practical
precise
precision
prerogative
prohibition
prosperous
psychology

Q

quandary
quantity
questionnaire

R

readily
reciprocate
recollect
reconciliation
reimburse
remembrance
renewable
repetition
resources
restaurant
ridiculous
revenue
routine

S

sabotage

safety
schedule
scientific
scrutinize
seize
sense
sensible
serviceable
siege
similar
sincerely
sizable
solely
specifically
specimen
sponsor
statistical
statistician
status

substantial
summarize
superficial
superfluous
supervisor
surgeon
susceptible
symmetry

T

tariff
technical
tenancy
thorough
through
traceable

U

unscrupulous

until
urgent
usable
utilize

V

vacuum
vague
valid
validate
valuable
velocity
vendor
vengeance
ventilator
villain
visitor
visualize
volume

W

waive
warehouse
weather
Wednesday
whereas
wherever
whether
wholly
wield
withhold

Y

yacht
yield

Z

zealous

Forms of Address for
Official Correspondence

GOVERNMENT OFFICIALS—FEDERAL, STATE, AND MUNICIPAL

The President

The President
The White House
Washington, D. C. 20501
Mr. President:
or *The President:*
or *My dear Mr. President:*

The Vice-President

The Honorable . . .
President of the Senate
United States Senate
Washington, D. C. 20510
Sir:

or

The Honorable . . .
Vice-President of the United States
Washington, D. C. 20501
Mr. Vice President:
or *Sir:*
or *My dear Mr. Vice-President:*

Cabinet Member

The Honorable . . .
Secretary of . . .
Washington, D. C.

or

The Secretary of . . .
Washington, D. C.
Sir:
or *Dear Sir:*
or *My dear Mr. Secretary:*

Members of Congress

The Honorable . . .
The United States Senate
Washington, D. C. 20510
Dear Sir:
or *My dear Senator:*
The Honorable . . .
House of Representatives
Washington, D. C. 20515

or

The Honorable . . .

Representative in Congress
City, State
Sir:
or *Dear Sir:*

or

My dear Mr. . . . :

Chief Justice of the United States

The Chief Justice of the United
States
Washington, D. C. 20543

or

The Chief Justice
The Supreme Court
Washington, D. C. 20543
Sir:
or *My dear Mr. Chief Justice:*

**Associate Justice of the Supreme Court
of the United States**

The Honorable . . .
United States Supreme Court
Washington, D. C. 20543

or

Mr. Justice . . .
United States Supreme Court
Washington, D. C. 20543
My dear Mr. Justice:
or *Dear Justice . . . :*

Ambassador

From Foreign Countries to the
United States
His Excellency . . .
The Ambassador of . . .
Washington, D. C.
Sir:
From United States to Foreign
Countries
The Honorable . . .
American Ambassador
Foreign Capital, Foreign Country
Sir:
or *Excellency:*

or use personal title, as *Your Grace:*

ROMAN CATHOLIC CLERGY

Governor

*His Excellency . . .
The Governor of . . .
State Capital, State

*In Massachusetts and New Hampshire.

or

The Honorable . . .
Governor of . . .
State Capital, State
Sir:
or *Dear Sir:*

State Senator

The Honorable . . .
(State) Senate
State Capital, State
Dear Sir:
or *My dear Senator:*

State Assemblyman, Representative, or Delegate

Note: Title varies, depending on the
official name of the lower house in
the respective state.
Assemblyman (or Representative or
Delegate) . . .
The State Assembly (or House of
Representatives or House of
Delegates)
State Capital, State

or

Use the second form for a state
senator, with appropriate changes.
Sir:
or *Dear Sir:*
or *My dear Mr. . . . :*

Mayor

The Honorable . . .
Mayor of . . .
City, State

or

The Mayor of the City of . . .
City, State
Sir:
or *Dear Sir:*
or *Dear Mr. Mayor:*
or *My dear Mr. Mayor:*

Cardinal

His Eminence . . . (insert given
name) Cardinal . . . (insert
surname)
Address
Your Eminence:

Archbishop

The Most Reverend . . .
Archbishop of . . .
Address
Your Excellency:

Bishop (in the U.S.)

The Most Reverend . . .
Bishop of . . .
Address
Your Excellency:

Monsignor

The Right (or Very) Reverend
Monsignor . . .
Address
My dear Monsignor:
or *Right Reverend Monsignor:*
or *Dear Monsignor . . . :*
or *Right (or Very) Reverend and
dear Monsignor:*

Priest

Reverend . . . , . . . (add initials
of order)
Address
Dear Father . . . :

Mother Superior

The Reverend Mother Superior . . . ,
(add initials of order)
Convent of . . .
Address
Reverend Mother:
or *Dear Reverend Mother:* (informal)
or *My dear Reverend Mother . . . :*

Sister

Sister . . . , (add initials of order)
Address
Dear Sister:

or *My dear Sister:*
or *Dear Sister . . . :*
or *My dear Sister . . . :*

PROTESTANT CLERGY

Protestant Episcopal Bishop
The Right Reverend . . .
Bishop of . . .
Address
Right Reverend and Dear Sir:
or *Dear Bishop . . . : (informal)*
or *My dear Bishop . . . :*

Protestant Episcopal Dean
The Very Reverend the Dean of . . . :
Address
or

The Very Rev. . . . , D. D., Dean of . . .
Address
Very Reverend Sir:
or *My dear Mr. Dean:*

Methodist Episcopal Bishop
The Reverend . . . , D.D.
Bishop of . . .
Address
Reverend Sir:
or *Dear Sir:*
or *Dear Bishop . . . :*
or *My dear Bishop . . . :*

OTHER CLERGYMEN

The Reverend Mr. (or Dr., if
entitled to a degree) . . .
Address
Dear Sir:
or *Reverend Sir:*
or *My dear Mr. (or Dr.) . . . :*
or *Dear Mr. (or Dr.) . . .:*

Jewish Rabbi
Rabbi . . . (or Reverend . . .)
Address
Reverend Sir:
or *Dear Sir:*
or *My dear Rabbi:*
or *Dear Rabbi . . .:*

MILITARY AND NAVAL PERSONNEL (U.S.)

Commanding Officers (Examples)
The Commander in Chief
Army of the United States
Address
or

Lieutenant General (or other rank) . . .
Commanding Officer
Army of the United States
Address

The Admiral of the Navy of
the United States
Address
or

Admiral . . .
Commanding United States Navy
Address
Sir:
or *My dear (rank) . . .: (informal)*
*Dear Mr. . . .: (for naval officers below
the rank of commander)*
*My dear (rank) . . .: (for military officers
below the rank of captain)*
NOTE: In addressing an officer by rank,
use *General* even though his rank is
Major General;
Commander even though his rank is
Lieutenant Commander; etc.

State Abbreviations

Recently the U.S. Post Office Department introduced two-letter abbreviations for all states and possessions of the United States. These abbreviations consist of two capital letters, with no space or periods. The ZIP Code number *must* be used with the new abbreviations.

The two-letter abbreviations have several advantages. They can be read faster by optical scanners (automated equipment that "reads" addresses and sorts mail at high speeds). They also save space if the address area is limited, as it is in most automated addressing systems used by bulk mailers.

However, the optical scanners can also read the full state names and the traditional state abbreviations. Hence, mailers are not required to use the new abbreviations; they may still use the preferred style of spelling out state names or they may use the traditional abbreviations.

The following list shows the correct traditional abbreviations as well as the new abbreviations introduced by the Post Office.

State	Traditional Abbreviation	Post Office Abbreviation
Alabama	Ala.	AL
Alaska	—	AK
Arizona	Ariz.	AZ
Arkansas	Ark.	AR
California	Calif.	CA
Canal Zone	C.Z.	CZ
Colorado	Colo.	CO
Connecticut	Conn.	CT
Delaware	Del.	DE
District of Columbia	D.C.	DC
Florida	Fla.	FL
Georgia	Ga.	GA
Guam	—	GU
Hawaii	—	HI
Idaho	—	ID
Illinois	Ill.	IL
Indiana	Ind.	IN

State	Traditional Abbreviation	Post Office Abbreviation
Iowa	—	IA
Kansas	Kans.	KS
Kentucky	Ky.	KY
Louisiana	La.	LA
Maine	—	ME
Maryland	Md.	MD
Massachusetts	Mass.	MA
Michigan	Mich.	MI
Minnesota	Minn.	MN
Mississippi	Miss.	MS
Missouri	Mo.	MO
Montana	Mont.	MT
Nebraska	Nebr.	NB
Nevada	Nev.	NV
New Hampshire	N.H.	NH
New Jersey	N.J.	NJ
New Mexico	N. Mex.	NM
New York	N.Y.	NY
North Carolina	N.C.	NC
North Dakota	N. Dak.	ND
Ohio	—	OH
Oklahoma	Okla.	OK
Oregon	Ore.	OR
Pennsylvania	Pa.	PA
Puerto Rico	P.R.	PR
Rhode Island	R.I.	RI
South Carolina	S.C.	SC
South Dakota	S. Dak.	SD
Tennessee	Tenn.	TN
Texas	Tex.	TX
Utah	—	UT
Vermont	Vt.	VT
Virginia	Va.	VA
Virgin Islands	V.I.	VI
Washington	Wash.	WA
West Virginia	W. Va.	WV
Wisconsin	Wis.	WI
Wyoming	Wyo.	WY

Index

Reports *(cont.)*
  informal, 373-381
    outline form, 379
    paragraph form, 379
    planning of, 377-378
    tabulated form, 379-380
    unsolicited, 380
    writing of, 374-375, 377-378
      by administrative assistant, 501
Request letters, 273-281, 488 *(see also*
    Letters)
Research, 498-501
Reservation letters, 276, 487
Response letters, 282-295 *(see also*
    Letters)
  printed responses, 291-293
Retroactive to, 134
Rise, raise, 74-75
Round numbers, 201

Sales letters, 236-241, 328-339 *(see also*
    Letters)
  action, driving for, 337-338
  attention, attracting of, 333-335
  audience for, 329-332
  buying motives and, 332-333
  comfort incentive in, 238
  desire, creating of, 335-337
  financial-gain incentive in, 236-237
  health and security and, 237-238
  interest, arousal of, 335-337
  mailing lists for, 250, 329-332
  status symbols and, 240-241
  "yes" attitude, development of, 337
Seasons of the year, not capitalized, 187
Secretarial duties, 484-492
  dictation and transcription, 485-486
  letter writing, 487-491
  mail handling, 486-487
  message taking, 491; *illus.*, 490
Secretarial handbooks, 499, 500
Self-ending pronouns, 96
Semiblocked letter style, *illus.*, 269
Semicolon, 153-154
  for comma, 153, 161, 162
  vs. dash, 156
  with enumeration, 153
  with parentheses, 183
  with quotation marks, 179, 181
Sentences, 62-65
  balanced, 142-143, 219-222, 225-226
  compound, punctuation of, 153, 160-
    161
  control of, 227-228
  dangling, 211-212
  declarative, 146
  fragmentary, 62, 148
  ideas in, subordination of, 229-230
  imperative, 146
  inverted, 64
    agreement in, 103
    who or *whom* in, 98
  length of, 227-228
  Memory Hook, 62

Sentences *(cont.)*
  parallel structure, 142-143, 219-222,
    225-226
  predicate of, 63
  shifts in voice, tense, person, and num-
    ber in, 225-226
  subject of, 63-64
    agreement *(see* Agreement of sub-
      ject and predicate)
    compound, 64
    simple, 63
  thought units in, 208-215
  variety in structure of, 230
Series, punctuation with, 162-163
Set, sit, 74-75
Ships, names of, 181
Simple adverbs, 124
Since, 140
Slang, quotation marks for, 180
So,
  and *as,* 141
  misused, 218
Social-business letters, 353-363 *(see also*
    Letters)
  condolence, 361-362
  congratulatory, 354-357
  format, 353
  invitations and replies, 360-361
  stationery for, 353
  thank-you, 284, 358-359
Some, somewhat, 128-129
Sort, 121
SOS, 195
Sounds in words, 217
South, capitalization of, 190
Specific words, 24-25
Speech,
  emphasis in, 422
  enunciation, 425-430
    exercises, 427-429
      jaw, 427-428
      lips, 428-429
      tongue, 429
  force (volume), 421
  pitch (level), 422
  pronunciation *(see* Pronunciation)
  quality of, 421-423
  rate (tempo), 422-423
  words per minute, 44, 422
Speeches, 447-459
  anecdotes and stories in, 456-457
  audiovisual materials for, 452
  conclusion of, 452, 458
  delivery of, 453-457
    appearance in, 419-421, 454
    confidence and, 453-454
    notes, use of in, 456
    reading or reciting, 456
    stage presence and, 454-457
  information sources for, 449-450
  introduction of speaker, 457-458
  introductory remarks in, 450-451
  memorized, 456
  note-taking for, 449-450
  organization of, 450-452